T4-ACU-992

WITHDRAWN
Stafford Library
Columbia College
1001 Rogers Street
Columbia, Missouri 65216

The
Encyclopedia of
MISSOURI
INDIANS

The

Encyclopedia of

MISSOURI

INDIANS

VOLUME TWO

TREATIES

*   *   *

Stafford Library
Columbia College
1001 Rogers Street
Columbia, Missouri 65216

SOMERSET PUBLISHERS, INC.

P.O. BOX 160

ST. CLAIR SHORES, MI. 48080

Copyright© 2001 by Somerset Publishers, Inc.

All rights reserved. No part of this work may be reproduced or utilized in any form or by any means, electronic or mechanical, or by any information storage and retrieval system, without permission in writing from the publisher.

Printed in the United States of America

ISBN 0-403-08891-7

CONTENTS

VOLUME ONE

HISTORY 1

A to Z ENCYCLOPEDIA 69

TREATY COMMITMENTS. 305

PICTORIAL SECTIONS
    BIOGRAPHY. P1
    TRIBES AND DAILY LIFE P35

AREA MAPS. P44

VOLUME TWO

TREATIES 1

INDIAN TREATIES
of The American Plains, West and Northwest Plateau

TREATY WITH THE EEL RIVER, ETC. {1803, Aug. 7}
Proclamation, Dec. 23, 1803.

At a council held at Vincennes on the seventh day of August, one thousand eight hundred and three, under the direction of William Henry Harrison, governor of the Indiana territory, superintendent of Indian affairs, and commissioner plenipotentiary of the United States for concluding any treaty or treaties which may be found necessary with any of the Indian nations north west of the river Ohio, at which were present the chiefs and warriors of the Eel River, Wyandot, Piankashaw and Kaskaskia nations, and also the tribe of the Kikapoes, by their representatives, the chiefs of the Eel River nation.

The fourth article of the treaty holden and concluded at Fort Wayne, on the seventh day of June, one thousand eight hundred and three, being considered, the chiefs and warriors of the said nations give their free and full consent to the same, and they do hereby relinquish and confirm to the United States the privilege and right of locating three several tracts of land of one mile square each, on the road leading from Vincennes to Kaskaskia, and also one other tract of land of one mile square on the road leading from Vincennes to Clarksville; which locations shall be made in such places on the aforesaid roads as shall best comport with the convenience and interest of the United States in the establishment of houses of entertainment for the accommodation of travellers.

In witness whereof, the said William Henry Harrison, and the said chiefs and warriors of the before-mentioned nations and tribe of Indians, have hereunto set their hands and affixed their seals, the day and year first above written.

William Henry Harrison.

La Boussier, his x mark, Ka Tunga, or Charly, his x mark, Akaketa, or ploughman, his x mark, Ducoigne edagogue, his x mark, Saconquaneva, or tired legs, his x mark, Gros Bled or big corn, his x mark, Black Dog, is x mark.

Signed, sealed, and delivered, in the presence of:
John Rice Jones, B. Parke, Joseph Barron, interpreter.

Plains, West and Northwest Plateau Indian Treaties

TREATY WITH THE KASKASKIA {1803, Aug 13 }
Proclamation, Dec. 3, 1803

Articles of a treaty made at Vincennes in the Indiana territory, between William Henry Harrison, governor of the said territory, superintendent of Indian affairs and commissioner plenipotentiary of the United States for concluding any treaty or treaties which may be found necessary with any of the Indian tribes north west of the river Ohio of the one part, and the head chiefs and warriors of the Kaskaskia tribe of Indians so called, but which tribe is the remains and rightfully represent all the tribes of the Illinois Indians, originally called the Kaskaskia, Mitchigamia, Cahokia and Tamaroi of the other part:

ARTICLE 1. Whereas from a variety of unfortunate circumstances the several tribes of Illinois Indians are reduced to a very small number, the remains of which have been long consolidated and known by the name of the Kaskaskia tribe, and finding themselves unable to occupy the extensive tract of country which of right belongs to them and which was possessed by their ancestors for many generations, the chiefs and warriors of the said tribe being also desirous of procuring the means of improvement in the arts of civilized life, and a more certain and effectual support for their women and children, have, for the considerations hereinafter mentioned, relinquished and by these presents do relinquish and cede to the United States all the lands in the Illinois country, which the said tribe has heretofore possessed, or which they may rightfully claim, reserving to themselves however the tract of about three hundred and fifty acres near the town of Kaskaskia, which they have always held and which was secured to them by the act of Congress of the third day of March, one thousand seven hundred and ninety-one, and also the right of locating one other tract of twelve hundred and eighty acres within the bounds of that now ceded, which two tracts of land shall remain to them forever.

ARTICLE 2. The United States will take the Kaskaskia tribe under their immediate care and patronage, and will afford them a protection, as effectual against the other Indian tribes and against all other persons whatever as is enjoyed by their own citizens. And the said Kaskaskia tribe do hereby engage to refrain from making war or giving any insult or offence to any other Indian tribe or to any foreign nation, without having first obtained the approbation and consent of the United States.

ARTICLE 3. The annuity heretofore given by the United States to the said tribe shall be increased to one thousand dollars, which is to be paid to them either in money, merchandise, provisions or domestic animals, at the option of the said tribe: and when the said annuity or any part thereof is paid in merchandise, it is to be delivered to them either at Vincennes, Fort Massac or Kaskaskia, and the first cost of the goods in the sea-port where they may be pro-

Plains, West and Northwest Plateau Indian Treaties

cured is alone to be charged to the said tribe free from the cost of transportation, or any other contingent expense. Whenever the said tribe may choose to receive money, provisions or domestic animals for the whole or in part of the said annuity, the same shall be delivered at the town of Kaskaskia.

The United States will also cause to be built a house suitable for the accommodation of the chief of the said tribe, and will enclose for their use a field not exceeding one hundred acres with a good and sufficient fence. And whereas, The greater part of the said tribe have been baptised and received into the Catholic church to which they are much attached, the United States will give annually for seven years one hundred dollars towards the support of a priest of that religion, who will engage to perform for the said tribe the duties of his office and also to instruct as many of their children as possible in the rudiments of literature.

And the United States will further give the sum of three hundred dollars to assist the said tribe in the erection of a church. The stipulations made in this and the preceding article, together with the sum of five hundred and eighty dollars, which is now paid or assured to be paid for the said tribe for the purpose of procuring some necessary articles, and to relieve them from debts which they have heretofore contracted, is considered as a full and ample compensation for the relinquishment made to the United States in the first article.

ARTICLE 4. The United States reserve to themselves the right at any future period of dividing the annuity now promised to the said tribe amongst the several families thereof, reserving always a suitable sum for the great chief and his family. Observing the boundary between their respective claims, the chiefs and head warriors of the said Kaskaskia tribe do hereby declare that their rightful claim is as follows, viz: Beginning at the confluence of the Ohio and the Mississippi, thence up the Ohio to the mouth of the Saline creek, about twelve miles below the mouth of the Wabash, thence along the dividing ridge between the said creek and the Wabash until it comes to the general dividing ridge between the waters which fall into the Wabash, and those which fall into the Kaskaskia river; and thence along the said ridge until it reaches the waters which fall into the Illinois river, thence in a direct course to the mouth of the Illinois river, and thence down the Mississippi to the beginning.

ARTICLE 6. As long as the lands which have been ceded by this treaty shall continue to be the property of the United States, the said tribe shall have the privilege of living and hunting upon them in the same manner that they have hitherto done.

ARTICLE 7. This treaty is to be in force and binding upon the said parties, as soon as it shall be ratified by the President and Senate of the United States.

Plains, West and Northwest Plateau Indian Treaties

In witness whereof, the said commissioner plenipotentiary, and the head chiefs and warriors of the said Kaskaskia tribe of Indians, have hereunto set their hands and affixed their seals, the thirteenth day of August, in the year of our Lord one thousand eight hundred and three, and of the Independence of the United States the twenty-eighth.

William Henry Harrison,

The mark x of Ocksinga, a Mitch-inn, The mark x of Jean Baptiste Ducoigne, The mark x of Pedagogue, The mark x of Micolas or Nicholas, Louis Decoucigne

Sealed and delivered in the presence of
J. R. Jones, secretary to commission. H. Vanderburgh, judge of Indiana Territory. T. F. Rivet, Indian Miss. Vigo, colonel Knox County Militia. Cor. Lyman, Captain First Infantry Regiment., Ins. Johnson, of Indiana territory. B. Parke, of the Indiana Territory. Joseph Barron, interpreter.

TREATY WITH THE SIOUX {1805, Sept. 23}
Ratified Apr. 16, 1808.
Never proclaimed by the President.

Whereas, a conference held between the United States of America and the Sioux Nation of Indians, Lieut. Z. M. Pike, of the Army of the United States, and the chiefs and warriors of the said tribe, have agreed to the following articles, which when ratified and approved of by the proper authority, shall be binding on both parties:

ARTICLE 1. That the Sioux Nation grants unto the United States for the purpose of the establishment of military posts, nine miles square at the mouth of the river St. Croix, also from below the confluence of the Mississippi and St. Peters, up the Mississippi, to include the falls of St. Anthony, extending nine miles on each side of the river. That the Sioux Nation grants to the United States, the full sovereignty and power over said districts forever, without any let or hindrance whatsoever.

ARTICLE 2. That in consideration of the above grants the United States (shall, prior to taking possession thereof, pay to the Sioux two thousand dollars, or deliver the value thereof in such goods and merchandise as they shall choose).

ARTICLE 3. The United States promise on their part to permit the Sioux to pass, repass, hunt or make other uses of the said districts, as they have formerly done, without any other exception, but those specified in article first.

Plains, West and Northwest Plateau Indian Treaties

In testimony hereof, we, the undersigned, have hereunto set our hands and seals, at the mouth of the river St. Peters, on the 23rd day of September, one thousand eight hundred and five.

Z. M. Pike, First Lieutenant and Agent at the above conference.
Le Petit Carbeau, his x mark. Way Aga Enogee, his x mark,

(*This treaty does not appear among those printed in the United States Statutes at Large. It was, however, submitted by the President to the Senate, March 29, 1808. The Senate committee reported favorably, on the 13th of April, with the following amendment to fill the blank in article 2, viz: "After the word States' in the second article insert the following words: shall, prior to taking possession thereof, pay to the Sioux two thousand dollars, or deliver the value thereof in such goods and merchandise as they shall choose."' In this form the Senate, on the 16th of April, 1808, advised and consented to its ratification by a unanimous vote.

An examination of the records of the State Department fails to indicate any subsequent action by the President in proclaiming the ratification of this treaty; but more than twenty-five years subsequent to its approval by the Senate the correspondence of the War Department speaks of the cessions of land described therein as an accomplished fact.)

TREATY WITH THE OSAGE {1808, Nov. 10}
Ratified Apt. 28, 1810.

Articles of a treaty made and concluded at Fort Clark, on the right bank of the Missouri, about five miles above the Fire Prairie, in the territory of Louisiana, the tenth day of November, in the year of our Lord one thousand eight hundred and eight, between Peter Chouteau, esquire, agent for the Osage, and specially commissioned and instructed to enter into the same by his excellency Meriwether Lewis, governor and superintendent of Indian affairs for the territory aforesaid, in behalf of the United States of America, of the one part, and the chiefs and warriors of the Great and Little Osage, for themselves and their nations respectively, on the other part.

ARTICLE 1. The United States being anxious to promote peace, friendship and intercourse with the Osage tribes, to afford them every assistance in their power, and to protect them from the insults and injuries of other tribes of Indians, situated near the settlements of the white people, have thought proper to build a fort on the right bank of the Missouri, a few miles above the Fire Prairie, and do agree to garrison the same with as many regular troops as the President of the United States may, from time to time, deem necessary for the protection of all orderly, friendly and well disposed Indians of the Great and Little

Plains, West and Northwest Plateau Indian Treaties

Osage nations, who reside at this place, and who do strictly conform to, and pursue the counsels or admonitions of the President of the United States through his subordinate officers.

ARTICLE 2. The United States being also anxious that the Great and Little Osage, resident as aforesaid, should be regularly supplied with every species of merchandise, which their comfort may hereafter require, do engage to establish at this place, and permanently to continue at all seasons of the year, a well assorted store of goods, for the purpose of bartering with them on moderate terms for their peltries and furs.

ARTICLE 3. The United States agree to furnish at this place, for the use of the Osage nations, a black-smith, and tools to mend their arms and utensils of husbandry, and engage to build them a horse mill, or water mill; also to furnish them with ploughs, and to build for the great chief of the Great Osage, and for the great chief of the Little Osage, a strong block house in each of their towns, which are to be established near this fort.

ARTICLE 4. With a view to quiet the animosities which at present exist between the inhabitants of the territory of Louisiana, and the Osage nations, in consequence of the lawless depredations of the latter, the United States do further agree to pay to their own citizens, the full value of such property as they can legally prove to have been stolen or destroyed by the said Osage, since the acquisition of Louisiana by the United States, provided the same does not exceed the sum of five thousand dollars.

ARTICLE 5. In consideration of the lands relinquished by the Great and Little Osage to the United States as stipulated in the sixth article of this treaty, the United States promise to deliver at Fire Prairie, or at St. Louis, yearly, to the Great Osage nation, merchandise to the amount or value of one thousand dollars, and to the Little Osage nation, merchandise to the amount or value of five hundred dollars, reckoning the value of said merchandise at the first cost thereof, in the city or place in the United States, where the same shall have been procured.

And in addition to the merchandise aforesaid, the United States have, at and before the signature of these articles, paid to the Great Osage nation, the sum of eight hundred dollars, and to the Little Osage nation, the sum of four hundred dollars.

ARTICLE 6. And in consideration of the advantages which we derive from the stipulations contained in the foregoing articles, we, the chiefs and warriors of the Great and Little Osage, for ourselves and our nations respectively, covenant and agree with the United States, that the boundary line between our nations and the United States shall be as follows, to wit: beginning at fort Clark, on the

Plains, West and Northwest Plateau Indian Treaties

Missouri, five miles above Fire Prairie, and running thence a due south course to the river Arkansas, and down the same to the Mississippi; hereby ceding and relinquishing forever to the United States, all the lands which lie east of the said line, and north of the southwardly bank of the said river Arkansas, and all lands situated northwardly of the river Missouri. And we do further cede and relinquish to the United States forever, a tract of two leagues Square, to embrace fort Clark, and to be laid off in such manner as the President of the United States shall think proper.

ARTICLE 7. And it is mutually agreed by the contracting parties, that the boundary lines hereby established, shall be run and marked at the expense of the United States, as soon as circumstances or their convenience will permit; and the Great and Little Osage promise to depute two chiefs front each of their respective nations, to accompany the commissioner, or commissioners who may be appointed on the part of the United States, to settle and adjust the said boundary line.

ARTICLE 8. And the United States agree that such of the Great and Little Osage Indians, as may think proper to put themselves under the protection of fort Clark, and who observe the stipulations of this treaty with good faith, shall be permitted to live and to hunt, without molestation, on all that tract of country, west of the north and south boundary line, on which they, the said Great and Little Osage, have usually hunted or resided: Provided, The same be not the hunting grounds of any nation or tribe of Indians in amity with the United States; and on any other lands within the territory of Louisiana, without the limits of the white settlements, until the United States may think proper to assign the same as hunting grounds to other friendly Indians.

ARTICLE 9. Lest the friendship which is now established between the United States and the said Indian nations should be interrupted by the misconduct of individuals, it is hereby agreed that for injuries done by individuals, no private revenge or retaliation shall take place, but instead thereof complaints shall be made by the party injured to the other, by the said nations or either of them, to the superintendent or other person appointed by the President to the chiefs of the said nation; and it shall be the duty of the said chiefs, upon complaints being made as aforesaid, to deliver up the person or persons against whom the complaint is made, to the end that he or they may be punished agreeably to the laws of the state or territory, where the offence may have been committed; and in like manner, if any robbery, violence or murder shall be committed on any Indian or Indians belonging to either of said nations, the person or persons so offending shah be tried, and if found guilty, shall be punished in like manner as if the injury had been done to a white man.

And it is agreed that the chiefs of the Great and Little Osage, shall to the utmost of their power exert themselves to recover horses or other property which may

Plains, West and Northwest Plateau Indian Treaties

be stolen from any citizen or citizens of the United States, by any individual or individuals of either of their nations; and the property so recovered shall be forthwith delivered to the superintendent or other person authorized to receive it, that it may be restored to the proper owner; and in cases where the exertions of the chiefs shall be ineffectual in recovering the property stolen as aforesaid, if sufficient proof can be adduced that such property was actually stolen by any Indian or Indians belonging to the said nations, or either of them, the superintendent, or other proper officer, may deduct from the annuity of the said nations respectively a sum equal to the value of the property which has been stolen.

And the United States hereby guarantee to any Indian or Indians of the said nations respectively, a full indemnification for any horses or other property which may be stolen from them by any of their citizens: Provided, That the property so stolen cannot be recovered, and that sufficient proof is produced that it was actually stolen by a citizen of the United States. And the said nations of the Great and Little Osage engage, on the requisition or demand of the President of the United States, or of the superintendent, to deliver up any white man resident among them.

ARTICLE 10. The United States receive the Great and Little Osage nations into their friendship and under their protection; and the said nations, on their part, declare that they will consider themselves under the protection of no other power whatsoever; disclaiming all right to cede, sell or in any manner transfer their lands to any foreign power, or to citizens of the United States or inhabitants of Louisiana, unless duly authorized by the President of the United States to make the said purchase or accept the said cession on behalf of the government.

ARTICLE 11. And if any person or persons, for hunting or other purpose, shall pass over the boundary lines, as established by this treaty, into the country reserved for the Great and Little Osage nations, without the license of the superintendent or other proper officer, they, the said Great and Little Osage, or either of them, shall be at liberty to apprehend such unlicensed hunters or other persons, and surrender them together with their property, but without other injury, insult or molestation, to the superintendent of Indian affairs, or to the agent nearest the place of arrest, to be dealt with according to law.

ARTICLE 12. And the chiefs and warriors as aforesaid, promise and engage that neither the Great nor Little Osage nation will ever, by safe, exchange or as presents, supply any nation or tribe of Indians, not in amity with the United States, with guns, ammunitions or other implements of war.

ARTICLE 13. This treaty shall take effect and be obligatory on the contracting parties, as soon as the same shall have been ratified by the President, by and with the advice and consent of the Senate of the United States.

Plains, West and Northwest Plateau Indian Treaties

In testimony whereof, the said Peter Chouteau, commissioned and instructed as aforesaid, and the chiefs and warriors of the Great and Little Osage nation of Indians, have hereunto set their hands and affixed their seals.

Done at fort Clark the day above mentioned.

P. Chouteau, E. B. Clemson, captain First Regiment Infantry, L. Lorimer, lieutenant First Regiment ,Infantry, Reazen Lewis, sub-agent Indian Affairs, Papuisea, the grand chief of the Big Osage, his x mark, Nichu Malli, the grand chief of the Little Osage, his x mark, Voithe Voihe, the second chief of the Big sage, his x mark, Voithe Chinga, the second chief of the Little Osage, his x mark, Ta Voingare, the little hief of the Big Osage, his x mark, Osogahe, the little chief of the Little Osage, his x mark, Voichinodhe, the little chief of the Big Osage, his x mark, Voi Nache, the little chief of the Little Osage, his mark, Vol Nonpache, the little chief of the Big Osage, his x mark, Quihi Ramaki, the little chief of the Little Osage, his x mark, Vol Nache, the little chief of the Big Osage, his x mark, Ponla Voitasuga, the little chief of the Little Osage, his x mark, Caygache, the little chief of the Big Osage, his x mark, Pahuroguesie, the little chief of the Little Osage, his x mark,

Miaasa, the little chief of the Big Osage, his x mark, Manjaguida, the little chief of the Little Osage, his x mark, Mantsa, the little chief of the Big Osage, his x mark, Nicagaris, the little chief of the Big Osage, his x mark, Dogachinga, the little chief of the Big Osage, his x mark, Tavaingare, the little chief of the Little Osage, his x mark, Tavainthere, the little chief of the Big Osage, his x mark, Naguemani, the war chief of the Big Osage, his x mark, Nicanauthe, the war chief of the Little Osage, his x mark, Chonmelase, the war chief of the Big Osage, his x mark, Nenonbas, the war chief of the Little Osage, his x mark, The Pograngue, the war chief of the Big Osage, his x mark, The Cayque, warrior, L. O. his x mark, Nonpevoite, do. B. O. his x mark, Vesasche, do. L. O. his x mark, Tonchenanque, do. B. O. his x mark, Caygache, do. L. O. his x mark, Lihibi, do. B. O. his x mark, Grinache, do. L. O. his x mark, Ni Couil Bran, do. B. O. his x mark, Chonnonsogue, do. L. O. his x mark,

Lisansandhe, do. B. O. his x mark, Mequaque, do. L. O. his x mark, Manhegare, do. B. O. his x mark, Megahe, do. L. O. his x mark, Meyhe, do. B. O. his x mark, Nudhetavoi do. L. O. his x mark, Thecayque, o. B. O. his x mark, Voitasean, do. L. O. his x mark, Cahapiche, do. B. O. his x mark, Manhevoi, do. L. O. his x mark, Talechiga, do. B. O. his x mark, Pedhechiga, do. L. O. his x mark, Cheganonsas, do. B. O. his x mark, Nesaque, do. L. O. his x mark, Lolechinga, do. B. O. his x mark, Panevoiguanda, do. L. O. his x mark, Tavoinhihi, do. B. O. his x mark, Mithechinga, do. L. O. his x mark, Voidhenache, do. B. O. his x mark, Manquesi, do. L. O. his x mark, Chingavoisa, do. B. O. his x mark, TaleVoile, do. L. O. his x mark, Voiengran, do. B. O. his x

Plains, West and Northwest Plateau Indian Treaties

mark, Scamani, do. L. O. his x mark, Nura Hague, do. B. O. his x mark, Me Chinga, do. L. O. his x mark,

Pachigue, little chief, B. O. his x mark, Rouda Nique, warrior, L. O. his x mark, Ne Paste, do. B. O. his x mark, Voibisandhe, do. L. O. his x mark, Nehi Zanga, do. B. O. his x mark, Nehudhe, warrior, L. O. his x mark, The Pagranque, do. B. O. his x mark, Chahetonga, do. L. O. his x mark, Manguepee Mani, do. B. O. his x mark, Voi Balune, do. L. O. his x mark, Ponea Voitaniga, do. B. O. his x mark, Taslondhe, do. L. O. his x mark.

Nequevoile, do. L. O. his x mark, Chonguehanga, do. B. O. his x mark, Ponlachinga, do. L. O. his x mark, Aguigueda, do. B. O. his x mark, Manjaguida, do. L. O. his x mark, Voidoguega, do. B. O. his x mark, The Sindhe, do. L. O. his x mark, Ninchagari, do. B. O. his x mark, Voihadani, do. L. O. his x mark, Voigaspeche, do. B. O. his x mark, Manyvofie, do. L. O. his x mark, Quinihonigue, do. B. O. his mark, Nognithe Chinga, do. L. O. his x .

We, the undersigned chiefs and warriors of the band of Osages, residing on the river Arkansas, being a part of the Great Osage nation, having this day had the foregoing treaty read and explained to us, by his excellency Meriwether Lewis, esquire, do hereby acknowledge, consent to, and confirm all the stipulations therein contained, as fully and as complctely as though we had been personally present at the signing, sealing, and delivering the same on the 10th day of November, 1808, the same being the day on which the said treaty was signed, sealed, and delivered, as will appear by a reference thereto.

In witness whereof, we have, for ourselves and our band of the Great Osage nation residing on the river Arkansas, hereunto set our hands and affixed our seals.

Done at St. Louis, in the territory of Louisiana, this thirty-first day of August, in the year of our Lord one thousand eight hundred and nine, and of the independence of the United States the thirty-fourth.

Tawangahuh, or Builder of Towns, his x mark, Honencache,. or the Terrible, his x mark, Talahu, or Deer's Pluck, his x mark, Cahigiagreh, or Good Chief, his x mark, Baughonghcheh, or Cutter, his x mark, Basonchinga, or Little Pine, his x mark,

In presence of us, and before signature attached to the original:
John G. Comegys, George Man, John W. Honey, Samuel Solomon, jun. John P. Gates, Interpreter, Noel Mongrain Marque, Indian Interpreter, Bazil Nassier Marque, Indian Interpreter.

Plains, West and Northwest Plateau Indian Treaties

TREATY WITH THE POTAWATOMI {1815, July 18}
Ratified, Dec. 26, 1815.

A treaty of peace and friendship, made and concluded at Portage des Sioux between William Clark, Ninian Edwards, and Auguste Chouteau, Commissioners Plenipotentiary of the United States of America, on the part and behalf of the said States, of the one part; and the undersigned Chiefs and Warriors of the Poutawatamie Tribe or Nation, residing on the river Illinois, on the part and behalf of the said Tribe or Nation, of the other part.

The parties being desirous of re-establishing peace and friendship between the United States and the said tribe or nation, and of being placed in all things, and in every respect, on the same footing upon which they stood before the war, have agreed to the following articles:

ARTICLE 1. Every injury or act of hostility by one or either of the contracting parties against the other, shall be mutually forgiven and forgot.

ARTICLE 2. There shall be perpetual peace and friendship between all the citizens of the United States of America, and all the individuals composing the said Poutawatamie tribe or nation.

ARTICLE 3. The contracting parties hereby agree, promise, and bind themselves, reciprocally, to deliver up all the prisoners now in their hands, (by what means soever the same may have come into their possession) to the officer commanding at Fort Clarke, on the Illinois river, as soon as it may be practicable.

ARTICLE 4. The contracting parties, in the sincerity of mutual friendship, recognize, re-establish and confirm, all and every treaty, contract, and agreement, heretofore concluded between the United States and the Poutawatamie tribe or nation.

In witness of all and every thing herein determined between the United States of America, and the said Poutawatamie tribe or nation, residing on the river Illinois: we, their underwritten commissioners and chiefs aforesaid, by virtue of our full powers, have signed this definitive treaty, and have caused our seals to be hereunto affixed. Done at Portage des Sioux, this eighteenth day of July, in the year of our Lord one thousand eight hundred and fifteen, and of the independence of the United States the fortieth.

William Clark, Ninian Edwards, Auguste Chouteau, Sunawchewome, his x mark, Mucketepoke, or Black Partridge, his x mark, Neggeneshkek, his x mark, Chawcawbeme, his x mark, Bendegakewa, his x mark, Wapewy, or White Hair, his x mark, Outawa, his x mark

Plains, West and Northwest Plateau Indian Treaties

In the presence of
R. Wash, secretary of the commission, Thomas Forsyth, Indian ag , N. Boilvin, agent, T. Paul, C. M. Maurice Blondeaux, Manuel Lisa, agent, John Miller, colonel Third Infantry, Richard Chitwood, Major M. Wm. Irvine Adair, captain Third Regiment U. S. Infantry, Cyrus Edwards, Samuel Solomon, Jacques Mette, Louis Decouagne, John A. Camero,sworn interpreters.

TREATY WITH THE TETON {1815, July 19}
Ratified, Dec. 26, 1815.

A treaty peace and friendship made and concluded at Portage des Sioux, between William Clark, Ninian Edwards, and Auguste Chouteau, Commissioners Plenipotentiary of the United States of America, on the part and behalf of the said States, of the one part; and the undersigned Chiefs and Warriors of the Teeton Tribe of Indians, on the part and behalf of their said Tribe, of the other part.

The parties being desirous of re-establishing peace and friendship between the United States and the said tribe, and of being placed in all things, and in every respect, on the same footing upon which they stood before the late war between the United States and (Great Britain, have agreed to the following articles:

ARTICLE 1. Every injury, or act of hostility, committed by one or either of the contracting parties against the other, shall be mutually forgiven and forgot.

ARTICLE 2. There shall be perpetual peace and friendship between all the citizens of the United States of America and all the individuals composing the said Teeton tribe; and the friendly relations that existed between them before the war, shall be, and the same are hereby, renewed.

ARTICLE 3. The undersigned chiefs and warriors, for themselves and their said tribe, do hereby acknowledge themselves and their aforesaid tribe to be under the protection of the United States of America, and of no other nation, power, or sovereign, whatsoever.

In witness whereof, the said William Clark, Ninian Edwards, and Auguste Chouteau, commissioners as aforesaid, and the chiefs and warriors of the said tribe, have hereunto subscribed their names, and affixed their seals this nineteenth day of July, one thousand eight hundred and fifteen, and of the independence of the United States the fortieth.

William Clark, Ninian Edwards, Auguste Chouteau, Eskatapia, the Player, his x mark, Tantanga, the True Buffaloe; his x mark, Weechachamanza, the Man of

Plains, West and Northwest Plateau Indian Treaties

Iron, his x mark, Ikmouacoulai, the Shooting Tiger, his x mark, Uakahincoukai, the Wind that Passes, his x mark, Mazamanie, the Walker in Iron, his x mark, Wanakagmamee, the Stamper, his x mark, Washeejonjrtga, the Left-handed Frenchman, his x mark, Monetowanari, the Bear's Soul, his x mark,

Done at Portage des Sioux, in the presence of
R. Wash, secretary to the commission, John Miller, colonel Third Infantry, H. Dodge, brigadier-general Missouri Militia, T. Paul, C. T. of the C. Manuel Lisa, agent, Thomas Forsyth, Indian agent, Maurice Blondeaux, John A. Cameron, Louis Decouagne, Louis Dorion, Cyrus Edwards, John Hay.

TREATY WITH THE SIOUX OF THE LAKES, {1815, July 19}
Ratified Dec. 26, 1815.

A treaty of friendship, made and concluded at portage des Sioux between, William, Clark, Ninian Edwards, and Auguste Chouteau, Commissioners Plenipotentiary of the United States of America, on the part and behalf of the said States, of the one art; and the of the Siouxs of the Lakes on the one undersigned Chiefs and Warriors of part and behalf of their Tribe, of the other part.

The parties being desirous of re-establishing peace and friendship between the United States and the said tribe, and of being placed in all things, and in every respect, on the same footing upon which they stood before the late war between the United States and Great Britain, have agreed to the following articles:

ARTICLE 1. Every injury, or act of hostility, committed by one or either of the contracting parties against the other, shall be mutually forgiven and forgot.

ARTICLE 2. There shall be perpetual peace and friendship between all the citizens of the United States of America and all the individuals composing the said tribe of the Lakes, and all the friendly relations that existed between them before the war, shall be, and the same are hereby, renewed.

ARTICLE 3. The undersigned chiefs and warriors, for themselves and their said tribe, do hereby acknowledge themselves and their aforesaid tribe to be under the protection of the United States, and of no other-nation, power, or sovereign, whatsoever.

In witness whereof, the said William Clark, Ninian Edwards, and Auguste Chouteau, commissioners aforesaid, and the chiefs and warriors of the aforesaid tribe, have hereunto subscribed their names and affixed their seals this nineteenth day of July, in the year of our Lord one thousand eight hundred and fifteen, and of the independence of the United States the fortieth.

Plains, West and Northwest Plateau Indian Treaties

William Clark, Ninian Edwards, Auguste Chouteau,

Tatangamania, the Walking Buffaloe, his x mark, Haisanwee, the Horn, his x mark, Aampahaa, the Speaker, his x mark, Nareesagata, the Hard Stone, his x mark, Haibohaa, the Branching Horn, his x mark,

Done at Portage des Sioux, in the presence of
R. Wash, secretary to the commission, John Miller, colonel Third Infantry, T. Paul, C. T. of the C., Edmund Hall, lieutenant late Twenty-eighth Infantry, J. B. Clark, adjutant Third Infantry, Manuel Lisa, agent, Thomas Forsyth, Indian agent, Jno. W. Johnson, United States factor and Indian agent, Mauriee Blondeaux, Lewis Decouagne, Louis Dorion, John A. Cameron, Jacques Mette, John Hay.

TREATY WITH THE SIOUX OF ST. PETER'S RIVER {1815, July 19} Ratified Dec. 26, 1815.

A treaty of peace and friendship, made and concluded at Portage des Sioux between William Clark, Ninian Edwards, and Auguste Chouteau, Commissioners Plenipotentiary of the United States of America, on the part and behalf of the said States, of the one part; and the. Chiefs and Warriors of the Siouxs of the river St. Peter's, on tire part and behalf of their said Tribe, on the other part.

THE parties being desirous of re-establishing peace and friendship between the United States and the said tribe, and of being placed in all things, and in every respect, on the same footing upon which they stood before the late war between the United States and Great Britain, have agreed to the following articles:

ARTICLE 1. Every injury or act of hostility committed by one or either of the contracting parties against the other, shall be mutually forgiven and forgot.

ARTICLE 2. There shall be perpetual peace and friendship between all the citizens of the United States of America and all the individuals composing the tribe of the Siouxs of the river St. Peter's; and all the friendly relations that existed between them before the war, shall be, and the same are hereby, renewed.

ARTICLE 3. The undersigned chiefs and warriors, for themselves and their said tribe, do hereby acknowledge themselves and their tribe to be under the protection of the United States, and of no other power, nation, or sovereign, whatsoever.

In testimony whereof, the said William Clark, Ninian Edwards and Auguste Chouteau, commissioners as aforesaid, and the chiefs and warriors of the aforesaid tribe, have hereunto subscribed their names and affixed their seals, this

Plains, West and Northwest Plateau Indian Treaties

nineteenth day of July, in the year of our Lord one thousand eight hundred and fifteen, and of the independence of the United States the fortieth.

William Clark, Ninian Edwards, Auguste Chouteau,

Enigmanee, that Flies as he Walks, his x mark, Wasoukapaha, the Falling Hail, his x mark, Champisaba, the Black War Club, his x mark, Manpinsaba, the Black Cloud, his x mark, Tatarnaza, the Iron Wind, his x mark, Nankanandee, who puts his foot in it, his x mark,

Done at Portage des Sioux, in the presence of
R. Wash, secretary of the commission, John Miller, colonel Third Infantry, H. Paul, C. T. of the C.John T. Chunn, brevet major of the U. S., Army, Edmund Hall, lieutenant late Twenty-eighth Infantry, Manuel Lisa, agent,Thomas Forsyth, Indian agent, J. W. Johnson, United States Factor and Indian agent. Maurice Blondeaux, Louis Decouagne, John A. Cameron, Louis Dorion, Jacques Matte, sworn interpreters.

TREATY WITH THE YANKTON SIOUX {1815, July 19} Ratified Dec. 26, 1815.

A treaty of peace and friendship, made and concluded at Portage des Sioux between William Clark, Ninian Edwards, and Auguste Chouteau, Commissioners Plenipotentiary of the United States of America, on the part and behalf of the said States, of the one part; and the undersigned Chiefs and Warriors of the Yancton Tribe of Indians, on the part and behalf of their said Tribe, of the other part.

THE parties being desirous of re-establishing peace and friendship between the United States and the said tribe, and of being placed in all things, and in every respect, on the same footing upon which they stood before the late war between the United States and Great Britain, have agreed to the following articles:

ARTICLE 1. Every injury or act of hostility committed by one or either of the contracting parties against the other, shall be mutually forgiven and forgot.

ARTICLE 2. There shall be perpetual peace and friendship between all the citizens of the United States of America, and all the individuals composing the said Yancton tribe, and all the friendly relations that existed between them before the war shall be, and the same are hereby, renewed.

ARTICLE 3. The undersigned chiefs and warriors, for themselves and their said tribe, do hereby acknowledge themselves to be under the protection of the

Plains, West and Northwest Plateau Indian Treaties

United States of America, and of no other nation, power, or sovereign, whatsoever.

In witness whereof, the said William Clark. Ninian Edwards, and Auguste Chouteau, commissioners as aforesaid, and the chiefs aforesaid, have hereunto subscribed their names and affixed their seals, this nineteenth day of July, in the year of our Lord one thousand eight hundred and fifteen, and of the independence of the United States the fortieth.

Wm. Clark, Ninian Edwards, Auguste Chouteau,

Monlori, or white bear, his x mark, Waskaijingo, or little dish, his x mark, Padamape, or panis sticker, his x mark, Chaponge, or musqui toe, his x mark, Mindalonga, partisan, or war chief, Weopaatowechashla, or sun set,Tokaymhominee, or the rock that turns, his x mark, Keonorunco, or fast flyer, his x mark, Mazo, or the iron, his x mark, Haiwongeeda, or one horn, his x mark, Mazehaio, or arrow sender, his x mark,

Done at the Portage des Sioux, in the presence of
R. Wash, secretary to the commission, John Miller, colonel, Third Infantry, H. Dodge, brigadier-general Missouri Militia, Manuel Lisa, agent, Thomas Forsyth, Indian agent, Maurice Blondeaux, Jacques Mette, John A. Cameron, R. Paul, C. T. of the commission, Louis Decouagne, Cyrus Edwards, Lewis Dorion, John Hay, interpreter.

TREATY WITH THE MAKAH {1815, July 20}
Ratified Dec. 26, 1815.

A treaty of peace and friendship, made and concluded between William Clark, Ninian Edwards, and Auguste Chouteau, Commissioners Plenipotentiary of the United States of America, on the part and behalf of the said States, of the one part, and the Chiefs and Warriors of the Mahas, on the part and behalf of said Tribe or Nation, of the other part.

THE parties being desirous of re-establishing peace and friendship between the United States and the said tribe or nation, and of being placed in all things, and in every respect, on the same footing upon which they stood before the late war between the United States and Great Britain, have agreed to the following articles:

ARTICLE 1. Every injury or act of hostility committed by one or either of the contracting parties against the other, shall be mutually forgiven and forgot.

Plains, West and Northwest Plateau Indian Treaties

ARTICLE 2. There shall be perpetual peace and friendship between all the citizens of the United States of America and all the individuals composing the tribe or nation of the Mahas, and all friendly relations that existed between them before the war, shall be, and the same are hereby, renewed.

ARTICLE 3. The undersigned chiefs and warriors, for themselves and their said tribe or nation, do hereby acknowledge themselves and their tribe or nation to be under the protection of the United States, and of no other nation, power, or sovereign, whatsoever.

In witness whereof, the said William Clark, Ninian Edwards, and Auguste Chouteau, commissioners as aforesaid, and the chiefs and warriors of the aforesaid tribe or nation, have hereunto subscribed their names and affixed their seals, this twentieth day of July, in the year of our Lord one thousand eight hundred and fifteen, and of the Independence of the United States the fortieth.

William Clark, Ninian Edwards, Auguste Chouteau,

Oupaatanga, or the big elk, his x mark, Washcamanie, or the hard walker, his x mark, Kaaheeguia, or the old chief, his x mark, Waanowrabai, or the blackbird's grandson, his x mark, Osogagee, or the point maker, his x mark, Toireeehee, or the cow's rib, his x mark, Manshaquita, or the little soldier, his x mark, Pissinguai, or he who has no gall, his x mark,

Done at Portage des Sioux, in presence of:
R. Wash, secretary to the commission, Thos. Forsyth, Indian agent, John Miller, colonel Third Infantry, J.W. Johnson, Indian :agent, R. Paul, C. T. of the C. Louis Decouagne, Edw. Hall, lieutenant late Twenty-eighth Infantry, Louis Dorion, John A. Cameron, John B. Clark, adjutant Third Infantry, Jacques Mette, Manuel Lisa, agent

TREATY WITH THE OSAGE {1815, Sept. 12}
Ratified Dec. 26, 1815.

A treaty of peace and friendship, made and concluded between William Clark Ninian Edwards, and Auguste Chouteau, Commissioners Plenipotentiary of the United States of America, on the part and behalf of the said States, of the one part; and the undersigned King, Chiefs, and Warriors, of the Great and Little Osage Tribes or Nations, on the part and behalf of their said Tribes or Nations, of the other part.

THE parties being desirous of re-establishing peace and friendship between the United States and the said tribes or nations, and of being placed in all things,

Plains, West and Northwest Plateau Indian Treaties

and in every respect, on the same footing upon which they stood before the war, have agreed to the following articles:

ARTICLE 1. Every injury, or act of hostility, by one or either of the contracting parties against the other, shall be mutually forgiven and forgot.

ARTICLE 2. There shall be perpetual peace and friendship between all the citizens of the United States of America and all the individuals composing the said Osage tribes or nations.

ARTICLE 3. The contracting parties, in the sincerity of mutual friendship recognize, re-establish, and confirm, all and every treaty, contract, and agreement, heretofore concluded between the United States and the said Osage tribes or nations.

In witness whereof, the said William Clark, Ninian Edwards, and Auguste Chouteau, commissioners as aforesaid, and the king, chiefs, and warriors of the said tribes or nations have hereunto subscribed their names and affixed their seals, this twelfth day of September, in the year of our Lord one thousand eight hundred and fifteen, and of the independence of the United States the fortieth.

Wm. Clark, Ninian Edwards, Auguste Chouteau,

Teshuhimga, or white hair, his x mark, Caygaywachepeche, or the bad chief, his x mark, Couchestawasta, The one who sees far, his x mark, Gradamnsa, or iron kite, his x mark, Mahsa, his x mark, Wanougpacha, or he who fears not, his x mark,

The Little Osages:
Caggatanagga, the great chief, his x mark, Nechoumanu, the walking rain, his x mark, Watashinga, he who s done little, his x mark, Nehujamega, without ears, his x mark, Wahadanoe, of the Missouri tribe, his x ark, Asooga, the little horn, his x mark, Mathagrhra, the cutter, his x mark,

Done at Portage des Sioux, in the presence of
R. Wash, secretary of the commission, Thomas Levers, lieutenant colonel, commanding First Regiment, I. T., P. Chouteau, agent Osages, T. Paul, C. C. T., James B. Moore, captain. Samuel Whiteside, captain. Jno. W. Johnson, United States, factor and Indian agent, Maurice Blondeaux. Samuel Solomon, Noel Mograine, Interpreters. P. L. Chouteau, Daniel Converse, third lieutenant.

Plains, West and Northwest Plateau Indian Treaties

TREATY WITH THE SAUK {1815, Sept. 13}
Ratified Dec. 26, 1815.

A treaty of peace and friendship, made and concluded between William Clark, Ninian Edwards, and Auguste Chouteau, Commissioners Plenipotentiary of the United States of America, of the part and behalf of the said States, of the one part; and the undersigned Chiefs and Warriors of that portion of the Sac Nation of Indians now residing on the Missouri river, of the other part.

WHEREAS the undersigned chiefs and warriors, as well as that portion of the nation which they represent, have at all times been desirous of fulfilling their treaty with the United States, with perfect good faith; and for that purpose found themselves compelled, since the commencement of the late war, to separate themselves from the rest of their nation, and remove to the Missouri river, where they have continued to give proofs of their friendship and fidelity; and whereas the United States, justly appreciating the conduct of said Indians, are disposed to do them the most ample justice that is practicable; the said parties have agreed to the following articles:

ARTICLE 1. The undersigned chiefs and warriors, for themselves and that portion of the Sacs which they represent, do hereby assent to the treaty between the United States of America and the united tribes of Sacs and Foxes, which was concluded at St. Louis, on the third day of November, one thousand eight hundred and four; and they moreover promise to do all in their power to re-establish and enforce the same.

ARTICLE 2. The said chiefs and warriors, for themselves and those they represent, do further promise to remain distinct and separate from the Sacs of Rock river, giving them no aid or assistance whatever, until peace shall also be concluded between the United States and the said Sacs of Rock river.

ARTICLE 3. The United States, on their part, promise to allow the said Sacs of the Missouri river all the rights and privileges secured to them by the treaty of St. Louis beforementioned, and also, as soon as practicable, to furnish them with a just proportion of the annuities stipulated to be paid by that treaty; provided they shall continue to comply with this and their former treaty.

In witness whereof, the said William Clark, Ninian Edwards, and Auguste Chouteau, commissioners as aforesaid, and the aforesaid chiefs and warriors, have hereunto subscribed their names and affixed their seals, this thirteenth day of September, in the year of our Lord one thousand eight hundred and fifteen, and of the independence of the United States the fortieth.

Wm. Clark, Ninian Edwards, Auguste Chouteau,

Plains, West and Northwest Plateau Indian Treaties

Shamaga, or the lance, his x mark, Weesaka, or the Devil, his x mark, Catchemackeseo, the big Lagle, his x mark, Chekaqua, or he that stands by the tree, his x mark, Kataka, or the sturgeon, his x mark, Mecaitch, or the eagle, his x mark,

Done at Portage des Sioux, in the presence of-
R. Wash, secretary of the commission, Thomas Levers, lieutenant colonel commanding First Regiment I. T.
P. Chouteau, agent. T. Paul, C. C. T.,James B. Moore, captain, Noel Mograine, Interpreters, Daniel Converse, third lieutenant.

TREATY WITH THE FOXES {1815, Sept. 14}
Ratified Dec. 26, 1815.

A treaty of peace and friendship, made and concluded at Portage des Sioux between William Clark, Ninian Edwards, and Auguste Chouteau, Commissioners Plenipotentiary of the United States of America, on the part and behalf of the said States, of the one part; and the undersigned King, Chiefs, and Warriors, of the Fox Tribe or Nation, on the part and behalf of the said Tribe or nation, of the other part.

The parties being desirous of re-establishing peace and friendship between the United States and the said tribe or nation, and of being placed in all things, and in every respect, on the same footing upon which they stood before the war, have agreed to the following articles:

ARTICLE 1. Every injury or act of hostility by one or either of the contracting parties against the other, shall be mutually forgiven and forgot.

ARTICLE 2. There shall be perpetual peace and friendship between the citizens of the United States of America and all the individuals composing the said Fox tribe or nation.

ARTICLE 3. The contracting parties do hereby agree, promise, and oblige themselves, reciprocally, to deliver up all the prisoners now in their hands, (by what means soever the same may have come into their possession) to the officer commanding at Fort Clark, on the Illinois river, to be by him restored to their respective nations as soon as it may be practicable.

ARTICLE 4. The said Fox tribe or nation do hereby assent to, recognize, reestablish, and confirm, the treaty of St. Louis, which was concluded on the third day of November, one thousand eight hundred and four, to the full extent of their interest in the same, as well as all other contracts and agreements be-

Plains, West and Northwest Plateau Indian Treaties

tween the parties; and the United States promise to fulfil all the stipulations contained in the said treaty in favor of the said Fox tribe or nation.

In witness whereof, the said William Clark, Ninian Edwards, and Auguste Chouteau, commissioners as aforesaid, and the aforesaid king, chiefs and warriors of the Fox tribe or nation, aforesaid, have hereunto subscribed their names and affixed their seals this fourteenth day of September, in the year of our Lord one thousand eight hundred and fifteen, and of the independence of the United States the fortieth.

Wm. Clark, Ninian Edwards, Auguste Chouteau, Pierremaskkin, the fox who walks crooked, his x mark, Muckkatawagout, black cloud, his x mark, Namasosanamet, he who surpasses all others, his x mark, Waapaca, his x mark, Mackkatananamakee, the black thunder, his x mark, Pashechenene, the liar, his x mark, Aquoqua, the kettle, his x mark, Nemarqua, his x mark, Machenamau, the bad fish, his x mark, Pesotaka, the flying fish, his x mark,

Done at Portage des Sioux, in the presence of:
R. Wash, secretary to the commission, Thomas Levens, lieutenant colonel, commandant First Regiment, I. T., Samuel Whiteside, captain, Jno. W. Johnson, United States factor and Indian agent, Maurice Blondeaux.
Samuel Solomon, Noel Mograine, Interpreters. Daniel Converse, third lieutenant.

TREATY WITH THE IOWA {1815, Sept. 16}
Ratified Dec. 26,1815.

A treaty of peace and friendship, made and concluded at Portage des Sioux, between William Clark, Ninian Edwards, and Auguste Chouteau, Commissioners Plenipotentiary of the United States of America, on the part and behalf of the said States, of the one part; and the undersigned, King, Chiefs, and Warriors, of the Iaway Tribe or Nation, on the part and behalf of the said Tribe or Nation, of the other part.

The parties being desirous of re-establishing peace and friendship between the United States and the said tribe or nation, and of being placed in all things, and in every respect, on the same footing upon which they stood before the war, have agreed to the following articles:

ARTICLE 1. Every injury, or act of hostility, by one or either of the contracting parties against the other shall be mutually forgiven and forgot.

Plains, West and Northwest Plateau Indian Treaties

ARTICLE 2. There shall be perpetual peace and friendship between all the citizens of the United States and all the individuals composing the said Iaway tribe or nation.

ARTICLE 3. The contracting parties do hereby agree, promise, and oblige themselves, reciprocally to deliver up all the prisoners now in their hands, (by what means soever the same may have come into their possession) to the officer commanding at St. Louis, to be by him restored to their respective nations, as soon as it may be practicable.

ARTICLE 4. The contracting parties, in the sincerity of mutual friendship, recognize, re-establish, and confirm, all and every treaty, contract, and agreement, heretofore concluded between the United States and the said Iaway tribe or nation.

In witness whereof, the said William Clark, Ninian Edwards, and Auguste Chouteau, commissioners as aforesaid, and the aforesaid king, chiefs, and warriors, have hereunto subscribed their names and affixed their seals, this sixteenth day of September, in the year of our Lord one thousand eight hundred and fifteen, and of the independence of the United States the fortieth.

William Clark, Ninian Edwards, Auguste Chouteau,

Wyingwaha, or hard heart, his x mark, Wongehehronyne, or big chief, his x mark, Wonehee, or the slave, his x mark, Wohomppee, the broth, his x mark, Shongatong, the horse jockey, his x mark, Nahocheininugga, without ears, his x mark, Conja, the plumb, his x mark, Chahowhrowpa, the dew-lap, his x mark, Manuhanu, the great walker, his x mark,

Done at Fortage des Sioux, in the presence of
R. Wash, secretary to the commission. D.L.Bissel, brigadier-general. R. Paul, C. C. T. Samuel Brady, lieutenant. Geo. Fisher, surgeon, Illinois regiment. P. Chouteau, agent. Jno. W. Johnson, United States factor and Indian agent. Samuel Solomon, interpreter. Maurice Blondeaux. Louis Dorion. Dennis Julien. Jas. McCulloch, captain.

Plains, West and Northwest Plateau Indian Treaties

TREATY WITH THE KANSA {1815, Oct. 28}
Ratified Dec. 26,1818.

A treaty of peace and friendship, made and concluded at St. Louis between Ninian Edwards and Auguste Chouteau, Commissioners Plenipotentiary of the United States of America, on the part and behalf of the said States, of one part; and the undersigned Chiefs and Warriors of the Kanzas Tribe of Indians, on the part and behalf of their said Tribe, of the other part.

THE parties being desirous of re-establishing peace and friendship between the United States and their said tribe, and of being placed, in all things, and in every respect, upon the same footing upon which they stood before the late war between the United States and Great Britain, have agreed to the following articles:

ARTICLE 1. Every injury or act of hostility by one or either of the contracting parties against the other, shall be mutually forgiven and forgot.

ARTICLE 2. There shall be perpetual peace and friendship between all the citizens of the United States of America and all the individuals composing the said Kanzas tribe, and all the friendly relations that existed between them before the war shall be, and the same are hereby, renewed.

ARTICLE 3. The undersigned chiefs and warriors, for themselves and their said tribe, do hereby acknowledge themselves to be under the protection of the United States of America, and of no other nation, power, or sovereign, whatsoever.

In witness whereof, the said Ninian Edwards and Auguste Chouteau, commissioners as aforesaid, and the chiefs aforesaid, have hereunto subscribed their names and affixed their seals, this twenty-eighth day of October, in the year of our Lord one thousand eight hundred and fifteen, and of the independence of the United States the fortieth.

Ninian Edwards, Auguste Chouteau,

Cayezettanzaw, or the big chief, his x mark, Needapy, his x mark, Hazeware, or the buck elk running after the doe, his x mark, Wahanzasby, or the endless, his x mark, Cayebasneenzaw, or the little chief, his x mark, Manshenscaw, or the white plume, his x mark, Necolebran, or he who can smell a man, his x mark, Mannanedze, his x mark, Watankezaw, his x mark, Taritchu, or the cow's rib.

Done at St. Louis, in presence of:
R. Wash, secretary to the commission., R. Paul, C. T. of the C., Ja. Kennerly, C. Indian Department, Christian Witt, Gabriel S. Chouteau, ensign M. M., G.

Plains, West and Northwest Plateau Indian Treaties

H. Kennerly, Thomas Forsyth, Indian agent, Taylor Berry., Antoine Barada, Paul Desjardins, Interpreters.

TREATY WITH THE SAUK {1816, May 13}
Proclamation, Dec. 30, 1816.

A treaty of peace and friendship made and concluded at St.???? between William Clark, Ninian Edwards, and Auguste Chouteau, commissioners plenipotentiary of the United States of America, on the part and behalf of the said states, of the one part, and the undersigned chiefs and warriors of the Sacs of Rock river and the adjacent country, of the other part.

WHEREAS by the ninth article of the treaty of peace, which was concluded on the twenty-fourth day of December, eighteen hundred and fourteen, between the United States and Great Britain, at Ghent, and which was ratified by the president, with the advice and consent of the senate, on the seventeenth day of February, eighteen hundred and fifteen, it was stipulated that the said parties should severally put an end to all hostilities with the Indian tribes, with whom they might be at war, at the time of the ratification of said treaty; and to place the said tribes inhabiting their respective territories, on the same footing upon which they stood before the war: Provided, they should agree to desist from all hostilities against the said parties, their citizens or subjects respectively, upon the ratification of the said treaty being notified to them, and should so desist accordingly.

And whereas the United States being determined to execute every article of the treaty with perfect good faith, and wishing to be particularly exact in the execution of the article above alluded to, relating to the Indian tribes: The president, in consequence thereof, for that purpose, on the eleventh day of March, eighteen hundred and fifteen, appointed the undersigned William Clark, governor of Missouri territory, Ninian Edwards, governor of Illinois territory, and Auguste Chouteau, esq. of the Missouri territory, commissioners, with full power to conclude a treaty of peace and amity with all those tribes of Indians, conformably to the stipulations contained in the said article, on the part of the United States, in relation to such tribes.

And whereas the commissioners, in conformity with their instructions in the early part of last year, notified the Sacks of Rock river, and the adjacent country, of the time of the ratification of said treaty; of the stipulations it contained in relation to them; of the disposition of the American government to fulfil those stipulations, by entering into a treaty with them, conformably thereto; and invited the said Sacs of Rock river, and the adjacent country, to send forward a deputation of their chiefs to meet the said commissioners at Portage des Sioux, for the purpose of concluding such a treaty as aforesaid, between the United

Plains, West and Northwest Plateau Indian Treaties

States and the said Indians, and the said Sacs of Rock river, and the adjacent country, having not only declined that friendly overture, but having continued their hostilities, and committed many depredations thereafter, which would have justified the infliction of the severest chastisement upon them; but having earnestly repented of their conduct, now imploring mercy, and being anxious to return to the habits of peace and friendship with the United States; and the latter being always disposed to pursue the most liberal and humane policy towards the Indian tribes within their territory, preferring their reclamation by peaceful measures, to their punishment, by the application of the military force of the nationNow, therefore,

The said William Clark, Ninian Edwards, and Auguste Chouteau, commissioners as aforesaid, and the undersigned chiefs and warriors, as aforesaid, for the purpose of restoring peace and friendship between the parties, do agree to the following articles:

ARTICLE 1. The Sacs of Rock river, and the adjacent country, do hereby unconditionally assent to recognize, re-establish, and confirm the treaty between the United States of America and the United tribes of Sacs and Foxes, which was concluded at St. Louis, on the third day of November, one thousand eight hundred and four; as well as all other contracts and agreements, heretofore made between the Sac tribe or nation, and the United States.

ARTICLE 2. The United States agree to place the aforesaid Sacs of Rock river, on the same footing upon which they stood before the war; provided they shall, on or before the first day of July next, deliver up to the officer commanding at cantonment Davis, on the Mississippi, all the property they, or any part of their tribe, have plundered or stolen from the citizens of the United States, since they were notified, as aforesaid, of the time of the ratification of the late treaty between the United States and Great Britain.

ARTICLE 3. If the said tribe shall fail or neglect to deliver up the property aforesaid, or any part thereof, on or before the first day of July aforesaid, they shall forfeit to the United States all right and title to their proportion of the annuities which, by the treaty of St. Louis, were covenanted to be paid to the Sac tribe; and the United States shall for ever afterwards be exonerated from the payment of so much of said annuities as upon a fair distribution, would fall to the share of that portion of the Sacs who are represented by the undersigned chiefs and warriors.

ARTICLE 4. This treaty shall take effect and be obligatory on the contracting parties, unless the same shall be disapproved by the president and senate of the United States, or by the president only: and in the mean time all hostilities shall cease from this date.

Plains, West and Northwest Plateau Indian Treaties

In testimony whereof, the said William Clark, Ninian Edwards, and Auguste Chouteau, commissioners as aforesaid, and the undersigned chiefs and warriors as aforesaid, have hereunto set their hands and affixed their seals, this thirteenth day of May, one thousand eight hundred and sixteen.

Wm. Clark,Ninian Edwards, Auguste Chouteau,

Anowart, or the One who speaks, his x mark, Namawenanu, Or Sturgeon Man, his x mark, Nasawarku, or the Forks, his x mark, Namatchesa, or the Jumping Sturgeon, his x mark, Mealeseta, or Bad Weather, his x mark, Caskupwa, or the Swan whose wings crack when he flies, his x mark, Napetaka, or he who has a Swan's throat around his neck, his x mark, Mashashe, or the Fox, his x mark, Wapamukqua, or the White Bear, his x mark,

St. Louis, May 13th, 1816, Done in the presence of:
R. Wash, secretary to the commission, R. Paul, C. T. of the C., J. Bt. Caron, Samuel Solomon, Interpreters., Charles Wm.Hunter, Cerre, M. La Croix, Gayol de Guirano, Boon Ingels, Moses Scott, James Sawyer.

TREATY WITH THE SIOUX {1816, June 1}
Proclamation, Dec. 30, 1816.

A treaty of peace and friendship made and concluded at St. Louis, between William Clark, Ninian Edwards, and Auguste Chouteau, commissioners plenipotentiary of the United States of America, on the part and behalf of the said states, of the one part, and the undersigned chiefs and warriors, representing eight bands of the Siouxs, composing the three tribes called the Siouxs of the Leaf, the Siouxs of the Broad Leaf, and the Siouxs who shoot in the Pine Tops, on the part and behalf of their said tribes, of the other part.

The parties being desirous of re-establishing peace and friendship between the United States and the said tribes, and of being placed in all things, and in every respect, on the same footing upon which they stood before the late war between the United States and Great Britain, have agreed to the following articles:

ARTICLE 1. Every injury or act of hostility, committed by one or either of the contracting parties against the other, shall be mutually forgiven and forgot.

ARTICLE 2. There shall be perpetual peace and friendship between all the citizens of the United States, and all the individuals composing the aforesaid tribes; and all the friendly relations that existed between them before the war shall be, and the same are hereby, renewed.

26

Plains, West and Northwest Plateau Indian Treaties

ARTICLE 3. The undersigned chiefs and warriors, for themselves and their tribes respectively, do, by these presents, confirm to the United States all and every cession, or cessions, of land heretofore made by their tribes to the British, French, or Spanish government, within the limits of the United States or their territories; and the parties here contracting do, moreover, in the sincerity of mutual friendship, recognize, re-establish, and confirm, all and every treaty, contract, and agreement, heretofore concluded between the United States and the said tribes or nations.

ARTICLE 4. The undersigned chiefs and warriors as aforesaid, for themselves and their said tribes, do hereby acknowledge themselves to be under the protection of the United States, and of no other nation, power, or sovereign, whatsoever.

In witness whereof, the commissioners aforesaid, and the undersigned chiefs and warriors as aforesaid, have hereunto subscribed their names and affixed their seals, this first day of June, in the year of our Lord one thousand eight hundred and sixteen, and of the independence of the United States the fortieth.

William Clark, Ninian Edwards, Auguste Chouteau,

Oocus, the Watchman, his x mark, Pahataka, the Humming Bird, his x mark, Eaohungko, the Man who marches quick, his x mark, Medermee, the Muddy Lake, his x mark, Tatawaka, the Medicine Wind, his x mark, Warshushasta, the Bad Hail, his x mark, Eoshark, the Belly-Ache, his x mark, Tuquaacundup, the Doctor, his x mark, Onudokea, the Fluttering Eagle, his x mark, Tusarquarp, he that walks with a Cane, his x mark, Hapula, the fourth Son, his x mark, Marc4wachup, the Dancer, his x mark, Shantanggaup, the Big Tree, his x mark, Shongkaska, the White Big-cared Dog, his x mark,

Done at St. Louis, in the presence of:
R. Wash, secretary to the commission, R. Paul, C. T. of the C. Wm. O. Allen, captain U. S. Corps Artillery, H. S. Geyer, Joshua Norvell, judge advocate M. M. N. Boilvin, agent, Thomas Forsyth, India agent, Maurice Blondeaux, Henry Delorier, interpreter, Pierre Lapointe, interpreter

Plains, West and Northwest Plateau Indian Treaties

TREATY WITH THE WINNEBAGO {1816, June 3}
Proclamation, Dec. 30, 1816.

A treaty of peace and friendship made and concluded between William Clark, Ninian Edwards, and Auguste Chouteau commissioners plenipotentiary of the United States of America, on the part and behalf of the said states, of the one part, and the undersigned chiefs and warriors of that portion of the Winnebago tribe or nation residing on the Ouiscosin river, of the other part.

Whereas the undersigned chiefs and warriors, as well as that portion of the nation which they represent, have separated themselves from the rest of their nation, and reside in a village on the Ouisconsin river, and are desirous of returning to a state of friendly relations with the United States, the parties hereto have agreed to the following articles.

ARTICLE 1. Every injury or act of hostility, committed by one or either of the contracting parties against the other, shall be mutually forgiven and forgot; and all the friendly relations that existed between them before the late war, shall be, and the same are hereby, renewed.

ARTICLE 2. The undersigned chiefs and warriors, for themselves and those they represent, do by these presents, confirm to the United States all and every cession of land heretofore made by their nation to the British, French, or Spanish government, within the limits of the United States, or their territories; and also, all and every treaty, contract, and agreement, heretofore concluded between the United States and the said tribe or nation, as far as their interest in the same extends.

ARTICLE 3. The undersigned chiefs and warriors as aforesaid, for themselves and those they represent, do hereby acknowledge themselves to be under the protection of the United States, and of no other nation, power, or sovereign, whatsoever.

ARTICLE 4. The aforesaid chiefs and warriors, for themselves and those they represent, do further promise to remain distinct and separate from the rest of their tribe or nation, giving them no aid or assistance whatever, until peace shall also be concluded between the United States and the said tribe or nation.

ARTICLE 5. The contracting parties do hereby agree, promise, and oblige themselves, reciprocally, to deliver up all prisoners now in their hands (by what means soever the same may have come into their possession) to the officer commanding at Prairie du Chien, to be by him restored to the respective parties hereto, as soon as it may be practicable.

Plains, West and Northwest Plateau Indian Treaties

In witness whereof, the commissioners aforesaid, and the undersigned chiefs and warriors as aforesaid, have hereunto subscribed their names, and affixed their seals, this third day of June, in the year of our Lord one thousand eight hundred and sixteen, and of the independence of the United States, the fortieth.

William Clark, Ninian Edwards, Aug. Chouteau,

Nekousaa, the Main Channel, his x mark, Wapanoneker, theBear, his x mark, Opwarchickwaka, the Rain, is x mark, Chepurganika, the little Buffalo Head, his x mark,

Done at St. Louis, in the presence of:
R. Wash, secretary to the commission, R. Paul, C. T. of the C. Wm. O. Allen, captain U. S. Corps of Artillery, N. Boilvin, agent, Jacques Mette, interpreter.

TREATY WITH THE MENOMINEE {1817, March 30}
Proclamation, Dec. 26, 1817.

A treaty of peace and friendship made and concluded at St. Louis by and between William Clark, Ninian Edwards, and Auguste Chouteau, commissioners on the part and behalf of the United States of America, of the one part, and the undersigned chiefs and warriors, deputed by the Menomenee tribe or nation of Indians, on the part and behalf of their said tribe or nation, of the other part.

THE parties, being desirous of re-establishing peace and friendship between the United States and the said tribe or nation, and of being placed in all things, and in every respect, on the same footing upon which they stood before the late war, have agreed to the following articles:

ARTICLE 1. Every injury, or act of hostility, by one or either of the contracting parties, against the other, shall be mutually forgiven and forgot.

ARTICLE 2. There shall be perpetual peace and friendship between all the citizens of the United States and all the individuals composing the said Menomenee tribe or nation.

ARTICLE 3. The undersigned chiefs and warriors, on the part and behalf of their said tribe or nation, do, by these presents, confirm to the United States all and every cession of land heretofore made by their tribe or nation to the British, French, or Spanish, government, within the limits of the United States, or their territories; and also, all and every treaty, contract, and agreement, heretofore concluded between the said United States and the said tribe or nation.

Plains, West and Northwest Plateau Indian Treaties

ARTICLE 4. The contracting parties do hereby agree, promise, and oblige themselves, reciprocally, to deliver up all prisoners now in their hands (by what means soever the same may have come into their possession) to the officer commanding at Prairie du Chien, to be by him restored to the respective parties hereto, as soon as it may be practicable.

ARTICLE 5. The undersigned chiefs and warriors as aforesaid, for themselves and those they represent, do hereby acknowledge themselves to be under the protection of the United States, and of no other nation, power, or sovereign, whatsoever.

In witness whereof, the commissioners aforesaid, and the undersigned chiefs and warriors, as aforesaid, have hereunto subscribed their names and affixed their seals, this thirtieth day of March, in the year of our Lord one thousand eight hundred and seventeen, and of the independence of the United States the forty-first.

William Clark, Auguste Chouteau,

Towanapee, Roaring Thunder, his x mark, Weekay, the Calumet Eagle, his x mark, Muequomota, the Fat of the Bear, his x mark, Shashamanee, the Elk, his x mark, Penoname, the Running Wolf, his x mark,

Done at St. Louis, in the presence of
R. Wash, secretary to the commissioners, R. Graham, U. S. Indian agent for Illinois Territory, Nathaniel Mills, Samuel Solomon.

TREATY WITH THE OTO {1817, June 24}
Proclamation, Dec. 26, 1817.

A treaty of peace and friendship made and concluded between William Clark and Augusta Chouteau, commissioners on the part, and behalf of the United States of America, of the one part; and the undersigned chiefs and warriors, of the Ottoes tribe of Indians, on the part and behalf of their said tribe, of the other part.

THE parties being desirous of re-establishing peace and friendship between the United States and their said tribe and of being placed, in all things, and in every respect, upon the same footing upon which they stood before the late war between the United States and Great Britain, have agreed to the following articles:

ARTICLE 1. Every injury or act of hostility by one or either of the contracting parties against the other, shall be mutually forgiven and forgot.

Plains, West and Northwest Plateau Indian Treaties

ARTICLE 2. There shall be perpetual peace and friendship between all the citizens of the United States of America and all the individuals composing the said Ottoes tribe, and all the friendly relations that existed between them before the war, shall be, and the same are hereby, renewed.

ARTICLE 3. The undersigned chiefs and warriors, for themselves and their said tribe, do hereby acknowledge themselves to be under the protection of the United States of America, and of no other nation, power, or sovereign, whatsoever,

In witness whereof, the said William Clark and Auguste Chouteau, commissioners as aforesaid, and the chiefs aforesaid, have hereunto subscribed their names and affixed their seals, this twenty-fourth day of June, in the year of our Lord one thousand eight hundred and seventeen, and of the independence of the United States the forty-first.

William Clark, Auguste Choteau,
Ottoes: Chongatonga, Big Horse, his x mark, Histashone, Big Eyes, his x mark, Mihahande, Eldest daughter, his x mark, Mantoeignet, the Little Bow, his x mark, Wapontraska, White Nostrils, his x mark,
Missouries: Tarposta, Son of the Priest, his x mark, Kahhehpah, Crow Head, his x mark, Harahkraton, the Sparrow Hawk, his x mark, Chanohato, Buffalo Hump, his x mark,

Witnesses present:
Lewis Bissell, acting secretary, Manuel Lisa, United States Indian agent. Benjamin O'Fallon, United States Indian agent, Stephen Julien, United States Indian interpreter, Gabriel S. Chouteau, second Lutenant,M.M., Joseph Lafleche, interpreter, his x mark

TREATY WITH THE PONCA {1817, June 25}
Proclamation, Dec. 26, 1817.

Treaty of peace and friendship made and concluded between William Clark and Auguste Chouteau, commissioners on the part and behalf of the United States of America, of the one part, and the undersigned chiefs and warriors of the Poncarar tribe of Indians, on (their) part and of their said tribe of the other part.

THE parties being desirous of re-establishing peace and friendship between the United States and their said tribe, and of being placed, in all things and every respect, upon the same footing upon which they stood before the late war between the United States and Great Britain, have agreed to the following articles:

Plains, West and Northwest Plateau Indian Treaties

ARTICLE 1. Every injury or act of hostility by one or either of the contracting parties against the other, shall be mutually forgiven and forgot.

ARTICLE 2. There shall be perpetual peace and friendship between all the citizens of the United States of America and all the individuals composing the said Poncarar tribe; and all the friendly relations that existed between them before the war shall be, and the same are hereby, renewed.

ARTICLE 3. The undersigned chiefs and warriors, for themselves and their said tribe, do hereby acknowledge themselves to be under the protection of the United States of America, and of no other nation, power, or sovereign, whatever.

In witness whereof, the said William Clark and Auguste Chouteau, commissioners as aforesaid, have hereunto subscribed their names and affixed their seals, this twenty-fifth day of June, in the year of our Lord one thousand eight hundred and seventeen, and of the independence of the United States the forty-first.

William Clark, Auguste Chouteau,

Aquelaba, the Fighter, his xmark, Showeno, the Comer, his x mark, Bardegara, he who stands fire, his x mark,

Witnesses present:
Lewis Bissel, acting secretary to the commissioners, Manual Lisa, United States Indian agent, Benja. O'Fallon, United States Indian agent, Stephen Julien, United States Indian interpreter, Joseph Lafleche, interpreter.

TREATY WITH THE GRAND PAWNEE {1815, Aug. 17}

A treaty of peace and friendship made and concluded, by and between, William Clark and Auguste Chouteau, Commissioners of the United States of America, on the part and behalf of the said States, of the one part, and the undersigned chiefs and warriors of the Grand Pawnee tribe, on the part and behalf of their settled tribe, of the other part.

THE parties, being desirous of establishing peace and friendship between the United States and the said tribe, have agreed to the following articles:

ARTICLE 1. Every injury, or act of hostility, by one or either of the contracting parties against the other, shall be mutually forgiven and forgot.

32

Plains, West and Northwest Plateau Indian Treaties

ARTICLE 2. There shall be perpetual peace and friendship between all the citizens of the United States of America, and all the individuals composing the said Grand Pawnee tribe.

ARTICLE 3. The undersigned chiefs and Warriors, for themselves and their said tribe, do hereby acknowledge themselves to be under the protection of the United States of America and of no other nation, power, or sovereign, whatsoever.

ARTICLE 4. The undersigned chiefs and warriors, for themselves and the tribe they represent, do moreover promise and oblige themselves to deliver up, or cause to be delivered up, to the authority of the United States, (to be punished according to law) each and every individual of the said tribe, who shall, at any time hereafter, violate the stipulations of the treaty this day concluded between the said tribe and the said United States.

In witness whereof, the said William Clark and Auguste Chouteau, commissioners as aforesaid, and the said chiefs and warriors as aforesaid, have hereunto subscribed their names and affixed their seals, this eighteenth day of June, in the year of our Lord one thousand eight hundred and eighteen, and of the independence of the United States the forty-second.

Wm. Clark, Aug. Chouteau,

Teratuewit, the Bald Eagle, his x mark, Taheerish, the Soldier, his x mark, Petaperishta, Who wants to go to War, his x mark, Talawehouree, the Follower, his x mark, Tarraricarrawaa, the Grand Chief Big Hair, his x mark, Kagakereeouk, the Crow's Eye, his x mark, Latatorishhara, the Chief of the Shield, his x mark,

Done at St. Louis, in the presence of
R. Wash, secretary to the commission. R. Paul, colonel M. M. John O'Fallon, R. R. Jno. Rutland, sub-agent and trans., etc., A. L. Papin, interpreter. Wm. Grayson, I. T. Honore, interpreter. Stephin Julian, United States interpreter., Josiah Ramsey, Th. Robedout.

Plains, West and Northwest Plateau Indian Treaties

TREATY WITH THE NOISY PAWNEE {1818, June 19}
Proclamation, Jan. 7, 1819.

A treaty of peace and friendship, made and concluded by, and between, William Clark and Auguste Chouteau, Commissioners of the United States of America, on the part and behalf of the said States, of the one part, and the undersigned, chiefs and warriors of the Pitavirate Noisy Pawnee tribe, on the part and behalf of their said tribe, of the other part.

The parties, being desirous of establishing peace and friendship between the United States and the said tribe, have agreed to the following articles:

ARTICLE 1. Every injury or act of hostility by one or either of the contracting parties, against the other, shall be mutually forgiven and forgot.

ARTICLE 2. There shall be perpetual peace and friendship between all the citizens of the United States of America, and all the individuals composing the said Noisy Pawnee tribe.

ARTICLE 3. The undersigned chiefs and warriors, for themselves and their said tribe, do hereby acknowledge themselves to be under the protection of the United States of America, and of no other nation, power, or sovereign, whatsoever.

ARTICLE 4. The undersigned chiefs and warriors, for themselves and the tribe they represent, do moreover promise and oblige themselves to deliver up, or cause to be delivered up, to the authority of the United States, (to be punished according to law) each and every individual of the said tribe, who shall, at any time hereafter, violate the stipulations of the treaty this day concluded between the said Noisy Pawnee tribe and the said States.

In witness whereof, the said William Clark and Auguste Chouteau, commissioners as aforesaid, and the chiefs and warriors aforesaid, have hereunto subscribed their names, and affixed their seals, this nineteenth day of June, in the year of our Lord one thousand eight hundred and eighteen, and of the independence of the United States the forty-second.

Wm. Clark, Aug. Chouteau,

Taarakarukaishta, the Handsome Bird, his x mark, Lecoutswaroushtu, the Buffaloe Doctor, his x mark, Tacacatahekou, the Running Wolf, his x mark, Kewatookoush, the Little Fox, his x mark.

Plains, West and Northwest Plateau Indian Treaties

Done at St. Louis, in the presence of : R. Wash, secretary to the commission, R. Paul, colonel M. M. C. Interpreter, I. T. Honore, Indian Interpreter, S. Julian, United States Indian Interpreter, Josiah Ramsey, Wm. Grayson, John Robedout.

TREATY WITH THE PAWNEE REPUBLIC {1818, June 20}
Proclamation, Jan. 17, 1819.

A treaty of peace and friendship, made and concluded by, and between, William Clark and Auguste Chouteau, Commissioners of the United States of America, on the part and behalf of the said States, of the one art, and the undersigned, chiefs and warriors on the Pawnee Republic, on the part and behalf of their tribe, of the other part.

The parties, being desirous of establishing peace and friendship between the United States and the said tribe, have agreed to the following articles:

ARTICLE 1. Every injury or act of hostility, by one or either of the contracting parties, against the other, shall be mutually forgiven and forgot.

ARTICLE 2. There shall be perpetual peace and friendship between all the citizens of the United States of America, and all the individuals composing the said Pawnee tribe.

ARTICLE 3. The undersigned, chiefs and warriors, for themselves and their said tribe, do hereby acknowledge themselves to be under the protection of the United States of America, and of no other nation, power, or sovereign, whatsoever.

ARTICLE 4. The undersigned chiefs and warriors, for themselves and the tribe they represent, do moreover promise and oblige themselves to deliver up, or to cause to be delivered up, to the authority of the United States, (to be punished according to law) each and every individual of the said tribe who shall, at any time hereafter, violate the stipulations of the treaty this day concluded between the said Pawnee Republic and the said States.

In witness whereof, the said William Clark, and Auguste Chouteau, commissioners as aforesaid, and the chiefs and warriors aforesaid, have hereunto subscribed their names and affixed their seals, this twentieth day of June, in the year of our Lord one thousand eight hundred and eighteen, and of the independence of the United States the forty-second.

William Clark, Aug. Chouteau,
Petaheick, the Good Chief, his x mark, Pa, or the Elk. his x mark, Tetawiouche, Wearer of Shoes, his x mark,

Plains, West and Northwest Plateau Indian Treaties

Done at St. Louis, in the presence of
R. Wash, secretary of the commission, J.T. Honore, Indian interpreter, T. Paul, colonel M. M. C. Interpreter, S. Julian, United States Indian interpreter,- John Robedout.

TREATY WITH THE PAWNEE MARHAR {1818, June 22}
Proclamation, Jan. 5,1819.

A treaty of peace and friendship, made and concluded by, and between, William Clark and Auguste Chouteau, Commissioners of the United States of America, on the part and behalf of the said States, of the one part, and the undersigned, chiefs and warriors of the Pawnee Marhar tribe, on the part and behalf of their said tribe, of the other part.

THE parties, being desirous of establishing peace and friendship between the United States and the said tribe, have agreed to the following articles:

ARTICLE 1. Every injury or act of hostility, by one or either of the contracting parties, against the other, shall be mutually forgiven and forgot.

ARTICLE 2. There shall be perpetual peace and friendship between all the citizens of the United States of America, and all the individuals composing the said Pawnee tribe.

ARTICLE 3. The undersigned chiefs and warriors, for themselves and their said tribe, do hereby acknowledge themselves to be under the protection of the United States of America, and of no other nation, power, or sovereign, whatsoever.

ARTICLE 4. The undersigned chiefs and warriors, for themselves and the tribe they represent, do moreover promise and oblige themselves to deliver up, or to cause to be delivered up, to the authority of the United States, (to be punished according to law) each and every individual of the said tribe, who shall, at any time hereafter, violate the stipulations of the treaty this day concluded between the said Pawnee Marhar tribe and the said States.

In witness whereof, the said William Clark, and Auguste Chouteau, commissioners as aforesaid, and the chiefs and warriors aforesaid, have hereunto subscribed their names and affixed their seals, this twenty-second day of June, in the year of our Lord one thousand eight hundred and eighteen, and of the independence of the United States the forty-second.

Plains, West and Northwest Plateau Indian Treaties

Wm. Clark, Aug. Chouteau, Tarahautacaw, White Bull, his x mark, Tearilari Sacki, Red Hawk, his x mark, Lahehozrashea, the Presence Striker, his x mark, Tarara, the Scalp Bearer, his x mark, Teripakoo, the First of Soldiers, his x mark, Irarikau, the White Cow, his x mark,

Done at St. Louis, in the presence of
R. Wash, secretary to the commission, J. T. Honore, Indian interpreter, S. Julian, United States Indian interpreter, Wm. Grayson, Josiah Ramsey, John Robedout.

TREATY WITH THE QUAPAW {1818, Aug. 24}
Proclamation Jan. 5, 1819

A treaty of friendship, cession, and limits, made and entered into, this twenty-fourth day of August, eighteen hundred and eighteen, by, and between, William Clark and Auguste Chouteau, Commissioners on the part and behalf of the United States, of the one part, and the undersigned, chiefs and warriors of the Quapaw tribe or nation, on the part and behalf of their said tribe or nation, of the other part.

ARTICLE 1. The undersigned chiefs and warriors, for themselves and their said tribe or nation, do hereby acknowledge themselves to be under the protection of the United States, and of no other state, power, or sovereignty, whatsoever.

ARTICLE 2. The undersigned chiefs and warriors, for themselves and their said tribe or nation, do hereby, for, and in consideration of, the promises and stipulations hereinafter named, cede and relinquish to the United States, forever, all the lands within the following boundaries, viz: Beginning at the mouth of the Arkansaw river; thence extending up the Arkansaw, to the Canadian fork, and up the Canadian fork to its source; thence south, to Big Red river, and down the middle of that river, to the Big Raft; thence, a direct line, so as to strike the Mississippi river, thirty leagues in a straight line, below the mouth of Arkansaw; together with all their claims to land east of the Mississippi, and north of the Arkansaw river, included within the coloured lines 1, 2, and 3, on the above map,(*) with the exception and reservation following, that is to say: the tract of country bounded as follows:

Beginning at a point on the Arkansaw river, opposite the present post of Arkansaw, and running thence, a due southwest course, to the Washita river; thence, up that river, to the Saline fork; and up the Saline fork to a point, from whence a due north course would strike the Arkansaw river at the Little Rock; and thence, down the right bank of the Arkansaw, to the place of beginning: which said tract of land, last above designated and reserved, shall be surveyed and

Plains, West and Northwest Plateau Indian Treaties

marked off, at the expense of the United States, as soon as the same can be done with convenience, and shall not be sold or disposed of, by the said Quapaw tribe or nation, to any individual whatever, nor to any state or nation, without the approbation of the United States first had and obtained.

ARTICLE 3. It is agreed, between the United States and the said tribe or nation, that the individuals of the said tribe or nation shall be at liberty to hunt within the territory by them ceded to the United States, without hindrance or molestation, so long as they demean themselves peaceably, and offer no injury or annoyance to any of the citizens of the United States, and until the said United States may think proper to assign the same, or any portion thereof, as hunting grounds to other friendly Indians.

ARTICLE 4. No citizen of the United States, or any other person, shall be permitted to settle on any of the lands hereby allotted to, and reserved for, the said Quapaw tribe or nation, to live and hunt on; yet it is expressly understood and agreed on, by, and between, the parties aforesaid, that, at all times, the citizens of the United States shall have the right to travel and pass freely, without toll or exaction, through the Quapaw reservation, by such roads or routes as now are, or hereafter may be, established.

ARTICLE 5. In consideration of the cession and stipulations aforesaid, the United States do hereby promise and bind themselves to pay and deliver to the said Quapaw tribe or nation, immediately upon the execution of this treaty, goods and merchandise to the value of four thousand dollars, and to deliver, or cause to be delivered, to them, yearly, and every year, goods and merchandise to the value of one thousand dollars, to be estimated in the city or place, in the United States, where the same are procured or purchased.

ARTICLE 6. Least the friendship which now exists between the United States and the said tribe or nation, should be interrupted by the misconduct of individuals, it is hereby agreed, that, for injuries done by individuals, no private revenge or retaliation shall take place; but, instead thereof, complaints shall be made by the party injured, to the other; by the tribe or nation aforesaid, to the governor, superintendent of Indian affairs, or some other person authorized and appointed for that purpose; and by the governor, superintendent, or other person authorized, to the chiefs of the said tribe or nation. And it shall be the duty of the said tribe or nation, upon complaint being made, as aforesaid, to deliver up the person or persons, against whom the complaint is made, to the end that he or they may be punished, agreeably to the laws of the state or territory where the offence may have been committed; and, in like manner, if any robbery, violence, or murder, shall be committed on any Indian or Indians, belonging to the said tribe or nation, the person or persons so offending shall be tried, and, if found guilty, punished in like manner as if the injury had been done to a white man.

Plains, West and Northwest Plateau Indian Treaties

And it is further agreed, that the chiefs of the said tribe or nation shall, to the utmost of their power, exert themselves to recover horses, or other property, which may be stolen from any citizen or citizens of the United States, by any individual or individuals of the said tribe or nation; and the property so recovered, shall be forthwith delivered to the governor, superintendent, or other person authorized to receive the same, that it may be restored to the proper owner.

And in cases where the exertions of the chief shall be ineffectual in recovering the property stolen, as aforesaid, if sufficient proof can be obtained that such property was actually stolen by an Indian or Indians, belonging to the said tribe or nation, a sum, equal to the value, of the property which has been stolen, may be deducted, by the United States, from the annuity of said tribe or nation. And the United States hereby guaranty to the individuals of the said tribe or nation, a full indemnification for any horse or horses, or other property, which may be taken from them by any of their citizens: Provided, the property so stolen cannot be recovered, and that sufficient proof is produced that it was actually stolen by a citizen or citizens of the United States.

ARTICLE 7. This treaty shall take effect, and be obligatory on the contracting parties, as soon as the same shall have been ratified by the President of the United States, by and with the advice and consent of the Senate.

William Clarke, Aug. Chouteau,
Krakaton, or the Dry Man, his x mark, Hradapaa, or the Eagle's Bill, his x mark, Mahraka, or Buck Wheat, his x mark, Hontikani, his x mark, Tataonsa, or the Whistling Wind, his x mark, Mozatete, his x mark,

Done at St. Louis in the presence of-
R. Wash, Secretary to the commission, J. T. Honore, Indian Interpreter, Joseph Bonne, Interpreter, Julius Pescay, Stephen Julian, U. S. Indian Interpreter, James Loper, William P. Clark.

TREATY WITH THE PEORIA, ETC. {1818, Sept. 25}
Proclamation, Jan. 5, 1819.

A treaty made and concluded by, and between Ninian Edwards and Auguste Chouteau, commissioners on the part and behalf of the United States of America, of the one part, and the undersigned, principal chiefs and warriors of the Peoria, Kaskaskia, Mitchigamia, Cahokia, and Tamarois, tribes of the Illinois nation of Indians, on the part and behalf of the said tribes, of the other part.

WHEREAS, by the treaty made at Vincennes, on the thirteenth day of August, in the year of our Lord one thousand eight hundred and three, between the

Plains, West and Northwest Plateau Indian Treaties

United States, of the one part, and the head chiefs and warriors of the tribe of Indians commonly called the Kaskaskia tribe, but which was composed of, and rightfully represented, the Kaskaskia, Mitchigamia, Cahokia, and Tamarois, tribes of the Illinois nation of Indians, of the other part, a certain tract of land was ceded to the United States, which was supposed to include all the land claimed by those respective tribes, but which did not include, and was not intended to include, the land which was rightfully claimed by the Peoria Indians, a tribe of the Illinois nation, who then did, and still do, live separate and apart from the tribes abovementioned, and who were not represented in the treaty referred to above, nor ever received any part of the consideration given for the cession of land therein mentioned.

And whereas the said tribe of Peoria are now also disposed to cede all their land to the United States, and, for the purpose of avoiding any dispute with regard to the boundary of their claim, are willing to unite with the Kaskaskia, Mitchigamia, Cahokia, and Tamarois, tribes, in confirming the cession of land to the United States, which was made by the treaty above referred to, and in extending the cession so as to include all the land claimed by those tribes, and themselves, respectively:

ARTICLE 1. For which purpose the undersigned, head chiefs and warriors of the Peoria, Kaskaskia, Mitchigamia, Cahokia, and Tamarois, tribes of the Illinois nation of Indians, for the considerations hereinafter mentioned, do hereby relinquish, cede, and confirm, to the United States, all the land included within the following boundaries, viz: Beginning at the confluence of the Ohio and Mississippi rivers.

Thence, up the Ohio, to the mouth of Saline creek, about twelve miles below the mouth of the Wabash; thence, along the dividing ridge between the waters of said creek and the Wabash, to the general dividing ridge between the waters which fall into the Wabash and those which fall into the Kaskaskia river; thence, along the said ridge, until it reaches the waters which fall into the Illinois river; thence, a direct line to the confluence of the Kankakee and Maple rivers; thence, down the Illinois river, to its confluence with the Mississippi river, and down the latter to the beginning.

ARTICLE 2. It is mutually agreed, by the parties hereto, that all the stipulations contained in the treaty, above referred to, shall continue binding and obligatory on both parties.

ARTICLE 3. The United States will take the Peoria tribe, as well as the other tribes herein abovementioned, under their immediate care and patronage, and will afford them a protection as effectual, against any other Indian tribes, and against all other persons whatever, as is enjoyed by the citizens of the United States. And the said Peoria tribe do hereby engage to refrain from making war,

Plains, West and Northwest Plateau Indian Treaties

or giving any insult or offence, to any other Indian tribe, or to any foreign nation, without first having obtained the approbation and consent of the United States.

ARTICLE 4. In addition to two thousand dollars' worth of merchandize, this day paid to the abovementioned tribes of Indians, the receipt whereof is hereby acknowledged, the United States promise to pay to the said Peoria tribe, for the term of twelve years, an annuity of three hundred dollars, in money, merchandize, or domestic animals, at the option of the said tribe; to be delivered at the village of St. Genevieve, in the territory of Missouri.

ARTICLE 5. The United States agree to cede, to the said Peoria tribe, six hundred and forty acres of land, including their village on Black-water river, in the territory of Missouri; provided that the said tract is not included within a private claim; but should that be the case, then some other tract of equal quantity and value shall be designated for said tribe, at such place as the President of the United States may direct. And the said Peoria tribe hereby agree to accept the same, together with the presents now given them, and the annuity hereby promised them, as a full equivalent for all and every tract of land to which they have any pretence of right or title.

In testimony whereof, the commissioners aforesaid, and the undersigned chiefs and warriors as aforesaid, have hereunto subscribed their names and affixed their seals. Done at Edwardsville, in the State of Illinois, this twenty-fifth day of September, in the year of our Lord one thousand eight hundred and eighteen, and of the independence of the United States the forty-third.

Ninian Edwards, Aug. Chouteau,
Peorias:
Waw Peeshawkawnan, Shield, his x mark, Wassawcosangaw, Shine, his x mark, Wecomawkawnaw, his x mark, Keeshammy, or Cut off a Piece, his his x mark,
Kaskaskias: Louis Jefferson Decouagne, his x mark, Wawpamahwhawaw, or White Wolf, hisxmark, Awrawmapingeaw, or Whale, his x mark, Keemawassaw, of Little Chief, his x mark,
Mitchigamias:
Wackshinggaw, or Crooked Moon, his x mark, Keetawkeemawwaw, or Andrew, his x mark, Manggonssaw, his x mark,
Cahokias: Mooyawkacke, or Mercier, his x mark, Pemmeekawwattaw, or Henry, his x mark, Papenegeesawwaw, his x mark, Shopinnaw, or Pint, his x mark, Maysheeweerattaw, or Big Horn, his x mark,
Tamarois:
Mahkattamawweeyaw, Black Wolf, his x mark, Queckkawpeetaw, or Round Seat, his x mark,

Plains, West and Northwest Plateau Indian Treaties

In presence of
Pascal Cerre, secretary to the commissioners, N. Bucknett, Jacob Prickett,
Abraham Prickett, Josias Randie, Richard Brevoofield, Ebenezer Baldwin,
Robert Bogue, John H. Randie, R. Pulliam, Edmund Randie. John Gaither,

TREATY WITH THE OSAGE {1818, Sept. 25}
Proclamation, Jan. 7, 1819.

A treaty made and concluded by, and between, William Clark, governor of the
Missouri Territory, superintendent of Indian affairs, and commissioner in behalf of the United States, of the one part, and a full and complete deputation of
considerate men, chiefs, and warriors, of all the several bands of the Great and
Little Osaka nation, assembled in behalf of their said nation, of the other part,
have agreed to the following articles:

ARTICLE 1. WHEREAS the Osage nations have been embarrassed by the
frequent demands for property taken from the citizens of the United States, by
war parties, and other thoughtless men of their several bands, (both before and
since their war with the Cherokees) and as the exertions of their chiefs have
been ineffectual in recovering and delivering such property, conformably with
the condition of the ninth article of a treaty, entered into with the United States,
at Fort Clark, the tenth of November, one thousand eight hundred and eight;
and as the deductions from their annuities, in conformity to the said article,
would deprive them of any for several years, and being destitute of funds to do
that justice to the citizens of the United States which is calculated to promote a
friendly intercourse, they have agreed, and do hereby agree, to cede to the
United States, and forever quit claim to, the tract of country included within the
following bounds, to wit: Beginning at the Arkansaw river, at where the present
Osage boundary line strikes the river at Frog Bayou; then up the Arkansaw and
Verdigris, to the falls of Verdigris river; thence, eastwardly, to the said Osage
boundary line, at a point twenty leagues north from the Arkansaw river; and,
with that line, to the place of beginning.

ARTICLE 2. The United States, on their part, and in consideration of the
above cession, agree, in addition to the amount which the Osage do now receive in money and goods, to pay their own citizens the full value of such property as they can legally prove to have been stolen or destroyed by the said Osage, since the year one thousand eight hundred and fourteen: provided the same
does not exceed the sum of four thousand dollars.

ARTICLE 3. The articles now stipulated will be considered as permanent ad-
ditions to the treaties, now in force, between the contracting parties, as soon as
they shall have been ratified by the President of the United States of America,
by and with the advice and consent of the Senate of the said United States.

Plains, West and Northwest Plateau Indian Treaties

In witness whereof, the said William Clark, commissioner as aforesaid, and the considerate men and chiefs aforesaid, have hereunto subscribed their names, and affixed their seals, at St. Louis, this twenty-fifth day of September, in the year of our Lord one thousand eight hundred and eighteen, and of the independence of the United States the forty-third.

William Clark,
Theoucoudhe, his x mark, Nihecounache, his x mark, Voidenoche, his x mark, Conchestuvoilla, his x mark, Naquidatonga, his x mark, Voitanigau, his x mark, Huquevoire, his x mark, Honhonquecon, his x mark, Tanhemonny, his x mark,Sandhecaan, his x mark, Paheksaw, or the White Hairs, his x mark, Kohesegre, or the Great Tract, his x mark, Nichenmanee, or the Walking Rain, his x mark, Tadhesajaudesor, or the Wind, his x mark, Tahechiga, his x mark,

Signed, sealed, and delivered, in the presence of
Pierre Chouteau, Paul Loise, interpreter Osage, Pierre Menard, Indian agent, J.T. Honore, Indian interpreter, John Ruland, sub-agent, Meriwether Lewis Clark. P. L. Chouteau, interpreter,

TREATY WITH THE POTAWATOMI {1818, Oct. 2}
Proclamation, Jan., 15, 1819.

Articles of a treaty made and concluded at St. Mary's, in the state of Ohio, between Jonathan Jennings, Lewis Cass, and Benjamin Parke, commissioners of the United States, and the Potawatamie nation of Indians.

ARTICLE 1. The Potawatamie nation of Indians cede to the United States all the country comprehended within the following limits: Beginning at the mouth of the Tippecanoe river, and running up the same to a point twenty-five miles in a direct line from the Wabash riverthence, on a line as nearly parallel to the general course of the Wabash river as practicable, to a point on the Vermilion river, twenty-five miles from the Wabash river; thence, down the Vermilion river to its mouth, and thence, up the Wabash river, to the place of beginning. The Potawatamies also cede to the United States all their claim to the country south of the Wabash river.

ARTICLE 2. The United States agree to purchase any just claim which the Kickapoos may have to any part of the country hereby ceded below Pine creek.

ARTICLE 3. The United States agree to pay to the Potawatamies a perpetual annuity of two thousand five hundred dollars in silver; one half of which shall be paid at Detroit, and the other half at Chicago; and all annuities which, by

Plains, West and Northwest Plateau Indian Treaties

any former treaty, the United States have engaged to pay to the Potawatamies, shall be hereafter paid in silver.

ARTICLE 4. The United States agree to grant to the persons named in the annexed schedule, and their heirs, the quantity of land therein stipulated to be granted; but the land so granted shall never be conveyed by either of the said persons, or their heirs, unless by the consent of the President of the United States.

In testimony whereof, the said Jonathan Jennings, Lewis Cass, and Benjamin Parke, commissioners as aforesaid, and the sachems, chiefs, and warriors, of the Pattawatima tribe of Indians, have hereunto set their hands, at St. Mary's in the State of Ohio, this second day of October, in the year of our Lord one thousand eight hundred and eighteen, and of the independence of the United States the forty-third.

Jonathan Jennings, Lewis Cass, B. Parke,
Meetenwa, his x mark, Scomack, his x mark, Chewago, his x mark, Tuthinepee, his x mark, Jowish, his x mark, Cheebaas, his x mark, Checalk, his x mark, Metamice, his x mark, Eshcam, his x mark, Winemakoos, his x mark, Wistea, his x mark, Mowa, or Black Wolf, his x mark,

In presence of
James Dill, secretary tothe commissioners, William Turner, secretary, Jno. Johnson, Indian agent, B. F. Stickney, S. I. A., William Prince, Indian agent, John Conner, William Conner, interpreter, R. A. Forsyth, secretary of Indian affairs, Isaac Burnett, Benedict Th. Flaget, Bishop of Bardstown, G. Godfroy, Indian agent, John T. Chunn, major Third Infantry. P. Hackley, captain Third Infantry.

Schedule referred to in the foregoing treaty.
There shall be granted to James Burnett, Isaac Burnett, Jacob Burnett, and Abraham Burnett, two sections of land each; and to Rebecca Burnett and Nancy Burnett, one section of land each; which said James, John, Isaac, Jacob, Abraham, Rebecca, and Nancy, are children of Cakimi, a Potawatamie woman, sister of Topinioe, principal chief of the nation; and six of the sections herein granted, shall be located from the mouth of the Tippecanoe river, down the Wabash river, and the other six (five) sections shall be located at the mouth of Flint river. There shall be granted to Perig, a Potawatamie chief, one section of land on the Flint river, where he now lives. There shall also be granted to Mary Chatalie, daughter of Neebosh, a Potawatamie chief, one section of land, to be located below the mouth of Pine river.

Jonathan Jennings, Lewis Cass, B. Parke.

Plains, West and Northwest Plateau Indian Treaties

TREATY WITH THE OSAGE {1822, Aug. 31}
Proclamation, Feb. 13, 1823.

Articles of a Treaty, entered into and concluded at the United States Factory on the M. De Cigue Augt. by and between Richard Graham, Agent of Indian Affairs, authorized on the part of the United States for that purpose, and the Chiefs, Warriors, and Head Men, of the Tribes of Great and Little Osage Indians, for themselves and their respective Tribes, of the other part.

WHEREAS, by the second article of the Treaty made and entered into between the United States and the Great and Little Osage nation of Indians, concluded and signed at Fort Clark, on the Missouri, on the tenth day of November, one thousand eight hundred and eight, it is stipulated that the United States shall establish at that place, and permanently continue, at all seasons of the year, a well assorted store of goods, for the purpose of bartering with them on moderate terms for their peltries and furs: Now, we, the said Chiefs, Warriors, and Head Men, in behalf of our said Tribes, for and in consideration of two thousand three hundred and twenty-nine dollars and forty cents to us now paid in merchandise, out of the United States Factory, by said Richard Graham, on behalf of the United States, the receipt whereof is hereby acknowledged, do exonerate, release, and forever discharge, the United States from the obligation contained in the said second article above mentioned; and the aforesaid second article is, from the date hereof, abrogated and of no effect.

In witness whereof, the said Richard Graham and the chiefs, warriors, and head men, of the Great and Little Osage tribes, have hereunto set their hands and affixed their seals, this thirty-first day of August, in the year of our Lord one thousand eight hundred and twenty-two.

R. Graham,
Pahuska, or White Hair, head chief, B.O., his x mark, Neshmnoiny, or Walk in Rain, head chief, L. O., his x mark, Kahegewashinpisheh, his x mark, Wahchewahheh, his x mark, Grenatheh, his x mark, Neocheninkeh, his x mark, Tanwanhehe, his x mark, Wasabewangoudake, his x mark, Wathinsabbeh, his x mark,

In presence of
Paul Baillio, Robert Dunlap, C. De La Croix.

45

Plains, West and Northwest Plateau Indian Treaties

TREATY WITH THE SAUK AND FOXES {1822, Sept. 3}
Proclamation, Feb. 13, 1823.

Articles of a Treaty entered into and concluded at Fort Armstrong, by and between Thomas Forsyth, Agent of Indian affairs, authorized on the part of the United States for that purpose, of the one part, and the Chiefs, warriors, and Head Men, of the United Sac and Fox Tribes, for themselves and their Tribes, of the other part.

WHEREAS by the ninth article of the Treaty made and entered into between the United States and the Sac and Fox Tribes of Indians, con-chided and signed at Saint Louis, in the District of Louisiana, on the third day of November, one thousand eight hundred and four, it is stipulated, in order to put a stop to the abuses and impositions which are practised upon the said Tribes by the private traders, the United States will, at a convenient time, establish a trading house or factory, where the individuals of the said Tribes can be supplied with goods at a more reasonable rate than they have been accustomed to procure them. Now, We, the said Chiefs, Warriors, and head men of the said Tribes, for and in consideration of the sum of one thousand dollars to us, now paid in merchandise out of the United States Factory, by said Thomas Forsyth, on behalf of the United States, the receipt whereof is hereby acknowledged, do exonerate, release, and forever discharge, the United States from the obligation contained in the said ninth article above recited, and the aforesaid ninth article is, from the date hereof, abrogated and of no effect.

In witness whereof, the said Thomas Forsyth, and the chiefs, warriors, and head men, of the Sac and ,Fox tribes, have hereunto set their hands, and affixed their seals, this third day of September, in the year of our Lord one thousand eight hundred and twenty-two.

Thomas Forsyth, United States Indian Agent,
Pushee Paho, his x mark, Quash Quamince, his x mark, Nesowakee, his x mark, Keeocuck, his x mark,
In the presence of
S, Burbank, major, U. S. Army, P. Craig, assistant surgeon, U. S. Army, John Connelly, Louis Betelle, interpreter.

TREATY WITH THE SAUK AND FOXES {1824, Aug. 4}
Proclamation, Jan. 18, 1825.

To perpetuate peace and friendship between the United States and the Sock and Fox tribes or nations of Indians, and to remove all future cause of dissensions which may arise from undefined territorial boundaries, the President of the United States of America, by William Clark, Superintendent of Indian Affairs,

Plains, West and Northwest Plateau Indian Treaties

and sole Commissioner specially appointed for that purpose, of the one part, and the undersigned Chiefs and Head Men of the Sock and Fox tribes or nations, fully deputized to act for and in behalf of their said nations, of the other part, have entered into the following articles and conditions, viz:

ARTICLE 1. The Sock and Fox tribes or nations of Indians, by their deputations in council assembled, do hereby agree, in consideration of certain sums of money, &c. to be paid to the said Sock and Fox tribes, by the Government of the United States, as hereinafter stipulated, to cede and for ever quit claim, and do, in behalf of their said tribes or nations, hereby cede, relinquish, and forever quit claim, unto the United States, all right, title, interest, and claim, to the lands which the said Sock and Fox tribes have, or claim, within the limits of the state of Missouri, which are situated, lying, and being, between the Mississippi and Missouri rivers, and a line running from the Missouri, at the entrance of Kansas river, north one hundred miles to the Northwest corner of the state of Missouri, and from thence east to the Mississippi. It being understood, that the small tract of land lying between the rivers Desmoin and the Mississippi, and the section of the above line between the Mississippi and the Desmoin, is intended for the use of the half-breeds belonging to the Sock and Fox nations; they holding it, however, by the same title, and in the same manner, that other Indian titles are held.

ARTICLE 2. The Chiefs and Head Men who sign this convention, for themselves and in behalf of their tribes, do acknowledge the lands east and south of the lines described in the first article, so far as the Indians claimed the same, to belong to the United States, and that none of their tribes shall be permitted to settle or hunt upon any part of it, after the first day of ,January, 1826, without special permission from the Superintendent of Indian Affairs.

ARTICLE 3. It is hereby stipulated and agreed, on the part of the United States, as a full consideration for the claims and lands ceded by the Sock and Fox tribes in the first article, there shall be paid to the Sock and Fox nations, within the present year, one thousand dollars in cash, or merchandize; and in addition to the annuities stipulated to be paid to the Sock and Fox tribes by a former treaty, the United States do agree to pay to the said Sock tribe, five hundred dollars, and to the Fox tribe five hundred dollars, annually, for the term of ten succeeding years; and, at the request of the Chiefs of the said Sock and Fox nations, the Commissioner agrees to pay to Morice Blondeau, a half Indian of the Fox tribe, the sum of five hundred dollars, it being a debt due by the said nation to the aforesaid Blondeaux, for property taken from him during the late war.

ARTICLE 4. The United States engage to provide and support a Blacksmith for the Sock and Fox nations, so long as the President of the United States may think proper, and to furnish the said nations with such farming utensils and cat-

Plains, West and Northwest Plateau Indian Treaties

tle, and to employ such persons to aid them in their agriculture, as the President may deem expedient.

ARTICLE 5. The annuities stipulated to be paid by the 3d article, are to be paid either in money, merchandise, provisions, or domestic animals, at the option of the aforesaid tribes, and when the said annuities or part thereof is paid in merchandise, it is to be delivered to them at the first cost of the goods at St. Louis, free from cost of transportation.

ARTICLE 6. This treaty shall take effect and be obligatory on the contracting parties so soon as the same shall be ratified by the President of the United States, by and with the advice and consent of the Senate thereof.

In testimony whereof, the said William Clark, commissioner as aforesaid, and the chiefs and head men of the Sock and Fox tribes of Indians as aforesaid, have hereunto set their hands, at Washington City, this fourth day of August, in the year of our Lord one thousand eight hundred and twenty-four.

William Clark,
Socks:
Pah-sah-pa-ha, or Stubbs, his x mark, Kah-kee-kai-maik, or All Fish, his mark, Wash-kee-chai,or Crouching Eagle, his x mark, Kee-o-kuck, or Watchful Fox, his x mark, Kah-kee-kai-maik, or All Fish, his x mark, Sah-col-o-quoit, or Rising Cloud, his x mark,

Foxes:
Fai-mah, or the Bear, his x mark, Ka-pol-e-qua, or White Nosed Fox, Pea-mash-ka, or the Fox winding his x mark,his horn, his x mark, Kee-sheswa, or the Sun, his x mark,
Witnesses at signing:
Thomas L. McKenney, Maurice Blondeau, Jno. W. Johnson, Meriwether Lewis Clark, Noal Dashnay.

TREATY WITH THE IOWA {1824, Aug. 4}
Proclamation, Jan. 18, 1825.

Articles of a treaty made and concluded at the City of Washington, on the fourth day of August, one thousand eight hundred and twenty-four, between William Clark, Superintendent of Indian Affairs, being specially authorized by the President of the United States thereto, and the undersigned Chiefs and Head men, of the Ioway Tribe or Nation, duly authorized and empowered by the said nation.

Plains, West and Northwest Plateau Indian Treaties

ARTICLE 1. THE Ioway Tribe or Nation of Indians by their deputies, Ma-hos-kah, (or White Cloud)and Mah-ne-hah-nah, (or Great Walker) in Council assembled, do hereby agree, in consideration of a certain sum of money, &c. to be paid to the said Ioway Tribe, by the government of the United States, as hereinafter stipulated, to cede and forever, quit claim, and do, in behalf of their said Tribe, hereby cede, relinquish, and forever quit claim, unto the United States, all right, title, interest, and claim, to the lands which the said Ioway Tribe have, or claim, within the State of Missouri, and situated between the Mississippi and Missouri rivers and a line running from the Missouri, at the mouth or entrance of Kanzas river, north one hundred miles, to the northwest corner of the limits of the state of Missouri, and, from thence, east to the Mississippi.

ARTICLE 2. It is hereby stipulated and agreed, on the part of the United States, as a full compensation for the claims and lands ceded by the Ioway Tribe in the preceding article, there shall be paid to the said Ioway tribe, within the present year, in cash or merchandise, the amount of five hundred dollars, and the United States do further agree to pay to the Ioway Tribe, five hundred dollars, annually, for the term of ten succeeding years.

ARTICLE 3. The Chiefs and Head Men who sign this Treaty, for themselves, and in behalf of their Tribe, do acknowledge that the lands east and south of the lines described in the first article, (which has been run and marked by Colonel Sullivan) so far as the Indians claimed the same, to belong to the United States, and that none of their tribe shall be permitted to settle or hunt upon any part of it, after 1st day of January, one thousand eight hundred and twenty-six, without special permission from the Superintendent of Indian Affairs.

ARTICLE 4. The undersigned Chiefs, for themselves, and all parts of the Ioway tribe, do acknowledge themselves and the said Ioway Tribe, to be under the protection of the United States of America, and of no other sovereign whatsoever; and they also stipulate, that the said Ioway tribe will not hold any treaty with any foreign powers, individual state, or with individuals of any state.

ARTICLE 5. The United States engage to provide and support a blacksmith for the Ioway Tribe, so long as the President of the United States may think proper, and to furnish the said Tribe with such farming utensils and cattle, and to employ such persons to aid them in their agriculture, as the President may deem expedient.

ARTICLE 6. The annuities stipulated to be paid by the second article, to be paid either in money, merchandise, provisions, or domestic animals, at the option of the aforesaid Tribe; and when the said annuities, or any part thereof, is paid in merchandise, it is to be delivered to them at the first cost of the goods at St. Louis, free from cost of transportation.

Plains, West and Northwest Plateau Indian Treaties

ARTICLE 7. This Treaty shall take effect, and be obligatory on the contracting parties, so soon as the same shall be ratified by the President of the United States, by and with the advice and consent of the Senate thereof.

In testimony whereof, the said William Clark, commissioner as aforesaid, and the chiefs and head men of the Ioway tribe of Indians, as aforesaid, have hereunto set their hands the day and year first before written.

Wm. Clark,
Ma-hos-kah, (White Cloud) his x mark, Mah-ne-hah-nah, (Great Walker) his x mark,
Witnesses present:
Thos. L. McKenney, G. W. Kennerly, Indian agent, Law. Taliaferro, Indian agent at St. Peter's,

TREATY WITH THE QUAPAW {1824, Nov. 15}
Proclamation, Feb. 19, 1825.

Articles of a treaty between the United States of America and Quapaw Nation of Indians.

ARTICLE 1. The Quapaw Nation of Indians cede to the United States of America, in consideration of the promises and stipulations hereinafter made, all claim or title which they may have to lands in the Territory of Arkansas, comprised in the following boundaries, to wit: Beginning at a point on the Arkansas river, opposite to the Post of Arkansas, and running thence a due south-west course to the Ouachita river; and thence, up the same, to the Saline Fork; and up the Saline Fork, to a point from whence a due north-east course will strike the Arkansas river at Little Rock: and thence down the right (or south bank) of the Arkansas river to the place of beginning.

ARTICLE 2. In consideration of the cession made in the first article of this Treaty, by the aforesaid Chiefs and Warriors, the United States engage to pay to the four head Chiefs of the Quapaw Nation, the sum of five hundred dollars each, in consideration of the losses they will sustain by removing from their farms and improvements. The payment to be made at the time they receive their annuity for the year 1825. And, also, to the said nation, the sum of four thousand dollars, to be paid in goods, at the signing of this Treaty. And the United States also engage to pay to the Quapaw Nation, one thousand dollars in specie, annually, for the term of eleven years, in addition to their present annuity.

ARTICLE 3. The United States hereby guaranty to the said Nation of Indians, the same right to hunt on the lands by them hereby ceded, as was guarantied to

50

Plains, West and Northwest Plateau Indian Treaties

them by a Treaty, concluded at St. Louis, on the 24th of August, 1818, between the said Quapaw Nation of Indians and WILLIAM CLARK and AUGUSTE CHOTEAU, Commissioners on the part of the United States.

ARTICLE 4. The Quapaw Tribe of Indians will hereafter be concentrated and confined to the district of country inhabited by the Caddo Indians, and form a part of said Tribe. The said nation of Indians are to commence removing to the district allotted them, before the twentieth day of January, one thousand eight hundred and twenty-six.

ARTICLE 5. For the purpose of facilitating the removal of the said Tribe, to the district of country allotted them, and as a compensation for the losses sustained, and the inconveniences to which they may be exposed by said removal, the United States will furnish them with corn, meat, and salt, for six months, from the first day of January, one thousand eight hundred and twenty-six. The United States further agree to furnish a sum not exceeding one thousand dollars, to be expended by their agent, to facilitate the transportation of the said Tribe to the district of country herein assigned them. An Agent, Sub Agent, or Interpreter, shall be appointed to accompany said tribe, and to reside among them.

ARTICLE 6. From the cession aforesaid, there shall be reserved to JAMES SCULL, in consideration of a debt of seven thousand five hundred dollars, due to him from the Quapaw Nation, and recognized in open Council, two sections of land commencing on the Arkansas river, opposite to Mrs. Embree's, and running up and back from said river for quantity. And the United States guaranty to the Quapaw Nation the payment of the said debt of seven thousand five hundred dollars, either by the ratification of the grant made in this article, or by the payment of said amount in money, exclusive of the amount stipulated to be paid to the said nation by this treaty.

ARTICLE 7. There shall be granted by the United States, to the following persons, being Indians by descent, the following tracts of Land: To Francois Imbeau, one quarter section of land, commencing at a point on the Arkansas river, opposite the upper end of Wright Daniel's farm, and thence, up and back from said river, for quantity. To Joseph Duchassien, one quarter section of land, commencing at the lower corner of the quarter section granted to Francois Imbeau, and running down and back from said river for quantity. To Saracen, a half breed Quapaw, eighty acres of land, to be laid off so as to include his improvement, where he now resides, opposite Vaugine's. To Batiste Socie, eighty acres of land, laying above and adjoining Saracen's grant.

To Joseph Bonne, eighty acres of land, lying above and adjoining Socie's grant. To Baptiste Bonne, eighty acres of land, lying above and adjoining Joseph Bonne's grant. To Lewis Bartelmi, eighty acres of land, lying above and ad-

51

Plains, West and Northwest Plateau Indian Treaties

joining Baptiste Bonne's grant. To Antoine Duchassin, eighty acres of land, lying above and adjoining Bartelmi's grant. To Baptiste Irabeau, eighty acres of land, lying above and adjoining A. Duchassin's grant. To Francois Coupot, eighty acres of land, lying above and adjoining Baptiste Imbeau's grant,. To Joseph Valliere, eighty acres of land, lying above and adjoining Francois Coupot's grant. All the said tracts of land shall be laid off, so as to conform to the lines of the United States surveys, and binding on the Arkansas river.

ARTICLE 8. This treaty shall take effect, and be obligatory on the contracting parties, so soon as the same shall be ratified by the Senate of the United States.

In testimony whereof, the commissioner on the part of the United States, Robert Crittenden, and the undersigned chiefs and warriors of the said nation, have hereunto subscribed their names and affixed their seals.

Done at Harrington's, in the territory of Arkansas, on the fifteenth day of November, A. D. one thousand eight hundred and twenty-four, and of the independence of the United States the forty-ninth.

Robert Crittenden, Commissioner on the part of the United States,
Hepahdagonneh, his x mark, Wahehsonjekah, his x mark, Gratonjekah, his x mark, Watuhtezka, his x mark, Dohkuhnonjeshu, his x mark, Kahtahkonku, his x mark, Hahcrontenah, his x mark,

Signed, sealed, and witnessed in presence of
Thomas W. Newton, secretary to the commission, Robert C. Oden, lieutenant-colonel Second Regiment Arkansas Militia, F. Farrelly, adjutant-general of Arkansas, Militia, B. Harrington., D. Barber, S. Agt. to the Osages, Joseph Duchassin, interpreter.

TREATY WITH THE OSAGE {1825, June 2}
Proclamation, Dec. 30, 1825.

Articles of a treaty made and concluded at St. Louis, in the State of Missouri, between William Clark, Superintendent of Indian Affairs, Commissioner on the part of the United States, and the undersigned, Chiefs, Head-Men, and Warriors, of the Great and Little Osage Tribes of Indians, duly authorized and empowered by their respective Tribes or Nations.

IN order more effectually to extend to said Tribes that protection of the Government so much desired by them, it is agreed as follows:

ARTICLE 1. The Great and Little Osage Tribes or Nations do, hereby, cede and relinquish to the United States, all their right, title, interest, and claim, to

Plains, West and Northwest Plateau Indian Treaties

lands lying within the State of Missouri and Territory of Arkansas, and to all lands lying West of the said State of Missouri and Territory of Arkansas, North and West of the Red River, South of the Kansas River, and East of a line to be drawn from the head sources of the Kansas, Southwardly through the Rock Saline, with such reservations, for such considerations, and upon such terms as are hereinafter specified, expressed, and provided for.

ARTICLE 2. Within the limits of the country, above ceded and relinquished, there shall be reserved, to, and for, the Great and Little Osage Tribes or Nations, aforesaid, so long as they may choose to occupy the same, the following described tract of land: beginning at a point due East of White Hair's Village, and twenty-five miles West of the Western boundary line of the State of Missouri, fronting on a North and South line, so as to leave ten miles North, and forty miles South, of the point of said beginning, and extending West, with the width of fifty miles, to the Western boundary of the lands hereby ceded and relinquished by said Tribes or Nations; which said reservations shall be surveyed and marked, at the expense of the United States, and upon which, the Agent for said Tribes or Nations and all persons attached to said agency, as, also, such teachers and instructors, as the President may think proper to authorize and permit, shall reside, and shall occupy, and cultivate, without interruption or molestation, such lands as may be necessary for them.

And the United States do, hereby, reserve to themselves, forever, the right of navigating, freely, all water courses and navigable streams, within or running through, the tract of country above reserved to said Tribes or Nations.

ARTICLE 3. In consideration of the cession and relinquishment, aforesaid, the United States do, hereby, agree to pay to the said tribes or nations, yearly, and every year, for twenty years, from the date of these presents, the sum of seven thousand dollars, at their Village, or at St. Louis, as the said tribes or nations may desire, either in money, merchandise, provisions, or domestic animals, at their option. And whenever the said annuity, or any part thereof, shall be paid in merchandise, the same is to be delivered to them at the first cost of the goods at St. Louis, free of transportation.

ARTICLE 4. The United States shall, immediately, upon the ratification of this convention, or as soon thereafter as may be, cause to be furnished to the tribes or nations, aforesaid, six hundred head of cattle, six hundred hogs, one thousand domestic fowls, ten yoke of oxen, and six carts, with such farming utensils as the Superintendent of Indian Affairs may think necessary, and shall employ such persons to aid them in their agricultural pursuits, as to the President of the United States may seem expedient, and shall, also, provide, furnish, and support for them, one blacksmith, that their farming utensils, tools, and arms, may be seasonably repaired; and shall build, for each of the four principal chiefs, at their respective villages, a comfortable and commodious dwelling house.

53

Plains, West and Northwest Plateau Indian Treaties

ARTICLE 5. From the above lands ceded and relinquished, the following reservations, for the use of the half-breeds, hereafter named, shall be made, to wit: One section, or six hundred and forty acres, for Augustus Clermont, to be located and laid off so as to include Joseph Rivar's residence, on the East side of the Neosho, a short distance above the Grand Saline, and not nearer than within one mile thereof; one section for each of the following half-breeds: James, Paul, Henry, Rosalie, Anthony, and Amelia, the daughter of She-me-hunga, and Amelia, the daughter of Mi-hun-ga, to be located two miles below the Grand Saline, and extending down the Neosho, on the East side thereof; and one section for Noel Mongrain, the son of Wa-taw-nagres, and for each of his ten children, Baptiste, Noel, Francis, Joseph, Mongrain, Louis, Victoria, Sophia, Julia, and Juliet: and the like quantity for each of the following named grandchildren, of the said Noel Mongrain, to wit: Charles, Francis, Louisson, and Wash, to commence on the Marias des Cygnes, where the Western boundary line of the State of Missouri crosses it at the fork of Mine river, and to extend up Mine river.

For quantity: one section for Mary Williams, and one for Sarah Williams, to be located on the North side of the Marias des Cygnet, at the Double Creek, above Harmony; one section, for Francis T. Chardon; one section, for Francis C. Tayon; one section, for James G. Chouteau; one section, for Alexander Chouteau; one section, for Pelagie Antaya; one section, for Celeste Antaya; one section, for Joseph Antaya; one section, for Baptiste St. Mitchelle, jr.; one section, for Louis St. Mitchelle; one section, for Victoria St. Mitchelle; one section, for Julia St. Mitchelle; one section, for Francis St. Mitchelle; one section, for Joseph Perra; one section, for Susan Larine; one section, for Marguerite Reneau; one section, for Thomas L. Balio; and one section, for Terese, the daughter of Paul Louise; which said several tracts are to be located on the North side of the Marias des Cygnes, extending up the river, above the reservations in favor of Mary and Sarah Williams, in the order in which they are herein above named.

ARTICLE 6. And also fifty-four other tracts, of a mile square each, to be laid off under the direction of the President of the United States, and sold, for the purpose of raising a fund to be applied to the support of schools, for the education of the Osage children, in such manner as the President may deem most advisable to the attainment of that end.

ARTICLE 7. Forasmuch as there is a debt due, from sundry individuals of the Osage tribes or nations, to the United States trading houses, of the Missouri and Osage rivers, amounting in the whole, to about the sum of four thousand one hundred and five dollars and eighty cents. which the United States do hereby agree to release; in consideration thereof, the said tribes or nations do, hereby, release and relinquish their claim upon the United States, for regular troops to

Plains, West and Northwest Plateau Indian Treaties

be stationed, for their protection, in garrison, at Fort Clark, and, also, for furnishing of a blacksmith, at that place, and the delivery of merchandise, at Fire Prairie, as is provided for in the first, third, and fifth, articles of the Treaty, concluded on the tenth day of November, one thousand eight hundred and eight.

ARTICLE 8. It appearing that the Delaware nation have various claims against the Osages, which the latter have not had it in their power to adjust, and the United States being desirous to settle, finally and satisfactorily, all demands and differences between the Delawares and Osages, do hereby agree to pay to the Delawares, in full satisfaction of all their claims and demands against the Osages, the sum of one thousand dollars.

ARTICLE 9. With a view to quiet the animosities, which at present exist between a portion of the citizens of Missouri and Arkansas and the Osage tribes, in consequence of the lawless depredations of the latter, the United States do, furthermore, agree to pay, to their own citizens, the full value of such property, as they can legally prove to have been stolen or destroyed, by the Osages, since the year eighteen hundred and eight, and for which payment has not been made under former treaties: Provided, The sum to be paid by the United States does not exceed the sum of five thousand dollars.

ARTICLE 10. It is furthermore agreed on, by and between the parties to these presents, that there shall be reserved two sections of land, to include the Harmony Missionary establishment, and their mill, on the Marias des Cygne; and one section, to include the Missionary establishment, above the Lick on the West side of Grand river, to be disposed of as the President of the United States shall direct, for the benefit of said Missions, and to establish them at the principal villages of the Great and Little Osage Nations, within the limits of the country reserved to them by this Treaty, and to be kept up at said villages, so long as said Missions shall be usefully employed in teaching, civilizing, and improving, the said Indians.

ARTICLE 11. To preserve and perpetuate the friendship now happily subsisting between the United States and the said tribes or nations, it is hereby agreed, that the provisions contained in the ninth article of the Treaty concluded and signed at fort Clark, on the tenth day of November, one thousand eight hundred and eight, between the United States and the said tribes or nations, shall, in every respect, be considered as in full force and applicable to the provisions of this Treaty, and that the United States shall take and receive, into their friendship and protection, the aforesaid tribes or nations, and shall guaranty to them, forever, the right to navigate, freely, all water-courses, or navigable streams, within the tract of country hereby ceded, upon such terms as the same are or may be navigated by the citizens of the United States.

55

Plains, West and Northwest Plateau Indian Treaties

ARTICLE 12. It is further agreed, that there shall be delivered as soon as may be, after the execution of this treaty, at the Osage villages, merchandise to the amount of four thousand dollars, first cost, in St. Louis, and two thousand dollars in merchandise, before their departure from this place; and horses and equipage, to the value of twenty-six hundred dollars; which, together with the sum of one hundred dollars, to be paid to Paul Loise, and the like sum to Baptiste Mongrain, in money, shall be in addition to the provisions and stipulations hereby above contained, in full satisfaction of the cession, hereinbefore agreed on.

ARTICLE 13. Whereas the Great and Little Osage tribes or nations are indebted to Augustus P. Chouteau, Paul Balio, and William S. Williams, to a large amount, for credits given to them, which they are unable to pay, and have particularly requested to have paid, or provided for, in the present negotiation; it is, therefore, agreed on, by and between the parties to these presents, that the United States shall pay to Augustus P. Chouteau, one thousand dollars; to Paul Balio, two hundred and fifty dollars, and to William S. Williams two hundred and fifty dollars, towards the liquidation of their respective debts due from the said tribes or nations.

ARTICLE 14. These articles shall take effect, and become obligatory on the contracting parties, so soon as the same shall be ratified by the President, by and with the advice and consent of the Senate of the United States.

In testimony whereof, the said William Clark, commissioner as aforesaid, and the deputation, chiefs, and head men, and warriors, of the Great and Little Osage nations of Indians, as aforesaid, have hereunto set their hands and seals, this second day of June, in the year of our Lord one thousand eight hundred and twenty-five, and of the independence of the United States the forty-ninth.

William Clark.

Clairmont, his x mark, Pahusca, or White Hair, his x mark, Chingawasa, or Handsome Bird, his x mark, Manchuhonga, his x mark, Chongaishonga, his x mark, Tawangahais, His x mark, Ponkchinga, his x mark, Nicohibran, his x mark, Panimonpachais, his x mark, Tawangahe, his x mark, Paigaismanie, or Big Soldier, his x mark,
Little Osages:
Nichumani, or Walking Rain, his x mark, Nihuchaisningaiswachinpichais, his x mark, Waruhagais, his x mark, Mangaisehis, his x mark, Mances'tpogran, his x mark, Nonbaaheri, his x mark,

Witnesses present:
R. Wash, secretary, Edward Coles, governor of Illinois, A. McNair, Osage agent, Pr. Chouteau, W. B. Alexander, sub Indian agent, Theodore Hunt, Cerre,

Plains, West and Northwest Plateau Indian Treaties

P. L. Chouteau sub agent, L. T. Honorie, interpreter, F. A. Chardon, Antonie Leclaire interpreter, James Coleman, Paul Louise, his x mark, interpreter, (Osages)

TREATY WITH THE KANSA {1825, June 3}
Proclamation, Dec. 30, 1825.

Articles of a treaty made and concluded at the City of Saint Louis, in the State of Missouri, between William Clark, Superintendent of Indian Affairs, Commissioner on the part of the United States of America, and the undersigned Chiefs, Head Men, and Warriors of the Kansas Nation of Indians, duly authorized and empowered by said Nation.

ARTICLE 1. THE Kansas do hereby cede to the United States all the lands lying within the State of Missouri, to which the said nation have title or claim; and do further cede and relinquish, to the said United States, all other lands which they now occupy, or to which they have title or claim, lying West of the said State of Missouri, and within the following boundaries: beginning at the entrance of the Kansas river into the Missouri river; from thence North to the North-West corner of the State of Missouri; from thence Westwardly to the Nodewa river, thirty miles from its entrance into the Missouri; from thence to the entrance of the big Nemahaw river into the Missouri, and with that river to its source; from thence to the source of the Kansas river, leaving the old village of the Pania Republic to the West; from thence, on the ridge dividing the waters of the Kansas river from those of the Arkansas, to the Western boundary of the State line of Missouri and with that line, thirty miles, to the place of beginning.

ARTICLE 2. From the cession aforesaid, the following reservation for the use of the Kansas nation of Indians shall be made, of a tract of land, to begin twenty leagues up the Kansas river, and to include their village on that river; extending West thirty miles in width, through the lands ceded in the first Article, to be surveyed and marked under the direction of the President, and to such extent as he may deem necessary, and at the expense of the United States. The agents for the Kansas, and the persons attached to the agency, and such teachers and instructors as the President shall authorize to reside near the Kansas, shall occupy, during his pleasure, such lands as may be necessary for them within this reservation.

ARTICLE 3. In consideration of the cession of land and relinquishments of claims, made in the first Articles, the United States agree to pay to the Kansas nation of Indians, three thousand five hundred dollars per annum, for twenty successive years, at their villages, or at the entrance of the Kansas river, either in money, merchandise, provisions, or domestic animals, at the option of the aforesaid Nation; and when the said annuities, or any part thereof., is paid in

Plains, West and Northwest Plateau Indian Treaties

merchandise, it shall be delivered to them at the first cost of the goods in Saint Louis, free of transportation.

ARTICLE 4. The United States, immediately upon the ratification of this convention, or as soon thereafter as may be, shall cause to be furnished to the Kansas Nation, three hundred head of cattle, three hundred hogs, five hundred domestic fowls, three yoke of oxen, and two carts, with such implements of agriculture as the Superintendant of Indian Affairs may think necessary; and shall employ such persons to aid and instruct them in their agriculture, as the President of the United States may deem expedient; and shall provide and support a blacksmith for them.

ARTICLE 5. Out of the lands herein ceded by the Kanzas Nation to the United States, the Commissioner aforesaid, in behalf of the said United States, doth further covenant and agree, that thirty-six sections of good lands, on the Big Blue river, shall be laid out under the direction of the President of the United States, and sold for the purpose of raising a fund, to be applied, under the direction of the President, to the support of schools for the education of the Kanzas children, within their Nation.

ARTICLE 6. From the lands above ceded to the United States, there shall be made the following reservations, of one mile square, for each of the half breeds of the Kanzas nation, viz: For Adel and Clement, the two children of Clement; for Josette, Julie, Pelagie, and Victoire, the four children of Louis Gonvil; for Marie and Lafleche, the two children of Baptiste of Gonvil; for Laventure, the son of Francis Laventure; for Elizabeth and Pierre Carbonau, the children of Pierre Brisa; for Louis Joncas; for Basil Joncas; for James Joncas; for Elizabeth Datcherute, daughter of Baptiste Datcherute; for Joseph Butler; for William Rodgers; for Joseph Coté; for the four children of Cicili Compáre, each one mile square; and one for Joseph James, to be located on the North side of the Kanzas river, in the order above named, commencing at the line of the Kanzas reservation, and extending down the Kanzas river for quantity.

ARTICLE 7. With the view of quieting all animosities which may at present exist between a part of the white citizens of Missouri and the Kanzas nation, in consequence of the lawless depredations of the latter, the United States do further agree to pay their own citizens, the full value of such property as they can legally prove to have been stolen or destroyed since the year 1815: Provided, The sum so to be paid by the United States shall not exceed the sum of three thousand dollars.

ARTICLE 8. And whereas the Kanzas are indebted to Francis G. Choteau, for credits given them in trade, which they are unable to pay, and which they have particularly requested to have included and settled in the present Treaty; it is, therefore, agreed on, by and between the parties to these presents, that the sum

Plains, West and Northwest Plateau Indian Treaties

of five hundred dollars, towards the liquidation of said debt, shall be paid by the United States to the said Francois G. Choteau.

ARTICLE 9. There shall be selected at this place such merchandise as may be desired, amounting to two thousand dollars, to be delivered at the Kanzas river, with as little delay as possible; and there shall be paid to the deputation now here, two-thousand dollars in merchandise and horses, the receipt of which is hereby acknowledged; which, together with the amount agreed on in the 3d and 4th articles, and the provisions made in the other articles of this Treaty, shall be considered as a full compensation for the cession herein made.

ARTICLE 10. Lest the friendship which is now established between the United States and the said Indian Nation should be interrupted by the misconduct of Individuals, it is hereby agreed, that for injuries done by individuals, no private revenge or retaliation shall take place, but instead thereof, complaints shall be made by the party injured, to the other by the said nation, to the Superintendent, or other person appointed by the President to the Chiefs of said nation. And it shall be the duty of the said Chiefs, upon complaints being made as aforesaid, to deliver up the person or persons against whom the complaint is made, to the end that he or they may be punished, agreeably to the laws of the State or Territory where the offence may have been committed.

And in like manner, if any robbery, violence, or murder, shall be committed on any Indian or Indians belonging to said nation, the person or persons so offending shall be tried, and, if found guilty, shall be punished in like manner as if the injury had been done to a white man. And it is agreed, that the Chiefs of the Kanzas shall, to the utmost of their power, exert themselves to recover horses or other property which may be stolen from any citizen or citizens of the United States, by any individual or individuals of the Nation; and the property so recovered shall be forthwith delivered to the Superintendent, or other person authorized to receive it, that it may be restored to its proper owner; and in cases where the exertions of the Chiefs shall be ineffectual in recovering the property stolen as aforesaid, if sufficient proof can be adduced that such property was actually stolen, by any Indian or Indians belonging to the said nation, the Superintendent or other officer may deduct from the annuity of the said nation a sum equal to the value of the property which has been stolen.

And the United States hereby guarantee, to any Indian or Indians, a full indemnification for any horses or other property which may be stolen from them by any of their citizens: Provided, That the property so stolen cannot be recovered, and that sufficient proof is produced that it was actually stolen by a citizen of the United States. And the said Nation of Kanzas engage, on the requisition or demand of the President of the United States, or of the Superintendent, to deliver up any white man resident amongst them.

Plains, West and Northwest Plateau Indian Treaties

ARTICLE 11. It is further agreed on, by and between the parties to these presents, that the United States shall forever enjoy the right to navigate freely all water courses or navigable streams within the limits of the tract of country herein reserved to the Kanzas Nation; and that the said Kanzas Nation shall never sell, relinquish, or in any manner dispose of the lands herein reserved, to any other nation, person or persons whatever, without the permission of the United States for that purpose first had and obtained. And shall ever remain under the protection of the United States, and in friendship with them.

ARTICLE 12. This Treaty shall take effect, and be obligatory on the contracting parties, as soon as the same shall be ratified by the President, by and with the consent and advice of the Senate of the United States.

In testimony whereof, the said William Clark, commissioner as aforesaid, and the deputation, chiefs, head men, and warriors of the Kanzas nation of Indians, as aforesaid, have hereunto set their hands and seals, this third day of June, in the year of our Lord eighteen hundred and twenty-five, and of the independence of the United States of America the forty-ninth year.

William Clark,
Nom-pa-wa-rah, or the White Plume, his x mark, Ky-he-ga-wa-ti-nin-ka, or the Full Chief, his x mark, Ky-he-ga-wa-che-he, his x mark, or the Chief of great valor,

Witnesses present:
R. Wash, secretary, W. B. Alexander, sub Indian agent, John F. A. Sanford, G. C. Sibley, United States Commissioner, O-pa-she-ga, his x mark, or the Cooper, Cha-ho-nush, his x mark, Paul Louise, his x mark, Osage interpreter, Noel Dashnay, interpreter, Ant. Le Claire.

TREATY WITH THE PONCA {1825, June 9}
Proclamation, Feb. 6, 1826.

FOR the purposes of perpetuating the friendship which-has heretofore existed, as also to remove all future cause of discussion or dissension, as it respects trade and friendship between the United States and their citizens, and the Poncar tribe of Indians, the President of the United States of America, by Brigadier General Henry Atkinson, of the United States Army, and Major Benjamin O'Fallon, Indian Agent, with full powers and authority, specially appointed and commissioned for that purpose of the one part, and the undersigned Chiefs, Headmen, and Warriors, of the Poncar tribe of Indians, on behalf of said tribe, of the other part, have made and entered into the following articles and conditions, which, when ratified by the President of the United States, by and with the advice and consent of the Senate, shall be binding on both parties to wit:

Plains, West and Northwest Plateau Indian Treaties

ARTICLE 1. It is admitted by the Poncar tribe of Indians, that they reside within the territorial limits of the United States, acknowledge their supremacy, and claim their protection. The said tribe also admit the right of the United States to regulate all trade and intercourse with them.

ARTICLE 2. The United States agree to receive the Poncar tribe of Indians into their friendship, and under their protection, and to extend to them, from time to time, such benefits and acts of kindness as may be convenient, and seem just and proper to the President of the United States.

ARTICLE 3. All trade and intercourse with the Poncar tribe shall be transacted at such place or places as may be designated and pointed out by the President of the United States, through his agents; and none but American citizens, duly authorized by the United States, shall be admitted to trade or hold intercourse with said tribe of Indians.

ARTICLE 4. That the Poncar tribe may be accommodated with such articles of merchandise, &c as their necessities may demand, the United States agree to admit and license traders to hold intercourse with said tribe, under mild and equitable regulations: in consideration of which, the Poncar tribe bind themselves to extend protection to the persons and the property of the traders, and the persons legally employed under them, whilst they remain within the limits of the Poncar district of country. And the said Poncar tribe further agree, that if any foreigner, or other person not legally authorized by the United States, shall come into their district of country, for the purposes of trade or other views, they will apprehend such person or persons, and deliver him or them to some United States superintendent, or agent of Indian Affairs, or to the Commandant of the nearest military post, to be dealt with according to law. And they further agree to give safe conduct to all persons who may be legally authorized by the United States to pass through their country; and to protect, in their persons and property, all agents or other persons sent by the United States to reside temporarily among them.

ARTICLE 5. That the friendship which is now established between the United States and the Poncar tribe should not be interrupted by the misconduct of individuals. It is hereby agreed, that for injuries done by individuals, no private revenge or retaliation shall take place, but instead thereof, complaints shall be made, by the party injured, to the superintendent or agent of Indian affairs, or other person appointed by the President; and it shall be the duty of the said Chiefs, upon complaint being made as aforesaid, to deliver up the person or persons against whom the complaint is made, to the end that he or they may be punished agreeably to the laws of the United States. And, in like manner, if any robbery, violence, or murder, shall be committed on any Indian or Indians belonging to said tribe, the person or persons so offending shall be tried, and if

61

Plains, West and Northwest Plateau Indian Treaties

found guilty shall be punished in like manner as if the injury had been done to a white man.

And it is agreed, that the Chiefs of said Poncar tribe shall, to the utmost of their power, exert themselves to recover horses or other property, which may be stolen or taken from any citizen or citizens of the United States, by any individual or individuals of said tribe; and the property so recovered shall be forthwith delivered to the agents or other person authorized to receive it, that it may be restored to the proper owner. And the United States hereby guaranty to any Indian or Indians of said tribe, a full indemnification for any horses or other property which may be stolen from them by any of their citizens: Provided, That the property so stolen cannot be recovered, and that sufficient proof is produced that it was actually stolen by a citizen of the United States. And the said Poncar tribe engage, on the requisition or demand of the President of the United States, or of the agents, to deliver up any white man resident among them.

ARTICLE 6. And the Chiefs and Warriors, as aforesaid, promise and engage, that their tribe will never, by sale, exchange, or as presents, supply any nation or tribe of Indians, not in amity with the United States, with guns, ammunition, or other implements of War.
Done at the Poncar Village, at the mouth of White Paint creek, the first below the Qui Carre river, this 9th day of June, A. D. 1825, and of the independence of the United States the forty-ninth.

In testimony whereof, the said commissioners, Henry Atkinson and Benjamin O'Fallon, and the chiefs, head men, and warriors, of the Poncar tribe, have hereunto set their hands and affixed their seals.

H. Atkinson, brigadier-general, U.S. Army, Benj. O'Fallon, United States agent Indian Affairs,
Shu-de-gah-he, or He who makes Smoke, his x mark, Ish-ca-da-bee, or Child Chief, his x mark, Wah-ha-nee-che, or He who hides something, his x mark, Wah, or The Hoe, his x mark, O-nam-ba-haa, or Lightning, his x mark, Ti-e-kee-ree, or Bi Head with tangled hair, his x mark,

Witnesses:
Woh-ge-a-mussee, or The flying iron, his x mark, Pee-la-ga, or Buffalo, his x mark, Wah-buc-kee, or The bull that leads, his x mark, Wah-ha-nega, or He that has no knife, his x mark, H. Leavenworth, colonel, U. S. Army., S. W. Kearny, brevet major First Infantry. D. Ketchum, major, U. S. Army. G. H. Kennerley, U. S. S. Indian agent. S. Wragg, adjutant, First Regiment Infantry. R. Holmes, lieutenant, Sixth Infantry. A. L. Langham, Secretary to the Commission.

Plains, West and Northwest Plateau Indian Treaties

TREATY WITH THE SIOUNE AND OGLALA TRIBES {1825, July 5} Proclamation, Feb. 6, 1826.

For the purpose of perpetuating the friendship which has heretofore existed, as also to remove all future cause of discussion or dissension, as it respects trade and friendship between the United States and their citizens, and the Sioune and Ogallala bands of the Sioux tribe of Indians, the President of the United States of America, by Brigadier-General Henry Atkinson, of the United States Army, and Major Benjamin O'Fallon, Indian Agent, with full powers and authority, specially appointed and commissioned for that purpose, of the one part, and the undersigned Chiefs, Head-men, and Warriors, of the said Sioune and Ogallala bands of Sioux Indians, on behalf of their bands, of the other part, have made and entered into the following articles and conditions, which, when ratified by the President of the United States, by and with the advice and consent of the Senate shall be binding on both parties, to wit:

ARTICLE 1. It is admitted by the Sioune and Ogallala bands of Sioux Indians, that they reside within the territorial limits of the United States, acknowledge their supremacy, and claim their protection. The said bands also admit the right of the United States to regulate all trade and intercourse with them.

ARTICLE 2. The United States agree to receive the Sioune and Ogallala bands of Sioux into their friendship, and under their protection, and to extend to them, from time to time, such benefits and acts of kindness as may be convenient, and seem just and proper to the President of the United States.

ARTICLE 3. All trade and intercourse with the Sioune and Ogallala bands shall be transacted at such place or places as may be designated and pointed out by the President of the United States, through his agents; and none but American citizens, duly authorized by the United States, shall be admitted to trade or hold intercourse with said bands of Indians.

ARTICLE 4. That the Sioune and Ogallala bands may be accommodated With such articles of merchandise, &c, as their necessities may demand, the United States agree to admit and license traders to hold intercourse with said bands, under mild and equitable regulations: in consideration of which, the Sioune and Ogallala bands bind themselves to extend protection to the persons and the property of the traders, and the persons legally employed under them, whilst they remain within the limits of their particular district of country. And the said Sioune and Ogallala bands further agree, that if any foreigner or other persons, not legally authorized by the United States, shall come into their district of country, for the purposes of trade or other views, they will apprehend such person or persons, and deliver him or them to some United States superintendent, or agent of Indian affairs, or to the commandant of the nearest military post, to

63

Plains, West and Northwest Plateau Indian Treaties

be dealt with according to law.And they further agree to give safe conduct to all persons who may be legally authorized by the United States to pass through their country; and to protect, in their persons and property, all agents or other persons sent by the United States to reside temporarily among them; nor will they, whilst on their distant excursions, molest or interrupt any American citizen or citizens who may be passing from the United States to New Mexico or returning from thence to the United States.

ARTICLE 5. That the friendship, which is now established between the United States and the Sioune and Ogallala bands should not be interrupted by the misconduct of individuals, it is hereby agreed, that for injuries done by individuals, no private revenge or retaliation shall take place, but instead thereof, complaints shall be made, by the injured party, to the superintendent or agent of Indian affairs, or other person appointed by the President; and it shall be the duty of said Chiefs, upon complaint being made as aforesaid, to deliver up the person or persons, against whom the complaint is made, to the end that he or they may be punished agreeably to the laws of the United States. And, in like manner, if any robbery, violence or murder, shall be committed on any Indian or Indians belonging to the said bands, the person or persons so offending shall be tried, and if found guilty shall be punished in like manner as if the injury had been done to a white man.

And it is agreed, that the chiefs of said Sioune and Ogallala bands shall, to the utmost of their power, exert themselves to recover horses or other property, which may be stolen or taken from any citizen or citizens of the United States, by any individual or individuals of said bands; and the property so recovered shall be forthwith delivered to the agents or other person authorized to receive it, that it may be restored to the proper owner. And the United States hereby guaranty to any Indian or Indians of said bands, a full indemnification for any horses or other property which may be stolen from them by any of their citizens: Provided, The property stolen cannot be recovered, and that sufficient proof is produced that it was actually stolen by a citizen of the United States. And the said Sioune and Ogallala bands engage, on the requisition or demand of the President of the United States, or of the agents, to deliver up any white man resident among them.

ARTICLE 6. And the Chiefs and Warriors, as aforesaid, promise and engage, that their bands will never, by sale, exchange, or as presents, supply any nation, tribe, or band of Indians, not in amity with the United States, with guns, ammunition, or other implements of war.

Done at the mouth of the Teton river, this 5th day of July, A. D. 1825, and of the independence of the United States the fiftieth.

Plains, West and Northwest Plateau Indian Treaties

In testimony whereof, the said commissioners, Henry Atkinson and Benjamin O'Fallon, and the chiefs, head men, and warriors, of the Sioune and Ogallala bands, have hereunto set their hands, and affixed their seals.

H. Atkinson, Brigadier-General, U. S. Army., Benj. O' Fallon, United States agent Indian Affairs.

Siounes chiefs: Wah-e-ne-ta, the Rushing Man, his x mark, Cah-re-we-ca-ca, the Crow Feather, his x mark, Ma-ra-sea, the White Swan, his x mark,
Warriors: Chan-ta-wah-nee-cha, the Notieart, his x mark, He-hum-pee, the one that has a voice in his neck, his x mark,
Ogallala chiefs: Ta-tun-ca-nash-sha, the Standing Buffalo, his x mark, He-a-long-ga, the Shoulder, his x mark,
Warriors: Ek-hah-ka-sap-pa, the Black Elk, his x mark, Tah-tong-ish-nan-na, the One Buffalo, his x mark,
Siounes of the Fire-hearts band, who sign at Camp Hidden Creek, on the 12th July, 1825:
Chiefs: Chan-ta-pa-ta, the Fire-heart, his x mark, Wah-con-ta-mon-ee, the one that shoots as he walks, his x mark, Ke-ah-ash-sha-pa, the one that makes a noise as he flies, his x mark,
Warriors: Mato-co-kee-pa, the one that is afraid of the White Bear, his x mark. Ho-ton-co-kee-pa, the one that is afraid of his voice, his x mark,

In the presence of
P. Wilson, U. S. S. Indian agent, John Gale, surgeon, U. S. Army, D. Ketchum, major, U. S. Army, Levi Nute, lieutenant, U. S. Army, G. C. Spencer, captain, First Infantry, M. W. Batman, lieutenant, Sixth Infantry, Wm. Armstrong, captain, Sixth Regiment Infantry, Jas. W. Kingsbury, lieutenant, First Regiment Infantry,

Witnesses to the signatures of the Fire-hearts band, as executed on the 12th July, 1825:
A. L. Langham, secretary to the Commission, G. H. Kennerly, U. S. S. Indian agent, H. Leavenworth, colonel, U. S. Army, S. W. Kearny, brevet major, First Infantry, P. Wilson, U. S. S. Indian agent, R. M. Coleman, U. S. Army, Wm. Armstrong, captain, Sixth Regiment Infantry, J. Gantt, captain, Sixth Infantry.

TREATY WITH THE CHEYENNE TRIBE {1825, July 6}
Proclamation, Feb. 6, 1826.

FOR the Purpose of perpetuating the friendship which has heretofore existed, as also to remove all future cause of discussion or dissension, as it respects trade and friendship between the United States and their citizens, and the Chayenne tribe of Indians, the President of the United States of America, by Briga-

Plains, West and Northwest Plateau Indian Treaties

dier-General Henry Atkinson, of the United States army, and Major Benjamin O'Fallon, Indian agent, with full powers and authority, specially appointed and commissioned for that purpose of the one part, and the undersigned Chiefs, Headmen and Warriors, of the Chayenne tribe of Indians, on behalf of said tribe, of the other part, have made and entered into the following Articles and Conditions; which, when ratified by the President of the United States, by and with the advice and consent of the Senate, shall be binding on both parties to wit:

ARTICLE 1. It is admitted by the Chayenne tribe of Indians, that they reside within the territorial limits of the United States, acknowledge their supremacy, and claim their protection,The said tribe also admit the right of the United States to regulate all trade and intercourse with them.

ARTICLE 2. The United States agree to receive the Chayenne tribe of Indians into their friendship, and under their protection, and to extend to them, from time to time, such benefits and acts of kindness as may be convenient, and seem just and proper to the President of the United States.

ARTICLE 3. All trade and intercourse with the Chayenne tribe shall be transacted at such place or places as may be designated and pointed out by the President of the United States, through his agents; and none but American citizens, duly authorized by the United. States, shall be admitted to trade or hold intercourse with said tribe of Indians.

ARTICLE 4. That the Chayenne tribe may be accommodated with such articles of merchandise, &c, as their necessities may demand, the United States agree to admit and license traders to hold intercourse with said tribe, under mild and equitable regulations: in consideration of which, the Chayenne tribe bind themselves to extend protection to the persons and the property of the traders, and the persons legally employed under them, whilst they remain within the limits of their particular district of country. And the said Chayenne tribe further agree, that if any foreigner or other person, not legally authorized by the United States, shall come into their district of country, for the purposes of trade or other views, they will apprehend such person or persons, and deliver him or them to some United States superintendent or agent of Indian Affairs, or to the commandant of the nearest military post, to be dealt with according to law.

And they further agree to give safe conduct to all persons who may be legally authorized by the United States to pass through their country, and to protect in their persons and property all agents or other persons sent by the United States to reside temporarily among them; nor will they, whilst on their distant excursions, molest or interrupt any American citizen or citizens, who may be passing from the United States to New Mexico, or returning from thence to the United States.

Plains, West and Northwest Plateau Indian Treaties

ARTICLE 5. That the friendship which is now established between the United States and the Chayenne tribe, should not be interrupted by the misconduct of individuals, it is hereby agreed, that for injuries done by individuals, no private revenge or retaliation shall take place, but instead thereof, complaints shall be made, by the party injured, to the superintendent or agent of Indian affairs, or other person appointed by the President; and it shall be the duty of the said chiefs, upon complaint being made as aforesaid, to deliver up the person or persons against whom the complaint is made, to the end that he or they may be punished, agreeably to the laws of the United States. And, in like manner, if any robbery, violence, or murder, shall be committed on any Indian or Indians belonging to said tribe, the person or persons so offending shall be tried, and, if found guilty, shall be punished in like manner as if the injury had been done to a white man. And it is agreed, that the Chiefs of said Chayenne tribe shall, to the utmost of their power, exert themselves to recover horses or other property, which may be stolen or taken from any citizen or citizens of the United States, by any individual or individuals of said tribe.

And the property so recovered shall be forthwith delivered to the agents or other person authorized to receive it, that it may be restored to the proper owner. And the United States hereby guarranty to any Indian or Indians of said tribe, a full indemnification for any horses or other property which may be stolen from them by any of their citizens: Provided, That the property so stolen cannot be recovered, and that sufficient proof is produced that it was actually stolen by a citizen of the United States. And the said Chayenne tribe engage, on the requisition or demand of the President of the United States, or of the agents, to deliver up any white man resident among them.

ARTICLE 6. And the Chiefs and Warriors, as aforesaid, promise and engage that their tribe will never, by sale, exchange, or as presents, supply any nation or tribe of Indians, not in amity with the United States, with guns, ammunition, or other implements of war.

Done at the mouth of the Teton River, this sixth day of July, A. D. 1825, and of the independence of the United States the fiftieth.

In testimony whereof, the said commissioners, Henry Atkinson and Benjamin O'Fallon, and the chiefs, head men, and warriors, of the Chayenne tribe, have hereunto set their hands and affixed their seals.

H. Atkinson, brigadier general, U. S. Army, Benj. O'Fallon, United States Agent Indian Affairs,
Sho-e-mow-e-to-chaw-ca-we-wah-ca-to-we, or the wolf with the high back, his x mark, We-che-gal-la, or the Little Moon, his x mark, Ta-ton-ca-pa, or the Buffalo Head, his x mark, J-a-pu, or the one who walks against the others, his x mark,

Plains, West and Northwest Plateau Indian Treaties

In presence of
G. H. Kennerly, U. S. special Indian agent, John Gale, surgeon, U. S. Army, D. Ketchum, major, U. S. Army, Oh-kee-che-ta, or the Soldier, his x mark, Tah-hi-o-ta, or the Lousy Man, his x mark, Wm. Armstrong, captain, Sixth Regiment Infantry, S. W. Kearny, brevet major, First Infantry, H. Leavenworth, brevet colonel, Sixth Infantry, Thos. P. Gwynn, lieutenant, First Infantry.

TREATY WITH THE HUNKPAPA BAND OF THE SIOUX TRIBE
{1825, July 16}
Proclamation, Feb. 6, 1826

For the purpose of perpetuating the friendship which has heretofore existed, as also to remove all future cause of discussion or dissension, as it respects trade and friendship between the United States and their citizens, and the Hunkpapas band of the Sioux tribe of Indians, the President of the United States of America, by Brigadier-General Henry Atkinson, of the United States Army, and Major Benjamin O'Fallon, Indian agent, with full powers and authority, specially appointed and commissioned for that purpose, of the one part, and the undersigned Chiefs, Headmen, and Warriors of the said Hunkpapas band of Sioux Indians, on behalf of their band, of the other part, have made and entered into the following Articles and Conditions; which, when ratified by the President of the United States, by and with the advice and consent of the Senate, shall be binding on both parties.

ARTICLE 1. It is admitted by the Hunkpapas band of Sioux Indians that they reside within the territorial limits of the United States, acknowledge their supremacy, and claim their protection. The said band also admit the right of the United States to regulate all trade and intercourse with them.

ARTICLE 2. The United States agree to receive the Hunkpapas band of Sioux into their friendship, and under their protection, and to extend to them from time to time such benefits and acts of kindness as may be convenient, and seem just and proper to the President of the United States.

ARTICLE 3. All trade and intercourse with the Hunkpapas band shall be transacted at such place or places as may be designated and pointed out by the President of the United States, through his agents; and none but American citizens, duly authorized by the United States, shall be admitted to trade or hold intercourse with said band of Indians.

ARTICLE 4. That the Hunkpapas band may be accommodated with such articles of merchandise, &c., as their necessities may demand, the United States agree to admit and license traders to hold intercourse with said band under mild

68

Plains, West and Northwest Plateau Indian Treaties

and equitable regulations: in consideration of which, the Hunkpapas band bind themselves to extend protection to the persons and the property of the traders, and the persons legally employed under them, whilst they remain within the limits of their particular district of country. And the said Hunkpapas band further agree, that if any foreigner, or other person not legally authorized by the United States, shall come into their district of country, for the purposes of trade or other views, they will apprehend such person or persons, and deliver him or them to some United States superintendent or agent of Indian affairs, or to the commandant of the nearest military post, to be dealt with according to law.

And they further agree to give safe conduct to all persons who may be legally authorized by the United States to pass through their country, and to protect in their persons and property all agents or other persons sent by the United States to reside temporarily among them.

ARTICLE 5. That the friendship which is now established between the United States and the Hunkpapas band should not be interrupted by the misconduct of individuals, it is hereby agreed that, for injuries done by individuals, no private revenge or retaliation shall take place, but instead thereof, complaints shall be made, by the injured party, to the superintendent or agent of Indian affairs, or other person appointed by the President: and it shall be the duty of said Chiefs, upon complaint being made as aforesaid, to deliver up the person or persons against whom the complaint is made, to the end that he or they may be punished agreeably to the laws of the United States.

And in like manner, if any robbery, violence, or murder, shall be committed on any Indian or Indians belonging to the said band, the person or persons so offending shall be tried, and if found guilty, shall be punished in like manner as if the injury had been done to a white man. And it is agreed, that the chiefs of said Hunkpapas band shall, to the utmost of their power, exert themselves to recover horses or other property, which may be stolen or taken from any citizen or citizens of the United States, by any individual or individuals of said band; and the property so recovered shall be forthwith delivered to the agents or other person authorized to receive it, that it may be restored to the proper owner. And the United States hereby guarranty to any Indian or Indians of said band, a full indemnification for any horses or other property which may be stolen from them by any of their citizens: Provided, That the property stolen cannot be recovered, and that sufficient proof is produced that it was actually stolen by a citizen of the United States. And the said Hunkpapas band engage, on the requisition or demand of the President of the United States, or of the-agents, to deliver up any white man resident among them.

ARTICLE 6. And the Chiefs and Warriors, as aforesaid, promise and engage that their band will never, by sale, exchange, or as presents, supply any nation

Plains, West and Northwest Plateau Indian Treaties

or tribe of Indians, not in amity with the United States, with guns, ammunition, or other implements of war.

Done at the Auricara Village, this sixteenth day of July, A. D. 1825, and of the independence of the United States the fiftieth.

In testimony whereof, the said commissioners, Henry Atkinson, and Benjamin O'Fallon, and the chiefs, head men, and warriors of the Hunkpapas tribe of Indians, have hereunto set their hands and affixed their seals.

H. Atkinson, brigadier-general, U. S. Army, Benj. O' Fallon, United States agent Indian affairs,
Mato-che-gal-lah, Little White Bear, his x mark, Cha-sa-wa-ne-che, the one that has no name, his x mark, Tah-hah-nee-ah, the on e that scares the game, his x mark,

In presence of
A. L. Langham, secretary to the commission, H. Leavenworth, colonel, U. S. Army, Levi Nute, lieutenant, U. S. Army, Collin Campbell.

TREATY WITH THE ARIKARA TRIBE {1825, July 18}
Proclamation, Feb. 6, 1826

To put an end to an unprovoked hostility on the part of the Ricara Tribe of Indians against the United States, and to restore harmony between the parties, the President of the United States, by Brigadier-general Henry Atkinson, of the United States Army, and Major Benjamin O'Fallon, Indian Agent, Commissioners duly appointed and commissioned to treat with the Indian tribes beyond the Mississippi river, give peace to the said Ricara Tribe; the Chiefs and Warriors thereof having first made suitable concessions for the offence. And, for the purpose of removing all further or future cause of misunderstanding as respects trade and friendly intercourse between the parties, the above named Commissioners on the part of the United States, and the undersigned Chiefs and Warriors of the Ricara Tribe of Indians on-the part of said Tribe, have made and entered into the following articles and conditions, which, when ratified by the President of the United States, by and with the advice and consent of the Senate, shall be binding on both parties, to wit:

ARTICLE 1. Henceforth there shall be a firm and lasting peace between the United States and the Ricara tribe of Indians; and a friendly intercourse shall immediately take place between the parties.

ARTICLE 2. It is admitted by the Ricara tribe of Indians, that they reside within the territorial limits of the United States, acknowledge their supremacy,

Plains, West and Northwest Plateau Indian Treaties

and claim their protection. The said tribe also admit the right of the United States to regulate all trade and intercourse with them.

ARTICLE 3. The United States agree to receive the Ricara tribe of Indians into their friendship, and under their protection, and to extend to them, from time to time, such benefits and acts of kindness as may be convenient and seem just and proper to the President of the United States.

ARTICLE 4. All trade and intercourse with the Ricara tribe shall be transacted at such place or places as may be designated and pointed out by the President of the United States, through his agents; and none but American citizens, duly authorized by the United States, shall be admitted to trade or hold intercourse with said tribe of Indians.

ARTICLE 5. That the Ricara tribe may be accommodated with such articles of merchandise, &c, as their necessities may demand, the United States agree to admit and license traders to hold intercourse with said tribe, under mild and equitable regulations: in consideration of which, the Ricara tribe bind themselves to extend protection to the persons and the property of the traders, and the persons legally employed under them, while they remain within the limits of their district of country. And the said Ricara tribe further agree, that if any foreigner or other person, not legally authorized by the United States, shall come into their district of country for the purposes of trade or other views, they will apprehend such person or persons, and deliver him or them to some United States superintendent or agent of Indian Affairs, or to the commandant of the nearest military post, to be dealt with according to law.

And they further agree to give safe conduct to all persons who may be legally authorized by the United States to pass through their country, and to protect in their persons and property all agents or other persons sent by the United States to reside temporarily among them.

ARTICLE 6. That the friendship which is now established between the United States and the Ricara tribe, shall not be interrupted by the misconduct of individuals, it is hereby agreed, that for injuries done by individuals, no private revenge or retaliation shall take place, but instead thereof, complaints shall be made, by the party injured, to the superintendent or agent of Indian affairs or other person appointed by the President; and it shall be the duty of the said Chiefs, upon complaint being made as aforesaid, to deliver up the person or persons against whom the complaint is made, to the end that he or they may be punished, agreeably to the laws of the United States.

And, in like manner, if any robbery, violence, or murder, shall be committed on any Indian or Indians belonging to said tribe, the person or persons so offending shall be tried, and, if found guilty, shall be punished in like manner as if the

Plains, West and Northwest Plateau Indian Treaties

injury had been done to a white man. And it is agreed, that the Chiefs of the said Ricara tribe shall, to the utmost of their power, exert themselves to recover horses or other property, which may be stolen or taken from any citizen or citizens of the United States, by any individual or individuals of said tribe; and the property so recovered shall be forthwith delivered to the agents or other person authorized to receive it, that it may be restored to the proper owner. And the United States hereby guaranty to any Indian or Indians of said tribe, a full indemnification for any horses or other property which may be stolen from them by any of their citizens.

Provided, That the property so stolen cannot be recovered, and that sufficient proof is produced that it was actually stolen by a citizen of the United States. And the said Ricara tribe engage, on the requisition or demand of the President of the United States, or of the agents, to deliver up any white man resident among them.

ARTICLE 7. And the Chiefs and Warriors, as aforesaid, promise and engage that their tribe will never, by sale, exchange, or as presents, supply any nation, tribe, or bands of Indians, not in amity with the United States, with guns, ammunition, or other implements of war.
Done at the Ricara village, this eighteenth day of July, A. D. 1825, and of the independence of the United States the fiftieth.

In testimony whereof, the said commissioners, Henry Atkinson and Benjamin O'Fallon, and the chiefs, head men, and warriors of the Ricara tribe of Indians, have hereunto set their hands and affixed their seals.

H. Atkinson, brigadier-general U. S. Army, Benj. O'Fallon, United States agent Indian affairs,
Stan-au-pat, the bloody hand, his x mark, Ca-car-we-ta, the little bear, his x mark, Scar-e-naus, the skunk, his x mark, Ne-sha-non-nack, the chief by himself, his x mark,

In the presence of
A. L. Langham, secretary to the commission, H. Leavenworth, colonel U. S. Army, S. W. Kearny, brevet major First Infantry, W. L. Harris, lieutenant First Infantry, G. H. Kennerly, U. S. special Indian agent, P. Wilson, U. S. special Indian agent, Antoine Garreau, his x mark, interpreter, Joseph Garreau, his x mark, interpreter, Pierre Garreau, his x mark,

Plains, West and Northwest Plateau Indian Treaties

TREATY WITH THE BELANTSE-ETOA OR MINITAREE TRIBE
{1825, July 20}
Proclamation, Feb. 6, 1826

WHEREAS acts of hostility have been committed, by some restless men of the Belantse-etea or Minnetaree tribe of Indians, upon some of the citazens of the United States: therefore, to put a stop to any further outrages of the sort, and to establish a more friendly understanding between the United States and the said Belantse-etea or Minnetaree tribe, the President of the United States, by Henry Atkinson, Brigadier-general of the United States army, and Major Benjamin O'Fallon, Indian Agent, commissioners duly appointed and commissioned to treat with the Indian tribes beyond the Mississippi river, forgive the offences which have been committed, the Chiefs and Warriors having first made satisfactory explanations touching the same.

And, for the purpose of removing all future cause of misunderstanding, as respects trade and friendly intercourse, between the parties, the above-named Commissioners, on the part of the United States, and the undersigned chiefs and Warriors of the Belantse-etea or Minnetaree tribe of Indians, on the part of said tribe, have made and entered into the following Articles and Conditions; which, when ratified by the President of the United States, by and with the advice and consent of the Senate, shall be binding on both parties to wit:

ARTICLE 1. Henceforth there shall be a firm and lasting peace between the United States and the Belantse-etea or Minnetaree tribe of Indians; and a friendly intercourse shall immediately take place between the parties.

ARTICLE 2. It is admitted by the Belantse-etea or Minnetaree tribe of Indians, that they reside within the territorial limits of the United States, acknowledge their supremacy, and claim their protection.The said tribe also admit the right of the United States to regulate all trade and intercourse with them.

ARTICLE 3. The United States agree to receive the Belantse-etea or Minnetaree tribe of Indians into their friendship, and under their protection, and to extend to them, from time to time, such benefits and acts of kindness as may be convenient, and seem just and proper to the President of the United States.

ARTICLE 4. All trade and intercourse with the Belantse-eta or Minnetaree tribe shall be transacted at such place or places as may be designated and pointed out, by the President of the United States, through his agents; and none but American citazens, duly authorized by the United States, shall be admitted to trade or hold intercourse with said tribe of Indians.

ARTICLE 5. That the Belantse-eta or Minnetaree tribe may be accommodated with such articles of merchandise, &c., as their necessities may demand, the

Plains, West and Northwest Plateau Indian Treaties

United States agree to admit and license traders to hold intercourse with said tribe, under mild and equitable regulations: in consideration of which, the Belantse-eta or Minnetaree tribe bind themselves to extend protection to the persons and the property of the traders, and the persons legally employed under them, whilst they remain within the limits of their district of country. And the said Belantse-eta or Minnetaree tribe further agree, that if any foreigner or other person, not legally authorized by the United States, shall come into their district of country, for the purposes of trade or other views, they will apprehend such person or persons, and deliver him or them to some United States superintendent or agent of Indian affairs, or to the commandant of the nearest military post, to be dealt with according to law. And they further agree to give safe conduct to all persons who may be legally authorized by the United States to reside temporarily among them.

ARTICLE 6. That the friendship which is now established between the United States and the Belantse-eta or Minnetaree tribe shall not be interrupted by the misconduct of individuals, it is hereby agreed, that for injuries done by individuals, no private revenge or retaliation shall take place, but instead thereof complaints shall be made, by the party injured, to the superintendent or agent of Indian affairs or other person appointed by the President; and it shall be the duty of the said Chiefs, upon complaint being made as aforesaid, to deliver up the person or persons against whom the complaint is made, to the end that he or they may be punished, agreeably to the laws of the United States. And, in like manner, if any robbery, violence, or murder, shall be committed on any Indian or Indians belonging to said tribe, the person or persons so offending shall be tried, and if found guilty, shall be punished in like manner as if the injury had been done to a white man.

And it is agreed that the Chiefs of the said Belantse-eta or Minnetaree tribe shall, to the utmost of their power, exert themselves to recover horses or other property, which may be stolen or taken from any citizen or citizens of the United States, by any individual or individuals of said tribe; and the property so recovered shall be forthwith delivered to the agents or other person authorized to receive it, that it may be restored to the proper owner. And the United States hereby guarranty to any Indian or Indians of said tribe, a full indemnification for any horses or other property which may be stolen from them by any of their citizens: Provided, That the property so stolen cannot be recovered, and that sufficient proof is produced that it was actually stolen by a citizen of the United States. And the said Belantse-eta or Minnetaree tribe engage, on the requisition or demand of the President of the United States, or of the agents, to deliver up any white man resident among them.

ARTICLE 7. And the Chiefs and Warriors, as aforesaid, promise and engage that their tribe will never, by sale, exchange, or as presents, supply any nation,

Plains, West and Northwest Plateau Indian Treaties

tribe, or band of Indians, not in amity with the United States, with guns, ammunition, or other implements of war.

Done at the Lower Mandan Village, this thirtieth day of July, A. D. 1825, and of the independence of the United States the fiftieth.

In testimony whereof, the commissioners, Henry Atkinson and Benjamin O'Fallon, and the chiefs and warriors of the said Belantse-etea or Minnetaree tribe of Indians, have hereunto set their hands and affixed their seals.

H. Atkinson, brigadier-general U. S. Army, Benj. O' Fallon, United States agent, Indian affairs,
Shan-sa-bat-say-e-see, the wolf chief, his x mark, E-re-ah-ree, the one that make the road, his x mark, Pas-ca-ma-e-ke-ree, the crow that looks, his x mark, E-tah-me-nah-ga-e-she, the guard of the red arrows, his x mark, San-jah-oe-tee, the wolf that has no tail, his x mark, E-sha-kee-te-ah, the big fingers, his x mark, Mah-shu-kah-e-te-ah, the big dog, his x mark, Be-ra-ka-ra-ah, the rotten wood, his x mark, E-ta-ro-sha-pa, the big brother, his x mark,
In the presence of
A. L. Langham, secretary to the commission, H. Leavenworth, colonel, U. S. Army, R. B. Mason, captain, First Infantry, Jas. W. Kingbury, lieutenant, First Regiment Infantry, R. Holmes, lieutenant, Sixth Infantry, J. Rogers, lieutenant, Sixth Infantry, W. S. Harney, lieutenant, First Infantry, Levi Nute, lieutenant, Sixth Infantry, B. Riley, captain, Sixth Infantry, R. M. Coleman, assistant surgeon, U. S. Army, George C. Hutter, lieutenant, Sixth Infantry, Colin Campbell, P. Wilson, United States sub-Indian agent, Touissant Chaboneau, interpreter, his x mark, S. W. Kearny, brevet major, First Infantry. Wm. Armstrong, captain, Sixth Regiment Infantry.

TREATY WITH THE MANDAN TRIBE {1825, July 30}
Proclamation, Feb. 1826.

WHEREAS acts of hostility have been committed by some restless men of the Mandan Tribe of Indians, upon some of the citizens of the United States: Therefore, to put a stop to any further outrages of the sort; and to establish a more friendly understanding between the United States and the said Mandan Tribe, the President of the United States, by Henry Atkinson, Brigadier General of the United States, Army, and Major Benjamin O'Fallon, Indian Agent, Commissioners duly appointed and commissioned to treat with the Indian Tribes beyond the Mississippi river, forgive the offences which have been committed, the Chiefs and Warriors having first made satisfactory explanations touching the same.

Plains, West and Northwest Plateau Indian Treaties

And, for the purpose of removing all future cause of misunderstanding as respects trade and friendly intercourse between the parties, the above named Commissioners on the part of the United States, and the undersigned Chiefs and Warriors of the Mandan tribe of Indians on the part of said Tribe, have made and entered into the following articles and conditions, which, when ratified by the President of the United States, by and with the advice and consent of the Senate, shall be binding on both parties to wit:

ARTICLE 1. Henceforth there shall be a firm and lasting peace between the United States and the Mandan tribe of Indians; and a friendly intercourse shall immediately take place between the parties.

ARTICLE 2. It is admitted by the Mandan tribe of Indians, that they reside within the territorial limits of the United States, acknowledge their supremacy, and claim their protection. The said tribe also admit the right of the United States to regulate all trade and intercourse with them.

ARTICLE 3. The United States agree to receive the Mandan tribe of Indians into their friendship, and under their protection, and to extend to them, from time to time, such benefits and acts of kindness as may be convenient, and seem just and proper to the President of the United States.

ARTICLE 4. All trade and intercourse with the Mandan tribe shall be transacted at such place or places as may be designated and pointed out by the President of the United States, through his agents; and none but American citizens, duly authorized by the United States, shall be admitted to trade or hold intercourse with said tribe of Indians.

ARTICLE 5. That the Mandan tribe may be accommodated with such articles of merchandise, &c., as their necessities may demand, the United States agree to admit and license traders to hold intercourse with said tribe, under mild and equitable regulations: in consideration of which, the Mandan tribe bind themselves to extend protection to the persons and the property of the traders, and the persons legally employed under them, whilst they remain within the limits of their district of country. And the said Mandan tribe further agree, that if any foreigner or other person, not legally authorized by the United States, shall come into their district of country, for the purposes of trade or other views, they will apprehend such person or persons, and deliver him or them to some United States superintendent or agent of Indian Affairs, or to the commandant of the nearest military post, to be dealt with according to law.

And they further agree to give safe conduct to all persons who may be legally authorized by the United States to pass through their country, and to protect in their persons and property all agents or other persons sent by the United States to reside temporarily among them.

Plains, West and Northwest Plateau Indian Treaties

ARTICLE 6. That the friendship which is now established between the United States and the Mandan tribe, shall not be interrupted by the misconduct of individuals, it is hereby agreed, that for injuries done by individuals, no private revenge or retaliation shall take place, but instead thereof, complaints shall be made, by the party injured, to the superintendent or agent of Indian affairs, or other person appointed by the President; and it shall be the duty of the said Chiefs, upon complaint being made as aforesaid, to deliver up the person or persons against whom the complaint is made, to the end that he or they may be punished, agreeably to the laws of the United States.

And, in like manner, if any robbery, violence, or murder, shall be committed on any Indian or Indians belonging to said tribe, the person or persons so offending shall be tried, and if found guilty, shall be punished in like manner as if the injury had been done to a white man. And it is agreed, that the Chiefs of the said Mandan tribe shall, to the utmost of their power, exert themselves to recover horses or other property, which may be stolen or taken from any citizen or citizens of the United States, by any individual or individuals of said tribe; and the property so recovered shall be forthwith delivered to the agents or other person authorized to receive it, that it may be restored to the proper owner.

And the United States hereby guarranty to any Indian or Indians of said tribe, a full indemnification for any horses or other property which may be stolen from them by any of their citizens: Provided, That the property so stolen cannot be recovered, and that sufficient proof is produced that it was actually stolen by a citizen of the United States. And the said Mandan tribe engage, on the requisition or demand of the President of the United States, or of the agents, to deliver up any white man resident among them.

ARTICLE 7. And the Chiefs and Warriors as aforesaid, promise and engage that their tribe will never, by sale, exchange, or as presents, supply any nation, tribe, or band of Indians, not in amity with the United States, with guns, ammunition, or other implements of war.

Done at the Mandan Village, this thirtieth day of July, A. D. 1825, and of the independence of the United States the fiftieth.

In testimony whereof, the commissioners, Henry Atkinson and Benjamin O'Fallon, and the chiefs and warriors of the Mandan tribe of Indians, have hereunto set their hands and affixed their seals.

H. Atkinson, brigadier-general U.S. Army, Benj. O' Fallen, United States agent Indian affairs;

Plains, West and Northwest Plateau Indian Treaties

Mat-sa-to-pas-pah-hah-pah, the chiefs of four men, his x mark, San-jah-mat-sa-eta, the wolf chiefs, his x mark, Ah-ra-na-shis, the one that has no arm, his x mark, Bot-sa-a-pa, the color of the wolf, his x mark, Con-ke-sheesse, the good child, his x mark, Lah-pa-see-ta-re-tah, the bear that does not walk, his x mark, Par-res-kah-eah-rush-ta, the little crow, his x mark, Ba-rah-rah-ca-tah, the broken pot, his x mark, Me-ra-pa-sha-po, the five beavers, his x mark, Bout-sa-ca-ho-ka, the crouching prairie wolf, his x mark,

In the presence of
A. L. Langham, secretary to the commission, H. Leavenworth, colonel U. S. Army, S. Mac Ree, lieutenant, aid-de-camp, R. B. Mason, captain, First Infantry,
A. S. Miller, lieutenant, First Infantry, Colin Campbell, Touissant Chaboneau, his x mark, interpreter.

TREATY WITH THE CROW TRIBE {1825, Aug. 4}
Proclamation, Feb. 6, 1826.

For the purpose of perpetuating the friendship which has heretofore existed, as also to remove all future cause of discussion or dissension, as it respects trade and friendship between the United States and their citizens, and the Crow tribe of Indians, the President of the United States of America, by Brigadier-General Henry Atkinson, of the United States army, and Major Benjamin O'Fallon, Indian agent, with full powers and authority, specially appointed and commissioned for that purpose, of the one part, and the undersigned Chiefs, Head men and Warriors of the said Crow tribe of Indians, on behalf of their tribe, of the other part, have made and entered into the following Articles and Conditions; which, when ratified by the President of the United States, by and with the advice and consent of the Senate, shall be binding on both partiesto wit:

ARTICLE 1. It is admitted by the Crow tribe of Indians, that they reside within the territorial limits of the United States, acknowledge their supremacy, and claim their protection.The said tribe also admit the right of the United States to regulate all trade and intercourse with them.

ARTICLE 2. The United States agree to receive the Crow tribe of Indians into their friendship, and under their protection, and to extend to them, from time to time, such benefits and acts of kindness as may be convenient, and seem just and proper to the President of the United States.

ARTICLE 3. All trade and intercourse with the Crow tribe shall be transacted at such place or places as may be designated and pointed out by the President of the United States, through his agents; and none but American citizens, duly

Plains, West and Northwest Plateau Indian Treaties

authorized by the United States, shall be admitted to trade or hold intercourse with said tribe of Indians.

ARTICLE 4. That the Crow tribe may be accommodated with such articles of merchandise, &c, as their necessities may demand, the United States agree to admit and license traders to hold intercourse with said tribe, under mild and equitable regulations: in consideration of which, the Crow tribe bind themselves to extend protection to the persons and the property of the traders, and the persons legally employed under them, whilst they remain within the limits of their district of country.

And the said Crow tribe further agree, that if any foreigner or other person, not legally authorized by the United States, shall come into their district of country, for the purposes of trade or other views, they will apprehend such person or persons, and deliver him or them to some United States Superintendent or Agent of Indian Affairs, or to the commandant of the nearest military post, to be dealt with according to law. And they further agree to give safe conduct to all persons who may be legally authorized by the United States to pass through their country, and to protect in their persons and property all agents or other persons sent by the United States to reside temporarily among them; and that they will not, whilst on their distant excursions, molest or interrupt any American citizen or citizens, who may be passing from the United States to New Mexico, or returning from thence to the United States.

ARTICLE 5. That the friendship which is now established between the United States and the Crow tribe, should not be interrupted by the misconduct of individuals, it is hereby agreed, that for injuries done by individuals, no private revenge or retaliation shall take place, but instead thereof, complaints shall be made, by the party injured, to the superintendent or agent of Indian affairs, or other person appointed by the President; and it shall be the duty of said Chiefs, upon complaint being made as aforesaid, to deliver up the person or persons against whom the complaint is made, to the end that he or they may be punished, agreeably to the laws of the United States. And, in like man-her, if any robbery, violence, or murder, shall be committed on any Indian or Indians belonging to the said tribe, the person or persons so offending shall be tried, and, if found guilty, shall be punished in like manner as if the injury had been done to a white man.

And it is agreed, that the Chiefs of said Crow tribe shall, to the utmost of their power, exert themselves to recover horses or other property, which may be stolen or taken from any citizen or citizens of the United States, by any individual or individuals of said tribe; and the property so recovered shall be forthwith delivered to the agents or other person authorized to receive it, that it may be restored to the proper owner. And the United States hereby guarranty to any Indian or Indians of said tribe, a full indemnification for any horses or other

Plains, West and Northwest Plateau Indian Treaties

property which may be stolen from them by any of their citizens: Provided, That the property stolen cannot be recovered, and that sufficient proof is produced that it was actually stolen by a citizen of the United States. And the said tribe engage, on the requisition or demand of the President of the United States, or of the agents, to deliver up any white man resident among them.

ARTICLE 6. And the Chiefs and Warriors, as aforesaid, promise and engage that their tribe will never, by sale, exchange, or as presents, supply any nation, tribe, or band of Indians, not in amity with the United States, with guns, ammunition, or other implements of war.

Done at the Mandan Village, this fourth day of August, A. D. 1825, and of the independence of the United States the fiftieth.

In testimony whereof, the said commissioners, Henry Atkinson and Benjamin O'Fallon, and the chiefs and warriors of the said tribe, have hereunto set their hands and affixed their seals.

H. Atkinson, brigadier-general U. S. Army, Benj. O'Fallon, U. S. agent Indian Affairs,
Chiefs: E-she-huns-ka, or the long hair, his x mark, She-wo-cub-bish, one that sings bad, his x mark, Har-rar-shash, one that rains, his x mark, Chay-ta-pah-ha, wolf's paunch, his x mark, Huch-che-rach, little black dog, his x mark, Mah-pitch, bare shoulder, his x mark, Esh-ca-ca-mah-hoo, the standing lance, his x mark, Che-rep-con-nes-ta-chea, the little white bull, his x ,
In presence of
A. L. Langham, secretary to the commission, H. Leavenworth, colonel U. S. Army, S. W. Kearny, brevet major First Infantry, D. Ketchum, major U. S. Army, R. B. Mason, captain First Infantry,pG.
C. Spencer, captain First Infantry, John Gantt, captain Sixth Infantry, Thos. P. Gwynne, lieutenant First Infantry, S. MacRee, lieutenant and aid-de-camp, Thomas Noel, lieutenant Sixth Infantry, William L. Harris, First Infantry, John Gale, surgeon U. S. Army,

Mash-pah-hash, the one that is not right, R. Holmes, lieutenant Sixth Infantry, M. W. Batman, lieutenant Sixth Infantry, R. M. Coleman, U. S. Army, J. Rogers, lieutenant Sixth Infantry, Wm. Day, lieutenant First Infantry, G. H. Kennerly, U. S. Indian agent, B. Riley, captain Sixth Infantry, Wm. S. Harney, lieutenant First Infantry, James W. Kingsbury, lieutenant First Regiment Infantry, George C. Hutter, lieutenant Sixth Infantry, Wm. Armstrong, captain Sixth Regiment Infantry.

Plains, West and Northwest Plateau Indian Treaties

TREATY WITH THE GREAT AND LITTLE OSAGE {1825, Aug. 10}
Proclamation, May 3, 1826.

WHEREAS the Congress of the United States of America, being anxious to promote a direct commercial and friendly intercourse between the citizens of the United States and those of the Mexican Republic, and, to afford protection to the same, did, at their last session, pass an act, which was approved the 3d March, 1825, "to authorize the President of the United States to cause a road to be marked out from the Western frontier of Missouri to the confines of New Mexico," and which authorizes the President of the United States to appoint Commissioners to carry said act of Congress into effect, and enjoins on the Commissioners, so to be appointed, that they first obtain the consent of the intervening tribes of Indians, by treaty, to the marking of said road, and to the unmolested use thereof to the citizens of the United States and of the Mexican Republic; and Benjamin H. Reeves, Geo. C. Sibley, and Thomas Mather, Commissioners duly appointed as aforesaid, being duly and fully authorized, have this day met the Chiefs and Head men of the Great and Little Osage Nations, who being all duly authorized to meet and negotiate with the said Commissioners upon the premises, and being specially met for that purpose, by the invitation of said Commissioners, at the place called the Council Grove, on the river Nee-o-zho, one hundred and sixty miles southwest from Fort Osage; have, after due deliberation and consultation, agreed to the following treaty, which is to be considered binding on the said Great and Little Osages, from and after this day:

ARTICLE 1. The Chiefs and Head Men of the Great and Little Osages, for themselves and their nations, respectively, do consent and agree that the Commissioners of the United States shall and may survey and mark out a road, in such manner as they may think proper, through any of the territory owned or claimed by the said Great and Little Osage Nations.

ARTICLE 2. The Chiefs and Head Men, as aforesaid, do further agree that the road authorized in article 1, shall, when marked, be forever free for the use of the citizens of the United States and of the Mexican Republic, who shall at all times pass and repass thereon, without any hindrance or molestation on the part of the said Great and Little Osages.

ARTICLE 3. The Chiefs and Head Men as aforesaid, in consideration of the friendly relations existing between them and the United States, do further promise, for themselves and their people, that they will, on all fit occasions, render such friendly aid and assistance as may be in their power, to any of the citizens of the United States, or of the Mexican Republic, as they may at any time happen to meet or fall in with on the road aforesaid.

Plains, West and Northwest Plateau Indian Treaties

ARTICLE 4. The Chiefs and Head Men, as aforesaid, do further consent and agree that the road aforesaid shall be considered as extending to a reasonable distance on either side, so that travellers thereon may, at any time, leave the marked tract, for the purpose of finding subsistence and proper camping places.

ARTICLE 5. In consideration of the privileges granted by the Chiefs of the Great and Little Osages in the three preceding articles, the said Commissioners on the part of the United States, have agreed to pay to them, the said Chiefs for themselves and their people the sum of five hundred dollars; which sum is to be paid them as soon as may be, in money or merchandise, at their option, at such place as they may desire.

ARTICLE 6. And the said Chiefs and Head Men, as aforesaid, acknowledge to have received from the Commissioners aforesaid, at and before the signing of this Treaty, articles of merchandise to the value of three hundred dollars; which sum of three hundred dollars, and the payment stipulated to be made to the said Osages in Article 5, shall be considered, and are so considered by said Chiefs, as full and complete compensation for every privilege herein granted by said Chiefs.

In testimony whereof, the said Benjamin H. Reeves, George C. Sibley, and Thomas Mather, commissioners as aforesaid, and the chiefs and head men of the Great and Little Osage tribes of Indians, have hereunto set their hands and seals, at Council Grove, this tenth day of August, in the year of our Lord one thousand eight hundred and twenty-five.

B. H. Reeves, G. C. Sibley, Thomas Mather, Pa-hu-sha, (white hair) head chief of the G. O., his x mark, Ca-hc-ga-wa-tonega, (foolish chief) head chief of the L. O., his x mark, Shin-gawassa, (handsome bird) chief of the G. O., his x mark, his x mark, Ta-ha-mo-nee, (swift walker) chief L. O., his x mark, Ca-he-ga-wash-im-pee-she (bad chief) chief G. O., his x mark, Wee-ho-je-ne-fare, (without ears) chief L. O., his x mark, Ca-he-ga-shinga, (little chief) G. O., his x mark, Waw-bur-cou, warrior Little Osages, his x mark,

Maw-sho-hun-ga, warrior Great Osages, his x mark, Waw-lo-gah, (Owl) warrior Little Osages, his x mark, Maw-she-to-mo-nee, warrior Great Osages, his x mark, Che-he-kaw, warrior Little Osages, his x mark, Ne-ha-wa-she-tun-ga, warrior Great Osages, his x mark, Ho-no-posse, warrior Little Osages, his x mark, Waw-kun-ehee, warrior Little Osages, his x mark, Pwa-ne-no-push-re, warrior Little Osages, his x mark,
In the presence of

Archibald Gamble, secretary, Jos. C. Brown, surveyor, W. S. Williams, interpreter, Stephen Cooper, Samuel Givens, Richard Brannan, Garrison Patrick,

Plains, West and Northwest Plateau Indian Treaties

Daniel J. Bahan, I. R. Walker, Singleton Vaughn, Benjamin Jones, Bradford Barbie, Hendley Cooper, John M. Walker, Joseph Davis, George West, Thomas Adams, James Brotherton.

TREATY WITH THE KANSAS {1825, Aug. 16}
Proclamation, May 3, 1826.

WHEREAS the Congress of the United States of America being anxious to promote a direct commercial and friendly intercourse between the citizens of the United States and those of the Mexican Republic, and, to afford protection to the same, did, at their last session, pass an act, which was approved the 3d of March, 1825, "to authorize the President of the United States to cause a road to be marked out from the Western frontier of Missouri to the confines of New Mexico," and which authorizes the President of the United States to appoint Commission-era to carry said act of Congress into effect, and enjoins on the Commissioners, so to be appointed, that they first obtain the consent of the in-tervening tribes of Indians, by treaty, to the marking of said road and to the unmolested use thereof to the citizens of the United States and of the Mexican Republic; and Benjamin H. Reeves, Geo. C. Sibley, and Thomas Mather, being duly appointed Commissioners as aforesaid, and being duly and fully author-ized, have this day met the Chiefs and Head Men of the Kansas tribe of Indians, who, being all duly authorized to meet and negotiate with the said Commis-sioners upon the premises, and being specially met for that purpose, by the in-vitation of said Commissioners, on the Sora Kansas Creek, two hundred and thirty-eight miles Southwestwardly from Fort Osage; have, after due delibera-tion and consultation, agreed to the following Treaty, which is to be considered binding on the said Kansas Indians, from and after this day:

ARTICLE 1. The Chiefs and Head Men of the Kansas Nation, or tribe of Indi-ans, for themselves and their nation, do consent and agree that the Commis-sioners of the United States shall, and may survey and mark out a road, in such manner as they may think proper, through any of the territory owned or claimed by the said Kansas Tribe or nation of Indians.

ARTICLE 2. The Chiefs and Head Men, as aforesaid, do further agree that the road authorized in article 1, shall, when marked, be forever free for the use of the citizens of the United States and of the Mexican Republic, who shall at all times pass and repass thereon, without any hindrance or molestation on the part of the said Kansas Indians.

ARTICLE 3. The Chiefs and Head Men as aforesaid, in consideration of the friendly relations existing between them and the United States, do further promise, for themselves and their people, that they will, on all fit occasions, render such friendly aid and assistance as may be in their power, to any of the

Plains, West and Northwest Plateau Indian Treaties

citizens of the United States, or of the Mexican Republic, as they may at any time happen to meet or fall in with on the road aforesaid.

ARTICLE 4. The Chiefs and Head Men, as aforesaid, do further consent and agree that the road aforesaid shall be considered as extending to a reasonable distance on either side, so that travellers thereon may, at any time, leave the marked track, for the purpose of finding subsistence and proper camping places.

ARTICLE 5. In consideration of the privileges granted by the Chiefs of Kansas Tribe in the three preceding articles, the said commissioners, on the part of the United States, have agreed to pay to them, the said Chiefs, for themselves and their people, the sum of five hundred dollars; which sum is to be paid them as soon as may be, in money or merchandise, at their option, at such place as they may desire.

ARTICLE 6. And the said Chiefs and Head Men, as aforesaid, acknowledge to have received from the Commissioners aforesaid, at and before the signing of this Treaty, articles of merchandise to the value of three hundred dollars; which sum of three hundred dollars and the payment stipulated to be made to the said Kansas in article 5, shall be considered, and are so considered by said Chiefs, as full and complete compensation for every privilege herein granted by said Chiefs.

In testimony whereof, the said Benjamin H. Reeves, George C. Sibley, and Thomas Mather, commissioners as aforesaid, and the chiefs and head men of the Kanzas tribe or nation of Indians, have hereunto set their hands and seals, on the Sora Kanzas Creek aforesaid, this sixteenth day of August, in the year of our Lord one thousand eight hundred and twenty-five.

B. H. Reeves, G. C. Sibley, Thomas Mather,
Shone-gee-ne-garethe great chief of the Kanzas nationhis x mark,
Ke-hea-bash-eeeldest son of the great chief, (a warrior and leader) his x mark,
Hu-ra-soo-gee, (the red eagle) a chief and warrior, his x mark, Opa-she-ga, (the unready) a warrior, his x mark, Nun-gee-saggy, (the hard heart) a warrior and counsellor, his x mark, Nee-a-ke-shalla chief, brother of the great chief, his x mark, Ee-be-seen-geea warrior, his x mark, Wa-rig-ni-ne-garea warrior, his x mark,

In presence of
Archibald Gamble, secretary, Jos. G. Brown, surveyor, W. S. Williams, interpreter, Stephen Cooper, Daniel T. Bahan, Benjamin Robertson, David Murphy, Singleton Vaughn, John M. Walker, Hah-ee-see-she (white plume's deputy) warrior, his x mark, Nee-ha-wash-in-tun-ga (the passionate) warrior, his x mark, Has-ska-mo-nee (white horns that walk) warrior, his x mark, To-ka-mee-

Plains, West and Northwest Plateau Indian Treaties

ra (the scalper) warrior, his x mark, Mee-ra-ta-mo-nee (the midway walker) warrior, his x mark,
Mo-nee-ra-ta (he who walks off) chief, his x ,

TREATY WITH THE SIOUX, ETC. {1825, Aug. 19}
Proclamation. Feb. 6, 1826.

Treaty with the Sioux and Chippewa, Sacs and Fox, Menominie, Ioway, Sioux, Winnebago, and a portion of the Ottawa, Chippewa, Potawattomie, Tribes.

THE United States of America have seen with much regret, that wars have for many years been carried on between the Sioux and the Chippewas, and more recently between the confederated tribes of Sacs and Foxes, and the Sioux; and also between the Ioways and Sioux; which, if not terminated, may extend to the other tribes, and involve the Indians upon the Missouri, the Mississippi, and the Lakes, in general hostilities. In order, therefore, to promote peace among these tribes, and to establish boundaries among them and the other tribes who live in their vicinity, and thereby to remove all causes of future difficulty, the United States have invited the Chippewa, Sac, and Fox, Menominie, Ioway, Sioux, Winnebago, and a portion of the Ottowa, Chippewa and Potawatomie Tribes of Indians living upon the Illinois, to assemble together, and in a spirit of mutual conciliation to accomplish these objects; and to aid therein, have appointed William Clark and Lewis Cass, Commissioners on their part, who have met the Chiefs, Warriors, and Representatives of the said tribes, and portion of tribes, at Prairie des Chiens, in the Territory of Michigan, and after full deliberation, the said tribes, and portions of tribes, have agreed with the United States, and with one another, upon the following articles:

ARTICLE 1. There shall be a firm and perpetual peace between the Sioux and Chippewas; between the Sioux and the confederated tribes of Sacs and Foxes; and between the Ioways and the Sioux.

ARTICLE 2. It is agreed between the confederated Tribes of the Sacs and Foxes, and the Sioux, that the Line between their respective countries shall be as follows: Commencing at the mouth of the Upper Ioway River, on the west bank of the Mississippi, and ascending the said Ioway river, to its left fork; thence up that fork to its source; thence crossing the fork of Red Cedar River, in a direct line to the second or upper fork of the Desmoines river; and thence in a direct line to the lower fork of the Calumet river; and down that river to its juncture with the Missouri river.

But the Yancton band of the Sioux tribe, being principally interested in the establishment of the line from the Forks of the Desmoines to the Missouri, and not being sufficiently represented to render the definitive establishment of that line proper, it is expressly declared that the line from the forks of the Des-

85

Plains, West and Northwest Plateau Indian Treaties

moines to the forks of the Calumet river, and down that river to the Missouri, is not to be considered as settled until the assent of the Yancton band shall be given thereto. And if the said band should refuse their assent, the arrangement of that portion of the boundary line shall be void, and the rights of the parties to the country bounded thereby, shall be the same as if no provision had been made for the extension of the line west of the forks of the Desmoines. And the Sacs and Foxes relinquish to the tribes interested therein, all their claim to land on the east side of the Mississippi river.

ARTICLE 3. The Ioways accede to the arrangement between the Sacs and Foxes, and the Sioux; but it is agreed between the Ioways and the confederated tribes of the Sacs and Foxes, that the Ioways have a just claim to a portion of the country between the boundary line described in the next preceding article, and the Missouri and Mississippi; and that the said Ioways, and Sacs and Foxes, shall peaceably occupy the same, until some satisfactory arrangement can be made between them for a division of their respective claims to country.

ARTICLE 4. The Ottoes not being represented at this Council, and the Commissioners for the United States being anxious that justice should be done to all parties, and having reason to believe that the Ottoes have a just claim to a portion of the country upon the Missouri, east and south of the boundary line dividing the Sacs and Foxes and the Ioways, from the Sioux, it is agreed between the parties interested therein, and the United States, that the claim of the Ottoes shall not be affected by any thing herein contained; but the same shall remain as valid as if this treaty had not been formed.

ARTICLE 5. It is agreed between the Sioux and the Chippewas, that the line dividing their respective countries shall commence at the Chippewa River, half a day's march below the falls; and from thence it shall run to Red Cedar River, immediately below the falls; from thence to the St. Croix River, which it strikes at a place called the standing cedar, about a day's paddle in a canoe, above the Lake at the mouth of that river; thence passing between two lakes called by the Chippewas "Green Lakes," and by the Sioux "the lakes they bury the Eagles in," and from thence to the standing cedar that "the Sioux Split;" thence to Rum River, crossing it at the mouth of a small creek called choaking creek, a long day's march from the Mississippi; thence to a point of woods that projects into the prairie, half a day's march from the Mississippi; thence in a straight line to the mouth of the first river which enters the Mississippi on its west side above the mouth of Sac river; thence ascending the said river (above the mouth of Sac river) to a small lake at its source; thence in a direct line to a lake at the head of Prairie river, which is supposed to enter the Crow Wing river on its South side; thence to Otter-tail lake Portage; thence to said Otter tail lake, and down through the middle thereof, to its outlet; thence in a direct line, so as to strike Buffalo river, half way from its source to its mouth, and down the said river to Red River; thence descending Red river to the mouth of Outard or Goose creek:

Plains, West and Northwest Plateau Indian Treaties

The eastern boundary of the Sioux commences opposite the mouth of Ioway river, on the Mississippi, runs back two or three miles to the bluffs, follows the bluffs, crossing Bad axe river, to the mouth of Black river, and from Black river to half a day's march below the Falls of the Chippewa River.

ARTICLE 6. It is agreed between the Chippewas and Winnebagoes, so far as they are mutually interested therein, that the southern boundary line of the Chippewa country shall commence on the Chippewa river aforesaid, half a day's march below the falls on that river, and run thence to the source of Clear Water river, a branch of the Chippewa; thence south to Black river; thence to a point where the woods project into the meadows, and thence to the Plover Portage of the Ouisconsin.

ARTICLE 7. It is agreed between the Winnebagoes and the Sioux, Sacs and Foxes, Chippewas and Ottawas, Chippewas and Potawatomies of the Illinois, that the Winnebago country shall be bounded as follows: south easterly by Rock River, from its source near the Winnebago lake, to the Winnebago village, about forty miles above its mouth; westerly by the east line of the tract, lying upon the Mississippi, herein secured to the Ottawa, Chippewa and Potawatomie Indians, of the Illinois; and also by the high bluff, described in the Sioux boundary, and running north to Black river: from this point the Winnebagoes claim up Black river, to a point due west from the source of the left fork of the Ouisconsin; thence to the source of the said fork, and down the same to the Ouisconsin; thence down the Ouisconsin to the portage, and across the portage to Fox river; thence down Fox river to the Winnebago lake, and to the grand Kan Kanlin, including in their claim the whole of Winnebago lake; but, for the causes stated in the next article, this line from Black river must for the present be left indeterminate.

ARTICLE 8. The representatives of the Menominies not being sufficiently acquainted with their proper boundaries, to settle the same definitively, and some uncertainty existing in consequence of the cession made by that tribe upon Fox River and Green Bay, to the New York Indians, it is agreed between the said Menominie tribe, and the Sioux, Chippewas, Winnebagoes, Ottawa, Chippewa and Potawatomie Indians of the Illinois, that the claim of the Menominies to any portion of the land within the boundaries allotted to either of the said tribes, shall not be barred by any stipulation herein; but the same shall remain as valid as if this treaty had not been concluded. It is, however, understood that the general claim of the Menominies is bounded on the north by the Chippewa country, on the east by Green Bay and lake Michigan extending as far south as Millawaukee river, and on the West they claim to Black River.

ARTICLE 9. The country secured to the Ottawa, Chippewa, and Potawatomie tribes of the Illinois, is bounded as follows: Beginning at the Winnebago village, on Rock river, forty miles from its mouth and running thence down the

Plains, West and Northwest Plateau Indian Treaties

Rock river to a line which runs from Lake Michigan to the Mississippi, and with that line to the Mississippi, opposite to Rock Island; thence up that river to the United States reservation, at the mouth of the Ouisconsin; thence with the south and east lines of the said reservation to the Ouisconsin; thence, southerly, passing the heads of the small streams emptying into the Mississippi, to the Rock river at the Winnebago village. The Illinois Indians have also a just claim to a portion of the country bounded south by the Indian boundary line aforesaid, running from the southern extreme of lake Michigan, east by lake Michigan, north by the Menominie country, and north-west by Rock river. This claim is recognized in the treaty concluded with the said Illinois tribes at St. Louis, August 24, 1816, but as the Millewakee and Manctoowalk bands are not represented at this Council, it cannot be now definitively adjusted.

ARTICLE 10. All the tribes aforesaid acknowledge the general controlling power of the United States, and disclaim all dependence upon, and connection with, any other power. And the United States agree to, and recognize, the preceding boundaries, subject to the limitations and restrictions before provided. It being, however, well understood that the reservations at Fever River, at the Ouisconsin, and St. Peters, and the ancient settlements at Prairie des Chiens and Green Bay, and the land property thereto belonging, and the reservations made upon the Mississippi, for the use of the half breeds, in the treaty concluded with the Sacs and Foxes, August 24, 1824, are not claimed by either of the said tribes.

ARTICLE 11. The United States agree, whenever the President may think it necessary and proper, to convene such of the tribes, either separately or together, as are interested in the lines left unsettled herein, and to recommend to them an amicable and final adjustment of their respective claims, so that the work, now happily begun, may be consummated. It is agreed, however, that a Council shall be held with the Yancton band of the Sioux, during the year 1826, to explain to them the stipulations of this treaty, and to procure their assent thereto, should they be disposed to give it, and also with the Ottoes, to settle and adjust their title to any of the country claimed by the Sacs, Foxes, and Ioways.

ARTICLE 12. The Chippewa tribe being dispersed over a great extent of country, and the Chiefs of that tribe having requested, that such portion of them as may be thought proper, by the Government of the United States, may be assembled in 1826, upon some part of Lake Superior, that the objects and advantages of this treaty may be fully explained to them, so that the stipulations thereof may be observed by the warriors. The Commissioners of the United States assent thereto, and it is therefore agreed that a council shall accordingly be held for these purposes.

Plains, West and Northwest Plateau Indian Treaties

ARTICLE 13. It is understood by all the tribes, parties hereto, that no tribe shall hunt within the acknowledged limits of any other without their assent, but it being the sole object of this arrangement to perpetuate a peace among them, and amicable relations being now restored, the Chiefs of all the tribes have expressed a determination, cheerfully to allow a reciprocal right of hunting on the lands of one another, permission being first asked and obtained, as before provided for.

ARTICLE 14. Should any causes of difficulty hereafter unhappily arise between any of the tribes, parties hereunto, it is agreed that the other tribes shall interpose their good offices to remove such difficulties; and also that the government of the United States may take such measures as they may deem proper, to effect the same object.

ARTICLE 15. This treaty shall be obligatory on the tribes, parties hereto, from and after the date hereof, and on the United States, from and after its ratification by the government thereof.

Done, and signed, and scaled, at Prairie des Chiens, in the territory of Michigan, this nineteenth day of August, one thousand eight hundred and twenty-five, and of the independence of the United States the fiftieth.

William Clark, Lewis Cass,
Sioux:
Wa-ba-sha, x or the leaf, Pe-tet-te x Corbeau, little crow, The Little x of the Wappitong tribe, Tartunka-nasiah x Sussitong, Sleepy Eyes, x Sossitong, Two faces x Sossitong, French Crow x Wappacoota, Kee-jec x Wappacoota, Tar-se-ga x Wappacoota, Wa-ma-de-tun-ka x black dog, Wan-na-ta x Yancton, or he that charges on his enemies, Red Wing x

The Little Crow, x Sussetong, Po-e-ha-pa x Me-da-we-con-tong, or eagle head, Ta-ke-wa-pa x Wappitong, or medicine blanket, Tench-ze-part, x his bow, Masc-pu-lo-chas-tosh, x the white man, Te-te-kar-munch,x the buffalo man, Wa-sa-o-ta x Sussetong, or a great of hail, Oeyah-ko-ca, x the crackling tract, Mak-to-
Wa-non-che-qua, x the merchant, Chon-que-pa, x or dog's head, Cha-rat-chon, x the smoker, Ca-ri-ca-si-ca,
Watch-kat-o-que, x the grand canoe, Ho-wa-mick-a, x the little elk,
Men omi nees:
Ma-can-me-ta, x medicine bear, Chau-wee-nou-mi-tai, x medicine south wind, Char-o-nee, x
Ma-wesh-a, x the little wolf, A-ya-pas-mis-ai, x the thunder that turns, Cha-ne-pau, x the riband, La-me-quon, x the spoon, En-im-e-tas, x the barking wolf, Pape-at, x the one just arrived, O-que-men-ce, x the little chief,

Plains, West and Northwest Plateau Indian Treaties

Chippewas:
Shinguaba x W'Ossin, 1st chief of the Chippewa nation, Saulte St. Marie, Gitspee x Jiauba, 2d chief, Gitspee x Waskee, or le boeuf of la pointe lake Superior, Nain-a-boozhu, x of lapointe lake Superior, Monga, x Zid or loon's foot of Fond du Lac, Weescoup, x or sucre of Fond du Lac, Mush-Koas, x or the elk of Fond du Lac, Nau-bun x Aqeezhik, of Fond du Lac, Kau-ta-waubeta, x or broken tooth of Sandy lake, Pugisaingegen, x or broken arm of Sandy lake, Kweeweezaishish, x or gross guelle of Sandy lake,
Ba-ba-see-kundade, x or curling hair of Sandy lake, Paashineep, x or man shooting at the mark of Sandy lake, Pu-ga-a-gik, x the little beef, Leech lake, Pee-see-ker, x or buffalo, St. Croix band, Nau-din, x or the wind, St. Croix band, Nau-quan-a-bee, x of Mille lac,
Ottawas:
Chaboner, x or Chambly, Shaw-fau-wick, x the mink,
Potawatomies:
Ignace, x
Ke-o-kuk, x
Che-chan-quose, x the little crane, Taw-wa-na-nee, x the trader,
Sacs:
Na-o-tuk, x the stabbing chief, Pish-ken-au-nee, x all fish, Po-ko-nau-qua, x or broken arm, Wau-kau-che, x eagle nose, Quash-kaume, x jumping fish, Ochaach, x the fisher, Ke-o-kuck, x the watchful fox, Skin-gwin-ee-see, the x ratler, Was-ar-wis-ke-no, x the yellow bird, Pau-ko-tuk, x the open sky, Aukaak-wan-e-suk, x he that vaults on the earth, Mu-ku-taak-wan-wet, x
Mis-ke-bee, x the standing hair,
Foxes:
Wan-ba-law, x the playing fox, Ti-a-mah, x the bear that makes the rocks shake, Pee-ar-maski, x the jumping sturgeon, Shagwa-na-tekwishu, x the thunder that is heard all over the world, Mis-o-win, x moose deer horn, No-ko-wot, x the down of the fur, Nau-sa-wa-quot, x the bear that sleeps on the forks, Shinquirt-is, x the ratler, O-lo-pee-aau, x or Mache-paho-ta, the bear, Keesis, x the sun, No-wank, x he that gives too little, Kan-ka-mote, x
Neck-wad, x

Witnesses:
Thomas Biddie, secretary, R. A. McCabe, Captain Fifth Infantry, R. A. Forsyth, N. Boilvin, United States Indian agent, C. C. Trowbridge, sub Indian agent, Henry R. SchoolCraft, United States Indian agent, B. F. Harney, Surgeon U. S. Army, W. B. Alexander, sub Indian agent, Thomas Forsyth, agent Indian affairs, Marvien Blondau, David Bailey, James M'Ilvaine, lieutenant U. S. Army, Law.
Taliaferro, Indian agent for Upper Mississippi, John Holiday, William Dickson, S. Campbell, United States interpreter, J. A. Lewis, William Holiday, Dunable Denejlevy, Bela Chapman.

Plains, West and Northwest Plateau Indian Treaties

TREATY WITH THE OTO AND MISSOURI TRIBE {1825, Sept. 26}
Proclamation, Feb. 6, 1826.

For the purpose of perpetuating the friendship which has heretofore existed, as also to remove all future cause of discussion or dissension, as it respects trade and friendship between the United States and their citizens, and the Ottoe and Missouri tribe of Indians, the President of the United States of America, by Brigadier-General Henry Atkinson, of the United States army, and Major Benjamin O'Fallon, Indian Agent, with full powers and authority, specially appointed and commissioned for that purpose, of the one part, and the undersigned Chiefs, Head-men, and Warriors, of the said Ottoe and Missouri tribe of Indians, on behalf of their tribe, of the other part, have made and entered into the following articles and conditions, which, when ratified by the President of the United States, by and with the advice and consent of the Senate, shall be binding on both partiesto wit:

ARTICLE 1. It is admitted by the Ottoe and Missouri tribe of Indians, that they reside within the territorial limits of the United States, acknowledge their supremacy, and claim their protection. The said tribe also admit the right of the United States to regulate all trade and intercourse with them.

ARTICLE 2. The United States agree to receive the Ottoe and Missouri tribe of Indians into their friendship, and under their protection, and to extend to them, from time to time, such benefits and acts of kindness as may be convenient, and seem just and proper to the President of the United States.

ARTICLE 3. All trade and intercourse with the Ottoe and Missouri tribe shall be transacted at such place or places as may be designated and pointed out by the President of the United States, through his agents; and none but American citizens, duly authorized by the United States, shall be admitted to trade or hold intercourse with said tribe of Indians.

ARTICLE 4. That the Ottoe and Missouri tribe may be accommodated with such articles of merchandise, etc, as their necessities may demand, the United States agree to admit and license traders to hold intercourse with said tribe, under mild and equitable regulations: in consideration of which, the said Ottoe and Missouri tribe bind themselves to extend protection to the persons and the property of the traders, and the persons legally employed under them, whilst they remain within the limits of their particular district of country. And the said Ottoe and Missouri tribe further agree, that if any foreigner or other person, not legally authorized by the United States, shall come into their district of country, for the purposes of trade or other views, they will apprehend such person or persons, and deliver him or them to some United States superintendent or agent

Plains, West and Northwest Plateau Indian Treaties

of Indian Affairs, or to the Commandant of the nearest military post, to be dealt with according to law.

And they further agree to give safe conduct to all persons who may be legally authorized by the United States to pass through their country: and to protect, in their persons and property, all agents or other persons sent by the United States to reside temporarily among them; nor will they, whilst on their distant excursions, molest or interrupt any American citizen or citizens who may be passing from the United States to New Mexico, or returning from thence to the United States.

ARTICLE 5. That the friendship which is now established between the United States and the Ottoe and Missouri tribe should not be interrupted by the misconduct of individuals, it is hereby agreed, that for injuries done by individuals, no private revenge or retaliation shall take place, but instead thereof, complaint shall be made, by the party injured, to the superintendent or agent of Indian affairs, or other person appointed by the President; and it shall be the duty of said Chiefs, upon complaint being made as aforesaid, to deliver up the person or persons against whom the complaint is made, to the end that he or they may be punished agreeably to the laws of the United States. And, in like manner, if any robbery, violence, or murder, shall be committed on any Indian or Indians belonging to said tribe, the person or persons so offending shall be tried, and if found guilty shall be punished in like manner as if the injury had been done to a white man. And it is agreed, that the Chiefs of said Ottoe and Missouri tribe shall, to the utmost of their power, exert themselves to recover horses or other property, which may be stolen or taken from any citizen or citizens of the U hired States, by any individual or individuals of said tribe; and the property so recovered shall be forthwith delivered to the agents or other person authorized to receive it, that it may be restored to the proper owner.

And the United States hereby guarranty to any Indian or Indians of said tribe, a full indemnification for any horses or other property which may be stolen from them by any of their citizens: Provided, That the property stolen cannot be recovered, and that sufficient proof is produced that it was actually stolen by a citizen of the United States. And the said Ottoe and Missouri tribe engage, on the requisition or demand of the President of the United States, or of the agents, to deliver up any white man resident among them.

ARTICLE 6. And the Chiefs and Warriors, as aforesaid, promise and engage, that, their tribe will never, by sale, exchange, or as presents, supply any nation, tribe, or band of Indians, not in amity with the United States, with guns, ammunition, or other implements of war.
Done at Fort Atkinson, Council Bluffs, this 26th day of September, A. D. 1825, and of the independence of the United States the fiftieth.

Plains, West and Northwest Plateau Indian Treaties

In testimony whereof, the said commissioners, Henry Atkinson and Benjamin O'Fallon, and the chiefs, head men, and warriors, of the Ottoe and Missouri tribe, have hereunto set their hands, and affixed their seals.

H. Atkinson, brigadier-general U. S. Army, Benj. O' Fallon, United States agent, Indian affairs,
Chiefs:
Ish-na-wong-ge-ge-he, the only chief, his x mark, Me-ha-hun-jah, the big female, his x mark, Skunk-so-pe, his x mark, Sho-mon-e-ka-sa, the prairie wolf, his x mark, Wong-ge-ge-he, the chief, his x mark, Waw-so-e-ing ge, the little black bear, his x mark, Eho-che-nung-a, the mad man, his x mark, E-ke-shaw-mon-ne, the walking bear, his x mark, Waw-ne-sung-e, the one who bears down, his x mark, Waw-ro-ne-sa, the bullet, his x mark, Wa-do-ke-ga, his x mark, Waw-paw-si-ae, his x mark,
Taw-ing-ee, the little dear, his x mark, Gray-tan-in-ca, the sparrow hawk, his x mark, Raw-no-way-braw, the broken pipe, his x mark, Non-jah-ning-e, the no heart, his x mark, Mon-to-ing-ge, the little bear, his x mark, mosk-ca-gaw-ha, his x mark,

In presence of
A. L. Langham, secretary to the commission, A. R. Woolley, lieutenant-colonel, U. S. Army, B. Riley, captain, Sixth Infantry, J. Gantt, captain, Sixth Infantry, John Gale, surgeon, U. S. Army, Wm. N. Wickliffe, lieutenant, U. S. Army, G. W. Folger, lieutenant, Sixth U. S.Infantry, J. Rogers, lieutenant, Sixth Infantry, Levi Nute, lieutenant, Sixth Infantry, M. W. Batman, lieutenant, Sixth Infantry, A. Richardson, lieutenant, Sixth Infantry, J. Nichols, lieutenant, Sixth Infantry,
G. H. Crosman, lieutenant, Sixth Infantry, G. H. Kennerly, U. S. S. Indian agent, W. W. Eaton, lieutenant, Sixth Infantry, Michael Burdeau, his x mark, Maha interpreter, William Rogers.

TREATY WITH THE PAWNEE TRIBE {1825, Sept. 3}
Proclamation, Feb. 6, 1826.

FOR the purpose of perpetuating the friendship which has heretofore existed, as also to remove all future cause of discussion or dissension, as it respects trade and friendship between the United States and their citizens, and the Pawnee tribe of Indians, the President of the United States of America, by Brigadier General Henry Atkinson, Of the United States army, and Major Benjamin O'Fallon, Indian Agent, with full powers and authority, specially appointed and commissioned for that purpose, of the one part, and the undersigned Chiefs, head men and Warriors of said Pawnee tribe of Indians, on behalf of their tribe of the other part, have made and entered into the following Articles and Condi-

Plains, West and Northwest Plateau Indian Treaties

tions; which, when ratified by the President of the United States, by and with the advice and consent of the Senate, shall be binding on both parties to wit:

ARTICLE 1. It is admitted by the Pawnee tribe of Indians, that they reside within the territorial limits of the United States, acknowledge their supremacy, and claim their protection. The said tribe also admit the right of the United States to regulate all trade and intercourse with them.

ARTICLE 2. The United States agree to receive the Pawnee tribe of Indians into their friendship, and under their protection, and to extend to them, from time to time, such benefits and acts of kindness as may be convenient, and seem just and proper to the President of the United States.

ARTICLE 3. All trade and intercourse with the Pawnee tribe shall be transacted at such place or places as may be designated and pointed out by the President of the United States, through his agents; and none but American citizens, duly authorized by the United States, shall be admitted to trade or hold intercourse with said tribe of Indians.

ARTICLE 4. That the Pawnee tribe may be accommodated with such articles of merchandise, &c, as their necessities may demand, the United States agree to admit and license traders to hold intercourse with said tribe, under mild and equitable regulations: in consideration of which, the said Pawnee tribe bind themselves to extend protection to the persons and the property of the traders, and the persons legally employed under them, whilst they remain within the limits of their particular district of country. And the said Pawnee tribe further agree, that if any foreigner or other person, not legally authorized by the United States, shall come into their district of country, for the purpose of trade or other views, they will apprehend such person or persons, and deliver him or them to some United States superintendent, or agent, of Indian Affairs, or to the commandant of the nearest military post, to be dealt with according to law.

And they further agree to give safe conduct to all persons who may be legally authorized by the United States to pass through their country, and to protect in their persons and, property all agents or other persons sent by the United States to reside temporarily among them; nor will they, whilst on their distant excursions, molest or interrupt any American citizen or citizens, who may be passing from the United States to New Mexico, or returning from thence to the United States.

ARTICLE 5. That the friendship which is now established between the United States and the Pawnee tribe, shall not be interrupted by the misconduct of individuals, it is hereby agreed, that for injuries done by individuals, no private revenge or retaliation shall take place, but instead thereof, complaints shall be made, by the party injured, to the superintendent, or agent of Indian affairs, or

Plains, West and Northwest Plateau Indian Treaties

other person appointed by the President; and it shall be the duty of said Chiefs, upon complaint being made as aforesaid, to deliver up the person or persons against whom the complaint is made, to the end that he or they may be punished, agreeably to the laws of the United States.

And, in like manner, if any robbery, violence, or murder, shall be committed on any Indian or Indians belonging to said tribe, the person or persons so offending shall be tried, and if found guilty, shall be punished in like manner as if the injury had been done to a white man. And it is agreed, that the Chiefs of said Pawnee tribe shall, to the utmost of their power, exert themselves to recover horses or other property, which may be stolen or taken from any citizen or citizens of the United States, by any individual or individuals of said tribe; and the property so recovered shall be forthwith delivered to the agents or other person authorized to receive it, that it may be restored to the proper owner. And the United States hereby guaranty to any Indian or Indians of said tribe, a full indemnification for any horses or other property which may be stolen from them by any of their citizens: Provided, That the property stolen cannot be recovered, and that sufficient proof is produced that it was actually stolen by a citizen of the United States.

And the said Pawnee tribe engage, on the requisition or demand of the President of the United States, or of the agents, to deliver up any white man resident among them.

ARTICLE 6. And the Chiefs and Warriors, as aforesaid, promise and engage that their tribe will never, by sale, exchange, or as presents, supply any nation, tribe, or band of Indians, not in amity with the United States, with guns, ammunition, or other implements of war.

Done at Fort Atkinson, Council Bluffs, this thirtieth day of September, A. D. 1825, and of the independence of the United States the fiftieth.

In testimony whereof, the said commissioners, Henry Atkinson and Benjamin O'Fallon, and the chiefs, head men, and warriors, of the Pawnee tribe, have hereunto set their hands and affixed their seals.

H. Atkinson, brigadier-general, U. S. Army, Benj. O'Fallon, United States agent, Indian affairs,
Esh-ca-tar-pa, the bad chief, his x mark, Shar-co-ro-la-shar, the sun chief, his x mark,
La-cota-ve-co-choqa-shar, the eagle chief, his x mark, La-tah-cartsqa-shar, the war eagle chief, his x mark, La-ta-le-shar, the knife chief, his x mark, Scar-lar-la-shar, the ,nan chief, his x mark, La-ke-tar-la-shar, the partizan chief, his x

Plains, West and Northwest Plateau Indian Treaties

mark, Lark-tar-ho-ra-la-shar, the pipe chief, his x mark, Esh-ca-tar-pa, the bad chief, republican band, his x mark,

In presence of
A. L. Langham, secretary to the commission. A. R. Woolley, lieutenant-colonel, U. S. Army.John Gale, surgeon, U. S. Army. John Gantt, captain, Sixth infantry.S. MacRee, aide de camp. Thomas Noel, adjutant, Sixth regiment.

TREATY WITH THE MAKAH TRIBE {1825, Oct. 6}
Proclamation, Feb. 6, 1826.

FOR the purpose of perpetuating the friendship which has heretofore existed, as also to remove all future cause of discussion or dissension, as it respects trade and friendship between the United States and their citizens, and the Maha tribe of Indians, the President of the United States of America, by Brigadier General Henry Atkinson, of the United States Army, and Major Benjamin O'Fallon, Indian Agent, with full powers and authority, specially appointed and commissioned for that purpose, of the one part, and the undersigned Chiefs, Head-men and Warriors, of the said Maha tribe of Indians, on behalf of their tribe, of the other part, have made and entered into the following articles and conditions, which, when ratified by the President of the United States, by and with the advice and consent of the Senate, shall be binding on both partiesto wit:

ARTICLE 1. It is admitted by the Maha tribe of Indians, that they reside within the territorial limits of the United States, acknowledge their supremacy, and claim their protection. The said tribe also admit the right of the United States to regulate all trade and intercourse with them.

ARTICLE 2. The United States agree to receive the Maha tribe of Indians into their friendship, and under their protection, and to extend to them, from time to time, such benefits and acts of kindness as may be convenient, and seem just and proper to the President of the United States.

ARTICLE 3. All trade and intercourse with the Maha tribe shall be transacted at such place or places as may be designated and pointed out by the President of the United States, through his agents: and none but American citizens, duly authorized by the United States, shall be admitted to trade or hold intercourse with said tribe of Indians.

ARTICLE 4. That the Maha tribe may be accommodated with such articles of merchandise, &c, as their necessities may demand, the United States agree to admit and license traders to hold intercourse with said tribe, under mild and equitable regulations: in consideration of which, the Maha tribe bind themselves to extend protection to the persons and the property of the traders, and

Plains, West and Northwest Plateau Indian Treaties

the persons legally employed under them, whilst they remain within the limits of their particular district of country.

And the said Maha tribe further agree, that if any foreigner, or other person not legally authorized by the United States, shall come into their district of country, for the purposes of trade or other views, they will apprehend such person or persons, and deliver him or them to some United States superintendent or agent of Indian Affairs, or to the Commandant of the nearest military post, to be dealt with according to law.And they further agree to give safe conduct to all persons who may be legally authorized by the United States to pass through their country; and to protect in their persons and property, all agents or other persons sent by the United States to reside temporarily among them; nor will they, whilst on their distant excursions, molest or interrupt any American citizen or citizens who may be passing from the United States to New Mexico, or returning from thence to the United States.

ARTICLE 5. That the friendship which is now established between the United States and the Maha tribe should not be interrupted by the misconduct of individuals, it is hereby agreed, that, for injuries done by individuals, no private revenge or retaliation shall take place, but instead thereof, complaints shall be made by the party injured, to the superintendent or agent of Indian affairs, or other person appointed by the President; and it shall be the duty of said Chiefs, upon complaint being made as aforesaid, to deliver up the person or persons against whom the complaint is made, to the end that he or they may be punished agreeably to the laws of the United States. And, in like manner, if any robbery, violence, or murder, shall be committed on any Indian or Indians belonging to said tribe, the person or persons so offending shall be tried, and if found guilty shall be punished in like manner as if the injury had been done to a white man.

And it is agreed, that the Chiefs of said Maha tribe shall, to the utmost of their power, exert themselves to recover horses or other property, which may be stolen or taken from any citizen or citizens of the United States, by any individual or individuals of said tribe; and the property so recovered shall be forthwith delivered to the agents or other person authorized to receive it, that it may be restored to the proper owner. And the United States hereby guarranty to any Indian or Indians of said tribe, a full indemnification for any horses or other property which may be stolen from them by any of their citizens: Provided, That the property stolen cannot be recovered, and that sufficient proof is produced that it was actually stolen by a citizen of the United States. And the said Maha tribe engage, on the requisition or demand of the President of the United States, or of the agents, to deliver up any white man resident among them.

ARTICLE 6. And the Chiefs and Warriors, as aforesaid, promise and engage, that their tribe will never, by sale, exchange, or as presents, supply any nation,

Plains, West and Northwest Plateau Indian Treaties

tribe, or band of Indians, not in amity with the United States, with guns, ammunition, or other implements of war.

Done at fort Atkinson, Council Bluffs, this 6th day of October, A. D. 1825, and of the independence of the United States the fiftieth.

In testimony whereof, the said commissioners, Henry Atkinson and Benjamin O'Fallon, and the chiefs, head men, and warriors of the Maha tribe, have hereunto set their hands, and affixed their seals.

H. Atkinson, brigadier-general U. S. Army, Benj. O'Fallon, U. S. agent Indian affairs,
Opa-ton-ga, the big elk, his x mark, Oho-shin-ga, the man that cooks little in a small kettle, his x mark, Wash-ca-ma-nee, the fast walker, his x mark, Shon-gis-cah, the white horse, his x mark, We-du-gue-noh, the deliberator, his x mark, Wa-shing-ga-sabba, the black bird, his x mark,

In the presence of
A. L. Langham, secretary to the commission, A. R. Wooley, lieutenant-colonel U. S.
Army, J. Gantt, captain Sixth Infantry, John Gale, surgeon U. S. Army, Ta-noh-ga, the buffalo bull, his x mark, Esh-sta-ra-ba, , his x mark, Ta-reet-tee, the side of a buffalo, his x mark, Sa-da-ma-ne, he that arrives, his x mark, Mo-pe-ma-nee, the walking cloud, his x mark, Momee-shee, he who lays on the arrows from the number that pierce him, his x mark, Ma-sha-ke-ta, the soldier, his x mark,
Te-sha-va-gran, the door of the lodge, his x mark, George C. Hutter, lieutenant Sixth Infantry, M. W. Batman, lieutenant Sixth Infantry, G. H. Kennerly, U. S. S. Indian agent, Michael Burdeau, his x mark, interpreter, William Rodgers.

TREATY WITH THE POTAWATOMI {1827, Sept. 19}
Proclamation, Feb. 23, 1829.

A treaty between the United States and the Potawatamie Tribe of Indians.

IN order to consolidate some of the dispersed bands of the Potawatamie Tribe in the Territory of Michigan at a point removed from the road leading from Detroit to Chicago, and as far as practicable from the settlements of the Whites, it is agreed that the following tracts of land, heretofore reserved for the use of the said Tribe, shall be, and they are hereby, ceded to the United States.

Two sections of land on the river Rouge at Seginsairn's village.
Two sections of land at Tonguish's village, near the river Rouge.

Plains, West and Northwest Plateau Indian Treaties

That part of the reservation at Macon on the river Raisin, which vet belongs to the said tribe, containing six sections, excepting therefrom one half of a section where the Potawatamie Chief Moran resides, which shall be reserved for his use.

One tract at Mang ach qua village, on the river Peble, of six miles square.
One tract at Mickesawbe, of six miles square.
One tract at the village of Prairie Rondo, of three miles square. One tract at the village of Match e be nash she wish, at the head of the Kekalamazoo river, of three miles square, which tracts contain in the whole ninety nine sections and one half section of land.

And in consideration of the preceding cession, there shall be reserved for the use of the said tribe, to be held upon the same terms on which Indian reservations are usually held, the following tracts of land.
Sections numbered five, six seven and eight, in the fifth township, south of the base line, and in the ninth range west of the principal meridian in the Territory of Michigan.
The whole of the fifth township, south, in the tenth range, west, not already included in the Nottawa Sape reservation.

Sections numbered one, two, eleven, twelve, thirteen, fourteen, twenty-three, twenty-four, twenty-five, twenty-six, thirty-five, and thirty-six, in the fifth township, south, and eleventh range, west.
The whole of the fourth township, south, in the ninth range, west. Sections numbered eight, seventeen, eighteen, nineteen, twenty, twenty-nine, thirty, thirty-one and thirty-two, in the fourth township, south, and ninth range, west.

Sections numbered one, two, eleven, twelve, thirteen, fourteen, twenty-three, twenty-four, twenty-five, twenty-six, thirty-five and thirty-six, in the fourth township, south, and eleventh range, west.

Which tracts of land will form a continuous reservation, and contain ninety-nine sections.
After this treaty shall be ratified by the President and Senate, the same shall be obligatory on the United States and the said tribe of Indians.

In testimony whereof, Lewis Cass, commissioner on the part of the United States, and the chiefs and warriors of the said tribe, have hereunto set their hands at St. Joseph, in the territory of Michigan, this nineteenth day of September, A. D. one thousand eight hundred and twenty-seven.

Lewis Cass,
Mixs-a-bee, his x mark, Shee-ko-maig, or marsh fish, his x mark, Pee-nai-sheish, or little bird, his x mark, Kne-o-suck-o-wah, his x mark, Mais-ko-see,

Plains, West and Northwest Plateau Indian Treaties

his x mark, A-bee-ta-que-zic, or half day, his x mark, Ko-jai-waincc, his x mark, Sa-kec-maus, his x mark, Mitch-c-pe-nain-she-wish, or bad bird, his x mark, Ma-tsai-bat-to, his x mark, Ne-kee-quin-nish-ka, his x mark, Wa-kai-she-maus, his x mark, Peerish Moran, his x mark, Mee-she-pe-she-wa-non, his x mark, O-tuck-quen, his x mark,

In presence of
John L. Leib, R. A. Forsyth, Benj. B. Kercheval, Isaac McCoy, G. W. Silliman, James J. Godfroy, Joseph Bertrand, T. T. Smith.

TREATY WITH THE WINNEBAGO, ETC {1828, Aug. 25}
Proclamation, Jan. 7, 1829.

Articles of agreement with the Winnebago Tribe and the United Tribes of Po-tawatamie, Chippewa and Ottawa Indians.

THE Government of the United States having appointed Commissioners to treat with the Sac, Fox, Winebago, Potawatamie, Ottawa, and Chippewa, tribes of Indians, for the purpose of extinguishing their title to land within the State of Illinois, and the Territory of Michigan, situated between the Illinois river and the Lead Mines on Fever River, and in the vicinity of said Lead Mines, and for other purposes; and it having been found impracticable, in consequence of the lateness of the period when the instructions were issued, the extent of the country occupied by the Indians, and their dispersed situation, to convene them in sufficient numbers to justify a cession of land on their part; and the Chiefs of the Winnebago tribe, and of the united tribes of the Potawatamies, Chippewas, and Ottawas, assembled at Green Bay, having declined at this time to make the desired cession, the following temporary arrangement, subject to the ratifica-tion of the President and Senate of the United States, has this day been made, between Lewis Cass and Pierre Menard, Commissioners of the United States, and the said Winnebago tribe, and the United tribes of Potawatamie, Chippewa, and Ottawa, Indians, in order to remove the difficulties which nave arisen in consequence of the occupation, by white persons, of that part of the mining country which has not been heretofore ceded to the United States.

ARTICLE 1. It is agreed that the following shall be the provisional boundary between the lands of the United States and those of the said Indians: The Ouis-consin river, from its mouth to its nearest approach to the Blue Mounds; thence southerly, passing east of the said mounds, to the head of that branch of the Pocatolaka creek which runs near the Spotted Arm's village; thence with the said branch to the main forks of Pocatolaka creek; thence southeasterly, to the ridge dividing the Winebago country from that of the Potawatamie, Chippewa, and Ottawa tribes; thence southerly, with the said ridge, to the line running from Chicago to the Mississippi, near Rock Island. And it is fully understood,

Plains, West and Northwest Plateau Indian Treaties

that the United States may freely occupy the country between these boundaries and the Mississippi river, until a treaty shall be held with the Indians for its cession; which treaty, it is presumed, will be held in the year 1829.

But it is expressly understood and agreed, that if any white persons shall cross the line herein described, and pass into the Indian country, for the purpose of mining, or for any other purpose whatever, the Indians shall not interfere with nor molest such persons, but that the proper measures for their removal shall be referred to the President of the United States. In the mean time, however, it is agreed, that any just compensation to which the Indians may be entitled for any injuries committed by white persons on the Indian side of the said line, shall be paid to the said Indians at the time such treaty may be heldIt is also agreed by the Indians that a ferry may be established over the Rock River, where the Fort Clark road crosses the same; and, also, a ferry over the same river at the crossing of the Lewiston road.

ARTICLE 2. The United States agree to pay to the Winebago, Potawatamie, Chippewa, and Ottawa Indians, the sum of twenty thousand dollars, in goods, at the time and place when and where the said treaty may be held: which said sum shall be equitably divided between the said tribes, and shall be in full compensation for all the injuries and damages sustained by them, in consequence of the occupation of any part of the mining country by white persons, from the commencement of such occupation until the said treaty shall be held. Excepting, however, such compensation as the Indians may be entitled to, for any injuries hereafter committed on their side of the line hereby established.

In testimony whereof, the said commissioners and the chiefs of the said tribes have hereunto set their hands at Green bay, in the territory of Michigan, this 25th day of August, in the year of our Lord one thousand eight hundred and twenty-eight.

Lewis Cass
Pierre Menard.

Winnebagoes:
Nan-kaw, or wood, his x mark, Koan-kaw, or chief, his x mark, Hoo-wam-ee-kaw, or little elk, his x mark, Tshay-ro-tsboan-kaw, or smoker, his x mark, Hatmp-ee-man-ne-kaw, or he who walks by day, his x mark, Hoo-tshoap-kaw, or four legs, his x mark, Morah-tshay-kaw, or little priest, his x mark, Kau-ree-kau-saw-kaw, or white crow, his x mark, Wan-kaun-haw-kaw, or snake skin, his x mark, Man-ah-kee-tshump-kaw, or spotted arm, his x mark, Wee-no-shee-kaw, his x mark,
Tshaw-wan-shaip-shootsh-kaw, his x mark, Hoootshoap-kaw, or four legs, (senior) his x mark, Nau-soo-ray-risk-kaw, his x mark, Shoank-tshunsk-kaw, or black wolf, his x mark, Wau-tshe-roo-kun-ah-kaw, or he who is master of the

101

Plains, West and Northwest Plateau Indian Treaties

lodge, his x mark, Kay-rah-tsho-kaw, or clear weather, his x mark, Hay-ro-kaw-kaw, or he without horns, his x mark, Wau-kaum-kam, or snake, his x mark, Kan-kaw-saw-kaw, his x mark, Man-kay-ray-kau, or spotted earth, his x mark, Thaun-wan-kaw, or wild cat, his x mark,
Span-you-kaw, or Spaniard, his x mark, Shoank-skaw-kaw, or white dog, his x mark,

Witnesses present:
W.B. Lee, secretary, H.
J. B. Brevoort, United States Indian agent, R. A. Forsyth, Jno. H. Kinzie, John Marsh, E. A.Brush, G. W. Silliman, C.Chouteau, Peter Menard, jun. , Indian subagent, Henry Gratiot, Pierre Paquet, Winnebago interpreter, J. Ogee, Potawatamie interpreter.

TREATY WITH THE POTAWATOMI {1828, Sept. 20}
Proclamation, Jan. 7, 1829.

Articles of a treaty made and concluded at the Missionary Establishments upon the St. Joseph, of Lake Michigan, in the Territory of Michigan, this 20th day of September, in the year of our Lord one thousand eight hundred and twenty-eight, between Lewis Cass and Pierre Ménard, Commissioners, on the part of the United States, and the Potowatami tribe of Indians.

ARTICLE 1. The Potowatami tribe of Indians cede to the United States the tract of land included within the following boundaries:

First. Beginning at the mouth of the St. Joseph, of Lake Michigan, and thence running up the said river to a point on the same river, half way between Lavache-qui-pisse and Macousin village: thence in a direct line, to the 19th mile tree, on the northern boundary line of the State Indiana; thence, with the same, west, to Lake Michigan; and thence, with the shore of the said Lake, to the place of beginning.

Second. Beginning at a point on the line run in 1817, due east from the southern extreme of Lake Michigan, which point is due south from the head of the most easterly branch of the Kankekee river, and from that point running south ten miles; thence, in a direct line, to the northeast corner of Flatbelly's reservation; thence, to the northwest corner of the reservation at Seek's village; thence, with the lines of the said reservation, and of former cessions, to the line between the States of Indiana and Ohio; thence, with the same to the former described line, running due east from the southern extreme of Lake Michigan; and thence, with the said line, to the place of beginning.

102

Plains, West and Northwest Plateau Indian Treaties

ARTICLE 2. In consideration of the cessions aforesaid, there shall be paid to the said tribe an additional permanent annuity of two thousand dollars; and also an additional annuity of one thousand dollars, for the term of twenty years; goods, to the value of thirty thousand dollars, shall be given to the said tribe, either immediately after signing this treaty, or as soon thereafter as they can be procured; an additional sum of ten thousand dollars, in goods, and another of five thousand dollars, in specie, shall be paid to them in the year 1829.

The sum of seven thousand five hundred dollars shall be expended for the said tribe, under the direction of the President of the United States, in clearing and fencing land, erecting houses, purchasing domestic animals and farming utensils, and in the support of labourers to work for them. Two thousand pounds of tobacco, fifteen hundred weight of iron, and three hundred and fifty pounds of steel, shall be annually delivered to them. One thousand dollars per annum shall be applied for the purposes Congress may think the appropriation may be of education, as long as useful.

One hundred dollars, in goods, shall be annually paid to To-pen-i-be-the, principal chief of the said tribe, during his natural life. The blacksmith, stipulated by the treaty of Chicago to be provided for the term of fifteen years, shall be permanently supported by the United States.
Three labourers shall be provided, during four months of the year, for ten years, to work for the band living upon the reservation South of the St. Joseph.

ARTICLE 3. There shall be granted to the following persons, all of whom are Indians by descent, the tracts of land hereafter mentioned, which shall be located upon the second cession above described, where the President of the United States may direct, after the country may be surveyed, and to correspond with the surveys, provided that no location shall be made upon the Elkheart Prairie, nor within five miles of the same; nor shall the tracts there granted be conveyed by the grantees, without the consent of the President of the United States.

To Sah-ne-mo-quay, wife of Jean B. Dutrist, one-half section of land.
To Way-pe-nah-te-mo-quay, wife of Thomas Robb, one half section of land.
To Me-no-ka-mick-quay, wife of Edward McCarty, one half section of land.
To Ship-pe-shick-quay, wife of James Wyman, one half section of land.
To Assapo, wife of Antoine Gamlin, one half section of land.
To Moahquay, wife of Richard Chabert, one half section of land. To Me-shaw-ke-to-quay, wife of George Cicot, two sections of land.

To Mary Préjean, wife of Louis St. Combe, one section of land
To To-pe-naw-koung, wife of Peter Langlois, one section of land. To Au-bee-nan-bee, a Potowatami chief, two sections of land. To Me-che-hee, wife of Charles Minie, a half section of land.

103

Plains, West and Northwest Plateau Indian Treaties

To Louison, a Potowatamie, a reservation of one section, to include his house and cornfield.

To Kes-he-wa-quay, wife of Pierre F. Navarre, one section of land. To Benac, a Potowatami, one section of land. To Pe-pe-nc-way, a chief, one section of land. To Pierre Le Clair, one section of land.

To Betsey Ducharme, one half section of land. The section of land granted by the treaty of Chicago to Nancy Burnett, now Nancy Davis, shall be purchased by the United States, if the same can be done for the sum of one thousand dollars.

To Madeleine Bertrand, wife of Joseph Bertrand, one section of land.

ARTICLE 4. The sum of ten thousand eight hundred and ninety-five dollars shall be applied to the payments of certain claims against the Indians, agreeably to a schedule of the said claims hereunto annexed.

ARTICLE 5. Circumstances rendering it probable that the missionary establishment now located upon the St. Joseph, may be compelled to remove west of the Mississippi, it is agreed that when they remove, the value of their buildings and other improvements shall be estimated, and the amount paid by the United States. But, as the location is upon the Indian reservation, the Commissioners are unwilling to assume the responsibility, of making this provision absolute, and therefore its rejection is not to affect any other part of the treaty.

ARTICLE 6. This treaty shall be obligatory, after the same has been ratified by the President and Senate of the United States.

In testimony whereof, the commissioners, and the chiefs and warriors of the said tribe have hereunto set their hands, at the place and upon the day aforesaid.

Lewis Cass, Pierre Menard,

To-pen-e-bee, his x mark, A-bee-ha-bee, his x mark, Po-ka-gon, his x mark, Ship-she-wa-non, his x mark, Quai-quai-ta, his x mark, Mixs-a-be, his x mark, Mo-sack, his x mark, Wa-ban-see, his x mark, Pe-nan-shies, his x mark, Mish-ko-see, his x mark, Moran, his x mark, Shaw-wa-nan-see, his x mark, Mank-see, his x mark, Shee-qua, his x mark, Ash-kun, his x mark, Louison, his x mark, Che-chalk-koos, his x mark, Pee-pee-nai-wa, his x mark, Moc-conse, his x mark, Kaush-quaw, his x mark, Sko-mans, his x mark, Au-tiss, his x mark, Me-non-quet, his x mark, Sack-a-roans, his x mark, Kin-ne-kose, his x mark, No-shai-e-quon, his x mark, Pe-tee-nans, his x mark, Jo-saih, his x mark, Mo-teille, his x mark, Wa-pee-kai-non, his x mark, Pack-quin, his x mark, Pash-po-oo, his x mark, Mans-kee-os, his x mark, Pee-shee-wai, his x mark, O-kee-au, his x mark, Nau-kee-o-nuck, his x mark, Me-she-ken-ho, his x mark, Non-ai, his x mark,

Wa-shais-skuck, his x mark, Pai-que-sha-bai, his x mark, Mix-a-roans, his x mark, Me-tai-was, his x mark, Mis-qua-buck, his x mark, A-bee-tu-que-zuck,

Plains, West and Northwest Plateau Indian Treaties

his x mark, Kee-ai-so-qua, his x mark, A-bee-tai-que-zuck, his x mark, Wau-shus-kee-zuck, his x mark, Kee-kee-wee-nus-ka, his x mark, Nichee-poo-sick, his x mark, Wa-sai-ka, his x mark, Mee-quen, his x mark, Num-quai-twa, his x mark, Mee-kee-sis, his x mark, Sans-gen-ai, his x mark, Wish-kai, his x mark, She-she-gon, his x mark, Pee-pee-au, his x mark, O-tuck-quin, his x mark, Moo-koos, his x mark, Louison, his x mark, Pchee-koo, his x mark, Sha-wai-no-kuck, his x mark, Zo-zai, his x mark, Wai-za-we-shuck, his x mark, Me-chee-pee-nai-she-insh, his x mark, Com-o-zoo, his x mark, Je-bause, his x mark, Le Boeuf, his x mark, Wash-e-on-ause, his x mark,

After the signature of the Treaty, and at the request of the Indians, it was agreed, that of the ten thousand, dollars stipulated to be delivered in goods, in 1829, three thousand dollars shall be delivered immediately, leaving seven thousand dollars in goods to be delivered in 1829.

The reservation of Pe. Langlois' wife to be located upon the north side of Eel river, between Peerish's village and Louison's reservation.

The reservation of Betsey Ducharme to be located at Louison's run.

Lewis Cass, Pierre Menard.

Ratified, with the exception of the following paragraph in the third article: "To Joseph Barron, a white man, who has long lived with the Indians, and to whom they are much attached, two sections of land; but the rejection of this grant is not to affect any other part of the treaty."

Signed in the presence of-
Alex. Wolcott, Indian agent, John Tipton, Indian agent, Charles Noble, secretary to commissioners, A. Edwards, president of the legislative council, R. A. Forsyth, D. G. Jones, Walter Wilson, major general Indiana Militia, Calvin Britain, E. Reed.

APPENDIX II.
Sept. 20, 1828.
7 Stat., 603.

Schedule of claims referred to in the fourth article of the treaty of the 20th September, 1828, with the Pottawatamie Indians.

Thomas Robb $200, for goods heretofore sold to the Indians. McGeorge $300, for provisions sold to the Indians.
Jno. B. Godfroy $200, for goods heretofore sold to the Indians. Jno. P. Hedges $200, for goods heretofore delivered to the Indians.

Plains, West and Northwest Plateau Indian Treaties

Joseph Alien $145, for horses stolen from him by the Indians while he was surveying.

Jean B. Bourre $700, for goods furnished the Indians, a part of them in relation to this treaty.

Thomas Forsyth $200, for goods heretofore sold to the Indians. S. Hanna & Co. $100, for goods heretofore sold to the Indians. Gabriel Godfroy, jr., $500, for goods heretofore sold to the Indians. Timothy S. Smith $100, for goods heretofore sold to the Indians.

W. G. and G. W. Ewings $200, for goods heretofore sold to the Indians. Joseph Bertrand $2,000, for goods heretofore sold to the Indians.

To Eleanor Kinzie and her four children, by the late John Kinzie, $3,500, in consideration of the attachment of the Indians to her deceased husband, who was long an Indian trader, and who lost a large sum in the trade by the credits given to them, and also by the destruction of his property. The money is in lieu of a tract of land which the Indians gave the late John Kinzie long since, and upon which he lived.

Robert A. Forsyth $1,250, in consideration of the debts due from the Indians to his late father, Robert A. Forsyth, who was long a trader among them, and who was assisted by his son, the present R. A. Forsyth. The money is in lieu of a tract of land which the Indians gave to the late R. A. Forsyth, since renewed to the present R. A. Forsyth, upon which both of them heretofore lived.

Jean B. Comparet $500, for goods heretofore sold to the Indians. C. and D. Dousseau $100, for goods heretofore sold to the Indians.

P.F. Navarre $100, for goods heretofore sold to the Indians. Francis Paget $100, for goods heretofore sold to the Indians. G. O. Hubbard $200, for goods heretofore sold to the Indians. Alexis Coquillard $200, for goods heretofore sold to the Indians.

Amounting, in the whole, to the sum of ten thousand eight hundred and ninety-five dollars.

LEW. CASS, PIERRE MENARD

TREATY WITH THE WINNEBAGO, ETC {1828, Aug. 25}
Proclamation, Jan. 7, 1829.

Articles of agreement with the Winnebago Tribe and the United Tribes of Potawatamie, Chippewa and Ottawa Indians.

THE Government of the United States having appointed Commissioners to treat with the Sac, Fox, Winebago, Potawatamie, Ottawa, and Chippewa, tribes of Indians, for the purpose of extinguishing their title to land within the State of Illinois, and the Territory of Michigan, situated between the Illinois river and

Plains, West and Northwest Plateau Indian Treaties

the Lead Mines on Fever River, and in the vicinity of said Lead Mines, and for other purposes; and it having been found impracticable, in consequence of the lateness of the period when the instructions were issued, the extent of the country occupied by the Indians, and their dispersed situation, to convene them in sufficient numbers to justify a cession of land on their part.

And the Chiefs of the Winnebago tribe, and of the united tribes of the Potawatamies, Chippewas, and Ottawas, assembled at Green Bay, having declined at this time to make the desired cession, the following temporary arrangement, subject to the ratification of the President and Senate of the United States, has this day been made, between Lewis Cass and Pierre Menard, Commissioners of the United States, and the said Winnebago tribe, and the United tribes of Potawatamie, Chippewa, and Ottawa, Indians, in order to remove the difficulties which nave arisen in consequence of the occupation, by white persons, of that part of the mining country which has not been heretofore ceded to the United States.

ARTICLE 1. It is agreed that the following shall be the provisional boundary between the lands of the United States and those of the said Indians: The Ouisconsin river, from its mouth to its nearest approach to the Blue Mounds; thence southerly, passing east of the said mounds, to the head of that branch of the Pocatolaka creek which runs near the Spotted Arm's village; thence with the said branch to the main forks of Pocatolaka creek; thence southeasterly, to the ridge dividing the Winebago country from that of the Potawatamie, Chippewa, and Ottawa tribes; thence southerly, with the said ridge, to the line running from Chicago to the Mississippi, near Rock Island.

And it is fully understood, that the United States may freely occupy the country between these boundaries and the Mississippi river, until a treaty shall be held with the Indians for its cession; which treaty, it is presumed, will be held in the year 1829. But it is expressly understood and agreed, that if any white persons shall cross the line herein described, and pass into the Indian country, for the purpose of mining, or for any other purpose whatever, the Indians shall not interfere with nor molest such persons, but that the proper measures for their removal shall be referred to the President of the United States. In the mean time, however, it is agreed, that any just compensation to which the Indians may be entitled for any injuries committed by white persons on the Indian side of the said line, shall be paid to the said Indians at the time such treaty may be heldIt is also agreed by the Indians that a ferry may be established over the Rock River, where the Fort Clark road crosses the same; and, also, a ferry over the same river at the crossing of the Lewiston road.

ARTICLE 2. The United States agree to pay to the Winebago, Potawatamie, Chippewa, and Ottawa Indians, the sum of twenty thousand dollars, in goods, at the time and place when and where the said treaty may be held: which said sum

Plains, West and Northwest Plateau Indian Treaties

shall be equitably divided between the said tribes, and shall be in full compensation for all the injuries and damages sustained by them, in consequence of the occupation of any part of the mining country by white persons, from the commencement of such occupation until the said treaty shall be held. Excepting, however, such compensation as the Indians may be entitled to, for any injuries hereafter committed on their side of the line hereby established.

In testimony whereof, the said commissioners and the chiefs of the said tribes have hereunto set their hands at Green bay, in the territory of Michigan, this 25th day of August, in the year of our Lord one thousand eight hundred and twenty-eight.

Lewis Cass
Pierre Menard.

Winnebagoes:
Nan-kaw, or wood, his x mark, Koan-kaw, or chief, his x mark, Hoo-wam-ee-kaw, or little elk, his x mark, Tshay-ro-tsboan-kaw, or smoker, his x mark, Hatmp-ee-man-ne-kaw, or he who walks by day, his x mark, Hoo-tshoap-kaw, or four legs, his x mark, Morah-tshay-kaw, or little priest, his x mark, Kau-ree-kau-saw-kaw, or white crow, his x mark, Wan-kaun-haw-kaw, or snake skin, his x mark, Man-ah-kee-tshump-kaw, or spotted arm, his x mark, Wee-no-shee-kaw, his x mark,

Tshaw-wan-shaip-shootsh-kaw, his x mark, Hoootshoap-kaw, or four legs, (senior) his x mark, Nau-soo-ray-risk-kaw, his x mark, Shoank-tshunsk-kaw, or black wolf, his x mark, Wau-tshe-roo-kun-ah-kaw, or he who is master of the lodge, his x mark, Kay-rah-tsho-kaw, or clear weather, his x mark, Hay-ro-kaw-kaw, or he without horns, his x mark, Wau-kaum-kam, or snake, his x mark, Kan-kaw-saw-kaw, his x mark, Man-kay-ray-kau, or spotted earth, his x mark, Thaun-wan-kaw, or wild cat, his x mark,
Span-you-kaw, or Spaniard, his x mark, Shoank-skaw-kaw, or white dog, his x mark,
Nee-hoo-kaw, or whirlpool, his x mark, Nath-kay-saw-kaw, or fierce heart, his x mark, Wheank-kaw, or duck, his x mark, Saw-waugh-kee-wau, or he that leaves the yellow track, his x mark, Sin-a-gee-wen, or ripple, his x mark, Shush-que-nau, his x mark, Sa-gin-hai-nee-pee, his x mark, Nun-que-wee-bee, or thunder sitting, his x mark, O-bwa-gunn, or thunder turn back, his x mark,

Witnesses present:
W.B. Lee, secretary, H.
J. B. Brevoort, United States Indian agent, R. A. Forsyth, Jno. H. Kinzie, John Marsh, E. A.Brush, G. W. Silliman, C.Chouteau, Peter Menard, jun. , Indian subagent, Henry Gratiot, Pierre Paquet, Winnebago interpreter, J. Ogee, Potawatamie interpreter

Plains, West and Northwest Plateau Indian Treaties

TREATY WITH THE POTAWATOMI {1828, Sept. 20}
Proclamation, Jan. 7, 1829.

Articles of a treaty made and concluded at the Missionary Establishments upon the St. Joseph, of Lake Michigan, in the Territory of Michigan, this 20th day of September, in the year of our Lord one thousand eight hundred and twenty-eight, between Lewis Cass and Pierre Ménard, Commissioners, on the part of the United States, and the Potowatami tribe of Indians.

ARTICLE 1. The Potowatami tribe of Indians cede to the United States the tract of land included within the following boundaries:

First. Beginning at the mouth of the St. Joseph, of Lake Michigan, and thence running up the said river to a point on the same river, half way between La-vache-qui-pisse and Macousin village: thence in a direct line, to the 19th mile tree, on the northern boundary line of the State Indiana; thence, with the same, west, to Lake Michigan; and thence, with the shore of the said Lake, to the place of beginning.

Second. Beginning at a point on the line run in 1817, due east from the southern extreme of Lake Michigan, which point is due south from the head of the most easterly branch of the Kankekee river, and from that point running south ten miles; thence, in a direct line, to the northeast corner of Flatbelly's reservation; thence, to the northwest corner of the reservation at Seek's village; thence, with the lines of the said reservation, and of former cessions, to the line between the States of Indiana and Ohio; thence, with the same to the former described line, running due east from the southern extreme of Lake Michigan; and thence, with the said line, to the place of beginning.

ARTICLE 2. In consideration of the cessions aforesaid, there shall be paid to the said tribe an additional permanent annuity of two thousand dollars; and also an additional annuity of one thousand dollars, for the term of twenty years; goods, to the value of thirty thousand dollars, shall be given to the said tribe, either immediately after signing this treaty, or as soon thereafter as they can be procured; an additional sum of ten thousand dollars, in goods, and another of five thousand dollars, in specie, shall be paid to them in the year 1829.

The sum of seven thousand five hundred dollars shall be expended for the said tribe, under the direction of the President of the United States, in clearing and fencing land, erecting houses, purchasing domestic animals and farming utensils, and in the support of labourers to work for them. Two thousand pounds of tobacco, fifteen hundred weight of iron, and three hundred and fifty pounds of steel, shall be annually delivered to them. One thousand dollars per annum shall

Plains, West and Northwest Plateau Indian Treaties

be applied for the purposes Congress may think the appropriation may be of education, as long as useful.

One hundred dollars, in goods, shall be annually paid to To-pen-i-be-the, principal chief of the said tribe, during his natural life. The blacksmith, stipulated by the treaty of Chicago to be provided for the term of fifteen years, shall be permanently supported by the United States.

Three labourers shall be provided, during four months of the year, for ten years, to work for the band living upon the reservation South of the St. Joseph.

ARTICLE 3. There shall be granted to the following persons, all of whom are Indians by descent, the tracts of land hereafter mentioned, which shall be located upon the second cession above described, where the President of the United States may direct, after the country may be surveyed, and to correspond with the surveys, provided that no location shall be made upon the Elkheart Prairie, nor within five miles of the same; nor shall the tracts there granted be conveyed by the grantees, without the consent of the President of the United States.

To Sah-ne-mo-quay, wife of Jean B. Dutrist, one-half section of land.
To Way-pe-nah-te-mo-quay, wife of Thomas Robb, one half section of land.
To Me-no-ka-mick-quay, wife of Edward McCarty, one half section of land.
To Ship-pe-shick-quay, wife of James Wyman, one half section of land.
To Assapo, wife of Antoine Gamlin, one half section of land.
To Moahquay, wife of Richard Chabert, one half section of land. To Me-shaw-ke-to-quay, wife of George Cicot, two sections of land.

To Mary Préjean, wife of Louis St. Combe, one section of land
To To-pe-naw-koung, wife of Peter Langlois, one section of land. To Au-bee-nan-bee, a Potowatami chief, two sections of land. To Me-che-hee, wife of Charles Minie, a half section of land.
To Louison, a Potowatamie, a reservation of one section, to include his house and cornfield.
To Kes-he-wa-quay, wife of Pierre F. Navarre, one section of land. To Benac, a Potowatami, one section of land. To Pe-pe-nc-way, a chief, one section of land. To Pierre Le Clair, one section of land.

To Betsey Ducharme, one half section of land. The section of land granted by the treaty of Chicago to Nancy Burnett, now Nancy Davis, shall be purchased by the United States, if the same can be done for the sum of one thousand dollars.
To Madeleine Bertrand, wife of Joseph Bertrand, one section of land.

110

Plains, West and Northwest Plateau Indian Treaties

ARTICLE 4. The sum of ten thousand eight hundred and ninety-five dollars shall be applied to the payments of certain claims against the Indians, agreeably to a schedule of the said claims hereunto annexed.

ARTICLE 5. Circumstances rendering it probable that the missionary establishment now located upon the St. Joseph, may be compelled to remove west of the Mississippi, it is agreed that when they remove, the value of their buildings and other improvements shall be estimated, and the amount paid by the United States. But, as the location is upon the Indian reservation, the Commissioners are unwilling to assume the responsibility, of making this provision absolute, and therefore its rejection is not to affect any other part of the treaty.

ARTICLE 6. This treaty shall be obligatory, after the same has been ratified by the President and Senate of the United States.
In testimony whereof, the commissioners, and the chiefs and warriors of the said tribe have hereunto set their hands, at the place and upon the day aforesaid.

Lewis Cass, Pierre Menard,
To-pen-e-bee, his x mark, A-bee-ha-bee, his x mark, Po-ka-gon, his x mark, Ship-she-wa-non, his x mark, Quai-quai-ta, his x mark, Mixs-a-be, his x mark, Mo-sack, his x mark, Wa-ban-see, his x mark, Pe-nan-shies, his x mark, Mish-ko-see, his x mark, Moran, his x mark, Shaw-wa-nan-see, his x mark, Mank-see, his x mark, Shee-qua, his x mark, Ash-kun, his x mark, Louison, his x mark, Che-chalk-koos, his x mark, Pee-pee-nai-wa, his x mark, Moc-conse, his x mark,
Kaush-quaw, his x mark, Sko-mans, his x mark, Au-tiss, his x mark, Me-non-quet, his x mark, Sack-a-roans, his x mark, Kin-ne-kose, his x mark, No-shai-e-quon, his x mark, Pe-tee-nans, his x mark, Jo-saih, his x mark, Mo-teille, his x mark, Wa-pee-kai-non, his x mark, Pack-quin, his x mark, Pash-po-oo, his x mark, Mans-kee-os, his x mark, Pee-shee-wai, his x mark, O-kee-au, his x mark, Nau-kee-o-nuck, his x mark, Me-she-ken-ho, his x mark, Non-ai, his x mark,
After the signature of the Treaty, and at the request of the Indians, it was agreed, that of the ten thousand, dollars stipulated to be delivered in goods, in 1829, three thousand dollars shall be delivered immediately, leaving seven thousand dollars in goods to be delivered in 1829.
The reservation of Pe. Langlois' wife to be located upon the north side of Eel river, between Peerish's village and Louison's reservation.
The reservation of Betsey Ducharme to be located at Louison's run.

Lewis Cass, Pierre Menard.

Ratified, with the exception of the following paragraph in the third article: "To Joseph Barron, a white man, who has long lived with the Indians, and to whom

Plains, West and Northwest Plateau Indian Treaties

they are much attached, two sections of land; but the rejection of this grant is not to affect any other part of the treaty."

Signed in the presence of-
Alex. Wolcott, Indian agent, John Tipton, Indian agent, Charles Noble, secretary to commissioners, A. Edwards, president of the legislative council, R. A. Forsyth, D. G. Jones, Walter Wilson, major general Indiana Militia, Calvin Britain, E. Reed.

APPENDIX II.
Sept. 20, 1828.
7 Stat., 603.

Schedule of claims referred to in the fourth article of the treaty of the 20th September, 1828, with the Pottawatamie Indians.

Thomas Robb $200, for goods heretofore sold to the Indians. McGeorge $300, for provisions sold to the Indians.
Jno. B. Godfroy $200, for goods heretofore sold to the Indians. Jno. P. Hedges $200, for goods heretofore delivered to the Indians.
Joseph Alien $145, for horses stolen from him by the Indians while he was surveying.
Jean B. Bourre $700, for goods furnished the Indians, a part of them in relation to this treaty.
Thomas Forsyth $200, for goods heretofore sold to the Indians. S. Hanna & Co. $100, for goods heretofore sold to the Indians. Gabriel Godfroy, jr., $500, for goods heretofore sold to the Indians. Timothy S. Smith $100, for goods heretofore sold to the Indians.

W. G. and G. W. Ewings $200, for goods heretofore sold to the Indians. Joseph Bertrand $2,000, for goods heretofore sold to the Indians.
To Eleanor Kinzie and her four children, by the late John Kinzie, $3,500, in consideration of the attachment of the Indians to her deceased husband, who was long an Indian trader, and who lost a large sum in the trade by the credits given to them, and also by the destruction of his property. The money is in lieu of a tract of land which the Indians gave the late John Kinzie long since, and upon which he lived.

Robert A. Forsyth $1,250, in consideration of the debts due from the Indians to his late father, Robert A. Forsyth, who was long a trader among them, and who was assisted by his son, the present R. A. Forsyth. The money is in lieu of a tract of land which the Indians gave to the late R. A. Forsyth, since renewed to the present R. A. Forsyth, upon which both of them heretofore lived.

Plains, West and Northwest Plateau Indian Treaties

Jean B. Comparet $500, for goods heretofore sold to the Indians. C. and D. Dousseau $100, for goods heretofore sold to the Indians.

P.F. Navarre $100, for goods heretofore sold to the Indians. Francis Paget $100, for goods heretofore sold to the Indians. G. O. Hubbard $200, for goods heretofore sold to the Indians. Alexis Coquillard $200, for goods heretofore sold to the Indians.

Amounting, in the whole, to the sum of ten thousand eight hundred and ninety-five dollars.

LEW. CASS, PIERRE MENARD.

TREATY WITH THE WINNEBAGO {1829, Aug. 1}
Proclamation, Jan. 2, 1830.

Articles of a treaty made and concluded at the Village of Prairie du Chien, Michigan Territory, on this first day of August, in the year one thousand eight hundred and twenty-nine, between the United States of America, by their Commissioners, General John M'Neil, Colonel Pierre Menard, and Caleb Atwater, Esq., for and on behalf of said States, of the one part, and the Nation of Winnebaygo Indians of the other part.

ARTICLE 1. THE said Winnebaygo nation hereby, forever, cede and relinquish to the said United States, all their right, title, and claim, to the lands and country contained within the following limits and boundaries, to wit: beginning on Rock River, at the mouth of the Pee-kee-ta-tau-no or Pee-kee-tol-a-ka, a branch thereof; thence, up the Pee-kee-tol-a-ka, to the mouth of Sugar Creek; thence, up the said creek, to the source of the Eastern branch thereof; thence, by a line running due North, to the road leading from the Eastern blue mound, by the most Northern of the four lakes, to the portage of the Wisconsin and Fox rivers; thence, along the said road, to the crossing of Duck Creek; thence, by a line running in a direct course to the most Southeasterly bend of Lake Puck-a-way, on Fox River; thence, up said Lake and Fox River, to the Portage of the Wisconsin; thence, across said portage, to the Wisconsin river; thence, down said river, to the Eastern line of the United States' reservation at the mouth of said river, on the south side thereof, as described in the second article of the treaty made at St. Louis, on the twenty-fourth day of August, in the year eighteen hundred and sixteen, with the Chippewas, Ottawas, and Potawatamies; thence, with the lines of a tract of country on the Mississippi river, (secured to the Chippewas, Ottawas, and Potawatamies, of the Illinois, by the ninth article of the treaty made at Prairie du Chien, on the nineteenth day of August, in the year eighteen hundred and twenty-five) running Southwardly, passing the heads of the small streams emptying into the Mississippi to the Rock river, at the

Plains, West and Northwest Plateau Indian Treaties

Winnebaygo village, forty miles above its mouth; thence, up Rock river, to the mouth of the Pee-kee-tol-a-ka river, the place of beginning.

ARTICLE 2. In consideration of the above cession, it is hereby stipulated, that the said United States shall pay to the said Winnebaygo nation of Indians the sum of eighteen thousand dollars in specie, annually, for the period of thirty years; which said sum is to be paid to said Indians at Prairie du Chien and Fort Winnebaygo, in proportion to the numbers residing within the most convenient distance of each place, respectively; and it is also agreed, that the said United States shall deliver immediately to said Indians, as a present, thirty thousand dollars in goods; and it is further agreed, that three thousand pounds of tobacco, and fifty barrels of salt, shall be annually delivered to the said Indians by the United States, for the period of thirty years; half of which articles shall be delivered at the Agency at Prairie du Chien, and the other half at the Agency of Fort Winnebaygo.

ARTICLE 3. And it is further agreed between the parties, that the said United States shall provide and support three blacksmiths' shops, with the necessary tools, iron, and steel, for the use of the said Indians, for the term of thirty years; one at Prairie du Chien, one at Fort Winnebaygo, and one on the waters of Rock river; and furthermore, the said United States engage to furnish, for the use of the said Indians, two yoke of oxen, one cart, and the services of a man at the portage of the Wisconsin and Fox rivers, to continue at the pleasure of the Agent at that place, the term not to exceed thirty years.

ARTICLE 4. The United States (at the request of the Indians aforesaid) further agree to pay to the persons named in the schedule annexed to this treaty, (and which forms part and parcel thereof) the several sums as therein specified, amounting, in all, to the sum of twenty-three thousand five hundred and thirty-two dollars and twenty-eight cents; which sum is in full satisfaction of the claims brought by said persons against said Indians, and by them acknowledged to be justly due.

ARTICLE 5. And it is further agreed, that, from the land herein before ceded, there shall be granted by the United States to the persons herein named, (being descendants of said Indians) the quantity of land as follows, to be located without the mineral country, under the direction of the President of the United States, that is to say: to Catherine Myott, two sections; to Mary, daughter of Catharine Myott, one section; to Michael St. Cyr, son of Hee-no-kau, (a Winnebaygo woman) one section; to Mary, Ellen, and Brigitte, daughters of said Hee-no-kau, each one section; to Catherine and Olivier, children of Olivier Amelle, each one section; to Francois, Therese, and Joseph, children of Joseph Thibault, each one section; to Sophia, daughter of Joshua Palen, one section.

Plains, West and Northwest Plateau Indian Treaties

To Pierre Pacquette, two sections; and to his two children, Therese and Moses, each one section; to Pierre Grignon L'Avoine, Amable, Margaret, Genevieve, and Mariette, children of said Pierre, each one section; to Mauh-nah-tee-see, (a Winnebaygo woman) one section; and to her eight children, viz: Therese, Benjamin, James, Simeon, and Phelise Leciiyer, Julia and Antoine Grignon, and Alexis Peyet, each one section; to John Baptiste Pascal, Margaret, Angelique, Domitille, Therese, and Lisette, children of the late John Baptiste Pacquette, each one section; to Madeline Brisbois, daughter of the late Michel Brisbois, Jr. one section; to Therese Gagnier and her two children, François and Louise, two sections; to Mary, daughter of Luther Gleason, one section; and to Theodore Lupien, one section; all which aforesaid grants are not to be leased or sold by said grantees to any person or persons whatever, without the permission of the President of the United States; and it is further agreed, that the said United States shall pay to Therese Gagnier the sum of fifty dollars per annum, for fifteen years, to be deducted from the annuity to said Indians.

ARTICLE 6. (Not ratified by Senate.)

ARTICLE 7. This Treaty, after the same shall be ratified by the President of the United States, by and with the advice and consent of the Senate thereof, shall be obligatory on the contracting parties.

In testimony whereof, the said John McNiel, Pierre Menard, and Caleb Atwater, commissioners as aforesaid, and the chiefs and warriors of the said Winnebago nation of Indians, have hereunto set their hands and seals, at the time and place first herein above written.

John McNiel, Pierre Menard, Caleb Atwater, Commissioners,
Hay-ray-tshon-sarp, black hawk, his x mark, Tshay-o-skaw-tsho-kaw, who plays with the ox, his x mark, Woank-shik-rootsh-kay, man eater, his x mark, Kau-rah-kaw-see-kan, crow killer, his x mark, Maunk-shaw-ka, white breast, his x mark, Hah-pau-koo-see-kaw, his x mark, Maun-kaw-kaw, earth, his x mark, Ah-sheesh-kaw, broken arm, his x mark, Waw-kaun-kaw, rattle snake, his x mark, Chey-skaw-kaw, white ox, his x mark, Nautch-kay-suck, the quick heart, his x mark, Wau-kaun-tshaw-way-kee-wen-kaw, whirling thunder, his x mark,

Thoap-nuzh-ee-kaw, four who stand, his x mark, Hay-nah-ah-ratsh-kay, left handed, his x mark, Woan-knaw-hoap-ee-ne-kaw, big medicine man, his x mark, Pey-tshun-kaw, the crane, his x mark, Jarot, or Jarrot, his x mark, Thay-hoo-kau-kaw, his x mark, Koy-se-ray-kaw, his x mark, Nau-kaw-kary-maunie, wood, his x mark, Hee-tshah-wau-shaip-soots-kau, red war eagle, his x mark, Hee-tsha-wau-sharp-skaw-kau, white war eagle, his x mark, Tsh u-o-nuzh-ee-kau, he who stands in the house, his x mark,

115

Plains, West and Northwest Plateau Indian Treaties

WaU-kaun-hah-kaw, snakeskin, his x mark, Hoo-wau-noo-kaw, little elk, his x mark, Shoank-tshunk-saip-kau, black wolf, his x mark, Kay-rah-tsho-kau, clear Sky, his x mark, Hee-tshaum-wau-kaw, wild cat, his x mark, Hoo-tshoap-kau, four legs, Jr., his x mark, Maunk-kay-ray-kau, crooked tail, his x mark, Wau-kaum-kaw, rattle snake, his x mark, Wau-tshee-roo-kun-o-kau, master of the lodge, his x mark, Menne-kam, the bear who scratches, his x mark, Waun-kaun-tshaw-zee-kau, yellow thunder, his x mark,
Kay-my-mau-nee, walking turtle, his x mark, Ni-si-wau-roosh-kun, the bear, his x mark, Kau-kau-saw-kaw, his x mark,

In presence of
Charles S. Hempstead, secretary to the commission, Joseph M. Street, Indian agent, Thomas Forsyth, Indian agent, Alex. Wolcott, Indian agent, John H. Kenzie, subagent Indian affairs, Z. Taylor, lieutenant-colonel, U. S. Army, H. Dodge, A. Hill, Henry Gratiot, Wm. Beaumont, surgeon, U. S. Army, G. W. Garey, Richard Gentry, James Turner, Richard H. Bell, John W. Johnson, Wm. M. Read, G. H. Kennerly, R. Holmes, U. S. Army, John Dallam, J. R. B. Gardenier, lieutenant, U. S. Infantry, Charles Chouteau, John Messersmith, John L. Chastain, Wm. D. Smith, Charles K. Henshaw, James B. Estis, Jesse Benton, Jr., Jacob Hambleton, John Quaill, John Garland, Henry Crossle, J. L. Bogardus, B. B. Kerchevai, Luther Glenson, Pierre Paquet, his x mark, Winnebago, interpreter, J. PaleR, Jacques Mette, Antoine Le Claire, Joge, M. Brisbois.

TREATY WITH THE SAUK AND FOXES, ETC. {1830, July 15}
Proclamation, Feb. 24,1831.

Articles of a treaty made and concluded by William Clark Superintendent of Indian Affairs and Willoughby Morgan, Col. of the United States 1st Regt. Infantry, Commissioners on behalf of the United States of the one part, and the undersigned Deputations of the Confederated Tribes of the Sacs and Foxes; the Medawah-Kanton, Wah-pacoota, Wahpeton and Sissetong Bands or Tribes of Sioux, the Omahas, Ioways, Ottoes and Missourians on the other part.

THE said Tribes being anxious to remove all causes which may hereafter create any unfriendly feeling between them, and being also anxious to provide other sources for supplying their wants besides those of hunting, which they are sensible must soon entirely fail them; agree with the United States on the following Articles.

ARTICLE 1. The said Tribes cede and relinquish to the United States forever all their right and title to the lands lying within the following boundaries, to wit: Beginning at the upper fork of the Demoine River, and passing the sources of the Little Sioux, and Floyds Rivers, to the fork of the first creek which falls into the Big Sioux or Calumet on the east side; thence, down said creek, and

Plains, West and Northwest Plateau Indian Treaties

Calumet River to the Missouri River; thence down said Missouri River to the Missouri State line, above the Kansas; thence along said line to the north west corner of the said State, thence to the high lands between the waters falling into the Missouri and Desmoines, passing to said high lands along the dividing ridge between the forks of the Grand River; thence along said high lands or ridge separating the waters of the Missouri from those of the Demoine, to a point opposite the source of Boyer River, and thence in a direct line to the upper fork of the Demoine, the place of beginning.

But it is understood that the lands ceded and relinquished by this Treaty, are to be assigned and allotted under the direction of the President of the United States, to the Tribes now living thereon, or to such other Tribes as the President may locate thereon for hunting, and other purposes.

ARTICLE 2. The confederated Tribes of the Sacs and Foxes, cede and relinquish to the United States forever, a tract of Country twenty miles in width, from the Mississippi to the Demoine; situate south, and adjoining the line between the said confederated Tribes of Sacs and Foxes, and the Sioux; as established by the second article of the Treaty of Prairie du Chien of the nineteenth of August one thousand eight hundred and twenty-five.

ARTICLE 3. The Medawah-Kanton, Wah-pa-coota, Wahpeton and Sisseton Bands of the Sioux cede and relinquish to the United States forever, a Tract of Country twenty miles in width, from the Mississippi to the Demoine River, situate north, and adjoining the line mentioned in the preceding article.

ARTICLE 4. In consideration of the cessions and relinquishments made in the first, second, and third articles of this Treaty, the United States agree to pay to the Sacs, three thousand dollars,-and to the Foxes three thousand dollars; To the Sioux of the Mississippi two thousand dollars ;To the Yancton and Santie Bands of Sioux three thousand dollars;To the Omahas, two thousand five hundred dollars;-To the Ioways two thousand five hundred dollars;To the Ottoes and Missourias two thousand five hundred dollars, and to the Sacs of the Missouri River five hundred dollars; to be paid annually for ten successive years at such place, or places on the Mississippi or Missouri, as may be most convenient to said Tribes, either in money, merchandise, or domestic animals, at their option; and when said annuities or any portion of them shall be paid in merchandise, the same is to be delivered to them at the first cost of the goods at St. Louis free of transportation.

And the United States further agree to make to the said Tribes and Bands, the following allowances for the period of ten years, and as long thereafter as the President of the United States may think necessary and proper, in addition to the sums herein before stipulated to be paid them; that is to say; To the Bands of the Sioux mentioned in the third article, one Blacksmith at the expense of the

117

Plains, West and Northwest Plateau Indian Treaties

United States, and the necessary tools; also instruments for agricultural purposes, and iron and steel to the amount of seven hundred dollars;To the Yancton and Santie Bands of Sioux, one Blacksmith at the expense of the United States, and the necessary tools, also instruments for agricultural purposes to the amount of four hundred dollars; To the Omahas one Blacksmith at the expense of the United States, and the necessary tools, also instruments for agricultural purposes to the amount of five hundred dollars.

To the Ioways an assistant Blacksmith at the expense of the United States, also instruments for agricultural purposes to the amount of six hundred dollars; To the Ottoes and Missourias one Blacksmith at the expense of the United States, and the necessary tools, also instruments for agricultural purposes to the amount of five hundred dollars; and to the Sacs of the Missouri River, one Blacksmith at the expense of the United States and the necessary tools; also instruments for agricultural purposes to the amount of two hundred dollars.

ARTICLE 5. And the United States further agree to set apart three thousand dollars annually for ten successive years, to be applied in the discretion of the President of the United States, to the education of the children of the said Tribes and Bands, parties hereto.

ARTICLE 6. The Yanckton and Santie Bands of the Sioux not being fully represented, it is agreed, that if they shall sign this Treaty, they shall be considered as parties thereto, and bound by all its stipulations.

ARTICLE 7. It is agreed between the parties hereto, that the lines shall be run, and marked as soon as the President of the United States may deem it expedient.

ARTICLE 8. The United States agree to distribute between the several Tribes, parties hereto, five thousand, one hundred and thirty-two dollars worth of merchandise, the receipt whereof, the said Tribes hereby acknowledge; which, together with the amounts agreed to be paid, and the allowances in the fourth and fifth articles of this Treaty, shall be considered as a full compensation for the cession and relinquishments herein made.

ARTICLE 9. The Sioux Bands in Council having earnestly solicited that they might have permission to bestow upon the half breeds of their Nation, the tract of land within the following limits, to wit: Beginning at a place called the barn, below and near the village of the Red Wing Chief, and running back fifteen miles; thence in a parallel line with Lake Pepin and the Mississippi, about thirty-two miles to a point opposite Beef or O-Boeuf River; thence fifteen miles to the Grand Encampment opposite the River aforesaid; The United States agree to suffer said half Breeds to occupy said tract of country; they holding by the same title, and in the same manner that other Indian Titles are held.

Plains, West and Northwest Plateau Indian Treaties

ARTICLE 10. The Omahas, Ioways and Ottoes, for themselves, and in behalf of the Yanckton and Santie Bands of Sioux, having earnestly requested that they might be permitted to make some provision for their half-breeds, and particularly that they might bestow upon them the tract of country within the following limits, to Wit; Beginning at the mouth of the Little Ne-mohaw River, and running up the main channel of said River to a point which will be ten miles from its mouth in a direct line; from thence in a direct line, to strike the Grand Ne-mohaw ten miles above its mouth, in a direct line (the distance between the two Ne-mohaws being about twenty miles)thence down said River to its mouth; thence up, and with the Meanders of the Missouri River to the point of beginning, it is agreed that the half-breeds of said Tribes and Bands may be suffered to occupy said tract of land; holding it in the same manner, and by the same title that other Indian titles are held; but the President of the United States may hereafter assign to any of the said half-breeds, to be held by him or them in fee simple, any portion of said tract not exceeding a section, of six hundred and forty acres to each individual. And this provision shall extend to the cession made by the Sioux in the preceding Article.

ARTICLE 11. The reservation of land mentioned in the preceding Article having belonged to the Ottoes, and having been exclusively ceded by them; it is agreed that the Omahas, the Ioways and the Yanckton and Santie Bands of Sioux shall pay out of their annuities to the said Ottoe Tribe, for the period of ten years, Three hundred Dollars annually; of which sum the Omahas shall pay one hundred Dollars, the Ioways one hundred Dollars, and the Yanckton and. Santie Bands one hundred dollars.

ARTICLE 12. It is agreed that nothing contained in the foregoing Articles shall be so construed as to affect any claim, or right in common, which has heretofore been held by any Tribes, parties to this Treaty, to any lands not embraced in the cession herein made; but that the same shall be occupied and held by them as heretofore.

ARTICLE 13. This Treaty, or any part thereof, shall take effect, and be obligatory upon the Contracting parties, so soon as the same shall be ratified by the President of the United States, by and with the advice and consent of the Senate thereof.

Done, and signed, and sealed at Prairie du Chien, in the Territory of Michigan, this fifteenth day of July, in the year of our Lord one thousand eight hundred and thirty, and of the independence of the United States, the fifty-fifth.

Wm. Clark, superintendent Indian affairs, Willoughby Morgan, colonel First Infantry U. S. Army,.commissioners.

Plains, West and Northwest Plateau Indian Treaties

Sacs:
Mash-que-tai-paw, or red head, his x mark, Sheco-Calawko, or turtle shell, his
x mark, Kee-o-cuck, the watchful fox, his x mark, Poi-o-tahit, one that has no
heart, his x mark, Os-hays-kee, ridge, his x mark, She-shee-quanince, little
gourd, his x mark, O-saw-wish-canoe, yellow bird, his x mark, I-onin, his x
mark, Am-oway, his x mark, Niniwow-qua-saut, he that fears mankind, his x
mark, Chaukee Manitou, the little spirit, his x mark, Moso-inn, the scalp, his x
mark, Wapaw-chicannuck, fish of the white marsh, his x mark, Mesico, jic, his
x mark,

Foxes
Wapalaw, the prince, his x mark, Taweemin, strawberry, his x mark, Pasha-
sakay, son of Piemanschie, his x mark, Keewausette, he who climbs everywhere, his x mark, Naw-mee, his x mark, Appenioce, or the grand child, his x
mark, Waytee-rains, his x mark, Nawayaw-cosi, his x mark, Manquo-pwam,
the bear's hip, (Morgan) his x mark, Kaw-Kaw-Kee, the crow, his x mark,
Mawcawtay-ee-quoiquenake, black neck, his x mark, Watu-pawnonsh, his x
mark, Meshaw-nuaw-peetay, the large teeth, his x mark,
Cawkee-Kamack, always fish, his x mark, Mussaw-wawquott, his x mark,

Sioux of the Mississippi, Medawakanton band
Wabishaw, or red leaf, his x mark, Tchataqua Manie, or little crow, his x mark,
Waumunde-tunkar, the great calu- met eagle, his x mark, Taco-coqui-pishnee,
he that fears nothing, his x mark, Wah-coo-ta, that shoots arrows, his x mark,
Pay-taw-whar, the fire owner, his x mark, Kaugh-Mohr, the floating log, his x
mark, Etarz-e-pah, the bow, his x mark, Teeah-coota, one that fires at the yellow, his x mark, Toh-kiah-taw-kaw, he who bites the enemy, his x mark, Nasi-
umpah, or the early riser, his x mark,

Am-pa-ta-tah-wah, his day, his x mark, Wah-kee-ah-tunkar, big thunder, his x
mark, Tauchaw-cadoota, the red road, his x mark, Tchaws-kesky, the elder, his
x mark, Mauzau-hautau, the grey iron, his x mark, Wazee-o-monie, the walking
pine, his x mark, Tachaw-cooash-tay, the good road, his x mark, Kie-ank-kaw,
the mountain, his x mark, Mah-peau-mansaw, iron cloud, his x mark, E-taych-
o-caw, half face, his x mark, Anoug-genaje, one that stands on both sides, his x
mark, Hough-appaw, the eagle head, his x mark, Hooka-mooza, the iron limb,
his x mark, Hoatch-ah-cadoota, the red voice, his x mark, Wat-chu-da, the
dancer.

Wah-pah-coota band
Wiarh-hoh-ha, french crow, his x mark, Shans-konar, moving shadow, his x
mark, Ah-pe-hatar, the grey mane, his x mark, Wahmedecaw-cahn-bohr, one
that prays for the land, his x mark, Wah-con-de-kah-har, the one that makes the
lightning, his x mark, Mazo-manie, or the iron that walks, his x mark, Mah-

Plains, West and Northwest Plateau Indian Treaties

kah-ke-a-munch, one that flies on the land, his x mark, Mauzau-haut-amundee, the walk-ing bell, his x mark, Kah-hih, the Menominie, his x mark,
Sussiton band
Ete-tahken-bah, the sleeping eyes, his x mark, Ho-toh-monie, groans when he walks, his x mark,

Omahahs
Opau-tauga, or the big elk, his x mark, Chonques-kaw, the white horse, his x mark, Tessan, the white crow, his x mark, Ishtan-mauzay, iron-eye, chief's son, his x mark, Waw-shin-ga-sau-bais, black bird, his x mark, Waugh-pay-shan, the one who scalps but a small part from the crown of the head, his x mark, Au-gum-an, the chief, his x mark, Age-en-gaw, the wing, his x mark, Non-bau-manie, the one that walks double, his x mark, Way-cosh-ton, the frequent feast giver, his x mark, Eh-que-naus-hus-kay, the second, his x mark, IoSey, (the son of Kawsay) his x mark,

Ioways
Wassau-nie, or the medicine club, his x mark, Mauhoos Kan, white cloud, his x mark, Wo-hoompee, the broth, his x mark, Tah-roh-na, a good many deer, his x mark, Wa-nau-quash-coonie, without fear, his x mark, Pah-a-manie, one who walks on the snow, his x mark, Pie-kan-ha-igne, the little star, his x mark, Niayoo Manie, walking rain, his x mark, Nautah-hoo, burnt-wood, his x mark, Pai-tansa, the white crane, his x mark,

Ottoes
I-atan, or Shaumanie-Cassan, or prairie wolf, his x mark, Mehah-hun-jee, sec-ond daughter, his x mark, Wawronesan, the encircler, hisx mark, Kansa-tauga, the big Kansas, his x mark, Noe-kee-sa-kay, strikes two, his x mark, Tchai-au-grai, the shield, his x mark, Mantoigne, the little bow, his x mark, Thee-rai-tchai-neehgrai, wolf-tail at the heel, his x mark, Oh-haw-kee-wano, that runs on the hills, his x mark, Rai-grai-a, speckled turtle, his x mark, Tchai-wah-tchee-ray, going by, his x mark, Krai-taunica, the hawk, his x mark, Mauto-a Kee-pah, that meets the bear, his x mark, Kai-wan-igne, little turtle, his x mark,

Missourias
Eh-shaw-manie, or the one who walks laughing, his x mark, Ohaw-tchee-ke-sakay, one who strikes the Little Osages, his x mark, Wamshe-katou-nat, the great man, his x mark, Shoug-resh-kay, the horse fly, his x mark, Tahmegrai-Soo-igne, little deer's dung, his x mark,

Missouri Sacs
Sau-kis-quoi-pee, his x mark, She-she-quene, the gourd, his x mark, Nochewai-tasay, his x mark, Mash-quaw-siais, his x mark, Nawai-yak-oosce, his x mark, Wee-tay-main, one that goes with the rest, his x mark,

Plains, West and Northwest Plateau Indian Treaties

The assent of the Yancton and Santie Bands of Sioux, to the foregoing treaty is given in testimony whereof, the chiefs, braves, and principal men of said bands have hereunto signed their names and acknowledge the same, at St. Louis, this 13th October, 1830.

Yancton and Santie Bands of Siouxs
Matto-Sa-Becha, the black bear, his x mark, Pa-con-okra, his x mark, Citta-eutapishma, he who dont eat buffalo, his x mark, To-ki-e-ton, the stone with horns, Ins x mark, Cha-pon-ka, or mosquitoe, his x mark, To-ki-mar-ne, he that walks ahead, his x mark, Woek-ta-ken-dee, kills and comes back, his x mark, Ha Sazza, his x mark, Chigga Wah-shu-she, little brave, his x mark, Wah-gho-num-pa, cotton wood on the neck, his x mark, Zuyesaw, warrior, his x mark,

Tokun Ohomenee, revolving stone, his x mark, Eta-ga-nush-kica, mad face, his x mark, Womendee Dooter, red war eagle, his x mark, Mucpea A-har-ka, cloud elk, his x mark, To-ka-oh, wounds the enemy, his x mark, Pd-ta-sun eta worn-per, white buffalo with two faces, his x mark, Cha-tun-kia, sparrow hawk, his x mark, Ke-un-chun-ko, swift flyer, his x mark, Ti-ha-uhar, he that carries his horn, his x mark, Sin-ta-nomper, two tails, his x mark, Wo-con Cashtaka, the whipt spirit, his x mark, Ta Shena Pater, fiery blanket, his x mark,

In presence of
Jno. Ruland, secretary to the commission.
Jon. L. Bean, special agent, Law Taliaferro, Indian agent at St. Peters, R. B. Mason, captain, First Infantry, G. Loomis, captain, First Infantry, James Peterson, lieutenant and adjutant, H. B. M., Thirty-third Regiment, N. S. Harris, lieutenant and adjutant, regiment, U. S. Infantry, Henry Bainbridge, lieutenant, U. S. Army, John Gale, surgeon, U. S. Army, J. Archer, lieutenant, U. S. Army, J. Dougherty, Indian agent, Thos. A. Davies, lieutenant, infantry, Wm. S. Williamson, sub-Indian agent, S. Hughes, sub Indian agent, A. G. Baldwin, lieutenant, Third Infantry, David D. Mitchell, H. L. Donsman, Wynkoop Warner, Geo. Davenport, Wm. Hempstead, Benjamin Mills, Wm. H. Warfield, lieutenant,

Witnesses to the signatures of the Yancton and Santie bands of Sioux, at Fort Tecumseh, Upper Missouri, on the fourth day of September, 1830:
Wm. Gordon, James Archdale Hamilton, David D. Mitchell, Wm. Saidlau, Jacob Halsey.

Witnesses present at the signing and acknowledgment of the Yancton and Santie Deputations:
Jno. Ruland, secretary to Commissioners.
Jon. L. Bean, sub-Indian agent for Upper Missouri, Felix F. Wain, Indian agent for Sacs and Foxes, John F. A. Sanford, United States Indian agent.

Plains, West and Northwest Plateau Indian Treaties

William C. Heyward, U. S. Army, D. J. Royster, U. S. Infantry, Samuel Kinney, U. S. Army, Merewether Lewis Clark, Sixth Regiment Infantry, Jacques Mette.

TREATY WITH THE MENOMINEE {1831, Feb. 8}
Proclamation, July 9, 1832.

Articles of agreement made and concluded at the City of Washington, this eighth day of February, one thousand eight hundred and thirty-one, between John H. Eaton, Secretary of War, and Samuel C. Stambaugh, Indian Agent at Green Bay, specially authorized by the President of the United States, and the undersigned chiefs and head men of the Menomonee nation of Indians, fully authorized and empowered by the said nation, to conclude and settle all matters provided for by this agreement.

THE Menomonee Tribe of Indians, by their delegates in council, this day, define the boundaries of their country as follows, to wit;

On the east side of Green Bay, Fox river, and Winnebago lake; beginning at the south end of Winnebago lake; thence southeastwardly to the Milwauky or Manawauky river; thence down said river to its mouth at lake Michigan; thence north, along the shore of lake Michigan, to the mouth of Green Bay thence up Green Bay Fox river and Winnebago lake, to the place of beginning. And on the rest side of Fox river as follows: beginning at the mouth of Fox river, thence down the east shore of Green bay, and across its mouth, so as to include all the islands of the "'Grand Traverse;" thence westerly, on the highlands between the lake Superior and Green bay, to the upper forks of the Menomonee river; thence to the Plover portage of the Wisconsin river; thence up the Wisconsin river, to the Soft Maple river; thence to the source of the Soft Maple river; thence west to the Plume river, which falls into the Chippeway river; thence down said Plume river to its mouth; thence down the Chippeway river thirty miles; thence easterly to the forks of the Manoy river, which falls into the Wisconsin river; thence down the said Manoy river to its mouth; thence down the Wisconsin river to the Wisconsin portage; thence across the said portage to the Fox river; thence down Fox river to its mouth at Green bay, or the place of beginning.

The country described within the above boundaries, the Menomonees claim as the exclusive property of their tribe. Not yet having disposed of any of their hands, they receive no annuities from the United States: whereas their brothers the Pootowottomees on the south, and the Winnebagoes on the west, have sold a great portion of their country, receive large annuities, and are now encroaching upon the lands of the Menomonees. For the purposes, therefore, of establishing the boundaries of their country, and of ceding certain portions of their

Plains, West and Northwest Plateau Indian Treaties

lands to the United States, in order to secure great and lasting benefits to themselves and posterity, as well as for the purpose of settling the long existing dispute between themselves and the several tribes of the New York Indians, who claim to have purchased a portion of their lands, the undersigned, chiefs and headmen of the Menomonee tribe, stipulate and agree with the United States, as follows:

First. The Menomonee tribe of Indians declare themselves the friends and allies of the United States, under whose parental care and protection they desire to continue; and although always protesting that they are under no obligation to recognize any claim of the New York Indians to any portion of their country; that they neither sold nor received any value, for the land claimed by these tribes; yet, at the solicitation of their Great Father, the President of the United States, and as an evidence of their love and veneration for him, they agree that such part of the land described, being within the following boundaries, as he may direct, may be set apart as a home to the several tribes of the New York Indians, who may remove to, and settle upon the same, within three years from the date of this agreement, viz: beginning on the west side of Fox river, near the "Little Kackalin," at a point known as the "Old Mill Dam;" thence northwest forty miles; thence northeast to the Oconto creek, falling into Green bay; thence down said Oconto creek to Green bay; thence up and along Green bay and Fox river to the place of beginning; excluding therefrom all private land claims confirmed, and also the following reservation for military purposes; beginning on the Fox river, at the mouth of the first creek above Fort Howard; thence north sixty-four degrees west to Duck creek; thence down said Duck creek to its mouth; thence up and along Green bay and Fox river to the place of beginning. The Menomonee Indians, also reserve, for the use of the United States, from the country herein designated for the New York Indians, timber and firewood for the United States garrison, and as much land as may be deemed necessary for public highways, to be located by the direction, and at the discretion of the President of the United States.

The country hereby ceded to the United States, for the benefit of the New York Indians, contains by estimation about five hundred thousand acres, and includes all their improvements on the west side of Fox river. As it is intended for a home for the several tribes of the New York Indians, who may be residing upon the lands at the expiration of three years from this date, and for none others, the President of the United States is hereby empowered to apportion the lands among the actual occupants at that time, so as not to assign to any tribe a greater number of acres than may be equal to one hundred for each soul actually settled upon the lands: and if, at the time of such apportionment, any lands shall remain unoccupied by any tribe of the New York Indians, such portion as would have belonged to said Indians, had it been occupied, shall revert to the United States.

Plains, West and Northwest Plateau Indian Treaties

That portion, if any, so reverting, to be laid off by the President of the United States. It is distinctly understood, that the lands hereby ceded to the United States for the New York Indians, are to be held by those tribes, under such tenure as the Menomonee Indians now hold their lands, subject to such regulations and alteration of tenure, as Congress and the President of the United States shall, from time to time, think proper to adopt.

Second. For the above cession to the United States, for the benefit of the New York Indians, the United States consent to pay the Menomonee Indians, twenty thousand dollars; five thousand to be paid on the first day of August next, and five thousand annually thereafter; which sums shall be applied to the use of the Menomonees, after such manner as the President of the United States may direct.

Third. The Menomonee tribe of Indians, in consideration of the kindness and protection of the Government Of the United States, and for the purpose of securing to themselves and posterity, a comfortable home, hereby cede and forever relinquish to the United States, all their country on the southeast side of Winnebago lake, Fox river, and Green bay, which they describe in the following boundaries, to wit: beginning at the south end of Winnebago lake, and running in a southeast direction to Milwauky or Manawauky river; thence down said river to its mouth; thence north, along the shore of lake Michigan, to the entrance of Green bay; thence up and along Green bay, Fox river, and Winnebago lake, to the place of beginning; excluding all private land claims which the United States have heretofore confirmed and sanctioned. It is also agreed that all the islands which lie in Fox river and Green bay, are likewise ceded; the whole comprising by estimation, two million five hundred thousand acres.

Fourth. The following described tract of land, at present owned and occupied by the Menomonee Indians, shall be set apart, and designated for their future homes, upon which their improvements as an agricultural people are to be made: beginning on the West side of Fox river, at the "Old Mill Dam" near the "Little Kackalin," and running up and along said river, to the Winnebago lake; thence along said lake to the mouth of Fox river; thence up Fox river to the Wolf river; thence up Wolf river to a point southwest of the west corner of the tract herein designated for the New York Indians; thence northeast to said west corner; thence southeast to the place of beginning. The above reservation being made to the Menomonee Indians for the purpose of weaning them from their wandering habits, by attaching them to comfortable homes, the President of the United States, as a mark of affection for his children of the Menomonee tribe, will cause to be employed five farmers of established character for capacity, industry, and moral habits, for ten successive years, whose duty it shall be to assist the Menomonee Indians in the cultivation of their farms, and to instruct their children in the business and occupation of farming.

125

Plains, West and Northwest Plateau Indian Treaties

Also, five females shall be employed, of like good character, for the purpose of teaching young Menomonee women, in the business of useful housewifery, during a period of ten years. The annual compensation allowed to the farmers, shall not exceed five hundred dollars, and that of the females three hundred dollars. And the United States will cause to be erected, houses suited to their condition, on said lands, as soon as the Indians agree to occupy them, for which ten thousand dollars shall be appropriated; also, houses for the farmers, for which three thousand dollars shall be appropriated; to be expended under the direction of the Secretary of War. Whenever the Menomonees thus settle their lands, they shall be supplied with useful household articles, horses, cows, hogs, and sheep, farming utensils, and other articles of husbandry necessary to their comfort, to the value of six thousand dollars; and they desire that some suitable device may be stamped upon such articles, to preserve them from sale or barter, to evil disposed white persons: none of which, nor any other articles with which the United States may at any time furnish them, shall be liable to sale, or be disposed of or bargained, without permission of the agent.

The whole to be under the immediate care of the farmers employed to remain among said Indians, but subject to the general control of the United States' Indian Agent at Green Bay acting under the Secretary of War. The United States will erect a grist and saw mill on Fox river, for the benefit of the Menomonee Indians, and employ a good miller, subject to the direction of the agent, whose business it shall be to grind the grain, required for the use of the Menomonee Indians, and saw the lumber necessary for building on their lands, as also to instruct such young men of the Menomonee nation, as desire to, and conveniently can be instructed in the trade of a miller.

The expenses of erecting such mills, and a house for the miller to reside in, Shall not exceed six thousand dollars, and the annual compensation of the miller shall be six hundred dollars, to continue for ten years. And if the mills so erected by the United States, can saw more lumber or grind more grain, than is required for the proper use of said Menomonee Indians, the proceeds of such milling shall be applied to the payment of other expenses occurring in the Green bay agency, under the direction of the Secretary of War.

In addition to the above provision made for the Menomonee Indians, the President of the United States will cause articles of clothing to be distributed among their tribe at Green bay, within six months from the date of this agreement, to the amount of eight thousand dollars and flour and wholesome provisions, to the amount of one thousand dollars, one thousand dollars to be paid in specie. The cost of the transportation of the clothing and provisions, to be included in the sum expended. There shall also be allowed annually thereafter, for the space of twelve successive years, to the Menomonee tribe, in such manner and form as the President of the United States shall deem most beneficial and advantageous to the Indians, the sum of six thousand dollars.

Plains, West and Northwest Plateau Indian Treaties

As a matter of great importance to the Menomonees, there shall be one or more gun and blacksmith's shops erected, to be supplied with a necessary quantity of iron and steel, which, with a shop at Green bay, shall be kept up for the use of the tribe, and continued at the discretion of the President of the United States. There shall also be a house for an interpreter to reside in, erected at Green bay, the expenses not to exceed five hundred dollars.

Fifth. In the treaty of Butte des Morts, concluded in August 1827, an article is contained, appropriating one thousand five hundred dollars annually, for the support of schools in the Menomonee country. And the representatives of the Menomonee nation, who are parties hereto, require, and it is agreed to, that said appropriation shah be increased five hundred dollars, and continued for ten years from this date, to be placed in the hands of the Secretary at War, in trust for the exclusive use and benefit of the Menomonee tribe of Indians, and to be applied by him to the education of the children of the Menomonee Indians, in such manner as he may deem most advisable.

Sixth. The Menomonee tribe of Indians shall be at liberty to hunt and fish on the lands they have now ceded to the United States, on the east side of Fox river and Green bay, with the same privileges they at present enjoy, until it be surveyed and offered for sale by the President; they conducting themselves peaceably and orderly. The chiefs and Warriors of the Menomonee nation, acting under the authority and on behalf of their tribe, solemnly pledge themselves to preserve peace and harmony between their people and the Government of the united States forever. They neither acknowledge the power nor protection of any other State or people. A departure from this pledge by any portion of their tribe, shah be a forfeiture of the protection of the United States' Government, and their annuities will cease. In thus declaring their friendship for the United States, however, the Menomonee tribe of Indians, having the most implicit confidence in their great father, the President of the United States, desire that he will, as a kind and faithful guardian of their welfare, direct the provisions of this compact to be carried into immediate effect. The Menomonee chiefs request that such part of it as relates to the New York Indians, be immediately submitted to the representatives of their tribes.

And if they refuse to accept the provision made for their benefit, and to remove upon the lands set apart for them, on the west side of Fox river, that he will direct their immediate removal from the Menomonee country; but if they agree to accept of the liberal offer made to them by the parties to this compact, then the Menomonee tribe as dutiful children of their great father the President, will take them by the hand as brothers, and settle down with them in peace and friendship.

127

Plains, West and Northwest Plateau Indian Treaties

The boundary as stated and defined in this agreement, of the Menomonee country, with the exception of the cessions herein before-made to the United States, the Menomonees claim as their country; that part of it adjoining the farming country, on the west side of Fox river, will remain to them as heretofore, for a hunting ground, until the President of the United States, shall deem it expedient to extinguish their title. In that case, the Menomonee tribe promise to surrender it immediately, upon being notified of the desire of Govern-merit to possess it. The additional annuity then to be paid to the Menomonee tribe, to be fixed by the President of the United States. It is conceded to the United States that they may enjoy the right of making such roads, and of establishing such military posts, in any part of the country now occupied by the Menomonee nation, as the President at any time may think proper.

As a further earnest of the good feeling on the part of their great father, it is agreed that the expenses of the Menomonee delegation to the city of Washington, and of returning, will be paid, and that a comfortable suit of clothes will be provided for each; also, that the United States will cause four thousand dollars to be expended in procuring fowling guns, and ammunition for them; and likewise, in lieu of any garrison rations, hereafter allowed or received by them, there shall be procured and given to said tribe one thousand dollars worth of good and wholesome provisions annually, for four years, by which time it is hoped their hunting habits may cease, and their attention be turned to the pursuits of agriculture.

In testimony whereof, the respective parties to this agreement have severally signed the same, this 8th February, 1831.

John H. Eaton, S.C. Stambaugh,
Kaush-kau-no-naive, grizzly bear, his x mark, A-ya-mah-taw, fish spawn, his x mark, Ko-ma-ni-kin, big wave, his x mark, Ko-ma-ni-kee-no-shah, little wave, his x mark, O-ho-pa-shah, little whoop, his x mark, Ah-ke-ne-pa-weh, earth standing, his x mark, Shaw-wan-noh, the south, his x mark, Mash-ke-wet, his x mark, Pah-she-nah-sheu, his x mark, Chi-mi-na-na-quet, great cloud, his x mark, A-na-quet-to-a-peh, setting in a cloud, his x mark, Sha-ka-cho-ka-mo, great chief, his x mark,

Signed, sealed, and delivered in presence of
R. A. Forsyth, William Wilkins, of Pennsylvania, C. A. Grignon, Samuel Swartwout, of N. York, Interpreters, John T. Mason, Michigan, A. G. Ellis, Rh. M. Johnson, Kentucky.
Richard Pricket, United States Interpreter, his x mark,

Plains, West and Northwest Plateau Indian Treaties

TREATY WITH THE MENOMINEE {1831, Feb. 17}
Proclamation, July 9, 1832.

WHEREAS certain articles of agreement were entered into and concluded at the city of Washington, on the 8th day of February instant, between the undersigned, Commissioners on behalf of the United States, and the chiefs and warriors, representing the Menomonee tribe of Indians, whereby a portion of the Menomonee country, on the northwest side of Fox river and Green bay, was ceded to the United States, for the benefit of the New York Indians, upon certain conditions and restrictions therein expressed: And whereas it has been represented to the parties to that agreement, who are parties hereto, that it would be more desirable and satisfactory to some of those interested that one or two immaterial changes be made in the first and sixth articles, so as not to limit the number of acres to one hundred for each soul who may be settled upon the land when the President apportions it, as also to make unlimited the time of removal and settlement upon these lands by the New York Indians, but to leave both these matters discretionary with the President of the United States.

Now, therefore, as a proof of the sincerity of the professions made by the Menomonee Indians, when they declared themselves anxious to terminate in an amicable manner, their disputes with the New York Indians, and also as a further proof of their love and veneration for their great father, the President of the United States, the undersigned, representatives of the Menomonee tribe of Indians, unite and agree with the Commissioners aforesaid, in making and acknowledging the following supplementary articles a part of their former aforesaid agreement.

First. It is agreed between the undersigned, commissioners on behalf of the United States, and the chiefs and warriors representing the Menomonee tribe of Indians, that, for the reasons above expressed, such parts of the first article of the agreement, entered into between the parties hereto, on the eighth instant, as limits the removal and settlement of the New York Indians upon the lands therein provided for their future homes, to three years, shall be altered and amended, so as to read as follows: That the President of the United States shall prescribe the time for the removal and settlement of the New York Indians upon the lands thus provided for them; and, at the expiration of such reasonable time, he shall apportion the land among the actual settlers, in such manner as he shall deem equitable and just.

And if, within such reasonable time, as the President of the United States shall prescribe for that purpose, the New York Indians, shall refuse to accept the provisions made for their benefit, or having agreed, shall neglect or refuse to remote from New York, and settle on the said lands, within the time prescribed for that purpose, that then, and in either of these events, the lands aforesaid shall be, and remain the property of the United States, according to said first

129

Plains, West and Northwest Plateau Indian Treaties

article, excepting so much thereof, as the President shall deem justly due to such of the New York Indians, as shall actually have removed to, and settled on the said lands.

Second. It is further agreed that the part of the sixth article of the agreement aforesaid, which requires the removal of those of the New York Indians, who may not be settled on the lands at the end of three years, shall be so amended as to leave such removal discretionary with the President of the United States. The Menomonee Indians having full confidence, that, in making his decision, he will take into consideration the welfare and prosperity of their nation.

Done and signed at Washington, this 17th of February, 1831.

John H. Eaton, S. C. Stambaugh,
Kaush-kau-no-naive, his x mark, A-ya-mah-taw, his x mark, Ko-ma-ni-kin, his x mark, Ko-ma-ni-kee-no-shah, his x mark, O-ho-pa-shah, his x mark, Ah-ke-ne-pa-weh, his x mark, Shaw-wan-noh, his x mark, Mash-ke-wet, his x mark, Pah-she-nah-sheu, his x mark, Chi-mi-na-na-quet, his x mark, A-na-quet-to-a-peh, his x mark, Sha-ka-cho-ka-mo, his x mark,

Signed in presence of
R. A. Forsyth, John T. Mason, C. A. Grignon, P.G. Randolph, Law. L. V. Kleeck, A.G. Ellis.

(NOTE.This treaty was ratified with the following Proviso contained in the Resolution of the Senate:
Provided, That for the purpose of establishing the rights of the New York Indians, on a permanent and just footing, the said treaty shall be ratified with the express understanding that two townships of land on the east side of the Winnebago lake, equal to forty-six thousand and eighty acres shall be laid off, (to commence at some point to be agreed on) for the use of the Stockbridge and Munsee tribes; and that the improvements made on the lands now in the possession of the said tribes, on the east side of the Fox river, which said lands are to be relinquished, shall, after being valued by a commissioner to be appointed by the President of the United States, be paid for by the Government: Provided, however, that the valuation of such improvements shall not exceed the sum of twenty-five thousand dollars; and that there shall be one township of land, adjoining the foregoing, equal to twenty-three thousand and forty acres, laid off and granted for the use of the Brothertown Indians, who are to be paid, by the Government the sum of one thousand six hundred dollars for the improvements on the lands now in their possession, on the east side of Fox river, and which lands are to be relinquished by said Indians.

Also, that a new line shall be run, parallel to the southwestern boundary line, or course of the tract of five hundred thousand acres described in the first article

Plains, West and Northwest Plateau Indian Treaties

of this treaty, and set apart for the New York Indians, to commence at a point on the west side of the Fox river, and one mile above the Grand Shute on Fox river, and at a sufficient distance from the said boundary line as established by the said first article, as shall comprehend the additional quantity of two hundred thousand acres of land, on and along the west side of Fox river, without including any of the confirmed private land claims on the Fox river, and which two hundred thousand acres shall be a part of the five hundred thousand acres intended to be set apart for the Six Nations of the New York Indians and the St. Regis tribe; and that an equal quantity to that which is added on the southwestern side shall be taken off from the northeastern side of the said tract, described in that article, on the Oconto Creek, to be determined by a Commissioner, to be appointed by the President of the United States; so that the whole number of acres to be granted to the Six Nations, and St. Regis tribe of Indians, shall not exceed the quantity originally stipulated by the treaty.")

TREATY WITH THE SAUK AND FOXES {1832, Sept. 21} Proclamation. Feb. 13, 1833.

Articles of a Treaty of Peace, Friendship and Cession, concluded at Fort Armstrong, Rock Island, Illinois, between the United Sates of America, by their Commissioners, Major General Winfield Scott, of the United States Army, and his Excellency John Reynolds, Governor of the State of Illinois, and the confederated tribes of Sac and Fox Indians, represented, in general Council, by the undersigned Chiefs, Headmen and Warriors.

WHEREAS, under certain lawless and desperate leaders, a formidable band, constituting a large portion of the Sac and Fox nation, left their country in April last, and, in violation of treaties, commenced an unprovoked war upon unsuspecting and defenceless citizens of the United States, sparing neither age nor sex; and whereas, the United States, at a great expense of treasure, have subdued the said hostile band, killing or capturing all its principal Chiefs and Warriorsthe said States, partly as indemnity for the expense incurred, and partly to secure the future safety and tranquillity of the invaded frontier, demand of the said tribes, to the use of the United States, a cession of a tract of the Sac and Fox country, bordering on said frontier, more than proportional to the numbers of the hostile band who have been so conquered and subdued.

ARTICLE 1. Accordingly, the confederated tribes of Sacs and Foxes hereby cede to the United States forever, all the lands to which the said tribes have title, or claim, (with the exception of the reservation hereinafter made) included within the following bounds, to wit: Beginning on the Mississippi river, at the point where the Sac and Fox northern boundary line, as established by the second article of the treaty of Prairie du Chien, of the fifteenth of July, one thousand eight hundred and thirty, strikes said river; thence, up said boundary line

Plains, West and Northwest Plateau Indian Treaties

to a point fifty miles from the Mississippi, measured on said line; thence, in a right line to the nearest point on the Red Cedar of the Ioway, forty miles from the Mississippi river; thence, in a right line to a point in the northern boundary line of the State of Missouri, fifty miles, measured on said boundary, from the Mississippi river; thence, by the last mentioned boundary to the Mississippi river, and by the western shore of said river to the place of beginning. And the said confederated tribes of Sacs and Foxes hereby stipulate and agree to remove from the lands herein ceded to the United States, on or before the first day of June next; and, in order to prevent any future misunderstanding, it is expressly understood, that no band or party of the Sac or Fox tribes shall reside, plant, fish, or hunt on any portion of the ceded country after the period just mentioned.

ARTICLE 2. Out of the cession made in the preceding article, the United States agree to a reservation for the use of the said confederated tribes, of a tract of land containing four hundred square miles, to be laid off under the directions of the President of the United States, from the boundary line crossing the Ioway river, in such manner that nearly an equal portion of the reservation may be on both sides of said river, and extending downwards, so as to include Ke-o-kuck's principal village on its right bank, which village is about twelve miles from the Mississippi river.

ARTICLE 3. In consideration of the great extent of the foregoing cession, the United States stipulate and agree to pay to the said confederated tribes, annually, for thirty successive years, the first payment to be made in September of the next year, the sum of twenty thousand dollars in specie.

ARTICLE 4. It is further agreed that the United States shall establish and maintain within the limits, and for the use and benefit of the Sacs and Foxes, for the period of thirty years, one additional black and gun smith shop, with the necessary tools, iron and steel; and finally make a yearly allowance for the same period, to the said tribes, of forty kegs of tobacco, and forty barrels of salt, to be delivered at the mouth of the Ioway river.

ARTICLE 5. The United States, at the earnest request of the said confederated tribes, further agree to pay to Farnham and Davenport, Indian traders at Rock island, the sum of forty thousand dollars without interest, which sum will be in full satisfaction of the claims of the said traders against the said tribes, and by the latter was, on the tenth day of July, one thousand eight hundred and thirty-one, acknowledged to be justly due, for articles of necessity, furnished in the course of the seven preceding years, in an instrument of writing of said date, duly signed by the Chiefs and Headmen of said tribes, and certified by the late Felix St. Vrain, United States' agent, and Antoine Le Claire, United States' Interpreter, both for the said tribes.

Plains, West and Northwest Plateau Indian Treaties

ARTICLE 6. At the special request of the said confederated tribes, the United States agree to grant, by patent, in fee simple, to Antoine Le Claire, Interpreter, a part Indian, one section of land opposite Rock Island, and one section at the head of the first rapids above said Island, within the country herein ceded by the Sacs and Foxes.

ARTICLE 7. Trusting to the good faith of the neutral bands of Sacs and Foxes, the United States have already delivered up to those bands the great mass of prisoners made in the course of the war by the United States, and promise to use their influence to procure the delivery of other Sacs and Foxes, who may still be prisoners in the hands of a band of Sioux Indians, the friends of the United States; but the following named prisoners of war, now in confinement, who were Chiefs and Headmen, shall be held as hostages for the future good conduct of the late hostile bands, during the pleasure of the President of the United States, viz: Muk-ka-ta-mish-a-ka-kaik (or Black Hawk) and his two sons; Wau-ba-kee-shik (the Prophet) his brother and two sons; Na-pope; We-sheet Ioway; Pamaho; and Cha-kee-pa-Shi-pa-ho (the little stabbing Chief).

ARTICLE 8. And it is further stipulated and agreed between the parties to this treaty, that there shall never be allowed in the confederated Sac and Fox nation, any separate band, or village, under any chief or warrior of the late hostile bands; but that the remnant of the said hostile bands shall be divided among the neutral bands of the said tribes according to bloodthe Sacs among the Sacs, and the Foxes among the Foxes.

ARTICLE 9. In consideration of the premises, peace and friendship are declared, and shall be perpetually maintained between the United States and the whole confederated Sac and Fox nation, excepting from the latter the hostages before mentioned.

ARTICLE 10. The United States, besides the presents, delivered at the signing of this treaty, wishing to give a striking evidence of their mercy and liberality, will immediately cause to be issued to the said confederated tribes, principally for the use of the Sac and Fox women and children, whose husbands, fathers and brothers, have been killed in the late war, and generally for the use of the whole confederated tribes, articles of subsistence as follows :thirty-five beef cattle; twelve bushels of salt; thirty barrels of pork; and fifty barrels of flour, and cause to be delivered for the same purposes, in the month of April next, at the mouth of the lower Ioway, six thousand bushels of maize or Indian corn.

ARTICLE 11. At the request of the said confederated tribes, it is agreed that a suitable present shall be made to them on their pointing out to any United States agent, authorized for the purpose, the position or positions of one or more mines, supposed by the said tribes to be of a metal more valuable than lead or iron.

Plains, West and Northwest Plateau Indian Treaties

ARTICLE 12. This treaty shall take effect and be obligatory on the contracting parties, as soon as the same shall be ratified by the President of the United States, by and with the advice and consent of the Senate thereof.

Done at Fort Armstrong, Rock Island, Illinois, this twenty-first day of September, in the year of our Lord one thousand eight hundred and thirty-two, and of the independence of the United States the fifty-seventh.

Winfield Scott, John Reynolds.

Sacs. Kee-o-kuck, or he who has been every where, his x mark, Pa-she-pa-ho, or the stabber, his x mark, Pia-tshe-noay, or the noise maker, his x mark, Wawk-kum-mee, or clear water, his x mark, O-sow-wish-kan-no, or yellow bird, his x mark, Pa-ca-tokee, or wounded lip, his x mark, Winne-wun-quai-saat, or the terror of man, his x mark, Mau-noa-tuck, or he who controls many, his x mark, Wau-we-au-tun, or the curling wave, his x mark, Foxes. Wau-pel-la, or he who is painted white, his x mark,

Tay-wee-mau, or medicine man, (strawberry) his x mark, Pow-sheek, or the roused bear, his x mark, An-nau-mee, or the running fox, his x mark, Ma-tow-e-qua, or the jealous woman, his x mark, Me-shee-wau-quaw, or the dried tree, his x mark,

May-kee-sa-mau-ker, or the wampum fish, his x mark, Chaw-co-saut, or the prowler, his x mark, Kaw-kaw-kce, or the crow, his x mark, Mau-que-tee, or the bald eagle, his x mark, Ma-she-na, or cross man, his x mark, Kaw-kaw-ke-monte, or the pouch, (running bear) his x mark, Wee-she-kaw-k-a-skuck, or he who steps firmly, his x mark,

Wee-ca-ma, or good fish, his x mark, Paw-qua-nuey, or the runner, his x mark, Ma-hua-wai-be, or the wolf skin, his x mark, Mis-see-quaw-kaw, or hairy neck, his x mark, Waw-pee-shaw-kaw, or white skin, his x mark, Mash-shen-waw-pee-tch, or broken tooth, his x mark, Nau-nah-que-kee-shee-ko, or between two days, his x mark, Paw-puck-ka-kaw, or stealing fox, his x mark, Tay-e-sheek, or the falling bear, his x mark, Wau-pee-maw-ker, or the white loon, his x mark, Wau-co-see-nee-me, or fox man, his x mark,

In presence of
R. Bache, captain ordnance, secretary to the commission, Abrm. Eustis, Alex. Cummings, lieutenant-colonel Second Infantry, Alex. R. Thompson, major U. S. Army, Sexton G. Frazer, P. H. Galt, Assistant Adjutant-General, Benj. F. Pike, Wm. Henry, James Craig, John Aukeney, J. B. F. Russell, Isaac Chambers, .John Clitz, adjutant infantry, John Pickell, lieutenant Fourth Artillery, A. G. Miller, lieutenant First Infantry, Geo. Davenport, assistant quartermaster-

Plains, West and Northwest Plateau Indian Treaties

general Illinois Militia, A. Drane, AEneas Mackay, captain U. S. Army, J. R. Smith, first lieutenant Second Infantry, Wm. Maynadier, lieutenant and aid-de-camp, J. S. Gallaghcr, first lieutenant, acting commissary subsistence, N. B. Bennett, lieutenant Third Artillery, B. Riley, major U. S. Army, H. Dodge, major, W. Campbell, Hy. Wilson, major Fourth U. S. Infantry, Donald Ward, Thos. Black Wolf, Horatio A. Wilson, lieutenant Fourth Artillery, H. Day, lieutenant Second Infantry, Jas. W. Penrose, lieutenant Second Infantry, J. E. Johnston, lieutenant Fourth Artillery, S. Burbank, lieutenant First Infantry, J. H. Prentiss, lieutenant First Artillery, L. J. Bcall, lieutenant First Infantry, Addison Philleo, Thomas L. Alexander, lieutenant Sixth Infantry, Horace Beale, acting surgeon U. S. Army, Oliver W. Kellogg, Jona Leighton, acting surgeon U. S. Army, Robt. C. Buchanan, lieutenant Fourth Infantry, Jas. S. Williams, lieutenant Sixth Infantry, John W. Spencer, Antoine Le Claire, interpreter.

TREATY WITH THE POTAWATOMI {1832, Oct. 26}
Proclamation, Jan. 21, 1833.

Articles of a treaty made and concluded on Tippecanoe River, in the State of Indiana, between Jonathan Jennings, John W. Davis and Marks Crume Commissioners on the part of the United States, and the Chiefs, Headmen and Warriors, of the Pottawatimie Indians, this twenty-sixth day of October, in the year eighteen hundred and thirty-two.

ARTICLE 1. The Chiefs, Headmen and Warriors, aforesaid, agree to cede to the United States their title and interest to lands in the State of Indiana, (to wit:) beginning at a point on Lake Michigan, where the line dividing the States of Indiana and Illinois intersects the same; thence with the margin of said Lake, to the intersection of the southern boundary of a cession made by the Pottawatimies, at the treaty of the Wabash, of eighteen hundred and twenty-six; thence east, to the northwest corner of the cession made by the treaty of St. Joseph's, in eighteen hundred and twenty-eight; thence south ten miles; thence with the Indian boundary line to the Michigan road; thence south with said road to the northern boundary line, as designated in the treaty of eighteen hundred and twenty-six, with the Pottawatimies; thence west with the Indian boundary line to the river Tippecanoe; thence with the Indian boundary line, as established by the treaty of eighteen hundred and eighteen, at St. Mary's to the line dividing the States of Indiana and Illinois; and thence north, with the line dividing the said States, to the place of beginning.

ARTICLE 2. From the cession aforesaid, the following reservations are made, (to wit:)
For the band of Aub-be-naub-bee, thirty-six sections, to include his village.
For the bands of Men-o-mi-nee, No-taw-kah, Muck-kah-tah-mo-way and Pee-pin-oh-waw, twenty-two sections.

Plains, West and Northwest Plateau Indian Treaties

For the bands of O-kaw-wause, Kee-waw-nay and Nee-bosh, eight sections.
For J. B. Shadernah, one section of land in the Door Prairie, where he now lives.

For the band of Com-o-za, two sections. For the band of Mah-che-saw, two sections. For the band of Mau-ke-kose, six sections.
For the bands of Nees-waugh-gee and Quash-qua, three sections.

ARTICLE 3. In consideration of the cession aforesaid, the United States agree to pay to the Pottawatimie Indians, an annuity for the term of twenty years, of twenty thousand dollars; and will deliver to them goods to the value of one hundred thousand dollars, so soon after the signing of this treaty as they can be procured; and a further sum of thirty thousand dollars, in goods, shall be paid to them in the year eighteen hundred and thirty-three, by the Indian agent at Eel river.

ARTICLE 4. The United States agree to pay the debts due by the Pottawatimies, agreeably to a schedule hereunto annexed; amounting to sixty-two thousand four hundred and twelve dollars.

ARTICLE 5. The United States agree to provide for the Pottawatimies, if they shall at any time hereafter wish to change their residence, an amount, either in goods, farming utensils, and such other articles as shall be required and necessary, in good faith, and to an extent equal to what has been furnished any other Indian tribe or tribes emigrating, and in just proportion to their numbers.

ARTICLE 6. The United States agree to erect a saw mill on their lands, under the direction of the President of the United States.
In testimony whereof, the said Jonathan Jennings, John W. Davis, and Marks Crume, commissioners as aforesaid, and the chiefs, head men, and warriors of the Pottawatimies, have hereunto set their hands at Tippecanoe river, on the twenty-sixth day of October, in the year eighteen hundred and thirty-two.

Jonathan Hennings, John W. Davis, Mark Crume

Witness: Geo. B. Walker.

Louison, his x mark, Che-chaw-cose, his x mark, Banack, his x mark, Man-o-quett. his x mark, Kin-kosh, his x mark, Pee-shec-waw-no,. his x mark, Min-o-xnin-ee, his x mark, Mis-sah-kaw-way, his x mark, Kee-waw-nay, his x mark, Sen-bo-go, his x mark, Che-quaw-ma-caw-co, his x mark, Muak-kose, his x mark, Ah-you-way, his x mark, Po-kah-kause, his x mark, So-po'-tie, his x mark, Che-man, his x mark, No-taw-kah, his x mark, Nas-waw-kee, his x mark, Pec-pin-a-h, aw, his x mark, Ma-che-saw, his x mark, O-kitch-chee, his x mark,

136

Plains, West and Northwest Plateau Indian Treaties

Pee-pish-kab, his x mark, Com-mo-yo, his x mark, Chick-kose, his x mark, Mis-qua-buck, his x mark, Mo-tie-ah, his x mark, Muck-ka-tah-mo-way, his x mark, Mah-quaw-shee, his X mark, O-sheh-wch, his x mark, Mah-ziek, his x mark, Queh-kah-pah, his x mark, Quash-quaw, his x mark, Louisor Perish, his x mark, Pam-bo-go, his x mark, Bee-yaw-yo, his x mark, Pah-ciss, his x mark, Mauck-co-paw-waw, his x mark, Mis-sah-qua, his x mark, Kawk, his x mark, Miee-kiss, his x mark, Shaw-bo, his x mark, Aub-be-naub-bee, his x mark, Mau-maut-wah, his x mark, O-ka-mause, his x mark, Pash-ee-po, his x mark, We-wiss-lah, his x mark, Ash-kum, his x mark, Waw-zee-o-nes, his x mark,

Witnesses:
William Marshall, Indian agent, Henry Hoover, secretary, H. Lasselle, interpreter, E. V. Cicott, Sint. interpreter, J. B. Bourie, interpreter, J. B. Jutra, Sint. interpreter, Edward McCartney, interpreter, Luther Rice, interpreter.

After the signing of this Treaty, and at the request of the Indians, five thousand one hundred and thirty-five dollars were applied to the purchase of horses, which were purchased and delivered to them, under our direction, leaving ninety-four thousand eight hundred and sixty-five dollars to be paid in merchandise.

Jonathan Jennings, John W. Davis, Marks Crume.

It is agreed, that the United States will satisfy the claims mentioned in the following schedule, as provided for in the fourth article of the foregoing treaty, viz:

To Andrew Waymire, forty dollars.
Zacheriah Cicott, nine hundred and fifty dollars. H. Lassell, senior, four thousand dollars.
Silas Atchinson, two hundred and twenty dollars. Alexander McAllister, two hundred and twenty dollars. Walker and Davis, fifteen hundred dollars.
Walker, Carter & Co. five thousand six hundred dollars. Edward McCartney, one thousand dollars.

F. R. Kintner, six hundred and twenty dollars. Joseph Trucky, one hundred dollars.
J. Vigus & C. Taber, eight hundred and fifty dollars. James Burnit, six hundred dollars.
Samuel Hanna, executor of Abraham Burner, three hundred and fifty dollars.
,lames Hickman, sixty dollars.
William Scott, two hundred and fifty dollars. M. Harse, seventy dollars.
Emmerson and Huntington, assignees of Willis Fellows, four thousand five hundred dollars.
W. G. and G. W. Ewing, one thousand dollars.

Plains, West and Northwest Plateau Indian Treaties

Peter Barron, seventeen hundred and sixty-six dollars. Hamilton & Taber, seven hundred and thirty-seven dollars. Skelton & Scott, six hundred and fifty dollars. Cyrus Taber, three hundred and fifty dollars. G. S. Hubbard, one thousand dollars. Moses Rice, one hundred dollars.
John E. Hunt, three thousand two hundred and sixteen dollars. John Baldwin, one thousand dollars. Louis Drouillard, sixty-eight dollars. George Crawford, eighty dollars. Thomas Hall, forty dollars.

John B. Duret, four hundred dollars. Anthony Gainbin, three hundred dollars.
Joseph Barron, seven hundred and ninety-six dollars. James H. Kintner, three hundred and fifty-seven dollars. John B. Bourie, five hundred dollars. Henry Ossum, nine hundred dollars. Samuel Hanna, fifteen hundred dollars.
Barnet & Hanna, three thousand five hundred dollars.
Todd & Vigus, six thousand five hundred and thirteen dollars. Allen Hamilton, seven hundred dollars.
W. G. and G. W. Ewing, three thousand dollars. George F. Turner, two hundred dollars.

Peter Longlois, two thousand five hundred dollars. Thomas Robb, eight hundred and forty dollars.
The estate of George Cicott, deceased, fifteen hundred dollars. George C. Spencer, one hundred and fifty-seven dollars. John T. Douglass, one hundred dollars.
W. G. and G. W. Ewing, seven hundred and sixteen dollars. H. B. M'Keen, six hundred dollars.
Joseph Bertrand, senior, fifteen hundred dollars. George C. Spencer, three hundred dollars.
Pease Buzann, three hundred and sixteen dollars. Joseph Douglass, four hundred and fifty dollars. John Smith, four hundred and eighty dollars. Moses Barnett, eight hundred and forty-five dollars. Harison Barnett, two hundred and sixty-seven dollars. Lot Bozarth, ninety dollars.

Silas Alchison, two hundred and forty-four dollars.
Harison Barnett & Co. one hundred and seventy-eight dollars. James Elliott, one hundred and nineteen dollars. Alexander Smith, one hundred dollars.
Walker, Garter & Co. four hundred and four dollars.
John Forsyth, amr. &c. of Thomas Forsyth, four hundred and seventy-three dollars.
John Forsyth, six hundred dollars.

Plains, West and Northwest Plateau Indian Treaties

TREATY WITH THE POTAWATOMI {1832, Oct. 27}
Proclamation, Jan. 21, 1833.

Articles of a Treaty, made and concluded on the Tippecanoe River, the State of Indiana, on the twenty-seventh day of October, in the year of our Lord eighteen hundred and thirty-two, between Jonathan Jennings, John W. Davis and Marks Crume, Commissioners on the part of the United States, and the Chiefs and Warriors of the Potowatomies, of the State of Indiana and Michigan Territory.

ARTICLE 1. The Chiefs and Warriors aforesaid cede to the United States, their title and interest to lands in the States of Indiana and Illinois, and in the Territory of Michigan, south of Grand river.

ARTICLE 2. From the cession aforesaid, the following reservations are made, (to wit:) The reservation at Po-ca-gan's village for his band, and a reservation for such of the Potowatomies as are resident at the village of Notta-we-sipa, agreeably to the treaties of the nineteenth of September, eighteen hundred and twenty-seven, and twentieth of September, 1828.

For the band of Kin-Kash, four sections: For O-ca-thee, one section:
For the band Mes-qua-buck, four sections, to include his village: For the band of Che-kase, four sections, to include his village:
For the band of Che-Chaw-kose ten sections, to include his village:
For the Potowatomies, two sections, to include their mills on Tippecanoe river.
For the band of To-i-sas brother Me-mot-way, and Chc-quam-ka-ko, ten sections to include their village:
For the band of Ma-sac, four sections:

For the band of Ash-kum and Wee-si-o-nas, sixteen sections, to include their villager
For the band of Wee-sau, five sections of land, including one section, granted to him by the Treaty of eighteen hundred and twenty-eight, and to include his present residence:
For the bands of Mo-ta and Men-o-quet, four sections, each, to include their villages:
For Be-si-ah, four sections.

ARTICLE 3. The United States agree to grant to each of the following persons, the quantity of land annexed to their names, which lands shall be conveyed to them by patent:

For Mon-i-taw-quah, daughter of Swa-gaw, one section, to include Wi-me-gos village:
For Wee-saw, three sections:
For Po-quia, the sister of Jose, one section: For Ben-ack, eight sections:

Plains, West and Northwest Plateau Indian Treaties

For Ursule Du-quin-dre, one section: For Ge-ncir, one section:
To To-pen-nc-bee, principal chief, one section: To Poch-a-gan, second Chief,
one section: To Pet-chi-co, two sections: To Sau-gana, one section:
To Louis Barnett, one section:
To Mare-qua, daughter of Sau-ga-na, one section:

To Mish-a-wa, adopted daughter of Pit-e-chew, one section: To Kesis-Shadana,
one section:
To Louis Chadann, one half section: To Charles Chadana one half section: To
John B. Chadann, one section: To Pier Navarre's wife, one section: To John B.
Ducharm, one section: To Mic-saw-bee, one quarter section: To Baptiste L.
Clare, one half section:
To Mary Lacombe's children, one half section:
To Joseph Bertrand's, jr. children, one half section jointly: To Francis Page, jr.
one half section:

To Alexander Rollane, a half blood, one half section:
To Re-re-mo-sau, (alias) Panlab, one section and one half section, on the
McCou, on the river Raison, in the Michigan Territory, which was reserved to
his use at St. Joseph's treaty, of eighteen hundred and twenty-eight:
To Mary Nedeau, one quarter section:
To Saw-greta, son of Pier Moran, one half section:
To Isadore Mo-mence and Wa-be-ga, sons of Pier Morans, one quarter section
each:
To Poch-a-gan's wife, one section:

To Pet-qua and Kee-see, sons of Ma-kee-sa-be, one half section: To Pe-nem-
chis, one half section: To Neu-a-tau-naut, one half section: To Francis de Jean,
one section:
To Mary Ann Ben-ack, wife of Edward McCartney, three sections
of land, to be located on the south side of the Turkey creek prairie: For Francis
Besion, one half section:
For Miss-no-qui, a chieftess, four sections: For Luther Rice, one quarter section:
For Med-lin Aucharm, one quarter section: For Sheaupo Truckey, one section:
For Ju-be Actrois, one section: For Ash-kum, two sections: For Pee-pees-kah
one section:

For Po-ka-kause, one half section: For Nas-wau-kee, one section:
For Man-me-nass, one half section: For Paul Longlois, one half section:
For Peter Longlois, junr., one half section: For Shaw-bo-wah-tuck, one quarter
section: For Betsev Rousau, one quarter section: For John Davis, one half sec-
tion:
For Nancy Cicott, one quarter section
For Amelia Cicott, one quarter section: For Lazette Allen, one quarter section:

Plains, West and Northwest Plateau Indian Treaties

For Polly Griffith, daughter of Ne-bosh, two sections: For Chop-y-tuck, or John Payne, one section: For Joe Borisau, one quarter section: For Quash-man, one quarter section: For Mas-co, one quarter section: For Mis-sink-qu-quah, six sections: For Aub-e-naub-bee, ten sections:

For Nee-kaw Dizzardee, one quarter section: For Mog-see, one half section: To Kaubee, one half section:
To old Ann Mac-i-to, one half section: To old Wee-saw, one half section: To Pe-te-no-on, one half section:
To Tou-se-qua, the wife of Joe Baily, one section:
To Au-taw-co-num, daughter of the Crane, one section: To Sen niss-quah and her daughter Nancy, two sections: To James Burnett, one section:
To To-gah, a Potawatomie woman, one quarter section: To Mary Ann Bruner, one quarter section.

The foregoing reservations shall be selected, under the direction of the President of the United States, after the lands shall have been surveyed, and the boundaries to correspond with the public surveys.

ARTICLE 4. In consideration of the aforesaid cession, the United States will pay fifteen thousand dollars annually for twelve years; Thirty-two thousand dollars, in goods, will be paid as soon after the signing of these articles, as they can be procured, and ten thousand dollars, in goods, will be paid next spring, at Notta-wa-si-pa, and to be paid to that band, and pay their just debts, agreeably to a schedule hereunto annexed, amounting to twenty thousand seven hundred and twenty-one dollars.

The section of land granted by the treaty of St. Joseph to To-pe-nau-koung, wife of Peter Longlois, shall be purchased by the United States, if the same can be done for the sum of eight hundred dollars.
The United States agree to appropriate, for the purpose of educating Indian youths, the annual sum of two thousand dollars, as long as the Congress of the United States may think proper, to be expended as the President may direct.

This treaty shall take effect and be obligatory on the contracting parties, as soon as the same shall have been ratified, by the President of the United States, by and with the advice and consent of the Senate.

In testimony whereof, the said Jonathan Jennings, John W. Davis, and Marks Crume, commissioners as aforesaid, and the chiefs, head men, and warriors of the Potowatomies, have hereunto set their hands at Tippecanoe, on the twenty-seventh day of October, in the year eighteen hundred and thirty-two.

Jonathan Jennings, J. W. Davis, To-pe-ne-be, his x mark, Po-ka-gou, his x mark, Sa-ga-nah, his x mark, Pe-che-co, his x mark, We-is-saw, his x mark,

Plains, West and Northwest Plateau Indian Treaties

Che-shaw-gun, his x mark, Ghe-bause, his x mark, O-saw-o-wah-co-ne-ah, his x mark, Mah-gah-guk, his x mark, Sa-gue-na-nah, his x mark, Louison Burnet, his x mark, Shaw-wah-nuk-wuk, his x mark, Mix-san-bah, his x mark, Ne-wah-ko-to, his x mark, Che-bah, his x mark, Wah-cose, his x mark, Ship-she-wa-no, his x mark, Kaw-kaw-bee, his x mark, O-ge-mah-caw-so, his x mark, Mash-kee, his x mark, Saw-ge-maw, his x mark, Nah-che-ke-zhie, his x mark, Mis-ke-qua-tah, his x mark, Now-o-le-naw, his x mark, Tuck-e-now, his x mark, Marks Crume.

Mo-nis, his x mark, O-go-maw-be-tuk, his x mark, Kaw-kaw-ke-moke, his x mark, Ke-swah-bay, his x mark, Win-keese, his x mark, To-posh, his x mark, Kawk-moc-a-sin, his x mark, Sa-maw-cah, his x mark, Ko-mack, his x mark, O-guon-cote, his x mark, Quis-sin, his x mark, Chou-a-ma-see, his x mark, Pat-e-ca-sha, his x mark, Pe-nah-seh, his x mark, Mix-e-nee, his x mark, Pe-na-shee, his x mark, So-wah-quen, his x mark, Gib-e-nash-wish, his x mark, Louison, his x mark, Che-chaw-cose, his x mark, Bee-zaw-yo, his x mark, O-shah-yaw, his x mark, Ash-kato, his x mark, O-ketch-chee, his x mark, Weh-zee-oness, his x mark, Aub-bee-noub-bee, his x mark,

Witness:
H. Hoover, secretary, Th. J. V. Owen, United States Indian agent, Marius Willet, J. Stewart, subagent, J. Bt. Chandonnais, J. E. Aunt, Peter Godfroy, G. A. Everts, Robert Simerwell, L. M. Taylor, Francis Comparret, E. N. Cicott, sint.
J. B. Baure, sint.
H. Lasselle, Henry 0ssem.

After the signing of this treaty, and at the request of the Indians, two thousand seven hundred dollars were applied to the purchasing of horses, which were purchased and delivered to the Indians under our direction, leaving the sum to be paid in merchandise, at this time, twenty-nine thousand three hundred dollars.

Jonathan Jennings, J. W. Davis, Marks Crume, Commissioners.

It is agreed on the part of the United States, that the following claims shall be allowed, agreeable to the fourth article of the foregoing treaty, viz:
To Erasmus Winslow, three hundred dollars, Squire Thompson, one hundred dollars, L. Johnson, three hundred and seventy-five dollars, Francis Comperret, two thousand four hundred and fifty dollars, Ica Rice, fifteen hundred dollars, T. P. and J. J. Godfroy, two hundred and fifty dollars, Joseph Smith, twenty-six dollars,
James Aveline, ninety-eight dollars, Edward Smith, forty-seven dollars, Gustavus A. Everts, two hundred dollars, Alexis Coquillard, five thousand one hundred dollars, Lathrop M. Taylor, two thousand two hundred and eighty dollars, Peter and J. J. Godfroy, three thousand five hundred dollars, R. A. Forsyth,

Plains, West and Northwest Plateau Indian Treaties

eighteen hundred dollars, Louis Dupuis, forty dollars, Timothy S. Smith, three hundred and ninety dollars, William Huff, one hundred dollars, Thomas Jones, two hundred and seventy-five dollars,
Michael Cadieux, four hundred and ninety dollars, Arthur Patterson, nine hundred dollars, Samuel McGeorge, three hundred and fifty dollars, D. H. Colerick, one hundred and fifty dollars, James Conner, one thousand dollars.

Jonathan Jennings, J. W. Davis, Marks Crume, Commissioners.

TREATY WITH THE KASKASKIA, ETC. {1832, Oct. 27} Proclamation, Feb. 12, 1833.

Articles of a treaty made and entered into at Castor Hill, in the country of St. Louis in the State of Missouri, the twenty-seventh day of October, one thousand eight hundred and thirty-two, between William Clark, Frank J. Allen and Nathan Kouns, Commissioners on the part of the United States, the one part; and the Kaskaskia and Peoria tribes, which, with the Michigamia, Cahokia and Tamarois bands, now united with the two first named tribes, formerly composed the Illinois nation of Indians, of the other part.

WHEREAS, the Kaskaskia tribe of Indians and the bands aforesaid united therewith, are desirous of uniting with the Peorias, (composed as aforesaid) on lands west of the State of Missouri, they have therefore for that purpose agreed with the commissioners aforesaid, upon the following stipulations:

ARTICLE 1. The Kaskaskia tribe of Indians and the several bands united with them as aforesaid, in consideration of the stipulations herein made on the part of the United States, do forever cede and release to the United States the lands granted to them forever by the first section of the treaty of Vincennes of 13th August 1803, reserving however to Ellen Decoigne the daughter of their late Chief who has married a white man, the tract of land of about three hundred and fifty acres near the town of Kaskaskia, which was secured to said tribe by the act of Congress of 3d March 1793.

ARTICLE 2. The Kaskaskia tribe further relinquishes to the United States the permanent annuity of one thousand dollars which they receive under the third article of the aforesaid treaty, and their salt annuity due by treaty of Fort Wayne of 7th June 1803.

ARTICLE 3. The Peoria tribe and the bands aforesaid, united therewith, cede and relinquish to the United States, all their claims to land heretofore reserved by, or assigned to them in former treaties, either in the State of Illinois or Missouri.

Plains, West and Northwest Plateau Indian Treaties

ARTICLE 4. The United States cede to the combined tribes of Kaskaskias and Peorias, and the bands aforesaid united with them, one hundred and fifty sections of land forever, or as long as they live upon it as a tribe, to include the present Peoria village, west of the State of Missouri, on the waters of Osage river, to be bounded as follows, to wit: North by the lands assigned to the Shawanoes; west, by the western line of the reservation made for the Piankeshaws, Weas, and Peorias; and east by lands assigned the Piankeshaws and Weas.

ARTICLE 5. In consideration of the foregoing cessions and relinquishments, the United (States) agree to pay to the said united Kaskaskia and Peoria tribes (composed as aforesaid) an annuity of three thousand dollars for ten successive years, to be paid on the lands assigned them in common, either in money, merchandise, or domestic stock, at their option; if in merchandise, to be delivered to them free of transportation.

ARTICLE 6. And whereas, the said Peoria tribe, and the bands united with them as aforesaid, assert in Council that they never understood the 5th article of the treaty of Edwardsville of 25th September 1818 (1825), as ceding to the United States their claims to lands in Missouri, on which they had been settled for a length of time previous to that treaty, and of which they had had possession for more than sixty years,and now demand an equivalent for those claims.

The Commissioners with a view of quieting forever the said claims and all demands of whatever nature which said Peoria tribe and the several bands united therewith as aforesaid, have against the government or citizens of the United States, agree to pay, viz:To the Peorias in common with the Kaskaskias, the sum of sixteen hundred dollars; to the Kaskaskias alone, for seven horses lost by them, and for salt annuities due to them by the treaty of Fort Wayne aforesaid, three hundred and fifty dollars; to the Peorias alone for improvements on the lands they moved from, two hundred and fifty dollars; to the united Peorias and Kaskaskias, there shall be paid and delivered on their land as soon as practicable after the ratification of this treaty, cows and calves and other stock to the amount of four hundred dollars, three iron bound carts, three yoke of oxen, and six ploughs.

There shall also be built for arid tribes, four log houses;for breaking up ground and fencing the same, three hundred dollars ;for agricultural implements, iron, and steel, fifty dollars per annum for four years. There shall also be paid to the said united tribes, on the signing of this treaty, eight hundred dollars in goods suited to their wants. Assistance shall also be given the Kaskaskias in moving to their lands, and provisions for one year after their removal to the amount of one thousand dollars. It is understood that any stipulations in this or the preceding articles, for the benefit of the Peorias or Kaskaskias separately, or united, shall embrace, in either case the bands before mentioned, united with either, or both tribes, as the case may be.

Plains, West and Northwest Plateau Indian Treaties

ARTICLE 7. In consideration of the stipulations contained in the preceding articles, the Peoria and Kaskaskia tribes and the bands of Michigamia, Cahokia and Tamarois Indians united with them, hereby forever cede and relinquish to the United States, their claims to lands within the States of Illinois and Missouri, and all other claims of whatsoever nature which they have had or preferred against the United States or the citizens thereof, up to the signing of this treaty.

ARTICLE 8. This treaty after the same shall be ratified by the President and Senate of the United States, shall be obligatory on the contracting parties.
Done at Castor Hill, in the county of St. Louis in the State of Missouri, the day and year above written, and of the independence of the United States the fifty-seventh.

Wm. Clark, Frank J. Allen, Nathan Kouns.

Peorias:
Wah-pe-sha-ka-na, white skin, his x mark, Ken-mah-re-ne-ah, his x mark, Pa-kee-sha-ma, cutter, his x mark, Pa-me-kaw-wa-ta, man' s track, his x mark, Al-le-ne-pe-sh-en-sha, his x mark,
Kaskaskias:
Ke-mon-sah, little chief, his x mark, Wah-kah-pe-se-wah, round flyer, Wa-pe-sae, white, his x mark, Pe-me-ka-wai, man's track, his x mark,

In presence of
James Kemmly, secretary, A. Shane, United States interpreter, Jacques Mette, United States interpreter, Jesse Oliver, Pierre Menard.
Wm. Radford, U. S. Navy, G. S. Rousseau, U. S. Army, Meriwether Lewis Clark, lieutenant, Sixth Infantry.

Plains, West and Northwest Plateau Indian Treaties

TREATY WITH THE MENOMINEE {1832, Oct. 27}
Proclamation, Mar. 13, 1833.

WHEREAS articles of agreement between the United States of America, and the Menominee Indians, were made and concluded at the city of Washington, on the eighth day of February A. D. one thousand eight hundred and thirty-one, by John H. Eaton, and Samuel C. Stambaugh, Commissioners on the part of the United States, and certain Chiefs and Headmen of the Menominee Nation, on the part of said nation; to which articles, an addition or supplemental article was afterwards made, on the seventeenth day of February in the same year, by which the said Menominee Nation agree to cede to the United States certain parts of their land; and that a tract of country therein defined shall be set apart for the New York Indians.

All which with the many other stipulations therein contained will more fully appear, by reference to the same. Which said agreements thus forming a Treaty, were laid before the Senate of the United States during their then session: but were not at said session acted on by that body. Whereupon a further agreement was on the fifteenth day of March, in the same year, entered into for the purpose of preserving the provisions of the treaty, made as aforesaid.

By which it was stipulated that the said articles of agreement, concluded as aforesaid, should be laid before the next Senate of the United States, at their ensuing session; and if sanctioned and confirmed by them, that each and every article thereof should be as binding and obligatory upon the parties respectively, as if they had been sanctioned at the previous session. And whereas the Senate of the United States, by their resolution of the twenty-fifth day of June, one thousand eight hundred and thirty-two, did advise and consent to accept, ratify and confirm the same, and every clause and article thereof upon the conditions expressed in the proviso, contained in their said resolution: which proviso is as follows: "Provided that for the purpose of establishing the rights of the New York Indians, on a permanent and just footing, the said treaty shall be ratified, with the express understanding that two townships of land on the east side of Winnebago Lake, equal to forty-six thousand and eighty acres shall be laid off (to commence at some point to be agreed on) for the use of the Stockbridge and Munsee tribes.

And that the improvements made on the lands now in the possession of the said tribes on the east side of the Fox river, which said lands are to be relinquished shall, after being valued by a commissioner to be appointed by the President of the United States, be paid for by the Government: Provided, however, that the valuation of such improvements shall not exceed the sum of twenty-five thousand dollars.

Plains, West and Northwest Plateau Indian Treaties

And that there shall be one township of land adjoining the foregoing, equal to twenty-three thousand and forty acres laid off and granted for the use of the Brothertown Indians, who are to be paid by the Government the sum of one thousand six hundred dollars for the improvements on lands now in their possession, on the east side of Fox river, and which lands are to be relinquished by said Indians: also that a new line shall be run, parallel to the southwestern boundary line or course of the tract of five hundred thousand acres, described in the first article of this treaty, and set apart for the New York Indians, to commence at a point on the west side of the Fox river, and one mile alcove the Grand Shute, on Fox river, and at a sufficient distance from the said boundary line as established by the said first article, as shall comprehend the additional quantity of two hundred thousand acres of land on and along the west side of Fox river, without including any of the confirmed private land claims on the Fox river

And which two hundred thousand acres shall be a part of the five hundred thousand acres, intended to be set apart for the Six Nations of the New York Indians and the St. Regis tribe; and that an equal quantity to that which is added to the southwestern side shall be taken off from the northeastern side of the said tract described in that article, on the Oconto creek, to be determined by a commissioner to be appointed by the President of the United States; so that the whole number of acres to be granted to the Six Nations, and St. Regis tribe of Indians, shall not exceed the quantity originally stipulated by the treaty." And whereas, before the treaty aforesaid, conditionally ratified, according to the proviso to the resolution of the Senate, above recited, could be obligatory upon the said Menominee nation, their assent to the same must be had and obtained.

And whereas the honorable Lewis Cass, Secretary of the Department of War, by his letter of instructions of the eleventh day of September, A. D. 1832, did authorize and request George B. Porter, Governor of the Territory of Michigan, to proceed to Green Bay, and endeavor to procure the assent of the Menominees to the change proposed by the Senate, as above set forth; urging the necessity of directing his first efforts to an attempt to procure the unconditional assent of the Menominees to the said treaty, as ratified by the Senate. But should he fail in this object that he would then endeavor to procure their assent to the best practicable terms, short of those proposed by the Senate; giving them to understand that he merely received such proposition as they might make, with a view to transmit it for the consideration of the President and Senate of the United States. And if this course became necessary that it would be very desirable that the New York Indians should also signify their acceptance of the modifications required by the Menominees.

And whereas, in pursuance of the said instructions the said George B. Porter proceeded to Green Bay and having assembled all the chiefs and headmen of the Menominee nation, in council, submitted to them, on the twenty-second day

Plains, West and Northwest Plateau Indian Treaties

of October A. D. one thousand eight hundred and thirty-two, the said proviso annexed to the resolution aforesaid of the Senate of the United States, for the ratification of the said treaty: and advised and urged on them the propriety of giving their assent to the same. And the said chiefs and headmen having taken time to deliberate and reflect on the proposition so submitted to them, and which they had been urged to assent to, did in the most positive and decided manner, refuse to give their assent to the same. (The many reasons assigned for this determination, by them, being reported in the journal of the said commissioner, which will be transmitted with this agreement.)

And whereas after failing in the object last stated, the said George B. Porter endeavored to procure the assent of the said chiefs and headmen of the Menominee nation to the best practicable terms short of those proposed by the Senate of the United States; and after much labor and pains, entreaty and persuasion, the said Menominees consented to the following, as the modifications which they would make; and which are reduced to writing, in the form of an agreement, as the best practicable terms which could be obtained from them, short of those proposed by the Senate of the United States, which they had previously positively refused to accede to. And as the modifications so made and desired, have been acceded to by the New York Indians, with a request that the treaty thus modified might be ratified and approved by the President and the Senate of the United States, it is the anxious desire of the Menominees also, that the treaty, with these alterations may be ratified and approved without delay, that they may receive the benefits and advantage secured to them by the several stipulations of the said treaty, of which they have so long been deprived.

The following is the article of agreement made between the said George B. Porter, commissioner on the part of the United States, specially appointed as aforesaid, and the said Menominee nation, through their chiefs and headmen on the part of their nation.

ARTICLE 1. The said chiefs and headmen of the Menominee nation of Indians do not object to any of the matters contained in the proviso annexed to the resolution of the Senate of the United States, so far as the same relate to the granting of three townships of land on the east side of Winnebago Lake, to the Stockbridge, Munsee and Brothertown tribes; to the valuation and payment for their improvements, &c. (ending with the words "and which lands are to be relinquished by said Indians.") They therefore assent to the same.

ARTICLE 2. The said chiefs and headmen of the Menominee nation of Indians, objecting to all the matters contained in the said proviso annexed to the resolution of the Senate of the United States, so far as the same relate to the running of a new line parallel to the southwestern boundary line or course of the tract of five hundred thousand acres, described in the first article of the

Plains, West and Northwest Plateau Indian Treaties

treaty, and set apart for the New York Indians, to commence at a point on the southwestern side of Fox river, and one mile above the Grand Shute, on Fox river, and at a sufficient distance from the said boundary line, as established by the said first article, as shall comprehend the additional quantity of two hundred thousand acres of land, on and along the west side of the Fox river, without including any of the confirmed private land claims, on the Fox river, to compose a part of the five hundred thousand acres intended to be set apart for the Six Nations of the New York Indians and St. Regis tribe, agree in lieu of this proposition, to set off a like quantity of two hundred thousand acres as follows: The said Menominee nation hereby agree to cede for the benefit of the New York Indians along the southwestern boundary line of the present five hundred thousand acres described in the first article of the treaty as set apart for the New York Indians, a tract of land; bounded as follows. Beginning on the said treaty line, at the old mill dam on Fox river, and thence extending up along Fox river to the little Rapid Croche.

From thence running a northwest course three miles; thence on a line running parallel with the several courses of Fox river, and three miles distant from the river, until it will intersect a line, running on a northwest course, commencing at a point one mile above the Grand Shute; thence on a line running northwest, so far as will be necessary to include, between the said last line and the line described as the southwestern boundary line of the five hundred thousand acres in the treaty aforesaid, the quantity of two hundred thousand acres; and thence running northeast until it will intersect the line, forming the southwestern boundary line aforesaid; and from thence along the said line to the old mill dam, or place of beginning, containing two hundred thousand acres. Excepting and reserving therefrom the privelege of Charles A. Grignon, for erecting a mill on Apple creek, &c., as approved by the Department of War on the twenty-second day of April one thousand eight hundred and thirty-one and all confirmed private land claims on the Fox river.

The lines of the said tract of land so granted to be run, marked and laid off without delay, by a commissioner to be appointed by the President of the United States. And that in exchange for the above, a quantity of land equal to that which is added to the southwestern side shall be taken off from the northeastern side of the said tract, described in that article, on the Oconto creek, to be run, marked and determined by the commissioner to be appointed by the President of the United States, as aforesaid, so that the whole number of acres to be granted to the Six Nations and St. Regis tribe of Indians, shall not exceed the quantity of five hundred thousand acres.

ARTICLE 3. The said chiefs and headmen of the Menominee nation agree, that in case the said original treaty, made as aforesaid, and the supplemental articles thereto, be ratified and confirmed at the ensuing session of the Senate of the United States, with the modifications contained in this agreement, that

Plains, West and Northwest Plateau Indian Treaties

each and every article thereof shall be as binding and obligatory upon the parties respectively, as if they had been sanctioned at the times originally agreed upon.

In consideration of the above voluntary sacrifices of their interest, made by the said Menominee nation, and as evidence of the good feeling of their great father, the President of the United States, the said George B. Porter commissioner as aforesaid, has delivered to the said chiefs, headmen, and the people of the said Menominee nation here assembled, presents in clothing to the amount of one thousand dollars: five hundred bushels of corn, ten barrels of pork, and ten barrels of flour, &c. &c.

In witness whereof, we have hereunto set our hands and seals, at the Agency House, at Green Bay, this twenty-seventh day of October, in the year of our Lord one thousand eight hundred and thirty-two.

G. B. Porter, Commissioner of the United States,
Kausk-kan-no-naive, grizzly bear, his x mark, Osh ~rosh, the brave, (by his brother fully empowered to act)
Osh-ke-e-na-neur, the young man, his x mark, A-ya-mah-ta, fish spawn, his x mark, Pe-wait-enaw, rain, his x mark, Che-na-po-mee, one that is looked at, his x mark, Ko-ma-ni-kin, big wave, his x mark, Ke-shee-a-quo-teur, the flying cloud, his x mark, Wain-e-saut, one who arranges the circle, (by his son, Wa-kee-che-on-a-peur) his x mark, Ke-shoh, the sun, (by his son, A-pa: ma-chao, shifting cloud) his x mark,
Ma-concee-wa-be-no-chee, bear's child, his x mark, Wa-bose, the rabbit, his x mark, Shaw-e-no-ge-shick, south sky, his x mark, Ac-camut, the prophet, his x mark, Mas-ka-ma-gee, his x mark, Sho-ne-on, silver, his x mark, Maw-baw-so, pale color, his x mark, Paw-a ko-neur, big soldier, (by his representative, Che-kaw-mah-kee-shen) his x mark,

Sealed and delivered, in the presence of
George Boyd, United States Indian agent, Charles A. Grignon, interpreter, Samuel Abbott, Joshua Boyer, secretary, James M. Boyd, Richard Pricket, his x mark, interpreter, Henry S. Baird, R. A. Forsyth, paymaster U. S. Army, B. B. Kercheval, Ebenezer Childs.

APPENDIX.
Oct. 27, 1832. 7 Stat., 409.

To all to whom these presents shall come, the undersigned, Chiefs and Headmen of the sundry tribes of New York Indians, (as set forth in the specifications annexed to their signatures) send greeting:

Plains, West and Northwest Plateau Indian Treaties

WHEREAS a tedious, perplexing and harassing dispute and controversy have long existed between the Menominee nation of Indians and the New York Indians, more particularly known as the Stockbridge, Munsee and Brothertown tribes, the Six Nations and St. Regis tribe. The treaty made between the said Menominee nation, and the United States, and the conditional ratification thereof by the Senate of the United States, being stated and set forth in the within agreement, entered into between the chiefs and headmen of the said Menominees, and George B. Porter, Governor of Michigan, commissioner specially appointed, with instructions referred to in the said agreement.

And whereas the undersigned are satisfied, and believe that the best efforts of the said commissioner were directed and used to procure, if practicable, the unconditional assent of the said Menominees to the change proposed by the Senate of the United States in the ratification of the said treaty: but without success. And whereas the undersigned further believe that the terms stated in the within agreement are the best practicable terms, short of those proposed by the Senate of the United States, which could be obtained from the said Menominees; and being asked to signify our acceptance of the modifications proposed as aforesaid by the Menominees, we are compelled, by a sense of duty and propriety to say that we do hereby accept of the same. So far as the tribes to which we belong are concerned, we are perfectly satisfied, that the treaty should be ratified on the terms proposed by the Menominees.

further believe that the tract of land which the Menominees in the within agreement, are willing to cede, in exchange for an equal quantity on the northeast side of the tract of five hundred thousand acres, contains a sufficient quantity of good land, favorably and advantageously situated, to answer all the wants of the New York Indians, and St. Regis tribe. For the purpose, then, of putting an end to strife, and that we may all sit down in peace and harmony, we thus signify our acceptance of the modifications proposed by the Menominees: and we most respectfully request that the treaty as now modified by the agreement this day entered into with the Menominees, may be ratified and approved by the President and Senate of the United States.

In witness whereof, we have hereunto set our hands and seals, at the Agency House at Green Bay, this twenty-seventh day of October, in the year of our Lord one thousand eighteen hundred and thirty-two.

G. B. Porter, commissioner on behalf of the United States,
For, and on behalf of, the Stockbridges and Munsees:
John Metoxen, John W. Quinny, Austin Quinny, Jacob Chicks, Robert Konkopa, his x , John Anthony Brant, his x mark, Thos. J. Hendrick, Benjamin Palmer, his x mark, Nathaniel Neddy, his x mark, Sampson Medyard, Capt. Porter, his x mark, Thomas Neddy, his x mark,
For, and on behalf of, the Brother-towns:

Plains, West and Northwest Plateau Indian Treaties

William Dick, Daniel Dick, Eleanah Dick, his x mark,
For, and on behalf of, the Six Nations and St. Regis tribe:
Daniel Bread, Henry Powles, his x mark, Cornelius Stevens, his x mark,

Sealed, and delivered, in the presence of
George Boyd, United States Indian agent, Eben. Childs, R. A. Forsyth, paymaster U. S. Army, Henry S. Baird, Charles A. Grignon, interpreter, Peter B. Grignon, Samuel Abbott, Hanson Johnson, Joshua Boyer, secretary, James M. Boyd, B. B. Kercheval, Richard Pricket, his x mark, interpreter.

TREATY WITH THE QUAPAW {1833, May 13}
Proclamation, Apt. 12, 1834.

Articles of agreement or a treaty between the United States and the Quapaw Indians entered into by John F. Schermerhorn, commissioner of Indian affairs west on the part of the United States and the chiefs and warriors of the Quapaw Indians.

WHEREAS, by the treaty between the United States and the Quapaw Indians, concluded November 15th, 1824, they ceded to the United States all their-lands in the Territory of Arkansas, and according to which they were "to be concentrated and confined to a district of country inhabited by the Caddo Indians and form a part of said tribe," and whereas they did remove according to the stipulations of said treaty, and settled on the Bayou Treache on the south side of Red River, on a tract of land given them by the Caddo Indians, but which was found subject to frequent inundations on account of the raft on Red River, and where their crops were destroyed by the water year after year, and which also proved to be a very sickly country and where in a short time, nearly one-fourth of their people died, and whereas they could obtain no other situation from the Caddoes and they refused to incorporate them and receive them as a constituent part of their tribe as contemplated by their treaty with the United States.

And as they saw no alternative but to perish if they continued there, or to return to their old residence on the Arkansas, they therefore chose the latter; and whereas they now find themselves very unhappily situated in consequence of having their little improvements taken from them by the settlers of the country; and being anxious to secure a permanent and peaceable home the following articles or treaty are agreed upon between the United States and the Quapaw Indians by John F. Schermerhorn, commissioners of Indian affairs west and the chiefs and warriors of said Quapaw Indians this (13th) thirteenth day of May 1833.--

152

Plains, West and Northwest Plateau Indian Treaties

ARTICLE 1. The Quapaw Indians hereby relinquish and convey to the United States all their right and title to the lands given them by the Caddo Indians on the Bayou Treache of Red River.--

ARTICLE 2. The United States hereby agree to convey to the Quapaw Indians one hundred and fifty sections of land west of the State line of Missouri and between the lands of the Senecas and Shawnees, not heretofore assigned to any other tribe of Indians, the same to be selected and assigned by the commissioners of Indian affairs west, and which is expressly designed to be (in) lieu of their location on Red River and to carry into effect the treaty of 1824, in order to provide a permanent home for their nation; the United States agree to convey the same by patent, to them and their descendants as long as they shall exist as a nation or continue to reside thereon, and they also agree to protect them in their new residence, against all interruption or disturbance from any other tribe or nation of Indians or from any other person or persons whatever.

ARTICLE 3. Whereas it is the policy of the United States in all their intercourse with the Indians to treat them liberally as well as justly, and to endeavour to promote their civilization and prosperity; it is further agreed that in consideration of the important and extensive cessions of lands made by the Quapaws to the United States and in view of their present impoverished and wretched condition, they shall be removed to their new homes at the expense of the United States and that they will supply them with one year's provision from the time of their removal, which shall be as soon as they receive notice of the ratification of this treaty by the President and Senate of the United States.

The United States will also furnish and deliver to them, after their arrival at their new homes, one hundred cows, one hundred breeding hogs, one hundred sheep, ten yoke of working cattle, twenty-five ploughs, one hundred axes, one hundred hoes, four ox carts, and one wagon, with all their necessary rigging, twenty iron hand corn-mills, tools of different descriptions to the amount of two hundred dollars, also looms, wheels, reels and wool-cards to the amount of two hundred dollars, one hundred blankets, fifty rifles, and five shot guns all with flint locks, ten kegs of powder, and six hundred pounds of lead,
The United States agree to provide a farmer to reside with them and to aid and instruct them in their agricultural pursuits and a blacksmith to do their necessary work, with a shop and tools and iron and steel not exceeding one ton per year. The United States also agree to appropriate one thousand dollars per year for education purposes to be expended under the direction of the President of the United States; the farmer and blacksmith and the above appropriation for education purposes to be continued only as long as the President of the United States deems necessary for the best interests of the Indians.

ARTICLE 4. It is hereby mutually agreed upon between the parties respectively to this treaty, that in lieu of and in full consideration of their present an-

153

Plains, West and Northwest Plateau Indian Treaties

nuities perpetual and limited, the United States will pay the debts of the Quapaw Indians according to the annexed schedule to the amount of four thousand one hundred and eighty dollars provided they can be discharged in full for that amount. They will also expend to the amount of one thousand dollars in hiring suitable labourers to build and aid them in erecting comfortable cabins and houses to live in; and also that they will pay them annually two thousand dollars for twenty years from the ratification of this treaty, and that out of said annuity there shall be allowed to their four principal chiefs, Hackatton, Sarassan, Tonnonjinka and Kaheketteda, and to their successors each, in addition to their distributive share of said annuity, the sum of fifty dollars per year.

ARTICLE 5. It is hereby agreed, and expressly understood, that this treaty is only supplementary to the treaty of 1824, and designed to carry into effect the views of the United States in providing a permanent and comfortable home for the Quapaw Indians; and also that all the stock and articles furnished the Indians by the United States as expressed in the fourth article shall be tinder the care and direction of the agent and farmer of said tribe, to see that the same is not squandered or sold, or any of the stock slain by the Indians, until such time as the natural increase of-the stock will warrant the same to be done without destroying the whole, and thus defeating the benevolent views of the Government in making this provision for them.

ARTICLE 6. The United States also agrees to employ an interpreter to accompany them on their removal and the same to continue with them during the pleasure of the President of the United StatesThe above treaty shall be binding on the United States whenever ratified and approved by the President and Senate of the United States.

John F. Schermerhorn,
Kunkadaquene, his x mark, Hackatton chief, his x mark, Wattekiane, his x mark, Sarrasin chief, his x mark, Hadaskamoncne, his x mark, Taunoujinka chief, his x mark, Hummonene, his x mark, Kaheketteda chief, his x mark, Hikaguedotton, his x mark, Monehunka', his x mark, Moussockane, his x mark, The above treaty was signed in open council, in the presence of
Richard M. Hannum, S.A.
Frederick Sangrain, Antoine Barraque, John D. Shaw, James W. Walker, Joseph Duchasin, interpreter.

The amount due from the Quapaw tribe of Indians to the following named persons
Frederic Notrabe $567.00
Joseph Dardene   300.00
Ignacc Bogy   170.00
Alexander Dickerson   28.00
William Montgomery   350.00

Plains, West and Northwest Plateau Indian Treaties

Joseph Bonne	30.00
Joseph Duchasin	30.00
Baptiste Bonne	20.00
Antoine Barraque	2,235.00
George W. Boyer	50.00
Weylon King	400.00
$4, 180.00	

TREATY WITH THE OTO AND MISSOURI {1833, Sept. 21}
Proclamation Apt. 12, 1834.

Articles of agreement and convention, made at the Otoe Village on the River Platte, between Henry L. Ellsworth, Commissioner, in behalf of the United States, and the united bands of Otoes, and Missourias dwelling on the said Platte this 21st day of September A. D. 1833.

ARTICLE 1. The said Otoes, and Missourias, cede and relinquish to the United States, all their right and title, to the lands lying south of the following line viz: Beginning, on the Little Nemohaw river, at the northwest corner of the land reserved by treaty at Prairie du Chien, on the 15th July 1830, in favor of certain half-breeds, of the Omahas, Ioways, Otoes, Yancton, and Santie bands of Sioux, and running westerly with said Little Nemohaw, to the head branches of the same; and thence running in a due west line as far west, as said Otoes and Missourias, have, or pretend to have any claim.

ARTICLE 2. The United States agree, to continue the present annuity of twenty-five hundred dollars, granted by said treaty of Prairie du Chien, to said Otoes and Missourias, ten years from the expiration of the same viz: ten years from 15th July 1840.

ARTICLE 3. The United States agree to continue for ten years from said 15th July, 1840, the annuity of five hundred dollars, granted for instruments for agricultural purposes.

ARTICLE 4. The United States agree, to allow annually five hundred dollars, for five years, for the purposes of education, which sum shall be expended under the direction of the President; and continued longer if he deems proper. The schools however, shall be kept within the limit of said tribe or nation.

ARTICLE 5. The United States agree, to erect a horse-mill for grinding corn, and to provide two farmers to reside in the nation, to instruct and assist said tribe, for the term of five years, and longer if the President thinks proper.

Plains, West and Northwest Plateau Indian Treaties

ARTICLE 6. The United States agree to deliver to said Otoes and Missourias, one thousand dollars value in stock, which shall be placed in the care of the agent, or farmer, until the President thinks the same can safely be intrusted to the Indians.

ARTICLE 7. It is expressly agreed and understood, that the stipulations contained in the 3d, 4th, 5th, and 6th articles are not to be fulfilled by the United States, until the Otoes and Missourias shall locate themselves in such convenient agricultural districts, as the President may think proper, nor shall the payments be continued, if the Otoes and Missourias shall abandon such location as the President shall think best for their agricultural interest.

ARTICLE 8. The Otoes and Missourias declare their entire willingness to abandon the chase for the agricultural lifetheir desire for peace with all other tribes, and therefore agree not to make war against any tribe with whom they now are, or shall be, at peace; but should any difficulty arise between them and any other tribe, they agree to refer the matter in dispute, to some arbiter, whom the President shall appoint to adjust the same.

ARTICLE 9. The United States agree to deliver the said. Otoes and Missourias the value of four hundred dollars in goods and merchandise; which said Otoes and Missourias hereby acknowledge to have received.

ARTICLE 10. This convention, or agreement, to be obligatory, when ratified by the President and Senate of the United States.

In testimony whereof, the commissioners aforesaid, and the undersigned chiefs and warriors have hereunto subscribed their names, and affixed their seals, at the Otoe village on the said Platte river, the date first above written.

Henry L. Ellsworth,
Jaton, his x mark, Big Kaw, his x mark, The Thief, his x mark, Wah-ro-ne-saw, his x mark, Rah-no-way-wah-ha-rah, his x mark, 'Gra-tah-ni-kah, his x mark, Mah-skah-gah-ha, his x mark, Nan-cha-si-zay, his x mark, A-Sha-bah-hoo, his x mark, Kah-he-ga, his x mark, Wah-ne-min-nah, his x mark, Cha-wa-che-ra, his x mark, Pa-che-ga-he, his x mark, Wah-tcha-shing-a, his x mark, Mon-to-ni-a, his x mark, Gra-da-nia, his x mark, Mock-shiga-tona, his x mark, Wah-nah-sha, his x mark, Wash-kah-money, his x mark, Cha-ah-gra, his x mark, To-he, his x mark, O-rah-kah-pe, his x mark, Wah-a-ge-hi-ru-ga-rah, his x mark, O-ha-ah-che-gi-sug-a, his x mark, Ish-kah-tap-a, his x mark, Meh-say-way, his x mark,

In presence of: Edward A. Ellsworth, secretary pro tempore, Jno. Dougherty, Indian agent, Ward S. May, M.D., John Dunlop, John T. Irving, jr., J. D. Blanchard, Charlo Mobrien, his x mark, Oloe, Interpreter.

156

Plains, West and Northwest Plateau Indian Treaties

TREATY WITH THE PAWNEE {1833, Oct. 9}
Proclamation, Apr. 12, 1834.

Articles of agreement and convention, made this ninth day of October, A. D. 1833, at the Grand Pawnee village, on the Platte river between Henry L. Ellsworth, commissioner in behalf of the United States, and the chiefs and head-men of the four confederated bands of Pawnees, viz:Grand Pawnees, Pawnee Loups, Pawnee Republicans, and Pawnee Tappaye, residing on the Platte and the Loup fork.

ARTICLE 1. The confederated bands of Pawnees aforesaid hereby cede and relinquish to the United States all their right, interest, and title in and to all the land lying south of the Platte river.

ARTICLE 2. The land ceded and relinquished hereby, so far as the same is not and shall not be assigned to any tribe or tribes, shall remain a common hunting ground, during the pleasure of the President, for the Pawnees and other friendly Indians, who shall be permitted by the President to hunt on the same.

ARTICLE 3. The United States, in consideration of said cession and for the purpose of advancing the welfare of the said Pawnees, agree to pay said bands annually, for the term of twelve years, the sum of forty-six hundred dollars in goods, at not exceeding St. Louis prices, as follows: to the Grand Pawnees and Republican villages, each thirteen hundred dollars, and to the Pawnee Loups and Tappaye Pawnee villages each one thousand dollars, and said annuity to said Grand Pawnees is in full remuneration for removal from the south to the north side of the Platte, and building again.

ARTICLE 4. The United States agree to pay to each of said four bands, for five years, the sum of five hundred dollars in agricultural implements; and to be continued longer if the President thinks proper.

ARTICLE 5. The United States agree to allow one thousand dollars a year for ten years, for schools to be established for the benefit of said four bands at the discretion of the President.

ARTICLE 6. The United States agree to furnish two blacksmiths and two strikers, with shop, tools and iron, for ten years, for said four bands, at an expense not exceeding two thousand dollars in the whole annually.

ARTICLE 7. The United States agree to furnish each of said four tribes with a farmer for five years, and deliver to said farmers for the benefit of said nation, one thousand dollars value in oxen and other stock. But said stock is not to be

157

Plains, West and Northwest Plateau Indian Treaties

delivered into the hands of the said Pawnees, until the President thinks the same can be done with propriety and safety.

ARTICLE 8. The United States agree to erect, for each of said four bands, a horse-mill for grinding corn.

ARTICLE 9. The Pawnee nation renew their assurance of friendship for the white men, their fidelity to the United States, and their desire for peace with all neighboring tribes of red men. The Pawnee nation therefore agree not to molest or injure the person or property of any white citizen of the United States, wherever found, nor to make war upon any tribe with whom said Pawnee nation now are, or may be, at peace; but should any difficulty arise between said nation and any other tribe, they agree to refer the matter in dispute to such arbiter as the President shall appoint to settle the same.

ARTICLE 10. It is agreed and understood that the United States shall not be bound to fulfil the stipulations contained in the fifth, seventh, and eighth articles, until said tribes shall locate themselves in convenient agricultural districts, and remain in these districts the whole year, so as to give protection to the teachers, the farmers, stock and mill.

ARTICLE 11. The United States, desirous to show the Pawnees the advantages of agriculture, engage, in case the Pawnees cannot agree to remain to protect their domestic interest, to break up for each village a piece of land suitable for corn and potatoes for one season; and should either village at any time agree to give the protection required, said village shall be entitled to the benefits conferred in said fifth, seventh, and eighth articles.

ARTICLE 12. In case the Pawnee nation will remain at home during the year, and give the protection specified, the United States agree to place twenty-five guns, with suitable ammunition, in the hands of the farmers of each village, to be used in case of an attack from hostile bands.

ARTICLE 13. The United States further agree to deliver to said four bands collectively, on the execution of this treaty, the amount of sixteen hundred dollars in goods and merchandise, and the receipt of the same is hereby acknowledged by said bands.

ARTICLE 14. These articles of agreement and convention shall be obligatory and binding when ratified by the President and Senate of the United States.
In testimony whereof the said Henry L. Ellsworth, commissioner, and the chiefs and head men of the four confederated bands of the Grand Pawnees, Pawnee Loups, Pawnee Republicans, and Tappaye Pawnees, have hereunto signed their names and affixed their seals on the day and year above written.

Plains, West and Northwest Plateau Indian Treaties

Henry L. Ellsworth, Grand Pawnees:
Shah-re-tah-riche, his x mark, Shon-gah-kah-he-gah, his x mark, Pe-tah-lay-shah-rho, his x ,hark, Ah-sha-kah-tah-kho, his x mark,
Pawnee Republicans:
Blue Coat, his x mark, Lay-shah-rho-lah-re-ho-rho, his x mark, Ah-shah-lay-kah-sah-hah, his x mark, Lay-shah-ke-re-pahs-kay, his x mark,
Tappaye Pawnees:
Little Chief, his x mark, Lah-ho-pah-go-lah-lay-shah-rho, his x mark, Ah-ke-tah-we-he-kah-he-gay, his x mark,
Pawnee Loups:
Big Axe, his x mark, Middle Chief, his x mark, Spotted Horse, his x mark, Big Soldier, his x mark,

Signed, sealed, and delivered in the presence of
Edward A. Ellsworth, secretary pro tempore, Jno. Dougherty, Indian agent, A. L. Papin, Ware S. May, M.D., ohn Dunlop, John T. Irving, jr., Lewis La Chapelle, interpreter.

TREATY WITH THE POTAWATOMI {1834, Dec. 4}
Proclamation, Mar. 16, 1835.

Articles of a Treaty, made and concluded at a camp, on Lake Max-ee-nie-kue-kee, in the State of Indiana, between William Marshall, Commissioner on the part of the United States, and Com-o-za, a Chief of the Potawattimie tribe of Indians and his band, on, the fourth day of Decent her, in the year eighteen hundred and thirty-four.

ARTICLE 1. The above named chief and his band hereby cede to the United States, the two sections of land reserved for them by the 2d article of the treaty between the United States and the Pottawattimie Indians on Tippecanoe river on the 26th day of October, in the year eighteen hundred and thirty-two.

ARTICLE 2. The above named chief and his band agree to yield peaceable possession of said sections within three years from the date of the ratification of said treaty of eighteen hundred and thirty-two.

ARTICLE 3. In consideration of the cession aforesaid the United States stipulate to pay the above named chief and his band the sum of four hundred dollars in goods at the signing of this treaty, and an annuity of four hundred dollars for one year, the receipt of which former sum of (four hundred dollars in goods) is hereby acknowledged.

ARTICLE 4. This treaty shall be binding upon both parties, from the date of its ratification by the President and Senate of the United States.

159

Plains, West and Northwest Plateau Indian Treaties

In testimony whereof, the said William Marshall, commissioner, on the part of the United States, and the above named chief and headmen, for themselves and their band, have hereunto subscribed their names, the day and year above written.

William Marshall,
Com-o-za, his x mark, Ah-ke-pah-am-sa, his x mark, Nee-so-aw-quet, his x mark, Paw-pee, his x mark,
Witnesses:
J. B. Duret, secretary to commission, Cyrus Taber, Joseph Barron, interpreter.

TREATY WITH THE POTAWATOMI {1834, Dec. 10}
Proclamation, Mar. 16, 1835.

Articles of a Treaty made and concluded at a camp on Tippecanoe river, in the State of Indiana, between William Marshall, Commissioner on the part of the United States and Muck Rose, a Chief of the Potawattamie tribe of Indians, and his band, on the tenth day of December, in the year eighteen hundred and thirty-four.

ARTICLE 1. The above flamed chief and his baud hereby cede to the United States sections of land reserved for them by the second article of the treaty between the United States and the Pottawattamie Indians on Tippecanoe river, on the twenty-sixth day of October, in the year, eighteen hundred and thirty-two.

ARTICLE 2. The above named chief and his band agree to yield peaceable possession of the said-sections of land to the United States within three years from the date of the ratification of said treaty of eighteen hundred and thirty-two.

ARTICLE 3. In consideration of the cession aforesaid the United States stipulate to pay to the above named chief and his band, four hundred dollars in goods at the signing of this treaty, and an annuity of one thousand dollars for two years, the receipt of which former sum of (four hundred dollars in goods) is hereby acknowledged.

ARTICLE 4. This treaty shall be binding upon both parties from the date of its ratification by the President and Senate of the United States.

In testimony whereof, the said William Marshall, commissioner on the part of the United States, and the above named chief and his band, have hereunto subscribed their names the day and year above written.

Plains, West and Northwest Plateau Indian Treaties

William Marshall, Muck Rose, his x mark, Paw-tisse, his x mark, Sis-see-yaw, his x mark, Wau-pish-shaw, his x mark, Koo-tah-waun-nay, hisx mark,
Witnesses:
J. B. Duret, secretary, Cyrus Taber, Henry Ossem, interpreter, J. B. Boure, interpreter, John B. Intrais, Joseph Barron, principal interpreter, Jesse Vermilya.

TREATY WITH THE POTAWATOMI {1834, Dec. 16}
Proclamation, Mar. 16, 1835.

Articles of a treaty, made and concluded at the Potawattimie mills, in the State of Indiana, on the sixteenth day of December, in the year of our Lord one thousand eight hundred and thirty-four, between William, Marshall Commissioner on the part of the United States and the Chiefs, headmen, and warriors of the Potawattamis Indians.

ARTICLE 1. The chiefs, head men and warriors aforesaid agree to cede to the United States their title and interest to a reservation made to them at the treaty on the Tippecanoe river on the 27th day of October 1832 of two sections of land to include their mills on said river.

ARTICLE 2. In consideration of the cession aforesaid the United States agree to pay the Potawattimie Indians, at the payment of their annuities in 1835, the sum of seven hundred dollars in cash, and pay their just debts agreeably to a schedule hereunto annexed, amounting to nine hundred dollars.

ARTICLE 3. The miller provided for by the 3rd article of the treaty with the Potawattimie tribe of Indians on the sixteenth day of October, in the year eighteen hundred and twenty-six, is not to be supported by the United States, and to cease from and after the signing of this treaty.

ARTICLE 4. This treaty shall be binding upon both parties, from the date of its ratification by the President and Senate of the United States.
In testimony whereof, the said William Marshall, commissioner on the part of the United States, and the chiefs, head men, and warriors of the Potawatamie tribe of Indians, have hereunto subscribed their names, the day and year above written.

William Marshall, Ash-kum, his x mark, Ku-waw-nay, his x mark, Pash-po-ho, his x mark, Che-quawm-a-kaw-ko, his x mark, Nas-waw-kay, his x mark, Quaush-quaw, his x ,
Witnesses:
J. B. Duret, secretary, Cyrus Taber, J. B. Boure, interpreter, Joseph Barron, principal interpreter.

Plains, West and Northwest Plateau Indian Treaties

It is agreed that the United States will satisfy the claims mentioned in the following schedule as provided for in the second article of the foregoing treaty. viz:

To J. B. Duret, four hundred dollars.
To Cyrus Taber, one hundred dollars.
To Ewing Walker & Co., three hundred dollars.
To Cyrus Vigus, one hundred dollars.

TREATY WITH THE POTAWATOMI {1834, Dec. 17}
Proclamation, Mar. 16, 1835.

Articles of a treaty made and concluded at the Indian Agency, Logansport Indiana between William Marshall, Commissioner on the part of the United States and Mota, a chief of the Potawattimie tribe of Indians, and his band on the 17th day of December, in the year eighteen hundred and thirty-four.

ARTICLE 1. The above-named Chief and his band hereby cede to the United States the four sections of land reserved for them by the second article of the treaty between the United States and the Potawattimie Indians on the twenty-seventh day of October in the year eighteen hundred and thirty-two.

ARTICLE 2. The above named chief and head men and their band, do hereby agree to yield peaceable possession of said sections, and to remove, with their families, to a country provided for them by the United States, west of the Mississippi river, within three years or less from the date of the ratification of said treaty of eighteen hundred and thirty-two.

ARTICLE 3. The United States, in consideration of the cession, made in the first article of this treaty, do hereby stipulate to remove the above named chief and headmen and their bands to the new country provided for them, and to furnish them either goods, farming utensils or other articles necessary for them, agreeably to the provisions of the fifth article of the treaty of October twenty-sixth, eighteen hundred and thirty-two.

ARTICLE 4. The United States further stipulate to pay to the above named chief, and head men and their bands, the sum of six hundred and eighty dollars in goods, at the signing of this treaty, and the further sum of six hundred dollars in cash at the payment of their annuities in 1835, the receipt of which former sum of (six hundred and eighty dollars in goods) is hereby acknowledged.

ARTICLE 5. This treaty shall be binding upon both parties, from the date of its ratification by the Senate of the United States.

162

Plains, West and Northwest Plateau Indian Treaties

In testimony whereof, the said William Marshall, commissioner on the part of the United States, and the above named chief and head men, for themselves and their bands, have hereunto subscribed their names, the day and year above written.

William Marshall,
Mo-ta, his x , Ta-puck-koo-nee-nee, his x , Shah-yauc-koo-pay, his x , To-tauk-gaus, his x , Poke-kee-to, his x , Waus-no-guen, his x , Ship-pe-she-waw-no, his x , Mtaw-mah, his x , Ship-pe-shick-quah, his x , Aw-sho-kish-ko-quah, his x , Pash-kum-ma-ko-quah, his x , Me-naun-quah, his x , Pee-nas-quah, his x , Mee-shah-ke-to-quah, his x , Waw-pee-shah-me-to-quah, his x , Mat-che-ke-no-quah, his x , 'Wau-waus-sa-mo-quah, his x mark, Saw-moke-quaw, his x mark,
Witnesses:
J. B. Duret, secretary to commissioner, Jesse Vermilya, Joseph Barron, inter-preter.

TREATY WITH THE CADDO {1835, July 1}
Proclamation, Feb. 1836.

Articles of a treaty made at the Agency-house in the Caddo nation and State of Louisiana, on the first day of July in the year of our Lord one thousand eight hundred and thirty-five, between Jehiel Brooks, Commissioner on the part of the United States, and the Chiefs, head men, and Warriors of the Caddo nation of Indians.

ARTICLE 1. The chiefs, head men, and warriors of the said nation agree to cede and relinquish to the United States all their land contained in the following boundaries: to-wit
Bounded on the west by the north and south line which separates the said United States from the Republic of Mexico, between the Sabine and Red rivers wheresoever the same shall be defined and acknowledged to be by the two governments. On the north and east by the Red river from the point where the said north and south boundary line shall intersect the Red river whether it be in the Territory of Arkansas or the State of Louisiana, following the meanders of the said river down to its junction with the Pascagoula bayou. On the south by the said Pascagoula bayou to its junction with the Bayou Pierre, by said bayou to its junction with Bayou Wallace, by said bayou and Lake Wallace to the mouth of the Cypress bayou thence up said bayou to the point of its intersection with the first mentioned north and south line following the meanders of the said water-courses.

But if the said Cypress bayou be not clearly definable so far then from a point which shah be definable by a line due west till it intersects the said first men-

163

Plains, West and Northwest Plateau Indian Treaties

tioned north and south boundary line, be the content of land within said boundaries more or less.

ARTICLE 2. The said chiefs head men and warriors of the said nation do voluntarily relinquish their possession to the territory of land aforesaid and promise to remove at their own expense out of the boundaries of the United. States and the territories belonging and appertaining thereto within the period of one year from and after the signing of this treaty and never more return to live settle or establish themselves as a nation tribe or community of people within the same.

ARTICLE 3. In consideration of the aforesaid cession relinquishment and removal it is agreed that the said United States shall pay to the said nation of Caddo Indians the sums in goods, horses, and money hereinafter mentioned, to wit:

Thirty thousand dollars to be paid in goods, and horses, as agreed upon to be delivered on the signing of this treaty.
Ten thousand dollars in money to be paid within one year from the first day of September next.
Ten thousand dollars, per annum in money for the four years next following so as to make the whole sum paid and payable eighty thousand dollars.

ARTICLE 4. It is further agreed that the said Caddo nation of Indians shall have authority to appoint an agent or attorney in fact, resident within the United States for the purpose of receiving for them from the said United States all of the annuities stated in this treaty as the same shall become due to be paid to their said agent or attorney in fact at such place or places within the said United States as shall be agreed on between him and the proper Officer of the Government of the United States.

ARTICLE 5. This treaty, after the same shall have been ratified and confirmed by the President and Senate of the United States, shall be binding on the contracting parties.
In testimony whereof, the said Jehiel Brooks, commissioner as aforesaid, and the chiefs, head men, and warriors of the said nation of Indians, have hereunto set their hands, and affixed their seals at the place and on the day and year above written.

J. Brooks,
Tarshar, his x mark, Tsauninot, his x mark, Satiownhown, his x mark, Tennehinum, his x mark, Oat, his x mark, Tinnowin, his x mark, Chowabah, his x mark, Kianhoon, his x mark, Tiatesum, his x mark, Tehowawinow, his x mark, Tewinnum, his x mark, Kardy, his x mark, Tiohtow, his x mark, Tehowahinno, his x mark, Tooeksoach, his x mark, Tehowainia, his x mark, Sauninow, his x

Plains, West and Northwest Plateau Indian Treaties

mark, Saunivoat, his x mark, Highahidock, his x mark, Mattan, his x mark, Towabinneh, his x mark, Aach, his x mark, Sookiantow, his x mark, Sohone, his x mark, Ossinse, his x mark,

In presence of-
T. J. Harrison, captain, Third Regiment Infantry, commanding detachment, J. Bonnell, first lieutenant., Third Regiment U. S. Infantry, J. P. Frile, brevet second lieutenant, Third Regiment U. S. Infantry, D. M. Heard, M.D., acting assistant surgeon U. S. Army, Isaac Williamson, Henry Queen, John W. Edwards, interpreter.

Agreeably to the stipulations in the third article of the treaty, there have been purchased at the request of the Caddo Indians, and delivered to them, goods and horses to the amount of thirty thousand dollars.
As evidence of the purchase and delivery as aforesaid, under the direction of the commissioner, and that the whole of the same have been received by the said Indians, the said commissioner, Jehiel Brooks, and the undersigned, chiefs and head men of the whole Caddo nation of Indians, have hereunto set their hands, and affixed their seals, the third day of July, in the year of our Lord one thousand eight hundred and thirty-five.

J. Brooks,
Tarshar, his x mark, Tsauninot, his x mark, Satiownhown, his x mark, Oat, his x mark, Ossinse, his x mark, Tiohtow, his x mark, Chowawanow, his x mark,

In presence of
Larkin Edwards, Henry Queen, John W. Edwards, interpreter, James Finncrty.

July 1, 1835.
Articles supplementary to the treaty made at the agency house in the Caddo nation and State of Louisiana on the first day of July, one thousand eight hundred and thirty-five between Jehiel Brooks Commissioner on the part of the United States, and the Chiefs head men, and Warriors of the Caddo nation of Indians concluded at the same place, and on the same day between the said Commissioner on the part of the United States and the Chiefs Head men and Warriors of the said nation of Indians, to wit

WHEREAS the said nation of Indians did in the year one thousand eight hundred and one, give to one Francois Grappe and to his three sons then born and still living, named Jacques, Dominique and Beltha-zar, for reasons stated at the time and repeated in a memorial which the said nation addressed to the President of the United States in the month of January last, one league of land to each, in accordance with the Spanish custom of granting land to individuals.

165

Plains, West and Northwest Plateau Indian Treaties

That the chiefs and head men, with the knowledge and approbation of the whole Caddo people did go with the said François Grappe, accompanied by a number of white men, who were invited by the said chiefs and head men to be present as witnesses, before the Spanish authority at Natchitoches, and then and there did declare their wishes touching the said donation of land to the said Grappe and his three sons, and did request the same to be written out in form and ratified and confirmed by the proper authorities agreeably to law.

And WHEREAS Larkin Edwards has resided for many years to the present time in the Caddo Nation was a long time their true and faithful interpreter, and though poor he has never sent the Red man away from his door hungry. He is now old and unable to support himself by manual labor, and since his employment as their interpreter has ceased possesses no adequate means by which to live: Now therefore

ARTICLE 1. It is agreed that the legal representatives of the said François Grappe deceased and his three sons Jacques, Dominique, and Belthazar Grappe, shall have their right to the said four leagues of land reserved to them and their heirs and assigns for ever. The said land to be taken out of the lands ceded to the United States by the said Caddo Nation of Indians as expressed in the treaty to which this article is supplementary. And the said four leagues of land shall be laid off in one body in the southeast corner of their lands ceded as aforesaid, and bounded by the Red river four leagues and by the Pascagoula bayou one league, running back for quantity from each, so as to contain four square leagues of land, in conformity with the boundaries established and expressed in the original Deed of Gift made by the said Caddo nation of Indians to the said Francois Grappe and his three sons Jacques, Dominique, and Belthazar Grappe.

ARTICLE 2. And it is further agreed that there shall be reserved to Larkin Edwards his heirs and assigns for ever one section of-land to be selected out of the lands ceded to the United States by the said nation of Indians as expressed in the treaty to which this article is supplementary in any part thereof not otherwise appropriated by the provisions contained in these supplementary articles.

ARTICLE 3. These supplementary articles, or either of them, after the same shall have been ratified and confirmed by the President and Senate of the United States, shall be binding on the contracting parties, otherwise to be void and of no effect upon the validity of the original treaty to which they are supplementary.

In testimony whereof, the said Jehiel Brooks, commissioner as aforesaid, and the chiefs, head men, and warriors of the said nation of Indians, have hereunto

Plains, West and Northwest Plateau Indian Treaties

set their hands and affixed their seals at the place, and on the day and year above written.

J. Brooks,
Tarshar, his x , Tsauninot, his x , Satiownhown, his x , Tinnehinan, his x , Oat, his x , Tinnowin, his x , Chowabah, his x , Kianhoon, his x , Tiatesun, his x , Tehowawinow, his x , Tewinnun, his x , Kardy, his x , Tiohtow, his x , Tehawahinno, his x , Toackooch, his x , Tchowainin, his x , Sanninow, his x , Sauninot, his x , Hiahidock, his x , Mattan, his x , Towahinnek, his x , Aach, his x , Soakiantow, his x , Sohone, his x , Ossinse, his x mark,

In presence of:
T. J. Harrison, captain, Third Regiment, commanding detachment, J. Bonnell, first lieutenant, Third Regiment U. S. Infantry, G. P. Field, brevet second lieutenant, Third Regiment U. S. Infantry, D. M. Heard, M. D., acting assistant surgeon, U. S. Army, Isaac C. Williamson, Henry Queen, John W. Edwards, interpreter.

TREATY WITH THE COMANCHE, ETC. {1835, Aug. 24}
Proclamation, May 1836.

Treaty with, the Comanche and Witchetaw Indians and their associated Bands.

For the purpose of establishing and perpetuating peace and friendship between the United States of America and the Comanche and Witchetaw nations, and their associated bands or tribes of Indians, and between these nations or tribes, and the Cherokee Muscogee, Choctaw, Osage, Seneca and Quapaw nations or tribes of Indians, the President of the United States has, to accomplish this desirable object, and to aid therein, appointed Governor M. Stokes, M. Arbuckle Brigdi.-Genl. United States army, and F. W. Armstrong, Actg. Supdt. Western Territory, commissioners on the part of the United States; and the said Governor M. Stokes and M. Arbuckle, Brigdi. Genl. United States army, with the chiefs and representatives of the Cherokee, Muscogee, Choctaw, Osage, Seneca, and Quapaw nations or tribes of Indians, have met the chiefs, warriors, and representatives of the tribes first above named at Camp Holmes, on the eastern border of the Grand Prairie, near the Canadian river, in the Muscogee nation, and after full deliberation, the said nations or tribes have agreed with the United States, and with one another upon the following articles:

ARTICLE 1. There shall be perpetual peace and friendship between all the citizens of the United States of America, and all the individuals composing the Comanche and Witchetaw nations and their associated bands or tribes of Indians, and between these nations or tribes and the Cherokee, Muscogee, Choctaw, Osage, Seneca and Quapaw nations or tribes of Indians.

Plains, West and Northwest Plateau Indian Treaties

ARTICLE 2. Every injury or act of hostility by one or either of the contracting parties on the other, shall be mutually forgiven and forever forgot.

ARTICLE 3. There shall be a free and friendly intercourse between all the contracting parties hereto, and it is distinctly understood and agreed by the Comanche and Witchetaw nations and their associated bands or tribes of Indians, that the citizens of the United States are freely permitted to pass and repass through their settlements or hunting ground without molestation or injury on their way to any of the provinces of the Republic of Mexico, or returning therefrom, and that each of the nations or tribes named in this article, further agree to pay the full value for any injury their people may do to the goods or property of the citizens of the United States taken or destroyed, when peaceably passing through the country they inhabit, or hunt in, or elsewhere. And the United States hereby guaranty to any Indian or Indians of either of the said Comanche or Witchetaw nations, and their associated bands or tribes of Indians, a full indemnification for any horses or other property which may be stolen from them: Provided, that the property so stolen cannot be recovered, and that sufficient proof is produced that it was actually stolen by a citizen of the United States, and within the limits thereof.

ARTICLE 4. It is understood and agreed by all the nations or tribes of Indians parties to this treaty, that each and all of the said nations or tribes have free permission to hunt and trap in the Great Prairie west of the Cross Timber, to the western limits of the United States.

ARTICLE 5. The Comanche and Witchetaw nations and their associated bands or tribes of Indians, severally agree and bind themselves to pay full value for any injury their people may do to the goods or other property of such traders as the President of the United States may place near to their settlements or hunting ground for the purpose of trading with them.

ARTICLE 6. The Comanche and Witchetaw nations and their associated bands or tribes of Indians, agree, that in the event any of the red people belonging to the nations or tribes residing south of the Missouri river and west of the State of Missouri, not parties to this treaty, Should visit their towns or be found on their hunting ground, that they will treat them with kindness and friendship and do no injury to them in any way whatever.

ARTICLE 7. Should any difficulty hereafter unfortunately arise between any of the nations or tribe; of Indians parties hereunto, in consequence of murder, the stealing of horses, cattle, or other cause, it is agreed that the other tribes shall interpose their good offices to remove such difficulties, and also that the Government of the United States may take such measures as they may deem

Plains, West and Northwest Plateau Indian Treaties

proper to effect the same object, and see that full justice is done to_the injured party.

ARTICLE 8. It is agreed by the commissioners of the United States, that in consequence of the Comanche and Witchetaw nations and their associated bands or tribes of Indians having freely and willingly entered into this treaty, and it being the first they have made with the United States or any of the contracting parties, that they shall receive presents immediately after signing, as a donation from the United States; nothing being asked from these nations or tribes in return, except to remain at peace with the parties hereto, which their own good and that of their posterity require.

ARTICLE 9. The Commanche and Witchetaw nations and their associated bands or tribes, of Indians, agree, that their entering into this treaty shall in no respect interrupt their friendly relations with the Republic of Mexico, where they all frequently hunt and the Comanche nation principally inhabit; and it is distinctly understood that the Government of the United States desire that perfect peace shall exist between the nations or tribes named in this article and the said republic.

ARTICLE 10. This treaty shall be obligatory on the nations or tribes parties hereto from and after the date hereof, and on the United States from and after its ratification by the Government thereof.
Done, and signed, and sealed at Camp Holmes, on the eastern border of the Grand Prairie, near the Canadian river, in the Muscogee nation, this twenty-fourth day of August, one thousand eight hundred and thirty-five, and of the independence of the United States the sixtieth.

Montfort Stokes, M.Arbuckle, Brigadier-General U. S. Army,
Comanches:
Ishacoly, or the wolf, his x mark, Queenashano, or the war eagle, his x mark, Tabaqueena, or the big eagle, his x mark, Pohowetowshah, or the brass man, his x mark, Shabbakasha, or the roving wolf, his x mark, Neraquassi, or the yellow horse, his x mark, Toshapappy, or the white hare, his x mark, Pahohsareya, or the broken arm, his x mark, Pahkah, or the man who draws the bow, his x mark, Witsitony, or he who sucks quick, his x mark, Leahwiddikah, or one who stirs up water, his x mark,

Esharsotsiki, or the sleeping wolf, his x mark, Pahtrisula, or the dog, his x mark, Ettah, or the gun, his x mark, Tennowikah, or the boy who was soon a man, his x mark, Kumaquai, or the woman who cuts buffalo meat, his x mark, Taqquanno, or the amorous man, his x mark, Kowa, or the stinking tobacco box, his x mark, Soko, or the old man, his x mark, Witchetaws: Kanostowah, or the man who don't speak, his x mark, Kosharokah, or the man who marries his wife twice, his x mark,

169

Plains, West and Northwest Plateau Indian Treaties

Terrykatowatix, the riding chief, his x mark, Tahdaydy, or the travellet, his x mark, Hahkahpillush, or the drummer, his x mark, Lachkah, or the first man in four battles. his x mark; Learhehash, or the man who weans children too soon, his x mark, Lachhardich, or the man who sees things done in the wrong way, his x mark, Noccuttardaditch, or the man who tries to excel the head chief, his x mark, Katardedwadick, or the man who killed an enemy in the water, his x mark, Losshah, or the twin, his x , Taytsaaytah, or the ambitious adulterer, his x mark, Tokaytah, or the summer, his x mark, Musshakratsatady, or the man with the dog skin cap, his x , Kipsh, or the man with one side of his head shaved, his x ,

Cherokees:
Dutch, his x mark, David Melton, his x mark,
Muscogees:
Roley Mcintosh, his x mark, Chilly Mclntosh, Cho-co-te-tuston-nogu, or marshalof the Cho-eo-te-elan, his x mark, Tus-ca-ne-ha, or the marshal, his x mark, Tusly Hatjoe, or crazy town, his x mark, Alexander Lasley, his x , Neha Harjoe, or crazy marshal, his x mark, Tustunucke Hatjoe, or crazy warrior, his x mark, Powes Emarlo, or marshal of Powes clan, his x mark, Cosa Yehola, or marshal of Cosa clan, his x mark, Powes Yehola, or marshal of Powes clan, his x mark,

Toma Yehola, or marshal of Toma clan, his x mark, Cosado Harjoe, or crazy Cosada, his x mark, Neha Harjoe, or crazy marshal, his x mark, Cosaria Tustonnogee, or the Cosada warrior, his x mark, Octiyachee Yehola, or marshal of Octiyachee clan, his x , Nulthcup Tustonnogee, or the middle warrior, his x mark, Ufala Harjoe, or crazy Ufala, his x mark, Cholafixico, or a fox without a heart, his x mark, Joseph Miller, his x mark, Samuel Brown, his x mark, Archi Kennard, his x mark,

Towannay, or the slender man, his x mark, Saccasumky, or to be praised, his x mark, Siah Hardridge, his x mark, Warrior Hardridge, his x mark, George Stedham, his x mark, Itchhas Harjoe, or crazy beaver, his x mark, Itchofake Harjoe, or crazy deer's heart, his x mark, Satockhaky, or the broad side, his x mark, Semehechee, or hide it away, his x mark, Hoyane, or passed by, his x , Melola, or waving, his x , Mateter, or the man who missed it, his x mark, Billy, his x mark,

Tuskia Harjoe, or crazy brave, his x mark, Aussy, or the pursuer, his x , Tohoithla, or standing upon, his x mark, John Hambly, K. Lewis, John Wynn, David McKillap,

Choctaws:
Mnshada-tubbee, or the man killer, his x mark, Na-tuck-a-chee, or fair day, his x mark, Par-chee-ste-cubbee, or the scalpholder, his x mark, To-pi-a-chee-

Plains, West and Northwest Plateau Indian Treaties

hubbee, or the painted face, his x mark, Ya-cha-a-o-pay, or the leader of the warriors, his x mark, Tus-qui-hola-tah, or the travelling warrior, his x mark, Tic-eban-jo-hubbee, or the first for war, his x mark, Nucke Stubbee, or the bullet that has killed, his x mark, Toqua, orwhat you say, his x , Po-sha-ma-stubbee, or the killer, his x mark, A-fa-ma-tubbee, or the man who kills every thing he meets, his x mark,

Osages:
Fah-ha-la, or the leaping deer, his x mark, Shone-ta-sah-ba, or the black dog, his x mark, Wah-shin-pee-sha, or the wicked man, his x mark, Tun-wan-le-he, or the town mover, his x mark, Whoa-har-tee, or the war eagle, his x mark, Me-tah-ne-gah, or the crazy robe, his x , Wah-she-sho-hee, or the smart spirit, his x mark, Ah-ke-tah, or the soldier, his x mark, Weir-sah-bah-sha, or the hidden black, his x mark, Ne-ko-jah, or the man hunter, his x mark, Hor-tea-go, or like night, his x mark,

Senecas:
Thomas Brant, his x mark, Small Crout Spicer, his x mark, Isaac, his x mark, Mingo Carpenter, his x mark, John Sky, his x mark, Henry Smith, his x mark, Little Town Spicer, his x mark, Young Henry, his x mark, Peter Pork, his x mark, William Johnston, his x mark, Big Bone, his x mark, Big Isaac, his x mark, Civil Jack, his x mark, Ya-ga-ha, or the water in the apple, his x mark, Cau-ya-que-neh, or the snow drift, his x mark, Ya-ta-ato, or the little lake, his x mark, Douglass, his x mark, George Herring, his x mark,

Quapaws:
Hi-ka-toa, or the dry man, his x mark, Wa-ga-de-tone, or the maggot, his x mark, Wa-to-va, or the spider, his x mark, Ca-ta-hah, or the tortoise, his x mark, Ma-towa-wah-cota, or the dug out, his x mark, Wa-go-dah-hou-kah, or the plume, his x mark, Ma-com-pa, or the doctor of the nose, his x mark, Cassa, or the black tortoise, his x mark, Haw-tez-chee-ka, or the little cedar, his x mark, Ma-so-goda-toah, or the hawk, his x mark, Wa-ka-toa-nosa, or the standing man, his x mark, Motosa, or the black bear, his x mark, Mor-bre-tone, or the little hawk, his x mark, Mar-to-ho-ga, or the

In presence of
R. B. Mason, major of dragoons, G. Birch, major, U. S. Army, Francis Lee, captain, Seventh Infantry, Samuel G. I. DeCamp, surgeon, W. Seawell, lieutenant and aid de camp; secretary to the commissioners, Thomas B. Ballard, Augustine A. Chouteau, John Hambly, United States interpreter to the Creeks, George Herron, Leonard C. McPhail, assistant surgeon, U. S. Army
Robert M. French.

Plains, West and Northwest Plateau Indian Treaties

TREATY WITH THE POTAWATOMI {1836, Mar. 26}
Proclamation, June 4, 1836.

Articles of a treaty made and concluded at camp in Turkey Creek Prairie in the State of Indiana between Abel C Pepper commissioner of the United States and Mes-quaw-buck, a chief of the Pottawatamy tribe of Indians and his band, on twenty-sixth day of March, in the year eighteen hundred and thirty-six.

ARTICLE 1. The above named chief and his band hereby cede to the United States the four sections of land reserved for them by the second article of the treaty between the United States and the Pottawatamy Indians, on Tippecanoe river on the twenty-seventh day of October 1832.

ARTICLE 2. In consideration of the cession aforesaid the United States stipulate to pay the above named chief and his band the sum of twenty-five hundred and sixty dollars in specie at the next payment of annuity after the ratification of this treaty.

ARTICLE 3. The United States stipulate to provide for the payment of the necessary expenses attending the making and concluding this treaty.

ARTICLE 4. The above named chief and his band agree to yield peaceable possession of the above sections of land and remove to the country west of the Mississippi provided for the Pottawatamy nation by the United States, within two years from this date.

ARTICLE 5. This treaty shall be binding upon both parties from the date of its ratification by the President and Senate of the United States.

ARTICLE 6. (Stricken out by Senate.)

In testimony whereof, the said A. C. Pepper, commissioner on the part of the United States, and the above named chief and head men for themselves and their band, hereunto subscribed their names, the day and year above written.

A. C. Pepper, Waw-baw-que-ke-aw, his x mark, Mes-quaw-buck, his x mark, Naush-waw-pi-tant, his x mark, Mess-Sett, his x mark, Che-qua-sau-quah, his x mark, Muck Rose, his x mark,

Witnesses:
C. Garter, secretary, Edward McCartney, interpreter.

172

Plains, West and Northwest Plateau Indian Treaties

TREATY WITH THE POTAWATOMI {1836, Apr. 11}
Proclamation, May 25, 1836.

Articles of a treaty made and concluded at a camp on Tippecanoe river, in the State of Indiana, between Abel C. Pepper commissioner on the part of the United States, and Pau-koo-shuck, Aub-ba-naub-ba's oldest son and the head men of Aub-ba-naub-ba's band of Potawattimie Indians, this eleventh day of April in the year, eighteen hundred and thirty-six.

ARTICLE 1. The aforesaid Pau-koo-shuck and the head men of Aub-ba-naub-ba's band, hereby cede to the United States the thirty-six sections of land reserved for them by the second article of the Treaty between the United States and the Potawattimie Indians on Tippecanoe river on the twenty-sixth day of October, in the year eighteen hundred and thirty-two,

ARTICLE 2. In consideration of the cession aforesaid, the United States stipulate to pay to the aforesaid band the sum of twenty-three thousand and forty dollars in specie, one half at the first payment of annuity, after the ratification of this Treaty, and the other half at the succeeding payment of annuity.

ARTICLE 3. The above-named Pau-koo-shuck and his band agree to remove to the country west of the Mississippi river, provided for the Potawattimie nation by the United States within two years.

ARTICLE 4. (Stricken out by Senate.)

ARTICLE 5. This Treaty, after the same shall be ratified by the President and Senate of the United States shall be binding upon both parties.

In testimony whereof, the said Abel C. Pepper, commissioner as aforesaid, and the said Pau-koo-shuck, and his band, have hereunto set their hands, this eleventh day of April, in the year of our Lord one thousand eight hundred and thirty-six.

Abel C. Pepper,
Pau-koo-shuck, his x mark, Taw-wah-quah, her x mark, Shah-quaw-ko-shuck, Aub-ba-naub-ba's son, his x mark, Mat-taw-mira, his x mark, Si-nis-quah, her x mark, Dah-moosh-ke-keaw, her x mark, Nan-wish-ma, his x mark,

Witnesses:
E. O. Cicott, secretary, Henry Ossem, Thos. Robb, Wm. Polke, O-Sauk-kay, his x mark, Ke-waw-o-nuck, his x mark, Aun-tuine, his x mark, Sin-ba-nim, his x mark, Nees-se-ka-tah, his x mark, Kaw-ke-me, her x mark, Pe-waw-ko, her x mark, O-ket-chee, her x mark, Nan-cee, her x mark, Joseph Bamont, principal interpreter, Joseph Truckey, George W. Ewing, Cyrus Tober.

Plains, West and Northwest Plateau Indian Treaties

TREATY WITH THE POTAWATOMI {1836, Apr. 22}
Proclamation, May 25, 1836.

Articles of a treaty made and concluded at the Indian Agency, in the State of Indiana, between Abel C. Pepper, commissioner on the part of the United States and O-kah-mause, Kee-waw-nay, Nee-boash, and Mat-chis-jaw, chiefs and head men of the Patawattimie tribe of Indians and their bands, on the twenty-second day of April, in the year eighteen hundred and thirty-six.

ARTICLE 1. The above named chiefs and head men and their bands, hereby cede to the United States, ten sections of land, reserved for them by the second article of the treaty, between the United States and the Patawattimie tribe of Indians, on Tippecanoe river, on the 26th day of October, in the year 1832.

ARTICLE 2. In consideration of the cession aforesaid, the United States stipulate to pay to the above-named chiefs and head men and their bands, the sum of six thousand four hundred dollars, at the first payment of annuity, after the ratification of this treaty.

ARTICLE 3. The above-named chiefs and head men and their bands agree to remove to the country west of the Mississippi river, provided for the Patawattimie nation by the United States, within two years. ART. 4. (Stricken out by Senate.)

ARTICLE 5. The United States stipulate to provide for the payment of the necessary expenses attending the making and concluding this treaty.

ARTICLE 6. This treaty, after the same shall be ratified by the President and Senate of the United States, shall be binding upon both parties.

In testimony thereof, the said Abel C. Pepper, commissioner as aforesaid, and the said chiefs and head men and their bands, have hereunto set their hands, this 22d day of April, A. D. 1836.

Abel C. Pepper,
Nee-boash, or twisted head, his x mark, Pash-po-ho, his x mark, I-o-weh, or nation's name, his x mark, O-kaw-mause, his x mark, Miss-no-qui, female fish, his x mark, Kee-waw-nee, his x mark, Kaw-che-noss, his x mark, Cho-quiss, fishes entrails, his x mark, Ma-che-saw, bleating fawn, his x mark, Waw-po-ko-ne-aw, white night, his x mark, Ah-muck, his x mark, Kohe-kah-me, his x mark, Que-que-nuk, his x mark,
Witnesses:
Geo. W. Ewing, Cyrus Tober, J. B. Duret, secretary, Peter Barron, Joseph Bamont, interpreter.

174

Plains, West and Northwest Plateau Indian Treaties

TREATY WITH THE POTAWATOMI {1836, Apr. 22}
Proclamation, May 25, 1836.

Articles of a treaty made and concluded at the Indian agency, in the State of Indiana between Abel C. Pepper commissioner on the part of the United States, and Nas-waw-kee and Quash-quaw chiefs and head men of the Patawattimie tribe of Indians and their bands on the 22d day of April, 1836.

ARTICLE 1. The above named chiefs and head men and their bands hereby cede to the United States three sections of land reserved for them by the second article of the treaty between the United States and the Patawattimie tribe of Indians on Tippecanoe river on the 26th day of October, 1832.

ARTICLE 2. In consideration of the cession aforesaid the United States stipulate to pay the above chiefs and head men and their bands nineteen hundred and twenty dollars at the first payment of annuity after the ratification of this treaty.

ARTICLE 3. The above named chiefs and head men and their bands agree to give possession of the aforesaid three sections of land, and remove to the country west of the Mississippi river provided by the United States for the Potawattimie nation of Indians within two years from this date.

ARTICLE 4. (Stricken out by Senate.)

ARTICLE 5. The United States stipulate to provide for the payment of the necessary expenses attending the making and concluding this treaty.

ARTICLE 6. This treaty, after the same shall be ratified by the President and Senate of the United States, shall be binding upon both parties.
In testimony whereof, the said Abel C. Pepper, commissioner as aforesaid, and the said chiefs and head men and their bands, have hereunto set their hands, this 22d day of April, A. D. 1836.

A. C. Pepper,
Quash-quaw, his x mark, Me-cos-ta, his x mark, Nas-waw-kee, his x mark, Wem-se-ko, his x mark, Ah-quaush-she, his x mark,

Witnesses:
J. B. Duret, secretary to commissioner, Joseph Bamont, interpreter, Cyrus Tober, Geo. W. Ewing, Peter Barron.

Plains, West and Northwest Plateau Indian Treaties

TREATY WITH THE POTAWATOMI {1836, Aug. 5}
Proclamation, Feb. 18, 1837.

Articles of a treaty made and concluded at a camp near Yellow river, in the State of Indiana, between Abel C. Pepper, commissioner on the part of the United States and Pe-pin-a-waw, No-taw-kah & Mac-kah-tah-mo-ah, chiefs and headmen of the Potawattimie tribe of Indians, and their bands on the fifth day of August in the year eighteen hundred and thirty-six.

ARTICLE 1. The above named chiefs and headmen and their bands hereby cede to the United States twenty-two sections of land reserved for them by the second article of the treaty between the United States and the Potawattimie tribe of Indians on Tippecanoe river, on the twenty-sixth day of October in the year eighteen hundred and thirty-two.

ARTICLE 2. In consideration of the cession aforesaid, the United States stipulate to pay to the above named chiefs and headmen and their bands, the sum of fourteen thousand and eighty dollars in specie after the ratification of this treaty, and on or before the first day of May next ensuing the date hereof.

ARTICLE 3. The above named chiefs and headmen and their bands agree to remove to the country west of the Mississippi river, provided for the Potawattimie nation by the United States within two years.

ARTICLE 4. At the request of the above named band it is stipulated that after the ratification of this treaty, the United States shall appoint a commissioner, who shall be authorized to pay such debts of the said band as may be proved to his satisfaction to be just, to be deducted from the amount stipulated in the second article of this treaty.

ARTICLE 5. The United States stipulate to provide for the payment of the necessary expences attending the making and concluding this treaty.

ARTICLE 6. This treaty, after the same shall be ratified by the President and Senate of the United States, shall be binding upon both parties.
In testimony whereof, the said Abel C. Pepper, commissioner as aforesaid, and the said chiefs, and headmen, and their bands, have hereunto set their hands, this fifth day of August, in the year of our Lord one thousand eight hundred and thirty-six.

A. C. Pepper,
Pee-pin-ah-waw, his x mark, No-taw-kah, his x mark, Te-cum-see, his x mark, Pam-bo-go, his x mark, Mup-paw-hue, his x mark, See-co-ass, his x mark, Co-quah-wah, his x mark, Mack-kah-tah-mo-may, his x mark, Wi-aw-koos-say, his

176

Plains, West and Northwest Plateau Indian Treaties

x mark, Quah-taw, his x mark, Kaw-kawk-kay, his x mark, Pis-saw, his x mark, Nas-waw-kay, his x mark,
Proper chiefs of the Wabash Patawattamiss:
Pash-pb-ho, his x mark, I-o-wah, his x mark, O-kah-maus, his x mark, Jo-quiss, his x mark, We-wis-sah, his x mark, Nas-waw-kah, his x mark, Ash-kum, his x mark, Ku-waw-nay, his x mark, Nu-bosh, his x mark, Pah-siss, his x mark, Mat-chis-saw, his x mark, Mas-saw, his x mark, Me-shaw-ki-to-quah, his x mark,

Witnesses:
J. B. Duret, secretary, E. O. Cicott, Geo. W. Ewing, Jos. Barron, interpreter.

TREATY WITH THE MENOMINEE {1836, Sept. 3}
Proclamation, Feb. 15, 1837.

Articles of agreement made and concluded at Cedar Point, on Fox river, near Greenbay, in the Territory of Wisconsin, this third day of September in the year of our Lord one thousand eight hundred and thirty-six between Henry Dodge, Governor of said Territory of Wisconsin, commissioner on the part of the United States, on the one part; and the chiefs and head men of the Menomonie nation of Indians, of the other part.

ARTICLE 1. The said Menomonie nation agree to cede to the United States, all of that tract or district of country included within the following boundaries, viz: Beginning at the mouth of Wolf river, and running up and along the same, to a point on the north branch of said river where it crosses the extreme north or rear line of the five hundred thousand acre tract heretofore granted to the New York Indians: thence following the line last mentioned, in a northeastwardly direction, three mines: thence in a northwardly course, to the upper forks of the Menomonie river, at a point to intersect the boundary line between the Menomonie and Chippewa nation of Indians: thence following the said boundary line last mentioned, in an eastwardly direction as defined and established by the treaty of the Little Bate des Mort, in 1827, to the Smooth rock or Shos-kin-aubie river.

Thence down the said river to where it empties into Green bay, between the Little and Great bay de Noquet: thence up and along the west side of Green bay, (and including all the islands therein, not heretofore ceded) to the mouth of Fox river: thence up and along the said Fox river, and along the west side of Winnebago lake (including the islands therein) to the mouth of Fox river, where it empties into said lake: thence up and along said Fox river to the place of beginning, (saving and reserving out of the district of country above ceded and described, all that part of the five hundred thousand acre tract, granted by the treaties between the Menomonies and the United States, made on the eighth

177

Plains, West and Northwest Plateau Indian Treaties

day of February A. D. 1831, and on the twenty-seventh day of October A. D. 1832, which may be situated within the boundaries hereinbefore described)the quantity of land contained in the tract hereby ceded, being estimated at about four millions of acres.

And the said Menomonie nation do further agree to cede and relinquish to the United States all that tract or district of country lying upon the Wisconsin river, in said territory; and included within the following boundaries; vizBeginning at a point upon said Wisconsin river two miles above the grant or privilege heretofore granted by said nation and the United States, to Amable Grignon; thence running up and along said river forty-eight miles in a direct line: and being three miles in width on each side of said river; this tract to contain eight townships or one hundred and eighty-four thousand three hundred and twenty acres of land.

ARTICLE 2. In consideration of the cession of the aforesaid tract of land, the United States agree to pay to the said Menomonie nation, at the lower end of Wah-ne-kun-nah lake in their own country, or at such other place as may be designated by the President of the United States the sum of twenty thousand dollars, per annum for the term of twenty years.

The United States further agree to pay and deliver to the said Indians, each and every year during the said term of twenty years, the following articlesThree thousand dollars worth of provisions; two thousand pounds of tobacco; thirty barrels of salt; also the sum of five hundred dollars, per year, during the same term, for the purchase of farming utensils, cattle, or implements of husbandry, to be expended under the direction of the superintendent or agent. Also to appoint ands pay two blacksmiths to be located at such places as may be designated by the said superintendent or agent, to erect (and supply with the necessary quantity of iron, steel, and tools) two blacksmith shops; during the same term.

The United States shall also pay the just debts of the said Menomonie Indians, agreeably to the schedule hereunto annexed, amounting to the sum of ninety-nine thousand seven hundred and ten dollars and fifty cents. Provided, always, That no portion of said debts shall be paid until the validity and justice of each of them, shall have been required into by the Commissioner of Indian Affairs, who shall in no instance increase the amount specified in said schedule, but who shall allow the sum specified, reject it entirely, or reduce it as upon examination and proof may appear just, and if any part of said sum is left after paying said debts so adjudged to be just, then such surplus shall be paid to the said Indians for their own use.

And whereas the said Indians are desirous of making some provision and allowance to their relatives and friends of mixed blood; the United States do fur-

178

Plains, West and Northwest Plateau Indian Treaties

ther agree to pay the sum of eighty thousand dollars, to be divided among all such persons of mixed blood as the chiefs shall hereafter designate: said sum to be apportioned and divided under the direction of a commissioner to be appointed by the President. Provided always, That no person shall be entitled to any part of said fund unless he is of Indian descent and actually resident within the boundaries described in the first article of this treaty, nor shall anything be allowed to any such person who may have received any allowance under any previous treaty. The portion of this fund allowed by the Commissioner to those half breeds who are orphans, or poor or incompetent to make a proper use thereof, shall be paid to them in installments or otherwise as the President may direct.

ARTICLE 3. The said Menomonie nation do agree to release the United States from all such provisions of the treaty of 1831 and 1832, aforesaid, as requires the payment of farmers, blacksmiths, millers &c. They likewise relinquish all their right under said treaty to appropriation for education, and to all improvements made or to be made upon their reservation on Fox river and Winnebago lake; together with the cattle, farming utensils or other articles furnished or to be furnish(ed) to them under said treaty. And in consideration of said release and relinquishment, the United States stipulate and agree that the sum of seventy-six thousand dollars, shall be allowed to the said Indians and this sum shall be invested in some safe stock and the interest thereof as it accrues shall also be so vested until such time as in the judgment of the President, the income of the aggregate sum can be usefully applied to the execution of the provisions in the said fourth article, or to some other purposes beneficial to the said Indians.

ARTICLE 4. The above annuities shall be paid yearly and every year, during the said term, in the month of June or July, or as soon thereafter as the amount shall be received; and the said Menomonie nation do agree to remove from the country ceded, within one year after the ratification of this treaty.
This treaty shall be binding and obligatory on the contracting parties, as soon as the same shall be ratified by the President and Senate of the United States.
Done at Cedar Point, in said territory of Wisconsin, this third day of September, in the year of our Lord one thousand eight hundred and thirty-six, and in the year of the Independence of the United States

H. Dodge, Osh-kosh, his x mark, Aya-ma-taw, his x mark, Ko-ma-ni-kin, his x mark, Wain-e-saut, his x mark, Kee-sis, his x mark, Carron-Glaude, his x mark, Say-ga-toke, his x mark, Shee-o-ga-tay, his x mark, Wah-pee-min, his x mark, Isk-ki-ninew, his x mark, Ko-ma-ni-kee-no-shah, his x mark, Wah-bee-ne-mickee, his x mark;

Signed and sealed in the presence of
Henry S. Baird, secretary to the commissioner.

Plains, West and Northwest Plateau Indian Treaties

Charles R. Brush, Louis Philipson, United States
George Boyd, L. Grignon, Indian agent, Agt. Grignon, David Blish, jr.,Charles
A. Grignon, sworn interpreter, Samuel Ryan, William Powell, sworn inter-
preter, William Bruce, George M. Brooke, brevet brigadier-general, John
Drake, R. E. Clary, U. S. Army, J. Jourdain, D. Jones, T.T. Porlier.
John P. Arndt,

Schedule.
It is agreed on the part of the United States, that the following claims shall be
allowed and paid, agreeably to the second article of the foregoing treaty, viz:
To John Lawe, twelve thousand five hundred dollars; Augustine Grignon ten
thousand dollars;
William Powell and Robert Grigon four thousand two hundred and fifty dollars; Charles A. Grignon ten thousand dollars; John Lawe & Co., six thousand
dollars; Walter T. Webster one hundred dollars; John P. Arndt five hundred and
fifty dollars;

William Farnsworth and Charles R. Brush two thousand five hundred dollars;
James Porlier, seven thousand five hundred dollars;
Heirs of Louis Beaupre one thousand five hundred dollars; Dominick Brunette
two hundred and thirty-one dollars and fifty cents; Alexander J. Irwin, one
thousand two hundred and fifty dollars; American Fur Co. (western outfit) four
hundred dollars; Charles Grignon one thousand two hundred dollars;
Joseph Rolette one thousand seven hundred and fifty dollars; Charles A. and
Alexander Grignon seven hundred and fifty dollars; James Reed seven hundred
dollars;

Peter Powell one thousand seven hundred and fifty dollars; Paul Grignon five
thousand five hundred dollars; William Dickinson three thousand dollars; Robert M. Eberts seventy-four dollars; Joseph Jourdain fifty dollars;
James Knaggs five hundred and fifty dollars ($550;) Ebenezer Childs two hun-
dred dollars; Lewis Rouse five thousand dollars;
William Farnsworth two thousand five hundred dollars; Sanft. Irwin & Geo.
Boyd jr. one hundred and five dollars; Aneyas Grignon two thousand five hundred dollars;

Pierre Grignon decd. by Rob. & Peter B. Grignon six thousand dollars; Stanis-
lius Chappue one hundred dollars;
John Lawe one thousand two hundred dollars; William Dickinson two hundred
and fifty dollars; Stanislius Chappue two thousand five hundred dollars;
Lewis Grignon seven thousand two hundred and fifty dollars.
H. Dodge, Commissioner.
All the above accts were sworn to before me the 3d day of September, 1836.
John P. Arndt, A Justice of the Peace.

Plains, West and Northwest Plateau Indian Treaties

TREATY WITH THE SIOUX {1836, Sept. 10}
Proclamation, Feb. 15, 1837.

Convention with the Sioux of Wa-ha-shaw's tribe.

In a convention held this tenth day of September 1836, between Col. Z. Taylor Indian Agent, and the chiefs, braves, and principal men of the Sioux of Wa-ha-shaw's tribe of Indians, it has been represented, that according to the stipulations of the first article of the treaty of Prairie du Chien, of the 15th July 1830, the country thereby ceded is "to be assigned and allotted under the direction of the President of the United States, to the tribes now living thereon, or to such other tribes as the President may locate thereon for hunting and other purposes," and, whereas, it is further represented to us, the chiefs, braves, and principal men of the tribe aforesaid, to be desirable that the lands lying between the State of Missouri and the Missouri river should be attached to and become a part of said State, and the Indian title thereto be extinguished but that, notwithstanding, as these lands compose a part of the country embraced by the provisions of said first article of the treaty aforesaid, the stipulations thereof will be strictly observed, until the assent of the Indians interested, is given to the proposed measure.

Now we, the chiefs, braves, and principal men of the above named tribe of Indians, fully understanding the subject, and well satisfied from the local position of the lands in question that they can never be made available for Indian purposes, and that an attempt to place an Indian population on them must inevitably lead to collisions with the citizens of the United States; and further believing that the extension of the State line in the direction indicated, would have a happy effect, by presenting a natural boundary between the whites and Indians: and, willing moreover, to give the United States a renewed evidence of our attachment & friendship, do hereby for ourselves, and on behalf of our respective tribes, (having full power and authority to this effect) forever cede, relinquish, and quit claim to the United States, all our right, title and interest of whatsoever nature in, and to, the lands lying between the State of Missouri and the Missouri river, and do freely and fully exonerate the United States from any guarantee, condition, or limitation, expressed or implied under the treaty of Prairie du Chien aforesaid or otherwise, as to the entire and absolute disposition of the said lands, fully authorizing the United States to do with the same whatever shall seem expedient or necessary.

As a proof of the continued friendship and liberality of the United-States towards the above named tribe of Indians, and as an evidence of the sense entertained for the good will manifested by said tribes to the citizens and Government of the United States, as evinced in the preceding cession or relinquishment, the undersigned agrees on behalf of the United States, to cause said tribes

Plains, West and Northwest Plateau Indian Treaties

to be furnished with presents to the amount of four hundred dollarsin goods or in money.

In testimony whereof, we have hereunto set our hands and seals, the day and year above written.

Sau-tabe-say, Wa-ba-shaw's son, his x mark, Wau-kaun-hendee-oatah, his x mark, Nau-tay-sah-pah, his x mark, Mauk-pee-au-cat-paun, his x mark, Hoo-yah, the eagle, his x mark,

Executed in presence of
H. L. Donsman, W. R. Jouett, captain, First Infantry, J. M. Scott, lieutenant, First Infantry, Geo. H. Pegram, lieutenant, First Infantry.

As a proof of the continued friendship and liberality of the United States towards the above named tribe of Indians, and as an evidence of the sense entertained for the good will manifested by said tribes to the citizens and Government of the United States, as evinced in the preceding cession or relinquishment, the undersigned agrees on behalf of the United States, to cause said tribes to be furnished with presents to the amount of four hundred dollars, in goods or in money.

In testimony whereof, I have hereunto set my hand and seal, this tenth day of September, 1836.

Z. Taylor, Colonel, U. S. Army, and Acting U. S. Indian Agent.

TREATY WITH THE IOWA, ETC. {1836, Sept. 17}
Proclamation, Feb. 15, 1837.

Articles of a treaty made and concluded at Fort Leavenworth, on the Missouri river, between William Clark, Superintendent of Indian Affairs, on the part of the United States, of the one part, and the undersigned chiefs, warriors, and counsellors of the Ioway tribe and the band of Sacks and Foxes of the Missouri, (residing west of the State of Missouri) in behalf of their respective tribes, of the other part.

ARTICLE 1. By the first article of the treaty of Prairie du Chien, held the fifteenth day of July eighteen hundred and thirty, with the confederated tribes of Sacks, Foxes, Ioways, Omahaws, Missourias, Ottoes, and Sioux, the country ceded to the United States by that treaty, is to be assigned and allotted under the direction of the President of the United States to the tribes living thereon, or to such other tribes as the President may locate thereon for hunting and other purposes.And whereas it is further represented to us the chiefs, warriors, and coun-

Plains, West and Northwest Plateau Indian Treaties

sellors of the Ioways and Sack and Fox band aforesaid, to be desirable that the lands lying between the State of Missouri and the Missouri river, should be attached to and become a part of said State, and the Indian title thereto, be entirely extinguished; but that, notwithstanding, as these lands compose a part of the country embraced by the provisions of said first article of the treaty aforesaid, the stipulations thereof will be strictly observed until the assent of the Indians interested is given to the proposed measures.

Now we the chiefs, warriors, and counsellors of the Ioways, and Missouri band of Sacks and Foxes, fully understanding the subject, and well satisfied from the local position of the lands in question, treat they never can be made available for Indian purposes, and that an a tempt to place an Indian population on them, must inevitably lead to collisions with the citizens of the United States; and further believing that the extension of the State line in the direction indicated would have a happy effect, by presenting a natural boundary between the whites and Indians; and willing, moreover, to give the United States a renewed evidence of our attachment and friendship, do hereby for ourselves, and on behalf of our respective tribes, (having full power and authority to this effect) forever cede, relinquish, and quit claim, to the United States, all our right, title, and interest of whatsoever nature in, and to, the lands lying between the State of Missouri and the Missouri river; and do freely and fully exonerate the United States from any guarantee; condition or limitation, expressed or implied, under the treaty of Prairie du Chien aforesaid, or otherwise, as to the entire and absolute disposition of the said lands, fully authorizing the United States to do with the same whatever shall seem expedient or necessary.

As a proof of the continued friendship and liberality of the United States towards the Ioways and band of Sacks and Foxes of the Missouri, and as an evidence of the sense entertained for the good will manifested by said tribes to the citizens and Government of the United States, as evinced in the preceding cession or relinquishment, the undersigned, William Clark, agrees on behalf of the United States, to pay as a present to the said Ioways and band of Sacks and Foxes, seven thousand five hundred dollars in money, the receipt of which they hereby acknowledge.

ARTICLE 2. As the said tribes of Ioways and Sacks and Foxes, have applied for a small piece of land, south of the Missouri, for a permanent home, on which they can settle, and request the assistance of the Government of the United States to place them on this land, in a situation at least equal to that they now enjoy on the land ceded by them: Therefore I, William Clark, Superintendent of Indian Affairs, do further agree on behalf of the United States, to assign to the Ioway tribe, and Missouri band of Sacks and Foxes, the small strip of land on the south side of the Missouri river, lying between the Kickapoo northern boundary line and the Grand Nemahar river, and extending from the Missouri back and westwardly with the said Kickapoo line and the Grand

Plains, West and Northwest Plateau Indian Treaties

Nemahar, making four hundred sections; to be divided between the said Ioways and Missouri band of Sacks and Foxes, the lower half to the Sacks and Foxes, and the upper half to the Ioways.

ARTICLE 3. The Ioways and Missouri band of Sacks and Foxes further agree, that they will move and settle on the lands assigned them in the above article, as soon as arrangements can be made by them; and the undersigned William Clark, in behalf of the United States, agrees, that as soon as the above tribes have selected a site for their villages, and places for their fields, and moved to them, to erect for the Ioways five comfortable houses, to enclose and break up for them two hundred acres of ground; to furnish them with a farmer, a black-smith, schoolmaster, and interpreter, as long as the President of the United States may deem proper; to furnish them with such agricultural implements as may be necessary, for five years; to furnish them with rations for one year, commencing at the time of their arrival at their new homes; to furnish them with one ferry-boat; to furnish them with one hundred cows and calves and five bulls and one hundred stock hogs when they require them; to furnish them with a mill and assist in removing them, to the extent of five hundred dollars.

And to erect for the Sacks and Foxes three comfortable houses; to enclose and break up for them two hundred acres of ground; to furnish them, with a farmer, blacksmith, schoolmaster, and interpreter, as long as the President of the United States may deem proper; to furnish them with such agricultural implements as may be necessary, for five years; to furnish them with rations for one year, commencing at the time of their arrival at their new home; to furnish them with one ferry-boat; to furnish them with one hundred cows and calves and five bulls, one hundred stock hogs when they require them; to furnish them with a mill; and to assist m moving them, to the extent of four hundred dollars.

ARTICLE 4. This treaty shall be obligatory on the tribes, parties hereto, from and after the date hereof, and on the United States from and after its ratification by the Government thereof.
Done, and signed, and sealed, at fort Leavenworth, on the Missouri, this seventeenth day of September, one thousand eight hundred and thirty-six, and of the independence of the United States the sixty-first.

Wm. Clark, Superintendent Indian Affairs.

Ioways: Mo-hos-ca, or white cloud, his x mark, Nau-che-ning, or no heart, his x mark, Wa-che-mo-ne, or the orator, his x mark, Ne-o-mo-ne, or raining cloud, his x mark, Mau-o-mo-ne, or pumpkin, his x mark,
Sacks and Foxes:
Cau-ca-car-mack, rock bass, his x mark, Sea-sa-ho, sturgeon, his x mark, Pe-a-chin-a-car-mack, bald headed eagle, his x mark, Pe-a-chin-a-car-mack, jr., bald headed eagle, his x mark, Ca-ha-qua, red fox, his x mark, Pc-shaw-ca, bear, his

Plains, West and Northwest Plateau Indian Treaties

x mark, Po-cau-ma, deer, his x mark, Ne-bosh-ca-wa, wolf, his x mark, Ne-squi-in-a, deer, his x mark, Ne-sa-au-qua, bear, his x mark, Qua-co-ou-si, wolf, his x mark, Se-quil-la, deer, his x mark, As-ke-pa-ke-ka-as-a, green lake, his x mark,

Witnesses:
S. W. Kearny, colonel First Regiment First Dragoons, Wm. Bowman, sergeant-major Dragoons, Jno. Dougherty, Indian Agent, Jeffrey Dorion, his x mark, sworn interpreter, Andrew S. Hughes, Sub-agent

TREATY WITH THE POTAWATOMI {1836, Sept. 20}
Proclamation, Feb. 18, 1837.

Articles of a treaty made and concluded at Chippewanaug in the State of Indiana, between Abel C. Pepper, commissioner on the part of the United States, and To-i-sa's brother Me-mat-way and Che-quaw-ka-ko, chiefs and headmen of the Patawattimie tribe of Indians and their band on the twentieth day of September, in the year eighteen hundred and thirty-six.

ARTICLE 1. The above-named chiefs and headmen and their band hereby cede to the United States, ten sections of land reserved for them by the second article of the treaty between the United States, and the Patawattimie tribe of Indians, on Tippecanoe river, on the 27th day of October, in the year 1832.

ARTICLE 2. In consideration of the cession aforesaid the United States stipulate to pay the above-named chiefs and headmen and their band the sum of eight thousand dollars on or before the first day of May next.

ARTICLE 3. The above-named chiefs and headmen and their band agree to remove to the country west of the Mississippi river, provided for the Patawattimie nation by the United States, within two years.

ARTICLE 4. At the request of the above-named band, it is stipulated that after the ratification of this treaty the United States shall appoint a commissioner who shall be authorized to pay such debts of the said band as may be proved to his satisfaction to be just, to be deducted from the amount stipulated in the second article of this treaty.

ARTICLE 5. The United States stipulate to provide for the payment of the necessary expenses attending the making and concluding this treaty.

ARTICLE 6. This treaty, after the same shall be ratified by the President and Senate of the United States, shall be binding upon both parties.

Plains, West and Northwest Plateau Indian Treaties

In testimony whereof, the said Abel C. Pepper, commissioner as aforesaid, and the said chiefs, and head men, and their band, have hereunto set their hands, this twentieth day of September, in the year eighteen hundred and thirty-six.

Abel C. Pepper,
We-we-sah, or To-i sa's brother, his x mark, Me-mot-way, his x mark, Che-quaw-ka-ko, his x mark, Min-tom-in, his x mark, Shaw-gwok-skuk, his x mark, Mee-kiss, or Kawk's widow, her x mark,

Witnesses:
J. B. Duret, secretary.
Allen Hamilton, Cyrus Taber, Geo. W. Ewing, James Moree, Abram Burnett.

TREATY WITH THE POTAWATOMI {1836, Sept. 22}
Proclamation, Feb. 16, 1837.

Articles of a treaty made and concluded at Chippewanaungin the State of Indiana between A. C. Pepper, commissioner on the part of the United States and Mo-sack, chief of the Potawattimie tribe of Indians and his band, on the twenty-second day of September, in the year eighteen hundred and thirty-six.

ARTICLE 1. The above-named chief and his band hereby cede to the United States four sections of land reserved for him and his band by the 2nd article of the treaty between the United States, and the Potawattimie tribe of Indians, on Tippecanoe river, on the 27th day of October, in the year eighteen hundred and thirty-two.

ARTICLE 2. In consideration of the cession aforesaid, the United States stipulate to pay the above-named chief and his band the sum of three thousand two hundred dollars, on or before the first of May next,
ARTICLE 3. The above-named chief and his band agree to remove to the country west of the Mississippi river provided for the Potawattimie nation by the United States within two years.

ARTICLE 4. At the request of the above-named chief and his band, it is stipulated that after the ratification of this treaty the United States shall appoint a commissioner-who shall be authorized to pay such debts of the said band as may be proved to his satisfaction to be just, to be deducted from the amount stipulated in the second article of this treaty.

ARTICLE 5. The United States stipulate to provide for the payment of the necessary expenses attending the making and concluding this treaty.

Plains, West and Northwest Plateau Indian Treaties

ARTICLE 6. This treaty after the same shall be ratified by the President and Senate of the United States, shall be binding upon both parties.
In testimony whereof, the said A. C. Pepper, commissioner as aforesaid, and the said chief and his band have hereunto set their hands, the day and year first above written.

A. C. Fepper, commissioner,
Mo-sack, his x mark, Nawb-bwitt, his x mark, Skin-cheesh, her x mark, Spo-tee, his x mark, Naw-squi-base, her x mark, Mose-so, his x mark,

Witnesses:
J. B. Duret, secretary, Geo. W. Ewing, Andrew Gosselin, his x mark, Benhack, his x mark,

TREATY WITH THE SAUK AND FOXES {1832, Sept. 21}
Proclamation. Feb. 13, 1833.

Articles of a Treaty of Peace, Friendship and Cession, concluded at Fort Armstrong, Rock Island, Illinois, between the United Sates of America, by their Commissioners, Major General Winfield Scott, of the United States Army, and his Excellency John Reynolds, Governor of the State of Illinois, and the confederated tribes of Sac and Fox Indians, represented, in general Council, by the undersigned Chiefs, Headmen and Warriors.

WHEREAS, under certain lawless and desperate leaders, a formidable band, constituting a large portion of the Sac and Fox nation, left their country in April last, and, in violation of treaties, commenced an unprovoked war upon unsuspecting and defenceless citizens of the United States, sparing neither age nor sex; and whereas, the United States, at a great expense of treasure, have subdued the said hostile band, killing or capturing all its principal Chiefs and Warriorsthe said States, partly as indemnity for the expense incurred, and partly to secure the future safety and tranquillity of the invaded frontier, demand of the said tribes, to the use of the United States, a cession of a tract of the Sac and Fox country, bordering on said frontier, more than proportional to the numbers of the hostile band who have been so conquered and subdued.

ARTICLE 1. Accordingly, the confederated tribes of Sacs and Foxes hereby cede to the United States forever, all the lands to which the said tribes have title, or claim, (with the exception of the reservation hereinafter made) included within the following bounds, to wit: Beginning on the Mississippi river, at the point where the Sac and Fox northern boundary line, as established by the second article of the treaty of Prairie du Chien, of the fifteenth of July, one thousand eight hundred and thirty, strikes said river; thence, up said boundary line to a point fifty miles from the Mississippi, measured on said line; thence, in a right line to the nearest point on the Red Cedar of the Ioway, forty miles from

187

Plains, West and Northwest Plateau Indian Treaties

the Mississippi river; thence, in a right line to a point in the northern boundary line of the State of Missouri, fifty miles, measured on said boundary, from the Mississippi river; thence, by the last mentioned boundary to the Mississippi river, and by the western shore of said river to the place of beginning.

And the said confederated tribes of Sacs and Foxes hereby stipulate and agree to remove from the lands herein ceded to the United States, on or before the first day of June next; and, in order to prevent any future misunderstanding, it is expressly understood, that no band or party of the Sac or Fox tribes shall reside, plant, fish, or hunt on any portion of the ceded country after the period just mentioned.

ARTICLE 2. Out of the cession made in the preceding article, the United States agree to a reservation for the use of the said confederated tribes, of a tract of land containing four hundred square miles, to be laid off under the directions of the President of the United States, from the boundary line crossing the Ioway river, in such manner that nearly an equal portion of the reservation may be on both sides of said river, and extending downwards, so as to include Ke-o-kuck's principal village on its right bank, which village is about twelve miles from the Mississippi river.

ARTICLE 3. In consideration of the great extent of the foregoing cession, the United States stipulate and agree to pay to the said confederated tribes, annually, for thirty successive years, the first payment to be made in September of the next year, the sum of twenty thousand dollars in specie.

ARTICLE 4. It is further agreed that the United States shall establish and maintain within the limits, and for the use and benefit of the Sacs and Foxes, for the period of thirty years, one additional black and gun smith shop, with the necessary tools, iron and steel; and finally make a yearly allowance for the same period, to the said tribes, of forty kegs of tobacco, and forty barrels of salt, to be delivered at the mouth of the Ioway river.

ARTICLE 5. The United States, at the earnest request of the said confederated tribes, further agree to pay to Farnham and Davenport, Indian traders at Rock island, the sum of forty thousand dollars without interest, which sum will be in full satisfaction of the claims of the said traders against the said tribes, and by the latter was, on the tenth day of July, one thousand eight hundred and thirty-one, acknowledged to be justly due, for articles of necessity, furnished in the course of the seven preceding years, in an instrument of writing of said date, duly signed by the Chiefs and Headmen of said tribes, and certified by the late Felix St. Vrain, United States' agent, and Antoine Le Claire, United States' Interpreter, both for the said tribes.

Plains, West and Northwest Plateau Indian Treaties

ARTICLE 6. At the special request of the said confederated tribes, the United States agree to grant, by patent, in fee simple, to Antoine Le Claire, Interpreter, a part Indian, one section of land opposite Rock Island, and one section at the head of the first rapids above said Island, within the country herein ceded by the Sacs and Foxes.

ARTICLE 7. Trusting to the good faith of the neutral bands of Sacs and Foxes, the United States have already delivered up to those bands the great mass of prisoners made in the course of the war by the United States, and promise to use their influence to procure the delivery of other Sacs and Foxes, who may still be prisoners in the hands of a band of Sioux Indians, the friends of the United States; but the following named prisoners of war, now in confinement, who were Chiefs and Headmen, shall be held as hostages for the future good conduct of the late hostile bands, during the pleasure of the President of the United States, viz: Muk-ka-ta-mish-a-ka-kaik (or Black Hawk) and his two sons; Wau-ba-kee-shik (the Prophet) his brother and two sons; Na-pope; We-sheet Ioway; Pamaho; and Cha-kee-pa-Shi-pa-ho (the little stabbing Chief).

ARTICLE 8. And it is further stipulated and agreed between the porties to this treaty, that there shall never be allowed in the confederated Sac and Fox nation, any separate band, or village, under any chief or warrior of the late hostile bands; but that the remnant of the said hostile bands shall be divided among the neutral bands of the said tribes according to bloodthe Sacs among the Sacs, and the Foxes among the Foxes.

ARTICLE 9. In consideration of the premises, peace and friendship are declared, and shall be perpetually maintained between the United States and the whole confederated Sac and Fox nation, excepting from the latter the hostages before mentioned.

ARTICLE 10. The United States, besides the presents, delivered at the signing of this treaty, wishing to give a striking evidence of their mercy and liberality, will immediately cause to be issued to the said confederated tribes, principally for the use of the Sac and Fox women and children, whose husbands, fathers and brothers, have been killed in the late war, and generally for the use of the whole confederated tribes, articles of subsistence as follows :thirty-five beef cattle; twelve bushels of salt; thirty barrels of pork; and fifty barrels of flour, and cause to be delivered for the same purposes, in the month of April next, at the mouth of the lower Ioway, six thousand bushels of maize or Indian corn.

ARTICLE 11. At the request of the said confederated tribes, it is agreed that a suitable present shall be made to them on their pointing out to any United States agent, authorized for the purpose, the position or positions of one or more mines, supposed by the said tribes to be of a metal more valuable than lead or iron.

Plains, West and Northwest Plateau Indian Treaties

ARTICLE 12. This treaty shall take effect and be obligatory on the contracting parties, as soon as the same shall be ratified by the President of the United States, by and with the advice and consent of the Senate thereof.

Done at Fort Armstrong, Rock Island, Illinois, this twenty-first day of September, in the year of our Lord one thousand eight hundred and thirty-two, and of the independence of the United States the fifty-seventh.

Winfield Scott, John Reynolds.

Sacs. Kee-o-kuck, or he who has been every where, his x mark, Pa-she-pa-ho, or the stabber, his x mark, Pia-tshe-noay, or the noise maker, his x mark, Wawk-kum-mee, or clear water, his x mark, O-sow-wish-kan-no, or yellow bird, his x mark, Pa-ca-tokee, or wounded lip, his x mark, Winne-wun-quai-saat, or the terror of man, his x mark, Mau-noa-tuck, or he who controls many, his x mark, Wau-we-au-tun, or the curling wave, his x mark, Foxes. Wau-pel-la, or he who is painted white, his x mark,
Waw-pee-shaw-kaw, or white skin, his x mark, Mash-shen-waw-pee-tch, or broken tooth, his x mark, Nau-nah-que-kee-shee-ko, or between two days, his x mark, Paw-puck-ka-kaw, or stealing fox, his x mark, Tay-e-sheek, or the falling bear, his x mark, Wau-pee-maw-ker, or the white loon, his x mark, Wau-co-see-nee-me, or fox man, his x mark,
In presence of
R. Bache, captain ordnance, secretary to the commission, Abrm. Eustis, Alex. Cummings, lieutenant-colonel Second Infantry, Alex. R. Thompson, major U. S. Army, Sexton G. Frazer, P. H. Galt, Assistant Adjutant-General, Benj. F. Pike, Wm. Henry, James Craig, John Aukeney, J. B. F. Russell, Isaac Chambers, .John Clitz, adjutant infantry, John Pickell, lieutenant Fourth Artillery, A. G. Miller, lieutenant
Artillery, H. Day, lieutenant Second Infantry, Jas. W. Penrose, lieutenant Second Infantry,

Plains, West and Northwest Plateau Indian Treaties

TREATY WITH THE SAUK AND FOX TRIBE {1836, Sept. 2}
Proclamation, Feb. 15,1837.

In a convention held this twenty-seventh day of September 1836, between Henry Dodge Superintendent of Indian Affairs, and the chiefs, braves, and principal men of the Sac and Fox tribe of Indians, it has been represented, that according to the stipulations of the first article of the treaty of Prairie du Chien, of the 15th July 1830, the country thereby ceded, is "to be assigned and allotted under the direction of the President of the United States, to the tribes now living thereon, or to such other tribes as the President may locate thereon for hunting and other purposes."

And, whereas, it is further represented to us, the chiefs, braves, and principal men of the tribe aforesaid, to be desirable that the lands lying between the State of Missouri and the Missouri river should be attached to, and become a part of said State, and the Indian title thereto be entirely extinguished; but that, notwithstanding, as these lands compose a part of the country embraced by the provisions of said first article of the treaty aforesaid, the stipulations thereof will be strictly observed until the assent of the Indians interested is given to the proposed measure.

Now, we the chiefs, braves, and principal men of the Sac and Fox tribes of Indians, fully understanding the subject, and well satisfied from the local position of the lands in question, that they can never be made available for Indian purposes, and that an attempt to place an Indian population on them must inevitably lead to collisions with the citizens of the United States; and further believing that the extension of the State line in the direction indicated, would have a happy effect, by presenting a natural boundary between the whites and Indians; and, willing moreover, to give the United States a renewed evidence of our attachment and friendship, do hereby, for ourselves, and on behalf of our respective tribes (having full power and authority to this effect) forever cede, relinquish, and quit claim to the United States, all our right, title, and interest of whatsoever nature in, and to, the lands lying between the State of Missouri and the Missouri river, and do freely and fully exonerate the United States from any guarantee, condition, or limitation, expressed or implied, under the treaty of Prairie du Chien aforesaid, or otherwise, as to the entire and absolute disposition of the said lands, fully authorizing the United States to do with the same whatever shall seem expedient or necessary.

In testimony whereof, we have hereunto set our hands and seals, the day and year first above written.

H. Dodge,
Wa-pa-ca, his x mark, Po-we-seek, his x mark, Qui-ya-ni-pe-na, his x mark, Au-sa-wa-kuk, his x mark, Wa-ko-sa-see, his x mark, Sa-sa-pe-ma, his x mark,

Plains, West and Northwest Plateau Indian Treaties

Ma-wha-wi, his x mark, Wa-pa-sa-kun, his x mark, Pa-ka-ka, his x mark, We-se-au-ke-no-huck, his x mark, Ka-ha-kee, his x mark, Na-a-huck, his x mark, Nau-a-wa-pit, his x mark, Keo-kuck, his x mark, Pa-she-pa-ho, his x mark, We-she-oa-ma-quit, his x mark, Ap-pi-nuis, his x mark, Pe-at-shin-wa, his x mark, Wa-po-pa-nas-kuek, his x mark,
Wa-ta-pe-naut, his x mark, Pa-na-see, his x mark, Ma-ke-no-na-see, his x mark, Na-che-min, his x mark,

In presence of us:
James W. Grimes, secretary of commission, Danniah Smith, Nathl. Knapp, Jos. M. Street, Indian agent., Daniel Geire, Ant. St. Clair, interpreter, Erastus H. Bassett, Frans. Labussir, interpreter, Geo. Catlin, James Craig, Robert Settell Wood.

TREATY WITH THE SAUK AND FOXES {1836, Sept. 28}
Proclamation, Dec. 13, 1837.

Articles of a treaty made and entered into at the treaty ground on the right bank of the Mississippi river in the county of Debuque and Territory of Wisconsin opposite Rock island, on the twenty-eighth day of September one thousand eight hundred and thirty-six, between Henry Dodge commissioner on the part of the United States, of the one part, and the confederated tribes of Sac and Fox Indians represented in general council by the undersigned chiefs, headmen and warriors of the said tribes, of the other part:

WHEREAS by the second article of the treaty made between the United States and the confederate tribes of the Sac and Fox Indians on the twenty-first day of September one thousand eight hundred and thirty-two, a reservation of four hundred sections of land was made to the Sac and Fox Indians to be laid off under the directions of the President of the United States in conformity to the provisions of said article, and the same having been so subsequently laid out accordingly, and the confederated tribes of Sacs and Foxes being desirous of obtaining additional means of support, and to pay their just creditors, have entered into this treaty, and make the following cession of land.

ARTICLE 1. The confederated tribes of Sacs and Foxes for the purposes above expressed, and for and in consideration of the stipulations and agreements hereinafter expressed, do hereby cede to the United States forever, the said reservation of four hundred sections of land as designated in the second article of the treaty made between the United States and the confederated tribes of Sacs and Foxes as the same has been surveyed and laid off by order of the President of the United States.

Plains, West and Northwest Plateau Indian Treaties

ARTICLE 2. In consideration of the cession contained in the preceding article, the United States hereby agree as follows, to wit; To pay to the confederated tribes of the Sac and Fox Indians in the month of June one thousand eight hundred and thirty-seven, the sum of thirty thousand dollars, and for ten successive years thereafter the sum of ten thousand dollars each year in specie, to be paid at the treaty ground opposite Rock island or such other place as may be designated by the President of the United States, to pay to the widow and children of Felix St. Vrain deceased former Indian agent who was killed by the Indians, one thousand dollars; to pay to the following named persons the sums set opposite to their names respectively, being the one half of the amount agreed to be due and owing by the confederated tribes of Sacs and Foxes to their creditors, provided said creditors will wait for the other half until the same can be paid out of their annuities, for which purpose the Sacs and Foxes will set apart the sum of five thousand dollars each year, beginning in one thousand eight hundred and thirty-eight, out of their annuities to be paid upon said debts in the proper proportion until the whole amount is discharged

To wit: to John Campbell ten thousand dollars, to Jeremiah Smith six hundred and forty dollars, to Stephen Dubois three hundred and five dollars and twenty cents, to Nathaniel Knapp one hundred dollars, to Wharton R. McPhearson two hundred and fifty dollars, to S. S. Phelps & Co. four thousand dollars, to Jesse W. Shull five hundred dollars, to James Jordan one hundred and fifty dollars.

To John R. Campbell fifteen dollars, to Amos Farrar one hundred dollars, to the owners of the S. boat Warrior, one hundred and sixty-two dollars and seventy-five cents, to George Davenport two thousand five hundred and sixty-three dollars and fifty cents, to Madame St. Ament five hundred dollars, to Madame Joseph Gunville five hundred dollars, to Madame Le Claire one hundred and twenty-five dollars, to Miss Blondeau one hundred and twenty-five dollars, to Antoine Le Claire two thousand four hundred and thirty-six dollars and fifty cents, to Francis Labachiere one thousand one hundred and sixty-seven dollars and seventy-five cents, to Pratte Chouteau & Co. twenty thousand three hundred and sixty-two dollars, and forty-two and a half cents, to Nathaniel Patterson four hundred and fifty-six dollars. The Iowa Indians having set up a claim to a part of the lands ceded by this treaty, it is therefore hereby provided, that the President of the United States shall cause the validity and extent of said claim to be ascertained, and upon a relinquishment of said claim to the United States, he shall cause the reasonable and fair value thereof to be paid to said Iowa Indians, and the same amount to be deducted from the sum stipulated to be paid to the Sacs and Foxes.

ARTICLE 3. The United States further agree to deliver to the confederated tribes of Sacs and Foxes two hundred horses, as near that number as can be procured with the sum of nine thousand three hundred and forty-one dollars, to

Plains, West and Northwest Plateau Indian Treaties

be delivered at the payment of the annuities in June one thousand eight hundred and thirty-seven.

ARTICLE 4. At the special request of the Sac and Fox Indians aforesaid, the United States agree to make the following provisions for the benefit and support of seven half-breeds of the Sac and Fox nation, to wit; The United States agree to pay to Wayman for the use and benefit of his half-breed child by a Fox woman-named Ni-an-no, one thousand dollars, to Wharton R. McPhearson for the use and benefit of his half-breed child by To-to-qua, a Fox woman, one thousand dollars, to James Thorn for the use and benefit of his half-breed child by Ka-kee-o-sa-qua, a Fox woman, one thousand dollars, to Joseph Smart for the use of his half-breed child by Ka-ti-qua a Fox woman one thousand dollars, to Nathan Smith for the use and benefit of his half-breed child by Wa-na-sa a Sac woman one thousand dollars, and to Joseph M. Street Indian agent, two thousand dollars for the use and benefit of two half-breed children, one the child of Niwa-ka-kee a Fox woman, by one Mitchell, the other the child of Ni-an-na by Amos Farrar, the two thousand dollars to be put at interest, and so much of said interest arising therefrom to be expended for the benefit of the children as said agent shall deem proper and necessary, and when each shall arrive at the age of twenty years, the said agent shall pay to each half-breed one thousand dollars and any balance of interest remaining in his hands at the time.

ARTICLE 5. At the special request of the said confederated tribes of Sac and Fox Indians it is further agreed by the United States, to pay to Joseph M. Street their agent, two hundred dollars for the use and benefit of Thompson Connoly and James Connoly children of their friend John Connoly deceased, to be by said agent put at interest and expended on the education of said Thompson and James Connoly children of said John Connoly deceased.

ARTICLE 6. The said confederated tribes of Sac and Fox Indians hereby stipulate and agree to remove from off the lands herein in the first article of this treaty ceded to the United States, by the first day of November next ensuing the date hereof, and in order to prevent any future misunderstanding, it is expressly agreed and understood that no band or party of the said confederated tribes of Sac and Fox Indians, shall plant, fish or hunt on any portion of the country herein ceded after the period just mentioned.

ARTICLE 7. This treaty shall be obligatory on the contracting parties after it shall be ratified by the President and Senate of the United States.
Done at the treaty ground on the right bank of the Mississippi in Debuque county Wisconsin Territory opposite Rock island this twenty-eighth day of September one thousand eight hundred and thirty-six.

A. Dodge,
A-sho-wa-huk, Ma-sha-na, Wa-ko-sha-she, Sa-sa-pe-man, Na-wo-huck, Pen-na

Plains, West and Northwest Plateau Indian Treaties

Foxes:
Wa-pella, Pow-a-sheek, Qua-qua-ha-pc-qua, Wa-pak-onas-kuck, Wa-tup-a-waut, Ma-kee-won-a-see, Ka-ka-no-an-na.

Sacs:
Kee-o-kuck, Pashapahoo, We-she-ko-ma-quit, Ap-a-noose, Pe-a-chin-wa, Mo-wha-wi, Wa-pe-sha-kon.

In presence of us-
James W. Grimes, secretary of commission, Jos. M. Street, Indian agent, L. Dorsey Stockton, jr., attorney at law, Ant. Leclaire, interpreter, Frans. Labussar, interpreter, James Craig, P. R. Chouteau, jr, Geo. Davenport, Nathl. Knapp.

To the Indian names are subjoined a mark and seal.

TREATY WITH THE OTO, ETC. {1836, Oct. 15}
Proclamation, Feb. 15, 1837.

Articles of a convention entered into and concluded at Bellevue Upper Missouri the fifteenth day of October one thousand eight hundred and thirty-six, by and between John Dougherty U. S. agt for Indian Affairs and Joshua Pilcher U. S. Ind. s. agt being specially authorized therefor; and the chiefs braves head men &c of the Otoes Missouries Omahaws and Yankton and Santee bands of Sioux, duly authorized by their respective tribes.

ARTICLE 1. Whereas it has been represented that according to the stipulations of the first article of the treaty of Prairie du Chien of the fifteenth of July eighteen hundred and thirty, the country ceded is "to be assigned and allotted under the direction of the President of the United States to the tribes now living thereon or to such other tribes as the President may locate thereon for hunting and other purposes," and whereas it is further represented to us the chiefs, braves and head men of the tribes aforesaid, that it-is desirable that the lands lying between the State of Missouri and the Missouri river, and south of a line running due west from the northwest corner of said State until said line strikes the Missouri river, should be attached to and become a part of said State, and the Indian title thereto be entirely extinguished; but that notwithstanding as these lands compose a part of the country embraced by the provisions of the said first article of the treaty aforesaid, the stipulations whereof will be strictly observed, until the assent of the Indians interested is given to the proposed measure.

Now we the chiefs braves and principal men of the Otoes Missouries Omahaws Yankton and Santee bands of Sioux aforesaid fully understanding the subject and well satisfied from the local position of the lands in question, that they

Plains, West and Northwest Plateau Indian Treaties

never can be made available for Indian purposes; and that an attempt to place an Indian population on them must inevitably lead to collisions with the citizens of the United States; and, further: believing that the extension of the State line in the direction indicated, would have a happy effect by presenting a natural boundary between the whites and Indians; and willing moreover to give the United States a renewed evidence of our attachment and friendship; do hereby for ourselves and on behalf of our respective tribes (having full power and authority to this effect) forever cede relinquish and quit claim to the United States all our right title and interest-of whatsoever nature in and to the lands lying between the State of Missouri and the Missouri river, and south of a line running due west from the northwest corner of the State to the Missouri river, as herein before mentioned, and freely and fully exonerate the United States from any guarantee condition or limitation expressed or implied under the treaty of Prairie du Chien aforesaid or otherwise, as to the entire and absolute disposition of said lands, fully authorizing the United States to do with the same whatever shall seem expedient or necessary.

ARTICLE 2. As a proof of the continued friendship and liberality of the United States towards the said Otoes Missouries Omahaws and Yankton and Santee bands of Sioux, and as an evidence of the sense entertained for the good will manifested by the said tribes to the citizens and Government of the United States as evinced in the preceding cession and relinquishment; and as some compensation for the great sacrifice made by the several deputations at this particular season, by abandoning their fall hunts and traveling several hundred miles to attend this convention the undersigned John Dougherty and Joshua Pileher agrees on behalf of the United States to pay as a present to the tribes herein before named the sum of four thousand five hundred and twenty dollars in merchandise, the receipt of which they hereby acknowledge having been distributed among them in the proportions following.

To the Otoes twelve hundred and fifty dollars, to the Missouries one thousand dollars to the Omahaws twelve hundred and seventy dolls. to the Yankton and Santee bands of Sioux one thousand dollars.

ARTICLE 3. In consequence of the removal of the Otoes and Missouries from their former situation on the river Platte to the place selected for them, and of their having to build new habitations last spring at the time which should have been occupied in attending to their crops, it appears that they have failed to such a degree as to make it certain that they will lack the means of subsisting next spring, when it will be necessary for them to commence cultivating the lands now preparing for their use. It is therefore agreed that the said Otoes, and Missouries (in addition to the presents herein before mentioned) shall be furnished at the expense of the United States with five hundred bushels of corn to be delivered at their village in the month of April next.

Plains, West and Northwest Plateau Indian Treaties

And the same causes operating upon the Omahaws, they having also abandoned their former situation, and established at the place recommended to them on the Missouri river, and finding it difficult without the aid of ploughs to cultivate land near their village where they would be secure from their enemies, it is agreed as a farther proof of the liberality of the Government and its disposition to advance such tribes in the cultivation of the soil as may manifest a disposition to rely on it for the future means of subsistence; that they shall have one hundred acres of ground broke up and put under a fence near their village, so soon as it can be done after the ratification of this convention.

ARTICLE 4. This convention shall be obligatory on the tribes parties hereto, from and after the date hereof, and on the United States from and after its ratification by the Government thereof.

Done, signed, and sealed at Bellevue, Upper Missouri, this fifteenth day of October, one thousand eight hundred and thirty-six, and of the independence of the United States, the sixty-first.

Jno. Dougherty, Indian agent, Joshua Pilcher, United States Indian subagent,

Otoes:
Jaton, his x mark, Big Kaw, his x mark, The Thief, his x mark, Wah-ro-ne-saw, his x mark, Buffalo Chief, his x mark, Shaking Handle, his x mark, We-ca-ru-ton, his x mark, Wash-shon-ke-ra, his x mark, Standing White Bear, his x mark, O-rah-car-pe, his x mark, Wah-nah-shah, his x mark, Wa-gre-ni-e, his x mark, Mon-nah-shu-jah, his x mark,

Missouries:
Hah-che-ge-sug-a, his x mark, Black Hawk, his x mark, No Heart, his x mark; Wan-ge-ge-he-ru-ga-ror, his x mark, The Arrow Fender, his x mark, Wah-ne-min-er, his x mark.Big Wing, his x mark, Omahaws: Big Elk, his x mark, Big Eyes, his x mark, Wash-kaw-mony, his x mark, White Horse, his x mark, White Caw, his x mark, Little Chief, his x mark, A-haw-paw, his x mark, Walking Cloud, his x mark, Wah-see-an-nee, his x mark, No tteart, his x mark,

Yankton and Santees
Pitta-eu-ta-pishna, his x mark, Wash-ka-shin-ga, his x mark, Mon-to-he, his x mark, Wah-kan-teau, his x mark,.

Witnesses:
J. Varnum Hamilton, sutler U. S. Dragoons and acting secretary, William Steele, John A. Ewell, William J. Martin, Martin Dorion, his x mark,

Plains, West and Northwest Plateau Indian Treaties

TREATY WITH THE SIOUX {1836, Nov. 30}
Proclamation, Feb. 18, 1837.

Convention with the Wahpaakootah, Susseton, and Upper Medawakanton tribes of Sioux Indians.

In a convention held this thirtieth day of November 1836 between Lawrence Taliaferro, Indian Agent at St. Peters, and the chiefs, braves, and principal men of the Wahpaakootah, Susseton, and Upper Medawakanton tribes of Sioux Indians, it has been represented, that according to the stipulations of the first article of the treaty of Prairie du Chien of the 15th July, 1830, the country thereby ceded is "to be assigned and allotted under the direction of the President of the United States to the tribes now living thereon, or to such other tribes as the President may locate thereon for hunting and other purposes." And, whereas, it is further represented to us, the chiefs, braves and principal men of the tribes aforesaid, to be desirable, that the lands lying between the State of Missouri, and the Missouri river should be attached to, and become a part of said State, and the Indian title thereto be entirely extinguished; but that, notwithstanding, as these lands compose a part of the country embraced by the provisions of said first article of the treaty aforesaid, the stipulations thereof will be strictly observed until the assent of the Indians interested is given to the proposed measure.

Now we, the chiefs, braves, and principal men of the Wahpaakootah, Susseton and Upper Medawakanton tribes of Sioux Indians, fully understanding the subject, and well satisfied from the local position of the lands in question that they can never be made available for Indian purposes, and that an attempt to place an Indian population on them must inevitably lead to collisions with the citizens of the United States; and further believing that the extension of the State line in the direction indicated, would have a happy effect, by presenting a natural boundary between the whites and Indians.

And willing, moreover, to give the United States a renewed evidence of our attachment and friendship, do hereby for ourselves, and on behalf of our respective tribes (having full power and authority to this effect) forever cede, relinquish and quit claim to the United States all our right, title and interest of whatsoever nature in, and to, the lands lying between the State of Missouri, and the Missouri river, and do freely and fully exonerate the United States from any guarantee, condition, or limitation, expressed or implied, under the treaty of Prairie du Chien aforesaid, or otherwise, as to the entire and absolute disposition of the said lands, fully authorizing the United States to do with the same whatever shall seem expedient or necessary.

As a proof of the continued friendship and liberality of the United States towards the Wahpaakootah, Susseton and Upper Medawakanton tribes of Sioux

Plains, West and Northwest Plateau Indian Treaties

Indians, and as an evidence of the sense entertained for the good will manifested by said tribes to the citizens and Government of the United States, as evinced in the preceding session or relinquishment, the undersigned agrees, on behalf of the United States, to cause said tribes to be furnished with presents to the amount of five hundred and fifty dollars in goods, the receipt of which is hereby acknowledged.

In testimony whereof, we have hereunto set our hands and seals, the day and year first above written.

Law. Taliaferro,

Sussetons:
Ese-tah-ken-bah, or the sleepy eyes, his x mark, Kahe-maa-doh-kah, or the male rover, his x mark, Tunkah-munnee, or the great walk-er, his x mark, Hohwah-munnee, or the walking crier, his x mark,

Wah paakootas:
Tah-sau-ga, orthe cane, his x mark, Wahmaadee-sappah, orblack eagle, his x mark, Skushkahnah, or moving shadow, his x mark, Ahppaa-hoh-tah, or the gray mane, his x mark,

Upper Medawakantons:
Wahkon-Tunkah, or the big thun-der, his x mark, Wahmadee-tunkah, or big eagle, his x mark, Marcpeeah-mah-zah, or iron cloud, his x mark, Koc-ko-moc-ko, or afloat, his x mark, Tah-chunk-pee-sappah, or the black tomahawk, his x mark, Marc-pee-wee-chas-tah, or chiefs of the clouds, his x mark, Tah-chunk-washtaa, or the good road, his x mark, Mah-zah-hoh-tah, or the gray iron, his x mark, Patah-eu-hah, or he that holds the five, his x mark,

Executed in presence of-
J. McClure, lieutenant, First Infantry, J.N. Nicollet, S. M. Plummer, lieutenant, First Infantry, Scott Campbell, United States interpreter.

TREATY WITH THE POTAWATOMI {1837, Feb. 11}
Proclamation, Feb. 18, 1837.

Articles of a treaty concluded in the city of Washington on the eleventh day of February eighteen hundred and thirty-seven between John T. Douglass, commissioner on the part of the United States and Chee-chaw-kose, Ash-kum, Wee-saw or Louison, Muck-kose and Qui-qui-to, chiefs of the Potawatomie tribe of Indians.

Plains, West and Northwest Plateau Indian Treaties

ARTICLE 1. The chiefs and head men above named do, for themselves and their respective bands sanction and give their assent to the provisions of the treaties concluded between A. C. Pepper, commissioner on the part of the United States and certain chiefs and young men of the Potawatomie tribe of Indians, on the 5th day of August and 23d day of September 1836, in which were ceded to the United States certain lands in the State of Indiana, in which the chiefs and head men above named have an interest, the same having been reserved for them and their bands respectively in the treaties of October 26th and 27th 1832. And the chiefs and head men above named, for themselves and their bands, do hereby cede to the United States all their interest in said lands, and agree to remove to a country that may be provided for them by the President of the United States, southwest of the Missouri river, within two years from the ratification of this treaty.

ARTICLE 2. The United States agree that the several sums, for the payment of which provision is made in the treaties of August and September 1836, referred to in the preceding article, shall be paid to the respective chiefs and bands, for whose benefit the lands, ceded by said treaties, were reserved.

ARTICLE 3. The United States further agree to convey by patent to the Potawatomies of Indiana, a tract of country, on the Osage river southwest of the Missouri river, sufficient in extent, and adapted to their habits and wants; remove them to the same; furnish them with one year's subsistence after their arrival there, and pay the expenses of this treaty, and of the delegation now in this city.

ARTICLE 4. It is further stipulated, that the United States will purchase the "five sections in the prairie, near Rock Village" reserved for Qui-qui-to, in the second article of the treaty of October 20th 1832 for the sum of $4,000; to be paid to said chief at such times and places as the President of the United States may think proper.

ARTICLE 5. This treaty to be obligatory upon the contracting parties when ratified by the President and Senate of the United States.

In witness whereof, the contracting parties have hereunto set their hands and seals, the day and year above written.

John T. Douglass, Commmissioner, Qui-qui-taw, his x mark, Che-chaw-kose, his x mark, Ash-kmn, his x mark, We-saw, or Louison, his x , Muck-kose, his x , Sin-qui-waugh, his x , Po-ga-kose, his x mark, John C. Barnett, Abram B. Burnett, William Turner, Interpreters.

Signed in presence of
G. C. Johnson, Isaac McCoy.

Plains, West and Northwest Plateau Indian Treaties

TREATY WITH THE KIOWA, ETC. {1837, May 26}
Proclamation, Feb. 21, 1838.

Treaty with the Kioway, Ka-ta-ka and Ta-wa-ka-ro, Nations of Indians.

Whereas a treaty of peace and friendship was made and signed on the 24th day of August 1835, between Montfort Stokes and Brigadier General Matthew Arbuckle, commissioners on behalf of the United States on the one part; and the chiefs, and head-men and representatives of the Comanche, Witehetaw, Cherokee Muscogee, Choctaw, Osage, Seneca and Quapaw nations or tribes of Indians on the other part: and whereas the said treaty has been duly ratified by the Government of the United States; now know all whom it may-concern, that the President of the United States, by letter of appointment and instructions of the 7th day of April 1837, has authorized Col. A. P. Chouteau to make a convention or treaty between the United States and any of the nations or tribes of Indians of the Great Western Prairie; we the said Montfort Stokes, and A. P. Chouteau, commissioners of Indian treaties, have this day made and concluded a treaty of peace and friendship, between the United States of America, and the chiefs, headmen and representatives of the Kioway, Ka-ta-ka, and Ta-wa-ka-ro nations of Indians, on the following terms and conditions, that is to say:

ARTICLE 1. There shall be perpetual peace and friendship between all the citizens of the United States of America and all the individuals composing the Kioway, Ka-ta-ka, and Ta-wa-ka-ro nations and their associated bands or tribes of Indians, and between these nations or tribes and the Muscogee and Osage nations or tribes of Indians.

ARTICLE 2. Every injury or act of hostility by one or either of the contracting parties on the other, shall be mutually forgiven and for ever forgot.

ARTICLE 3. There shall be a free and friendly intercourse between all the contracting parties hereto; and it is distinctly understood and agreed by the Kioway, Ka-ta-ka and Ta-wa-ka-ro nations, and their associated bands or tribes of Indians, that the citizens of the United States are freely permitted to pass and repass through their settlements or hunting ground without molestation or injury, on their way to any of the provinces of the Republics of Mexico or Texas, or returning therefrom, and that the nations or tribes named in this article further agree to pay the full value of any injury their people may do to the goods or property of the Citizens of the United States, taken or destroyed when peaceably passing through the country they inhabit or hunt in, or elsewhere.

And the United States hereby guarantee to any Indian or Indians of the Kioway, Ka-ta-ka and Ta-wa-ka-ro nations, and their associated bands or tribes of Indi-

Plains, West and Northwest Plateau Indian Treaties

ans, a full indemnification for any horses or other property which may be stolen from them, Provided That the property so stolen cannot be recovered, and that sufficient proof is produced that it was actually stolen by a citizen of the United States, and within the limits thereof.

ARTICLE 4. It is understood and agreed by all the nations or tribes of Indians, parties to this treaty, that each and all of the said nations or tribes have free permission to hunt and trap in the Great Prairie west of the Cross Timber to the western limits of the United States.

ARTICLE 5. The Kioway, Ka-ta-ka and Ta-wa-ka-ro nations and their associated bands or tribes of Indians agree and bind themselves to pay full value for any injury their people may do to the goods or other property of such traders as the President of the United States may place near to their settlements or hunting ground for the purpose of trading with them.

ARTICLE 6. The Kioway, Ka-ta-ka and Ka-wa-ka-ro nations and their associated bands or tribes of Indians, agree, that in the event any of the red people belonging to the nations or tribes of Indians residing south of the Missouri river, and west of the States of Missouri and Arkansas, not parties to this treaty, should visit their towns, or be found on their hunting ground, that they will treat them with kindness and friendship, and do no injury to them in any way whatever.

ARTICLE 7. Should any difficulty hereafter unfortunately arise between any of the nations or tribes of Indians, parties hereunto, in consequence of murder, the stealing of horses, cattle, or other cause, it is agreed that the other tribes shall interpose their good offices to remove such difficulties; and also that the Government of the United States may take such measures as they may deem proper to effect the same object, and see that full justice is done to the injured party.

ARTICLE 8. It is agreed by the commissioners of the United States that in consequence of the Kioway, Ka-ta-ka and Ta-wa-ka-ro nations and their associated bands or tribes of Indians having freely and willingly entered into this treaty, and it being the first they have made with the United States, or any of the contracting parties, that they shall receive presents immediately after signing, as a donation from the United States; nothing being asked from the said nations or tribes in return, except to remain at peace with the parties hereto, which their own good and that of their posterity require.

ARTICLE 9. The Kioway, Ka-ta-ka and Ta-wa-ka-ro nations, and their associated bands or tribes of Indians, agree, that their entering into this treaty shall in no respect interrupt their friendly relations with the Republics of Mexico and Texas, where they all frequently hunt and the Kioway, Ka-ta-ka and Ta-wa-ka-

Plains, West and Northwest Plateau Indian Treaties

ro nations sometimes visit; and it is distinctly understood that the Government of the United States desire that perfect peace shall exist between the nations or tribes named in this article, and the said Republics.

ARTICLE 10. This treaty shall be obligatory on the nations or tribes, parties hereto, from and after the date hereof, and on the United States, from and after its ratification by the Government thereof.

Done and signed and sealed at Fort Gibson, this twenty-sixth day of May one thousand eight hundred and thirty-seven and of the independence of the United States the sixty-second.

M. Stokes, Commissioner of Indian treaties.
A. P. Chouteau, Commissioner Indian treaties.

Kioways:
Ta-ka-ta-couche, the Black Bird, Cha-hon-de-ton, the Flying Squirrel, Ta-ne-congais, the Sea Gull, Bon-congais, the Black Cap, To-ho-sa, the Top of the Mountain, Sen-son-da-cat, the White Bird, Con-a-hen-ka, the Horne Frog, He-pan-ni-gais, the Night, Ka-him-hi, the Prairie Dog, Pa-con-ta, My Young Brother.

Ka-ta-kas:
Hen-ton-te, the Iron Shoe, A-ei-kenda, the One who is Surrendered, Cet-ma-ni-ta, the Walking Bear.

Ta-wa-ka-ros:
Ka-ta-ca-karo, He who receives the Word of God, Ta-ce-hache, the One who Speaks to.the Chief, Ke-te-cara-con-ki, the White Cow, Ta-ka, the Hunter of Men.

Muscogees:
Holy McIntosh, Alex. Gillespie, Samuel Miller, Samuel Perryman, John Randam, To-me-yo-hola, Efi-e,nathla, Chis-coolaco-mici, Encotts Harjo, Ufalila Harjo.

Osages:
Clermont, the Principal Chief, Ka-hi-gair-tanga, the Big Chief, Ka-hi-gair-wa-chin-pi-chaisi, the Mad Chief, Chan-gais-mon-non, the Horse Thief, Wa-cri-cha, the Liberal, Ta-lais, the Going Deer, Chonta-sa-bais, the Black Dog, Wa-clum-pi-chais, the Mad Warrior

Witnesses:
Wm. Whistler, Lieutenant-Colonel Seventh Infantry, commanding.
B. L. E. Bonneville, captain, Seventh Infantry, Francis Lee, captain, Seventh Infantry, Jas. R. Stephenson, captain, Seventh Infantry. P.

203

Plains, West and Northwest Plateau Indian Treaties

S.G. Bell, captain, First Dragoons.
W. Seawell, captain, Seventh Infantry. and secretary to the commissioners.
S.W. Moore, first lientenant and adjutant, Seventh Infantry, Th. H. Holmes, first lieutentant, Seventh Infantry, R. H. Ross, first lieutenant, Seventh Infantry, J. H. Bailey, assistant surgeon, G. K. Paul, first lieutenant, Seventh Infantry, S. G. Simmons, first lieutenant, Seventh Infantry, J. G. Reed, second lieutenant, Seventh Infantry, J. M. Wells, second lieutenant, Seventh Infantry, R. L. Dodge.
F. Britton, lieutenant, Seventh, U. S. Army.
S. Hardage, Creek interpreter.

(To the Indian names are subjoined marks.)

TREATY WITH THE SIOUX {1837, Sept. 29}
Proclamation, June 15, 1838.

Articles of a treaty, made at the City of Washington, between Joel R. Poinsett, thereto specially authorized by the President of the United States, and certain chiefs and braves of the Sioux nation of Indians.

ARTICLE 1. The chiefs and braves representing the parties having an interest therein, cede to the United States all their land, east of the Mississippi river, and all their islands in the said river.

ARTICLE 2. In consideration of the cession contained in the preceding article, the United States agree to the following stipulations on their part.

First. To invest the sum of $300,000 (three hundred thousand dollars) in such safe and profitable State stocks as the President may direct, and to pay to the chiefs and braves as aforesaid, annually, forever, an income of not less than five per cent. thereon; a portion of said interest, not exceeding one third, to be applied in such manner as the President may direct, and the residue to be paid in specie, or in such other manner, and for such objects, as the proper authorities of the tribe may designate.

Second. To pay to the relatives and friends of the chiefs and braves, as aforesaid, having not less than one quarter of Sioux blood, $110,000 (one hundred and ten thousand dollars) to be distributed by the proper authorities of the tribe, upon principles to be determined by the chiefs and braves signing this treaty, and the War Department.

Third. To apply the sum of $90,000 (ninety thousand dollars)to the payment of Just debts of the Sioux Indians, interested in the lands herewith ceded.

204

Plains, West and Northwest Plateau Indian Treaties

Fourth. To pay to the chiefs and braves as aforesaid an annuity for twenty years of $10,000 (ten thousand dollars)in goods, to be purchased under the direction of the President, and delivered at the expense of the United States.

Fifth. To expend annually for twenty years, for the benefit of Sioux Indians, parties to this treaty, the sum of $8,250 (eight thousand two hundred and fifty dollars) in the purchase of medicines, agricultural implements and stock, and for the support of a physician, farmers, and blacksmiths, and for other beneficial objects.

Sixth. In order to enable the Indians aforesaid to break up and improve their lands, the United States will supply, as soon as practicable, after the ratification of this treaty, agricultural implements, mechanics' tools, cattle, and such other articles as may be useful to them, to an amount not exceeding $10,000, (ten thousand dollars.)

Seventh. To expend annually, for twenty years, the sum of $5.500 (five thousand five hundred dollars) in the, purchase of provisions, to be delivered at the expense of the United States.

Eighth. To deliver to the chiefs and braves signing this treaty, upon their arrival at St. Louis, $6,000 (six thousand dollars) in goods.

ARTICLE 3. (Stricken out by Senate.)

ARTICLE 4. This treaty shall be binding on the contracting parties as soda as it shall be ratified by the United States.

In testimony whereof, the said Joel R. Poinsett, and the undersigned chiefs and braves of the Sioux nation, have hereunto set their hands, at the City of Washington, this 29th day of September A. D. 1837.

J. R. Poinsett.

Medawakantons:
Tah-tape-saah, The Upsetting Wind, Wah-keah-tun-kah, Big Thunder, Mah-zah-hoh-tah, Grey Iron, Tautunga-munne, Walking Buffalo, Eu-hah-kaakow, He that comes last, Mah-kuah-pah, he that shakes the Earth, Tah-mah-zah-hoh-wash-taa, The Iron of handsome voice, Watt-chu-dah, The Dancer, Mah-zah-tunkah, The Big Iron, Mau-po-koah-munnee, He that runs after the clouds, Tah-chunk-wash-taa, Good Road, Mare-pu-ah-nasiah, Standing Cloud, Koi-moko, Afloat, Mau-pu-wee-chastah, White Man, Mau-pu-ah-mah-zah, Iron Cloud, Tah-chunek-oh-dutah, The Red Road, Wasson-wee-chastish-nee, The Bad Hail, Hoe-yah-pah, the Eagle Head Annon-ge-nasiah, He that Stands on

Plains, West and Northwest Plateau Indian Treaties

Both sides, Chaudus-ka-mumee, the Walking Circle, Tee-oh-du-tah, the Red Lodge.

In presence of
Chauncy Bush, secretary.
Mahlon Dickerson, Secretary of the Navy.
W. J. Worth, lieutenant-colonel.

(To the Indian names are subjoined marks.)

TREATY WITH THE SAUK AND FOXES {1837, Oct. 21}
Proclamation, Feb. 21, 1838.

Articles of a treaty made at the city of Washington, between Carey A. Harris, Commissioner of Indian Affairs, thereto authorized by the President of the United States, and the confederated tribes of Sacs and Foxes, by their chiefs and delegates.

ARTICLE 1. The Sacs and Foxes make to the United States the following cessions:

First. Of a tract of country containing 1,250,000 (one million two hundred and fifty thousand) acres lying west and adjoining the tract conveyed by them to the United States in the treaty of September 21st, 1832. It is understood that the points of termination for the present cession shall be the northern and southern points of said tract as fixed by the survey made under the authority of the United States, and that a line shall be drawn between them, so as to intersect a line extended westwardly from the angle of said tract nearly opposite to Rock Island as laid down in the above survey, so far as may be necessary to include the number of acres hereby ceded, which last mentioned line it is estimated will be about twenty-five miles.

Second. Of all right or interest in the land ceded by said confederated tribes on the 15th of July 1830, which might be claimed by them, under the phraseology of the first article of said treaty.

ARTICLE 2. In consideration of the cessions contained in the preceding article, the United States agree to the following stipulations on their part:

First. To cause the land ceded to be surveyed at the expense of the United States, and permanent and prominent land marks established, in the presence of a deputation of the chiefs of said confederated tribes.

Plains, West and Northwest Plateau Indian Treaties

Second. To pay the debts of the confederated tribes, which may be ascertained to be justly due, and which may be admitted by the Indians, to the amount of one hundred thousand dollars ($100,000) provided, that if all their just debts amount to more than this sum, then their creditors are to be paid pro rata upon their giving receipts in full; and if said debts fall short of said sum, then the remainder to be paid to the Indians. And provided also, That no claim for depredations shall be paid out of said sum.

Third. To deliver to them goods, suited to their wants, at cost, to the amount of twenty-eight thousand five hundred dollars ($28,500.)

Fourth. To expend, in the erection of two grist mills, and the support of two millers for five years, ten thousand dollars ($10,000.)

Fifth. To expend in breaking up and fencing in ground on the land retained by said confederated tribes, and for other beneficial objects, twenty-four thousand dollars ($24,000.)

Sixth. To expend in procuring the services of the necessary number of laborers, and for other objects connected with aiding them in agriculture, two thousand dollars ($2,000) a year, for five years.

Seventh. For the purchase of horses and presents, to be delivered to the chiefs and delegates on their arrival at St. Louis, four thousand five hundred dollars ($4,500) one thousand dollars ($1,000) of which is in full satisfaction of any claim said tribe may have on account of the stipulation for blacksmiths in the treaty of 1S32.

Eighth. To invest the sum of two hundred thousand dollars ($200,000) in safe State stocks, and to guarantee to the Indians, an annual income of not less than five per cent. the said interest to be paid to them each year, in the manner annuities are paid, at such time and place, and in money or goods as the tribe may direct. Provided, That it may be competent for the President to direct that a portion of the same may, with the consent of the Indians, be applied to education, or other purposes calculated to improve them.

ARTICLE 3. The two blacksmith's establishments, and the gunsmith's establishment, to which the Sacs and Foxes are entitled under treaties prior to this, shall be removed to, and be supported in the country retained by them, and all other stipulations in former treaties, inconsistent with this, or with their residence, and the transaction of their business on their retained land are hereby declared void.

Plains, West and Northwest Plateau Indian Treaties

ARTICLE 4. The Sacs and Foxes agree to remove from the tract ceded, with the exception of Keokuck's village, possession of which may be retained for two years, within eight months from the ratification of this treaty.

ARTICLE 5. The expenses of this negotiation and of the chiefs and delegates signing this treaty to this city, and to their homes, to be paid by the United States.

ARTICLE 6. This treaty to be binding upon the contracting parties when the same shall be ratified by the United States.

In witness whereof the said Carey A. Harris, and the undersigned chiefs and delegates of the said tribes, have hereunto set their hands at the city of Washington, this 21st October A. D. 1837.

C. A. Harris.

Sacs or Saukes:
Kee-o-kuck, The Watchful Fox, principal chief of the confederated tribes, Wau-cai-chai, Crooked Sturgeon, a chief, A-shee-au-kon, Sun Fish, a chief, Pa-nau-se, Shedding Elk, Wau-wau-to-sa, Great Walker, Pa-sha-ka-se, The Deer, Appan-oze-o-ke-mar, The Hereditary Chief, (or He who was a Chief when a Child)
Waa-co-me, Clear Water, a chief, Kar-ka-no-we-nar, The Long-horned Elk, Nar-nar-he-keit, the Self-made Man, As-ke-puck-a-wau, The Green Track, Wa-pella, the Prince, a principal chief,
Qua-qua-naa-pe-pua, the Rolling Eyes, a chief, Paa-ka-kar, the Striker, Waa-pa-shar-kon, the White Skin, Wa-pe-mauk, White Lyon, Nar-nar-wau-ke-hait, the Repenter, (or the Sorrowful)
Po-we-sheek, Shedding Bear, a (principal chief), Con-no-ma-co, Long Nose Fox, a chief, (wounded), Waa-co-shaa-shee, Red Nose Fox, a principal chief Fox tribe, (wounded), An-non-e-wit, The Brave Man, Kau-kau-kee, The Crow, Kish-kee-kosh, The Man with one leg off.

Signed in presence of
Chauncey Bush, Secretary.
Joseph M. Street, U. S. Indian Agent.

(To the Indian names are subjoined marks.)

Plains, West and Northwest Plateau Indian Treaties

TREATY WITH THE YANKTON SIOUX {1837, Oct. 21}
Proclamation, Feb. 1838

Articles of a treaty made at the city of Washington, between Carey A. Harris, thereto specially authorized by the President of the United States, and the Yankton tribe of Sioux Indians, by their chief and delegates.

ARTICLE 1. The Yankton tribe of Sioux Indians cede to the United States all the right and interest in the land ceded by the treaty, concluded with them and other tribes on the fifteenth of July, 1830, which they might be entitled to claim, by virtue of the phraseology employed in the second article of said treaty.

ARTICLE 2. In consideration of the cession contained in the preceding article, the United States stipulate to pay them four thousand dollars ($4,000.)

It is understood and agreed, that fifteen hundred dollars ($1,500) of this sum shall be expended in the purchase of horses and presents, upon the arrival of the chiefs and delegates at St. Louis; two thousand dollars ($2,000) delivered to them in goods, at the expense of the United States, at the time their annuities are delivered next year; and five hundred dollars ($500) be applied to defray the expense of removing the agency building and blacksmith shop from their present site.

ARTICLE 3. The expenses of this negotiation, and of the chiefs and delegates signing this treaty to this city and to their homes, to be paid by the United States.

ARTICLE 4. This treaty to be binding upon the contracting parties, when the same shall be ratified by the United States.

In witness whereof, the said Carey A. Harris, and the undersigned chiefs and delegates of said tribe, have hereunto set their hands at the city of Washington, this 21st day of October A. D. 1837.

C. A. Harris.

Ha-sa-za (The Elk's Horn), Mau-ka-ush-can (The Trembling Earth), Ha-sha-ta (The Forked Horn), Mort-to-he (White crane), To-ka-can (He that gives the First Wound)

In presence of
Chauncey Bush, Secretary.
Joshua Pilcher, Indian agent.
W. Thompson.

209

Plains, West and Northwest Plateau Indian Treaties

TREATY WITH THE SAUK AND FOXES {1837, Oct. 21}
Proclamation, Feb. 21, 1838.

Articles of a treaty made at the City of Washington, between Carey A. Harris, thereto specially authorized by the President of the United States, and the Sacs and Foxes of Missouri, by their Chiefs and Delegates.

ARTICLE 1. The Missouri Sac and Fox Indians make the following cessions to the United States:

First. Of all right or interest in the country between the Missouri and Mississippi rivers and the boundary line between the Sac and Fox and the Sioux Indians, described in the second article of the treaty made with these and other tribes on the 19th of August 1825, to the full extent to which said claim was recognized in the third article of said treaty; and of all interest or claim by virtue of the provisions of any treaties since made by the United States with the Sacs and Foxes.

Second. Of all the right to locate, for hunting or other purposes, on the land ceded in the first article of the treaty of July 15th 1830, which, by the authority therein conferred on the President of the United States they may be permitted by him to enjoy.

Third. Of all claims or interest under the treaties of November 3d, 1804, August 4th, 1824, July 15th, 1830, and September 17th, 1836, for the satisfaction of which no appropriations have been made.

ARTICLE 2. In consideration of the cession contained in the preceding article, the United States agree to the following stipulations on their part:

First. To pay to the said Sacs and Foxes of the Missouri, the sum of one hundred and sixty thousand dollars ($160,000.) It is understood and agreed that of the said sum of one hundred and sixty thousand dollars, ($160,000) there shall be expended in the purchase of merchandise to be delivered whenever in the judgment of the President it may be best for them twenty-five hundred dollars, ($2,500;) and there shall be paid to Jacques Mettez, their interpreter, for services rendered, and at their request, one hundred dollars, ($100.)

Second. To invest the balance of said sum amounting to one hundred and fifty-seven thousand four hundred dollars ($157,400) and to guaranty them an annual income of not less than five per cent. thereon.

210

Plains, West and Northwest Plateau Indian Treaties

Third. To apply the interest herein guaranteed, in the following manner:
For the support of a blacksmith's establishment, one thousand dollars ($1,000) per annum.

For the support of a farmer, the supply of agricultural implements and assistance, and other beneficial objects, sixteen hundred dollars ($1,600) per annum. For the support of a teacher and the incidental expenses of a school, seven hundred and seventy dollars ($770) per annum. The balance of the interest, amounting to forty-five hundred dollars ($4,500) shall be delivered at the cost of the United States, to said Sac and Fox Indians, in money or merchandise, at the discretion of the President, and at such time and place as he may direct.

ARTICLE 3. The expenses of this negotiation and of the chiefs and delegates signing this treaty to this city and to their homes to be paid by the United States.

ARTICLE 4. This treaty to be binding upon the contracting parties, when the same shall be ratified by the United States.
In witness whereof, the said Carey A. Harris and the undersigned chiefs and delegates of said tribe, have hereunto set their hands at the city of Washington, this 21st day of October A. D. 1837.

C. A. Harris.

Sacs:
Po-ko-mah (The Plum), Nes-mo-ea (The Wolf), Au-ni-mo-ni (The Sun Fish)

Foxes:
Sa-ka-pa (son of Quash-qua-mi), A-ka-ke (The Crow)

In presence of
Chauncey Bush, Secretary.
Joshua Pilcher, Indian Agent.
W. Thompson.

(To the Indian names are subjoined marks.)

TREATY WITH THE WINNEBAGO {1837, Nov. 1}
Proclamation, June 15, 1838.

Articles of a treaty made at the city of Washington, between Carey A. Harris, thereto specially directed by the President of the United States, and the Winnebago nation of Indians, by their chiefs and delegates.

Plains, West and Northwest Plateau Indian Treaties

ARTICLE 1. THE Winnebago nation of Indians cede to the United States all their land east of the Mississippi river.

ARTICLE 2. The said Indians further agree to relinquish the right to occupy, except for the purpose of hunting a portion of the land held by them west of the Mississippi, included between that river and a line drawn from a point twenty miles distant therefrom on the southern boundary of the neutral ground to a point, equidistant from the said river, on the northern boundary thereof. But this stipulation shall not be so construed, as to invalidate their title to the said tract.

ARTICLE 3. The said Indians agree to remove within eight months from the ratification of this treaty, to that portion of the neutral ground west of the Mississippi, which was conveyed to them in the second article of the treaty of September 15th, (21st) 1832, and the United States agree that the said Indians may hunt upon the western part of said neutral ground until they shall procure a permanent settlement.

ARTICLE 4. In consideration of the cession and relinquishment contained in the preceding articles, the United States agree to the following stipulations on their part.

First. To set apart the sum of two hundred thousand dollars ($200,000) for the following purposes:

To pay to the individuals herein named the sum specified for each; To Nicholas Boilvin, six thousand dollars ($6,000); to the other four children of Nicholas Boilvin, formerly agent for said nation, four thousand dollars ($4,000) each; to Catherine Myott, one thousand dollars, ($1,000); to Hyancinthe St. Cyr one thousand dollars ($1,000); to the widow of-Henry Gratiot, late sub-agent of the nation, in trust for her eight children, ten thousand dollars ($10,000).

To H. L. Dousman, in trust for the children of Pierre Paquette, late interpreter for the nation three thousand dollars ($3,000); to Joseph Brisbois, two thousand dollars ($2,000); to Satterlee Clark, junior, two thousand dollars ($2,000;) to John Roy, two thousand dollars ($2,000); to Antoine Grignon, two thousand dollars ($2,000); to Jane F. Rolette, two thousand dollars ($2,000); to George Fisher, one thousand dollars ($1,000); to Therese Roy, one thousand dollars ($1,000); to Domitille Brisbois, one thousand dollars ($1,000). These sums are allowed, at the earnest solicitation of the chiefs and delegates, for supplies and services to the nation, afforded by these individuals.

The balance of the above sum of two hundred thousand dollars ($200,000) shall be applied to the debts of the nation, which may be ascertained to be justly due, and which may be admitted by the Indians: Provided, That if all their just debts

Plains, West and Northwest Plateau Indian Treaties

shall amount to more than this balance, their creditors shall be paid pro rata, upon their giving receipts in full; and if the just debts shall fall short of said balance, the residue of it shall be invested for the benefit of the nation; And provided, also, That no claim for depredations shall be paid out of said balance.

Second. To may under the direction of the President to the relations and friends of said Indians, having not less than one quarter of Winnebago blood, one hundred thousand dollars ($100,000).

Third. To expend, for their removal to the lands assigned them, a sum not exceeding seven thousand dollars ($7,000).

Fourth. To deliver to the chiefs and delegates on their arrival at St. Louis, goods and horses to the amount of three thousand dollars ($3,000); and, also, to deliver to them, as soon as practicable after the ratification of this treaty, and at the expense of the United States goods to the amount of forty-seven thousand dollars ($47,000).

Fifth. To deliver to them provisions to the amount of ten thousand dollars, ($10,000); and horses to the same amount.

Sixth. To apply to the erection of a grist-mill, three thousand dollars, ($3,000).

Seventh. To expend, in breaking up and fencing in ground, after the removal of the said Indians, ten thousand dollars ($10,000).

Eighth. To set apart the sum of ten thousand dollars ($10,000) to defray contingent and incidental expenses in the execution of this treaty, and the expenses of an exploring party, when the said Indians shall express a willingness to send one to the country southwest of the Missouri river.

Ninth. To invest the balance of the proceeds of the lands ceded in the first article of the treaty, amounting to eleven hundred thousand dollars (1,100,000)and to guaranty to them an interest of not less than five per cent. Of this interest amounting to fifty-five thousand dollars ($55,000) it is agreed the following disposition shall be made; for purposes of education, twenty-eight hundred dollars ($2,800). For the support of an interpreter for the school, five hundred dollars, ($500.)

For the support of a miller, six hundred dollars ($600.)
For the supply of agricultural implements and assistance, five hundred dollars, ($500.)

For medical services and medicines, six hundred dollars ($600.)

Plains, West and Northwest Plateau Indian Treaties

The foregoing sums to be expended for the objects specified, for the term of twenty-two years, and longer at the discretion of the President. If at the expiration of that period, or any time thereafter, he shall think it expedient to discontinue either or all of the above allowances, the amount so discontinued shall be paid to the said Winnebago nation. The residue of the interest, amounting to fifty thousand dollars ($50,000) shall be paid to said nation, in the following manner; Ten thousand dollars ($10,000) in provisions, twenty thousand dollars ($20,000) in goods, and twenty thousand dollars ($20,000) in money.

ARTICLE 5. It is understood and agreed that so much of the stipulations in existing treaties with said Winnebago nation, as requires services to be performed, supplies furnished, or payments made, at designated times and places, shall be henceforth null and void; and those stipulations shall be carried into effect at such times and at such points in the country to which they are about to remove, as the President may direct.

ARTICLE 6. This treaty to be binding on the contracting parties when it shall be ratified by the United States.

In witness whereof, the said Carey A. Harris and the undersigned chiefs and delegates of the said Winnebago nation, have hereunto set their hands at the City of Washington, this first day of November, A. D. 1837.

C. A. Harris.

Watch-hat-ty-kan, (Big Boat), Keesh-kee-pa-kah, (Kar-i-mo-nee), Mo-ra-chay-kah, (Little Priest), Ma-na-pay-kah, (Litt.le Soldier), Wa-kaun-ha-kah, (Snake Skin)

In presence of
Thos. A. B. Boyd, U. S. S. Indian agent, N. Boilvin, Antoine Grinion, Jean Roy, Interpreters, Joseph Moore, J. Brisbois, Sat. Clark, jr., Conductors, Alexis Bailly.

(To the Indian names are subjoined a mark.)

TREATY WITH THE IOWA {1837, Nov. 23}
Proclamation, Feb. 21, 1838.

Articles of a treaty made at the city of Saint Louis, between Joshua Pilcher, thereto specially authorized by the President of the United States, and the Ioway Indians, by their chiefs and delegates.

Plains, West and Northwest Plateau Indian Treaties

ARTICLE 1. THE Ioway Indians cede to the United States all the right and interest in the land ceded by the treaty, concluded with-them and other tribes on the 15th of July 1830, which they might be entitled to claim, by virtue of the phraseology employed in the second article of said treaty.

ARTICLE 2. In consideration of the cession contained in the preceding article, the United States stipulate to pay them two thousand five hundred dollars ($2,500) in horses, goods and presents, upon their signing this treaty in the city of Saint Louis.

ARTICLE 3. The expenses of this negotiation and of the chiefs and delegates signing this treaty to the city of Washington and to their homes to be paid by the United States.

ARTICLE 4. This treaty to be binding upon the contracting parties when the same shall be ratified by the United States.

In witness whereof the said Joshua Pilcher and the undersigned chiefs and delegates of said Indians have hereunto set their hands at the city of Saint Louis, this twenty-third day of November A. D. 1837.

Joshua Pilcher, U. S. Indian agent.

Ne-o-mon-ni, Non-che-ning-ga, Wat-che-mon-ne, Tah-ro-hon.

Signed in presence of
E. A. Hitchcock, Captain U. S. Army
John B Farpy.
L. G. C. Bliss.

(To the Indian names are subjoined marks.)

TREATY WITH THE ONEIDA {1838, Feb. 3}
Proclamation, May 17, 1838.

Articles of a treaty made at the City of Washington between Carey A. Harris, thereto specially directed by the President of the United States and the First Christian and Orchard parties of the Oneida Indians residing at Green Bay, by their chiefs and representatives.

ARTICLE 1. The First Christian and Orchard parties of Indians cede to the United States all their title and interest in the land set apart for them in the 1st article of the treaty with the Menomonies of February 8th, 1831, and the 2d article of the treaty with the same tribe of October 27th, 1832.

215

Plains, West and Northwest Plateau Indian Treaties

ARTICLE 2. From the foregoing cession there shall be reserved to the said Indians to be held as other Indian lands are held a tract of land containing one hundred (100) acres, for each individual, and the lines of which shall be so run as to include all their settlements and improvements in the vicinity of Green Bay.

ARTICLE 3. In consideration Of the cession contained in the 1st article of this treaty, the United States agree to pay to the Orchard party of the Oneida Indians three thousand (3000) dollars, and to the First Christian party of Oneida Indians thirty thousand five hundred (30,500) dollars, of which last sum three thousand (3,000) dollars may be expended under the supervision of the Rev. Solomon Davis, in the erection of a church and parsonage house, and the residue apportioned, under the direction of the President among the persons having just claims thereto; it being understood that said aggregate sum of thirty-three thousand five hundred (33,500) dollars is designed to be in reimbursement of monies expended by said Indians and in remuneration of the services of their chiefs and agents in purchasing and securing a title to the land ceded in the 1st article. The United States further agree to cause the tracts reserved in the 2d article to be surveyed as soon as practicable.

ARTICLE 4. In consideration of the sum of live hundred (500) dollars to be paid to him by the chiefs and representatives of the said parties of Oneida Indians, John Denny (alias John Sundown) their interpreter agrees to relinquish to them all his title and interest in the tract reserved in the 2d article of this treaty.

ARTICLE 5. It is understood and agreed that the expenses of this treaty and of the chiefs and representatives signing it, in coming to and returning from this city, and while here, shall be paid by the United States.

ARTICLE 6. This treaty to be binding upon the contracting parties when the same shall be ratified by the United States.

In witness whereof, the said Carey A. Harris and the undersigned chiefs and representatives of the said parties of Oneida Indians have hereunto set their hands at the City of Washington, this third day of February 1838.

C. A. Harris.

First Christians:
Henry Powles, John Denny, alias John Sundown, Adam Swamp, Daniel Bread.

Orchard:
Jacob Cornelius.

Plains, West and Northwest Plateau Indian Treaties

In presence of
Geo. W, Jones, Delegate Wisconsin Territory, Solomon Davis, Alfred Iverson.
O. S. Hall.

(To the Indian names are subjoined marks.)

TREATY WITH THE IOWA {1838, Oct. 19}
Proclamation, Mar. 2, 1839.

Articles of a treaty made at the Great Nemowhaw sub-agency between John Dourberry Agent of Indian Affairs on the part of the United States, being specially authorized, and the chiefs and headmen of the Ioway tribe of Indians for themselves, and on the part of their tribe.

ARTICLE 1. The Ioway tribe of Indians cede to the United States, First. All right or interest in the country between the Missouri and Mississippi rivers, and the boundary between the Sacs and Foxes, and Sioux, described in the second article of the treaty made with these and other tribes, on the 19th of August 1825, to the full extent to which said claim is recognized in the third article of said treaty, and all interest or claim by virtue of the provisions of any treaties since made by the United States with the Sacs and Foxes of the Mississippi.

Second. All claims or interest under the treaties of August 4th 1824, July 15th 1830, and September 17th 1836, except so much of the last mentioned treaty as secures to them two hundred sections of land the erection of five comfortable houses, to enclose and break up for them two hundred acres of ground to furnish them with a ferry boat, one hundred cows and calves, five bulls, one hundred head of stock hogs a mill and interpreter.

ARTICLE 2. In consideration of the cession contained in the preceding article, the United States agree to the following stipulations on their part.

First. To pay to the said Ioway tribe of Indians the sum of one hundred and fifty-seven thousand five hundred ($157,500) dollars.

Second. To invest said sum of one hundred and fifty-seven thousand five hundred (157,500)dollars, and to guaranty them an annual income of not less than five per cent. thereon during the existence of their tribe.

Third. To set apart annually such amount of said income as the chiefs and headmen of said tribe may require, for the support of a blacksmith shop agricultural assistance, and education to be expended under the direction of the President of the United States.

Plains, West and Northwest Plateau Indian Treaties

Fourth. To pay out of said income to Jeffrey Derroin interpreter for said tribe for services rendered, the sum of fifty dollars annually during his natural life the balance of said income shall be delivered, at the cost of the United States, to said tribe of Ioway Indians in money or merchandise, at their own discretion, at such time and place as the President may direct, Provided always That the payment shall be made each year in the month of October.

ARTICLE 3. The United States further agree in addition to the above consideration to cause to be erected ten houses at such place or places on their own land as said Ioways may select, of the following description (viz) each house to be ten feet high from bottom sill to top plate eighteen by twenty feet in the clear the roof to be well sheeted and shingled, the gable ends to be weather boarded a good floor above and below, one door and two windows complete, one chimney of stone or brick, and the whole house to be underpined.

ARTICLE 4. This treaty to be binding upon the contracting parties when the same shall be ratified by the United States.

In witness whereof the said John Dougherty agent of Indian affairs and the undersigned chiefs and headmen of the Ioway tribe of Indians have hereunto set their hands this 19th day of October A. D. 1838.

Jno. Dougherty, Indian Agent.

Frank White Cloud, Non-gee-ninga, or No Heart, Kon-gee, or the Plum, Mock Shig a ton-ah, or the Great Man, Wah nun gua schoo ny, or He that has no Fear, Seenah ty yaa, or the Blistered Foot, Rahno way ing ga, or Little Pipe, Thraw ing ga, or Little War Eagle, Pak she ing ga, or the Cocked Nose, O yaw tche a, or Heard to Load, Ro to gra zey, or Speckled Rib, Mah za, or the Iron, Ta-ro-hah, or Pile of Meat.

TREATY WITH THE STOCKBRIDGE AND MUNSEE {1839, Sept. 3} Proclamation; May 16, 1840.

Articles of a treaty made at Stockbridge in the Territory of Wisconsin, on the third day of September in the year of our Lord one thousand eight hundred and thirty-nine, between the United States of America, by their commissioner Albert Gallup, and the Stockbridge and Munsee tribes of Indians, who reside upon Lake Winnebago in the territory of Wisconsin.

ARTICLE 1. The Stockbridge and Munsee tribes of Indians (formerly of New York) hereby cede and relinquish to the United States, the east half of the tract of forty-six thousand and eighty acres of land, which was laid off for their use, on the east side of Lake Winnebago, in pursuance of the treaty made by George

Plains, West and Northwest Plateau Indian Treaties

B. Porter commissioner on the part of the United States; and the Menominee nation of Indians, on the twenty-seventh day of October eighteen hundred and thirty-two. The said east half hereby ceded, to contain twenty-three thousand and forty acres of land; to be of equal width at the north and south ends, and to be divided from the west half of said tract of forty-six thousand and eighty acres, by a line to be run parallel to the east line of said tract. The United States to pay therefor, one dollar per acre at the time and in the manner hereinafter provided.

ARTICLE 2. Whereas a portion of said tribes, according to a census or roll taken, and hereunto annexed, are desirous to remove west and the others to remain where they now are; and whereas the just proportion of the emigrating party in the whole tract of forty-six thousand and eighty acres is eight thousand seven hundred and sixty-seven and three-fourths acres of land; it is agreed that the United States pay to the said emigrating party, the sum of eight thousand seven hundred and sixty-seven dollars and seventy-five cents, as a full compensation for all their interest in the lands held by the party who remain, as well as in the lands hereby ceded to the United States.

ARTICLE 3. Whereas the improvements of the emigrating party are all on that part of the original tract which is reserved and still held by the party who remain in Stockbridge, and it is but equitable that those who remain should pay those who emigrate for such improvements; it is agreed that the United States shall pay to the emigrating party the sum of three thousand eight hundred and seventy-nine dollars and thirty cents, the appraised value of said improvements; and it is hereby agreed and expressly understood, that the monies payable to the emigrating party shall be distributed among the heads of families according to the schedule hereunto annexed, the whole amount to be paid to the emigrating party under this and the preceding article being the sum of twelve thousand six hundred and forty-seven dollars and five cents.

ARTICLE 4. The balance of the consideration money for the lands hereby ceded, (after deducting the sums mentioned in the second and third articles) amounting to the sum of ten thousand three hundred and ninety-two dollars and ninety-five cents, is to be paid to, and invested for the benefit of such of the Stockbridge and Munsee tribes of Indians (numbering three hundred and forty-two souls) as remain at their present place of residence at Stockbridge on the east side Of Winnebago lake, as follows. Six thousand dollars of said sum to be invested by the United States in public stocks at an interest of not less than five per cent. per annum as a permanent school fund; the interest of which shall be paid annually to the sachem and counsellors of their tribes, or such other person as they may appoint to receive the same, whose receipt shall be a sufficient voucher therefor; and the balance thereof amounting to four thousand three hundred and ninety-two dollars and ninety-five cents, shall be paid to the said

Plains, West and Northwest Plateau Indian Treaties

sachem and counsellors, or to such person as they may appoint to receive the same, whose receipt shall be a sufficient voucher therefor.

ARTICLE 5. The monies herein secured to be paid by the United States to the Stockbridge and Munsee tribes amounting in all to twenty-three thousand and forty dollars, are to be paid in manner aforesaid, in one year from the date hereof, or sooner if practicable.

ARTICLE 6. It is agreed that an exploring party not exceeding three in number may visit the country west, if the Indians shall consider it necessary, and that whenever those who are desirous of emigrating shall signify their wish to that effect, the United States will defray the expenses of their removal west of the Mississippi and furnish them with subsistence for one year after their arrival at their new homes. The expenses of the exploring party to be borne by the emigrants.

ARTICLE 7. Whereas there are certain unliquidated claims and accounts existing between the emigrating party, and those who remain where they now are, which it is now impossible to liquidate and adjust; it is hereby agreed that the same shall be submitted to the agent of the United States who shall be appointed to make the payments under this treaty, and that his decision shall be final thereon.

In witness whereof we have hereunto set our hands and seals this third day of September in the year of our Lord one thousand eight hundred and thirty-nine.

Albert Gallup, Commissioner on the part of the United States.

Austin E. Quinny, Sachem, Thomas T. Hendrick, John Metoxen, Jacob Chicks, Robert Konkapot, Captain Porter, Munsee chief, James Rain, Munsee war chief.

Stockbridges:
Timothy Jourdan, Benjamin Palmer, Jno. N. Chicks, Jno. W. Quinney, John P. Quinney, John W. Newcom, Thomas S. Branch, Levi Konkapot, John Littlemon, Peter Sherman, J. L. Chicks.

Munsee:
John Killsnake.

Stockbridges:
Jeremiah Singerland, Jonas Thompson, Eli Hendrick, Elisha Konkapot, Henry Skicket, Simon S. Metoxen, Samuel Miller, Gerret Thompson, Daniel David, Ziba T. Peters, Simeon Konkapot, David Abrams, Jonas Konkapot, David Calvin, Benjamin Pye, sen.
Aaron Ninham.

Plains, West and Northwest Plateau Indian Treaties

Signed and sealed in presence
A. S. Kellogg, Cutting Marsh, Clark Whitney, John Deen, John Wilber.

(To the Indian names are subjoined a mark and seal.)

Roll and schedule referred to in articles two and three of the treaty hereunto annexed.

Done in presence of
Anthony L. Davis, Indian sub-agent.
Vance M. Campbell.

(To the Indian names are subjoined marks.)

TREATY WITH THE SAUK AND FOXES {1842, Oct. 11}
Proclamation, Mar, 23, 1843.

Articles of a treaty made and concluded at the agency of the Sac and Fox Indians, in the Territory of Iowa, between the United States of America, by John Chambers their commissioner thereto specially authorized by the President, and the confederated tribes of Sac and Fox Indians represented by their chiefs, headmen and braves:

ARTICLE 1. THE confederated tribes of Sacs and Foxes cede to the United States, forever, all the lands west of the Mississippi river, to which they have any claim or title, or in which they have any interest whatever; reserving a right to occupy for the term of three years from the time of signing this treaty, all that part of the land hereby ceded which lies west of a line running due north and south from the painted or red rocks on the White Breast fork of the Des Moines river, which rocks will be found about eight miles, when reduced to a straight line, from the junction of the White Breast with the Des Moines.

ARTICLE 2. In consideration of the cession contained in the preceding article, the United States agree to pay annually to the Sacs and Foxes, an interest of five per centum upon the sum of eight hundred thousand dollars, and to pay their debts mentioned in the schedule annexed to and made part of this treaty, amounting to the sum of two hundred and fifty-eight thousand, five hundred and sixty-six dollars and thirty-four cents; and the United States also agree,
First. That the President will as soon after this treaty is ratified on their part as may be convenient, assign a tract of land suitable and convenient for Indian purposes, to the Sacs and Foxes for a permanent and perpetual residence for them and their descendants, which tract of land shall be upon the Missouri river, or some of its waters.

Plains, West and Northwest Plateau Indian Treaties

Second. That the United States will cause the blacksmiths and gunsmiths' tools, with the stock of iron and steel on hand at the present agency of the Sacs and Foxes, to be removed, as soon after their removal as convenient, to some suitable point at or near their residences west of the north and south line mentioned in the first article of this treaty; and will establish and maintain two blacksmiths and two gunsmiths' shops convenient to their agency, and will employ two blacksmiths, with necessary assistance, and two gunsmiths to carry on the said shops for the benefit of the Sacs and Foxes; one blacksmiths and one gunsmiths' shop to be employed exclusively for the Sacs, and one of each to be employed exclusively for the Foxes, and all expenses attending the removal of the tools, iron and steel, and the erection of new shops, and the purchase of iron and steel, and the support and maintenance of the shops, and wages of the smiths and their assistants, are to be paid by the tribe, except such portion thereof as they are now entitled to have paid by the United States, under the 4th article of the treaty made with them on the 4th of August 1824, and the 4th article of the treaty of the 21st of September t832.

And When the said tribes shall remove to the land to be assigned them by the President of the United States, under the provisions of this treaty, the smiths' shops above stipulated for shall be re-established and maintained at their new residence, upon the same terms and conditions as are above provided for their removal and establishment west of the north and south line mentioned in the first article of this treaty.

Third. That the President of the United States will as soon as convenient after the ratification of this treaty, appoint a commissioner for the purpose, and cause a line to be run north from the painted or red rocks on the White Breast, to the southern boundary of the neutral ground, and south from the said rocks to the northern boundary of Missouri; and will have the said lines so marked and designated, that the Indians and white people may know the boundary which is to separate their possessions.

ARTICLE 3. The Sacs and Foxes agree that they will remove to the west side of the line running north and south from the painted or red rocks on the White Breast, on or before the first of May next, and that so soon after the President shall have assigned them a residence upon the waters of the Missouri, as their chiefs shall consent to do so, the tribe will remove to the land so assigned them; and that if they do not remove before the expiration of the term of three years, they will then remove at their own expense; and the United States agree, that whenever the chiefs shall give notice to the Commissioner of Indian Affairs of the time at which they will commence their removal to the land to be assigned them by the President, a quantity of provisions sufficient for their subsistence while removing, shall be furnished them at their agency, and an additional quantity, not exceeding one years supply shall be delivered to them upon their

Plains, West and Northwest Plateau Indian Treaties

arrival upon the lands assigned them; the cost and expenses of which supplies shall be retained out of any money payable to them by the United States.

ARTICLE 4. It is agreed that each of the principal chiefs of the Sacs and Foxes, shall hereafter receive the sum of five hundred dollars annually, out of the annuities payable to the tribe, to be used and expended by them for such purposes as they may think proper, with the approbation of their agent.

ARTICLE 5. It is further agreed that there shall be a fund amounting to thirty thousand dollars retained at each annual payment to the Sacs and Foxes, in the hands of the agent appointed by the President for their tribe, to be expended by the chiefs, with the approbation of the agent, for national and charitable purposes among their people; such as the support of their poor, burying their dead, employing physicians for the sick, procuring provisions for their people in cases of necessity, and such other purposes of general utility as the chiefs may think proper, and the agent approve. And if at any payment of the annuities of the tribe, a balance of the fund so retained from the preceding year shall remain unexpended, only so much shall be retained in addition as will make up the sum of thirty thousand dollars.

ARTICLE 6. It is further agreed that the Sacs and Foxes may, at any time, with the consent of the President of the United States, direct the application of any portion of the annuities payable to them, under this or any former treaty, to the purchase of goods or provisions, or to agricultural purposes, or any other object tending to their improvement, or calculated to increase the comfort and happiness of their people.

ARTICLE 7. The United States agree, that the unexpended balance of the fund created by the seventh paragraph of the second article of the treaty of the twenty-first of October, 1837, for agricultural purposes, or so much thereof as may be necessary, shall be used and employed in the cultivation of the, pattern farm near the present Sac and Fox agency, in the year 1843, for the exclusive use and benefit of the tribe. And they further agree, that such portion of the fund for erecting mills, and supporting millers, specified in the fourth paragraph of the second article of the aforesaid treaty of October 21st, 1837, as may be and remain unexpended on the 1st day of May next, shall be transferred to and made part of the sum designated in the fifth paragraph (as amended) of the article and treaty above named, for breaking up land and other beneficial objects, and become thereafter applicable to the same purposes, as were in the said fifth paragraph, originally intended.

ARTICLE 8. The Sacs and Foxes have caused the remains of their late distinguished chief Wa-pel-lo to be buried at their agency, near the grave of their late friend and agent General Joseph M. Street, and have put into the hands of their agent the sum of one hundred dollars to procure a tombstone to be erected over

223

Plains, West and Northwest Plateau Indian Treaties

his grave, similar to that which has been erected over the grave of General Street; and because they wish the graves of their friend and their chief to remain in the possession of the family of General Street, to whom they were indebted in his life-time for many acts of kindness, they wish to give to his widow Mrs. Eliza M. Street one section of land to include the said graves, and the agency-house and enclosures around and near it; and as the agency house was built at the expense of the United States, the Sacs and Foxes agree to pay them the sum of one thousand dollars the value of said building, assessed by gentlemen appointed by them, and Governor Chambers commissioner on the part of the United States, to be deducted from the first annuity payable to them under the provisions of this treaty.

And the United States agree to grant to the said Eliza M. Street by one or more patents, six hundred and forty acres of land in such legal subdivisions, as will include the said burial ground, the agency house, and improvements around, and near it, in good and convenient form, to be selected by the said E. M. Street or her duly authorized agent.

ARTICLE 9. It is finally agreed that this treaty shall be binding on the two contracting parties, so soon as it shall have been ratified by the President and Senate of the United States: Provided always, That should the Senate disagree to and reject, alter or amend any portion or stipulation thereof, the same must be again submitted to the Sacs and Foxes, and assented to by them, before it shall be considered valid and obligatory upon them, and if they disagree to such alteration or amendment, the treaty shall be returned to the Senate for ratification or rejection, in the form in which it was signed.

In witness whereof, the said John Chambers, commissioner on the part of the United States, and the undersigned chiefs, braves, and headmen of the Sac and Fox nation of Indians, have hereunto set their hands, at the Sac and Fox agency, in the Territory of Iowa, this eleventh day of October, Anno Domini one thousand eight hundred and forty-two.

John Chambers.

Sacs:
Ke o kuk, Ke o kuk, Jr., Wa ca cha, Che kaw que, Ka pon e ka, Pa me kow art, Ap pe noose, Wa pe, Wa sa men, Wis ko pe, As ke po ka won,
Foxes:
Pow a shick, Wa co sha she, An au e wit, Ka ka ke, Ma wha why, Ma che na ka me quat, Ka ka ke too, Kish ka naqua hok, Pea tau a quis, Ma ne ni sit, Mai con ne, I o nah, Wish e co ma que, Pash e pa ho, Ka pe koma, Tuk quos, Wis co sa, Ka kon we na, Na cote e we na, Sho wake, Mean ai to wa, Muk e ne
Pe she she lnone, Pe shaw koa, Puck aw koa, Qua co hose, Wa pasha kon, Kis ke kosh, Ale mo ne qua, Cha ko kow a, Wah ke mo wa ta pa,

Plains, West and Northwest Plateau Indian Treaties

Signed in presence of
John Beach, U. S. Indian agent and secretary.
Josiah Swart, U. S. interpreter.
J. Allen, captain, First Dragoons.

(To the Indian names are subjoined marks.)

Schedule of debts due from the confederated tribes of the Sac and Fox Indians to be paid by the United States under the provisions of a treaty made and concluded at the Sac and Fox agency in the Territory of Iowa on the eleventh day of October in the year 1842; to which this schedule is annexed as a part thereof.

Name of claimant. Place of residence. Amount.
Pierre Chouteau, jr. & Co   St. Louis, Missouri, licensed traders
    $112,109.47
W. G. & G. W. Erving   Indiana, do,do   66,371.83
J. P. Eddy & Co   Ioway, do, do   52,332.78
Thomas Charlton   Van Buren c'ty, Ioway   76.69
R. B. Willoughby   Dodo   25.00
Francis Withington Lincoln county, Missouri   4,212.58
Jesse B. Webber   Burlington, Ioway 116.60
J. C. Wear   Jefferson county, Ioway   50.00
W. C. Cameron, assignee of A. M. Bissel (bankrupt)   Burlington
    283.14
David Bailey   Lincoln c'ty, Missouri   75.00
Thomas W. Bradley   Ioway   20.00
John J. Grimes   Lincoln c'ty, Missouri   625.00
William Settles   Do, do   320.00
John S. David   Burlington, Ioway 20.00
F. Hancock   Van Buren, do   20.00
C. G. Pelton   Burlington, do   34.00
J. TolmanVan Buren, do   115.00
J. L. Burtiss   Lee county, do   715.00
Isaac A. Lefevre   Van Buren, do   348.00
Jeremiah Smith, jr Burlington, do   4,000.00
William & Sampson Smith   Jefferson county, do   60.00
John Koontz   6.50
Robert Moffet   New Lexington, Ioway   129.63
Antoine Leclair   Davenport, do   1,375.00
Margaret Price   Lee county, do   9.00
Jesse Sutton   Van Buren, do   22.00
Jefferson Jordon   Do , do   175.00
Jeremiah Wayland St. Francisville, Missouri   15.00

Plains, West and Northwest Plateau Indian Treaties

Robert Brown, assignee of Cutting & Gordon.   Van Buren c'ty, Ioway
    73.25
William Rowland Do, do   460.32
Edward Kilbourne Lee county, do   10,411.80
Perry & Best   Do   22.75
P. Chouteau, jr. & Co   St. Louis, Missouri 26.00
Job Garter   Van Buren c'ty   28.00
Francis Bosseron St. Louis, Mo   26.00
James Jordon   Van Buren, Ioway 1,775.00
Sampson Smith   do   54.00
Louis Laplant   Ioway   122.00
William Phelps   Clark county, Missouri   310.00
William B. Street Ioway   300.00
Julia Ann Goodell Do   855.00
George L. Davenport   Davenport, Ioway 320.00
G. C. R. Mitchell Do, do   100.00
David Noggle   Van Buren, do   20.00

Amount $258,566.34
John Chambers, Commissioner on the part of the U. S.
Alfred Hebard, Arthur Bridgman, Commissioners appointed by the commission on the part of the U. S. for examining and adjusting claims.

TREATY WITH KANSAS TRIBE {1846, Jan. 14}
Ratified Apr. 13, 1846.
Proclaimed, Apr. 15, 1846.

Articles of a treaty made and concluded at the Methodist Mission, in the Kansas country, between Thomas H. Harvey and Richard W. Cummins, commissioners of the United States, and the Kansas tribe of Indians.

ARTICLE 1. The Kansas tribe of Indians cede to the United States two millions of acres of land on the east part of their country, embracing the entire width, thirty miles, and running west for quantity.

ARTICLE 2. In consideration of the foregoing cession, the United States agree to pay to the Kansas Indians two hundred and two thousand dollars, two hundred thousand of which shall be funded at five per cent, the interest of which to be paid annually for thirty years, and thereafter to be diminished and paid pro rata, should their numbers decrease, but not otherwisethat is: the Government of the United States shall pay them the full interest for thirty years on the amount funded, and at the end of that time, should the Kansas tribe be less than at the first payment, they are only to receive pro rata the sums paid them at the first annuity payment.

Plains, West and Northwest Plateau Indian Treaties

One thousand dollars of the interest thus accruing shall be applied annually to the purposes of education in their own country; one thousand dollars annually for agricultural assistance, implements, &c.; but should the Kansas Indians at any time be so far advanced in agriculture as to render the expenditure for agricultural assistance unnecessary, then the one thousand dollars above provided for that purpose shall be paid them in money with the balance of their annuity; the balance, eight thousand dollars, shall be paid them annually in their own country.

The two thousand dollars not to be funded shall be expended in the following manner: first, the necessary expenses in negotiating this treaty; second, four hundred dollars shall be paid to the Missionary Society of the Methodist Episcopal Church for their improvements on the land ceded in the first article; third, six hundred dollars shall be applied to the erection of a mill in the country in which the Kansas shall settle for their use, it being in consideration of their mill on the land ceded in the first article. The balance to be placed in the hands of their agent, as soon after the ratification of this treaty as practicable, for the purpose of furnishing the said Kansas Indians with provisions for the present year.

ARTICLE 3. In order that the Kansas Indians may know the west line of the land which they have ceded by this treaty, it is agreed that the United States shall, as soon as may be convenient in the present year, cause the said line to be ascertained and marked by competent surveyors.

ARTICLE 4. The Kansas Indians are to move from the lands ceded to the United States, by the first article of this treaty, by the first day of May, 1847.

ARTICLE 5. As doubts exist whether there is a sufficiency of timber on the land remaining to the Kansas, after taking off the land ceded in the first article of this treaty, it is agreed by the contracting parties, that after the western line of the said cession shall be ascertained, (and) the President of the United States shall be satisfied that there is not a sufficiency of timber, he shall cause to be selected and laid off for the Kansas a suitable country, near the western boundary of the land ceded by this treaty, which shall remain for their use forever. In consideration of which, the Kansas nation cede to the United States the balance of the reservation under the treaty of June 3, 1825, and not ceded in the first article of this treaty.

ARTICLE 6. in consideration of the great distance which the Kansas Indians will be removed from the white settlements and their present agent, and their exposure to difficulties with other Indian tribes, it is agreed that the United States shall cause to reside among the Kansas Indians a sub-agent, who shall be especially charged with the direction of their farming operations, and general

Plains, West and Northwest Plateau Indian Treaties

improvement, and to be continued as long as the President of the United States should consider it advantageous to the Kansas.

ARTICLE 7. Should the Government of the United States be of opinion that the Kansas Indians are not entitled to a smith under the fourth article of the treaty of June 3, 1825, it is agreed that a smith shall be supported out of the one thousand dollars provided in the fourth article for agricultural purposes.
In testimony whereof, Thomas H. Harvey and Richard W. Cummins, Commissioners, (and) the Chiefs and Principal Men of the Kansas tribe of Indians have, this the 14th day of January one thousand eight hundred and forty-six, set their hands and seals at the Methodist Kansas Mission.

Th. H. Harvey, Rich. W. Cummins, Commissioners.

Ki-hi-ga-wah-chuffe, or Hard Chief, Me-cho-shin-gah, or Broken Thigh, Pi-is-cah-cah, Ish-tal-a-sa, or Speckled Eyes, Mah-gah-ha, Shin-gah-ki-hi-ga, Ca-ho-nah-she, Wa-shon-ge-ra, Ne-qui-bra, Ke-bucco-mah-e,
No-pa-war-ra, Was-sol-ba-shinga, Ke-hi-ga-wat-ti-in-ga, Big-no-years, Wah-pug-ja, Ah-ke-is-tah, Chi-ki-cah-rah, Ke-hah-ga-ch a-wah-go, Wah-hah-hah.

Witnesses:
James M. Simpson, secretary, Clement Lesserrs, interpreter, John T. Peery, John D. Clark, Chs. Choteau, Seth M. Hays, Nelson Henrys, R. M. Parrett.

(To the names of the Indians are added their marks.)

TREATY WITH THE COMANCHE, AIONAI, ANADARKO, CADDO, ETC. {1846, May 15}
Proclamation, Mar. 8, 1847.

Treaty with the Comanche, and other tribes. Articles of a treaty made and concluded at Council Springs, in the county of Robinson, Texas, near the Brazos River, this 15th day of May, A. D. 1846, between P. M. Butler and M. G. Lewis, commissioners on the part of the United States, of the one part, and the undersigned chiefs, counsellors, and Warriors of the Comanche, I-on-i, Ana-da-ca, Cadoe, Lepan, Long-wha, Keehy, Tah-wa-carro, Wichita, and Wacoe tribes of Indians, and their associate bands, in behalf of their said tribes on the other part.

ARTICLE 1. The undersigned chiefs, warriors, and counsellors, for themselves and their said tribes or nations, do hereby acknowledge themselves to be under the protection of the United States, and of no other power, state, or sovereignty whatever.

Plains, West and Northwest Plateau Indian Treaties

ARTICLE 2. It is stipulated and agreed by the said tribes or nations, and their associate bands, that the United States shall have the sole and exclusive right of regulating trade and intercourse with them, and they do hereby respectively engage to afford protection to such persons, with their property, as shall be duly licensed to reside among them for the purpose of trade and intercourse, and to their agents and servants, but no person shall be permitted to reside among them as a trader who is not furnished with a license for that purpose, under the hand and seal of the superintendent to be appointed by the President of the United States or such other person as the President shall authorize to grant such licenses, to the end that said Indians may not be imposed on in their trade; and if any licensed trader shall abuse his privilege by unfair dealing, upon complaint by the chiefs to their agents and proof thereof, his license shall be taken from him, and he shall be further punished according to the laws of the United States; and if any person shall intrude himself as a trader without such license, upon complaint he shall be dealt with according to law.

ARTICLE 3. (Stricken out.)

ARTICLE 4. The said tribes and their associate bands agree to deliver, by the first day of November next, to the superintendent of Indian affairs to be appointed by the President, at such place as he may direct, due notice of which shall be given to the said tribes, all white persons and negroes who are now prisoners among any of the said tribes or nations, for which the United States agree to make them a fair compensation; and the United States further agree to make (that) all the prisoners taken from said tribes by Texas or the United States, shall be delivered up to the said tribes, at the same time and place, without charge. And when any member of any of said tribes or nations, and their associate bands, having in his possession an American prisoner or prisoners, white or black, shall refuse to give them up, the President of the United States shall have the privilege of sending among said tribes or nations such force as he may think necessary to take them; and the chiefs of the nations or tribes, parties to this treaty, pledge themselves to give protection and assistance to such persons as may be sent among them for this purpose.

ARTICLE 5. (Stricken out.)

ARTICLE 6. The said tribes and their associate bands pledge themselves to give notice to the agent of the United States residing near them of any designs which they may know or suspect to (be) formed in any neighboring tribe, or by any person whatever, against the peace and interests of the United States.

ARTICLE 7. It is agreed that, if any Indian or Indians shall commit a murder or robbery on any citizen of the United States, the tribe or nation to which the offender belongs shall deliver up the person or persons so complained of, on complaint being made to their chief, to the nearest post of the United States, to

Plains, West and Northwest Plateau Indian Treaties

the end that he or they may be tried, and, if found guilty, punished, according to the law of the State or Territory where such offence may have been committed. In like manner, if any subject or citizen of the United States shall commit murder or robbery on any Indian or Indians of the said tribes or nations, upon complaint thereof to the agent residing near them, he or they shall be arrested, tried, and punished according to the law of the State or Territory where such offence may have been committed.

ARTICLE 8. The practice of stealing horses has prevailed very much to the great disquiet of the citizens of the United States, and, if per, slated in, cannot fail to involve both the United States and the Indians in endless strife. It is therefore agreed that it shall be put an entire stop to on both sides. Nevertheless, should bad men, in defiance of this agreement, continue to make depredations of that nature, the person convicted thereof shall be punished with the utmost severity, according to the laws of the State or Territory where the offence may have been committed; and all horses so stolen, either by the Indians from the citizens of the United States or by the citizens of the United States from any of the said tribes or nations, into whose possession soever they may have passed, upon due proof of rightful ownership, shall be restored; and the chiefs of said tribes or nations shall give all necessary aid and protection to citizens of the United States in reclaiming and recovering such stolen horses; and the civil magistrates of the United States, respectively, shall give all necessary aid and protection to Indians in claiming and recovering such stolen horses.

ARTICLE 9. For the protection of said Indians and for the purpose of carrying out the stipulations of this treaty more effectually, the President shall, at his discretion, locate upon their borders trading-houses, agencies, and posts. In consideration of the friendly disposition of said tribes, evidenced by the stipulations in the present treaty, the commissioners of the United States, in behalf of the said States, agree to give to the said tribes or nations goods, as presents, at this time, and agree to give presents in goods to them, to the amount of ten thousand dollars, at such time as the President of the United States may think proper, at the Council Springs, on the Brazos, where this council is now held, or at some other point to be designated, and of which due notice shall be given to said tribes.

ARTICLE 10. The said tribes or nations and their associate bands are now, and forever agree to remain, at peace with the United States. All animosities for past offences are hereby mutually forgiven and forgotten, and the parties to this treaty pledge themselves to carry it into full execution, in good faith and sincerity.

ARTICLE 11. And the said tribes and their associate bands are now, and agree to remain, friendly with such tribes as are now at peace with the United States, residing upon the waters of the Arkansas, Missouri, and Red Rivers.

230

Plains, West and Northwest Plateau Indian Treaties

ARTICLE 12. If any person or persons shall introduce ardent spirits or intoxicating liquors of any kind among said tribes or nations, such person or person (persons) shall be punished according to the laws of the United States, and the said tribes or nations agree to give immediate notice to the agent of the United States residing near them, and to prevent by any means in their power the violation of this article of treaty.

ARTICLE 13. It is further agreed that blacksmiths shall be sent to reside among the said tribes or nations, to keep their guns and farming-utensils in order, as long and in such manner as the President may think proper. It is further agreed that school-teachers, at the discretion of the President, shall be sent among the said tribes or nations for the purpose of instructing them; and the said tribes or nations agree that preachers of the gospel may travel or reside among them by permission of the President or his agents to be appointed, and that ample protection shall be afforded them in the discharge of their duties.

ARTICLE 14. The said tribes or nations, parties to this treaty, are anxious to be at peace with all other tribes or nations, and it is agreed that the President shall use his exertions, in such manner as he may think proper, to preserve friendly relations between the different tribes or nations parties to this treaty, and all other tribes of Indians under his jurisdiction.

Given under our hands and sells this day and date above.

P.M. Butler, M. G. Lewis, U. S. Commissioners.

Comanches:
Pah-ha-u-ca, (or the Amorous Man), Mo-pe-chu-co-pe, (or Old Owl), Cush-un-a-rah-ah, (or Ravisher), Ka-bah-ha-moo, (or Won't Smoke), O-ka-art-su, (or Rope Cutter), Moo-ra-que-top, (or Nasty Mule), Ta-bup-pua-ta, (or the Winner), Kai-tia-tah, (or Little), Kai-he-na-mou-rah, (Blind Man), Ho-chu-cah, (Birdshouse), Pah-moo-wah-tah, (No Tobacco), Mon-ne-con-nah-heh, (Ring), Po-che-na-qua-heip, (Buffalo Hump), Santa Anna, Sa-ba-heit, (Small Wolf), Quarah-ha-po-e, (Atelope Road), Ka-nah-u-mah-ka, (Nearly Dead, Ish-a-me-a-qui, (Travelling Wolf), Mo-he-ka, (Polecat), A-ka-chu-a-ta, (No Horn), Ka-he-ha-bo-ne, (Blind Man), Ma-war-ra, (The Lost), Ke-wid-da-wip-pa, (Tall Woman), Pa-na-che, (Mistletoe.)

Wacoes:
We-ar-ras, (Big Dog), Hed-e-cok-isk, (Double-Barrelled),

Keeches:
Sa-sed-da-qua, (Dead Man), A-ko-ha-rai-at, (Pursuer), Hens-ke-da-hick, (Long Frock), Uks-que-ra-qua-ar-da, (House Keeper), Ha-wi-da-sai-kish, (Man Kil-

Plains, West and Northwest Plateau Indian Treaties

ler), No-cur-ra-oh-to-a-wa, (Loud Talker), To-ka-rah, (Black House), Ken-di-ash-ush-sa, (Narrow Escape.)

Tonkaways:
Ha-set-ta, (Sitting by a River), Campo, Ha-shu-ka-nah, (Can't Kill Him), Place-don, Cha-al-lah, (Strong Man), Jose, Ka-sa, (A Worshipper), Tron-ke-la, (Thunder), Nic-co-na-nah, (Killed an Indian on the Hill), Hose-Marea, (or Aish), Be-cin-ta, Shell Chief, (or Tow-a-ash), Bin-chah, Chick-a-saw-che.

Wichetas:
To-sa-quas, (White Tail), Cho-wash-ta-ha-da, (Runner)
Kow-wah, (Shirt Tail), With-qua-sa-is, (Contrary), His-si-da-wah, (Stubborn.)

Towa-karroes:
Ke-chi-ko-ra-ko, (Stubborn), Nes-ho-chil-lash, (Traveller), Na-co-ah, (Danger-field), Ka-ra-ko-ris, (Deceiver), Ha-ke-di-ad-ah, (Gallant Man), Wha-cha-ash-da, (Looker-on), Wash-le-doi-ro-ka, (Don't you do so), Te-ah-kur-rah, (Light-man), Sar-rah-de-od-a-sa, (Straight Looker.)

Wacoes:
A-qua-gosh, (Short Tail), Ho-hed-orah, (Long Ways over the River), Chos-toch-ka-a-wah, (Charger), Cha-to-wait, (Ghost.)

Secretaries:
Thomas J. Wilson, Isaac H. Du Val.

Witnesses:
Robt. S. Neighbor, Hugh Rose, Jno. H. Rollins, Thomas J. Smith, E. More-house. interpreters:
Louis Sanches, John Conner, Jim Shaw.

(To each of the names of the Indians is affixed his mark.)

TREATY WITH THE POTAWATOMI NATION {1846, June 5 and 17}
Ratified, July 22, 1846.
Proclaimed, July 23, 1846.

Whereas the various bands of the Pottowautomie Indians, known as the Chip-pewas, Ottawas, and Pottowautomies, the Pottowautomies of the Prairie, the Pottowautomies of the Wabash, and the Pottowautomies of Indiana, have, sub-sequent to the year 1828, entered into separate and distinct treaties with the United States, by which they have been separated and located in different countries, and difficulties have arisen as to the proper distribution of the stipu-lations under various treaties, and being the same people by kindred, by feeling,

Plains, West and Northwest Plateau Indian Treaties

and by language, and having, in former periods, lived on and owned their lands in common; and being desirous to unite in one common country, and again become one people, and receive their annuities and other benefits in common, and to abolish all minor distinctions of bands by which they have heretofore been divided, and are anxious to be known only as the Pottowautomie Nation, thereby reinstating the national character; and

Whereas the United States are also anxious to restore and concentrate said tribes to a state so desirable and necessary for the happiness of their people, as well as to enable the Government to arrange and manage its intercourse with them:

Now, therefore, the United States and the said Indians do hereby agree that said people shall hereafter be known as a nation, to be called the Pottowautomie Nation; and to the following articles of a treaty made and concluded at the Agency on the Missouri River, near Council Bluffs, on the fifth day of June, and at Pottawatomie Creek, near the Osage River, south and west of the State of Missouri, on the seventeenth day of the same month, in the year of our Lord one thousand eight hundred and forty-six, between T P. Andrews, Thomas H. Harvey, and Gideon C. Matlock, commissioners on the part of the United States, on the one part, and the various bands of the Pottowautomie, Chippewas, and Ottowas Indians on the other part:

ARTICLE 1. It is solemnly agreed that the peace and friendship which so happily exist between the people of the United States and the Pottowautomie Indians shall continue forever; the said tribes of Indians giving assurance, hereby, of fidelity and friendship to the Government and people of the United States; and the United States giving, at the same time, promise of all proper care and parental protection.

ARTICLE 2. The said tribes of Indians hereby agree to sell and cede, and do hereby sell and cede, to the United States, all the lands to which they have claim of any kind whatsoever, and especially the tracts or parcels of lands ceded to them by the treaty of Chicago, and subsequent thereto, and now, in whole or in part, possessed by their people, lying and being north of the river Missouri, and embraced in the limits of the Territory of Iowa; and also all that tract of country lying and being on or near the Osage River, and west of the State of Missouri; it being understood that these cessions are not to affect the title of said Indians to any grants or reservations made to them by former treaties.

ARTICLE 3. In consideration of the foregoing cessions or sales of land to the United States, it is agreed to pay to said tribes of Indians the sum of eight hundred and fifty thousand dollars, subject to the conditions, deductions, and liabilities provided for in the subsequent articles of this treaty.

Plains, West and Northwest Plateau Indian Treaties

ARTICLE 4. The United States agree to grant to the said united tribes of Indians possession and title to a tract or parcel of land containing five hundred and seventy-six thousand acres, being thirty miles square, and being the eastern part of the lands ceded to the United States by the Kansas tribe or Indians, by treaty concluded on the 14th day of January, and ratified on the 15th of April of the present year, lying adjoining the Shawnees on the south, and the Delawares and Shawnees on the east, on both sides of the Kansas River, and to guarantee the full and complete possession of the same to the Pottowautomie Nation, parties to this treaty, as their land and home forever; for which they are to pay the United States the sum of eighty-seven thousand dollars, to be deducted from the gross sum promised to them in the 3d article of this treaty.

ARTICLE 5. The United States agree to pay said nation of Indians, at the first annuity payment after the ratification of this treaty, and after an appropriation shall have been made by Congress, the sum of fifty thousand dollars, out of the aggregate sum granted in the third article of this treaty to enable said Indians to arrange their affairs, and pay their just debts, before leaving their present homes; to pay for their improvements; to purchase wagons, horses, and other means of transportation, and pay individuals for the loss of property necessarily sacrificed in moving to their new homes; said sum to be paid, in open council, by the proper agents of the United States, and in such just proportions to each band as the President of the United States may direct.

ARTICLE 6. The said tribes of Indians agree to remove to their new homes on the Kansas River, within two years from the ratification of this treaty; and further agree to set apart the sum of twenty thousand dollars to the upper bands, (being ten dollars per head) and ten thousand dollars to the lower bands, (being five dollars per head) to pay the actual expenses of removing; and the sum of forty thousand dollars for all the bands, as subsistence money, for the first twelve months after their arrival at their new homes; to be paid to them so soon as their arrival at their new homes is made known to the Government, and convenient arrangements can be made to pay the same between the parties to this treaty; the aforesaid sums to be also deducted from the aggregate sum granted by the United States to said tribes of Indians by the 3d article of this treaty.

ARTICLE 7. The balance of the said sum of eight hundred fifty thousand dollars, after deducting the cost of removal and subsistence, &c., it is agreed shall remain with the United States, in trust for said Indians, and an interest of five per cent annually paid thereon, commencing at the expiration of one year after the removal of said Indians, and continuing for thirty years, and until the nation shall be reduced below one thousand souls. If, after the expiration of thirty years, or any period thereafter, it shall be ascertained that the nation is reduced below that number, the said annuity shall thenceforth be paid pro rata so long

Plains, West and Northwest Plateau Indian Treaties

as they shall exist as a separate and distinct nation, in proportion as the present number shall bear to the number then in existence.

ARTICLE 8. it is agreed upon by the parties to this treaty that, after the removal of the Pottowautomie Nation to the Kansas country, the annual interest of their "improvement fund" shall be paid out promptly and fully, for their benefit at their new homes. If, however, at any time thereafter, the President of the United States shall be of opinion that it would be advantageous to the Pottowautomie Nation, and they should request the same to be done, to pay them the interest of said money in lieu of the employment of persons or purchase of machines or implements, he is hereby authorized to pay the same, or any part thereof, in money, as their annuities are paid at the time of the general payments of annuities. It is also agreed that, after the expiration of two years from the ratification of this treaty, the school-fund of the Pottowautomies shall be expended entirely in their own country, unless their people, in council, should, at any time, express a desire to have any part of the same expended in a different manner.

ARTICLE 9. It is agreed by the parties to this treaty that the buildings occupied as a missionary establishment, including twenty acres of land now under fence, shall be reserved for the use of the Government agency; also the houses used for blacksmith house and shop shall be reserved for the use of the Pottowautomie smith; but should the property cease to be used for the aforementioned purposes, then it shall revert to the use of the Pottowautomie Nation.

ARTICLE 10. It is agreed that hereafter there shall be paid to the Pottowautomie Nation, annually, the sum of three hundred dollars, in lieu of the two thousand pounds of tobacco, fifteen hundred pounds of iron, and three hundred and fifty pounds of steel, stipulated to be paid to the Pottowautomies under the third article of the treaty of September 20, 1828.

In testimony whereof, T. P. Andrews, Thomas H. Harvey, and Gideon C. Matlock, aforesaid Commissioners, and the Chiefs and Principal Men of the Pottowautomie, Ottowa, and Chippewas tribes of Indians, have set their hands, at the time and place first mentioned.

T. P. Andrews, Th. H. Harvey, G. C. Matlock, Commissioners.

Mi-au-mise, (the Young Miami), Op-te-gee-shuck, (or Half Day), Wa-sow-o-ko-uck, (or the Lightning), Kem-me-kas, (or Bead), Mi-quess, (or the Wampum), Wab-na-ne-rne, (or White Pigeon), Na-no-no-uit, (or Like the Wind), Patt-co-shuck, junior, Cattc-nab-mee, (the Close Observer), Wap-que-shuck, (or White Cedar), Sah-ken-na-ne-be, Etwa-gee-shuck, Saass-pucks-kum, (or Green Leaf), Ke-wa-ko-to, (Black Cloud Turning),

235

Plains, West and Northwest Plateau Indian Treaties

Meek-sa-rnack, (the Wampum), Chau-cose, (Little Crane), Co-shae-wais, (Tree Top), Patt-qui, Me-shuk-to-no, Ween-co, Joseph Le Frambeau, Interpreter, Pierre or Perish Le Clerk, M. B. Beaubien, Interpreter, Pes-co-unk, (Distant Thunder), Naut-wish-cum, Ob-nob, (or He Looks Back), Pam-wa-mash-kuck, Pacq-qui-pa-chee, Ma-shaus, (the Cutter), Ci-co, Puck-quon, (or the Rib), Sena-tche-wan, (or Swift Current), Shaub-poi-tuck, (the Man goes through), Wab-sai, (or White Skin), Shaum-num-teh, (or Medicine Man), Nah-o-sah, (the Walker), Keahh, Ne-ah-we-quot, (the Four Faces), Wa-sash-kuck, (or the Grass Turner), Ke-ton-ne-co, (or the Kidneys), *Francois Bourbonnai, *Chas. H. Beaubien, *Shau-on-nees, *Paskal Miller, *Joseph Glaudeau, *Joseph Laughton,

Witnesses.
R. B. Mitchell, Indian sub-agent, Richard Pearson, A. G. Wilson, S. W. Smith, Edward Pore, John H. Whitehead, John Copeland, T. D. S. McDonnell, W. R. English, S. E. Wicks, Lewis Kennedy, L. T. Tate.

(To the names of the Indians, except where there is an asterisk, are added their marks.)

We, the undersigned, Chiefs and Head Men, and Representatives of the Wabash, St. Joseph, and Prairie bands of the Ottowa, Chippewas, and Pottowautomie Indians, do hereby accept, ratify, and confirm the foregoing articles of a treaty, in all particulars. Done at Pottowautomie Creek, near the Osage River, west and south of the State of Missouri, this seventeenth day of June, A. D., 1846.

To-pen-e-be, We-we-say, Gah-gah-amo, I-o-way, Mah-go-quick, Zhah-wee, Louison, Mash-kum-me, Crane, Esk-bug-ge, Noa-ah-kye, Abraham BUrner, Ma-gis-gize, Nas-wah-gay, Pok-to, Little Bird, Shim-nah, Ma-kda-wah, Black Wolf, Root, Niena-kto, Ma-je-sah, Mah-suck, Bade-je-zha, Kah-shqua, Little American, Match-kay, Wane-mage, Wah-wah-suck 2d, Black Bird, Wah-wah-suck 1st, Wab-mack, (Henry Clay)

(To the names of the Indians, except where there is an asterisk, are added their marks.)

Witnesses.
Joseph Bertrand, Jr., R. W. Cummins, Indian Agent, Leonidas A. Vaughan, Robert Simerwell, Thomas Hurlburt, J. W. Polk, J. Lykins, M. H. Scott, Washn. Bossman, John T. Jones, James A. Poage, Joseph Clymer, Jr., W. W. Cleghorn.

Plains, West and Northwest Plateau Indian Treaties

TREATY WITH THE WINNEBAGO {1846, Oct. 13}
Proclamation, Feb. 4, 1847.

Articles of a treaty made and concluded at the city of Washington, on the thirteenth day of October, in the year one thousand eight hundred and forty-six, between the United States, of the one part, by their commissioners, Albion K. Parris, John J. Abert, and T. P. Andrews, and the Winnebago tribe of Indians, of the other part, by a full delegation of said tribe, specially appointed by the chiefs, head-men, and warriors thereof.

ARTICLE 1. It is solemnly agreed that the peace and friendship which exist between the people of the United States and the Winnebago Indians shall be perpetual; the said tribe of Indians giving assurance, hereby, of fidelity and friendship to the Government and people of the United States, and the United States giving to them, at the same time, promise of all proper care and parental protection.

ARTICLE 2. The said tribe of Indians hereby agree to cede and sell, and do hereby cede and sell, to the United States, all right, title interest, claim, and privilege, to all lands, wherever situated, now or heretofore occupied or claimed by said Indians, within the States and Territories of the United States, and especially to the country now occupied, inhabited, or in any way used by them, called the "neutral ground," which tract of country was assigned to said Indians by the second article of the treaty of Fort Armstrong, concluded on the fifteenth day of September, 1832, and ratified on the thirteenth day of February following.

ARTICLE 3. In consideration of the foregoing purchase from, or cession by, the said Indians, the United States hereby agree to purchase and give to the said Indians, as their home, to be held as all Indians' lands are held, a tract of country north of St. Peter's and west of the Mississippi Rivers, of not less than eight hundred thousand acres, which shall be suitable to their habits, wants, and wishes: Provided, Such land can be obtained on just and reasonable terms.

ARTICLE 4:. The United States agree to pay to said tribe of Indians the sum of one hundred and fifty thousand dollars for the land, and the sum of forty thousand dollars for release of hunting privileges, on the lands adjacent to their present home, making the sum of one hundred and ninety thousand dollars, being in further consideration of the cession or sale made to the United States by the second article of this treaty; to be paid as follows: Forty thousand dollars to enable them to comply with their present just engagements, and to cover the expenses of exploring and selecting (by their own people, or by an agent of their own appointment) their new home; twenty thousand dollars in consideration of their removing themselves, and twenty thousand dollars in consideration of their subsisting themselves the first year after their removal; ten thousand

237

Plains, West and Northwest Plateau Indian Treaties

dollars to be expended for breaking up and fencing lands, under the direction of the President of the United States, at their new home; ten thousand dollars to be set apart and applied, under the direction of the President, to the creation and carrying on of one or more manual-labor schools for the benefit of said tribe of Indians; and five thousand dollars for building a saw and grist mill.

The balance of said sum of one hundred and ninety thousand dollars, viz, eighty-five thousand dollars, to remain in trust with the United States, and five per cent interest thereon to be paid annually to said tribe, or applied for their benefit, as the President of the United States may from time to time direct, for the period of thirty years, which shall be in full payment of the said balance: Provided, That no part of the said consideration moneys shall be paid until after the arrival of said tribe of Indians at their new home, and appropriations shall have been made by Congress; and that the sums for meeting their present engagements, for removal and subsistence, and for exploring their new home, shall be paid to the chiefs in open council, in such a manner as they in said council shall request.

ARTICLE 5. It is further agreed by the parties to this treaty that the said tribe of Indians shall remove to their new home within one year after the ratification of this treaty, and their new home shall have been procured for them, and they duly notified of the same.

ARTICLE 6. It is further agreed by the parties to this treaty, that the President may, at his discretion, (should he at any time be of opinion that the interest of the Indians would be thereby promoted) direct that any portion of the money, not exceeding ten thousand dollars per annum, now paid in goods, as provided for by the last clause of the fourth article of the treaty of the first of November, 1837, be applied to the purchase of additional provisions, or to other purposes.

In testimony whereof, the Commissioners, Albion K. Parris, John J. Abert, and T. P. Andrews, and the undersigned Chiefs, Head Men, and Delegates, of the Winnebago Tribe of Indians, have hereunto subscribed their names and affixed their seals, at the City of Washington, this thirteenth day of October, one thousand eight hundred and forty-six.

Albion K. Parris, John J. Abert, T. P. Andrews, Commissioners.

Hoong-ho-no-kaw, Is-jaw-go-bo-kaw, Co-no-ha-ta-kaw, Naw-hoo-skaw-kaw, Shoong-skaw-kaw, Kooz-a-ray-kaw, Waw-ma-noo-ka-kaw, Ha-naw-hoong-per-kaw, Wo-gie-qua-kaw, Waw-kon-chaw-she-shick-kaw, Chas-chun-kaw.
Naw-hey-kee-kaw, Ah-hoo-zheb-kaw, Waw-roo-jaw-h ee-kaw, Baptist-Lasalica, Waw-kon-chaw-per-kaw, Kaw-how-ah-kaw, Hakh-ee-nee-kaw, Waw-kon-chaw-ho-no-kaw, Maw-hee-ko-shay-naw-zhee-kaw, Maw-nee-ho-

Plains, West and Northwest Plateau Indian Treaties

no-nic, Maw-ho-kee-wee-kaw, Sho-go-nee-kaw, Watch-ha-ta-kaw-, (by Henry M. Rice, his delegate).

Witnesses:
John C. Mullay, secretary to board of commissioners.
J. E. Fletcher, subagent.
S. B. Lowry, Peter Mananaige, Antoine Grignon, interpreters. Simeon Lecure, H.L. Dousman, Richard Chute, John Haney, George Cahn, James Maher.

(To each of the names of the Indians are affixed a seal and mark.)

TREATY WITH THE MENOMINEE {1848, Oct. 18}
Ratified Jan. 23, 1849.

Articles of a treaty made and concluded at Lake Pow-aw-hay-kon-nay, in the State of Wisconsin, on the eighteenth day of October, one thousand eight hundred and forty-eight, between the United States of America, by William Medill, a commissioner duly appointed for that purpose, and the Menomonee tribe of Indians, by the chiefs, headmen, and warriors of said tribe.

ARTICLE 1. It is stipulated and solemnly agreed that the peace and friendship now so happily subsisting between the Government and people of the United States and the Menomonee Indians shall be perpetual.

ARTICLE 2. The said Menomonee tribe of Indians agree to cede, and do hereby cede, sell, and relinquish to the United States all their lands in the State of Wisconsin, wherever situated.

ARTICLE 3. In consideration of the foregoing cession, the United States agree to give, and do hereby give, to said Indians for a home, to be held as Indians' lands are held, all that country or tract of land ceded to the said United States by the Chippewa Indians of the Mississippi and Lake Superior, in the treaty Of August 2, 1847, and the Pillager band of Chippewa Indians, in the treaty of August 21, 1847, which may not be assigned to the Winnebago Indiana, under the treaty with that tribe of October 13, 1846, and which is guarantied to contain not less than six hundred thousand acres.

ARTICLE 4. In further and full consideration of said cession, the United States agree to pay the sum of three hundred and fifty thousand dollars, at the several times, in the manner, and for the purposes following, viz:

To the chiefs, as soon after the same shall be appropriated by Congress as may be convenient, to enable them to arrange and settle the affairs of their tribe pre-

239

Plains, West and Northwest Plateau Indian Treaties

paratory to their removal to the country set apart for and given to them as above, thirty thousand dollars.

To such person of mixed blood, and in such proportion to each as the chiefs in council, and a commissioner to be appointed by the President, shall designate and determine, and as soon after the appropriation thereof as may be found practicable and expedient, forty thousand dollars.

In such manner and at such times as the President shall prescribe, in consideration of their removing themselves, which they agree to do, without further cost or expense to the United States, twenty thousand dollars.

In such manner and at such times as the President shall prescribe, in consideration of their subsisting themselves the first year after their removal, which they agree to do, without further cost or expense on the part of the United States, twenty thousand dollars.

To be laid out and applied, under the direction of the President, in the establishment of a manual-labor school, the erection of a grist and saw mill, and other necessary improvements in their new country, fifteen thousand dollars.

To be laid out and applied, under the direction of the President, in procuring a suitable person, to attend and carry on the said grist and saw mill for a period of fifteen years, nine thousand dollars.

To be laid out and applied, under the direction of the President, in continuing and keeping up a blacksmith's shop, and providing the usual quantity of iron and steel for the use and benefit of said tribe, for a period of twelve years, commencing with the year one thousand eight hundred and fifty-seven, and when all provision for blacksmiths' shops under the treaty of 1836 shall cease, eleven thousand dollars.

To be set apart, applied, and distributed under the direction of the President, in payment of individual improvements of the tribe upon the lands above ceded to the United States, five thousand dollars.

And the balance, amounting to the sum of two hundred thousand dollars, to be paid over to the tribe, as Indian annuities are required to be paid, in ten equal annual instalments, commencing with the year one thousand eight hundred and fifty-seven, and when their annuities or annual instalments under the treaty of 1836 shall have ceased.

ARTICLE 5. it is stipulated and agreed, that the sum now invested in stocks, under the Senate's amendment to the treaty of 1836, with the interest due thereon at this time, shall be and remain invested, under the direction of the President, and that the interest hereafter arising therefrom shall be disposed of as follows: that is to say, so much thereof as may be necessary to the support and maintenance of the said manual-labor school, and other means of educa-

Plains, West and Northwest Plateau Indian Treaties

tion, and the balance be annually paid over in money as other annuities, or applied for the benefit and improvement of said tribe, as the President, on consultation with the chiefs, may, from time to time, determine.

ARTICLE 6. To enable the said Indians to explore and examine their new country, and as an inducement to an early removal thereto, it is agreed that the United States will pay the necessary expenses of a suitable delegation, to be selected for that purpose, under the direction of the President.

ARTICLE 7. It is alleged that there were less goods delivered to the said Indians at the annuity payment of 1837 than were due and required to be paid and delivered to them under the stipulations of their treaties with the United States then in force; and it is therefore agreed that the subject shall be properly investigated, and that full indemnity shall be made to them for any loss which they may be shown to have sustained.

ARTICLE 8. It is agreed that the said Indians shall be permitted, if they desire to do so, to remain on the lands hereby ceded for and during the period of two years from the date hereof, and until the President shall notify them that the same are wanted.

ARTICLE 9. It is stipulated that Robert Grignon, who has erected a saw-mill upon the Little Wolf River, at his own expense, for the benefit and at the request of said Indians, shall have the right of a pre-emptor to the lands upon which such improvements are situated, not exceeding in quantity on both sides of said river one hundred and sixty acres.

ARTICLE 10. This treaty to be binding on the contracting parties as soon as it is ratified by the President and Senate of the United States.

In testimony whereof, the said William Medill, Commissioner as aforesaid, and the chiefs, headmen, and warriors of the said Menomonee tribe of Indians, have hereunto set their hands and seals, at the place and on the day and year aforesaid.

W. Medill, Commissioner on the Part of the United States.

Signed and sealed in the presence of us
Albert G. Ellis, Sub-Agent, Chas. A. Grignon, U. S. Interpreter, F. J. Bonduel, Missionary Priest among the Menomonee Indians.
M. L. Martin, P. B. Grignon, Samuel Ryan, A. G. Grignon, John B. Jacobs.
Osh, Kush, Jau-ma-tau, Waw-kee-che-un, Sage-toke, Wy-tah-sauh, Kee-cheenew, Chee-cheequon-away, Corron Glaude, Sho-nee-nieu, Lamotte, Che-quotum;

Plains, West and Northwest Plateau Indian Treaties

Shaw-wan-on, Ah-ko-no-may, Shaw-poa-tuk, Wau-po-nan-ah, Sho-na-new, Jr., Pah-maw-po-may, Naw-kaw-chis-ka, Show-anno-penessee, Tah-ko, Osh-kish-he-nay-new, Little Wave, Muck-atah-penesse, Wa-pee-men-shaw, Ah-ke-na-pe-new, Ah-kaw-mut, Kee-she-teu-ke-tau, She-pau-na-ko, Naw-kaw-nish-kau-wa.

(To each of the names of the Indians is affixed his mark.)

Witnesses:
William Powell, John B. Dube, John G. Kittson, Robt. Grignon, Charles Caron, Antoine Gotheiu, F. Desnoyers, Louis G. Porhir, O. W. F. Bruce.

TREATY WITH THE STOCKBRIDGE TRIBE {1848, Nov. 2}
Ratified Mar. 1, 1849.

WHEREAS by an act of Congress entitled "An act for the relief of the Stock-bridge tribe of Indians, in the Territory of Wisconsin," approved on the third day of March, A. D. 1843, it was provided that the township of land on the east side of Winnebago Lake, secured to said tribe by the treaty with the Menomonee Indians of February 8th, 1831, as amended by the Senate of the United States, and not heretofore ceded by said tribe to the United States, should be divided and allotted among the individual members of said tribe, by commissioners to be elected for that purpose, who were to make report of such division and allotment, and thereupon the persons composing said tribe were to become citizens of the United States.

And whereas a portion of said tribe refused to recognize the validity of said act of Congress, or the proceedings which were had under it, or to be governed by its provisions, and upon their petition a subsequent act was passed by the Congress of the United States, on the 6th day of August, 1846, repealing the said act of March 3d, 1843, and providing, among other things, that such of said tribe as should enroll themselves with the subagent of Indian affairs at Green Bay, should be and remain citizens of the United States, and the residue of said tribe were restored to their ancient form of government as an Indian tribe. It was also provided that the said township of land should be divided into two districts, one of which was to be known as the "Indian district," the other as the "citizen district;" the former to be held in common by the party who did not desire citizenship, and the latter to be divided and allotted among such as were citizens and desired to remain so.

And whereas it has been found impracticable to carry into full effect the provisions of the act of August 6th, 1846, by dividing the said township of land in the manner specified in said act, without infringing upon private rights acquired in good faith under the act of 1843 hereinbefore referred to, with a view of re-

242

Plains, West and Northwest Plateau Indian Treaties

lieving both the Indian and citizen parties of said Stockbridge tribe of Indians from their present embarrassments, and to secure to each their just rights, articles of agreement and compromise have been entered into, as follows:

Articles of agreement and treaty made and concluded at Stockbridge, in the State of Wisconsin, on the 24th day of November, in the year of our Lord one thousand eight hundred and forty-eight, by and between the undersigned, acting commissioners on the part of the United States of America, and the Stockbridge tribe of Indians.

ARTICLE 1. The said Stockbridge tribe of Indians renounce all participation in any of the benefits or privileges granted or conferred by the act of Congress entitled "An act for the relief of the Stockbridge tribe of Indians, in the Territory of Wisconsin," approved March 3, 1843, and relinquish all rights secured by said act; and they do hereby acknowledge and declare themselves to be under the protection and guardianship of the United States, as other Indian tribes.

ARTICLE 2. That no misunderstanding may exist, now or hereafter, in determining who compose said tribe and are parties hereto, it is agreed that a roll or census shall be taken and appended to this agreement, and in like manner taken annually hereafter, and returned to the Secretary of the War Department of the United States, containing the names of all such as are parties hereto, and to be known and recognized as the Stockbridge tribe of Indians, who shall each be entitled to their due proportion of the benefits to be derived from the provisions made for their tribe by this and former agreements; and whenever any of them shall separate themselves from said tribe, or abandon the country Which may be selected for their future home, the share or portion of such shall cease, and they shall forfeit all claims to be recognized as members of said tribe.

ARTICLE 3. The said Stockbridge tribe of Indians hereby sell and relinquish to the United States the township of land on the east side of Lake Winnebago, (granted and secured to said tribe by the treaty with the Menomonee tribe of Indians of February 8, 1831, as amended by the resolution of the Senate of the United States) and situated in the State of Wisconsin.

ARTICLE 4. The said township of land shall be surveyed into lots, in conformity with the plan adopted by the commissioners elected under the act of March 3, 1843, and such of said lands as were allotted by said commissioners to members of said tribe who have become citizens of the United States (a schedule of which is hereunto annexed)are hereby confirmed to such individuals respectively, and patents therefor shall be issued by the United States. The residue of said lands belonging to the United States shall be brought into market but shall not be sold at less than the appraised value, unless the Senate of the United States shall otherwise determine.

Plains, West and Northwest Plateau Indian Treaties

ARTICLE 5. In consideration of the cession and relinquishment hereinbefore made by the said Stockbridge tribe of Indians, it is agreed that the United States shall pay to said tribe, within six months after the ratification of this agreement, the sum of sixteen thousand five hundred dollars, to enable them to settle their affairs, obtain necessaries, and make provision for establishing themselves in a new home.

ARTICLE 6. The United States shall also pay to said tribe, within six months after the ratification of this agreement, the sum of fourteen thousand five hundred and four dollars and eighty-five cents, being the appraised value of their improvements upon the lands herein ceded and relinquished to the United States, and to be paid to the individuals claiming said improvements according to the schedule and assessment herewith transmitted.

ARTICLE 7. It is further stipulated and agreed that the said Stockbridge tribe may remain upon the lands they now occupy for one year after the ratification of this agreement, and that they will remove to the country set apart for them, or such other west of the Mississippi River as they may be able to secure, where all their treaty stipulations with the Government shall be carried into effect.

ARTICLE 8. Whenever the said Stockbridge tribe shall signify their wish to emigrate, the United States will defray the expenses of their removal west of the Mississippi and furnish them with subsistence for one year after their arrival at their new home.

ARTICLE 9. It is further stipulated and agreed, that, for the purpose of making provision for the rising generation of said tribe, the sum of sixteen thousand five hundred dollars shall be invested by the United States in stock, bearing an interest of not less than five per cent. per annum, the interest of which shall be paid annually to said tribe, as other annuities are paid by the United States.

ARTICLE 10. It is agreed that nothing herein shall prevent a survey of said lands, at any time after the ratification of this agreement, and that said tribe shall commit no waste or do unnecessary damage upon the premises occupied by them.

ARTICLE 11. The United States will pay the expenses incurred by the sachem and head-men, amounting to three thousand dollars, in attending to the business of said tribe since the year 1843.

ARTICLE 12. This agreement to be binding and obligatory upon the contracting parties from and after its ratification by the Government of the United States.

Plains, West and Northwest Plateau Indian Treaties

In witness whereof, the said commissioners, and the sachem, councillors, and headmen of said tribe, have hereunto set their hands and seals, the day and year above written.

Morgan L. Martin, Albert G. Ellis,
Augustin E. Quinney, sachem, Zeba T. Peters, Peter D. Littleman, Councillors.
*Abram Pye, Joseph M. Quinney, Samuel Stephens, Jeremiah Slingerland,
*Benjamin Pye, 2d, Simon S. Metoxen, Daniel Metoxen, *Moses Charles,
*Benjamin Pye, 3d, *Jacob Jehoiakim,

To each of the names of the Indians marked with an asterisk is affixed his mark,

In presence of
Charles A. Grignon, U. S. Interpreter.
Lemuel Goodell, Eleazer Williams, Charles Poreuninozer.

SUPPLEMENTAL ARTICLE. Whereas the Stockbridge and Munsee Indians consider that they have a claim against the United States for indemnity for certain lands on White River in the State of Indiana, and for certain other lands in the State of Wisconsin, which they allege they have been deprived of by treaties entered into with the Miamies and Delawares, or to the lands claimed by them in Indiana, and with the Menomonees and Winnebagoes, or to the lands in Wisconsin, without their consent; and whereas the said Stockbridge and Munsee Indians, by their chiefs and agents, have continued to prosecute their said claims during the last twenty years at their own expense, except the sum of three thousand dollars paid them in 1821.

And whereas it is desirable that all ground of discontent on the part of said Indians shall be removed, the United States do further stipulate, in consideration of the relinquishment by them of said claims, and all others, except as provided in this treaty, to pay the sachems or chiefs of said Indians, on the ratification of this article by them, with the assent of their people, the sum of five thousand dollars, and the further sum of twenty thousand dollars, to be paid in ten annual instalments, to commence when the said Indians shall have selected and removed to their new homes, as contemplated by the seventh article of this treaty.

The President of the United States, within two years from the ratification of this treaty, shall procure for the use of said Stockbridge Indians a quantity of land west of the Mississippi River, upon which they shall reside, not less than seventy-two sections, said Indians to be consulted as to the location of said land, and to be holden by the same tenure as other Indian lands.

Roll or census of the Stockbridge tribe of Indians, taken, in conformity with the provisions of the second article of the within agreement.

245

Plains, West and Northwest Plateau Indian Treaties

Heads of families.	Male	Female	Boys	Girls	Total	
Austin E. Quinney	1	1	3	4	9	
John Metoxen	1			2	1	
Benjamin Pye, sen	1	1		1	3	
Garret Thompson	1	1	2		4	
Elisha Konkapot	1	1	1		3	
John W. Quinney	1				1	
John P. Quinney	1	1	1		3	
Peter D. Littleman	1	1	1	2	5	
Jonas Thompson	1	1	1	1	4	
James Joshua	1				1	
Joseph M. Quinney		1	1	2	1	5
Simon L. Metoxen	1	1	2	5	9	
Benjamin Pye, 2d	1	1	1	3	6	
Thomas Schenandoah		1	1			2
Aaron Turkey	1	1	2	2	6	
Abram Pye	1	1	4	1	7	
Benjamin Pye, 4th	1	1		1	3	
Benjamin Doxtater	1	1	1	1	4	
Moses Charles	1	1	1	1	4	
Benjamin Pye, 3d	1	1	1	1	4	
Eli Williams	1				1	
David Palmer	1	1	1		3	
Jacob Konkapot	1	1		1	3	
Daniel Metoxen	1	1			2	
Elizabeth Palmer (widow)		1	1	1		3
Elizabeth Aaron	1	1	2	4		
Catharine Butterfield		1		1		2
Samuel Miller	1	1	4	2	8	
Louisa Jamison		1			1	
Jacob Jahoicum	1				1	
Anna Turkey		1			1	
Jeremiah Slingerland		1		3		4
John Yocum	1	1		2	4	
Elizabeth Wilber		1	1	3	5	
John W. Quinney, jr., and sister 2		1		1		
Clarissa Miller and son		1	1			2
Elizabeth Pye		1		1	2	
Phoebe S. Ricket		1			1	
Josiah Abrams, wife, and sister 3			1	2		
Jeremiah Bennet	1	2		2	5	
Paul Pye	1	1	1		3	

Plains, West and Northwest Plateau Indian Treaties

Peter Bennet	1				1
Ziba T. Peters	1	1	2		4
Ezekiel Robinson and brother					2
2					
Lawrence Yocum	1				1
Moses Doxtater	1			1	2
Lucinda Quinney		1	2	1	4
Jemima Doxtater		1			1
Amelia Quinney		1	1		2
Peter Bennet, sen	1	1	1	3	6
John Bennet	1	1	1	1	4
Levi Konkapot	1				1
Samuel Stevens	1				1
John Killsnake	1				1
Lewis Hendricks	1				1
Diana Davids		1			1

M. L. Martin, Albert G. Ellis, Austin E. Quinney.

Stockbridge, November 24, 1848.

John Metoxen, John W. Quinney, Samuel Miller, Ziba T. Peters, Peter D. Littleman, Abram Pye, Joseph M. Quinney, Samuel Stephens, Jeremiah Slingerland, Benjamin Pye, 2d, Simon S. Metoxen, Daniel Metoxen, Moses Charles, Benjamin Pye, 3d.
Jacob Jehoiakim, David Palmer, Ezekiel Robinson, James Joshua, Garret Thompson, Laurens Yocum, Thomas Schanandoah, Joshua W. Quinney, jr
Nicholas Palmer, John P. Quinney, Washington Quinney, Aaron Turkey.

Schedule of lands to be patented to individuals under the 4th article of the above agreement.

Names	No. of lot	No. of acres	
Josiah Chicks	1		
Nancy Chicks	2		
John N. Chicks	4		
Jacob Davids	5		
Harvey Johnson	8		
Hannah P. Chicks	10		
Dindemia, Big Deer		½ E. end 14	22. 66
Puella Jourdain	16		
Jacobs Chicks	17		
John N. Chicks	18		
Josiah Chicks	20		
Jacob Chicks	21		
Jos. L. Chicks	22		

Plains, West and Northwest Plateau Indian Treaties

Jacob Chicks	23		
John N. Chicks	24		
Moses E. Merrill	25, 26, 27		
John N. Chicks	28, 29		
Jane Dean	30		
Mariette Abrams	31		
Catharine Mills	N. ½ 32 30. 62		
Joseph L. Chicks	33		
John Dick	37		
John More	38		
Isaac Jacobs	40		
Benjamin Welch	31		
Lucy Jacobs	44		
Daniel Davids	47		
Daniel Davids	N. ½ 48		
John W. Abrams	S. ½ 48		
Louisa Davids	50		
Harry E. Eastman	51		
Eunice Abrams	52		
Daniel Davids	53		
John N. Chicks	54		
Hoel S. Wright	S. part of 55	5	
Oscar Wright	N. part of 55	57½	
John Littleman	S ½ 56		
Daniel Davids	N ½ 56		
Darius Davids	57		
Margaret Davids	58		
Daniel Davids	60		
Erastus Welch, (a strip E. of road)	65	6 chains 25 lks. wide off S. side of lot.	
Richard Fiddler_	E. of road 65	Balance of the lot.	
Henry Modlin	part 65 W. of road, 54 3/8		
Henry Jacobs	63		
Lucy Jacobs	frac'l part of 66	W. of road, 50.50	
John W. Abrams	E ½ 68		
John Dick	70		
Eunice Abrams	N. ½ 76		
Mary Hendrick	E. ½ 78		
Isaac Jacobs and George Bennet	79		
John N. Chicks	81		
John N. Chicks and Jacob Davids.	82		
Nancy Hunt	W. ½ 83 31 1/4		
James Menagre and Betsy Menagre	part of 84 E.	end 15½	
Betsy Wyatt	W. 1/2 85 & 86	62 1/2	
William Gardner	87		

248

Plains, West and Northwest Plateau Indian Treaties

Timothy Jourdain	90			
Timothy Jourdain	S. ½ 91	31. 25		
Charles Stevens	92 & 94			
Nancy Homm	98			
Joseph L. Chicks	102			
John N. Chicks	103			
John Moore	105			
Josiah Chicks	106			
John N. Chicks	110			
Timothy Jourdain	111			
John Littleman	113			
Nathan Goodell	115			
Charles Stevens	S. part 119		50	
Catharine Littleman		E. part 128		54. 60
John Moore	129			
John W. Abrams	130			
Jacob Davids	131			
Adam Sheriff	W. 1/2 132		31.25	
Jacob Davids	133			
Joseph L. Chicks	134			
Catharine Mills	W. ½ 136			
Joseph Doxtater	144 & 145			
Isaac Jacobs	151			
Alexander Abrams	154			
Jacob Dayida	155			
Darius Dayida	156			
John Littleman	157			
Isaac Jacobs	158			
Hannah W. Chicks	159			
Catharine Mills	160			
Nathan Goodell	170			
John N. Chicks	173			
James N. Lane	174			
Jacob Davids	175			
Job Moore	176			
Thomas J. Chicks	179			
Harvey Johnson	180			
Nancy Gardner	181			
Abagail Jourdain	182			
Abram Chicks	184			
Bartholomew Bowman		186		
Harriet Jourdain	187			
Andrew Chicks	188			
Sarah Davids	189			
Job Moore	191			

William Gardner	S. part of 192, and 221	50
Mordy Mann	N. part of 192, and 221	70
Mary N. Chicks	194	
William Gardner	220	
Tripbane E. Jourdain		222
Caleb Moors	223	
Isaac Simons	224	
Isabel Chicks	225	
Sophia M. Jourdain	226	
Jesse Bownan	227	
Catharine Franks	228	
Jonathan Chicks	229	
Jonas Davids	231	
Adam Davids	232	
Linke Jourdain	233	
Elizabeth Moore	234	
Joseph Doxtater	235	
George Bennet	237	
Isaac Simmons	240	
Abigail Moore	263	
Henry Moore	264	
William Scott	265	
William Scott	S. 1/2 266	
George Bennet	N. ½ 266	
Reuben Johnson	267	
Silas Jourdain	268	
Jesse M. Jourdain	271	
Simon Gardner	274	
Hannah Moore	276	
Solomon Davids	277	
Edward Howell	279	
Harriet Johnson	280	
Lucinda Gardner	282	
Hope Moore	284	
Jemison C. Chicks	308	
Obadiah Gardner	309	
Rachael Davids	313	
Julius Davids	314	
Elizabeth Bowman	315	
Jeremiah Gardner	316	
Mary Jane Bowman		317
Nancy Johnson	319	
Jason Simmons	320	
Betsy Menagre	321	
Darius Davids	323	

Plains, West and Northwest Plateau Indian Treaties

Humble M. Jourdain		325
Stephen Gardner	326	
Francis T. Davids	327	
Mary McAllister	328	
Mary Hendrick	335	
Susannah Hendrick	349	
Jacob Moore	355	
David Gardner	357	
George Gardner	359	
Catharine Bowman	360	
Serepta Johnson	361	
Thankful Stephens	362	
William Gardner	364	
Joseph Chicks	365	
John Chicks	366	
Charles Stephens	367, 368	
Timothy Jourdain	369, 370, 371	
Jacob Chicks	372, 373	
Paul D. Hayward	375	
State of Wisconsin	383	School purposes.
Timothy Jourdain	384	
Jeremiah Johnson	385, 389	
American Board of Commissioners for Foreign Missions.		386,390
Jacob Chick	387, 391	
Timothy Jourdain	388	
John N. Chicks	392, 396	
William Gardner	393, 394, 397, 398	
Lemuel Goodell	N, end 395 2 acres.	
M. L. Martin.		
Albert G. Ellis.		

Valuation-of improvement. (vide ART. 6.)

	Acres	Dollars
Austin E. Quinney	163.38	2,760.63
	49.50	718.25
Joseph M. Quinney	30.90	617.15
Samuel Stevens	38.76	703.26
Moses Chicks	43.00	980.50
Elizabeth Palmer	29.06	512.41
Samuel Miller	55.62	880.87
Elisha Konkapot	5.00	142.50
Peter D. Littleman	3.25	168.88
John P. Quinney	15.50	267.50
Heirs of J. Yocum	5.78	78.03
Aaron Turkey	6.00	311.00

Plains, West and Northwest Plateau Indian Treaties

Benjamin Pye, 2d	40.00	640.00	
John Metoxen	50.00	825.00	
Mrs. B. Wright	5.00	67.50	
Abraham Pye	30.00	495.00	
Benjamin Pye, 4th		40.00	
Benjamin Pye, sr		40.00	
Benjamin Pye, 3d	20. 00	350.00	
Garrett Thompson	30. 00	485.00	
Ziba T. Peters	10. 00	215.00	
Betsy T. Aaron	3.00	85.00	
Thomas Skenandoah		17. 00	349.50
Simon S. Metoxen	30. 00	535.00	
Elizabeth Wilber	41.62	711.87	
Ezekiel Robinson	4. 00	60.00	
J. W. Quinney	60.00	1,315.00	
School-house		150.00	
		$14, 504.85	

M. L. Martin, Albert G. Ellis.

TREATY WITH THE NAVAHO {1849, Sept. 9}
Ratified Sept. 9, 1850.
Proclaimed Sept. 24, 1850.

THE following acknowledgements, declarations, and stipulations have been duly considered, and are now solemnly adopted and proclaimed by the undersigned; that is to say, John M. Washington, governor of New Mexico, and lieutenant-colonel commanding the troops of the United States in New Mexico, and James S. Calhoun, Indian agent, residing at Santa Fé, in New Mexico, representing the United States of America, and Mariano Martinez, head chief, and Chapitone, second chief, on the part of the Navajo tribe of Indians:

ARTICLE 1. The said Indians do hereby acknowledge that, by virtue of a treaty entered into by the United States of America and the United Mexican States, signed on the second day of February, in the year of our Lord eighteen hundred and forty-eight, at the city of Guadalupe Hidalgo, by N. P. Trist, of the first part, and Luis G. Cuevas, Bernardo Couto, and Mgl Atristain, of the second part, the said tribe was lawfully placed under the exclusive jurisdiction and protection of the Government of the said United States, and that they are now, and will forever remain, under the aforesaid jurisdiction and protection.

ARTICLE 2. That from and after the signing of this treaty, hostilities between the contracting parties shall cease, and perpetual peace and friendship shall exist; the said tribe hereby solemnly covenanting that they will not associate with, or give countenance or aid to, any tribe or band of Indians, or other persons or

Plains, West and Northwest Plateau Indian Treaties

powers, who may be at any time at enmity with the people of the said United States; that they will remain at peace, and treat honestly and humanely all persons and powers at peace with the said States; and all cases of aggression against said Navajoes by citizens or others of the United States, or by other persons or powers in amity with the said States, shall be referred to the Government of said States for adjustment and settlement.

ARTICLE 3. The Government of the said States having the sole and exclusive right of regulating the trade and intercourse with the said Navajoes, it is agreed that the laws now in force regulating the trade and intercourse, and for the preservation of peace with the various tribes of Indians under the protection and guardianship of the aforesaid Government, shall have the same force and efficiency, and shall be as binding and as obligatory upon the said Navajoes, and executed in the same manner, as if said laws had been passed for their sole benefit and protection; and to this end, and for all other useful purposes, the government of New Mexico, as now organized, or as it may be by the Government of the United States, or by the legally constituted authorities of the people of New Mexico, is recognized and acknowledged by the said Navajoes; and for the due enforcement of the aforesaid laws, until the Government of the United States shall otherwise order, the territory of the Navajoes is hereby annexed to New Mexico.

ARTICLE 4. The Navajo Indians hereby bind themselves to deliver to the military authority of the United States in New Mexico, at Santa Fé, New Mexico, as soon as he or they can be apprehended, the murderer or murderers of Micente Garcia, that said fugitive or fugitives from justice may be dealt with as justice may decree.

ARTICLE 5. All American and Mexican captives, and all stolen property taken from Americans or Mexicans, or other persons or powers in amity with the United States, shall be delivered by the Navajo Indians to the aforesaid military authority at Jemez, New Mexico, on or before the 9th day of October next ensuing, that justice may be meted out to all whom it may concern; and also all Indian captives and stolen property of such tribe or tribes of Indians as shall enter into a similar reciprocal treaty, shall, in like manner, and for the same purposes, be turned over to an authorized officer or agent of the said States by the aforesaid Navajoes.

ARTICLE 6. Should any citizen of the United States, or other person or persons subject to the laws of the United States, murder, rob, or otherwise maltreat any Navajo Indian or Indians, he or they shall be arrested and tried, and, upon conviction, shall be subjected to all the penalties provided by law for the protection of the persons and property of the people of the said States.

Plains, West and Northwest Plateau Indian Treaties

ARTICLE 7. The people of the United States of America shall have free and safe passage through the territory of the aforesaid Indians, under such rules and regulations as may be adopted by authority of the said States.

ARTICLE 8. In order to preserve tranquility, and to afford protection to all the people and interests of the contracting parties, the Government of the United States of America will establish such military posts and agencies, and authorize such trading-houses, at such time and in such places as the said Government may designate.

ARTICLE 9. Relying confidently upon the justice and the liberality of the aforesaid Government, and anxious to remove every possible cause that might disturb their peace and quiet, it is agreed by the aforesaid Navajoes that the Government of the United States shall, at its earliest convience, designate, settle, and adjust their territorial boundaries, and pass and execute in their territory such laws as may be deemed conducive to the prosperity and happiness of said Indians.

ARTICLE 10. For and in consideration of the faithful performance of all the stipulations herein contained by the said Navajo Indians, the Government of the United States will grant to said Indians such donations, presents, and implements, and adopt such other liberal and humane measures, as said Government may deem meet and proper.

ARTICLE 11. This treaty shall be binding upon the contracting parties from and after the signing of the same, subject only to such modifications and amendments as may be adopted by the Government of the United States; and, finally, this treaty is to receive a liberal construction, at all times and in all places, to the end that the said Navajo Indians shall not be held responsible for the conduct of others, and that the Government of the United States shall so legislate and act as to secure the permanent prosperity and happiness of said Indians.

In faith whereof, we, the undersigned, have signed this treaty, and affixed thereunto our seals, in the valley of Cheille, this the ninth day of September, in the year of our Lord one thousand eight hundred and forty-nine.

J. M. Washington, Brevet Lieutenant-Colonel Commanding.

Mariano Martinez, Head Chief, his x mark, Chapitone, Second Chief, his x mark, J. L. Collins.

Witnesses
H. L. Kendrick, Brevet Major U. S. Army, J. N. Ward, Brevet First Lieutenant Third Infantry, John Peck, Brevet Major U. S. Army.

Plains, West and Northwest Plateau Indian Treaties

J. F. Hammond, Assistant Surgeon U. S. Army.
H. L. Dodge, Captain commanding Eut. Regulars.

TREATY WITH THE UTAH {1849, Dec. 30}
Ratified, Sept. 9, 1850.
Proclaimed, Sept. 9, 1850.

THE following articles have been duly considered and solemnly adopted by the undersigned, that is to say, James S. Calhoun, Indian agent, residing at Santa Fé, acting as commissioner on the part of the United States of America, and Quixiachigiate, Nanito, Nincocunachi, Abaganixe, Ramahi, Subleta, Rupallachi, Saguasoxego, Paguisachi, Cobaxanor, Amuche, Puigigniachi, Panachi, Sichuga, Uvicaxinane, Cuchuticay,Nachitope, Pueguate, Guano Juas, Pacachi, Saguanchi, Acaguate nochi, Puibuquiacte, Quixache tuate, Saxiabe, Pithlute, Nochichigue, Uvive, principal and subordinate chiefs, representing the Utah tribe of Indians.

ARTICLE 1. The Utah tribe of Indians do hereby acknowledge and declare they are lawfully and exclusively under the jurisdiction of the Government of said States: and to its power and authority they now unconditionally submit.

ARTICLE 2. From and after the signing of this treaty, hostilities between the contracting parties shall cease, and perpetual peace and amity shall exist, the said tribe hereby binding themselves most solemnly never to associate with, or give countenance or aid to, any tribe or band of Indians, or other persons or powers, who may be, at any time, at enmity with the people or Government of said States; and that they will, in all future time, treat honestly and humanely every citizen of the United States, and all persons and powers at peace with the said States, and all cases of aggression against the said Utahs shall be referred to the aforesaid Government for adjustment and settlement.

ARTICLE 3. All American and Mexican captives, and others, taken from persons or powers at peace with the said States shall be restored and delivered by said Utahs to an authorized officer or agent of said States, at Abiquin, on or before the first day of March, in the year of our Lord one thousand eight hundred and fifty. And, in like manner, all stolen property, of every description, shall be restored by or before the aforesaid first day of March, 1850. In the event such stolen property shall have been consumed or destroyed, the said Utah Indians do agree and are hereby bound to make such restitution and under such circumstances as the Government of the United States may order and prescribe. But this article is not to be so construed or understood, as to create a claim against said States, for any losses or depredations committed by said Utahs.

255

Plains, West and Northwest Plateau Indian Treaties

ARTICLE 4. The contracting parties agree that the laws now in force, and such others as may be passed, regulating the trade and intercourse, and for the preservation of peace with the various tribes of Indians under the protection and guardianship of the Government of the United States, shall be as binding and obligatory upon the said Utahs as if said laws had been enacted for their sole benefit and protection. And that said laws may be duly executed, and for all other useful purposes, the territory occupied by the Utahs is hereby annexed to New Mexico as now organized or as it may be organized or until the Government of the United States shall otherwise order.

ARTICLE 5. The people of the United States, and all others in amity with the United States, shall have free passage through the territory of said Utahs, under such rules and regulations as may be adopted by authority of said States.

ARTICLE 6. In order to preserve tranquility, and to afford protection to all he people and interests of the contracting parties, the Government of he United States will establish such military posts and agencies, and authorize such trading-houses, at such time and in such places as the said Government may designate.

ARTICLE 7. Relying confidently upon the justice and liberality of the United States, and anxious to remove every possible cause that might disturb their peace and quiet, it is agreed by the Utahs that the aforesaid Government shall, at its earliest convenience, designate, settle, and adjust their territorial boundaries, and pass and execute such laws, in their territory, as the Government of said States may deem conducive to the happiness and prosperity of said Indians.

And the said Utahs, further, bind themselves not to depart from their accustomed homes or localities unless specially permitted by an agent of the aforesaid Government; and so soon as their boundaries are distinctly defined, the said Utahs are further bound to confine themselves to said limits, under such rules as the said Government may prescribe, and to build up pueblos, or to Settle in such other manner as will enable them most successfully to cultivate the soil, and pursue such other industrial pursuits as will best promote their happiness and prosperity: and they now deliberately and considerately, pledge their existence as a distinct tribe, to abstain, for all time to come, from all depredations; to cease the roving and rambling habits which have hitherto marked them as a people; to confine themselves strictly to the limits which may be assigned them; and to support themselves by their own industry, aided and directed as it may be by the wisdom, justice, and humanity of the American people.

ARTICLE 8. For, and in consideration of the faithful performance of all the stipulations contained in this treaty by the said Utahs, the Government of the United States will grant to said Indians such donations, presents, and imple-

Plains, West and Northwest Plateau Indian Treaties

ments, and adopt such other liberal and humane measures, as said Government may deem meet and proper.

ARTICLE 9. This treaty shall be binding upon the contracting parties from and after the signing of the same, subject, in the first place, to the approval of the civil and military governor of New Mexico, and to such other modifications, amendments, and orders as may be adopted by the Government of the United States.

In faith whereof, the undersigned have signed this treaty, and affixed thereunto their seals, at Abiquin, in New Mexico, this the thirtieth day of December, in the year of our Lord one thousand eight hundred and forty-nine.

James S. Calhoun, Indian Agent, Commissioner, U. S.

Quixiachigiate, his x mark, Principal Chief.
Nanito, his x mark, Nincocunachi, his x mark, Abaganixe, his x mark, Ramahi, his x mark, Subleta, his x mark, Rupallachi, his x mark, Saguasoxego, his x mark, Paguishachi, his x mark, Cobaxanor, his x mark, Amuche, his x mark, Puigniachi, his x mark, Panachi, his x mark, Sichuga, his x mark, Uvicaxinape, his x mark,

Witnesses:
Anto. Jesus Solosa, Franco Tomas Baco, Vicente Vilarde, his x mark, Interpreter, Antonio Leroux, Interpreter, James Conklin, Interpreter.
J. H. Whittlesey, First Lieutenant First Dragoons. Edward M. Kern, George W. Martin, Wm. H. Mitchell.

Approved:
John Munroe, Brevet Colonel U. S. Army, Civil and Military Governor.

TREATY WITH THE SIOUX SISSETON AND WAHPETON BANDS
{1851, July 23}
Proclamation, Feb. 24, 1853.

Articles of a treaty made and concluded at Traverse des Sioux, upon the Minnesota River, in the Territory of Minnesota, on the twenty-third day of July, eighteen hundred and fifty-one, between the United States of America, by Luke Lea, Commissioner of Indian Affairs, and Alexander Ramsey, governor and ex-officio superintendent of Indian affairs in said Territory, commissioners duly appointed for that purpose, and See-see-roan and Wah-pay-toan bands of Dakota or Sioux Indians.

Plains, West and Northwest Plateau Indian Treaties

ARTICLE 1. It is stipulated and solemnly agreed that the peace and friendship now so happily existing between the United States and the aforesaid bands of Indians, shall be perpetual.

ARTICLE 2. The said See-see-toan and Wah-pay-toan bands of Dakota or Sioux Indians, agree to cede, and do hereby cede, sell, and relinquish to the United States, all their lands in the State of Iowa; and, also all their lands in the Territory of Minnesota, lying east of the following line, to wit: Beginning at the junction of the Buffalo River with the Red River of the North; thence along the western bank of said Red River of the North, to the mouth of the Sioux Wood River; thence along the western bank of said Sioux Wood River to Lake Traverse; thence, along the western shore of said lake, to the southern extremity thereof; thence in a direct line, to the junction of Kampeska Lake with the Tchan-kas-an-data, or Sioux River; thence along the western bank of said river to its point of intersection with the northern line of the State of Iowa; including all the islands in said rivers and lake.

ARTICLE 3. (Stricken out.)

ARTICLE 4. In further and full consideration of said cession, the United States agree to pay to said Indians the sum of one million six hundred and sixty-five thousand dollars ($1,665,000) at the several times, in the manner and for the purposes following, to wit:

First. To the chiefs of the said bands, to enable them to settle their affairs and comply with their present just engagement; and in consideration of their removing themselves to the country set apart for them as above, which they agree to do within two years, or sooner, if required by the President, without further cost or expense to the United States, and in consideration of their subsisting themselves the first year after their removal, which they agree to do without further cost or expense on the part of the United States, the sum of two hundred and seventy-five thousand dollars, ($275,000): Provided, That said sum shall be paid to the chiefs in such manner as they, hereafter, in open council shall request, and as soon after the removal of said Indians to the home set apart for them, as the necessary appropriation therefor shall be made by Congress.

Second. To be laid out under the direction of the President for the establishment of manual-labor schools; the erection of mills and blacksmith shops, opening farms, fencing and breaking land, and for such other beneficial objects as may be deemed most conducive to the prosperity and happiness of said Indians, thirty thousand dollars, ($30,000.)

The balance of said sum of one million six hundred and sixty-five thousand dollars, ($1,665,000) to wit: one million three hundred and sixty thousand dollars ($1,360,000) to remain in trust with the United States, and five per cent

Plains, West and Northwest Plateau Indian Treaties

interest thereon to be paid, annually, to said Indians for the period of fifty years, commencing the first day of July, eighteen hundred and fifty-two (1852) which shall be in full payment of said balance, principal and interest, the said payment to be applied under the direction of the President, as follows, to wit:

Third. For a general agricultural improvement and civilization fund, the sum of twelve thousand dollars, Fourth. For educational purposes, the sum of six thousand dollars, ($6,000.)

Fifth. For the purchase of goods and provisions, the sum of ten thousand dollars, ($10,000.)

Sixth. For money annuity, the sum of forty thousand dollars, ($40,000.) ARTICLE 5. The laws of the United States prohibiting the introduction and sale of spirituous liquors in the Indian country shall be in full force and effect throughout the territory hereby ceded and lying in Minnesota until otherwise directed by Congress or the President of the United States.

ARTICLE 6. Rules and regulations to protect the rights of persons and property among the Indians, parties to this treaty, and adapted to their condition and wants, may be prescribed and enforced in such manner as the President or the Congress of the United States, from time to time, shall direct.
In testimony whereof, the said Commissioners, Luke Lea and Alexander Ramsey, and the undersigned Chiefs and Headmen of the aforesaid See-see-toan and Wah-pay-toan bands of Dakota or Sioux Indians, have hereunto subscribed their names and affixed their seals, in duplicate, at Traverse des Sioux, Territory of Minnesota, this twenty-third day of July, one thousand eight hundred and fifty-one.

L. Lea, Alex. Ramsey,
Een-yang-ma-nee, (Running Walker or "the Gun"), Wee-tchan-h'pee-ee-tay-toan, (the Star face or the "Orphan"), Ee-tay-wa-keen-yan, ("Limping Devil" or "Thunder Face"), Eesh-ta-hum-ba, ("Sleepy Eyes"), Oo-pee-ya-hen-day-a, (Extending his train), Hoak-shee-dan-wash-tay, (Good Boy), Ee-tay-tcho-ka, (Face in the midst), Hay-ha-hen-day-ma-za, (Metal Horn), Am-pay-too-sha, (Red Day), Eesh-ta-humba-koash-ka, (Sleepy Eyes young), A na-wang-ma-nee,

Signed in presence of
Thomas Foster, Secretary, Nathaniel McLean, Indian Agent, Alexander Faribault, Stephen R. Riggs, Interpreters.

To the Indian names are subjoined marks.

SUPPLEMENTAL ARTICLE. First. The United States do hereby stipulate to pay the Sioux bands of Indians, parties to this treaty, at the rate of ten cents per

Plains, West and Northwest Plateau Indian Treaties

acre, for the lands included in the reservation provided for in the third article of the treaty as originally agreed upon in the following words: "ARTICLE 3. In part consideration of the foregoing cession, the United States do hereby set apart for the future occupancy and home of the Dakota Indians, parties to this treaty, to be held by them as Indian lands are held, all that tract of country on either side of the Minnesota River, from the western boundary of the lands herein ceded, east, to the Tchay-tam-bay River on the north, and to Yellow Medicine River on the south side, to extend, on each side, a distance of not less than ten miles from the general course of said river; the boundaries of said tract to be marked out by as straight lines as practicable, whenever deemed expedient by the President, and in such manner as he shall direct:" Which article has been stricken out of the treaty by the Senate, the said payment to be in lieu of said reservation: the amount when ascertained under instructions from the Department of the Interior, to be added to the trust-fund provided for in the fourth article.

Second. It is further stipulated, that the President be authorized, with the assent of the said band of Indians, parties to this treaty, and as soon after they shall have given their assent to the foregoing article, as may be convenient, to cause to be set apart by appropriate landmarks and boundaries, such tracts of country without the limits of the cession made by the first (2d) article of the treaty as may be satisfactory for their future occupancy and home: Provided, That the President may, by the consent of these Indians, vary the conditions aforesaid if deemed expedient.

TREATY WITH THE SIOUX MDEWAKANTON AND WAHPAKOOTA BANDS {1851, Aug. 5}
Proclamation Feb. 24, 1853.

Articles of a treaty made and concluded at Mendora, in the Territory of Minnesota, on the fifth day of August, eighteen hundred and fifty-one, between the United States of America, by Luke Lea, Commissioner of Indian Affairs, and Alexander Ramsey, governor and ex-officio superintendent of Indian affairs in said Territory, commissioners duly appointed for that purpose, and the Med-ay-wa-kan-toan and Wah-pay-koo-tay bands of Dakota and Sioux Indians.

ARTICLE 1. The peace and friendship existing between the United States and the Med-ay-wa-kan-toan and Wah-pay-koo-tay bands of Dakota or Sioux Indians shall be perpetual.

ARTICLE 2. The said Med-ay-wa-kan-toan and Wah-pay-koo-tay bands of Indians do hereby cede and relinquish all their lands and all their right, title and claim to any lands whatever, in the Territory of Minnesota, or in the State of Iowa.

Plains, West and Northwest Plateau Indian Treaties

ARTICLE 3. (Stricken out.)

ARTICLE 4. In further and full consideration of said cession and relinquishment, the United States agree to pay to said Indians the sum of one million four hundred and ten thousand dollars, ($1,410,000) at the several times, in the manner and for the purposes following, to wit:

First. To the chiefs of the said bands, to enable them to settle their affairs and comply with their present just engagements; and in consideration of their removing themselves to the country set apart for them as above, (which they agree to do within one year after the ratification of this treaty, without further cost or expense to the United States) and in consideration of their subsisting themselves the first year after their removal, (which they agree to do without further cost or expense on the part of the United States) the sum of two hundred and twenty thousand dollars ($220,000.) Provided, That said sum shall be paid, one-half to the chiefs of the Med-ay-wa-kan-toan band, and one-half to the chief and headmen of the Wah-pay-koo-tay band, in such manner as they, hereafter, in open council, shall respectively request, and as soon after the removal of said Indians to the home set apart for them as the necessary appropriations therefor shall be made by Congress.

Second. To be laid out, under the direction of the President, for the establishment of manual labor schools; the erection of mills and blacksmith shops, opening farms, fencing and breaking land, and for such other beneficial objects as may be deemed most conducive to the prosperity and happiness of said Indians, thirty thousand dollars ($30,000.)

The balance of said sum of one million four hundred and ten thousand dollars, ($1,410,000) to wit: one million, one hundred and sixty thousand dollars ($1,160,000)to remain in trust with the United States, and five per cent interest thereon to be paid annually to said Indians for the period of fifty years, commencing on the first day of July, eighteen hundred and fifty-two (1852) which shall be in full payment of said balance, principal and interest: said payments to be made and applied, under the direction of the President as follows, to wit:

Third. For a general agricultural improvement and civilization fund, the sum of twelve thousand dollars, ($12,000.)

Fourth. For educational purposes, the sum of six thousand dollars, ($6,000.)

Fifth. For the purchase of goods and provisions, the sum of ten thousand dollars, ($10,000.)

Sixth. For money annuity, the sum of thirty thousand dollars, ($30,000.)

Plains, West and Northwest Plateau Indian Treaties

ARTICLE 5. The entire annuity, provided for in the first section of the second article of the treaty of September twenty-ninth, eighteen hundred and thirty-seven, (1837) including an unexpended balance that may be in the Treasury on the first of July, eighteen hundred and fifty-two, (1852) shall thereafter be paid in money.

ARTICLE 6. The laws of the United States prohibiting the introduction and sale of spirituous liquors in the Indian country shall be in full force and effect throughout the territory hereby ceded and lying in Minnesota until otherwise directed by Congress or the President of the United States.

ARTICLE 7. Rules and regulations to protect the rights of persons and property among the Indian parties to this Treaty, and adapted to their condition and wants, may be prescribed and enforced in such manner as the President or the Congress of the United States, from time to time, shall direct.

In witness whereof, the said Luke Lea and Alexander Ramsey, Commissioners on the part of the United States and the undersigned Chiefs and Headmen of the Med-ay-wa-kan-toan and Wah-pay-koo-tay bands of Dakota or Sioux Indians, have hereunto set their hands, at Mendota, in the Territory of Minnesota, this fifth day of August, Anno Domini, one thousand eight hundred and fifty-one.

L. Lea.
Alex. Ramsey.

Med-ay-wa-kan-toans:
Chief

Ta-oya-te-duta, (his scarlet people, or "Little Crow"),
Headmen
Wa-kan-o-zhan, (Sacred Light, or Medicine Bottle), Tee-tchay, (Top of the Lodge or "Jim," or "Old Thad"), Ta-tchan-h' pee-sa-pa, (His "Black Toma-hawk"), Ma-ka-na-ho-toan-ma-nee, (At whose tread the earth resounds), H'-da-ee-yan-kay, (he runs rattling), Too-kan-a-hena-ma-nee, (Walker on the Medi-cine Boulders or Stones), Wa-m' dee-doo-ta, (Scarlet War Eagle), Na-ghee-yoo-shkan, (He moves the Ghosts or Shadows), Shoank'-a-ska, ("White Dog"),
Headmen
Wa-kan-hendee-o-ta, (Many Lightnings), Tchan-h' pee-yoo-ka, (He has a war club), Heen-han-doo-ta, (Red Owl), Ma ka-ka-ee-day, (He sets the Earth on fire),
Headmen
Ma-h'pee-ya-ma za, (Metal cloud), Ta-ma-za-ho-wash-tay, (his good iron voice), Ma-ka ta-na-zheen, (He stands on the earth), Ee-wan-kam-ee-na-zhan, (He stands above), Wa-kan-ta-pay-ta, (The Spirit' s Fire), Na-ghee-mee-tcha-

262

Plains, West and Northwest Plateau Indian Treaties

keetay, (He kills the Ghosts), Een-yan-sha-sha, (Red Stones), Ee-day-wa-kan, (Sacred Blaze), Ta-sag-yay-ma-za, (His metal Staff),
Chief Ma-h' pee mee-tchash-tay,(man of the sky),
Headmen
Wee-tchan-h' pee, (The Star), Ta-tay-na-zhee-na, (Little standing Wind),
Headmen
Hoak-shee-dan-doo-ta, (Scarlet Boy), Am-pay-sho-ta, (Smoky Day), Ha-ha-ka-ma-za, (Metal Elk), Ta-ray-h'moo-he-ya-ya, ("Whistling Wind"), Wa-pa-ma-nee, (He strikes walking), Ma-h'pee-ya-wa-kan, (Sacred Cloud), Ta-tchan-
Headmen
Wa-soo-mee-tchash-ta-shnee, (Wicked or "Bad Hail"), Oan-ketay-hee-dan,(LittleWater-God or "Little Whale"), Tcha-noon-pay-sa, (The Smoker), Ta-tay-to-kay-tcha, (Other wind), Ka-ho, (The Rambler about),
Chief Ta-tchan-koo-wash-tay, (Good Road),
Headmen
Ta-tay-o-wo-teen-ma-nee, (Roaring Wind that walks), O-yay-tchan-ma-nee, (Track Maker),
Ta-shoark-ay, (His Dog),
Chief Sha-k'pay, ("Six"),
Headmen
A-no-ghee-ma-zheen, (He that stands on both sides),
Headmen
Ma-za-wa-menoo-ha, (Gourd shell metal medicine rattle),
Chief Hay-ee-tcha-h' moo-ma-nee, (Horn whistling walking), Ta-wo-ta-way-doo-ta, (His Scarlet Armor), Hay-pee, (Third Son),

In presence of
Thomas Foster, Secretary, Nathaniel McLean, Indian Agent, Alexander Fariboult, P. Prescott, G. H. Pond, Interpreters.

To the Indian names are subjoined marks.

SUPPLEMENTAL ARTICLE. First. The United States do hereby stipulate to pay the Sioux bands of Indians, parties to this treaty, at the rate of ten cents per acre, for the lands included in the reservation provided for in the third article of the treaty as originally agreed upon in the following words:

ARTICLE 3. In part consideration of the foregoing cession and relinquishment, the United States do hereby set apart for the future occupancy and home of the Dakota Indians, parties to this treaty, to be held by them as Indian lands are held, a tract of country of the average width of ten miles on either side of the Minnesota River, and bounded on the west by the Tchaytam-bay and Yellow Medicine Rivers, and on the east by the Little Rock River and a line running due south from its mouth to the Waraju River; the boundaries of said tract to be marked out by as straight lines as practicable, whenever and in such manner as

Plains, West and Northwest Plateau Indian Treaties

the President of the United States shall direct: Provided, That said tract shall be held and occupied by said bands in common, and that they shall hereafter participate equally and alike, m all the benefits derived from any former treaty between said bands, or either of them, and the United States," which article has been stricken out of the treaty by the Senate. The said payment to be in lieu of said reservation; the amount, when ascertained under instructions from the Department of the Interior, to be added to the trust fund provided for in the fourth article.

Second. It is further stipulated that the President be authorized, with the assent of the said bands of Indians, parties to this treaty, and as soon after they shall have given their assent to the foregoing article, as may be convenient, to cause to be set apart by appropriate landmarks and boundaries, such tracts of country without the limits of the cession made by the first article of the treaty as may be satisfactory for their future occupancy and home: Provided, That the President may, by the consent of these Indians, vary the conditions aforesaid if deemed expedient.

TREATY OF FORT LARAMIE WITH SIOUX, ETC. {1851, Sept. 17}

Articles of a treaty made and concluded at Fort Laramie, in the Indian Territory, between D. D. Mitchell, superintendent of Indian affairs, and Thomas Fitzpatrick, Indian agent, commissioners specially appointed and authorized by the President of the United States, of the first part, and the chiefs, headmen, and braves of the following Indian nations, residing south of the Missouri River, east of the Rocky Mountains, and north of the lines of Texas and New Mexico, viz, the Sioux or Dahcotahs, Cheyennes, Arrapahoes, Crows, Assinaboines, Gros-Ventre Mandans, and Arrickaras, parties of the second part, on the seventeenth day of September, A.D. one thousand eight hundred and fifty-one. (a)

ARTICLE 1. The aforesaid nations, parties to this treaty, having assembled for the purpose of establishing and confirming peaceful relations amongst themselves, do hereby covenant and agree to abstain in future from all hostilities whatever against each other, to maintain good faith and friendship in all their mutual intercourse, and to make an effective and lasting peace.

ARTICLE 2. The aforesaid nations do hereby recognize the right of the United States Government to establish roads, military and other posts, within their respective territories.

ARTICLE 3. In consideration of the rights and privileges acknowledged in the preceding article, the United States bind themselves to protect the aforesaid Indian nations against the commission of all depredations by the people of the said United States, after the ratification of this treaty.

Plains, West and Northwest Plateau Indian Treaties

ARTICLE 4. The aforesaid Indian nations do hereby agree and bind them-selves to make restitution or satisfaction for any wrongs committed, after the ratification of this treaty, by any band or individual of their people, on the peo-ple of the United States, whilst lawfully residing in or passing through their respective territories.

ARTICLE 5. The aforesaid Indian nations do hereby recognize and acknowl-edge the following tracts of country, included within the metes and boundaries hereinafter designated, as their respective territories, viz;
The territory of the Sioux or Dahcotah Nation, commencing the mouth of the White Earth River, on the Missouri River; thence in a southwesterly direction to the forks of the Platte River; thence up the north fork of the Platte River to a point known as the Red Buts, or where the road leaves the river; thence along the range of mountains known as the Black Hills, to the head-waters of Heart River; thence down Heart River to its mouth; and thence down the Missouri River to the place of beginning.

The territory of the Gros Ventre, Mandans, and Arrickaras Nations, commenc-ing at the month of Heart River; thence up the Missouri River to the mouth of the Yellowstone River; thence up the Yellowstone River to the mouth of Pow-der River in a southeasterly direction, to the head-waters of the Little Missouri River; thence along the Black Hills to the head of Heart River, and thence down Heart River to the place of beginning.

The territory of the Assinaboin Nation, commencing at the mouth of Yellow-stone River; thence up the Missouri River to the mouth of the Muscle-shell River; thence from the mouth of the Muscle-shell River in a southeasterly di-rection until it strikes the head-waters of Big Dry Creek; thence down that creek to where it empties into the Yellowstone River, nearly opposite the mouth of Powder River, and thence down the Yellowstone River to the place of beginning.

The territory of the Blackfoot Nation, commencing at the mouth of Muscle-shell River; thence up the Missouri River to its source; thence along the main range of the Rocky Mountains, in a southerly direction, to the head-waters of the northern source of the Yellowstone River; thence down the Yellowstone River to the mouth of Twenty-five Yard Creek; thence across to the head-waters of the Muscle-shell River, and thence down the Muscle-shell River to the place of beginning.

The territory of the Crow Nation, commencing at the mouth of Powder River on the Yellowstone; thence up Powder River to its source; thence along the main range of the Black Hills and Wind River Mountains to the head-waters of the Yellowstone River; thence down the Yellowstone River to the mouth of

265

Plains, West and Northwest Plateau Indian Treaties

Twenty-five Yard Creek; thence to the head waters of the Muscle-shell River; thence down the Muscle-shell River to its mouth; thence to the head-waters of Big Dry Creek, and thence to its mouth.

The territory of the Cheyennes and Arrapahoes, commencing at the Red Bute, or the place where the road leaves the north fork of the Platte River; thence up the north fork of the Platte River to its source; thence along the main range of the Rocky Mountains to the head-waters of the Arkansas River; thence down the Arkansas River to the crossing of the Santa Fe' road; thence in a northwesterly direction to the forks of the Platte River, and thence up the Platte River to the place of beginning.

It is, however, understood that, in making this recognition and acknowledgement, the aforesaid Indian nations do not hereby abandon or prejudice any rights or claims they may have to other lands; and further, that they do not surrender the privilege of hunting, fishing, or passing over any of the tracts of country heretofore described.

ARTICLE 6. The parties to the second part of this treaty having selected principals or head-chiefs for their respective nations, through whom all national business will hereafter be conducted, do hereby bind themselves to sustain said chiefs and their successors during good behavior.

ARTICLE 7. In consideration of the treaty stipulations, and for the damages which have or may occur by reason thereof to the Indian nations, parties hereto, and for their maintenance and the improvement of their moral and social customs, the United States bind themselves to deliver to the said Indian nations the sum of fifty thousand dollars per annum for the term of ten years, with the right to continue the same at the discretion of the President of the United States for a period not exceeding five years thereafter, in provisions merchandise, domestic animals, and agricultural implements, in such proportions as may be deemed best adapted to their condition by the President of the United States, to be distributed in proportion to the population of the aforesaid Indian nations.

ARTICLE 8. It is understood and agreed that should any of the Indian nations, parties to this treaty, violate any of the provisions thereof, the United States may withhold the whole or a portion of the annuities mentioned in the preceding article from the nation so offending, until, in the opinion of the President of the United States, proper satisfaction shall have been made.
In testimony whereof the said D. D. Mitchell and Thomas Fitzpatrick commissioners as aforesaid, and the chiefs, headmen, and braves, parties hereto, have set their hands and affixed their marks, on the day and at the place first above written.

D. D. Mitchell

Plains, West and Northwest Plateau Indian Treaties

Thomas Fitzpatrick Commissioners.

Sioux:
Mah-toe-wha-you-whey, his x mark, Mah-kah-toe-zah-zah, his x mark, Bel-o-ton-kah-tan-ga, his x mark, Nah-ka-pah-gi-gi, his x mark, Mak-toe-sah-bi-chis, his x mark, Meh-wha-tah-ni-hans-kah, his x mark,
Cheyennes:
Wah-ha-nis-satta, his x mark, Voist-ti-toe-vetz, his x mark, Nahk-ko-me-ien, his x mark, Koh-kah-y-wh-cum-est, his x mark,
Arrapahoes:
Bè-ah-té-a-qui-sah, his x mark, Neb-ni-bah-seh-it, his x mark, Beh-kah-jay-beth-sah-es, his x mark,
Crows:
Arra-tu-ri-sash, his x mark, Doh-chepit-seh-chi-es, his x mark,
Assinaboines:
Mah-toe-wit-ko, his x mark, Toe-tah-ki-eh-nan, his x mark, Mandans and Gros Ventres:
Nochk-pit-shi-toe-pish, his x mark, She-oh-mant-ho, his x mark,
Arickarees:
Koun-hei-ti-shan, his x mark, Bi-atch-tah-wetch, his x mark,

Witnesses:
A. B. Chambers, secretary S. Cooper, colonel, U. S. Army, R. H. Chilton,, Captain, First Drags, Thomas Duncan, captain, Mounted Riflemen.

(a) This treaty as signed was ratified by the Senate with an amendment changing the annuity in Article 7 from fifty to ten years, subject to acceptance by the tribes. Assent of all tribes except the Crows was procured (see Upper Platte C., 570, 1853, Indian Office) and in subsequent agreements this treaty has been recognized as in force.

Plains, West and Northwest Plateau Indian Treaties

TREATY WITH THE APACHE {1852, July 1}
Ratified Mar. 23, 1853.
Proclaimed Mar. 25, 1853.

Articles of a treaty made and entered into at Santa Fe, New Mexico, on the first day of July in the year of our Lord one thousand eight hundred and fifty-two, by and between Col. E. V. Sumner, U. S. A., commanding the 9th Department and in charge of the executive office of New Mexico, and John Greiner, Indian agent in and for the Territory of New Mexico, and acting superintendent of Indian affairs of said Territory, representing the United States, and Cuentas, Azules, Blancito, Negrito, Capitan Simon, Capitan Vuelta, and Mangus Colorado, chiefs, acting on the part of the Apache Nation of Indians, situate and living within the limits of the United States.

ARTICLE 1. Said nation or tribe of Indians through their authorized Chiefs aforesaid do hereby acknowledge and declare that they are lawfully and exclusively under the laws, jurisdiction, and government of the United States of America, and to its power and authority they do hereby submit.

ARTICLE 2. From and after the signing of this Treaty hostilities between the contracting parties shall forever cease, and perpetual peace and amity shall forever exist between said Indians and the Government and people of the United States; the said nation, or tribe of Indians, hereby binding themselves most solemnly never to associate with or give countenance or aid to any tribe or band of Indians, or other persons or powers, who may be at any time at war or enmity with the government or people of said United States.

ARTICLE 3. Said nation, or tribe of Indians, do hereby bind themselves for all future time to treat honestly and humanely all citizens of the United States, with whom they have intercourse, as well as all persons and powers, at peace with the said United States, who may be lawfully among them, or with whom they may have any lawful intercourse.

ARTICLE 4. All said nation, or tribe of Indians, hereby bind themselves to refer all cases of aggression against themselves or their property and territory, to the government of the United States for adjustment, and to conform in all things to the laws, rules, and regulations of said government in regard to the Indian tribes.

ARTICLE 5. Said nation, or tribe of Indians, do hereby bind themselves for all future time to desist and refrain from making any "incursions within the Territory of Mexico" of a hostile or predatory character; and that they will for the future refrain from taking and conveying into captivity any of the people or citizens of Mexico, or the animals or property of the people or government of

Plains, West and Northwest Plateau Indian Treaties

Mexico; and that they will, as soon as possible after the signing of this treaty, surrender to their agent all captives now in their possession.

ARTICLE 6. Should any citizen of the United States, or other person or persons subject to the laws of the United States, murder, rob, or otherwise maltreat any Apache Indian or Indians, he or they shall be arrested and tried, and upon conviction, shall be subject to all the penalties provided by law for the protection of the persons and property of the people of the said States.

ARTICLE 7. The people of the United States of America shall have free and safe passage through the territory of the aforesaid Indians, under such rules and regulations as may be adopted by authority of the said States.

ARTICLE 8. In order to preserve tranquility and to afford protection to all the people and interests of the contracting parties, the government of the United States of America will establish such military posts and agencies, and authorize such trading houses at such times and places as the said government may designate.

ARTICLE 9. Relying confidently upon the justice and the liberality of the aforesaid government, and anxious to remove every possible cause that night disturb their peace and quiet, it is agreed by the aforesaid Apache's that the government of the United States shall, at its earliest convenience designate, settle, and adjust their territorial boundaries, and pass and execute in their territory such laws as may be deemed conducive to the prosperity and happiness of said Indians.

ARTICLE 10. For and in consideration of the faithful performance of all the stipulations herein contained, by the said Apache's Indians, the government of the United States will grant to said Indians such donations, presents, and implements, and adopt such other liberal and humane measures as said government may deem meet and proper.

ARTICLE 11. This Treaty shall be binding upon the contracting parties from and after the signing of the same, subject only to such modifications and amendments as may be adopted by the government of the United States; and, finally, this treaty is to receive a liberal construction, at all times and in all places, to the end that the said Apache Indians shall not be held responsible for the conduct of others, and that the government of the United States shall so legislate and act as to secure the permanent prosperity and happiness of said Indians.

In faith whereof we the undersigned have signed this Treaty, and affixed thereunto our seals, at the City of Santa Fé, this the first day of July in the year of our Lord one thousand eight hundred and fifty-two.

Plains, West and Northwest Plateau Indian Treaties

E. V. Sumner, Bvt. Col. U. S. A. commanding Ninth Department In charge of
Executive Office of New Mexico, John Greiner, Act. Supt. Indian Affairs, New
Mexico.

Witnesses:
F. A. Cunningham, Paymaster, U. S. A.
J. C. McFerran, 1st Lt. 3d Inf. Act. Ast. Adj. Gen.
Caleb Sherman.

TREATY WITH THE COMANCHE, KIOWA, AND APACHE
{1853, July 27}
Ratified Apr. 12, 1854.

Articles of a treaty, made and concluded at Fort Atkinson, in the Indian Territory, of the United States of America, on the 27th day of July, anno Domini
eighteen hundred and fifty-three, between the United States of America, by
Thomas Fitzpatrick, Indian agent, and sole commissioner, duly appointed for
that purpose, and the Camanche, and Kiowa, and Apache tribes or nations of
Indians, inhabiting the said territory south of the Arkansas River.

ARTICLE 1.   Peace, friendship, and amity shall hereafter exist between the
United States and the Camanche and Kiowa, and Apache tribes of Indians, parties to this treaty, and the same shall be perpetual.

ARTICLE 2.   The Camanche, Kiowa, and Apache tribes of Indians do hereby
jointly and severally covenant that peaceful relations shall likewise be maintained amongst themselves in future; and that they will abstain from all hostilities whatsoever against each other, and cultivate mutual good-will and friendship.

ARTICLE 3.   The aforesaid Indian tribes do also hereby fully recognize and
acknowledge the right of the United States to lay off and mark out roads or
highwaysto make reservations of land necessary theretoto locate depots and to
establish military and other posts within the territories inhabited by the said
tribes; and also to prescribe and enforce, in such manner as the President or the
Congress of the United States shall from time to time direct, rules and regulations to protect the rights of persons and property among the said Indian tribes.

ARTICLE 4.   The Camanche, Kiowa, and Apache tribes, parties as before recited, do further agree and bind themselves to make restitution or satisfaction
for any injuries done by any band or any individuals of their respective tribes to
the people of the United States who may be lawfully residing in or passing
through their said territories; and to abstain hereafter from levying contribu-

Plains, West and Northwest Plateau Indian Treaties

tions from, or molesting them in any manner; and, so far as may be in their power, to render assistance to such as need relief, and to facilitate their safe passage.

ARTICLE 5. The Camanche, and Kiowa, and Apache tribes of Indians, parties to this treaty, do hereby solemnly covenant and agree to refrain in future from warlike incursions into the Mexican provinces, and from all depredations upon the inhabitants thereof; and they do likewise bind themselves to restore all captives that may hereafter be taken by any of the bands, war-parties, or individuals of the said several tribes, from the Mexican provinces aforesaid, and to make proper and just compensation for any wrongs that may be inflicted upon the people thereof by them, either to the United States or to the Republic of Mexico, as the President of the United States may direct and require.

ARTICLE 6. In consideration of the foregoing agreements on the part of the Camanche, and Kiowa, and Apache tribes, parties to this treatyof the losses which they may sustain by reason of the travel of the people of the United States through their territoriesand for the better support, and the improvement of the social condition of the said tribes the United States do bind themselves, and by these presents stipulate to deliver to the Camanche, Kiowa, and Apache tribes aforesaid, the sum of eighteen thousand dollars per annum, for and during the term of ten years next ensuing from this date, and for the additional term of five years, if, in the opinion of the President of the United States, such extension shall be advisable;the same to be given to them in goods, merchandise, provisions, or agricultural implements, or in such shape as may be best adapted to their wants, and as the President of the United States may designate, and to be distributed amongst the said several tribes in proportion to the respective numbers of each tribe.

ARTICLE 7. The United. States do moreover bind themselves, in consideration of the covenants contained in the preceding articles of this treaty, to protect and defend the Indian tribes, parties hereto, against the committal of any depredations upon them, and in their territories, by the people of the United States, for and during the term for which this treaty shall be in force, and to compensate them for any injuries that may result therefrom.

ARTICLE 8. It is also stipulated and provided, by and between the parties to this treaty, that should any of the Indian tribes aforesaid violate any of the conditions, provisions, or agreements herein con-rained, or fail to perform any of the obligations entered into on their part, then the United States may withhold the whole or a part of the annuities mentioned in the sixth article of this treaty, from the tribe so offending, until, in the opinion of the President or the Congress of the United States, proper satisfaction shall have been made, or until persons amongst the said Indians offending against the laws of the United States shall have been delivered up to justice.

Plains, West and Northwest Plateau Indian Treaties

ARTICLE 9. It is also consented to and determined between the parties hereto, that the annuities to be given on the part of the United States, as provided in the sixth article of this treaty, shall be delivered to the said Indian tribes collectively, at or in the vicinity of Beaver Creek, yearly, during the month of July in each year, until some other time and place shall have been designated by the President of the United States, in which event the said Indian tribes shall have due notice thereof, and the place of distribution which may be selected shall always be some point within the territories occupied by the said tribes.

ARTICLE 10. It is agreed between the United States and the Camanche, Kiowa, and Apache tribes of Indians, that, should it at any time hereafter be considered by the United States as a proper policy to establish farms among and for the benefit of said Indians, it shall be discretionary with the President, by and with the advice and consent of the Senate, to change the annuities herein provided for, or any part thereof, into a fund for that purpose.

In witness whereof, the said Thomas Fitzpatrick, Indian Agent, and sole commissioner on the part of the United States, and the undersigned chiefs and headmen of the Camanche and Kiowa, and Apache tribes or nations, have hereunto set their hands, at Fort Atkinson, in the Indian Territory of the United States, this twenty-seventh day of July, A. D. eighteen hundred and fifty-three.

Thomas Fitzpatrick, Indian Agent, and Commissioner on behalf of the United States.
B. Gratz Brown, Secretary.
R. H. Chilton.
B. T. Moylero.

Wulea-boo, his x mark (Shaved Head), chief Camanche.
Wa-ya-ba-tos-a, his x mark (White Eagle), chief of band.
Hai-nick-seu, his x mark (The Crow), chief of band.
Paro-sa-wa-no, his x mark (Ten Sticks), chief of band.

Witness:
B. B. Dayton, Geo. M. Alexander, T. Polk, Geo. Collier, jr.

We do hereby accept and consent to the Senate amendments to the treaty aforesaid, and agree that the same may be considered as a part thereof.
In testimony whereof we have hereunto set our hands and affixed our seals, this 21st day of July, A. D. 1854.

Camanches: To-che-ra-nah-boo, (Shaved Head), his x mark, Wa-ya-ba-to-sa, (White Eagle), his x mark, Hai-nick-seu, (Crow), his x mark, Ty-har-re-ty,

272

Plains, West and Northwest Plateau Indian Treaties

(One who runs after women), his x mark, Para-sar-a-man-no, (Ten Bears), his x mark,

Kiowas:
To-han-seu, (Little Mountain), his x mark, Ti-sank-ki, (Sitting Bear), his x mark, Ko-a-ty-ka, (Wolf outside), his x mark,

Executed in presence of
Aquilla T. Ridgely, assistant surgeon, U. S. Army, A. H. Plummer, brevet second lieutenant, Sixth Infantry, Paul Carrey, John Kinney, United States interpreter, H. E. Nixon, clerk.

I certify that the foregoing amendments to the treaty of 27th day of July, 1853, was read add explained to the chiefs, and that they consented to, and signed the same on the 21st day of July, 1854.

J. W. Whitfield, Indian Agent.

TREATY WITH THE ROGUE RIVER {1853, Sept. 10}
Ratified Apr. 12, 1854.
Proclaimed Feb. 5, 1855.

Whereas a treaty was made and entered into at Table Rock, near Rogue River, in the Territory of Oregon, this 10th day of September, A. D. 1853, by and between Joel Palmer, superintendent of Indian affairs, and Samuel H. Culver, Indian agent, on the part of the United States; and Jo-aps-er-ka-har, principal chief, Sam To-qua-he-ar, and Jim Ana-cha-a-rah, subordinate chiefs, and others, head-men of the bands of the Rogue River tribe of Indians, on the part of said tribe.

ARTICLE 1. The Rogue River tribe of Indians do hereby cede and relinquish, for the considerations hereinafter specified, to the United States, all their right, title, interest, and claim to all the lands lying in that part of the Territory of Oregon, and bounded by lines designated as follows, to wit:
Commencing at a point one mile below the mouth of Applegate Creek, on the south side of Rogue River, running thence southerly to the highlands dividing the waters of Applegate Creek from those of Althouse Creek, thence along said highlands to the summit of the Siskiyou range of mountains, thence easterly to Pilot Rock, thence northeasterly to the summit of the Cascade range, thence northerly along the said Cascade range to Pitt's Peak, continuing northerly to Rogue River, thence westerly to the head-waters of Jump-off-jo Creek, thence down said creek to the intersection of the same with a line due north from the place of beginning, thence to the place of beginning.

Plains, West and Northwest Plateau Indian Treaties

ARTICLE 2. It is agreed on the part of the United States that the aforesaid tribe shall be allowed to occupy temporarily that portion of the above-described tract of territory bounded as follows, to wit: Commencing on the north side of Rogue River, at the mouth of Evan's Creek; thence up said creek to the upper end of a small prairie bearing in a northwesterly direction from Table Mountain, or Upper Table Rock, thence through the gap to the south side of the cliff of the said mountain, thence in a line to Rogue River, striking the southern base of Lower Table Rock, thence down said river to the place of beginning. It being understood that this described tract of land shall be deemed and considered an Indian reserve, until a suitable selection shall be made by the direction of the President of the United States for their permanent residence and buildings erected thereon, and provision made for their removal.

ARTICLE 3. For and in consideration of the cession and relinquishment contained in article 1st, the United States agree to pay to the aforesaid tribe the sum of sixty thousand dollars, fifteen thousand of which sum to be retained, (according to the stipulations of article 4th of a "treat of peace made and entered into on the 8th day of September, 1853 {This agreement is unratified and a copy of the original agreement on file in the Indian Office (Oregon, 1844-1858, Ore. Sup. L., 323) has been included in the Appendix, post, p. 1049.} between Gen'l Jo. Lane, commanding forces of Oregon Territory, and Jo., principal chief, Sam and Jim, subordinate chiefs, on the part of the Rogue River tribe of Indians,") by the-superintendent of Indian affairs, to pay for the property of the whites destroyed by them during the late war, the amount of property so destroyed to be estimated by three disinterested commissioners, to be appointed by the superintendent of Indian affairs, or otherwise, as the President may direct.

Five thousand dollars to be expended in the purchase of agricultural implements, blankets, clothing, and such other goods as may be deemed by the superintendent, or agent most conducive to the comfort and necessities of said tribe, on or before the 1st day of September, 1854; and for the payment of such permanent improvements as may have been made by land claimants on the aforesaid reserve, the value of which to be ascertained by three persons appointed by the said superintendent.

The remaining forty thousand dollars to be paid in sixteen equal annual instalments, of two thousand five hundred dollars each, (commencing on or about the 1st day of September, 1854) in blankets, clothing, farming-utensils, stock, and such other articles as may be deemed most conducive to the interests of said tribe.

ARTICLE 4. It is further agreed that there shall be erected, at the expense of the United States, one dwelling-house for each of the three principal chiefs of the aforesaid tribe, the cost of which shall not exceed five hundred dollars each

Plains, West and Northwest Plateau Indian Treaties

the aforesaid buildings to be erected as soon after the ratification of this treaty as possible. And when the tribe may be removed to another reserve, buildings and other improvements shall be made on such reserve of equal value to those which may be relinquished; and upon such removal, in addition to the before-mentioned sixty thousand dollars, the United States agree to pay the further sum of fifteen thousand dollars, in five equal annual instalments, commencing at the expiration of the before-named instalments.

ARTICLE 5. The said tribe of Indians further agree to give safe-conduct to all persons who may be authorized to pass through their reserve, and to protect, in their person and property, all agents or other persons sent by the United States to reside among them; they further agree not to molest or interrupt any white person passing through their reserve.

ARTICLE 6. That the friendship which is now established between the United States and the Rogue River tribe of Indians shall not be interrupted by the misconduct of individuals, it is hereby agreed that for injuries done by individuals no private revenge or retaliation shall take place; but instead thereof, Complaint shall be made by the party injured to the Indian agent; and it shall be the duty of the chiefs of the said tribe, that upon complaint being made as aforesaid, to deliver up the person or persons against whom the complaint is made, to the end that he or they may be punished agreeably to the laws of the United States; and in like manner if any violation, robbery, or murder shall be committed on any Indian or Indians belonging to said tribe, the person or persons so offending shall be tried, and if found guilty, shall be punished according to the laws of the United States. And it is agreed that the chiefs of the said tribe shall, to the utmost of their power, exert themselves to recover horses or other property, which has or may be stolen or taken from any citizen or citizens of the United States, by any individual of said tribe; and the property so recovered shall be forthwith delivered to the Indian agent or other person authorized to receive the same, that it may be restored to the proper owner.

And the United States hereby guarantee to any Indian or Indians of the said tribe a full indemnification for any horses or other property which may be Stolen from them by any citizens of the United States: Provided, That the property stolen or taken cannot be recovered, and that sufficient proof is produced that it was actually stolen or taken by a citizen of the United States. And the chiefs and head-men of the said tribe engage, on the requisition or demand of the President of the United States, superintendent of Indian affairs, or Indian agent, to deliver up any white person or persons resident among them.

ARTICLE 7. It is agreed between the United States and the Rogue River tribe of Indians, that, should it at any time hereafter be considered by the United States as a proper policy to establish farms among and for the benefit of said Indians, it shall be discretionary with the President, by and with the advice and

Plains, West and Northwest Plateau Indian Treaties

consent of the Senate; to change the annuities herein provided for, or any part thereof, into a fund for that purpose.

ARTICLE 8. This treaty shall take effect and be obligatory on the contracting parties as soon as the same shall have been ratified by the President of the United States by and with the advice and consent of the Senate.

In testimony whereof the said Joel Palmer and Samuel H. Culver, on the part of the United States, and the chiefs and headmen of the Rogue River Indians aforesaid, have hereunto set their hands and seals, the day and year aforesaid.

Joel Palmer, Superintendent Indian Affairs.
Samuel H. Culver, Indian Agent.

Jo, his x mark, Aps-er-ka-har, Sam, his x mark, To-qua-he-ar, Jim, his x mark, Ana-chah-a-rah, John, his x mark, Lympe, his x mark,

Signed in presence of
J. W. Nesmith, Interpreter, R. B. Metcalf, John, his x mark, J. D. Mason, Secretary, T. T. Tierhey.

We the undersigned principal chief, subordinate chiefs and headmen of the bands of the Rogue River tribe of Indians, parties to the treaty concluded at Table Rock, near Rogue River, in the Territory of Oregon, on the 10th day of September, A. D. 1853, having had fully explained to us the amendment made to the same by the Senate of the United States, on the 12th day of April, 1854, do hereby accept and consent to the said amendment to the treaty aforesaid, and agree that the same shall be considered as a part thereof.

In testimony whereof we have hereunto set our hands and affixed our seals, this 11th day of November, A. D. 1854.

Aps-so-ka-hah, Horse-rider, or Jo, his x mark, Ko-ko-ha-wah, Wealthy, or Sam, his x mark, Te-cum-tom, Elk Killer, or John, his x mark, Chol-cul-tah, Joquah Trader, or George, his x mark,

Executed in presence of-
Edward H. Geary, Secretary, Cris.Taylor, John Flett, R. B. Metcalf, Interpreter, Joel Palmer, Superintendent.

Plains, West and Northwest Plateau Indian Treaties

TREATY WITH THE UMPQUA COW CREEK BAND {1853, Sept. 19}
Ratified Apt. 12, 1854.
Proclaimed Feb. 5, 1855.

Stipulations of a treaty made and entered into on Cow Creek, Umpqua Valley, in the Territory of Oregon, this 19th day of September, A. D. 1853, by and between Joel Palmer, superintendent of Indian Affairs, on the part of the United States, and Quin-ti-oo-san, or Bighead, principal chief, and My-n-e-letta, or Jackson; and Tom, son of Quin-ti-oo-san, subordinate chiefs, on the part of the Cow Creek band Umpqua Tribe of Indians.

ARTICLE 1. The Cow Creek band of Indians do hereby cede and relinquish, for the consideration hereinafter specified, to the United States, all their right, title, interest, and claim to all the lands lying in that part of the Territory of Oregon bounded by lines designated as follows, to wit:

Commencing on the north bank of the south fork of Umpqua River, at the termination of the high-lands, dividing the waters of Myrtle Creek from those of Day's Creek, thence running easterly along the summit of said range to the headwaters of Day's Creek, thence southerly, crossing the Umpqua River to the headwaters of Cow Creek, thence to the dividing ridge between Cow Creek and Grave Creek, thence southwesterly along the said divide to its junction with the ridge dividing the waters of Cow Creek from those of Rogue River, thence westerly and northerly around on said ridge to its connection with the spur terminating opposite the mouth of Myrtle Creek, thence along said spur to a point on the same northwest of the eastern line of Isaac Baily's land-claim, thence southeast to Umpqua River, thence up said river to place of beginning.

ARTICLE 2. It is agreed on the part of the United States that the aforesaid tribe shall be allowed to occupy temporarily that portion of the above-described tract of territory bounded as follows, to wit: Commencing on the south side of Cow Creek, at the mouth of Council Creek, opposite Wm. H. Riddle's land-claim, thence up said creek to the summit of Cañon Mountain, thence westerly along said summit two miles, thence northerly to Cow Creek at a point on the same one mile above the falls; thence down said creek to place of beginning. It being understood that this last-described tract of land shall be deemed and considered an Indian reserve until a suitable selection shall be made by the direction of the President of the United States for their permanent residence, and buildings erected thereon and other improvements made of equal value of those upon the above reserve at the time of removal.

ARTICLE 3. For and in consideration of the cession and relinquishment contained in article first, the United States agree to pay to the aforesaid band of Indians, the sum of twelve thousand dollars, in man-her to wit: one thousand dollars to be expended in the purchase of twenty blankets, eighteen pairs pants,

Plains, West and Northwest Plateau Indian Treaties

eighteen pairs shoes, eighteen hickory shirts, eighteen hats or caps, three coats, three vests, three pairs socks, three neck handkerchiefs, forty cotton flags, one hundred and twenty yards prints, one hundred yards domestic, one gross buttons, two lbs. thread, ten papers needles, and such other goods and provisions as may be deemed by the superintendent or agent most conducive to the comfort and necessities of said Indians, on or before the first day of October, A. D. 1854. The remaining eleven thousand dollars, to be paid in twenty equal annual instalments of five hundred and fifty dollars each, commencing on or about the first day of October, 1854, in blankets, clothing, provisions, stock, farming-implements, or such other articles, and in such manner as the President of the United States may deem best for the interests of said tribe.

ARTICLE 4. In addition to the aforesaid twelve thousand dollars there shall be erected for the use of said tribe, at the expense of the United States, two dwelling-houses, the cost of which shall not exceed two hundred dollars each, and a field of five acres fenced and ploughed, and suitable seed furnished for planting the same.

ARTICLE 5. The said band of Indians agree to give safe conduct to all persons passing through their reserve, and to protect in their person and property all agents or other persons sent by authority of the United States to reside among them.

ARTICLE 6. That the friendship which is now established between the United States and the Cow Creek band of Indians, shall not be interrupted by the misconduct of individuals, it is hereby agreed that for injuries done, no private revenge or retaliation shall take place; but instead thereof complaint shall be made by the party injured to the Indian agent; and it shall be the duty of the chiefs of said band of Indians, upon complaint being made as aforesaid, to deliver up the person against whom the complaint is made, to the end that he may be punished, agreeably to the laws of the United States.

And in like manner if any violation, robbery, or murder shall be committed on any Indian belonging to said band, the person so offending shall be tried, and if found guilty, shall be punished according to the laws of the United States. And it is further agreed that the chiefs shall, to the utmost of their ability, exert themselves to recover horses or other property which has or may hereafter be stolen from any citizen of the United States, by any individual of said tribe, and deliver the same to the agent or other person authorized to receive it; and the United States hereby guarantee to any Indian or Indians of said band, a full indemnification for any horses or other property which may be stolen or taken from them by any citizen of the United States, provided, the property stolen cannot be recovered, and that sufficient proof is produced that it was actually stolen or taken by a citizen of the U. S. And the chiefs further agree, that upon

Plains, West and Northwest Plateau Indian Treaties

the requisition of the President of the U. S., superintendent of Indian affairs, or Indian agent, to deliver up any person resident among them.

ARTICLE 7. It is agreed between the United States and the Cow Creek band of the Umpqua tribe of Indians, that, should it at any time hereafter be considered by the United States as a proper policy to establish farms among and for the benefit of said Indians, it shall be discretionary with the President, by and with the advice and consent of the Senate, to change the annuities herein provided for, or any part thereof, into a fund for that purpose.

ARTICLE 8. This treaty shall take effect and be obligatory on the contracting parties as soon as the same shall be ratified by the President of the United States, by and with the advice and consent of the Senate.

In testimony whereof the said Joel Palmer, Superintendent of Indian Affairs, on the part of the United States, and chiefs of the Cow Creek band of Umpqua Indians, before named, have hereunto set their hands and seals, the day and year aforesaid.

Joel Palmer, Superintendent Indian Affairs,
O. T. Bighead, Quin-ti-oo-san, his x mark, Jackson, My-n-e-letta, his x mark, Tom, son of Quin-ti-oo-san, his x mark, Tom, Tal-sa-pe-er, his x mark,

Signed in presence of
J. B. Nichols, E. Catching, Interpreters.
Theodore Tierney, Secretary.
John D. Bown, W. Starr, Witnesses.

TREATY WITH THE OTO AND MISSOURI {1854, Mar. 15}
Ratified Apr. 17, 1854
Proclaimed June 21, 1854.

Articles of agreement and convention made and concluded at the city Washington, this fifteenth day of March, one thousand digit hundred and fifty-four, by George W. Manypenny, as commissioner on the part of the United States, and the following-named Chiefs of the confederate tribes of the Ottoe and Missouria Indians, viz: Ar-ke-kee-tah, or Stay by It; Heh-cah-po, or Kickapoo; Shaw-ha-haw-wa, or Medicine Horse; Mi-ar-ke-tah-hun-she, or Big Soldier; Cha-won-a-he or Buffalo Chief; Ah-hah-che-ke-saw-ke, or Missouria Chief; and Maw-thra-ti-ne, or White Water; they being thereto duly authorized by said confederate tribes.

ARTICLE 1. The confederate tribes of Ottoe and Missouria Indians cede to the United States all their country west of the Missouri River, excepting a strip of

279

Plains, West and Northwest Plateau Indian Treaties

land on the waters of the Big Blue River, ten miles in width and bounded as follows: Commencing at a point in the mid-die of the main branch of the Big Blue River, in a west or southwest direction from Old Fort Kearney, at a place called by the Indians the "Islands;" thence west to the western boundary of the country hereby ceded; thence in a northerly course with said western boundary, ten miles; thence east to a point due north of the starting point and ten miles therefrom; thence to the place of beginning.

Provided, That in case the said initial point is not within the limits of the country hereby ceded, or that the western boundary of said country is not distant twenty-five miles or more from the initial point, in either case, there shall be assigned by the United States to said Indians, for their future home, a tract of land not less than ten miles wide by twenty-five miles long, the southeast corner of which tract shall be the initial point above named. And such portion of such tract, if any, as shall prove to be outside of the ceded country, shall be and the same is hereby granted and ceded to the confederate tribes of Ottoe and Missouria Indians by the United States, who will have said tract properly set off by durable monuments as soon after the ratification of this instrument as the same can conveniently be done.

ARTICLE 2. The said confederate tribes agree, that as soon after the United States shall make the necessary provision for fulfilling the stipulations of this instrument, as they can conveniently arrange their affairs, and not to exceed one year after such provision is made, they will vacate the ceded country, and remove to the lands herein reserved for them.

ARTICLE 3. The said confederate tribes relinquish to the United States, all claims, for money or other thing, under former treaties, and all claim which they may have heretofore, at any time, set up, to any land on the east side of the Missouri River; Provided, That said confederate tribes shall receive the unexpended balances of former appropriations now in the United States Treasury, of which, four thousand dollars shall at once be applied for the purchase of provisions and to farming purposes.

ARTICLE 4. In consideration of, and payment for the country herein ceded, and the relinquishments herein made, the United States agree to pay to the said confederate tribes of Ottoe and Missouria Indians, the several sums of money following, to wit:

First. Twenty thousand dollars, per annum, for the term of three years, commencing on the first day of January, one thousand eight hundred and fifty-five.

Second. Thirteen thousand dollars, per annum, for the term of ten years, next succeeding the three years.

Plains, West and Northwest Plateau Indian Treaties

Third. Nine thousand dollars, per annum, for the term of fifteen years, next succeeding the ten years.

Fourth. Five thousand dollars, per annum, for the term of twelve years, next succeeding the fifteen years.

All which several sums of money shall be paid to the said confederate tribes, or expended for their use and benefit under the direction of the President of the United States, who may, from time to time, determine, at his discretion, what proportion of the annual payments, in this article provided for, if any, shall be paid to them in money, and what proportion shall be applied to and expended, for their moral improvement and education; for such beneficial objects as in his judgment will be calculated to advance them in civilization; for buildings, opening farms, fencing, breaking land, providing stock, agricultural implements, seeds, &c., for clothing, provisions, and merchandise; for iron, steel, arms and ammunition; for mechanics, and tools; and for medical purposes.

ARTICLE 5. In order to enable the said confederate tribes to settle their affairs, and to remove, and subsist themselves for one year at their new home, (and which they agree to do without further expense to the United States) and to break up and fence one hundred and fifty acres of land at their new home, they shall receive from the United States the further sum of twenty thousand dollars, to be paid out and expended under the direction of the President, and in such manner as he shall approve.

ARTICLE 6. The President may, from time to time, at his discretion, cause the whole of the land herein reserved or appropriated west of the Big Blue River, to be surveyed off into lots, and assign to such Indian or Indians of said confederate tribes, as are willing to avail of the privilege, and who will locate on the same as a permanent home, if a single person over twenty-one years of age, one-eighth of a section; to each family of two, one-quarter section; to each family of three and not exceeding five, one-half section; to each family of six and not exceeding ten, one section; and to each family exceeding ten in number, one quarter section for every additional five members.

And he may prescribe such rules and regulations as will secure to the family, in case of the death of the head thereof, the possession and enjoyment of such permanent home and the improvements thereon. And the President may, at any time in his discretion, after such person or family has made a location on the land assigned for a permanent home, issue a patent to such person or family for such assigned land, conditioned that the tract shall not be aliened or leased for a longer term than two years; and shall be exempt from levy, sale, or forfeiture, which conditions shall continue in force, until a State constitution embracing such land within its boundaries shall have been formed, and the legislature of the State shall remove the restrictions.

Plains, West and Northwest Plateau Indian Treaties

If any such person or family shall at any time neglect or refuse to occupy and till a portion of the land assigned, and on which they have located, or shall rove from place to place, the President may, if the patent shall have been issued, revoke the same, or, if not issued, cancel the assignment, and may also withhold from such person or family, their proportion of the annuities or other moneys due them, until they shall have returned to such permanent home, and resumed the pursuits of industry; and in default of their return, the tract may be declared abandoned, and thereafter assigned to some other person or family of such confederate tribes, or disposed of as is provided for the disposal of the excess of said land. And the residue of the land hereby reserved, after all the Indian persons or families of such confederate tribes shall have had assigned to them permanent homes, may be sold for their benefit, under such laws, rules, or regulations as may hereafter be_prescribed by the Congress or President of the United States. No State legislature shall remove the restriction herein provided for, without the consent of Congress.

ARTICLE 7. The United States will erect for said confederate tribes at their new home a grist and saw mill, and keep the same in repair, and provide a miller for a term of ten years; also erect a good blacksmith shop, supply the same with tools, and keep it in repair for the term of ten years, and provide a good blacksmith for a like period, and employ an experienced farmer, for ten years, to instruct the Indians in agriculture.

ARTICLE 8. The annuities of the Indians shall not be taken to pay the debts of individuals.

ARTICLE 9. The said confederate tribes acknowledge their dependence on the Government of the United States, and promise to be friendly with all the citizens thereof, and pledge themselves to commit no depredations on the property of such citizens. And should any one or more of the Indians violate this pledge, and the fact be satisfactorily proven before the agent, the property taken shall be returned, or in default thereof, or if injured or destroyed, compensation may be made by the Government out of their annuities. Nor will they make war on any other tribe except in self-defence, but will submit all matters of difference between them and other Indians, to the Government of the United States, or its agent, for decision, and abide thereby. And if any of the said Indians commit any depredations on any other Indians, the same rule shall prevail as that prescribed in this article in cases of depredations against citizens.

ARTICLE 10. The Ottoes and Missourias are desirous to exclude from their country the use of ardent spirits, and to prevent their people from drinking the same; and therefore it is provided that any one of them who is guilty of bringing liquor into their country, or who drinks liquor, may have his or her propor-

282

Plains, West and Northwest Plateau Indian Treaties

tion of the annuities withheld from him or her for such time, as the President may determine.

ARTICLE 11. The said confederate tribes agree, that all the necessary roads and highways, and railways, which may be constructed as the country improves, and the lines of which may run through their land west of the Big Blue River, shall have a right of way through the reservation, a just compensation being made therefor in money.

ARTICLE 12. The United States will pay to Lewis Barnard the sum of three hundred dollars, he having been in the service of the said tribes and they being unable to pay him.

ARTICLE 13. This treaty shall be obligatory on the contracting parties as soon of the same shall be ratified by the President and Senate of the United States.

In testimony whereof the said George W. Manypenny, commissioner as aforesaid, and the undersigned, chiefs of the said confederate tribes of Ottoes and Missourias, have hereunto set their hands and seals, at the place and on the day and year hereinbefore written.

George W. Manypenny, Commissioner.

Ottoes:
Ar-ke-kee-tah, his x mark, Or Stay By It.
Heh-cah-po, his x mark, Or Kickapoo.
Shaw-ka-haw-wa, his x mark, Or Medicine Horse.

Missourias:
Ah-hah-che-ke'saw-ke, his x mark, Or Missouria Chief.
Maw-thra-ti-ne, his x mark, Or White Water.

Executed in the presence of us:
James M. Gatewood, Indian agent.
Thomas Maxfield.
Lewis Bernard, interpreter, his x mark,

TREATY WITH THE OMAHA {1854, March 16}
Ratified Apr. 17, 1854.
Proclaimed June 21, 1854.

Articles of agreement and convention made and concluded at the city of Washington this sixteenth day of March, one thousand eight hundred and fifty-four, by George W. Manypenny, as commissioner on the part of the United

Plains, West and Northwest Plateau Indian Treaties

States, and the following named chiefs of the Omaha tribe of Indians, viz: Shon-ga-sha, or Logan Fontenelle; E-sta-mah-za, or Joseph Le Flesche; Gratah-nah-je, or Standing Hawk; Gah-he-ga-gin-gah, or Little Chief; Ta-wah-gah-ha or Village Maker; Wah-no-ke-ga, or Noise; So-da-nah-ze, or Yellow Smoke; they being thereto duly authorized by said tribe.

ARTICLE 1. The Omaha Indians cede to the United States all their lands west of the Missouri River, and south of a line drawn due west from a point in the centre of the main channel of said Missouri River due east of where the Ayoway River disembogues out of the bluffs, to the western boundary of the Omaha country, and forever relinquish all right and title to the country south of said line: Provided, however, That if the country north of said due west line, which is reserved by the Omahas for their future home, should not on exploration prove to be a satisfactory and suitable location for said Indians, the President may, with the consent of said Indians, set apart and assign to them, within or outside of the ceded country, a residence suited for and acceptable to them.

And for the purpose of determining at once and definitely, it is agreed that a delegation of said Indians, in company with their agent, shall, immediately after the ratification of this instrument, proceed to examine the country hereby reserved, and if it please the delegation, and the Indians in counsel express themselves satisfied, then it shall be deemed and taken for their future home; but if otherwise, on the fact being reported to the President, he is authorized to cause a new location, of suitable extent, to be made for the future home of said Indians, and which shall not be more in extent than three hundred thousand acres, and then and in that case, all of the country belonging to the said Indians north of said due west line, shall be and is hereby ceded to the United States by the said Indians, they to receive the same rate per acre for it, less the number of acres assigned in lieu of it for a home, as now paid for the land south of said line.

ARTICLE 2. The Omahas agree, that so soon after the United States shall make the necessary provision for fulfilling the stipulations of this instrument, as they can conveniently arrange their affairs, and not to exceed one year from its ratification, they will vacate the ceded country, and remove to the lands reserved herein by them, or to the other lands provided for in lieu thereof, in the preceding article, as the case may be.

ARTICLE 3. The Omahas relinquish to the United States all claims, for money or other thing, under former treaties, and likewise all claim which they may have heretofore, at any time, set up, to any land on the east side of the Missouri River: Provided, The Omahas shall still be entitled to and receive from the Government, the unpaid balance of the twenty-five thousand dollars appropriated for their use, by the act of thirtieth of August, 1851.

284

Plains, West and Northwest Plateau Indian Treaties

ARTICLE 4. In consideration of and payment for the country herein ceded, and the relinquishments herein made, the United States agree to pay to the Omaha Indians the several sums of money following, to wit;
First. Forty thousand dollars, per annum, for the term of three years, commencing on the first day of January, eighteen hundred and fifty-five.
Second. Thirty thousand dollars per annum, for the term of ten years, next succeeding the three years.

Third. Twenty thousand dollars per annum, for the term of fifteen years, next succeeding the ten years.

Fourth. Ten thousand dollars per annum, for the term of twelve years, next succeeding the fifteen years.
All which several sums of money shall be paid to the Omahas, or expended for their use and benefit, under the direction of the President of the United States, who may from time to time determine at his discretion, what proportion of the annual payments, in this article provided for, if any, shall be paid to them in money, and what proportion shall be applied to and expended, for their moral improvement and education; for such beneficial objects as in his judgment will be calculated to advance them in civilization; for buildings, opening farms, fencing, breaking land, providing stock, agricultural implements, seeds, &c.; for clothing, provisions, and merchandise; for iron, steel, arms, and ammunition; for mechanics, and tools; and for medical purposes.

ARTICLE 5. In order to enable the said Indians to settle their affairs and to remove and subsist themselves for one year at their new home, and which they agree to do without further expense to the United States, and also to pay the expenses of the delegation who may be appointed to make the exploration provided for in article first, and to fence and break up two hundred acres of land at their new home, they shall receive from the United States, the further sum of forty-one thousand dollars, to be paid out and expended under the direction of the President, and in such manner as he shall approve.

ARTICLE 6. The President may, from time to time, at his discretion, cause the whole or such portion of the land hereby reserved, as he may think proper, or of such other land as may be selected in lieu thereof, as provided for in article first, to be surveyed into lots, and to assign to such Indian or Indians of said tribe as are willing to avail of the privilege, and who will locate on the same as a permanent home, if a single person over twenty-one years of age, one-eighth of a section; to each family of two, one quarter section; to each family of three and not exceeding five, one half section; to each family of six and not exceeding ten, one section; and to each family over ten in number, one quarter section for every additional five members. And he may prescribe such rules and regulations as will insure to the family, in case of the death of the head thereof, the

Plains, West and Northwest Plateau Indian Treaties

possession and enjoyment of such permanent home and the improvements thereon.

The President may, at any time, in his discretion, after such person or family has made a location on the land assigned for a permanent home, issue a patent to such person or family for such assigned land, conditioned that the tract shall not be aliened or leased for a longer term than two years; and shall be exempt from levy, sale, or forfeiture, which conditions shall continue in force, until a State constitution, embracing such lands within its boundaries, shall have been formed, and the legislature of the State shall remove the restrictions.

And if any such person or family shall at any time neglect or refuse to occupy and till a portion of the lands assigned and on which they have located, or shall rove from place to place, the President may, if the patent shall have been issued, cancel the assignment, and may also withhold from such person or family, their proportion of the annuities or other moneys due them, until they shall have returned to such permanent home, and resumed the pursuits of industry; and in default of their return the tract may be declared abandoned, and thereafter assigned to some other person or family of such tribe, or disposed of as is provided for the disposition of the excess of said land.

And the residue of the land hereby reserved, or of that which may be selected in lieu thereof, after all of the Indian persons or families shall have had assigned to them permanent homes, may be sold for their benefit, under such laws, rules or regulations, as may hereafter be prescribed by the Congress or President of the United States. No State legislature shall remove the restrictions herein provided for, without the consent of Congress.

ARTICLE 7. Should the Omahas determine to make their permanent home north of the due west line named in the first article, the United States agree to protect them from the Sioux and all other hostile tribes, as long as the President may deem such protection necessary; and if other lands be assigned them, the same protection is guaranteed.

ARTICLE 8. The United States agree to erect for the Omahas, at their new home, a grist and saw mill, and keep the same in repair, and provide a miller for ten years; also to erect a good blacksmith shop, supply the same with tools, and keep it in repair for ten years; and provide a good blacksmith for a like period; and to employ an experienced farmer for the term of ten years, to instruct the Indians in agriculture.

ARTICLE 9. The annuities of the Indians shall not be taken to pay the debts of individuals.

Plains, West and Northwest Plateau Indian Treaties

ARTICLE 10. The Omahas acknowledge their dependence on the Government of the United States, and promise to be friendly with all the citizens thereof, and pledge themselves to commit no depredations on the property of such citizens. And should any one or more of them violate this pledge, and the fact be satisfactorily proven before the agent, the property taken shall be returned, or in default thereof, or if injured or destroyed, compensation may be made by the Government out of their annuities. Nor will they make war on any other tribe, except in self-defence, but will submit all matters of difference between them and other Indians to the Government of the United States, or its agent, for decision, and abide thereby. And if any of the said Omahas commit any depredations on any other Indians, the same rule shall prevail as that prescribed in this article in cases of depredations against citizens.

ARTICLE 11. The Omahas acknowledge themselves indebted to Lewis Sounsosee, (a half-breed) for services, the sum of one thousand dollars, which debt they have not been able to pay, and the United States agree to pay the same.

ARTICLE 12. The Omahas are desirous to exclude from their country the use of ardent spirits, and to prevent their people from drinking the same, and therefore it is provided that any Omaha who is guilty of bringing liquor into their country, or who drinks liquor, may have his or her proportion of the annuities withheld from him or her for such time as the President may determine.

ARTICLE 13. The board of foreign missions of the Presbyterian Church have on the lands of the Omahas a manual-labor boarding-school, for the education of the Omaha, Ottoe, and other Indian youth, which is now in successful operation, and as it will be some time before the necessary buildings can be erected on the reservation, and (it is) desirable that the school should not be suspended, it is agreed that the said board shall have four adjoining quarter sections of land, so as to include as near as may be all the improvements heretofore made by them; and the President is authorized to issue to the proper authority of said board, a patent in fee-simple for such quarter sections.

ARTICLE 14. The Omahas agree that all the necessary roads, highways, and railroads, which may be constructed as the country improves, and the lines of which may run through such tract as may be reserved for their permanent home, shall have a right of way through the reservation, a just compensation being paid therefor in money.

ARTICLE 15. This treaty shall be obligatory on the contracting parties as soon as the same shall be ratified by the President and Senate of the United States.

In testimony whereof, the said George W. Manypenny, commissioner as aforesaid, and the undersigned chiefs, of the Omaha tribe of Indians, have hereunto

Plains, West and Northwest Plateau Indian Treaties

set their hands and seals, at the place and on the day and year hereinbefore written.

George W. Manypenny, Commissioner.

Shon-ga-ska, or Logan Fontenelle, his x mark, E-sta-mah-za, or Joseph Le Flesche, his x mark, Gra-tah-mah-je, or Standing Hawk, his x mark, Gah-he-ga-gin-gah, or Little Chief, his x mark, Tah-wah-gah-ha, or Village Maker, his x mark, Wah-no-ke-ga, or Noise, his x mark, So-da-nah-ze, or Yellow Smoke, his x mark,

Executed in the presence of us:
James M. Gatewood, Indian agent.
James Goszler.
Charles Calvert.

TREATY WITH THE MENOMINEE {1854, May 12}
Proclamation Aug. 2, 1854.

Articles of agreement made and concluded at the Falls of Wolf River, in the State of Wisconsin, on the twelfth day of May, one thousand eight hundred and fifty-four, between the United States of America, by Francis Huebschmann, superintendent of Indian Affairs, duly authorized thereto, and the Menomonee tribe Indians, by the chiefs, headmen, and warriors of said tribesuch articles being supplementary and amendatory to the treaty made between the United States and said tribe on the eighteenth day of October, one thousand hundred and forty-eight.

Whereas, among other provisions contained in the treaty in the caption mentioned, it is stipulated that for and in consideration of all the lands owned by the Menomonees, in the State of Wisconsin, wherever situated, the United States should give them all that country or tract of land ceded by the Chippewa Indians of the Mississippi and Lake Superior, in the treaty of the second of August, eighteen hundred and forty-seven, and by the Pillager band of Chippewa Indians in the treaty of the twenty-first of August, eighteen hundred and forty-seven, which had not been assigned to the Winnebagoes, guarantied not to contain less than six hundred thousand acres; should pay them forty thousand dollars for removing and subsisting themselves; should give them fifteen thousand dollars for the establishment of a manual-labor school, the erection of a grist and saw mill, and for other necessary improvements in their new country; should cause to be laid out and expended in the hire of a miller, for the period of fifteen years, nine thousand dollars; and for continuing and keeping up a blacksmith shop and providing iron and steel for twelve years, commencing on the first of January, eighteen hundred and fifty-seven, eleven thousand dollars.

288

Plains, West and Northwest Plateau Indian Treaties

And whereas, upon manifestation of great unwillingness on the part of said Indians to remove to the country west of the Mississippi River, upon Crow Wing, which had been assigned them, and a desire to remain in the State of Wisconsin, the President consented to their locating temporarily upon the Wolf and Oconto Rivers.

Now, therefore, to render practicable the stipulated payments herein recited, and to make exchange of the lands given west of the Mississippi for those desired by the tribe, and for the purpose of giving them the same for a permanent home, these articles are entered into.

ARTICLE 1. The said Menomonee tribe agree to cede, and do hereby cede, sell, and relinquish to the United States, all the lands assigned to them under the treaty of the eighteenth of October, eighteen hundred and forty-eight.

ARTICLE 2. In consideration of the foregoing cession the United States agree to give, and do hereby give, to said Indians for a home, to be held as Indian lands are held, that tract of country lying upon the Wolf River, in the State of Wisconsin, commencing at the southeast corner of township 28 north of range 16 east of the fourth principal meridian, running west twenty-four miles, thence north eighteen miles, thence east twenty-four miles, thence south eighteen miles, to the place of beginningthe same being townships 28, 29, and 30, of ranges 13, 14, 15, and 16, according to the public surveys.

ARTICLE 3. The United States agree to pay, to be laid out and applied under the direction of the President, at the said location, in the establishment of a manual-labor school, the erection of a grist and saw mill, and other necessary improvements, fifteen thousand dollars; in procuring a suitable person to attend and carry on the said grist and saw mill, for a period of fifteen years, nine thousand dollars, in continuing and keeping up a blacksmith shop, and providing the usual quantity of iron and steel for the use of said tribe, for a period of twelve years, commencing with the year eighteen hundred and fifty-seven, eleven thousand dollars; and the United States further agree to pay the said tribe, to be applied under the direction of the President, in such manner and at such times as he may deem advisable, for such purposes and uses as in his judgment will best promote the improvement of the Menomonees, the forty thousand dollars stipulated to be applied to their removal and subsistence west of the Mississippi. It being understood that all other beneficial stipulations in said treaty of 1848 are to be fulfilled as therein provided.

ARTICLE 4. In consideration of the difference in extent between the lands hereby ceded to the United States, and the lands given in exchange, and for and in consideration of the provisions hereinbefore recited, and of the relinquishment by said tribe of all claims set up by or for them, for the difference in

Plains, West and Northwest Plateau Indian Treaties

quantity of lands supposed by them to have been ceded in the treaty of eighteenth of October, eighteen hundred and forty-eight, and what was actually ceded, the United States agree to pay said tribe the sum of two hundred and forty-two thousand six hundred and eighty-six dollars, in fifteen annual instalments, commencing with the year 1867; each instalment to be paid out and expended under the direction of the President of the United States, and for such objects, uses, and purposes, as he shall judge necessary and proper for their wants, improvement, and civilization.

ARTICLE 5. It is further agreed that all expense incurred in negotiating this treaty shall be paid by the United States.

ARTICLE 6. This treaty to be binding on the contracting parties as soon as it is ratified by the President and Senate of the United States, and assented to by Osh-kosh and Ke-she-nah, chiefs of said tribe.
In testimony whereof, the said Francis Huebschmann, superintendent as aforesaid, and the chiefs, headmen, and warriors of the said Menomonee tribe, have hereunto set their hands and seals, at the place and on the day and year aforesaid.

Francis Huebschmann, Superintendent of Indian affairs.

Wau-ke-chon, his x mark, Wis-ke-no, his x mark, Way-tan-sah, his x mark, Carton, his x mark, Sho-ne-niew, his x mark, Lamotte, his x mark, Pe-quo-quon-ah, his x mark, Shaw-poa-tuk, his x mark, Wau-pen-na-nosh, his x mark, Sho-ne-on, his x mark, Shaw-wan-na-penasse, his x mark, Ta-ko, his x mark,

Signed and sealed in the presence of us:
John V. Suydam, sub-agent, Heman M. Cady, United States
Chas. H. White, deputy United States marshal,

TREATY WITH THE IOWA {1854, May 17}
Proclamation. July 17, 1854.

Articles of agreement and convention made and concluded at the city of Washington, this seventeenth day of May, one thousand eight hundred and fifty-four, by George W. Manypenny, commissioner on the part of the United States, and the following-named delegates of the Ioway tribe of Indians, viz: Nan-chee-ning-a, or No Heart; Shoon-ty-ing-a, or Little Wolf; Wah-moon-a-ka, or the Man who Steals; and Nar-ge-ga-rash, or British; they being thereto duly authorized by said tribe.

ARTICLE 1. The Ioway tribe of Indians hereby cede, relinquish, and convey to the United States, all their right, title, and interest in and to the country, with

Plains, West and Northwest Plateau Indian Treaties

the exception hereinafter named, which was assigned to them by the treaty concluded with their tribe and the Missouri band of Sacs and Foxes, by William Clark, superintendent of Indian affairs, on the seventeenth of September, one thousand eight hundred and thirty-six, being the upper half of the tract described in the second article thereof, as "the small strip of land on the south side of the Missouri River, lying between the Kickapoo northern boundary-line and the Grand Nemahaw River, and extending from the Missouri back and westwardly with the said Kickapoo line and the Grand Nemahaw, making four hundred sections; to be divided between the said Ioways and Missouri band of Sacs and Foxes; the lower half to the Sacs and Foxes, the upper half to the Ioways," but they except and reserve of said country, so much thereof as is embraced within and designated by the following metes and bounds, viz: Beginning at the mouth of the Great Nemahaw River where it empties into the Missouri; thence down the Missouri River to the mouth of Noland's Creek; thence due south one mile; thence due west to the south fork of the Nemahaw River; thence down the said fork with its meanders to the Great Nemahaw River, and thence with the meanders of said river to the place of beginning, which country, it is hereby agreed, shall be the future and permanent home of the Ioway Indians.

ARTICLE 2. In consideration of the cession made in the preceding article, the United States agree to pay in the manner hereinafter prescribed, to the Ioway Indians, all the moneys received from the sales of the lands which are stipulated in the third article hereof, to be surveyed and soldafter deducting therefrom the costs of surveying, managing, and selling the same.

ARTICLE 3. The United States agree to have surveys made of the country ceded by the Ioways in article first in the same manner that the public lands are surveyed, and as soon as it can conveniently be done; and the President, after the surveys shall have been made and approved, shall proceed to offer said surveyed land for sale, at public auction, being governed therein by the laws of the United States respecting sales of public lands; and such of said lands as may not be sold at public sales, shall be subject to private entry in the manner that private entries are made of United States land; and all the land remaining unsold after being for three years subject to private entry at the minimum Government price, may, by act of Congress, be graduated and reduced in price until the whole is disposed of, proper regard being had, in making such reduction, to the interests of the Ioways and the speedy settlement of the country. Until after the said land shall have been surveyed, and the surveys approved, no white persons or citizens shall be permitted to make thereon any location or settlement; and the provisions of the act of Congress, approved on the third day of March, one thousand eight hundred and seven relating to lands ceded to the United States, shall, so far as they are applicable, be extended over the lands herein ceded.

Plains, West and Northwest Plateau Indian Treaties

ARTICLE 4. It being understood that the present division-line between the Ioways and the Sacs and Foxes of Missouri, as run by Isaac McCoy, will, when the surveys are made, run diagonally through many of the sections, cutting them into fractions; it is agreed that the sections thus cut by said line, commencing at the junction of the Wolf with the Missouri River, shall be deemed and taken as part of the land hereinbefore ceded and directed to be sold for the benefit of the Ioways, until the quantity thus taken, including the before-recited reservation, and all the full sections north of said line, shall amount to two hundred sections of land. And should the Sacs and Foxes of Missouri consent to a change of their residence and be so located by the United States as to occupy any portion of the land herein ceded and directed to be sold for the benefit of the Ioways, west of the tract herein reserved, the Ioways hereby agree to t, he same, and consent to such an arrangement, upon the condition that a quantity of land equal to that which may be thus occupied by the Sacs and Foxes, and of as good quality, shall be set apart for them out of the country now occupied by the last-named tribe, contiguous to said division-line, and sold for their benefit as hereinbefore provided.

ARTICLE 5. As the receipts from the sales of the lands cannot now be determined, it is agreed that the whole subject shall be referred to the President of the United States, who may, from time to time, prescribe how much of the proceeds thereof shall be paid out to the Ioway people, and the time and mode of such payments, and also how much shall be invested in safe and profitable stocks, the principal of which to remain unimpaired, and the interest to be applied annually for the civilization, education, and religious culture of the Ioways and such other objects of a beneficial character as may be proper and essential to their well-being and prosperity: provided, that if necessary, Congress may, from time to time, by law, make such regulations in regard to the funds arising from the sale of said lands, and the application thereof for the benefit of the Ioways, as may in the wisdom of that body seem just and expedient.

ARTICLE 6. The President may cause the country the Ioways have reserved for their future home, to be surveyed, at their expense, and in the same way as the public lands are surveyed, and assign to each person or family such portion thereof as their industry and ability to manage business affairs may, in his opinion, render judicious and proper; and Congress may hereafter provide for the issuing to such persons, patents for the same, with guards and restrictions for their protection in the possession and enjoyment thereof.

ARTICLE 7. Appreciating the importance and the benefit derived from the mission established among them by the board of foreign missions of the Presbyterian Church, the Ioways hereby grant unto the said board a tract of three hundred and twenty acres of land, to be so located as to include the improvements at the mission, and also a tract of one hundred and sixty acres of tim-

Plains, West and Northwest Plateau Indian Treaties

bered land, to be selected by some agent of the board from the legal subdivisions of the surveyed land; and the President shall issue a patent or patents for the same, to such person or persons as said board may direct. They further grant to John B. Rev, their interpreter, a tract of three hundred and twenty acres of land, to be selected by him in "Wolf's Grove," for which the President shall also issue a patent.

ARTICLE 8. The debts of Indians contracted in their private dealings as individuals, whether to traders or otherwise, shall not be paid out of the general fund.

ARTICLE 9. As some time must elapse before any benefit can be derived from the proceeds of the sale of their land, and as it is desirable that the Ioways should at once engage in agricultural pursuits and in making improvements on the tract hereinbefore reserved for them, it is hereby agreed that, of the fund of one hundred and fifty-seven thousand five hundred dollars, set apart to be invested by the second clause of the second article of the treaty concluded on the nineteenth day of October, one thousand eight hundred and thirty-eight, a sum not exceeding one hundred thousand dollars shall be paid to the Indians, or expended under the direction of the President for the erection of houses, breaking and fencing lands, purchasing stock, farming utensils, seeds, and such other articles as may be necessary for their comfort. Fifty thousand dollars, or so much thereof as may be deemed expedient, to be paid during the year commencing on the first of October, one thousand eight hundred and fifty-four; and the other fifty thousand dollars, or so much thereof as shall be deemed expedient, to be paid during the year commencing on the first of October, one thousand eight hundred and fifty-five.

The residue of said fund of one hundred and fifty-seven thousand five hundred dollars on hand after the payments herein provided for have been made shall remain as a trust fund, the interest upon which, as well as the interest that may have accrued on the portion drawn out, shall be applied, under the direction of the President, to educational or other beneficial purposes among the Ioways.

ARTICLE 10. It is agreed that all roads and highways laid out by authority of law shall have a right of way through the lands herein reserved, on the same terms as are provided by law when roads and highways are made through the lands of citizens of the United States; and railroad companies, when the lines of their roads necessarily pass through the lands of the Ioways, shall have right of way on the payment of a just compensation therefor in money.

ARTICLE 11. The Ioways promise to renew their efforts to suppress the introduction and use of ardent spirits in their country, to encourage industry, thrift, and morality, and by every possible effort to promote their advancement in civilization. They desire to be at peace with all men, and they bind themselves

293

Plains, West and Northwest Plateau Indian Treaties

to commit no depredation or wrong upon either Indians or citizens; and whenever difficulties arise they will abide by the laws of the United States, in such cases made and provided, as they expect to be protected and to have their rights vindicated by them.

ARTICLE 12. The Ioway Indians release the United States from all claims and demands of every kind and description arising under former treaties, and agree to remove themselves within six months after the ratification of this instrument, to the lands herein reserved for their homes; in consideration whereof, the United States agree to pay to said Indians five thousand dollarstwo thousand of which with such portion of balances of former appropriations of interest-fund as may not now be necessary under specific heads, may be expended in the settlement of their affairs preparatory to removal.

ARTICLE 13. The object of this instrument being to advance the interests of the Ioway people, it is agreed, if it prove insufficient, from causes which cannot now be foreseen, to effect these ends, that the President may, by and with the advice and consent of the Senate, adopt such policy in the management of their affairs, as, in his judgment, may be most beneficial to them; or Congress may hereafter make such provision by law as experience shall prove to be necessary.

ARTICLE 14. This instrument shall be obligatory on the contracting parties whenever the same shall be ratified by the President and the Senate of the United States.
In testimony whereof, the said George W. Manypenny, commissioner as aforesaid, and the delegates of the Ioway tribe of Indians, have hereunto set their hands and seals, at the place and on the day and in the year hereinbefore written.

George W. Manypenny, Commissioner.

Nan-chee-ning-a, or No Heart, his x mark, Shoon-ty-ing-a, or Little Wolf, his x mark, Wah-moon-na-ka, or The Man who Steals, his x mark, Nar-ge-ga-rash, or British, his x mark,

Executed in the presence of
D. Vanderslice, Indian agent.
John B. Roy, his x mark, United States interpreter.
Wm. B. Waugh, witness to signing of John B. Roy.

Plains, West and Northwest Plateau Indian Treaties

TREATY WITH THE SAUK AND FOXES OF MISSOURI
{1854, May 18}
Ratified July 11, 1854.
Proclaimed July 17, 1854.

Articles of agreement and convention made and concluded at the city of Washington this eighteenth day of May, one thousand eight hundred and fifty-four, by George IV. Manypenny, commissioner on the part of the United States, and the following-named delegates of the Sacs and foxes of Missouri, viz: Pe-to-o-ke-mah, or Hard Fish; Mo-less or Wah-pe-nem-mah, or Sturgeon; Ne-son-quoit, or Bear; Mo-ho-ho-ko, or Jumping Fish; and No-ko-what, or Fox; they being thereto duly authorized by the said Sac and Fox Indians.

ARTICLE 1. The Sacs and Foxes of Missouri hereby cede, relinquish and convey to the United States all their right, title and interest in and to the country assigned to them by the treaty concluded on the seventeenth day of September, one thousand eight hundred and thirty-six, between William Clark, superintendent of Indian affairs, on the part of the United States, and the Ioways and Missouri Sacs and Foxes, being the lower half of the country described in the second article thereof as "the small strip of land on the south side of the. Missouri River, lying between the Kickapoo northern boundary-line and the Grand Nemahaw River, and extending from the Missouri back and westwardly with the said Kickapoo line and the Grand Nemahaw, making four hundred sections; to be divided between the said Ioways and Missouri band of Sacs and Foxes; the lower half to the Sacs and Foxes, the upper half to the Ioways;" saving and reserving fifty sections, of six hundred and forty acres each, which shall be selected in the western part of the cession by the delegates, parties hereto, and the agent for the tribe, after their return home, and which shall be located in one body and set off by metes and bounds: Provided, That the delegates and agent can find such an amount of land in one body within said specified section of country suitable to the wants and wishes of the Indians.

It is further provided, That should a suitable location, upon examination, to the full extent of fifty sections not be found within said western part of this cession, then the said delegates a d agent shall be permitted to extend the location west or northwest of the country herein ceded and south of the Great Nemahaw River, over so much of the public domain, otherwise unappropriated, as shall make up the deficiency; or to make a selection entirely beyond the limits of the country herein ceded upon any lands of the United States, not otherwise appropriated, lying as aforesaid west or northwest of the ceded country and south of the Great Nemahaw. And in either case they shall describe their selection, which must be made within six months from the date hereof, by metes and bounds, and transmit the description thereof signed by said delegates and agent, to the (Commissioner of Indian Affairs; and thereupon the selection so made,

295

Plains, West and Northwest Plateau Indian Treaties

shall be taken and deemed as the future permanent home of the Sacs and Foxes of Missouri.

It is expressly understood that these Indians shall claim under this article, no more than fifty sections of land, and if that quantity or any portion thereof shall be selected, as provided above, outside of the reservation herein made, then said reservation or a quantity equal to that which may be selected outside thereof, shall be and the same is hereby, ceded, relinquished, and conveyed to the United States.

ARTICLE 2. In consideration of the cession and relinquishment made in the preceding article, the United States agree to pay to the Sacs and Foxes of Missouri, the sum of forty-eight thousand dollars, in manner following, viz: Fifteen thousand dollars in the month of October in each of the years one thousand eight hundred and fifty-four and one thousand eight hundred and fifty-five; ten thousand dollars in the same month of the year one thousand eight hundred and fifty-six, and eight thousand dollars in the same month of the year one thousand eight hundred and fifty-seven; which several sums shall be paid directly to the Indians, or otherwise, as the President may deem advisable, for building houses, breaking and fencing lands, purchasing stock, farming-implements, seeds, and such other articles as may be necessary for their comfort and prosperity.

ARTICLE 3. The President may cause to be surveyed, in the same manner in which the public lands are surveyed, the reservation herein provided for the Sacs and Foxes of Missouri, and may assign to each person or family desiring it such quantity of land as, in his opinion, will be sufficient for such person or family, with the understanding that he or they will occupy, improve, and cultivate the same, and comply with such other conditions as the President may prescribe. The land thus assigned may hereafter be confirmed by patent to the parties, or their representatives, under such regulations and restrictions as Congress may prescribe.

ARTICLE 4. The said Indians reserve a tract of one section of land at the site of their present farm and mill, and to include the same; and if they desire it, said farm may be cultivated for them for a term not exceeding two yearsat the end of which time, or sooner if the Indians request it, the said tract and mill may be sold by the President to the highest bidder, and upon payment being made a patent to issue to the purchaser; the proceeds of the sale to be paid over to the Indians with their other moneys.

ARTICLE 5. At the request of the Indians, it is hereby agreed that the Board of Foreign Missions of the Presbyterian Church shall have a tract of one hundred and sixty acres of land, to be selected by said board at a distance not exceeding two miles in a westerly direction from the grant made to said board at their

Plains, West and Northwest Plateau Indian Treaties

mission by the Ioway Indiansand the President is authorized to issue a patent for the same to such person or persons as said board may designate.

ARTICLE 6. The said Indians release the United States from all claims or demands of any kind whatsoever arising, or which may hereafter arise, under former treaties, and agree to remove within six months after the ratification of this instrument, and to subsist themselves, without cost to the United States. In consideration of which release and agreement, the United States agree to pay them the sum of five thousand dollarsthree thousand of which may be applied to the settlement of their affairs preparatory to removal.

ARTICLE 7. The invested fund provided by the second clause of the second article of the treaty of twenty-first day of October, one thousand eight hundred and thirty-seven, (being one hundred and fifty-seven thousand four hundred dollars) shall remain with the United States at an annual interest of five per cent, which interest as it accumulates, shall be expended under the direction of the President in such manner as he may deem best for the interests of the Indians and a like disposition may be made of any unexpended balance of interest now on hand.

ARTICLE 8. No part of the moneys hereby stipulated to be paid to the Indians or for their benefit, or of their invested fund, shall be applied to the payment of debts contracted by them in their private dealings, as individuals, whether with traders or otherwise.

ARTICLE 9. It is agreed by said Indians that all roads and highways laid out by authority of law, shall have right of way through their reservation on the same terms as are provided by law when roads and highways are made through lands of citizens of the United States; and railroad companies, when the lines of their roads necessarily pass through the lands of these Indians, shall have right of way on the payment of a just compensation therefor in money.

ARTICLE 10. The said Indians promise to use their best efforts to prevent the introduction and use of ardent spirits in their country; to encourage industry, thrift and morality; and by every possible means to promote their advancement in civilization. They desire to be at peace with all men, and therefore bind themselves to commit no depredation or wrong upon either Indians or citizens, and whenever difficulties arise, to abide by the laws of the United States in such cases made and provided, as they expect to be protected and to have their own rights vindicated by them.

ARTICLE 11. The object of these articles of agreement and convention being to advance the true interests of the Sac and Fox Indians, it is agreed should they prove insufficient, from causes which cannot now be foreseen, to effect these ends, that the President may, by and with the advice and consent of the Senate,

Plains, West and Northwest Plateau Indian Treaties

adopt such policy in the management of their affairs, as in his judgment may be most beneficial to them; or Congress may hereafter make such provisions by law, as experience shall prove to be necessary.

ARTICLE 12. This instrument shall be obligatory on the contracting parties whenever the same shall be ratified by the President and the Senate of the United States.

In testimony whereof the said George W. Manypenny, commissioner aforesaid and the delegates of the Sacs and Foxes of Missouri, have hereunto set their hands and seals at the place, and on the day and year first above written.

George W. Manypenny, Commissioner.

Pe-to-o-ke-mah, or Hard Fish, his x mark, Me-less or Wah-pe-nem-mah, or Sturgeon, his x mark, Ne-son-quoit, or Bear, his x mark, Mo-ko-ho-ko, or Jumping Fish, his x mark, No-ko-what, or Fox, his x mark,

Executed in presence of
Charles Calvert.
Wm. B. Waugh, witness to signing of Peter Cadue.

TREATY WITH THE KASKASKIA, PEORIA, ETC. {1854, May 30}
Ratified August 2, 1854.
Proclaimed Aug. 10, 1854.

Articles of agreement and convention made and concluded at the city of Washington, this thirtieth day of May, one thousand eight hundred and fifty-four, by George W. Manypenny, commissioner on the part of the United States, and the following-named delegates representing the united tribes of Kaskaskia and Peoria, Piankeshaw and Wea Indians, viz: Kio-kaw-mo-zan, David Lykins; Sa-wa-ne-ke-ah, or Wilson; Sha-cah-quah, or Andrew Chick; Ta-ko-nah, or Mitchel; Che-swa-wa, or Rogers; and Yellow Beaver, they being duly authorized thereto by the said Indians.

ARTICLE 1. The tribes of Kaskaskia and Peoria Indians, and of Piankeshaw and Wea Indians, parties to the two treaties made with them respectively by William Clark, Frank J. Allen, and Nathan Kouns, commissioners on the part of the United States, at Castor Hill, on the twenty-seventh and twenty-ninth days of October, one thousand eight hundred and thirty-two, having recently in joint council assembled, united themselves into a single tribe, and having expressed a desire to be recognized and regarded as such, the United States hereby assent to the action of said joint council to this end, and now recognize the delegates

Plains, West and Northwest Plateau Indian Treaties

who sign and seal this instrument as the authorized representatives of said consolidated tribe.

ARTICLE 2. The said Kaskaskias and Peorias, and the said Piankeshaws and Weas, hereby cede and convey to the United States, all their right, title, and interest in and to the tracts of country granted and assigned to them, respectively, by the fourth article of the treaty of October twenty-seventh, and the second article of the treaty of October twenty-ninth, one thousand eight hundred and thirty-two, for a particular description of said tracts, reference being had to said articles; excepting and reserving therefrom a quantity of land equal to one hundred and sixty acres for each soul in said united tribe, according to a schedule attached to this instrument, and ten sections additional, to be held as the common property of the said tribeand also the grant to the American Indian Mission Association, hereinafter specifically set forth.

ARTICLE 3. It is agreed that the United States, shall as soon as it can conveniently be done, cause the lands hereby ceded to be surveyed as the public lands are surveyed; and, that the individuals and heads of families shall, within ninety days after the approval of the surveys, select the quantity of land therefrom to which they may be respectively entitled as specified in the second article hereof; and that the selections shall be so made as to include in each case, as far as possible, the present residences and improvements of eachand where that is not practicable, the selections shall fall on lands in the same neighborhood; and if by reason of absence or otherwise the above-mentioned selections shall not all be made before the expiration of said period, the chiefs of the said united tribe shall proceed to select lands for those in default; and shall also, after completing said last-named selections, choose the ten sections reserved to the tribe; and said chiefs in the execution of the duty hereby assigned them, shall select lands lying adjacent to or in the vicinity of those that have been previously chosen by individuals.

All selections in this article provided for, shall be made in conformity with the legal subdivisions of the United States lands, and shall be reported immediately in writing, with apt descriptions of the same, to the agent for the tribe. Patents for the lands selected by or for individuals or families may be issued subject to such restrictions respecting leases and alienation as the President or Congress of the United States may prescribe. When selections are so made or attempted to be made as to produce injury to, or controversies between individuals, which cannot be settled by the parties, the matters of difficulty shall be investigated, and decided on equitable terms by the council of the tribe, subject to appeal to the agent, whose decision shall be final and conclusive.

ARTICLE 4. After the aforesaid selections shall have been made, the President shall immediately cause the residue of the ceded lands to be offered for sale at public auction, being governed in all respects in conducting such sale by the

299

Plains, West and Northwest Plateau Indian Treaties

laws of the United States for the sale of public lands, and such of said lands as may not be sold at public sale, shall be subject to private entry at the minimum price of United States lands, for the term of three years; and should any thereafter remain unsold, Congress may, by law, reduce the price from time to time, until the whole of said lands are disposed of, proper regard being had in making the reduction to the interests of the Indians and to the settlement of the country. And in consideration of the cessions hereinbefore made, the United States agree to pay to the said Indians, as hereinafter provided, all the moneys arising from the sales of said lands after deducting therefrom the actual cost of surveying, managing, and selling the same.

ARTICLE 5. The said united tribes appreciate the importance and usefulness of the mission established in their country by the board of the American Indian Mission Association, and desiring that it shall continue with them, they hereby grant unto said board a tract of one section of six hundred and forty acres of land, which they, by their chiefs, in connection with the proper agent of the board, will select; and it is agreed that after the selections shall have been made, the President shall issue to such person or persons as the aforesaid board may designate, a patent for the same.

ARTICLE 6. The said Kaskaskias and Peorias, and the said Piankeshaws and Weas, have now, by virtue of the stipulations of former treaties, permanent annuities amounting in all to three thousand eight hundred dollars per annum, which they hereby relinquish and release, and from the further payment of which they forever absolve the United States; and they also release and discharge the United States from all claims or damages of every kind by reason of the non-fulfilment of former treaty stipulations, or of injuries to or losses of stock or other property by the wrongful acts of citizens of the United States; and in consideration of the relinquishments and releases aforesaid, the United States agree to pay to said united tribe, under the direction of the President, the sum of sixty-six thousand dollars, in six annual instalments, as follows: In the month of October, in each of the years one thousand eight hundred and fifty-four, one thousand eight hundred and fifty-five, and one thousand eight hundred and fifty-six, the sum of thirteen thousand dollars, and in the same month in each of the years one thousand eight hundred and fifty-seven, one thousand eight hundred and fifty-eight, and one thousand eight hundred and fifty-nine, nine thousand dollars, and also to furnish said tribe with an interpreter and a blacksmith for five years, and supply the smith-shop with iron, steel, and tools, for a like period.

ARTICLE 7. The annual payments provided for in article six are designed to be expended by the Indians, chiefly in extending their farming operations, building houses, purchasing stock, agricultural implements, and such other things as may promote their improvement and comfort, and shall so be applied by them. But at their request it is agreed that from each of the said annual pay-

300

Plains, West and Northwest Plateau Indian Treaties

ments the sum of five hundred dollars shall be reserved for the support of the aged and infirm, and the sum of two thousand dollars shah be set off and applied to the education of their youth; and from each of the first three there shall also be set apart and applied the further sum of two thousand dollars, to enable said Indians to settle their affairs. And as the amount of the annual receipt from the sales of their lands, cannot now be ascertained, it is agreed that the President may, from time to time, and upon consultation with said Indians, determine how much of the net proceeds of said sales shall be paid them, and how much shall be invested in safe and profitable stocks, the interest to be annually paid to them, or expended for their benefit and improvement.

ARTICLE 8. Citizens of the United States, or other persons not members of said united tribe, shall not be permitted to make locations or settlements in the country herein ceded, until after the selections provided for, have been made by said Indians; and the provisions of the act of Congress approved March third, one thousand eight hundred and seven, in relation to lands ceded to the United States, shall, so far as the same are applicable, be extended to the lands herein ceded.

ARTICLE 9. The debts of individuals of the tribe, contracted in their private dealings, whether to traders or otherwise, shall not be paid out of the general funds. And should any of said Indians become intemperate or abandoned, and waste their property, the President may withhold any moneys due or payable to such, and cause them to be paid, expended or applied, so as to ensure the benefit thereof to their families.

ARTICLE 10. The said Indians promise to renew their efforts to prevent the introduction and use of ardent spirits in their country, to encourage industry, thrift, and morality, and by every possible means to promote their advancement in civilization. They desire to be at peace with all men, and they bind themselves not to commit depredation or wrong upon either Indians or citizens; and, should difficulties at any time arise, they will abide by the laws of the United States in such cases made and provided, as they expect to be protected and to have their rights vindicated by those laws.

ARTICLE 11. The object of the instrument being to advance the interests of said Indians, it is agreed if it prove insufficient, from causes which cannot now be foreseen, to effect these ends, that the President may, by and with the advice and consent of the Senate, adopt such policy in the management of their affairs, as, in his judgment, may be most beneficial to them; or, Congress may hereafter make such provisions by law as experience shall prove to be necessary.

ARTICLE 12. It is agreed that all roads and highways, laid out by authority of law, shall have right of way through the lands herein ceded and reserved, on the same terms as are provided by law, when roads and highways are made through

Plains, West and Northwest Plateau Indian Treaties

lands of citizens of the United States; and railroad companies, when the lines of their roads necessarily pass through the lands of the said Indians, shall have right of way, on the payment of a just compensation therefor in money.

ARTICLE 13. It is believed that all the persons and families of the said combined tribe are included in the annexed schedule, but should it prove otherwise, it is hereby stipulated that such person or family shall select from the ten sections reserved as common property, the quantity due, according to the rules hereinbefore prescribed, and the residue of said ten sections or all of them, as the case may be, may hereafter, on the request of the chiefs, be sold by the President, and the proceeds applied to the benefit of the Indians.

ARTICLE 14. This instrument shall be obligatory on the contracting parties whenever the same shall be ratified by the President and the Senate of the United States.

In testimony whereof the said George W. Manypenny, commissioner as aforesaid, and the delegates of the said combined tribe, have hereunto set their hands and seals, at the place and on the day and year first above written.

George W. Manypenny, Commissioner.

Kio-kaw-mo-zan, his x mark, Ma-cha-ko-me-ah, or David Lykins.
Sa-wa-ne-ke-ah, or Wilson, his x mark, Sha-cah-quah, or Andrew Chick, his x mark, Ta-ko-nah, or Mitchel, his x mark, Che-swa-wa, or Rogers, his x mark, Yellow Beaver, his x mark,

Executed in the presence of
Charles Calvert, Jas. T. Wynne, Robert Campbell, Wm. B. Waugh, Ely Moore, Indian agent.

Schedule of persons or families composing the united tribes of Weas, Piankeshaws, Peorias, and Kaskaskias, with the quantity of land to be selected in each case as provided in the second and third articles.

Persons or families	Males	Females	Total	Number of acres		
Mash-she-we-lot-ta, or Joe Peoria		2	2	4		640
Marcus Lindsay	3	3	6	960		
Sam Slick	5	1	6	960		
Wah-ka-ko-nah, or Billy	1	0	1		160	
Wah-kah-ko-se-ah	1	1	2	320		
Luther Pascal	2	2	4	640		
Lewis Pascal	1	1	2	320		
John Pascal	1	0	1	160		
Edward Black	3	2	5	800		
Sha-cah-quah, or Andrew Chick		3	4	7		1,120

Che-swa-wa, or Rodgers	2	4	6	960
John Westley	1	1	2	320
Ma-co-se-tah, or F. Valley	3	1	4	640
Ma-cha-co-me-yah, or David Lykins	3	2	5	800
Sa-wa-na-ke-keah, or Wilson	1	2	3	480
Na-me-quah-wah	2	0	2	320
Pun-gish-e-no-qua	1	3	4	640
Ma-cen-sah	1	1	2	320
Yellow Beaver	3	3	6	960
John Charly	3	3	6	960
Bam-ba-cap-wa, or Battiste Charly	2	3	5	800
Pah-to-cah	2	2	4	640
Lee-we-ah, or Lewis	1	2	3	480
Mah-kon-sah, junior	2	2	4	640
Baptiste Peoria	3	5	8	1,280
Ma-qua-ko-non-ga, or Lewis Peckham	5	2	7	1,120
Captain Mark	2	2	4	640
Te-com-se, or Edward Dajexat	3	1	4	640
Thomas Hedges	1	1	2	320
Pah-ka-ko-se-qua	0	1	1	160
En-ta-se-ma-qua	0	1	1	160
Yon-za-na-ke-sa-gah	2	1	3	480
Aw-sap-peen-qua-zah	4	0	4	640
Kio-kaw-mo-zaw	4	2	6	960
Chin-qua-ke-ah	2	3	5	800
Peter Cloud	3	-	3	480
Au-see-pan-nah, or Coon	2	1	3	480
My-he-num-ba	3	3	6	960
Kish-e-koon-sah	1	2	3	480
Kish-e-wan-e-sah	3	1	4	640
Sho-cum-qua	-	2	2	320
Pe-ta-na-ke-ka-pa	2	0	2	320
Pa-kan-giah	2	1	3	480
Se-pah-ke-ah	1	1	2	320
Ngo-to-kop-wa	1	1	2	320
Kil-so-qua	2	2	4	640
Be-zio, or Ben	1	2	3	480
Kil-son-zah	1	2	3	480
Shaw-lo-lee	2	1	3	480
Ke-she-kon-sah, or Wea	1	2	3	480
Ah-shaw-we-se-wah	2	-	2	320
George Clinton	2	-	2	320
Ke-kaw-ke-to-qua	2	2	4	640
Sa-saw-kaw-qua-ga, or Kain Tuck	2	3	5	800
Wah-sah-ko-le-ah	1	3	4	640

Plains, West and Northwest Plateau Indian Treaties

Kin-ge-ton-no-zah,-or Red Bird	1	1	2	320
Paw-saw-qua, or Jack Booei	3	1	4	640
No-wa-ko-se-ah	2	-	2	320
Me-shin-qua-me-saw	1	3	4	640
Chen-gwan-zaw	3	-	3	480
Ke-che-kom-e-ah	2	-	2	320
Na-me-qua-wah, junior	2	-	2	320
Ta-pah-con-wah	1	1	2	320
Pa-pee-ze-sa-wah	1	1	2	320
Ta-ko-nah, or Mitchel	2	3	5	800
Pe-la-she	1	1	2	320
Wah-ke-shin-gah	2	2	4	640
Waw-pon-ge-quah, or Mrs. Ward	3	3	6	960
Paw-saw-kaw-kaw-maw	-	2	2	320
Ke-maw-lan-e-ah	2	3	5	800
Qua-kaw-me-kaw-trua, or J. Cox	2	2	4	640
Cow-we-shaw	2	-	2	320
Tah-wah-qua-ke-mon-ga	3	1	4	640

TREATY WITH THE ROGUE RIVER {1854, Nov. 15}
Ratified Mar. 3, 1855.
Proclaimed Apr. 7, 1855

Articles of agreement entered into and concluded this fifteenth day of November, one thousand eight hundred and fifty-four, between Joel Palmer, superintendent of Indian affairs, on the part of the United States, and the chiefs and headmen of the Rogue River tribe of Indians, on the part of said tribe.

ARTICLE 1. It is agreed on the part of said tribe, that the Table Rock reserve, described in the treaty of the 10th September, 1853, between the United States and the Rogue River tribe, shall be possessed and occupied jointly by said tribe and such other tribes and bands of Indians as the United States shall agree with by treaty stipulations, or the President of the United States shall direct, to reside thereupon, the place of residence of each tribe, part of tribe, or band on said reserve, to be designated by the superintendent of Indian affairs or Indian agent; that the tribes and bands hereafter to be settled on said reserve shall enjoy equal rights and privileges with the Rogue River tribe; and that the annuities paid to the Indians now residing, or hereafter to reside on said reserve, shall be shared by all alike, from and after said residence thereon: Provided, That the annuity of the Rogue River tribe, as agreed on in the treaty of the 10th September, 1853, shall not be diminished or in any way impaired thereby. It is also agreed, that the United States shall have the right to make such roads, highways, and railroads through said reserve as the public good may from time to time require, a just compensation being made therefor.

Plains, West and Northwest Plateau Indian Treaties

ARTICLE 2. In consideration of the foregoing stipulations, it is agreed on the part of the United States to pay to the Rogue River tribe, as soon as practicable after the signing of this agreement, two thousand one hundred and fifty dollars, in the following articles: twelve horses, one beef, two yokes of oxen, with yokes and chains, one wagon, one hundred men's coats, fifty pairs of pantaloons, and fifty hickory shirts; also, that in the treaties to be made with other tribes and bands, hereafter to be located on said reserve, that provision shall be made for the erection of two smith-shops; for tools, iron, and blacksmiths for the same; for opening farms and employing farmers; for a hospital, medicines, and a physician; and for one or more schools; the uses and benefits of all which shall be secured to said Rogue River tribe, equally with the tribes and bands treated with; all the improvements made, and schools, hospital, and shops erected, to be conducted in accordance with such laws, rules, and regulations as the Congress or the President of the United States may prescribe.

ARTICLE 3. It is further agreed, that when at any time hereafter the Indians residing on this reserve shall be removed to another reserve, or shall be elsewhere provided for, that the fifteen thousand dollars thereafter to be paid to said Rogue River tribe, as specified in the treaty of the 10th September, 1853, shall be shared alike by the members of all the tribes and bands that are, or hereafter shall be located on the said Table Rock reserve.

ARTICLE 4. It is also further provided that in the event that this agreement shall not be ratified by the President and Senate of the United States, or that no other tribe or band shall be located on said reserve, the two thousand one hundred and fifty dollars stipulated in article second of this agreement to be paid said Rogue River tribe, shall be deducted from their annuities hereafter to be paid said Indians.

In testimony whereof, the said Joel Palmer, superintendent as aforesaid, and the undersigned chiefs and headmen of the Rogue River Tribe of Indians, have hereunto set their hands and seals, at Even's Creek, on the Table Rock Reserve, on the day and year herein before written.

Joel Palmer, superintendent

Ap-sa-ka-hah, or Joe, first chief, his x mark, Ko-ko-ha-wah, or Sam, second chief, his x mark, Sambo, third chief, his x mark, Te-cum-tum, or John, fourth chief, his x mark, Te-wah-hait, or Elijah, his x mark, Cho-cul-tah, or George, his x mark, Telum-whah, or Bill, his x mark, Hart-tish, or Applegate John, his x mark, Qua-chis, or Jake, his x mark, Tom, his x mark, Henry, his x mark, Jim, his x mark,
Executed in presence of
Edward R. Geary, secretary.

Plains, West and Northwest Plateau Indian Treaties

Cris. Taylor, John Flett, interpreter.
R. B. Metcalfe.

TREATY WITH THE CHASTA, ETC. {1854, Nov. 18}
Ratified Mar. 3, 1855.
Proclaimed Apr. 10, 1855.

Articles of a convention, and agreement made and concluded at the council-ground, opposite the mouth of Applegate Creek, on Rogue River, in the Territory of Oregon, on the eighteenth day of November, one thousand eight hundred and fifty-four, by Joel Palmer, superintendent of Indian affairs, on the part of the United States, and the chiefs and head-men of the Quil-si-eton and Na-hel-ta bands, of the Chasta tribe of Indians, the Cow-nan-ti-co, Sa-cher-i-ton, and Na-al-ye bands of Scotons, and the Grave Creek band of Umpquas, to wit, Jes-tul-tut, or Little Chief, Ko-ne-che-quot, or Bill, Se-sel-che-tel, or Salmon Fisher, Kul-ki-am-i-na, or Bush-head, Te-po-kon-ta, or Sam, and Jo, they being duly authorized thereto by said united bands.

ARTICLE 1. The aforesaid united bands cede to the United States all their country, bounded as follows:
Commencing at a point in the middle of Rogue River, one mile below the mouth of Applegate Creek; thence northerly, on the western boundary of the country heretofore purchased of the Rogue River tribe by the United States, to the head-waters of Jump-Off-Jo Creek; thence westerly to the extreme northeastern limit of the country purchased of the Cow Creek band of Umpquas; thence along that boundary to its extreme southwestern limit; thence due west to a point from which a line running due south would cross Rogue River, midway between the mouth of Grave Creek and the great bend of Rogue River; thence south to the southern boundary of Oregon; thence east along said boundary to the summit of the main ridge of the Siskiou Mountains, or until this line reaches the boundary of the country purchased of the Rogue River tribe; thence northerly along the western boundary of said purchase to the place of beginning.

ARTICLE 2. The said united bands agree that as soon after the ratification of this convention as practicable, they will remove to such portion of the Table Rock reserve as may be assigned them by the superintendent of Indian affairs or agent, or to whatsoever other reserve the President of the United States may at any time hereafter direct.

ARTICLE 3. In consideration of and payment for the country herein ceded, the United States agree to pay to the said united bands the sum of two thousand dollars annually for fifteen years, from and after the first day of September, one thousand eight hundred and fifty-five, which annuities shall be added to those

Plains, West and Northwest Plateau Indian Treaties

secured to the Rogue River tribe by the treaty of the 10th September, 1853, and the amount shared by the members of the united bands and of the Rogue River tribe, jointly and alike; said annuities to be expended for the use and benefit of said bands and tribe in such manner as the President may from time to time prescribe; for provisions, clothing, and merchandise; for buildings, opening and fencing farms, breaking land, providing stock, agricultural implements, tools, seeds, and such other objects as will in his judgment promote the comfort and advance the prosperity and civilization of said Indians. The United States also agree to appropriate the additional sum of five thousand dollars, for the payment of the claims of persons whose property has been stolen or destroyed by any of the said united bands of Indians since the first day of January, 1849; such claims to be audited and adjusted in such manner as the President may prescribe.

ARTICLE 4. When said united bands shall be required to remove to the Table Rock reserve or elsewhere, as the President may direct, the further sum of six thousand five hundred dollars shall be expended by the United States for provisions to aid in their subsistence during the first year they shall reside thereon; for the erecting of necessary buildings, and the breaking and fencing of fifty acres of land, and providing seed to plant the same, for their use and benefit, in common with the other Indians on the reserve.

ARTICLE 5. The United States engage that the following provisions, for the use and benefit of all Indians residing on the reserve, shall be made:
An experienced farmer shall be employed to aid and instruct the Indians in agriculture for the term of fifteen years. Two blacksmith-shops shall be erected at convenient points on the reserve, and furnished with tools and the necessary stock, and skilful smiths employed for the same for five years. A hospital shall be erected, and proper provision made for medical purposes, and the care of the sick for ten years.

School-houses shall be erected, and qualified teachers employed to instruct children on the reserve, and books and stationery furnished for fifteen years. All of which provisions shall be controlled by such laws, rules, or regulations as Congress may enact or the President prescribe.

ARTICLE 6. The President may, from time to time, at his discretion, direct the surveying of a part or all of the agricultural lands on said reserve, divide the same into small farms of from twenty to eighty acres, according to the number of persons in a family, and assign them to such Indians as are willing to avail themselves of the privilege and locate thereon as a permanent home, and to grant them a patent therefor under such laws and regulations as may hereafter be enacted or prescribed.

Plains, West and Northwest Plateau Indian Treaties

ARTICLE 7. The annuities of the Indians shall not be taken to pay the debts of individuals.

ARTICLE 8. The said united bands acknowledge themselves subject to the Government of the United States, and engage to live in amity with the citizens thereof, and commit no depredations on the property of said citizens; and should any Indian or Indians violate this pledge, and the fact be satisfactorily proven, the property shall be returned, or if not returned, or if injured or destroyed, compensation may be made therefor out of their annuities. They also pledge themselves to live peaceably with one another, and with other Indians, to abstain from war and private acts of revenge, and to submit all matters of difference between themselves and Indians of other tribes and bands to the decision of the United States or the agent, and to abide thereby.

It is also agreed that if any individual shall be found guilty of bringing liquor into their country, or drinking the same, his or her annuity may be withheld during the pleasure of the President.

ARTICLE 9. This convention shall be obligatory on the contracting parties from and after its ratification by the President and Senate of the United States. In testimony whereof, Joel Palmer, superintendent aforesaid, and the undersigned chiefs and headmen of said united bands, have hereunto set their hands and seals at the place and on the day and year herein written.

(Signed in duplicate)

Joel Palmer, Superintendent.

Jes-tul-tut, or Little Chief, his x mark, Ko-ne-che-quot, or Bill, his x mark, Sesel-chetl, or Salmon Fisher, his x mark, Bas-ta-shin, his x mark, For Kul-ke-am-ina, or Bushland.

Executed in presence of
Edward R. Geary, Secretary.
John Flett, Interpreter.
Cris. Taylor.

TREATY WITH THE UMPQUA AND KALAPUYA {1854, Nov. 29}
Ratified Mar, 3, 1855.
Proclaimed Mar. 30, 1855.

Articles of agreement and convention made and concluded at Calapooia Creek Douglas County, Oregon Territory, this twenty-ninth day of November, one thousand eight hundred and fifty-four, by Joel Palmer, superintendent of Indian

Plains, West and Northwest Plateau Indian Treaties

affairs, on the part of the United States, and the following-named chiefs and heads of the confederated bands of the Umpqua tribe of Indians, and of the Calapooias residing in Umpqua Valley, to wit: Napesa, or Louis, head chief Peter, or Injice; Tas-yah, or General Jackson; Bogus; Nessick; Et-na-ma or William, Cheen-len-ten or George, Nas-yah or John, Absaquil or Chenook, Jo, and Tom, they being assembled in council with their respective bands.

ARTICLE 1. The confederated bands of Umpqua and Calapooia Indians cede to the United States all their country included within the following limits, to wit: Commencing at the northwest corner of the country purchased of the Galeese Creek and Illinois River Indians on the 18th day of November, 1854, and running thence east to the boundary of the Cow Creek purchase, thence northerly along said boundary to its northeastern extremity; thence east to the main ridge of the Cascade Mountains; thence northerly to the main falls of the North Umpqua River; thence to Scott's Peak, bearing easterly from the head-waters of Calapooia Creek; thence northerly to the connection of the Calapooia Mountains with the Cascade range; thence westerly along the summit of the Calapooia Mountains to a point whence a due south line would cross Umpqua River at the head of tide-water; thence on that line to the dividing ridge between the waters of Umpqua and Coose Rivers; thence along that ridge, and the divide between Coquille and Umpqua Rivers, to the western boundary of the country purchased of the Galeese Creek Indians, or of the Cow Creek Indians, as the case may be, and thence to the place of beginning.

Provided, however, That so much of the lands as are embraced within the following limits, shall be held by said confederated bands, and such other bands as may be designated to reside thereupon, as an Indian reservation. To wit: Commencing at a point three miles due south of the mouth of a small creek emptying into the Umpqua River, near the western boundary of John Churchell's land-claim, at the lower end of Cole's Valley; thence north to the middle of the channel of Umpqua River; thence up said river to a point due south of the highest peak of the ridge, immediately west of Allan Hubbard's land-claim; thence to said peak, thence along the summit of the ridge dividing the waters, to its termination at or near the mouth of Little Canyon Creek; thence, crossing the Umpqua River in a westerly direction to the high-lands opposite the mouth of said creek; thence following the divide until it reaches a point whence a line drawn to the place of beginning will run three miles south of the extreme southern bend in the Umpqua River between these two points: and thence to the place of beginning.

Should the President at any time believe it demanded by the public good and promotive of the best interests of said Indians to be located elsewhere, the said Indians agree peaceably, and without additional expense to the Government of the United States, to remove to such reserve as may be selected; provided that a

Plains, West and Northwest Plateau Indian Treaties

delegation of three or more of the principal men of said bands selected by them, Shall concur with the authorized agent or agents of the United States in the selection of said new reserve. And when said removal shah take place, the particular tracts then actually occupied by said Indians, on the reserve herein described, according to the provisions of this treaty, and those occupied by Indians of other bands that may be located thereon, shall be sold by order of the President of the United States, and the proceeds of such sales expended in permanent improvements on the new reserve, for the use and benefit of the holders of said tracts respectively.

ARTICLE 2. The confederated bands agree that as soon after the United States shall make the necessary provision for fulfilling the stipulations of this treaty as they conveniently can, and not to exceed one year after such provision is made, they will vacate the ceded territory and remove to the lands herein reserved for them.

ARTICLE 3. In consideration of and payment for the country herein ceded, the United States agree to pay the said confederated bands the several sums of money following, to wit: First, three thousand dollars per annum for the term of five years, commencing on the first day of September, 1855. Second, two thousand three hundred dollars per annum for the term of five years next succeeding the first five. Third, one thousand seven hundred dollars per annum for the term of five years next succeeding the second five years. Fourth, one thousand dollars per annum for the term of five years next succeeding the third five years.

All of which several sums of money shall be expended for the use and benefit of the confederated bands, under the direction of the President of the United States, who may from time to time, at his discretion, determine what proportion shall be expended for such beneficial objects as in his judgment will be calculated to advance them in civilization; for their moral improvement and education; for buildings, opening farms, fencing, breaking land, providing stock, agricultural implements, seeds, &c.; for clothing, provisions, and merchandise; for iron, steel, arms, and ammunition; for mechanics and tools, and for medical purposes.

ARTICLE 4. In order to enable the said Indians to remove to their new home, and subsist themselves for one year thereafter, (and which they agree to do without further expense to the United States) and to provide for the breaking up and fencing of fifty acres of land, and the erection of buildings on the reserve, the purchase of teams, farming-utensils, tools, &c., and for other purposes necessary to their comfort and subsistence, they shall receive from the United States the further sum of ten thousand dollars, to be paid out and expended under the direction of the President, and in such manner as he shall approve.

Plains, West and Northwest Plateau Indian Treaties

ARTICLE 5. The President may from time to time, at his discretion, cause the whole or such portion of the land hereby reserved as he may think proper, or of such other land as may be selected in lieu thereof, as provided for in the first article, to be surveyed into lots, and assigned to such Indian or Indians of said confederated bands as are willing to avail themselves of the privilege, and who will locate thereon as a permanent home, if a single person over twenty-one years of age, twenty acres; to each family of two persons, forty acres; to each family of three and not exceeding five persons sixty acres; to each family of six and not exceeding ten persons, eighty acres; and to each family over ten in number, forty acres for each additional five members.

And the President may provide such rules and regulations as will secure to the family, in case of the death of the head thereof, the possession and enjoyment of such permanent home, and the improvements thereon; and he may at any time at his discretion, after such person or family has made location on the land assigned for a permanent home, issue a patent to such person or family for such assigned land, conditioned that the tract shall not be aliened or leased for a longer term than two years, and shall be exempt from levy, sale, or forfeiture, which conditions shall continue in force until a State constitution, embracing such lands within its boundaries, shall have been formed, and the legislature of the State shall remove the restrictions.

If any such family shall at any time neglect or refuse to occupy or till a portion of the land assigned, and on which they have located, or shall rove from place to place, the President may, if the patent shall have been issued, revoke the same, or, if not issued, cancel the assignment, and may also withhold from such person or family their proportion of the annuities or other moneys due them, until they shall have returned to such permanent home, and resume the pursuits of industry; and in default of their return, the tract may be declared abandoned and thereafter assigned to some other person or family of the Indians residing on the reserve.

No State legislature shall remove the restrictions herein provided for, without the consent of Congress.

ARTICLE 6. The United States agree to erect for said Indians a good black-smith-shop, furnish it with tools, and keep it in repair for ten years, and provide a competent blacksmith for the same period; to erect suitable buildings for a hospital, supply medicines, and provide an experienced physician for fifteen years; to provide a competent farmer to instruct the Indians in agriculture for ten years; and to erect a school-house, and provide books, stationery, and a properly qualified teacher for twenty years.

ARTICLE 7. The annuities of the Indians shall not be taken to pay the debts of individuals.

Plains, West and Northwest Plateau Indian Treaties

ARTICLE 8. The said confederated bands acknowledge their dependence on the Government of the United States, and promise to be friendly with all the citizens thereof, and pledge themselves to commit no depredations on the property of such citizens. And should any one or more of the Indians violate this pledge, and the fact be satisfactorily proven before the agent, the property shall be returned, or in default thereof, or if injured or destroyed, compensation may be made by the Government out of their annuities. Nor will they make war on any other tribe except in self-defense, but will submit all matters of difference between them and other Indians to the Government of the United States or its agent, for decision, and abide thereby. And if any of the said Indians commit any depredations on any other Indians, the same rule shall prevail as that prescribed in this article in case of any depredations against citizens. Said Indians further engage to submit to, and observe all laws, rules, and regulations which may be prescribed by the United States for the government of said Indians.

ARTICLE 9. It is hereby provided, in order to prevent the evils of intemperance among said Indians, that any one of them who shall be guilty of bringing liquor into their reserve, or shall drink liquor, may have his or her proportion of the annuities withheld from him or her for such time as the President may determine.

ARTICLE 10. The said confederate bands agree, that all the necessary roads, highways, and railroads which may be constructed as the country improves, the lines of which may run through the reservation of said Indians, shall have the right of way therein, a just compensation being made therefor.

ARTICLE 11. The merchandise distributed to the members of the said confederate bands at the negotiation of this treaty shall be considered as in part payment of the annuities herein provided.

ARTICLE 12. This treaty shall be obligatory on the contracting parties as soon as the same shall be ratified by the President and Senate of the United States.
In testimony whereof, the said Joel Palmer, on the part of the United States as aforesaid, and the undersigned chiefs and heads of the said confederated bands of Umpquas and Calapooias, have hereunto set their hands and seals, at the place and on the day and year heretofore written.

Joel Palmer, superintendent.

Na-pe-sa, or Louis, his x mark, Injice, or Peter, his x mark, Tas-yah, or General Jackson, his x mark, Bogus, his x mark, Nessick, his x mark, Et-na-ma, or William, his x mark, Cheen-len-ten, or George, his x mark, Nas-yah, or John, his x mark, Absaquil, or Chenook, his x mark, Jo, his x mark, Tom, his x mark,

312

Plains, West and Northwest Plateau Indian Treaties

Executed in the presence of us
Edward R. Geary, secretary.
Cris. Taylor.
John Flett, interpreter.

TREATY WITH THE CONFEDERATED OTO AND MISSOURI
{1854, Dec. 9}
Ratified, Feb. 28, 1855.
Proclaimed Apr. 10, 1855.

Article of agreement and convention made and concluded at Nebraska City, in the Territory of Nebraska, on the ninth day of December, one thousand eight hundred and fifty-four, between tins United States of America, by George Hefner, United States' Indian agent, duly authorized thereto, and the chiefs and headmen of the confederate tribes of the Ottoe and Missouria Indians, to be taken and considered as a supplement to the treaty made between the United States and said confederate tribes, on the fifteenth day of March, one thousand eight hundred and fifty-four.

Whereas, by the first article of the treaty in the caption mentioned, it is stipulated that the confederate tribes of the Ottoe and Missouria Indians cede to the United States all their country west of the Missouri River, excepting a strip of land on the waters of the Big Blue River, ten miles in width, and bounded as follows: commencing at a point in the middle of the main branch of the Big Blue River, in a west or southwest direction from old Fort Kearney, at a place called by the Indians the "Islands;" thence west to the western boundary of the country hereby ceded; thence in a northerly course with said western boundary ten miles; thence east to a point due north of the starting point, and ten miles therefrom; thence to the place of beginning.

And whereas, upon exploration of said reservation by the said confederate tribes, it was found that they had been mistaken as to the location thereof, much the larger portion, or nearly the entirety of it, being to the west of the Big Blue River, and without sufficiency of timber, and they being dissatisfied therewith, and the United States being desirous of removing all cause of complaint, this article is entered into.

ARTICLE. It is agreed and stipulated, between the United States and the said confederate tribes of Ottoe and Missouria Indians, that the initial point of their reservation, in lieu of that stated in the treaty, in the caption hereof mentioned, shall be a point five miles due east thereof, thence west twenty-five miles, thence north ten miles, thence east to a point due north of the starting point and ten miles therefrom, thence to the place of beginning; and the country embraced within said boundaries shall be taken and considered as the reservation

Plains, West and Northwest Plateau Indian Treaties

and home of said confederate tribes, in lieu of that provided for them and described in the first article of said treaty.

In witness whereof the said George Hepner and the undersigned chiefs and head men of the said Confederate tribes of Ottoes and Missourias, have hereunto set their hands and seals, at the place and on the day and year above written.

George Hepner, United States Indian agent.

Hick Kapoo, his x mark, Bil Soldier, his x mark, Chi-an-a-ka, or Buffalo Chief, his x mark, Missouri Chief, his x mark, White Water, his x mark,

Executed in the presence of
Lewis Bernard, his x mark, U. S. interpreter.
H. P. Downs, John Baulware.

TREATY WITH THE NISQUALLI, PUYALLUP, ETC. {1854, Dec. 26}
Ratified Mar. 3, 1855.
Proclaimed Apr. 10, 1855.

Articles of agreement and convention made and concluded on the She-nab-ham, or Medicine Creek, in the Territory of Washington, this twenty-sixth day of December, in the year one thousand eight hundred and fifty-four, by Isaac I. Stevens, governor and superintendent of Indian affairs of the said Territory, on the part of the United States, and the undersigned chiefs, head-men, and delegates of the Nisqually, Puyallup, Steilacoom, Squawskin, S'Homamish, Stehchass, T'Peeksin, Squi-aitl, and Sa-heh-wamish tribes and bands of Indians, occupying the lands lying round the head of Puget's Sound and the adjacent inlets, who, for the purpose of this treaty, are to be regarded as one nation, on behalf of said tribes and bands, and duly authorized by them.

ARTICLE 1. The said tribes and bands of Indians hereby cede, relinquish, and convey to the United States, all their right, title, and interest in and to the lands and country occupied by them, bounded and described as follows, to wit: Commencing at the point on the eastern side of Admiralty Inlet, known as Point Pully, about midway between Commencement and Elliott Bays; thence running in a southeasterly direction, following the divide between the waters of the Puyallup and Dwamish, or White Rivers, to the summit of the Cascade Mountains; thence southerly, along the summit of said range, to a point opposite the main source of the Skookum Chuck Creek; thence to and down said creek, to the coal mine; thence northwesterly, to the summit of the Black Hills; thence northerly, to the upper forks of the Satsop River; thence northeasterly, through the portage known as Wilkes's Portage, to Point Southworth, on the western

Plains, West and Northwest Plateau Indian Treaties

side of Admiralty Inlet; thence around the foot of Vashon's Island, easterly and southeasterly, to the place of beginning.

ARTICLE 2. There is, however, reserved for the present use and occupation of the said tribes and bands, the following tracts of land, viz:

The small island called Klah-che-min, situated opposite the mouths of Hammersley's and Totten's Inlets, and separated from Hartstene Island by Peale's Passage, containing about two sections of land by estimation; a square tract containing two sections, or twelve hundred and eighty acres, on Puget's Sound, near the mouth of the She-nah-nam Creek, one mile west of the meridian line of the United States land survey, and a square tract containing two sections, or twelve hundred and eighty acres, lying on the south side of Commencement Bay; all which tracts shall be set apart, and, so far as necessary, surveyed and marked out for their exclusive use; nor shall any white man be permitted to reside upon the same without permission of the tribe and the superintendent or agent. And the said tribes and bands agree to remove to and settle upon the same within one year after the ratification of this treaty, or sooner if the means are furnished them. In the mean time, it shall be lawful for them to reside upon any ground not in the actual claim and occupation of citizens of the United States, and upon any ground claimed or occupied, if with the permission of the owner or claimant. If necessary for the public convenience, roads may be run through their reserves, and, on the other hand, the right of way with free access from the same to the nearest public highway is secured to them.

ARTICLE 3. The right of taking fish, at all usual and accustomed grounds and stations, is further secured to said Indians in common with all citizens of the Territory, and of erecting temporary houses for the purpose of curing, together with the privilege of hunting, gathering roots and berries, and pasturing their horses on open and unclaimed lands: Provided, however, That they shall not take shellfish from any beds staked or cultivated by citizens, and that they shall alter all stallions not intended for breeding-horses, and shall keep up and confine the latter.

ARTICLE 4. In consideration of the above session, the United States agree to pay to the said tribes and bands the sum of thirty-two thousand five hundred dollars, in the following manner, that is to say: For the first year after the ratification hereof, three thousand two hundred and fifty dollars; for the next two years, three thousand dollars each year; for the next three years, two thousand dollars each year; for the next four years fifteen hundred dollars each year; for the next five years twelve hundred dollars each year; and for the next five years one thousand dollars each year; all which said sums of money shall be applied to the use and benefit of the said Indians, under the direction of the President of the United States, who may from time to time determine, at his discretion, upon what beneficial objects to expend the same. And the superintendent of Indian

315

Plains, West and Northwest Plateau Indian Treaties

affairs, or other proper officer, shall each year inform the President of the wishes of said Indians in respect thereto.

ARTICLE 5. To enable the said Indians to remove to and settle upon their aforesaid reservations, and to clear, fence, and break up a sufficient quantity of land for cultivation, the United States further agree to pay the sum of three thousand two hundred and fifty dollars, to be laid out and expended under the direction of the President, and in such manner as he shall approve.

ARTICLE 6. The President may hereafter, when in his opinion the interests of the Territory may require, and the welfare of the said Indians be promoted, remove them from either or all of said reservations to such other suitable place or places within said Territory as he may deem fit, on remunerating them for their improvements and the expenses of their removal, or may consolidate them with other friendly tribes or bands. And he may further, at his discretion, cause the whole or any portion of the lands hereby reserved, or of such other land as may be selected in lieu thereof, to be surveyed into lots, and assign the same to such individuals or families as are willing to avail themselves of the privilege, and will locate on the same as a permanent home, on the same terms and subject to the same regulations as are provided in the sixth article of the treaty with the Omahas, so far as the same may be applicable. Any substantial improvements heretofore made by any Indian, and which he shall be compelled to abandon in consequence of this treaty, shall be valued under the direction of the President, and payment be made accordingly therefor.

ARTICLE 7. The annuities of the aforesaid tribes and bands shall not be taken to pay the debts of individuals.

ARTICLE 8. The aforesaid tribes and bands acknowledge their dependence on the Government of the United States, and promise to be friendly with all citizens thereof, and pledge themselves to commit no depredations on the property of such citizens. And should any one or more of them violate this pledge, and the fact be satisfactorily proved before the agent, the property taken shall be returned, or in default thereof, or if injured or destroyed, compensation may be made by the Government out of their annuities. Nor will they make war on any other tribe except in self-defence, but will submit all matters of difference between them and other Indians to the Government of the United States, or its agent, for decision, and abide thereby. And if any of the said Indians commit any depredations on any other Indians within the Territory, the same rule shall prevail as that prescribed in this article, in cases of depredations against citizens. And the said tribes agree not to shelter or conceal offenders against the laws of the United States, but to deliver them up to the authorities for trial.

ARTICLE 9. The above tribes and bands are desirous to exclude from their reservations the use of ardent spirits, and to prevent their people from drinking

Plains, West and Northwest Plateau Indian Treaties

the same; and therefore it is provided, that any Indian belonging to said tribes, who is guilty of bringing liquor into said reservations, or who drinks liquor, may have his or her proportion of the annuities withheld from him or her for such time as the President may determine.

ARTICLE 10. The United States further agree to establish at the general agency for the district of Puget's Sound, within one year from the ratification hereof, and to support, for a period of twenty years, an agricultural and industrial school, to be free to children of the said tribes and bands, in common with those of the other tribes of said district, and to provide the said school with a suitable instructor or instructors, and also to provide a smithy and carpenter's shop, and furnish them with the necessary tools, and employ a blacksmith, carpenter, and farmer, for the term of twenty years, to instruct the Indians in their respective occupations. And the United States further agree to employ a physician to reside at the said central agency, who shall furnish medicine and advice to their sick, and shall vaccinate them; the expenses of the said school, shops, employees, and medical attendance, to be defrayed by the United States, and not deducted from the annuities.

ARTICLE 11. The said tribes and bands agree to free all slaves now held by them, and not to purchase or acquire others hereafter.

ARTICLE 12. The said tribes and bands finally agree not to trade at Vancouver's Island, or elsewhere out of the dominions of the United States; nor shall foreign Indians be permitted to reside in their reservations without consent of the superintendent or agent.

ARTICLE 13. This treaty shall be obligatory on the contracting parties as soon as the same shall be ratified by the President and Senate of the United States.

In testimony whereof, the said Isaac I. Stevens, governor and superintendent of Indian Affairs, and the undersigned chiefs, headmen, and delegates of the aforesaid tribes and bands, have hereunto set their hands and seals at the place and on the day and year hereinbefore written.

Isaac I. Stevens, Governor and Superintendent Territory of Washington.

Ke-cha-hat, his x mark, Spee-peh, his x mark, Swe-yah-tum, his x mark, Cha-achsh, his x mark, Pich-kehd, his x mark, S'Klah-o-sum, his x mark, Sah-le-tatl, his x mark, See-lup, his x mark, E-la-kah-ka, his x mark, Slug-yeh, his x mark, Hi-nuk, his x mark, Ma-mo-nish, his x mark, Cheels, his x mark, Knutcanu, his x mark, Bats-ta-kobe, his x mark, Win-ne-ya, his x mark, Klo-out, his x mark, Se-uch-ka-nam, his x mark, Ske-mah-han, his x mark, Wuts-un-a-pum, his x mark, Quuts-a-tadm, his x mark, Quut-a-heh-mtsn, his x mark, Yah-leh-chn, his x mark, To-lahl-kut, his x mark

317

Plains, West and Northwest Plateau Indian Treaties

Executed in the presence of us
M. T. Simmons, Indian agent, James Dory, secretary of the commission, C. H. Mason, secretary Washington Territory, W. A. Slaughter, first lieutenant, Fourth Infantry, James McAlister, E. Giddings, jr.
George Shazer, Henry D. Cock, S. S. Ford, jr., John W. McAlister, Clovington Cushman, Peter Anderson, Samuel Klady, W. H. Pullen, P.O. Hough, E. R. Tyerall, George Gibbs, Benj. F. Shaw, interpreter, Hazard Stevens.

TREATY WITH THE KALAPUYA, ETC {1855, Jan. 22}
Ratified, Mar. 3, 1855.
Proclaimed, Apr. 10. 1855.

Articles of agreement and convention made and concluded at Dayton, Oregon Territory, by Joel Palmer, superintendent of Indian affairs, on the part of the United States, and the following-named chiefs of the confederated bands of Indians residing in the Willamette Valley, they being duly authorized thereto by their respective bands, to wit: Ki-a-kuts, Le Medecin, and Yat-Skaw, or Dave, chiefs of the Tualatin band of Calapooias; Shap-h, or William, Shel-ka-ah, or David, and Cha-ah, or Jesse, chiefs of the Yam Hill band; Dabo, or Jim, Sco-la-quit, or John, and Yah-kow or Kompetine, chiefs of the Che-luk-i-ma-uke band; Ah-mo, or George, Himpher, or Hubbard, and Oh-no, or Time, chiefs of the Chep-en-a-pho or Marysville band; Ma-mah-mo, or Charley Peter, Cha-che-clue, or Tom, and Quineflat, or Ben, chiefs of the Chem-a-pho or Maddy band; Luck-a-ma-foo, or Antoine, and Hoo-til, or Charley, chief of Che-lam-e-la or Long Tom band, all of the Calapooias; Qui-a-qua-ty, Yalkus, and Kow-ka-ma, or Long Hair, chiefs of Mo-lal-la band of Mo-lal-las; Kiles, or Jim, and Kow-ah-tough, or John, chiefs of the Calapooia band of Calapooias; Auto-quil-al-la, or John, and Mequah, of the Winnefelly and Mohawk bands; Yack-a-tee, or Sam, To-phor, or Jim Brown, and Hal-la-be, or Doctor, of the Tekopoa band; Pulk-tah, of the Chafan band of the Calapooia tribe; Tum-walth and O-ban-a-hah, chiefs of the Wah-lal-la band of Tum-waters; Watch-a-no, Te-ap-i-nick, and Wal-lah-pi-coto, chiefs of the Clack-a-mas tribe; Lallak and Cuck-a-man-na, or David, of the Clow-we-wal-la or Willamette Tum-water band; Tow-ye-col-la, or Louis; Yelk-ma, or Jo, La-ham, or Tom, Joseph Sanegertta, Pullican, Te-na, or Kiles, Pul-kup-li-ma, or John, Sallaf, or Silas, Hoip-ke-nek, or Jack, Yepta, and Sat-invose or James, chiefs and headmen of the Santiam bands of Calapooias.

ARTICLE 1.   The above-named confederated bands of Indians cede to the United States all their right, title, and claim to all and every part of the country included in the following boundaries, to wit:
Commencing in the middle of the main channel of the Columbia River, opposite the mouth of the first creek emptying into said river from the south below Oak Point, thence south to the first standard parallel north of the base-line in

318

Plains, West and Northwest Plateau Indian Treaties

the Government survey, thence west to the summit of the Coast Range of mountains, thence southerly along the summit of said range to the Calapooia Mountains, thence easterly along the summit of said mountains to the summit of the Cascade Mountains, thence along said summit northerly, to the middle of the Columbia River, at the Cascade Falls, and thence down the middle of said river to the place of beginning.

Provided, however, That said bands be permitted to remain within the limits of the country ceded, and on such temporary reserves as may be made for them by the superintendent of Indian affairs, until a suitable district of country shall be designated for their permanent home, and proper improvements made thereon: And provided, That the United States make proper provision for the security of their persons and property from the hostile attacks of Indians of other tribes and bands. At which time, or when thereafter directed by the superintendent of Indian affairs, or agent, said confederated bands engage peaceably, and without expense to the United States other than that provided for in this treaty, to vacate the country hereby ceded, and remove to the district which shall be designated for their permanent occupancy.

ARTICLE 2. In consideration of, and payment for the country herein described, the United States agree to pay to the bands and tribes of Indians claiming territory and residing in said country, the several sums of money following, to wit:
Ten thousand dollars per annum for the first five years, commencing on the first day of September, 1855.
Eight thousand dollars per annum for the term of five years next succeeding the first five.
Six thousand five hundred dollars per annum for the term of five years next succeeding the second five.

Five thousand five hundred dollars per annum for the term of five years next succeeding the third five.
All of which several sums of money shall be expended for the use and benefit of the confederated bands, under the direction of the President of the United States, who may, from time to time, at his discretion, determine what proportion thereof shall be expended for such objects as in his judgment will promote their well-being, and advance them in civilization, for their moral improvement and education, for buildings, opening and fencing farms, breaking land, providing stock, agricultural implements, seeds, &c.; for clothing, provisions, and tools; for medical purposes; providing mechanics and farmers, and for arms and ammunition.

The United States agree to pay said Indians the additional sum of fifty thousand dollars, a portion wherefore shall be expended for such articles as the superintendent of Indian affairs shall furnish the Indians, as soon as practicable after

Plains, West and Northwest Plateau Indian Treaties

the signing of this treaty; and in providing, after the ratification thereof, and while the Indians shall reside on the temporary reserves that may be assigned them, horses, oxen, and other stock, wagons, agricultural implements, clothing, and provisions, as the President may direct; and for erecting on the tract that may be selected as their permanent homes, mills, shops, school-houses, a hospital, and other necessary buildings, and making improvements; for seeds, stock, and farming operations thereon; for paying for the permanent improvements of settlers, should any such be on said tract at the time of its selection; to pay the expenses of the removal of the Indians thereto, and in providing for their subsistence thereon for the first year after their removal.

Provided, however, That if any band or bands of Indians, residing on or claiming any portion or portions of the country described in article first, shall not accede to the terms of this treaty, then the bands becoming parties hereunto agree to receive such part of the several annual and other payments herein named, as a consideration for the entire country described as aforesaid, as shall be in the proportion that their aggregate number may bear to the whole number of Indians residing in and claiming the entire country aforesaid, as consideration and payment in full for the tracts in said country claimed by them.

And, provided, Any of the bands becoming parties to this treaty establish a legitimate claim to any portion of the country north of the Columbia River, that the amount to which they may be entitled as a consideration for such country, in any treaties hereafter entered into with the United States, shall be added to the annuities herein provided for.

ARTICLE 3. In addition to the considerations specified, the United States agree to provide for the employment, for the term of five years from and after the removal of said Indians to their permanent reserve, of a physician, a school-teacher, a blacksmith, and a superintendent of farming operations.

ARTICLE 4. The President may, from time to time, at his discretion, cause the whole, or such portion as he may think proper, of the tract that may hereafter be set apart as the permanent home of these Indians, to be surveyed into lots, and assign them to such Indians of the confederated bands as may wish to enjoy the privilege, and locate thereon permanently; to a single person, over twenty-one years of age, twenty acres; to a family of two persons, forty acres; to a family of three, and not exceeding five persons, fifty acres; to a family of six persons, and not exceeding ten, eighty acres; and to each family over ten in number, twenty acres for each additional three members.

The President may provide such rules and regulations as will secure to the family, in case of the death of the head thereof, the possession and enjoyment of such permanent home, and the improvements thereon; and he may, at any time, at his discretion, after such person or family has made location on the

Plains, West and Northwest Plateau Indian Treaties

land assigned as a permanent home, issue a patent to such person or family, for such assigned land, conditioned that the tract shall not be aliened or leased for a longer time than two years, and shall be exempt from levy, sale, or forfeiture; which conditions shall continue in force until a State constitution, embracing such lands within its boundaries, shall have been formed, and the legislature of the State shall remove the restrictions: Provided, however, That no state legislature shall remove the restrictions herein provided for, without the consent of Congress.

And if any such family shall, at any time neglect or refuse to occupy or till a portion of the land assigned, and on which they have located, or shall rove from place to place, the President may, if the patent shall have been issued, revoke the same; or, if not issued, cancel the assignment; and may also withhold from such person or family their proportion of the annuities or other moneys due them, until they shall have returned to such permanent home, and resume the pursuits of industry; and in default of their return, the tract may be declared abandoned, and thereafter assigned to some other person or family of the Indians residing on the reserve.

ARTICLE 5. The annuities of the Indians shall not be taken to pay the debts of individuals.

ARTICLE 6. The confederated bands acknowledge their dependence on the government of the United States, and promise to be friendly with all the citizens thereof, and pledge themselves to commit no depredations on the property of such citizens. And should any one or more of the Indians violate this pledge, and the fact be satisfactorily proven before the agent, the property taken shall be returned, or in default thereof, or if injured or destroyed, compensation may be made by the Government out of their annuities. Nor will they make war on any other band or tribe of Indians, except in self-defence, but will submit all matters of difference between them and other Indians to the Government of the United States, or its agent, for decision, and abide thereby. And if any of said Indians commit any depredations on any other Indians, the same rule shall prevail as that prescribed in this article in case of depredations against citizens. Said Indians further engage to submit to and observe all laws, rules, and regulations which may be prescribed by the United States for the government of said Indians.

ARTICLE 7. In order to prevent the evils of intemperance among said Indians, it is hereby provided that any one of them who shall drink liquor, or procure it for other Indians to drink, may have his or her proportion of the annuities withheld from him or her for such time as the President may determine.

ARTICLE 8. The said confederated bands agree that when a permanent reserve shall be assigned them, all roads, highways, and railroads, demanded at

Plains, West and Northwest Plateau Indian Treaties

any time by the public convenience, shall have the right of way therein, a just compensation being made therefor.

ARTICLE 9. This treaty shall be obligatory on the contracting parties as soon as the same shall be ratified by the President and Senate of the United States. In testimony whereof the said Joel Palmer, on the part of the United States as aforesaid, and the undersigned chiefs of the said confederated bands, have hereunto set their hands and seals this fourth day of January, eighteen hundred and fifty-five, at Dayton, in Oregon Territory.

Joel Palmer, superintendent of Indian Affairs.

Ki-ac-kuts, first chief, his x mark, Le Medecin or Doctor, second chief, his x mark, Yats-kow, or Dave, third chief, his x mark, Shap-h, or William, first chief, his x mark, Shel-ke-ah, or David, second chief, his x mark, Che-ah, or Jesse, third chief, his x mark, Dabo, or Jim, first chief, his x mark, Sco-la-quit, or John, second chief, his x mark, Yah-kow, or Kompetine, third chief, his x mark,

Executed in the presence of us
Edward R. Geary, secretary.
John Flett, interpreter.

We, the chiefs of the Molalla band of Molallas, and of the Calapooia band of Calapooias, give our assent unto and agree to the provisions of the foregoing treaty.

In testimony whereof we have hereunto set our hands and seals, at Dayton, this ninth day of January, eighteen hundred and fifty-five.

Quia-quaty, first chief, his x mark, Yalkus, second chief, his x mark, Kaw-ka-ma, or Long Hair, third chief, his x mark, Kiles, or Jim, first chief, his x mark, Kowah-tough, or John, second chief, his x mark,

Executed in the presence of us
Edward R. Geary, secretary.
Cris. Taylor, assistant secretary.

We, the chiefs and headmen of the Nin-ne-felly, Mohawk, Chapen, and Te-co-pa bands of Calapooias, Wal-lal-lah band of Tum-waters, and the Clockamus tribe of Indians, being duly authorized by our respective bands, give our assent unto, and agree to the provisions of the foregoing treaty.

In testimony whereof we have hereunto set our hands and seals, at Dayton, Oregon Territory, this tenth day of January, eighteen hundred and fifty-five.

Plains, West and Northwest Plateau Indian Treaties

An-ta, first chief, his x mark, Quil-al-la, or John, second chief, his x mark, Me-quah, or Dick, his x mark, Yack-a-tee, or Sam, first chief, his x mark, To-phor, or Jim Brown, second chief, his x mark, Hal-lade, or Doctor, his x mark, Pulk-tah, second chief, his x mark, Tum-walth, first chief, his x mark, O-ban-a-hah, second chief, his x mark, Watch-a-no, first chief, his x mark, Te-ap-i-nick, second chief, his x mark,

Executed in the presence of
Cris. Taylor, assistant secretary.
Andrew Smith.
John Flett, interpreter.

We, the chiefs and headmen of the Clow-we-wal-la, or Willamette Tam-water band of Indians, being assembled in council, give our assent unto, and agree to the provisions of the foregoing treaty.

In testimony whereof we have hereunto set our hands and seals, at Linn city, Oregon Territory, this nineteenth day of January, eighteen hundred and fifty-five.

Lal-bick, or John, his x mark, Cuck-a-man-na, or David, his x mark,

Executed in the presence of us
Cris. Taylor, assistant secretary.
John Flett, interpreter.

We, the chiefs and headmen of the Santam bands of Calapooia Indians, being duly authorized by our respective bands, give our assent unto, and agree to the provisions of the foregoing treaty.

In testimony whereof we have hereunto set our hands and seals, at Dayton, Oregon Territory, this twenty-second day of January, eighteen hundred and fifty-five.

Tow-ye-colla, or Louis, first chief, his x mark, La-ham, or Tom, third chief, his x mark, Senegertta, his x mark, Pal-i-can, his x mark, Te-na, or Kiles, his x mark, Pul-kup-ti-ma, or John, his x mark, Sal-laf, or Silas, his x mark, Hoip-ke-nek, or Jack, his x mark, Yep-tah, his x mark, Satinvose, or James, his x mark,

Executed in the presence of us
Edward R. Geary, secretary.
Cris. Taylor.

Plains, West and Northwest Plateau Indian Treaties

TREATY WITH THE DWAMISH, SUQUAMISH, ETC. {1855, Jan. 22}
Ratified Mar. 8, 1859.
Proclaimed Apr. 11, 1859.

Articles of agreement and convention made and concluded at Múckl-te-óh, or Point Elliott, in the Territory of Washington, this twenty-second day of January, eighteen hundred and fifty-five, by Isaac I. Stevens, governor and superintendent of Indian affairs for the said Territory, on the part of the United States, and the undersigned chiefs, head-men and delegates of the Dwánish, Suquámish, Sk-táhl-mish, Sam-áhmish, Smalh-kamish, Skope-ámish, St-káhmish, Snoquálmoo, Skai-wha-mish, N'Quentl-má-mish, Sk-táh-le-jum, Stoluckwhá-mish, Sno-ho-mish, Skágit, Kik-i-állus, Swin-á-mish, Squin-áh-mish, Sahku-méhu, Noo-whá-ha, Nook-wa-cháh-mish, Mee-sée-qua-guilch, Cho-bah-áhbish, and other allied and subordinate tribes and bands of Indians occupying certain lands situated in said Territory of Washington, on behalf of said tribes, and duly authorized by them.

ARTICLE 1. The said tribes and bands of Indians hereby cede, relinquish, and convey to the United States all their right, title, and interest in and to the lands and country occupied by them, bounded and described as follows: Commencing at a point on the eastern side of Admiralty Inlet, known as Point Pully, about midway between Commencement and Elliott Bays; thence eastwardly, running along the north line of lands heretofore ceded to the United States by the Nisqually, Puyallup, and other Indians, to the summit of the Cascade range of mountains; thence northwardly, following the summit of said range to the 49th parallel of north latitude; thence west, along said parallel to the middle of the Gulf of Georgia; thence through the middle of said gulf and the main channel through the Canal de Arro to the Straits of Fuca, and crossing the same through the middle of Admiralty Inlet to Suquamish Head; thence southwesterly, through the peninsula, and following the divide between Hood's Canal and Admiralty Inlet to the portage known as Wilkes' Portage; thence northeastwardly, and following the line of lands heretofore ceded as aforesaid to Point Southworth, on the western side of Admiralty Inlet, and thence around the foot of Vashon's Island eastwardly and southeastwardly to the place of beginning, including all the islands comprised within said boundaries, and all the right, title, and interest of the said tribes and bands to any lands within the territory of the United States.

ARTICLE 2. There is, however, reserved for the present use and occupation of the said tribes and bands the following tracts of land, viz: the amount of two sections, or twelve hundred and eighty acres, surrounding the small bight at the head of Port Madison, called by the Indians Noo-sohk-um; the amount of two sections, or twelve hundred and eighty acres, on the north side Hwhomish Bay and the creek emptying into the same called Kwilt-seh-da, the peninsula at the southeastern end of Perry's Island, called Shais-quihl, and the island called

324

Plains, West and Northwest Plateau Indian Treaties

Chah-choo-sen, situated in the Lummi River at the point of separation of the mouths emptying respectively into Bellingham Bay and the Gulf of Georgia. All which tracts shall be set apart, and so far as necessary surveyed and marked out for their exclusive use; nor shall any white man be permitted to reside upon the same without permission of the said tribes or bands, and of the superintendent or agent, but, if necessary for the public convenience, roads may be run through the said reserves, the Indians being compensated for any damage thereby done them.

ARTICLE 3. There is also reserved from out the lands hereby ceded the amount of thirty-six sections, or one township of land, on the northeastern shore of Port Gardner, and north of the mouth of Snohomish River, including Tulalip Bay and the before-mentioned Kwilt-seh-da Creek, for the purpose of establishing thereon an agricultural and industrial school, as hereinafter mentioned and agreed, and with a view of ultimately drawing thereto and settling thereon all the Indians living west of the Cascade Mountains in said Territory. Provided, however, That the President may establish the central agency and general reservation at such other point as he may deem for the benefit of the Indians.

ARTICLE 4. The said tribes and bands agree to remove to and settle upon the said first above-mentioned reservations within one year after the ratification of this treaty, or sooner, if the means are furnished them. In the mean time it shall be lawful for them to reside upon any land not in the actual claim and occupation of citizens of the United States, and upon any land claimed or occupied, if with the permission of the owner.

ARTICLE 5. The right of taking fish at usual and accustomed grounds and stations is further secured to said Indians in common with all citizens of the Territory, and of erecting temporary houses for the purpose of curing, together with the privilege of hunting and gathering roots and berries on open and unclaimed lands. Provided, however, That they shall not take shell-fish from any beds staked or cultivated by citizens.

ARTICLE 6. In consideration of the above cession, the United States agree to pay to the said tribes and bands the sum of one hundred and fifty thousand dollars, in the following mannerthat is to say: For the first year after the ratification hereof, fifteen thousand dollars; for the next two year, twelve thousand dollars each year; for the next three years, ten thousand dollars each year; for the next four years, seven thousand five hundred dollars each years; for the next five years, six thousand dollars each year; and for the last five years, four thousand two hundred and fifty dollars each year. All which said sums of money shall be applied to the use and benefit of the said Indians, under the direction of the President of the United States, who may, from time to time, determine at his discretion upon what beneficial objects to expend the same; and the superinten-

325

Plains, West and Northwest Plateau Indian Treaties

dent of Indian affairs, or other proper officer, shall each year inform the President of the wishes of said Indians in respect thereto.

ARTICLE 7. The President may hereafter, when in his opinion the interests of the Territory shall require and the welfare of the said Indians be promoted, remove them from either or all of the special reservations hereinbefore made to the said general reservation, or such other suitable place within said Territory as he may deem fit, on remunerating them for their improvements and the expenses of such removal, or may consolidate them with other friendly tribes or bands; and he may further at his discretion cause the whole or any portion of the lands hereby reserved, or of such other land as may be selected in lieu thereof, to be surveyed into lots, and assign the same to such individuals or families as are willing to avail themselves of the privilege, and will locate on the same as a permanent home on the same terms and subject to the same regulations as are provided in the sixth article of the treaty with the Omahas, so far as the same may be applicable. Any substantial improvements heretofore made by any Indian, and which he shall be compelled to abandon in consequence of this treaty, shall be valued under the direction of the President and payment made accordingly therefor.

ARTICLE 8. The annuities of the aforesaid tribes and bands shall not be taken to pay the debts of individuals.

ARTICLE 9. The said tribes and bands acknowledge their dependence on the Government of the United States, and promise to be friendly with all citizens thereof, and they pledge themselves to commit no depredations on the property of such citizens. Should any one or more of them violate this pledge, and the fact be satisfactorily proven before the agent, the property taken shall be returned, or in default thereof, of if injured or destroyed, compensation may be made by the Government out of their annuities. Nor will they make war on any other tribe except in self-defence, but will submit all matters of difference between them and the other Indians to the Government of the United States or its agent for decision, and abide thereby. And if any of the said Indians commit depredations on other Indians within the Territory the same rule shall prevail as that prescribed in this article in cases of depredations against citizens. And the said tribes agree not to shelter or conceal offenders against the laws of the United States, but to deliver them up to the authorities for trial.

ARTICLE 10. The above tribes and bands are desirous to exclude from their reservations the use of ardent spirits, and to prevent their people from drinking the same, and therefore it is provided that any Indian belonging to said tribe who is guilty of bringing liquor into said reservations, or who drinks liquor, may have his or her proportion of the annuities withheld from him or her for such time as the President may determine.

326

Plains, West and Northwest Plateau Indian Treaties

ARTICLE 11. The said tribes and bands agree to free all slaves now held by them and not to purchase or acquire others hereafter.

ARTICLE 12. The said tribes and bands further agree not to trade at Vancouver's Island or elsewhere out of the dominions of the United States, nor shall foreign Indians be permitted to reside in their reservations without consent of the superintendent or agent.

ARTICLE 13. To enable the said Indians to remove to and settle upon their aforesaid reservations, and to clear, fence, and break up a sufficient quantity of land for cultivation, the United States further agree to pay the sum of fifteen thousand dollars to be laid out and expended under the direction of the President and in such manner as he shall approve.

ARTICLE 14. The United States further agree to establish at the general agency for the district of Puget's Sound, within one year from the ratification hereof, and to support for a period of twenty years, an agricultural and industrial school, to be free to children of the said tribes and bands in common with those of the other tribes of said district, and to provide the said school with a suitable instructor or instructors, and also to provide a smithy and carpenter's shop, and furnish them with the necessary tools, and employ a blacksmith, carpenter, and farmer for the like term of twenty years to instruct the Indians in their respective occupations. And the United States finally agree to employ a physician to reside at the said central agency, who shall furnish medicine and advice to their sick, and shall vaccinate them; the expenses of said school, shops, persons employed, and medical attendance to be defrayed by the United States, and not deducted from the annuities.

ARTICLE 15. This treaty shall be obligatory on the contracting parties as soon as the same shall be ratified by the President and Senate of the United States. In testimony whereof, the said Isaac I. Stevens, governor and superintendent of Indian affairs, and the undersigned chiefs, headmen, and delegates of the aforesaid tribes and bands of Indians, have hereunto set their hands and seals, at the place and on the day and year hereinbefore written.

Isaac I. Stevens, Governor and Superintendent.

Seattle, Chief of the Dwamish andSuquamish tribes, his x mark, Pat-ka-nam, Chief of the Snoqualmoo, Snohomish and other tribes, his x mark, Chow-its-hoot, Chief of the Lummiand other tribes, his x mark, Goliah, Chief of the Skagits andother allied tribes, his x mark, Kwallattum, or General Pierce, Sub-chief of the Skagit tribe, his x mark, S'hootst-hoot, Sub-chief of Snohomish, his x mark, Snah-talc, or Bonaparte, Sub-chief of Snohomish, his x mark, Squushum, or The Smoke, Sub-chief of the Snoqualmoo, his x mark,

Plains, West and Northwest Plateau Indian Treaties

Kut-ta-kanam, or John, Lummitribe, his x mark, Ch-lah-ben, Noo-qua-cha-mishband, his x mark, Noo-heh-oos, Snoqualmoo tribe, his x mark, Hweh-uk, Snoqualmoo tribe, his x mark, Peh-nus, Skai-whamish tribe, his x mark, Yim-ka-dam, Snoqualmoo tribe, his x mark, Twooi-as-kut, Skaiwhamish tribe, his x mark, Luch-al-kanam, Snoqualmoo tribe, his x mark, S'hoot-kanam, Snoqual-moo tribe, his x mark, Sme-a-kanam, Snoqualmoo tribe, his x mark, Sad-zis-keh, Snoqualmoo, his x mark,

Executed in the presence of us
M. T. Simmons, Indian agent, C. H. Mason, Secretary of Washington Territory, Benj. F. Shaw, Interpreter, Chas. M. Hitchcock, H. A. Goldsborough

TREATY WITH THE S'KLALLAM {1855, Jan. 26}
Ratified Mar. 8, 1859.
Proclaimed Apr. 29, 1859.

Articles of agreement and convention made and concluded at Hahdskus, or Point no Point, Suquamish Head, in the Territory of Washington, this twenty-sixth day of January, eighteen hundred and fifty-five, by Isaac I. Stevens, governor and superintendent of Indian affairs for the said Territory, on the part of the United States, and the undersigned chiefs, headmen, and delegates of the different villages of the S'Klallams, viz: Kah-tai, Squah-quaihtl Tch-queen Ste-tehtlum, Tsohkw, Yennis, Elh-wa, Pishtst, Hunnint, Klat-la-wash, and Oke-ho, and also of the Sko-ko-mish, To-an-hooch, and Chem-a-kum tribes, occupying certain lands on the Straits of Fuca and Hood's Canal, in the Territory of Washington, on behalf of said tribes, and duly authorized by them.

ARTICLE 1. The said tribes and bands of Indians hereby cede, relinquish, and convey to the United States all their right, title, and interest in and to the lands and country occupied by them, bounded and described as follows, viz: Commencing at the mouth of the Okeho River, on the Straits of Fuca; thence south-eastwardly along the westerly line of territory claimed by the Makah tribe of Indians to the summit of the Cascade Range; thence still southeastwardly and southerly along said summit to the head of the west branch of the Satsop River, down that branch to the main fork; thence eastwardly and following the line of lands heretofore ceded to the United States by the Nisqually and other tribes and bands of Indians, to the summit of the Black Hills, and northeastwardly to the portage known as Wilkes' Portage; thence northeastwardly, and following the line of lands heretofore ceded to the United States by the Dwamish, Suquamish, and other tribes and bands of Indians, to Suquamish Head; thence northerly through Admiralty Inlet to the Straits of Fuca; thence westwardly through said straits to the place of beginning; including all the right, title, and interest of the said tribes and bands to any land in the Territory of Washington.

Plains, West and Northwest Plateau Indian Treaties

ARTICLE 2. There is, however, reserved for the present use and occupation of the said tribes and bands the following tract of land, viz: The amount of six sections, or three thousand eight hundred and forty acres, situated at the head of Hood's Canal, to be hereafter set apart, and so far as necessary, surveyed and marked out for their exclusive use; nor shall any white man be permitted to reside upon the same without permission of the said tribes and bands, and of the superintendent or agent; but, if necessary for the public convenience, roads may be run through the said reservation, the Indians being compensated for any damage thereby done them. It is, however, understood that should the President of the United States hereafter see fit to place upon the said reservation any other friendly tribe or band, to occupy the same in common with those above mentioned, he shall be at liberty to do so.

ARTICLE 3. The said tribes and bands agree to remove to and settle upon the said reservation within one year after the ratification of this treaty, or sooner if the means are furnished them. In the mean time, it shall be lawful for them to reside upon any lands not in the actual claim or occupation of citizens of the United States, and upon any land claimed or occupied, if with the permission of the owner.

ARTICLE 4. The right of taking fish at usual and accustomed grounds and stations is further secured to said Indians, in common with all citizens of the United States; and of erecting temporary houses for the purpose of curing; together with the privilege of hunting and gathering roots and berries on open and unclaimed lands. Provided, however, That they shall not take shell-fish from any beds staked or cultivated by citizens.

ARTICLE 5. In consideration of the above cession the United States agree to pay to the said tribes and bands the sum of sixty thousand dollars, in the following manner, that is to say: during the first year after the ratification hereof, six thousand dollars; for the next two years, five thousand dollars each year; for the next three years, four thousand dollars each year; for the next four years, three thousand dollars each year; for the next five years, two thousand four hundred dollars each year; and for the next five years, one thousand six hundred dollars each year. All which said sums of money shall be applied to the use and benefit of the said Indians under the direction of the President of the United States, who may from time to time determine at his discretion upon what beneficial objects to expend the same. And the superintendent of Indian affairs, or other proper officer, shall each year inform the President of the wishes of said Indians in respect thereto.

ARTICLE 6. To enable the said Indians to remove to and settle upon their aforesaid reservations, and to clear, fence, and break up a sufficient quantity of land for cultivation, the United States further agree to pay the sum of six thou-

Plains, West and Northwest Plateau Indian Treaties

sand dollars, to be laid out and expended under the direction of the President, and in such manner as he shall approve.

ARTICLE 7. The President may hereafter, when in his opinion the interests of the Territory shall require, and the welfare of said Indians be promoted, remove them from said reservation to such other suitable place or places within said Territory as he may deem fit, on remunerating them for their improvements and the expenses of their removal; or may consolidate them with other friendly tribes or bands. And he may further, at his discretion, cause the whole or any portion of the lands hereby reserved, or of such other lands as may be selected in lieu thereof, to be surveyed into lots, and assign the same to such individuals or families as are willing to avail themselves of the privilege, and will locate thereon as a permanent home, on the same terms and subject to the same regulations as are provided in the sixth article of the treaty with the Omahas, so far as the same may be applicable. Any substantial improvements heretofore made by any Indian, and which he shall be compelled to abandon in consequence of this treaty, shall be valued under the direction of the President, and payment made therefor accordingly.

ARTICLE 8. The annuities of the aforesaid tribes and bands shall not be taken to pay the debts of individuals.

ARTICLE 9. The said tribes and bands acknowledge their dependence on the Government of the United States, and promise to be friendly with all citizens thereof; and they pledge themselves to commit no depredations on the property of such citizens. And should any one or more of them violate this pledge, and the fact be satisfactorily proven before the agent, the property taken shall be returned, or in default thereof, or if injured or destroyed, compensation may be made by the Government out of their annuities. Nor will they make war on any other tribe, except in self-defence, but will submit all matters of difference between them and other Indians to the Government of the United States, or its agent, for decision, and abide thereby. And if any of the said Indians commit any depredations on any other Indians within the Territory, the same rule shall prevail as that prescribed in this article in cases of depredations against citizens. And the said tribes agree not to shelter or conceal offenders against the United States, but to deliver them up for trial by the authorities.

ARTICLE 10. The above tribes and bands are desirous to exclude from their reservation the use of ardent spirits, and to prevent their people from drinking the same, and therefore it is provided that any Indian belonging thereto who shall be guilty of bringing liquor into said reservation, or who drinks liquor, may have his or her proportion of the annuities withheld from him or her for such time as the President may determine.

Plains, West and Northwest Plateau Indian Treaties

ARTICLE 11. The United States further agree to establish at the general agency for the district of Puget's Sound, within one year from the ratification hereof, and to support for the period of twenty years, an agricultural and industrial school, to be free to children of the said tribes and bands in common with those of the other tribes of said district, and to provide a smithy and carpenter's shop, and furnish them with the necessary tools, and employ a blacksmith, carpenter, and farmer for the term of twenty years, to instruct the Indians in their respective occupations. And the United States further agree to employ a physician to reside at the said central agency, who shall furnish medicine and advice to the sick, and shall vaccinate them; the expenses of the said school, shops, persons employed, and medical attendance to be defrayed by the United States, and not deducted from the annuities.

ARTICLE 12. The said tribes and bands agree to free all slaves now held by them, and not to purchase or acquire others hereafter.

ARTICLE 13. The said tribes and bands finally agree not to trade at Vancouver's Island, or elsewhere out of the dominions of the United States, nor shall foreign Indians be permitted to reside in their reservations without consent of the superintendent or agent.

ARTICLE 14. This treaty shall be obligatory on the contracting parties as soon as the same shall be ratified by the President of the United States.

In testimony whereof, the said Isaac I. Stevens, governor and superintendent of Indian affairs, and the undersigned chiefs, headmen, and delegates of the aforesaid tribes and bands of Indians have hereunto set their hands and seals at the place and on the day and year hereinbefore written.

Isaac I. Stevens, governor and superintendent.

Chits-a-mah-han, the Duke of York, Chief of the S'klallams, his x mark, Dah-whil-luk, Chief of the Sko-ko mush, his x mark, Kul-kah-han, or General Pierce, Chief of the Chem-a-kum, his x mark, Hool-hole-tan, or Jim, Sko-ko-mish, sub-chief, his x mark, Sai-a-kade, or Frank, Sko-ko-mish, sub-chief, his x mark, Loo-gweh-oos, or George, Sko-ko-mish, sub-chief, his x mark, E-dagh-tan, or Tom, Sko-ko-mish, sub-chief, his x mark, Kai-a-han, or Daniel Webster, Chem-a-kum, sub-chief, his x mark,

Executed in the presence of us
M. T. Simmons, C. H. Mason, secretary Washington Territory, Benj. F. Shaw, interpreter, John H. Scranton, Josiah P. Keller, C. M. Hitchcock, M.D., A. B. Gove, H. A. Goldsborough

Plains, West and Northwest Plateau Indian Treaties

TREATY WITH THE MAKAH {1855, Jan. 31}
Ratified Mar. 8, 1859.
Proclaimed Apr. 18, 1859.

Articles of agreement and convention made and concluded at Neah Bay, in the Territory of Washington, this thirty-first day of January, in the year eighteen hundred and fifty-five, by Isaac I. Stevens, governor and superintendent of Indian affairs for the said Territory, on the part of the United States, and the undersigned chiefs, head-men, and delegates of the several villages of the Makah tribe of Indians, viz: Neah Waatch, Tsoo-Yess, and Osett, occupying the country around Cape Classett or Flattery, on behalf of the said tribe and duly authorized by the same.

ARTICLE 1. The said tribe hereby cedes, relinquishes, and conveys to the United States all their right, title, and interest in and to the lands and country occupied by it, bounded and described as follows, viz: Commencing at the mouth of the Oke-ho River, on the Straits of Fuca; thence running westwardly with said straits to Cape Classett or Flattery; thence southwardly along the coast to Osett, or the Lower Cape Flattery; thence eastwardly along the line of lands occupied by the Kwe-déh-tut or Kwill-eh-yute tribe of Indians, to the summit of the coast-range of mountains, and thence northwardly along the line of lands lately ceded to the United States by the S'Klallam tribe to the place of beginning, including all the islands lying off the same on the straits and coast.

ARTICLE 2. There is, however, reserved for the present use and occupation of the said tribe the following tract of land, viz: Commencing on the beach at the mouth of a small brook running into Neah Bay next to the site of the old Spanish fort; thence along the shore round Cape Classett or Flattery, to the mouth of another small stream running into the bay on the south side of said cape, a little above the Waateh village; thence following said brook to its source; thence in a straight line to the source of the first-mentioned brook, and thence following the same down to the place of beginning; which said tract shall be set apart, and so far as necessary surveyed and marked out for their exclusive use; nor shall any white man be permitted to reside upon the same without permission of the said tribe and of the superintendent or agent; but if necessary for the public convenience, roads may be run through the said reservation, the Indians being compensated for any damage thereby done them. It is, however, understood that should the President of the United States hereafter see fit to place upon the said reservation any other friendly tribe or band to occupy the same in common with those above mentioned, he shall be at liberty to do so.

ARTICLE 3. The said tribe agrees to remove to and settle upon the said reservation, if required so to do, within one year after the ratification of this treaty, or sooner, if the means are furnished them. In the mean time it shall be lawful for them to reside upon any land not in the actual claim and occupation of citi-

332

Plains, West and Northwest Plateau Indian Treaties

zens of the United States, and upon any land claimed or occupied, if with the permission of the owner.

ARTICLE 4. The right of taking fish and of whaling or sealing at usual and accustomed grounds and stations is further secured to said Indians in common with all citizens of the United States, and of erecting temporary houses for the purpose of curing, together with the privilege of hunting and gathering roots and berries on open and unclaimed lands: Provided, however, That they shall not take shell-fish from any beds staked or cultivated by citizens.

ARTICLE 5. In consideration of the above cession the United States agree to pay to the said tribe the sum of thirty thousand dollars, in the following manner, that is to say: During the first year after the ratification hereof, three thousand dollars; for the next two years, twenty-five hundred dollars each year; for the next three years, two thousand dollars each year; for the next four years, one thousand five hundred dollars each year; and for the next ten years, one thousand dollars each year; all which said sums of money shall be applied to the use and benefit of the said Indians, under the direction of the President of the United States, who may from time to time determine at his discretion upon what beneficial objects to expend the same. And the superintendent of Indian affairs, or other proper officer, shall each year inform the President of the wishes of said Indians in respect thereto.

ARTICLE 6. To enable the said Indians to remove to and settle upon their aforesaid reservation, and to clear, fence, and break up a sufficient quantity of land for cultivation, the United States further agree to pay the sum of three thousand dollars, to be laid out and expended under the direction of the President, and in such manner as he shall approve. And any substantial improvements heretofore made by any individual Indian, and which he may be compelled to abandon in consequence of this treaty, shall be valued under the direction of the President and payment made therefor accordingly.

ARTICLE 7. The President may hereafter, when in his opinion the interests of the Territory shall require, and the welfare of said Indians be promoted thereby, remove them from said reservation to such suitable place or places within said Territory as he may deem fit, on remunerating them for their improvements and the expenses of their removal, or may consolidate them with other friendly tribes or bands; and he may further, at his discretion, cause the whole, or any portion of the lands hereby reserved, or such other land as may be selected in lieu thereof, to be surveyed into lots, and assign the same to such individuals or families as are willing to avail themselves of the privilege, and will locate thereon as a permanent home, on the same terms and subject to the same regulations as are provided in the sixth article of the treaty with the Omahas, so far as the same may be practicable.

333

Plains, West and Northwest Plateau Indian Treaties

ARTICLE 8. The annuities of the aforesaid tribe shall not be taken to pay the debts of individuals.

ARTICLE 9. The said Indians acknowledge their dependence on the Government of the United States, and promise to be friendly with all citizens thereof, and they pledge themselves to commit no depradations on the property of such citizens. And should any one or more of them violate this pledge, and the fact be satisfactorily proven before the agent, the property taken shall be returned, or in default thereof, or if injured or destroyed, compensation may be made by the Government out of their annuities. Nor will they make war on any other tribe except in self-defence, but will submit all matters of difference between them and other Indians to the Government of the United States or its agent for decision and abide thereby. And if any of the said Indians commit any depradations on any other Indians within the Territory, the same rule shall prevail as that prescribed in this article in case of depredations against citizens. And the said tribe agrees not to shelter or conceal offenders against the United States, but to deliver up the same for trial by the authorities.

ARTICLE 10. The above tribe is desirous to exclude from its reservation the use of ardent spirits, and to prevent its people from drinking the same, and therefore it is provided that any Indian belonging thereto who shall be guilty of bringing liquor into said reservation, or who drinks liquor, may have his or her proportion of the annuities withheld from him or her for such time as the President may determine.

ARTICLE 11. The United States further agree to establish at the general agency for the district of Puget's Sound, within one year from the ratification hereof, and to support for the period of twenty years, an agricultural and industrial school, to be free to children of the said tribe in common with those of the other tribes of said district and to provide a smithy and carpenter's shop, and furnish them with the necessary tools and employ a blacksmith, carpenter and farmer for the like term to instruct the Indians in their respective occupations. Provided, however, That should it be deemed expedient a separate school may be established for the benefit of said tribe and such others as may be associated with it, and the like persons employed for the same purposes at some other suitable place. And the United States further agree to employ a physician to reside at the said central agency, or at such other school should one be established, who shall furnish medicine and advice to the sick, and shall vaccinate them; the expenses of the said school, shops, persons employed, and medical attendance to be defrayed by the United States and not deducted from the annuities.

ARTICLE 12. The said tribe agrees to free all slaves now held by its people, and not to purchase or acquire others hereafter.

Plains, West and Northwest Plateau Indian Treaties

ARTICLE 13. The said tribe finally agrees not to trade at Vancouver's Island or elsewhere out of the dominions of the United States, nor shall foreign Indians be permitted to reside in its reservation without consent of the superintendent or agent.

ARTICLE 14. This treaty shah be obligatory on the contracting parties as soon as the same shall be ratified by the President of the United States.

In testimony whereof, the said Isaac I. Stevens, governor and superintendent of Indian affairs, and the undersigned, chiefs, headmen and delegates of the tribe aforesaid have hereunto set their hands and seals at the place and on the day and year hereinbefore written.

Isaac I. Stevens, governor and superintendent.

Tse-kauwtl, head chief of the Ma kah tribe, his x mark, Kal-chote, subchief of the Makahs, his x mark, Tah-a-howtl, subchief of the Ma kahs, his x mark, Kah-bach-sat, subchief of the Ma kahs, his x mark, Kets-kus-sum, subchief of the Ma kahs, his x mark, Haatse, subchief of the Makahs, his x mark, Keh-chook, subchief of the Ma kahs, his x mark, It-an-da-ha, subchief of the Ma kahs, his x mark, Klah-pe-an-hie, or Andrew Jack son, subchief of the Makahs, his x mark,

Executed in the presence of us.
The words "five hundred" being first interlined in the 5th article, and erasures made in the 8th and 9th articles.
M. T. Simmons, Indian agent, George Gibbs, secretary, B. F. Shaw, interpreter, C. M. Hitchcock, M.D, E Fowler, Orrington Cushman, Robt. Davis.

Plains, West and Northwest Plateau Indian Treaties

TREATY WITH THE WINNEBAGO {1855, Feb. 27}
Ratified Mar. 3, 1855.
Proclaimed Mar. 23, 1855.

Articles of agreement and convention, made and concluded at Washington City on the twenty-seventh day of February, eighteen hundred and fifty-five, between George W. Manypenny, commissioner on the part of the United States, and the following-named chiefs and delegates representing the Winnebago tribe of Indians, viz: Waw-kon-chaw-koo-haw, The Coming Thunder, or Kinnoshik; Sho-go-nik-kaw, or Little Hill; Maw-he-coo-shah-naw-zhe-kaw, One that Stands and Reaches the Skies, or Little Decorie; Waw-kon-chaw-hoo-no-haw, or Little Thunder; Hoonk-hoo-no-kaw, Little Chief, or Little Priest; Honch-hutta-kaw, or Big Bear; Wach-ha-ta-kaw, or Big Canoe; Ha-zum-kee-kaw, or One Horn; Ha-zee-kaw, or Yellow Bank; and Baptiste Lassallier, they being thereto duly authorized by said tribe:

ARTICLE 1. The Winnebago Indians hereby cede, sell, and convey to the United States all their right, title, and interest in, and to, the tract of land granted to them pursuant to the third article of the treaty concluded with said tribe, at Washington City, on the thirteenth day of October, one thousand eight hundred and forty-six, lying north of St. Peter's River and west of the Mississippi River, in the Territory of Minnesota, and estimated to contain about eight hundred and ninety-seven thousand and nine hundred (897,900) acres; the boundary-lines of which are thus described, in the second article of the treaty concluded between the United States and the Chippewa Indians of the Mississippi and Lake Superior, on the second day of August, one thousand eight hundred and forty seven, viz:

"Beginning at the junction of the Crow Wing and Mississippi Rivers; thence, up the Crow Wing River, to the junction of that river with the Long Prairie River; thence, up the Long Prairie River, to the boundary line between the Sioux and Chippewa Indians; thence, southerly, along the said boundary-line, to a lake at the head of Long Prairie River; thence, in a direct line, to the sources of the Watab River; thence, down the Watab to the Mississippi River; thence, up the Mississippi, to the place of beginning:" Provided, however, That the portions of said tract embracing the improved lands of the Indians, the grist and saw mill, and all other improvements made for or by them, shall be specially reserved from pre-emption, sale, or settlement until the said mills and improvements, including the improvements to the land, shall have been appraised and sold, at public sale, to the highest bidder, for the benefit of the Indians, but no sale thereof shall be made for less than the appraised value. And the President may prescribe such rules and regulations in relation to said sale as he may deem proper; and the person or persons purchasing said mills and improvements, shall have the right, when the land is surveyed, to enter the legal

Plains, West and Northwest Plateau Indian Treaties

subdivisions thereof, including the improvements purchased by them, at one dollar and twenty-five cents per acre.

ARTICLE 2. In consideration of the cessions aforesaid, and in full compensation therefor, the United States agree to pay to the said Indians, the sum of seventy thousand dollars, ($70,000) and to grant them, as a permanent home, a tract of land equal to eighteen miles square, on the Blue Earth River, in the Territory of Minnesota, which shall be selected and located by the agent of the Government and a delegation of the Winnebagoes, immediately after the ratification of this instrument, and after the necessary appropriations to carry it into effect shall have been made; and a report of such selection and location, shall be made in writing, to the superintendent of Indian affairs for the Territory of Minnesota, who shall attach his official signature to the same, and forward it to the Commissioner of Indian Affairs; and the country thus selected shall be the permanent home of the said Indians; Provided, Said tract shall not approach nearer the Minnesota River than the mouth of the La Serrer fork of the Blue Earth River.

ARTICLE 3. It is agreed, that the moneys received from the sale of the Indian improvements, as provided for in the first article, and the sum stipulated to be paid by the second article of this instrument, shall be expended under the direction of the President, in removing the Indians to their new homes, including those who are now severed from the main body of the tribe, living in Kansas Territory, Wisconsin, or elsewhere; in subsisting them a reasonable time after their removal; in making improvements, such as breaking and fencing land, and building houses; in purchasing stock, agricultural implements and household furniture, and for such other objects as may tend to promote their prosperity and advancement in civilization. And the said Winnebago Indians agree to remove to their new homes immediately after the selection of the tract hereinbefore provided for, is made.

ARTICLE 4. In order to encourage the Winnebago Indians to engage in agriculture, and such other pursuits as will conduce to their well-being and improvement, it is agreed: that, at such time or times as the President may deem advisable, the land herein provided to be selected as their future home, or such portions thereof as may be necessary, shall be surveyed; and the President shall, from time to time, as the Indians may desire it, assign to each head of a family, or single persons over twenty-one years of age, a reasonable quantity of land, in one body, not to exceed eighty acres in any case, for their separate use; and he may, at his discretion, as the occupants thereof become capable of managing their business and affairs, issue patents to them for the tract so assigned to them, respectively; said tracts to be exempt from taxation, levy, sale, or forfeiture, until otherwise provided by the legislature of the State in which they may be situated, with the assent of Congress; nor shall they be sold or alienated, in

Plains, West and Northwest Plateau Indian Treaties

fee, within fifteen years after the date of the patents, and not then, without the assent of the President of the United States being first obtained

Prior to the patents being issued, the President shall make such rules and regulations as he may deem necessary and expedient, respecting the disposition of any of said tracts, in case of the death of the person or persons to whom they may be assigned, so that the same shall be secured to the families of such deceased persons; and should any of the Indians to whom tracts may be assigned, thereafter abandon them, the President may take such action in relation to such abandoned tracts, as in his judgment may be necessary and proper.

ARTICLE 5. All unexpended balances now in the hands of the agent of the tribe, arising under former treaties, for schools, pay of interpreter therefor, support of blacksmiths and assistants; and also of the sum of ten thousand dollars set apart by the treaty of October thirteenth eighteen hundred and forty-six, for manual-labor schools, shall be expended and applied, in the opening of farms, building and furnishing of houses, and the purchase of stock for said Indians. And the stipulations in former treaties providing for the application or expenditure of particular sums of money for specific purposes, are hereby so far modified and changed, as to confer upon the President the power, in his discretion, to cause such sums of money, in whole or in part, to be expended for, or applied to such other objects and purposes and in such manner as he shall deem best calculated to promote the welfare and improvement of said Indians.

ARTICLE 6. No part of the moneys stipulated to be paid to the Winnebago Indians by these articles of agreement and convention, nor any of the future instalments due and payable under former treaties between them and the United States, shall ever be taken, by direction of the chiefs, to pay the debts of individual Indians, contracted in their private dealings, known as national or tribal debts.

ARTICLE 7. The missionaries, or other persons who are, by authority of law, now residing on the lands ceded by the first article of this agreement, shall each have the privilege of entering one hundred and sixty acres of the said ceded lands, to include any improvements they may have, at one dollar and twenty-five cents per acre: and such of the mixed-bloods, as are heads of families, and now have actual residences and improvements of their own, in the ceded country, shall each have granted to them, in fee, eighty acres of land, to include their improvements: Provided, however, That said entries and grants shall in no case be upon, or in any manner interfere with, any of the lands improved by the Government, or by or for the Indians, or on which the agency building, saw and grist mill, or other public or Indian improvements have been erected or made.

ARTICLE 8. The laws which have been or may be enacted by Congress, regulating trade and intercourse with the Indian tribes, shall continue and be in

Plains, West and Northwest Plateau Indian Treaties

force within the country herein provided to be selected as the future permanent home of the Winnebago Indians; and those portions of said laws which prohibit the introduction, manufacture, use of, and traffic in, ardent spirits in the Indian country, shall continue and be in force within the country herein ceded to the United States, until otherwise provided by Congress.

ARTICLE 9. All roads and highways authorized by law, the lines of which may be required to be laid through any part of the country herein provided as the future permanent home of the Winnebago Indians, shall have right of way through the same; a fair and just value of such right being paid to the Indians, in money, to be assessed and determined according to the laws in force for the appropriation of land for such purposes.

ARTICLE 10. The said tribe of Indians, jointly and severally, obligate and bind themselves, not to commit any depredation or wrong upon other Indians, or upon citizens of the United States; to conduct themselves at all times in a peaceable and orderly manner; to submit all difficulties between them and other Indians to the President, and to abide by his decision; to respect and observe the laws of the United States, so far as the same are to them applicable; to settle down in the peaceful pursuits of life; to commence the cultivation of the soil; to educate their children, and to abstain from the use of intoxicating drinks and other vices to which many of them have been addicted. And the President may withhold from such of the Winnebagoes as abandon their homes, and refuse to labor, and from the idle, intemperate, and vicious, the benefits they may be entitled to under these articles of agreement and convention, or under articles of former treaties, until they give evidences of amendment and become settled, and conform to, and comply, with the stipulations herein provided; or, should they be heads of families, the same may be appropriated, under the direction of the President, to the use and enjoyment of their families.

ARTICLE 11. These articles of agreement and convention, shall be in lieu of the "Articles of a convention made and concluded between Willis A. Gorman and Jonathan E. Fletcher, on the part of the United States, and the chiefs and head-men of the Winnebago tribe of Indians, on the 6th day of August, A. D. 1853," and the amendments of the Senate thereto, as expressed in its resolution of July twenty-first, eighteen hundred and fifty-four; to which amendments the said Winnebago Indians refused to give their assent, which refusal was communicated to the Commissioner of Indian Affairs, by the governor of Minnesota Territory, on the twenty-fourth of January, eighteen hundred and fifty-five.

ARTICLE 12. The United States will pay the necessary expenses incurred by the Winnebago delegates in making their present visit to Washington, while here, and in returning to their homes.

Plains, West and Northwest Plateau Indian Treaties

ARTICLE 13. This instrument shall be obligatory on the contracting parties as soon as the same shall be ratified by the President and the Senate of the United States.

In testimony whereof the said George W. Manypenny, commissioner as aforesaid, and the said chiefs and delegates of the Winnebago tribe of Indians, have hereunto set their hands and seals, at the place and on the day and year hereinbefore written.

George W. Manypenny, commissioner,
Waw-kon-chaw-koo-haw, the Coming Thunder, or Win-no-shik, his x mark, Sho-go-nik-kaw, or Little Hill his x mark, Maw-he-coo-shaw-naw-zhe-kaw, One that Stands and Reaches the Skies, or Little Decorie, his x mark, Waw-kon-chaw-hoo-no-kaw, or Little Thunder, his x mark, Hoonk-hoo-no-kaw, Little Chief or Little Priest his x mark, Honch-hutta-kaw, or Big Bear, his x mark, Watch-ha-ta-kaw, or Big Canoe, his x mark, Ha-zhun-kee-kaw, or One Horn, his x mark,

In presence of
Geo. Culver, Asa White, John Dowling, J. E. Fletcher, Peter Manaiy, United States interpreter.

TREATY WITH THE WALLAWALLA, CAYUSE, ETC. {1855, June 9}
Ratified Mar. 8, 1859.
Proclaimed Apt. 11, 1859.

Articles of agreement and convention made and concluded at the treaty-ground, Camp Stevens, in the Walla-Walla Valley, this Ninth day of June, in the year one thousand eight hundred and fifty-five, by and between Isaac I. Stevens, governor and superintendent of Indian affairs for the Territory of Washington, and Joel Palmer, superintendent of Indian affairs for Oregon Territory, on the part of the United States, and the undersigned chiefs, head-men, and delegates of the Walla-Wallas, Cayuses, and Umatilla tribes, and bands of Indians, occupying lands partly in Washington and partly in Oregon Territories, and who, for the purposes of this treaty, are to be regarded as one nation acting for and in behalf of their respective bands and tribes, they being duly authorized thereto; it being understood that Superintendent I. I. Stevens assumes to treat with that portion of the above-named bands and tribes residing within the Territory of Washington, and Superintendent Palmer with those residing within Oregon.

ARTICLE 1. The above-named confederated bands of Indians cede to the United States all their right, title, and claim to all and every part of the country claimed by them included in the following boundaries, to wit: Commencing at the mouth of the Tocannon River, in Washington Territory, running thence up

Plains, West and Northwest Plateau Indian Treaties

said river to its source; thence easterly along the summit of the Blue Mountains, and on the southern boundaries of the purchase made of the Nez Percés Indians, and easterly along that boundary to the western limits of the country claimed by the Shoshonees or Snake Indians; thence southerly along that boundary (being the waters of Powder River) to the source of Powder River, thence to the head-waters of Willow Creek, thence down Willow Creek to the Columbia River, thence up the channel of the Columbia River to the lower end of a large island below the mouth of Umatilla River, thence northerly to a point on the Yakama River, called Tomah-luke, thence to Le Lac, thence to the White Banks on the Columbia below Priest's Rapids, thence down the Columbia River to the junction of the Columbia and Snake Rivers, thence up the Snake River to the place of beginning: Provided, however, That so much of the country described above as is contained in the following boundaries shall be set apart as a residence for said Indians, which tract for the purposes contemplated shall be held and regarded as an Indian reservation; to wit:

Commencing in the middle of the channel of Umatilla River opposite the mouth of. Wild Horse Creek, thence up the middle of the channel of said creek to its source, thence southerly to a point in the Blue Mountains, known as Lee's Encampment, thence in a line to the head-waters of Howtome Creek, thence west to the divide between Howtome and Birch Creeks, thence northerly along said divide to a point due west of the southwest corner of William C. McKay's land-claim, thence east along his line to his southeast corner, thence in a line to the place of beginning; all of which tract shall be set apart and, so far as necessary, surveyed and marked out for their exclusive use; nor shall any white person be permitted to reside upon the same without permission of the agent and superintendent.

The said tribes and bands agree to remove to and settle upon the same within one year after the ratification of this treaty, without any additional expense to the Government other than is provided by this treaty, and until the expiration of the time specified, the said bands shall be permitted to occupy and reside upon the tracts now possessed by them, guaranteeing to all citizen(s) of the United States, the right to enter upon and occupy as settlers any lands not actually enclosed by said Indians.

Provided, also, That the exclusive right of taking fish in the streams running through and bordering said reservation is hereby secured to said Indians, and at all other usual and accustomed stations in common with citizens of the United States, and of erecting suitable buildings for curing the same; the privilege of hunting, gathering roots and berries and pasturing their stock on unclaimed lands in common with citizens, is also secured to them.

And provided, also, That if any band or bands of Indians, residing in and claiming any portion or portions of the country described in this article, shall

Plains, West and Northwest Plateau Indian Treaties

not accede to the terms of this treaty, then the bands becoming parties hereunto agree to reserve such part of the several and other payments herein named, as a consideration for the entire country described as aforesaid, as shall be in the proportion that their aggregate number may have to the whole number of Indians residing in and claiming the entire country aforesaid, as consideration and payment in full for the tracts in said country claimed by them.

And provided, also, That when substantial improvements have been made by any member of the bands being parties to this treaty, who are compelled to abandon them in consequence of said treaty, (they) shall be valued under the direction of the President of the United States, and payment made therefor.

ARTICLE 2. In consideration of and payment for the country hereby ceded, the United States agree to pay the bands and tribes of Indians claiming territory and residing in said country, and who remove to and reside upon said reservation, the several sums of money following, to wit: eight thousand dollars per annum for the term of five years, commencing on the first day of September, 1856; six thousand dollars per annum for the term of five years next succeeding the first five; four thousand dollars per annum for the term of five years next succeeding the second five, and two thousand dollars per annum for the term of five years next succeeding the third five; all of which several sums of money shall be expended for the use and benefit of the confederated bands herein named, under the direction of the President of the United States, who may from time to time at his discretion, determine what proportion thereof shall be expended for such objects as in his judgment will promote their well-being, and advance them in civilization, for their moral improvement and education, for buildings, opening and fencing farms, breaking land, purchasing teams, wagons, agricultural implements and seeds, for clothing, provision and tools, for medical purposes, providing mechanics and farmers, and for arms and ammunition.

ARTICLE 3. In addition to the articles advanced the Indians at the time of signing this treaty, the United States agree to expend the sum of fifty thousand dollars during the first and second years after its ratification, for the erection of buildings on the reservation, fencing and opening farms, for the purchase of teams, farming implements, clothing, and provisions, for medicines and tools, for the payment of employes, and for subsisting the Indians the first year after their removal.

ARTICLE 4. In addition to the consideration above specified, the United States agree to erect, at suitable points on the reservation, one saw-mill, and one flouring-mill, a building suitable for a hospital, two school-houses, one blacksmith shop, one building for wagon and plough maker and one carpenter and joiner shop, one dwelling for each, two millers, one farmer, one superintendent of farming operations, two school-teachers, one blacksmith, one wagon

Plains, West and Northwest Plateau Indian Treaties

and plough maker, one carpenter and joiner, to each of which the necessary out-buildings. To purchase and keep in repair for the term of twenty years all necessary mill fixtures and mechanical tools, medicines and hospital stores, books and stationery for schools, and furniture for employes.

The United States further engage to secure and pay for the services and subsistence, for the term of twenty years, (of) one superintendent of farming operations, one farmer, one blacksmith, one wagon and plough maker, one carpenter and joiner, one physician, and two school-teachers.

ARTICLE 5. The United States further engage to build for the head chiefs of the Walla-Walla, Cayuse, and Umatilla bands each one dwelling-house, and to plough and fence ten acres of land for each, and to pay to each five hundred dollars per annum in cash for the term of twenty years. The first payment to the Walla-Walla chief to commence upon the signing of this treaty. To give to the Walla-Walla chief three yoke of oxen, three yokes and four chains, one wagon, two ploughs, twelve hoes, twelve axes, two shovels, and one saddle and bridle, one set of wagon-harness, and one set of plough-harness, within three months after the signing of this treaty.

To build for the son of Pio-pio-mox-mox one dwelling-house, and plough and fence five acres of land, and to give him a salary for twenty years, one hundred dollars in cash per annum, commencing September first, eighteen hundred and fifty-six.

The improvement named in this section to be completed as soon after the ratification of this treaty as possible.

It is further stipulated that Pio-pio-mox-mox is secured for the term of five years, the right to build and occupy a house at or near the mouth of Yakama River, to be used as a trading-post in the sale of his bands of wild cattle ranging in that district: And provided, also, That in consequence of the immigrant wagon-road from Grand Round to Umatilla, passing through the reservation herein specified, thus leading to turmoils and disputes between Indians and immigrants, and as it is known that a more desirable and practicable route may be had to the south of the present road, that a sum not exceeding ten thousand dollars shall be expended in locating and opening a wagon-road from Powder River or Grand Round, so as to reach the plain at the western base of the Blue Mountain, south of the southern limits of said reservation.

ARTICLE 6. The President may, from time to time at his discretion cause the whole or such portion as he may think proper, of the tract that may now or hereafter be set apart as a permanent home for those Indians, to be surveyed into lots and assigned to such Indians of the confederated bands as may wish to enjoy the privilege, and locate thereon permanently, to a single person over

343

Plains, West and Northwest Plateau Indian Treaties

twenty-one years of age, forty acres, to a family of two persons, sixty acres, to a family of three and not exceeding five, eighty acres; to a family of six persons and not exceeding ten, one hundred and twenty acres; and to each family over ten in number, twenty acres to each additional three members; and the President may provide for such rules and regulations as will secure to the family in case of the death of the head thereof, the possession and enjoyment of such permanent home and improvement thereon; and he may at any time, at his discretion, after such person or family has made location on the land assigned as a permanent home, issue a patent to such person or family for such assigned land, conditioned that the tract shall not be aliened or leased for a longer term than two years, and shall be exempt from levy, sale, or forfeiture, which condition shall continue in force until a State constitution, embracing such land within its limits, shall have been formed and the legislature of the State shall remove the restriction.

Provided, however, That no State legislature shall remove the restriction herein provided for without the consent of Congress.

Provided, also, That if any person or family, shall at any time, neglect or refuse to occupy or till a portion of the land assigned and on which they have located, or shall roam from place to place, indicating a desire to abandon his home, the President may if the patent shall have been issued, cancel the assignment, and may also withhold from such person or family their portion of the annuities or other money due them, until they shall have returned to such permanent home, and resumed the pursuits of industry, and in default of their return the tract may be declared abandoned, and thereafter assigned to some other person or family of Indians residing on said reservation: And provided, also, That the head chiefs of the three principal bands, to wit, Pio-pio-mox-mox, Weyatenatemany, and Wenap-snoot, shall be secured in a tract of at least one hundred and sixty acres of land.

ARTICLE 7. The annuities of the Indians shall not be taken to pay the debts of individuals.

ARTICLE 8. The confederated bands acknowledge their dependence on the Government of the United States and promise to be friendly with all the citizens thereof, and pledge themselves to commit no depredation on the property of such citizens, and should any one or more of the Indians violate this pledge, and the fact be satisfactorily proven before the agent, the property taken shall be returned, or in default thereof, or if injured or destroyed, compensation may be made by the Government out of their annuities; nor will they make war on any other tribe of Indians except in self-defense, but submit all matter of difference between them and other Indians, to the Government of the United States or its agents for decision, and abide thereby; and if any of the said Indians commit any depredations on other Indians, the same rule shall prevail as that

Plains, West and Northwest Plateau Indian Treaties

prescribed in the article in case of depredations against citizens. Said Indians further engage to submit to and observe all laws, rules, and regulations which may be prescribed by the United States for the government of said Indians.

ARTICLE 9. In order to prevent the evils of intemperance among said Indians, it is hereby provided that if any one of them shall drink liquor, or procure it for others to drink, (such one) may have his or her proportion of the annuities withheld from him or her for such time as the President may determine.

ARTICLE 10. The said confederated bands agree that, whenever in the opinion of the President of the United States the public interest may require it, that all roads highways and railroads shall have the right of way through the reservation herein designated or which may at any time hereafter be set apart as a reservation-for said Indians.

ARTICLE 11. This treaty shall be obligatory on the contracting parties as soon as the same shall be ratified by the President and Senate of the United States. In testimony whereof, the said I. I. Stevens and Joel Palmer, on the part of the United States, and the undersigned chiefs, headmen, and delegates of the said confederated bands, have hereunto set their hands and seals, this ninth day of June, eighteen hundred and fifty-five.

Isaac I. Stevens, Governor and Superintendent Washington Territory
Joel Palmer, Superintendent Indian Affairs, O. T.

Pio-pio-mox-mox, his x mark, head chief of Walla-Wallas, Meani-teat or Pierre, his x mark, Weyatenatemany, his x mark, head chief of Cayuses, Wenap-snoot, his x mark, head chief of Umatilla

Signed in the presence of
James Doty, secretary treaties, Wm. C. McKay, secretary treaties, C. Chirouse, O. M. I, A. D. Pamburn, interpreter, John Whitford, his x mark, interpreter.

TREATY WITH THE YAKIMA {1855, June 9}
Ratified Mar. 8,1859.
Proclaimed Apr. 18, 1859.

Articles of agreement and convention made and concluded at the treaty-ground, Camp Stevens. Walla-Walla Valley, this ninth day of June, in the year one thousand eight hundred and fifty-five, by and between Isaac L Stevens, governor and superintendent of Indian affairs for the Territory of Washington, on the part of the United States, and the undersigned head chiefs, chiefs, head-men, and delegates of the Yakama, Palouse, Pisquose, Wenatshapam, Klikatat, Klinquit, Kow-was-say-ee, Li-ay-was, Skin-pah, Wish-ham, Shyiks, Oche-chores,

345

Plains, West and Northwest Plateau Indian Treaties

Kah-milt-pah, and Se-ap-cat, confederated tribes and bands of Indians, occupying lands hereinafter bounded and described and lying in Washington Territory, who for the purposes of this treaty are to be considered as one nation, under the name of "Yakama," with Kamaiakun as its head chief, on behalf of and acting for said tribes and bands, and being duly authorized thereto by them.

ARTICLE 1. The aforesaid confederated tribes and bands of Indians hereby cede, relinquish, and convey to the United States all their right, title, and interest in and to the lands and country occupied and claimed by them, and bounded and described as follows, to wit:

Commencing at Mount Ranier, thence northerly along the main ridge of the Cascade Mountains to the point where the northern tributaries of Lake Che-lan and the southern tributaries of the Methow River have their rise; thence southeasterly on the divide between the waters of Lake Che-lan and the Methow River to the Columbia River; thence, crossing the Columbia on a true east course, to a point whose longitude is one hundred and nineteen degrees and ten minutes, (119° 10') which two latter lines separate the above confederated tribes and bands from the Oakinakane tribe of Indians; thence in a true south course to the forty-seventh (47°) parallel of latitude; thence east on said parallel to the main Palouse River, which two latter lines of boundary separate the above confederated tribes and bands from the Spokanes; thence down the Palouse River to its junction with the Moh-hah-ne-she, or southern tributary of the same; thence in a southeasterly direction, to the Snake River, at the mouth of the Tucannon River, separating the above confederated tribes from the Nez Percé tribe of Indians; thence down the Snake River to its junction with the Columbia River; thence up the Columbia River to the "White Banks" below the Priest's Rapids; thence westerly to a lake called "La Lac;" thence southerly to a point on the Yakama River called Toh-mah-luke; thence, in a southwesterly direction, to the Columbia River, at the western extremity of the "Big Island," between the mouths of the Umatilla River and Butler Creek; all which latter boundaries separate the above confederated tribes and bands from the Walla-Walla, Cayuse, and Umatilla tribes and bands of Indians; thence down the Columbia River to midway between the mouths of White Salmon and Wind Rivers; thence along the divide between said rivers to the main ridge of the Cascade Mountains; and thence along said ridge to the place of beginning.

ARTICLE 2. There is, however, reserved, from the lands above ceded for the use and occupation of the aforesaid confederated tribes and bands of Indians, the tract of land included within the following boundaries, to wit: Commencing on the Yakama River, at the mouth of the Attah-nam River; thence westerly along said Attah-nam River to the forks; thence along the southern tributary to the Cascade Mountains; thence southerly along the main ridge of said mountains, passing south and east of Mount Adams, to the spur whence flows the waters of the Klickatat and Pisco Rivers; thence down said spur to the divide

Plains, West and Northwest Plateau Indian Treaties

between the waters of said rivers; thence along said divide to the divide separating the waters of the Satass River from those flowing into the Columbia River; thence along said divide to the main Yakama, eight miles below the mouth of the Satass River; and thence up the Yakama River to the place of beginning.

All which tract shall be set apart and, so far as necessary, surveyed and marked out, for the exclusive use and benefit of said confederated tribes and bands of Indians, as an Indian reservation; nor shall any white man, excepting those in the employment of the Indian Depart-meat, be permitted to reside upon the said reservation without permission of the tribe and the superintendent and agent. And the said confederated tribes and bands agree to remove to, and settle upon, the same, within one year after the ratification of this treaty. In the mean time it shall be lawful for them to reside upon any ground not in the actual claim and occupation of citizens of the United States; and upon any ground claimed or occupied, if with the permission of the owner or claimant.

Guaranteeing, however, the right to all citizens of the United States to enter upon and occupy as settlers any lands not actually occupied and cultivated by said Indians at this time, and not included in the reservation above named. And provided, That any substantial improvements heretofore made by any Indian, such as fields enclosed and cultivated, and houses erected upon the lands hereby ceded, and which he may be compelled to abandon in consequence of this-treaty, shall be valued, under the direction of the President of the United States, and payment made therefor in money; or improvements of an equal value made for said Indian upon the reservation. And no Indian will be required to abandon the improvements aforesaid, now occupied by him, until their value in money, or improvements of an equal value shall be furnished him as aforesaid.

ARTICLE 3.   And provided, That, if necessary for the public convenience, roads may be run through the said reservation; and on the other hand, the right of way, with free access from the same to the nearest public highway, is secured to them; as also the right, in common with citizens of the United States, to travel upon all public highways.

The exclusive right of taking fish in all the streams, where running through or bordering said reservation, is further secured to said confederated tribes and bands of Indians, as also the right of taking fish at all usual and accustomed places, in common with the citizens of the Territory, and of erecting temporary buildings for curing them; together with the privilege of hunting, gathering roots and berries, and pasturing their horses and cattle upon open and unclaimed land.

347

Plains, West and Northwest Plateau Indian Treaties

ARTICLE 4. In consideration of the above cession, the United States agree to pay to the said confederated tribes and bands of Indians, in addition to the goods and provisions distributed to them at the time of signing this treaty, the sum of two hundred thousand dollars, in the following manner, that is to say: Sixty thousand dollars, to be expended under the direction of the President of the United States, the first year after the ratification of this treaty, in providing for their removal to the reservation, breaking up and fencing farms, building houses for them, supplying them with provisions and a suitable outfit, and for such other objects as he may deem necessary, and the remainder in annuities, as follows: For the first five years after the ratification of the treaty, ten thousand dollars each year, commencing September first, 1856; for the next five years, eight thousand dollars each year; for the next five years, six thousand dollars per year; and for the next five years, four thousand dollars per year.

All which sums of money shall be applied to the use and benefit of said Indians, under the direction of the President of the United States, who may from time to time determine, at his discretion, upon what beneficial objects to expend the same for them. And the superintendent of Indian affairs, or other proper officer, shall each year inform the President of the wishes of the Indians in relation thereto.

ARTICLE 5. The United States further agree to establish at suitable points within said reservation, within one year after the ratification hereof, two schools, erecting the necessary buildings, keeping them in repair, and providing them with furniture, books, and stationery, one of which shall be an agricultural and industrial school, to be located at the agency, and to be free to the children of the said confederated tribes and bands of Indians, and to employ one superintendent of teaching and two teachers; to build two blacksmiths' shops, to one of which shall be attached a tin-shop, and to the other a gunsmith's shop; one carpenter's shop, one wagon and plough maker's shop, and to keep the same in repair and furnished with the necessary tools; to employ one superintendent of farming and two farmers, two blacksmiths, one tinnor, one gunsmith, one carpenter, one wagon and plough maker, for the instruction of the Indians in trades and to assist them in the same.

To erect one saw-mill and one flouring-mill, keeping the same in repair and furnished with the necessary tools and fixtures; to erect a hospital, keeping the same in repair and provided with the necessary medicines and furniture, and to employ a physician; and to erect, keep in repair, and provided with the necessary furniture, the building required for the accommodation of the said employees. The said buildings and establishments to be maintained and kept in repair as aforesaid, and the employees to be kept in service for the period of twenty years.

Plains, West and Northwest Plateau Indian Treaties

And in view of the fact that the head chief of the said confederated tribes and bands of Indians is expected, and will be called upon to perform many services of a public character, occupying much of his time, the United States further agree to pay to the said confederated tribes and bands of Indians five hundred dollars per year, for the term of twenty years after the ratification hereof, as a salary for such person as the said confederated tribes and bands of Indians may select to be their head chief, to build for him at a suitable point on the reservation a comfortable house, and properly furnish the same, and to plough and fence ten acres of land. The said salary to be paid to, and the said house to be occupied by, such head chief so long as he may continue to hold that office.

And it is distinctly understood and agreed that at the time of the conclusion of this treaty Kamaiakun is the duly elected and authorized head chief of the confederated tribes and bands aforesaid, styled the Yakama Nation, and is recognized as such by them and by the commissioners on the part of the United States holding this treaty; and all the expenditures and expenses contemplated in this article of this treaty shall be defrayed by the United States, and shall not be deducted from the annuities agreed to be paid to said confederated tribes and band of Indians. Nor shall the cost of transporting the goods for the annuity payments be a charge upon the annuities, but shall be defrayed by the United States.

ARTICLE 6. The President may, from time to time, at his discretion, cause the whole or such portions of such reservation as he may think proper, to be surveyed into lots, and assign the same to such individuals or families of the said confederated tribes and bands of Indians as are willing to avail themselves of the privilege, and will locate on the same as a permanent home, on the same terms and subject to the same regulations as are provided in the sixth article of the treaty with the Omahas, so far as the same may be applicable.

ARTICLE 7. The annuities of the aforesaid confederated tribes and bands of Indians shall not be taken to pay the debts of individuals.

ARTICLE 8. The aforesaid confederated tribes and bands of Indians acknowledge their dependence upon the Government of the United States, and promise to be friendly with all citizens thereof, and pledge themselves to commit no depredations upon the property of such citizens.
And should any one or more of them violate this pledge, and the fact be satisfactorily proved before the agent, the property taken shall be returned, or in default thereof, or if injured or destroyed, compensation may be made by the Government out of the annuities.

Nor will they make war upon any other tribe, except in self-defence, but will submit all matters of difference between them and other Indians to the Government of the United States or its agent for decision, and abide thereby. And if

Plains, West and Northwest Plateau Indian Treaties

any of the said Indians commit depredations on any other Indians within the Territory of Washington or Oregon, the same rule shall prevail as that provided in this article in case of depredations against citizens. And the said confederated tribes and bands of Indians agree not to shelter or conceal offenders against the laws of the United States, but to deliver them up to the authorities for trial.

ARTICLE 9. The said confederated tribes and bands of Indians desire to exclude from their reservation the use of ardent spirits, and to prevent their people from drinking the same, and, therefore, it is provided that any Indian belonging to said confederated tribes and bands of Indians, who is guilty of bringing liquor into said reservation, or who drinks liquor, may have his or her annuities withheld from him or her for such time as the President may determine.

ARTICLE 10. And provided, That there is also reserved and set apart from the lands ceded by this treaty, for the use and benefit of the aforesaid confederated tribes and bands, a tract of land not exceeding in quantity one township of six miles square, situated at the forks of the Pisquouse or Wenatshapam River, and known as the "Wenatisha-pain Fishery," which said reservation shall be surveyed and marked out whenever the President may direct, and be subject to the same provisions and restrictions as other Indian reservations.

ARTICLE 11. This treaty shall be obligatory upon the contracting parties as soon as the same shall be ratified by the President and Senate of the United States.

In testimony whereof, the said Isaac I. Stevens, governor and superintendent of Indian affairs for the Territory of Washington, and the undersigned head chief, chiefs, headmen, and delegates of the aforesaid confederated tribes and bands of Indians, have hereunto set their hands and seals, at the place and on the day and year hereinbefore written.

Isaac I. Stevens, Governor and Superintendent.

Kamaiakun, his x mark, Skloom, his x mark, Owhi, his x mark, Te-cole-kun, his x mark, La-hoom, his x mark, Me-ni-nock, his x mark, Elit Palmer, his x mark, Wish-och-kmpits, his x mark, Koo-lat-toose, his x mark, Shee-ah-cotte, his x mark, Tuck-quille, his x mark, Ka-loo-as, his x mark, Scha-noo-a, his x mark, Sla-kish, his x mark,

Signed and sealed in the presence of
James Doty, secretary of treaties, Mie. Cles. Pandosy, O. M. T., Wm. C. McKay, W. H. Tappan, sub Indian agent, W. T., C. Chirouse, O. M. T., Patrick McKenzie, interpreter, A. D. Pareburn, interpreter, Joel Palmer, superintendent Indian affairs, O. T., W. D. Biglow, A. D. Pamburn, interpreter.

Plains, West and Northwest Plateau Indian Treaties

TREATY WITH THE NEZ PERCÉS {1855, June 11}
Ratified Mar. 8, 1859.
Proclaimed Apr. 29, 1859.

Articles of agreement and convention made and concluded at the treaty ground, Camp Stevens, in the Walla-Walla Valley, this eleventh day of June, in the year one thousand eight hundred and fifty-five, by and between Isaac I. Stevens, governor and superintendent of Indian affairs for the Territory of Washington, and Joel Palmer, superintendent of Indian affairs for Oregon Territory, on the part of the United States, and the undersigned chiefs, head-men, and delegates of the Nez Percé tribe of Indians occupying lands lying partly in Oregon and partly in Washington Territories, between the Cascade and Bitter Root Mountains, on behalf of, and acting for said tribe, and being duly authorized thereto by them, it being understood that Superintendent Isaac I. Stevens assumes to treat only with those of the above-named tribe of Indians residing within the Territory of Washington, and Superintendent Palmer with those residing exclusively in Oregon Territory.

ARTICLE 1. The said Nez Percé tribe of Indians hereby cede, relinquish and convey to the United States all their right, title, and interest in and to the country occupied or claimed by them, bounded and described as follows, to wit: Commencing at the source of the Wo-na-ne-she or southern tributary of the Paleuse River; thence down that river to the main Paleuse; thence in a southerly direction to the Snake River, at the mouth of the Tucanon River; thence up the Tucanon to its source in the Blue Mountains; thence southerly along the ridge of the Blue Mountains; thence to a point on Grand Ronde River, midway between Grand Ronde and the mouth of the Well-low-how River; thence along the divide between the waters of the Well-low-how and Powder River; thence to the crossing of Snake River, at the mouth of Powder River; thence to the Salmon Rivet', fifty miles above the place known (as) the "crossing of the Salmon River;" thence due north to the summit of the Bitter Root Mountains; thence along the crest of the Bitter Root Mountains to the place of beginning.

ARTICLE 2. There is, however, reserved from the lands above ceded for the use and occupation of the said tribe, and as a general reservation for other friendly tribes and bands of Indians in Washington Territory, not to exceed the present numbers of the Spokane, Walla-Walla, Cayuse, and Umatilla tribes and bands of Indians, the tract of land included within the following boundaries, to wit: Commencing where the Moh ha-na-she or southern tributary of the Palouse River flows from the spurs of the Bitter Root Mountains; thence down said tributary to the mouth of the Ti-nat-pan-up Creek; thence southerly to the crossing of the Snake River ten miles below the mouth of the Al-po-wa-wi River; thence to the source of the Al-po-wa-wi River in the Blue Mountains;

351

Plains, West and Northwest Plateau Indian Treaties

thence along the crest of the Blue Mountains; thence to the crossing of the Grand Rondo River, midway between the Grand Ronde and the mouth of the Woll-low-how River; thence along the divide between the waters of the Woll-low-how and Powder Rivers; thence to the crossing of the Snake River fifteen miles below the mouth of the Powder River; thence to the Salmon River above the crossing; thence by the spurs of the Bitter Root Mountains to the place of beginning.

All which tract shall be set apart, and, so far as necessary, surveyed and marked out for the exclusive use and benefit of said tribe as an Indian reservation; nor shall any white man, excepting those in the employment of the Indian Department, be permitted to reside upon the said reservation without permission of the tribe and the superintendent and agent; and the said tribe agrees to remove to and settle upon the same within one year after the ratification of this treaty.

In the mean time it shall be lawful for them to reside upon any ground not in the actual claim and occupation of citizens of the United States, and upon any ground claimed or occupied, if with the permission of the owner or claimant, guarantying, however, the right to all citizens of the United States to enter upon and occupy as settlers any lands not actually occupied and cultivated by said Indians at this time, and not included in the reservation above named. And provided that any substantial improvement heretofore made by any Indian, such as fields enclosed and cultivated, and houses erected upon the lands hereby ceded, and which he may be compelled to abandon in consequence of this treaty, shall be valued under the direction of the President of the United States, and payment made therefor in money, or improvements of an equal value be made for said Indian upon the reservation, and no Indian will be required to abandon the improvements aforesaid, now occupied by him, until their value in money or improve-merits of equal value shall be furnished him as aforesaid.

ARTICLE 3. And provided that, if necessary for the public convenience, roads may be run through the said reservation, and, on the other hand, the right of way, with free access from the same to the nearest public highway, is secured to them, as also the right, in common with citizens of the United States, to travel upon all public highways. The use of the Clear Water and other streams flowing through the reservation is also secured to citizens of the United States for rafting purposes, and as public highways.

The exclusive right of taking fish in all the streams where running through or bordering said reservation is further secured to said Indians; as also the right of taking fish at all usual and accustomed places in common with citizens of the Territory; and of erecting temporary buildings-for curing, together with the privilege of hunting, gathering roots and berries, and pasturing their horses and cattle upon open and unclaimed land.

Plains, West and Northwest Plateau Indian Treaties

ARTICLE 4. In consideration of the above cession, the United States agree to pay to the said tribe in addition to the goods and provisions distributed to them at the time of signing this treaty, the sum of two hundred thousand dollars, in the following manner, that is to say, sixty thousand dollars, to be expended under the direction of the President of the United States, the first year after the ratification of this treaty, in providing for their removal to the reserve, breaking up and fencing farms, building houses, supplying them with provisions and a suitable outfit, and for such other objects as he may deem necessary, and the remainder in annuities, as follows: for the first five years after the ratification of this treaty, ten thousand dollars each year, commencing September 1, 1856; for the next five years, eight thousand dollars each year; for the next five years, six thousand each year, and for the next five years, four thousand dollars each year.

All which said sums of money shall be applied to the use and benefit of the said Indians, under the direction of the President of the United States, who may from time to time determine, at his discretion, upon what beneficial objects to expend the same for them. And the superintendent of Indian affairs, or other proper officer, shall each year inform the President of the wishes of the Indians in relation thereto.

ARTICLE 5. The United States further agree to establish, at suitable points within said reservation, within one year after the ratification hereof, two schools, erecting the necessary buildings, keeping the same in repair, and providing them with furniture, books, and stationery, one of which shall be an agricultural and industrial school, to be located at the agency, and to be free to the children of said tribe, and to employ one superintendent of teaching and two teachers; to build two blacksmiths' shops, to one of which shall be attached a tin-shop and to the other a gunsmith's shop; one carpenter's shop, one wagon and plough maker's shop, and to keep the same in repair, and furnished with the necessary tools; to employ one superintendent of farming and two farmers, two blacksmiths, one tinner, one gunsmith, one carpenter, one wagon and plough maker, for the instruction of the Indians in trades, and to assist them in the same; to erect one saw-mill and one flouring-mill, keeping the same in repair, and furnished with the necessary tools and fixtures, and to employ two millers; to erect a hospital, keeping the same in repair, and provided with the necessary medicines and furniture, and to employ a physician; and to erect, keep in repair, and provide with the necessary furniture the buildings required for the accommodation of the said employees. The said buildings and establishments to be maintained and kept in repair as aforesaid, and the employees to be kept in service for the period of twenty years.

And in view of the fact that the head chief of the tribe is expected, and will be called upon, to perform many services of a public character, occupying much of his time, the United States further agrees to pay to the Nez Percé tribe five hundred dollars per year for the term of twenty years, after the ratification hereof,

Plains, West and Northwest Plateau Indian Treaties

as a salary for such person as the tribe may select to be its head chief. To build for him, at a suitable point on the reservation, a comfortable house, and properly furnish the same, and to plough and fence for his use ten acres of land. The said salary to be paid to, and the said house to be occupied by, such head chief so long as he may be elected to that position by his tribe, and no longer.

And all the expenditures and expenses contemplated in this fifth article of this treaty shall be defrayed by the United States, and shall not be deducted from the annuities agreed to be paid to said tribes nor shall the cost of transporting the goods for the annuity-payments be a charge upon the annuities, but shall be defrayed by the United States.

ARTICLE 6. The President may from time to time, at his discretion, cause the whole, or such portions of such reservation as he may think proper, to be surveyed into lots, and assign the same to such individuals or families of the said tribe as are willing to avail themselves of the privilege, and will locate on the same as a permanent home, on the same terms and subject to the same regulations as are provided in the sixth article of the treaty with the Omahas in the year 1854, so far as the same may be applicable.

ARTICLE 7. The annuities of the aforesaid tribe shall not be taken to pay the debts of individuals.

ARTICLE 8. The aforesaid tribe acknowledge their dependence upon the Government of the United States, and promise to be friendly with all citizens thereof, and pledge themselves to commit no depredations on the property of such citizens; and should any one or more of them violate this pledge, and the fact be satisfactorily proved before the agent, the property taken shall be returned, or in default thereof, or if injured or destroyed, compensation may be made by the Government out of the annuities. Nor will they make war on any other tribe except in self-defence, but will submit all matters of difference between them and the other Indians to the Government of the United States, or its agent, for decision, and abide thereby; and if any of the said Indians commit any depredations on any other Indians within the Territory of Washington, the same rule shall prevail as that prescribed in this article in cases of depredations against citizens. And the said tribe agrees not to shelter or conceal offenders against the laws of the United States, but to deliver them up to the authorities for trial.

ARTICLE 9. The Nez Percés desire to exclude from their reservation the use of ardent spirits, and to prevent their people from drinking the same; and therefore it is provided that any Indian belonging to said tribe who is guilty of bringing liquor into said reservation, or who drinks liquor, may have his or her proportion of the annuities withheld from him or her for such time as the President may determine.

354

Plains, West and Northwest Plateau Indian Treaties

ARTICLE 10. The Nez Percé Indians having expressed in council a desire that William Craig should continue to live with them, he having uniformly shown himself their friend, it is further agreed that the tract of land now occupied by him, and described in his notice to the register and receiver of the land-office of the Territory of Washington, on the fourth day of June last, shall not be considered a part of the reservation provided for in this treaty, except that it shall be subject in common with the lands of the reservation to the operations of the intercourse act.

ARTICLE 11. This treaty shall be obligatory upon the contracting parties as soon as the same shall be ratified by the President and Senate of the United States.

In testimony whereof, the said Isaac I. Stevens, governor and superintendent of Indian affairs for the Territory of Washington, and Joel Palmer, superintendent of Indian affairs for Oregon Territory, and the chiefs, headmen, and delegates of the aforesaid Nez Percé tribe of Indians, have hereunto set their hands and seals, at the place, and on the day and year hereinbefore written.

Isaac I. Stevens, Governor and Superintendent Washington Territory.
Joel Palmer, Superintendent Indian Affairs.

Aleiya, or Lawyer, Head-chief of the Nez Percés, Appushwa-hite, or Looking-glass, his x mark, Joseph, his x mark, James, his x mark, Red Wolf, his x mark, Timothy, his x mark, U-ute-sin-male-cun, his x mark, Spotted Eage., his x mark, Stoop-toop-nm or Cut-hair, his x mark, Tah-moh-moh-kin, his x mark, Tippelanecbupooh, his x mark, Hah-hah-stilpilp, his x mark, Cool-cool-shua-nin, his x mark,

Signed and sealed in presence of
James Doty, secretary of treaties, W.T, Mie. Cles. Pandosy, Lawrence Kip, W. H. Pearson.

TREATY WITH THE TRIBES OF MIDDLE OREGON {1855, June 25}
Ratified Mar. 8, 1859.
Proclaimed Apr. 18, 1859.

Articles of agreement and convention made and concluded at Wasco, near the Dalles of the Columbia River, in Oregon Territory, by Joel Palmer, superintendent of Indian affairs, on the part of the United States, and the following-named chiefs and head-men of the confederated tribes and bands of Indians, residing in Middle Oregon, they being duly authorized thereto by their respective bands, to wit: Sym-tustus, Locks-quis-sa, Shick-a-me, and Kuck-up, chiefs of the Taih

Plains, West and Northwest Plateau Indian Treaties

or Upper De Chutes band of Walla-Wallas; Stocket-ly and Iso, chiefs of the Wyam or Lower De Chutes band of Walla-Wallas; Alexis and Talkish, chiefs of the Tenino band of Walla-Wallas; Yise, chief of the Dock-Spus or John Day's River band of Walla-Wallas; Mark, William Chenook, and Cush-Kella, chiefs of the Dalles band of the Wascoes; Toh-simph, chief of the Ki-gal-twal-la band of Wascoes; and Wal-la-chin, chief of the Dog River band of Wascoes.

ARTICLE 1. The above-named confederated bands of Indians cede to the United States all their right, title, and claim to all and every part of the country claimed by them, included in the following boundaries, to wit:

Commencing in the middle of the Columbia River, at the Cascade Falls, and running thence southerly to the summit of the Cascade Mountains; thence along said summit to the forty-fourth parallel of north latitude; thence east on that parallel to the summit of the Blue Mountains, or the western boundary of the Sho-sho-ne or Snake country; thence northerly along that summit to a point due east from the head-waters of Willow Creek; thence west to the head-waters of said creek; thence down said stream to its junction with the Columbia River; and thence down the channel of the Columbia River to the place of beginning. Provided, however, that so much of the country described above as is contained in the following boundaries, shall, until otherwise directed by the President of the United States, be set apart as a residence for said Indians, which tract for the purposes contemplated shall be held and regarded as an Indian reservation, to wit:

Commencing in the middle of the channel of the De Chutes River opposite the eastern termination of a range of high lands usually known as the Mutton Mountains; thence westerly to the summit of said range, along the divide to its connection with the Cascade Mountains; thence to the summit of said mountains; thence southerly to Mount Jefferson; thence down the main branch of De Chutes River; heading in this peak, to its junction with De Chutes River; and thence down the middle of the channel of said river to the place of beginning. All of which tract shall be set apart, and, so far as necessary, surveyed and marked out for their exclusive use; nor shall any white person be permitted to reside upon the same without the concurrent permission of the agent and superintendent.

The said bands and tribes agree to remove to and settle upon the same within one year after the ratification of this treaty, without any additional expense to the United States other than is provided for by this treaty; and, until the expiration of the time specified, the said bands shall be permitted to occupy and reside upon the tracts now possessed by them, guaranteeing to all white citizens the right to enter upon and occupy as settlers any lands not included in said reservation, and not actually inclosed by said Indians. Provided, however, That prior to the removal of said Indians to said reservation, and before any im-

Plains, West and Northwest Plateau Indian Treaties

provements contemplated by this treaty shall have been commenced, that if the three principal bands, to wit: the Wascopum, Tiah, or Upper De Chutes, and the Lower De Chutes bands of Walla-Wallas shall express in council, a desire that some other reservation may be selected for them, that the three bands named may select each three persons of their respective bands, who with the superintendent of Indian affairs or agent, as may by him be directed, shall proceed to examine, and if another location can be selected, better suited to the condition and wants of said Indians, that is unoccupied by the whites, and upon which the board of commissioners thus selected may agree, the same shall be declared a reservation for said Indians, instead of the tract named in this treaty.

Provided, also, That the exclusive right of taking fish in the streams running through and bordering said reservation is hereby secured to said Indians; and at all other usual and accustomed stations, in common with citizens of the United States, and of erecting suitable houses for curing the same; also the privilege of hunting, gathering roots and berries, and pasturing their stock on unclaimed lands, in common with citizens, is secured to them. And provided, also, That if any band or bands of Indians, residing in and claiming any portion or portions of the country in this article, shall not accede to the terms of this treaty, then the bands becoming parties hereunto agree to receive such part of the several and other payments herein named as a consideration for the entire country described as aforesaid as shall be in the proportion that their aggregate number may have to the whole number of Indians residing in and claiming the entire country aforesaid, as consideration and payment in full for the tracts in said country claimed by them. And provided, also, That where substantial improvements have been made by any members of the bands being parties to this treaty, who are compelled to abandon them in consequence of said treaty, the same shall be valued, under the direction of the President of the United States, and payment made therefor; or, in lieu of said payment, improvements of equal extent and value at their option shall be made for them on the tracts assigned to each respectively.

ARTICLE 2. In consideration of, and payment for, the country hereby ceded, the United States agree to pay the bands and tribes of Indians claiming territory and residing in said country, the several sums of money following, to wit:

Eight thousand dollars per annum for the first five years, commencing on the first day of September, 1856, or as soon thereafter as practicable.

Six thousand dollars per annum for the term of five years next succeeding the first five. Four thousand dollars per annum for the term of five years next succeeding the second five; and Two thousand dollars per annum for the term of five years next succeeding the third five.

Plains, West and Northwest Plateau Indian Treaties

All of which several sums of money shall be expended for the use and benefit of the confederated bands, under the direction of the President of the United States, who may from time to time, at his discretion determine what proportion thereof shall be expended for such objects as in his judgment will promote their well-being and advance them in civilization; for their moral improvement and education; for building, opening and fencing farms, breaking land, providing teams, stock, agricultural implements, seeds, &c.; for clothing, provisions, and tools; for medical purposes, providing mechanics and farmers, and for arms and ammunition.

ARTICLE 3. The United States agree to pay said Indians the additional sum of fifty thousand dollars, a portion whereof shall be applied to the payment for such articles as may be advanced them at the time of signing this treaty, and in providing, after the ratification thereof and prior to their removal, such articles as may be deemed by the President essential to their want; for the erection of buildings on the reservation, fencing and opening farms; for the purchase of teams, farming implements, clothing and provisions, tools, seeds, and for the payment of employees; and for subsisting the Indians the first year after their removal.

ARTICLE 4. In addition to the considerations specified the United States agree to erect, at suitable points on the reservation, one sawmill and one flouring-mill; suitable hospital buildings; one school-house; one blacksmith-shop with a tin and a gunsmith-shop thereto attached; one wagon and ploughmaker shop; and for one sawyer, one miller, one superintendent of farming operations, a farmer, a physician, a schoolteacher, a blacksmith, and a wagon and plough-maker, a dwelling house and the requisite outbuildings for each; and to purchase and keep in repair for the time specified for furnishing employees all necessary mill-fixtures, mechanics' tools, medicines and hospital stores, books and stationery for schools, and furniture for employees.

The United States further engage to secure and pay for the services and subsistence, for the term of fifteen years, of one farmer, one blacksmith, and one wagon and plough maker; and for the term of twenty years, of one physician, one sawyer, one miller, one superintendent of farming operations, and one school teacher.

The United States also engage to erect four dwelling-houses, one for the head chief of the confederated bands, and one each for the Upper and Lower De Chutes bands of Walla-Wallas, and for the Was-copum band of Wascoes, and to fence and plough for each of the said chiefs ten acres of land; also to pay the head chief of the confederated bands a salary of five hundred dollars per annum for twenty years, commencing six months after the three principal bands named in this treaty shall have removed to the reservation, or as soon thereafter as a head chief should be elected.

Plains, West and Northwest Plateau Indian Treaties

And provided, also, That at any time when by the death, resignation, or removal of the chief selected, there shall be a vacancy and a successor appointed or selected, the salary, the dwelling, and improvements shall be possessed by said successor, so long as he shall occupy the position as head chief; so also with reference to the dwellings and improvements provided for by this treaty for the head chiefs of the three principal bands named.

ARTICLE 5. The President may, from time to time, at his discretion, cause the whole, or such portion as he may think proper, of the tract that may now or hereafter be set apart as a permanent home for these Indians, to be surveyed into lots and assigned to such Indians of the confederated bands as may wish to enjoy the privilege, and locate thereon permanently. To a single person over twenty-one years of age, forty acres; to a family of two persons, sixty acres; to a family of three and not exceeding five, eighty acres; to a family of six persons, and not exceeding ten, one hundred and twenty acres; and to each family over ten in number, twenty acres for each additional three members. And the President may provide such rules and regulations as will secure to the family in case of the death of the head thereof the possession and enjoyment of such permanent home and the improvement thereon; and he may, at any time, at his discretion, after such person or family has made location on the land assigned as a permanent home, issue a patent to such person or family for such assigned land, conditioned that the tract shall not be aliened or leased for a longer term than two years and shall be exempt from levy, sale, or forfeiture, which condition shall continue in force until a State constitution embracing such lands within its limits shall have been formed, and the legislature of the State shall remove the restrictions.

Provided, however, That no State legislature shall remove the restrictions herein provided for without the consent of Congress. And provided, also, That if any person or family shall at any time neglect or refuse to occupy or till a portion of the land assigned and on which they have located, or shall roam from place to place indicating a desire to abandon his home, the President may, if the patent shall have been issued, revoke the same, and if not issued, cancel the assignment, and may also withhold from such person, or family, their portion of the annuities, or other money due them, until they shall have returned to such permanent home and resumed the pursuits of industry, and in default of their return the tract may be declared abandoned, and thereafter assigned to some other person or family of Indians residing on said reservation.

ARTICLE 6. The annuities of the Indians shall not be taken to pay the debts of individuals.

ARTICLE 7. The confederated bands acknowledge their dependence on the Government of the United States, and promise to be friendly with all the citi-

Plains, West and Northwest Plateau Indian Treaties

zens thereof, and pledge themselves to commit no depredation on the property of said citizens; and should any one or more of the Indians violate this pledge, and the fact be satisfactorily proven before the agent, the property taken shall be returned, or in default thereof, or if injured or destroyed, compensation may be made by the Government out of their annuities; nor will they make war on any other tribe of Indians except in self-defence, but submit all matters of difference between them and other Indians to the Government of the United States, or its agents for decision, and abide thereby; and if any of the said Indians commit any depredations on other Indians, the same rule shall prevail as that prescribed in the case of depredations against citizens; said Indians further engage to submit to and observe all laws, rules, and regulations which may be prescribed by the United States for the government of said Indians.

ARTICLE 8. In order to prevent the evils of intemperance among said Indians, it is hereby provided, that if any one of them shall drink liquor to excess, or procure it for others to drink, his or her proportion of the annuities may be withheld from him or her for such time as the President may determine.

ARTICLE 9. The said confederated bands agree that whensoever, in the opinion of the President of the United States, the public interest may require it, that all roads, highways, and railroads shall have the right of way through the reservation herein designated, or which may at any time hereafter be set apart as a reservation for said Indians.

This treaty shall be obligatory on the contracting parties as soon as the same shall be ratified by the President and Senate of the United States.

In testimony whereof, the said Joel Palmer, on the part of the United States, and the undersigned, chiefs, headmen, and delegates of the said confederated bands, have hereunto set their hands and seals, this twenty-fifth day of June, eighteen hundred fifty-five.

Joel Palmer, Superintendent of Indian Affairs, O.T.

Wasco: Mark, his x mark, William Chenook, his x mark, Cush Kella, his x mark,
Lower De Chutes: Stock-etley, his x mark, Iso, his x mark,
Upper De Chutes: Simtustus, his x mark, Locksquissa, his x mark, Shick-ame, his x mark, Kuck-up, his x mark,
Tenjno: Alexsee, his x mark, Talekish, his x mark,
Dog River Wasco: Walachin, his x mark, Tah Symph, his x mark, Ash-ha-chat, his x mark, Che-wot-nleth, his x mark, Te-cho, his x mark, Sha-qually, his x mark, Louis, his x mark, Yise, his x mark, Stamite, his x mark, Ta-cho, his x mark, Penop-teyot, his x mark, Elosh-kish-kie, his x mark, Am. Zelic, his x mark, Kc-chac, his x mark, Tanes Salmon, his x mark, Ta-kos, his x mark,

360

Plains, West and Northwest Plateau Indian Treaties

David, his x mark, Sowal-we, his x mark, Postie, his x mark, Yawan-shewit, his x mark, Own-aps, his x mark,

Signed in presence of
Wm. C. McKay, secretary of treaty, O. T, R.R. Thompson, Indian agent.

TREATY WITH THE QUINAIELT, ETC. {1855, July 1}
Ratified Mar. 8, 1859.
Proclaimed, Apr. 11, 1859.

Articles of agreement and convention made and concluded by and between Isaac I. Stevens, governor and superintendent of Indian affairs of the Territory of Washington, on the part of the United States, and the undersigned chiefs, headmen, and delegates of the different tribes and bands of the Qui-nai-elt and Quil-leh-ute Indians, on the part of said tribes and bands, and duly authorized thereto by them.

ARTICLE 1. The said tribes and bands hereby cede, relinquish, and convey to the United States all their right, title, and interest in and to the lands and country occupied by them, bounded and described as follows: Commencing at a point on the Pacific coast, which is the southwest corner of the lands lately ceded by the Makah tribe of Indians to the United States, and running easterly with and along the southern boundary of the said Makah tribe to the middle of the coast range of mountains; thence southerly with said range of mountains to their intersection with the dividing ridge between the Chehalis and Quiniatl Rivers; thence westerly with said ridge to the Pacific coast; thence northerly along said coast to the place of beginning.

ARTICLE 2. There shall, however, be reserved, for the use and occupation of the tribes and bands aforesaid, a tract or tracts of land sufficient for their wants within the Territory of Washington, to be selected by the President of the United States, and hereafter surveyed or located and set apart for their exclusive use, and no white man shall be permitted to reside thereon without permission of the tribe and of the superintendent of Indian affairs or Indian agent. And the said tribes and bands agree to remove to and settle upon the same within one year after the ratification of this treaty, or sooner if the means are furnished them. In the meantime it shall be lawful for them to reside upon any lands not in the actual claim and occupation of citizens of the United States, and upon any lands claimed or occupied, if with the permission of the owner or claimant. If necessary for the public convenience, roads may be run through said reservation, on compensation being made for any damage sustained thereby.

ARTICLE 3. The right of taking fish at all usual and accustomed grounds and stations is secured to said Indians in common with all citizens of the Territory,

361

Plains, West and Northwest Plateau Indian Treaties

and of erecting temporary houses for the purpose of curing the same; together with the privilege of hunting, gathering roots and berries, and pasturing their horses on all open and unclaimed lands. Provided, however, That they shall not take shell-fish from any beds staked or cultivated by citizens; and provided, also, that they shall alter all stallions not intended for breeding, and keep up and confine the stallions themselves.

ARTICLE 4. In consideration of the above cession, the United States agree to pay to the said tribes and bands the sum of twenty-five thousand dollars, in the following manner, that is to say: For the first year after the ratification hereof, two thousand five hundred dollars; for the next two years, two thousand dollars each year; for the next three years, one thousand six hundred dollars each year; for the next four years, one thousand three hundred dollars each year; for the next five years, one thousand dollars each year; and for the next five years, seven hundred dollars each year. All of which sums of money shall be applied to the use and benefit of the said Indians under the directions of the President of the United States, who may from time to time, determine at his discretion upon what beneficial objects to expend the same; and the superintendent of Indian affairs, or other proper officer, shall each year inform the President of the wishes of said Indians in respect thereto.

ARTICLE 5. To enable the said Indians to remove to and settle upon such reservation as may be selected for them by the President, and to clear, fence, and break up a sufficient quantity of land for cultivation, the United States further agree to pay the sum of two thousand five hundred dollars, to be laid out and expended under the direction of the President, and in such manner as he shall approve.

ARTICLE 6. The President may hereafter, when in his opinion the interests of the Territory shall require, and the welfare of the said Indians be promoted by it, remove them from said reservation or reservations to such other suitable place or places within said Territory as he may deem fit, on remunerating them for their improvements and the expenses of their removal, or may consolidate them with other friendly tribes or bands, in which latter case the annuities, payable to the consolidated tribes respectively, shall also be consolidated; and he may further, at his discretion, cause the whole or any portion of the lands to be reserved, or of such other land as may be selected in lieu thereof, to be surveyed into lots, and assign the same to such individuals or families as are willing to avail themselves of the privilege, and will locate on the same as a permanent home, on the same terms and subject to the same regulations as are provided in the sixth article of the treaty with the Omahas, so far as the same may be applicable. Any substantial improvements heretofore made by any Indians, and which they shall be compelled to abandon in consequence of this treaty, shall be valued under the direction of the President, and payment made accordingly therefor.

Plains, West and Northwest Plateau Indian Treaties

ARTICLE 7. The annuities of the aforesaid tribes and bands shall not be taken to pay the debts of individuals.

ARTICLE 8. The said tribes and bands acknowledge their dependence on the Government of the United States, and promise to be friendly with all citizens thereof, and pledge themselves to commit no depredations on the property of such citizens; and should any one or more of them violate this pledge, and the fact be satisfactorily proven before the agent, the property taken shall be returned, or in default thereof, or if injured or destroyed, compensation may be made by the Government out of their annuities. Nor will they make war on any other tribe except in self-defence, but will submit all matters of difference between them and other Indians to the Government of the United States, or its agent, for decision and abide thereby; and if any of the said Indians commit any depredations on any other Indians within the Territory, the same rule shall prevail as is prescribed in this article in case of depredations against citizens. And the said tribes and bands agree not to shelter or conceal offenders against the laws of the United States, but to deliver them to the authorities for trial.

ARTICLE 9. The above tribes and bands are desirous to exclude from their reservations the use of ardent spirits, and to prevent their people from drinking the same, and therefore it is provided that any Indian belonging to said tribes who is guilty of bringing liquor into said reservations, or who drinks liquor, may have his or her proportion of the annuities withheld from him or her, for such time as the President may determine.

ARTICLE 10. The United States further agree to establish at the general agency for the district of Puget Sound, within one year from the ratification hereof, and to support for a period of twenty years, an agricultural and industrial school, to be free to the children of the said tribes and bands in common with those of the other tribes of said district, and to provide the said school with a suitable instructor or instructors, and also to provide a smithy and carpenter's shop, and furnish them with the necessary tools, and to employ a blacksmith, carpenter, and farmer for a term of twenty years, to instruct the Indians in their respective occupations. And the United States further agree to employ a physician to reside at the said central agency, who shall furnish medicine and advice to their sick, and shall vaccinate them; the expenses of the said school, shops, employees, and medical attendance to be defrayed by the United States, and not deducted from their annuities.

ARTICLE 11. The said tribes and bands agree to free all slaves now held by them, and not to purchase or acquire others hereafter.

ARTICLE 12. The said tribes and bands finally agree not to trade at Vancouver's Island or elsewhere out of the dominions of the United States, nor shall

Plains, West and Northwest Plateau Indian Treaties

foreign Indians be permitted to reside on their reservations without consent of the superintendent or agent.

ARTICLE 13. This treaty shall be obligatory on the contracting, parties as soon as the same shall be ratified by the President and Senate of the United States.

In testimony whereof, the said Isaac I. Stevens, governor and superintendent of Indian affairs, and the undersigned chiefs, headmen, and delegates of the aforesaid tribes and bands of Indians, have hereunto set their hands and seals, at Olympia, January 25, 1856, and on the Qui-nai-elt River, July 1, 1855.

Isaac I. Stevens, Governor and Sup't of Indian Affairs.

Tah-ho-lah, Head Chief Qui-nite-'l tribe, his x mark, How-yat'l, Head Chief Quil-leyyute tribe, his x mark, Kal-lape, Sub-chief Quil-ley-hutes, his x mark, Tah-ah-ha-wht'l, Sub-chief Quilley-hutes, his x mark, Lay-le-whash-er, his x mark, E-mah-lah-cup, his x mark, Ash-chak-a-wick, his x mark, Ay-a-quan, his x mark, Yats-see-o-kop, his x mark, Karts-so-pe-ah, his x mark, Quat-a-de-tot'l, his x mark,

Executed in the presence of us; the words "or tracts," in the 2 article, and "next," in the 4th article, being interlined prior to execution.
M. T. Simmons, special Indian agent, H. A. Goldsborough, commissary, &c, B. F. Shaw, interpreter.

TREATY WITH THE FLATHEADS, ETC. {1855, July 16}
Ratified Mar. 8, 1859.
Proclaimed Apr. 18, 1859.

Articles of agreement and convention made and concluded at the treaty-ground at Hell Gate, in the Bitter Root Valley, this sixteenth day of July, in the year one thousand eight hundred and fifty-five, by and between Isaac I. Stevens, governor and superintendent of Indian affairs for the Territory of Washington, on the part of the United States, and the undersigned chiefs, head-men, and delegates of the confederated tribes of the Flathead, Kootenay, and Upper Pend d' Oreilles Indians, on behalf of and acting for said confederated tribes, and being duly authorized thereto by them. It being understood and agreed that the said confederated tribes do hereby constitute a nation, under the name of the Flathead Nation, with Victor, the head chief of the Flathead tribe, as the head chief of the said nation, and that the several chiefs, head-men, and delegates, whose names are signed to this treaty, do hereby, in behalf of their respective tribes, recognise Victor as said head chief.

Plains, West and Northwest Plateau Indian Treaties

ARTICLE 1. The said confederated tribe of Indians hereby cede, relinquish, and convey to the United States all their right, title, and interest in and to the country occupied or claimed by them, bounded and described as follows, to wit:

Commencing on the main ridge of the Rocky Mountains, at the forty-ninth (49th) parallel of latitude, thence westwardly on that parallel to the divide between the Flat-bow or Kootenay River and Clarke's Fork, thence southerly and southeasterly along said divide to the one hundred and fifteenth degree of longitude, (115°) thence in a southwesterly direction to the divide between the sources of the St. Regis Borgia and the Coeur d'Alene Rivers, thence southeasterly and southerly along the main ridge of the Bitter Root Mountains to the divide between the head-waters of the Koos-koos-kee River and of the southwestern fork of the Bitter Root River, thence easterly along the divide separating the waters of the several tributaries of the Bitter Root River from the waters flowing into the Salmon and Snake Rivers to the main ridge of the Rocky Mountains, and thence northerly along said main ridge to the place of beginning.

ARTICLE 2. There is, however, reserved from the lands above ceded, for the use and occupation of the said confederated tribes, and as a general Indian reservation, upon which may be placed other friendly tribes and bands of Indians of the Territory of Washington who may agree to be consolidated with the tribes parties to this treaty, under the common designation of the Flathead Nation, with Victor, head chief of the Flathead tribe, as the head chief of the nation, the tract of land included within the following boundaries, to wit:

Commencing at the source of the main branch of the Jocko River; thence along the divide separating the waters flowing into the Bitter Root River from those flowing into the Jocko to a point on Clarke's Fork between the Camash and Horse Prairies; thence northerly to, and along the divide bounding on the west the Flathead River, to a point due west from the point half way in latitude between the northern and southern extremities of the Flathead Lake; thence on a due east course to the divide whence the Crow, the Prune, the So-ni-el-em and the Jocko Rivers take their rise, and thence southerly along said divide to the place of beginning.

All which tract shall be set apart, and, so far as necessary, surveyed and marked out for the exclusive use and benefit of said confederated tribes as an Indian reservation. Nor shall any white man, excepting those in the employment of the Indian department, be permitted to reside upon the said reservation without permission of the confederated tribes, and the superintendent and agent. And the said confederated tribes agree to remove to and settle upon the same within one year after the ratification of this treaty. In the meantime it shall be lawful for them to reside upon any ground not in the actual claim and occupation of

Plains, West and Northwest Plateau Indian Treaties

citizens of the United States, and upon any ground claimed or occupied, if with the permission of the owner or claimant.

Guaranteeing however the right to all citizens of the United States to enter upon and occupy as settlers any lands not actually occupied and cultivated by said Indians at this time, and not included in the reservation above named. And provided, That any substantial improvements heretofore made by any Indian, such as fields enclosed and cultivated and houses erected upon the lands hereby ceded, and which he may be compelled to abandon in consequence of this treaty, shall be valued under the direction of the President of the United States, and payment made therefor in money, or improvements of an equal value be made for said Indian upon the reservation; and no Indian will be required to abandon the improvements aforesaid, now occupied by him, until their value in money or improvements of an equal value shall be furnished him as aforesaid.

ARTICLE 3. And provided, That if necessary for the public convenience roads may be run through the said reservation; and, on the other hand, the right of way with free access from the same to the nearest public highway is secured to them, as also the right in common with citizens of the United States to travel upon all public highways. The exclusive right of taking fish in all the streams running through or bordering said reservation is further secured to said Indians; as also the right of taking fish at all usual and accustomed places, in common with citizens of the Territory, and of erecting temporary buildings for curing; together with the privilege of hunting, gathering roots and berries, and pasturing their horses and cattle upon open and unclaimed land.

ARTICLE 4. In consideration of the above cession, the United States agree to pay to the said confederated tribes of Indians, in addition to the goods and provisions distributed to them at the time of signing this treaty the sum of one hundred and twenty thousand dollars, in the following mannerthat is to say: For the first year after the ratification hereof, thirty-six thousand dollars, to be expended under the direction of the President, in providing for their removal to the reservation, breaking up and fencing farms, building houses for them, and for such other objects as he may deem necessary. For the next four years, six thousand dollars each year; for the next five years, five thousand dollars each year; for the next five years, four thousand dollars each year; and for the next five years, three thousand dollars each year.

All which said sums of money shall be applied to the use and benefit of the said Indians, under the direction of the President of the United States, who may from time to time determine, at his discretion, upon what beneficial objects to expend the same for them, and the superintendent of Indian affairs, or other proper officer, shall each year inform the President of the wishes of the Indians in relation thereto.

Plains, West and Northwest Plateau Indian Treaties

ARTICLE 5. The United States further agree to establish at suitable points within said reservation, within one year after the ratification hereof, an agricultural and industrial school, erecting the necessary buildings, keeping the same in repair, and providing it with furniture, books, and stationery, to be located at the agency, and to be free to the children of the said tribes, and to employ a suitable instructor or instructors. To furnish one blacksmith shop, to which shall be attached a tin and gun shop; one carpenter's shop; one wagon and ploughmaker's shop: and to keep the same in repair, and furnished with the necessary tools. To employ two farmers, one blacksmith, one tinner, one gunsmith, one carpenter, one wagon and plough maker, for the instruction of the Indians in trades, and to assist then, in the same.

To erect one saw-mill and one flouring-mill, keeping the same in repair and furnished with the necessary tools and fixtures, and to employ two millers. To erect a hospital, keeping the same in repair, and provided with the necessary medicines and furniture, and to employ a physician; and to erect, keep in repair, and provide the necessary furniture the buildings required for the accommodation of said employees. The said buildings and establishments to be maintained and kept in repair as aforesaid, and the employees to be kept in service for the period of twenty years.

And in view of the fact that the head chiefs of the said confederated tribes of Indians are expected and will be called upon to perform many services of a public character, occupying much of their time, the United States further agree to pay to each of the Flathead, Kootenay, and Upper Pend d'Oreilles tribes five hundred dollars per year, for the term of twenty years after the ratification hereof, as a salary for such persons as the said confederated tribes may select to be their head chiefs, and to build for them at suitable points on the reservation a comfortable house, and properly furnish the same, and to plough and fence for each of them ten acres of land. The salary to be paid to, and the said houses to be occupied by, such head chiefs so long as they may be elected to that position by their tribes, and no longer.

And all the expenditures and expenses contemplated in this article of this treaty shall be defrayed by the United States, and shall not be deducted from the annuities agreed to be paid to said tribes. Nor shall the cost of transporting the goods for the annuity payments be a charge upon the annuities, but shall be defrayed by the United States.

ARTICLE 6. The President may from time to time, at his discretion, cause the whole, or such portion of such reservation as he may think proper, to be surveyed into lots, and assign the same to such individuals or families of the said confederated tribes as are willing to avail themselves of the privilege, and will locate on the same as a permanent home, on the same terms and subject to the

Plains, West and Northwest Plateau Indian Treaties

same regulations as are provided in the sixth article of the treaty with the Omahas, so far as the same may be applicable.

ARTICLE 7. The annuities of the aforesaid confederated tribes of Indians shall not be taken to pay the debts of individuals.

ARTICLE 8. The aforesaid confederated tribes of Indians acknowledge their dependence upon the Government of the United States, and promise to be friendly with all citizens thereof, and pledge themselves to commit no depredations upon the property of such citizens. And should any one or more of them violate this pledge, and the fact be satisfactorily proved before the agent, the property taken shall be returned, or, in default thereof, or if injured or destroyed, compensation may be made by the Government out of the annuities.

Nor will they make war on any other tribe except in self-defence, but will submit all matters of difference between them and other Indians to the Government of the United States, or its agent, for decision, and abide thereby. And if any of the said Indians commit any depredations on any other Indians within the jurisdiction of the United States, the same rule shall prevail as that prescribed in this article, in case of depredations against citizens. And the said tribes agree not to shelter or conceal offenders against the laws of the United States, but to deliver them up to the authorities for trial.

ARTICLE 9. The said confederated tribes desire to exclude from their reservation the use of ardent spirits, and to prevent their people from drinking the same; and therefore it is provided that any Indian belonging to said confederated tribes of Indians who is guilty of bringing liquor into said reservation, or who drinks liquor, may have his or her proportion of the annuities withheld from him or her for such time as the President may determine.

ARTICLE 10. The United States further agree to guaranty the exclusive use of the reservation provided for in this treaty, as against any claims which may be urged by the Hudson Bay Company under the provisions of the treaty between the United States and Great Britain of the fifteenth of June, eighteen hundred and forty-six, in consequence of the occupation of a trading-post on the Pru-in River by the servants of that company.

ARTICLE 11. it is, moreover, provided that the Bitter Root Valley, above the Loodo Fork, shall be carefully surveyed and examined, and if it shall prove, in the judgment of the President, to be better adapted to the wants of the Flathead tribe than the general reservation provided for in this treaty, then such portions of it as may be necessary shall be set apart as a separate reservation for the said tribe. No portion of the Bitter Root Valley, above the Loo-lo Fork, shall be opened to settlement until such examination is had and the decision of the President made known.

Plains, West and Northwest Plateau Indian Treaties

ARTICLE 12. This treaty shall be obligatory upon the contracting parties as soon as the same shall be ratified by the President and Senate of the United States.

In testimony whereof, the said Isaac I. Stevens, governor and superintendent of Indian affairs for the Territory of Washington, and the undersigned head chiefs, chiefs and principal men of the Flathead, Kootenay, and Upper Pend d'Oreilles tribes of Indians, have hereunto set their hands and seals, at the place and on the day and year hereinbefore written.

Isaac I. Stevens,Governor and Superintendent Indian Affairs

W. T. Victor, head chief of the Flathead Nation, his x mark, Alexander, chief of the Upper Pend d'Oreilles, his x mark, Michelle, chief of the Kootenays, his x mark, Ambrose, his x mark, Pah-soh, his x mark, Bear Track, his x mark, Adolphe, his x mark, Thunder, his x mark, Big Canoe, his x mark, Kootel Chah, his x mark, Paul, his x mark, Andrew, his x mark, Michelle, his x mark, James Doty, secretary, R.H. Lansdale, Indian Agent.

TREATY WITH THE BLACKFEET {1855, Oct. 17}
Ratified Apr. 15,1856.
Proclaimed Apr. 25, 1856.

Articles of agreement and convention made and concluded at the council ground on the Upper Missouri, near the mouth of the Judith River, in the Territory of Nebraska, this seventeenth day of October, in the year one thousand eight hundred and fifty-five, by and between A. Gumming and Isaac I. Stevens, commissioners duly appointed and authorized, on the part of the United States, and the undersigned chiefs, headmen, and delegates of the following nations and tribes of Indians, who occupy, for the purposes of hunting, the territory on the Upper Missouri and Yellowstone Rivers, and who have permanent homes as follows: East of the Rocky Mountains, the Blackfoot Nation, consisting of the Piegan, Blood, Blackfoot, and Gros Ventres tribes of Indians. West of the Rocky Mountains, the Flathead Nation, consisting of the Flathead, Upper Pend d'Oreille, and Kootenay tribes of Indians, and the Nez Perce tribe of Indians, the said chiefs, headmen and delegates, in behalf of and acting for said nations and tribes, and being duly authorized thereto by them.

ARTICLE 1. Peace, friendship and amity shall hereafter exist between the United States and the aforesaid nations and tribes of Indians, parties to this treaty, and the same shall be perpetual.

Plains, West and Northwest Plateau Indian Treaties

ARTICLE 2. The aforesaid nations and tribes of Indians, parties to this treaty, do hereby jointly and severally covenant that peaceful relations shall likewise be maintained among themselves in future; and that they will abstain from all hostilities whatsoever against each other, and cultivate mutual good-will and friendship. And the nations and tribes aforesaid do furthermore jointly and severally covenant, that peaceful relations shall be maintained with and that they will abstain from all hostilities whatsoever, excepting in self-defense, against the following-named nations and tribes of Indians, to wit: the Crows, Assineboins, Crees, Snakes, Blackfeet, Sans Arcs, and Aunce-pa-pas bands of Sioux, and all other neighboring nations and tribes of Indians.

ARTICLE 3. The Blackfoot Nation consent and agree that all that portion of the country recognized and defined by the treaty of Laramie as Blackfoot territory, lying within lines drawn from the Hell Gate or Medicine Rock Passes in the main range of the Rocky Mountains, in an easterly direction to the nearest source of the Muscle Shell River, thence to the mouth of Twenty-five Yard Creek, thence up the Yellowstone River to its northern source, and thence along the main range of the Rocky Mountains, in a northerly direction, to the point of beginning, shall be a common hunting-ground for ninety-nine years, where all the nations, tribes and bands of Indians, parties to this treaty, may enjoy equal and uninterupted privileges of hunting, fishing and gathering fruit, grazing animals, curing meat and dressing robes. They further agree that they will not establish villages, or in any other way exercise exclusive rights within ten miles of the northern line of the common hunting-ground, and that the parties to this treaty may hunt on said northern boundary line and within ten miles thereof.

Provided, That the western Indians, parties to this treaty, may hunt on the trail leading down the Muscle Shell to the Yellowstone; the Muscle Shell River being the boundary separating the Blackfoot from the Crow territory.

And provided, That no nation, band, or tribe of Indians, parties to this treaty, nor any other Indians, shall be permitted to establish permanent settlements, or in any other way exercise, during the period above mentioned, exclusive rights or privileges within the limits of the above-described hunting-ground. And provided further, That the rights of the western Indians to a whole or a part of the common hunting-ground, derived from occupancy and possession, shall not be affected by this article, except so far as said rights may be determined by the treaty of Laramie.

ARTICLE 4. The parties to this treaty agree and consent, that the tract of country lying within lines drawn from the Hell Gate or Medicine Rock Passes, in an easterly direction, to the nearest source of the Muscle Shell River, thence down said river to its mouth, thence down the channel of the Missouri River to the mouth of Milk River, thence due north to the forty-ninth parallel, thence due west on said parallel to the main range of the Rocky Mountains, and thence

Plains, West and Northwest Plateau Indian Treaties

southerly along said range to the place of beginning, shall be the territory of the Blackfoot Nation, over which said nation shall exercise exclusive control, excepting as may be otherwise provided in this treaty. Subject, however', to the provisions of the third article of this treaty, giving the right to hunt, and prohibiting the establishment of permanent villages and the exercise of any exclusive rights within ten miles of the northern line of the common hunting-ground, drawn from the nearest source of the Muscle Shell River to the Medicine Rock Passes, for the period of ninety-nine years.

Provided also, That the Assiniboins shall have the right of hunting, in common with the Blackfeet, in the country lying between the aforesaid eastern boundary line, running from the mouth of Milk River to the forty-ninth parallel, and a line drawn from the left bank of the Missouri River, opposite the Round Butte north, to the forty-ninth parallel.

ARTICLE 5. The parties to this treaty, residing west of the main range of the Rocky Mountains, agree and consent that they will not enter the common hunting ground, nor any part of the Blackfoot territory, or return home, by any pass in the main range of the Rocky Mountains to the north of the Hell Gate or Medicine Rock Passes. And they further agree that they will not hunt or otherwise disturb the game, when visiting the Blackfoot territory for trade or social intercourse.

ARTICLE 6. The aforesaid nations and tribes of Indians, parties to this treaty, agree and consent to remain within their own respective countries, except when going to or from, or whilst hunting upon, the "common hunting ground," or when visiting each other for the purpose of trade or social intercourse.

ARTICLE 7. The aforesaid nations and tribes of Indians agree that citizens of the United States may live in and pass unmolested through the countries respectively occupied and claimed by them. And the United States is hereby bound to protect said Indians against depredations and other unlawful acts which white men residing in or passing through their country may commit.

ARTICLE 8. For the purpose of establishing travelling thoroughfares through their country, and the better to enable the President to execute the provisions of this treaty, the aforesaid nations and tribes do hereby consent and agree, that the United States may, within the countries respectively occupied and claimed by them, construct roads of every description; establish lines of telegraph and military posts; use materials of every description found in the Indian country; build houses for agencies, missions, schools, farms, shops, mills, stations, and for any other purpose for which they may be required, and permanently occupy as much land as may be necessary for the various purposes above enumerated, including the use of wood for fuel and land for grazing, and that the navigation of all lakes and streams shall be forever free to citizens of the United States.

371

Plains, West and Northwest Plateau Indian Treaties

ARTICLE 9. In consideration of the foregoing agreements, stipulations, and cessions, and on condition of their faithful observance, the nited States agree to expend, annually, for the Piegan, Blood, Black-foot, and Gros Ventres tribes of Indians, constituting the Blackfoot Nation, in addition to the goods and provisions distributed at the time of signing the treaty, twenty thousand dollars, annually, for ten years, to be expended in such useful goods and provisions, and other articles, as the President, at his discretion, may from time to time determine; and the superintendent, or other proper officer, shall each year inform the President of the wishes of the Indians in relation thereto: Provided, however, That if, in the judgment of the President and Senate, this amount be deemed insufficient, it may be increased not to exceed the sum of thirty-five thousand dollars per year.

ARTICLE 10. The United States further agree to expend annually, for the benefit of the aforesaid tribes of the Blackfoot Nation, a sum not exceeding fifteen thousand dollars annually, for ten years, in establishing and instructing them in agricultural and mechanical pursuits, and in educating their children, and in any other respect promoting their civilization and Christianization: Provided, however, That to accomplish the objects of this article, the President may, at his discretion, apply any or all the annuities provided for in this treaty: And provided, also, That the President may, at his discretion, determine in what proportions the said annuities shall be divided among the several tribes.

ARTICLE 11. The aforesaid tribes acknowledge their dependence on the Government of the United States, and promise to be friendly with all citizens thereof, and to commit no depredations or other violence upon such citizens. And should any one or more violate this pledge, and the fact be proved to the satisfaction of the President, the property taken shall be returned, or, in default thereof, or if injured or destroyed, compensation may be made by the Government out of the annuities. The aforesaid tribes are hereby bound to deliver such offenders to the proper authorities for trial and punishment, and are held responsible, in their tribal capacity, to make reparation for depredations so committed.

Nor will they make war upon any other tribes, except in self-defense, but will submit all matter of difference, between themselves and other Indians, to the Government of the United States, through its agents, for adjustment, and will abide thereby. And if any of the said Indians, parties to this treaty, commit depredations on any other Indians within the jurisdiction of the United States, the same rule shall prevail as that prescribed in this article in case of depredations against citizens. And the said tribes agree not to shelter or conceal offenders against the laws of the United States, but to deliver them up to the authorities for trial.

Plains, West and Northwest Plateau Indian Treaties

ARTICLE 12. It is agreed and understood, by and between the parties to this treaty, that if any nation or tribe of Indians aforesaid, shall violate any of the agreements, obligations, or Stipulations, herein contained, the United States may withhold, for such length of time as the President and Congress may determine, any portion or all of the annuities agreed to be paid to said nation or tribe under the ninth and tenth articles of this treaty.

ARTICLE 13. The nations and tribes of Indians, parties to this treaty, desire to exclude from their country the use of ardent spirits or other intoxicating liquor, and to prevent their people from drinking the same. Therefore it is provided, that any Indian belonging to said tribes who is guilty of bringing such liquor into the Indian country, or who drinks liquor, may have his or her proportion of the annuities withheld from him or her, for such time as the President may determine.

ARTICLE 14. The aforesaid nations and tribes of Indians, west of the Rocky Mountains, parties to this treaty, do agree, in consideration of the provisions already made for them in existing treaties, to accept the guarantees of the peaceful occupation of their hunting-grounds, east of the Rocky Mountains, and of remuneration for depredations made by the other tribes, pledged to be secured to them in this treaty out of the annuities of said tribes, in full compensation for the concessions which they, in common with the said tribes, have made in this treaty.

The Indians east of the mountains, parties to this treaty, likewise recognize and accept the guarantees of this treaty, in full compensation for the injuries or depredations which have been, or may be committed by the aforesaid tribe's, west of the Rocky Mountains.

ARTICLE 15. The annuities of the aforesaid tribes shall not be taken to pay the debts of individuals.

ARTICLE 16. This treaty shall be obligatory upon the aforesaid nations and tribes of Indians, parties hereto, from the date hereof, and upon the United States as soon as the same shall be ratified by the President and Senate.

In testimony whereof the said A. Gumming and Isaac I. Stevens, commissioners on the part of the United States, and the undersigned chiefs, headmen, and delegates of the aforesaid nations and tribes of Indians, parties to this treaty, have hereunto set their hands and seals at the place and on the day and year hereinbefore written.

A. Cumming.
Isaac I. Stevens.

Plains, West and Northwest Plateau Indian Treaties

Piegans:
Nee-ti-nee, or "the only chief," now called the Lame Bull, his x mark, Mountain Chief, his x mark, Low Horn, his x mark, Little Gray Head, his x mark, Little Dog, his x mark, Big Snake, his x mark, The Skunk, his x mark, The Bad Head, his x mark, Kitch-eepone-istah, his x mark, Middle Sitter, his x mark,
Bloods:
Onis-tay-say-nah-que-im, his x mark, The Father of All Children, his x mark, The Bull's Back Fat, his x mark, Heavy Shield, his x mark, Nah-tose-onistah, his x mark, The Calf Shirt, his x mark, Gros Ventres:
Blackfeet:
The Three Bulls, his x mark, The Old Kootomais, his x mark, I Pow-ah-que, his x mark, Chief Rabbit Runner, his x mark, Nez Peters: Spotted Eagle, his x mark, Looking Glass, his x mark, The Three Feathers, his x mark, Eagle from the Light, his x mark, The Lone Bird, his x mark, Ip-shun-nee-wus, his x mark, Flathead Nation:
Victor, his x mark, Alexander, his x mark, Moses, his x mark, Big Canoe, his x mark, Ambrose, his x mark, Kootle-eha, his x mark, Miehelle, his x mark, Francis, his x mark, Vincent, his x mark, Andrew, his x mark,
Piegans:
Running Rabbit, his x mark, Chief Bear, his x mark, The Little White Buffalo, his x mark, The Big Straw, his x mark,
Flathead:
Bear Track, his x mark, Little Michelle, his x mark, Palchinah, his x mark,
Bloods:
The Feather, his x mark, The White Eagle, his x mark.

Executed in presence of
James Doty, secretary, Alfred J. Vaughan, jr, E. Alw. Hatch, agent for Blackfeet

TREATY WITH THE MOLALA {1855, Dec. 21}
Ratified Mar. 8,1859.
Proclaimed Apr. 27, 1859.

Articles of convention and agreement entered into this 21st day of December, 1855, between Joel Palmer, superintendent of Indian affairs, acting for and in behalf of the United States, and the chiefs and head-men of the Mo-lal-la-las or Molel tribe of Indians, they being authorized by their respective bands in council assembled.

ARTICLE 1. The above-named tribe of Indians hereby cede to the United States all their right, title, interest and claim to all that part of Oregon Territory situated and bounded as hereinafter described, the same being claimed by them. To wit: Beginning at Scott's Peak, being the northeastern termination of the

Plains, West and Northwest Plateau Indian Treaties

purchase made of the Umpaquah, and Calapooias of Umpaquah Valley on the 29th day of November, 1854; thence running southerly on the eastern boundary line of that purchase and the purchase of the Cow Creeks, on the 19th day of September, 1853, and the tract purchased of the Scotens, Chestas and Grave Creeks, on the nineteenth (eighteenth) day of November, 1854, to the boundary of the Rogue River purchase made on the tenth day of September, 1853; thence along the northern boundary of that purchase to the summit of the Cascade Mountains; thence northerly along the summit of said mountains to a point due east of Scott's Peak; thence west to the place of beginning.

ARTICLE 2. In consideration of the cession and relinquishment herein made, the United States agree to make the following provisions for said Indians and pay the sums of money as follows:
First. To secure to the members of said tribe all the rights and privileges guaranteed by treaty to the Umpaquah and Calapooias, of the Umpaquah Valley, jointly with said tribes, they hereby agreeing to confederate with those bands.

Second. To erect and keep in repair and furnish suitable persons to attend the same for the term of ten years, the benefits of which to be shared alike by all the bands confederated, one flouring-mill and one saw-mill.

Third. To furnish iron, steel, and other materials for supplying the smith's shop and tin-shop stipulated in the treaty of 29th November, 1854, and pay for the services of the necessary mechanics for that service for five years in addition to the time specified by that treaty.

Fourth. To establish a manual-labor school, employ and pay teachers, furnish all necessary materials and subsistence for pupils, of sufficient capacity to accommodate all the children belonging to said confederate bands, of suitable age and condition to attend said school.

Fifth. To employ and pay for the services of a carpenter and joiner for the term of ten years to aid in erecting buildings and making furniture for said Indians, and to furnish tools for use in said service.
Sixth. To employ and pay for the services of an additional farmer for the term of five years.

ARTICLE 3. In consequence of the existence of hostilities between the whites and a portion of the Indian tribes in Southern Oregon and Northern California, and the proximity of the Umpaquah reservation to the mining district, and the consequent fluctuating and transient population, and the frequent commission by whites and Indians of petty offences, calculated to disturb the peace and harmony of the settlement, it is hereby agreed, the Umpaquahs and Calapooias agreeing, that the bands thus confederated shall immediately remove to a tract of land selected on the head-waters of the Yamhill River adjoining the coast

Plains, West and Northwest Plateau Indian Treaties

reservation, thereon to remain until the proper improvements are made upon that reservation, for the accommodation of said confederate bands, in accordance with the provisions of this and the treaty of 29th November, 1854, and when so made, to remove to said coast reservation, or such other point as may, by direction of the President of the United States, be designated for the permanent residence of said Indians.

ARTICLE 4. For the purpose of carrying out in good faith the objects expressed in the preceding article, it is hereby agreed on the part of the United States, that the entire expense attending the removal of the bands named, including transportation and subsistence, and the erection of temporary buildings at the encampment designated, as well as medical attendance on the sick, shall be paid by the United States.

ARTICLE 5. It is further agreed that rations, according to the Army, regulations, shall be furnished the member's of the said confederated bands, and distributed to the heads of families, from the time of their arrival at the encampment on the head-waters of Yamhill River until six months after their arrival at the point selected as their permanent residence.

ARTICLE 6. For the purpose of insuring the means of subsistence for said Indians, the United States engage to appropriate the sum of twelve thousand dollars for the extinguishment of title and the payment of improvements made thereon by white settlers to lands in the Grand Round Valley, the point of encampment referred to, to be used as wheat-farms, or other purposes, for the benefit of said Indians, and for the erection of buildings upon the reservation, opening farms, purchasing of teams, tools and stock; the expenditure of which amounts, and, the direction of all the provisions of this convention, shall be in accordance with the spirit and meaning of the treaty of 29th November, 1854, with the Umpaquah and Calapooia tribes aforesaid.

In witness whereof, we, the several parties, hereto set our hands and seals, the day and date before written.

Joel Palmer, Superintendent Indian Affairs.

Steencoggy, his x mark, Lattchie, his x mark, Dugings, his x mark, Counisnase, his x mark,

Done in presence of the undersigned witnesses
C. M. Walker, T. R. Magruder, John Flett, interpreter.

We, the Chiefs and headmen of the Umpaquah and Calapooia tribes, treated with in the Umpaquah Valley, on the 29th day of November, 1854, referred to

Plains, West and Northwest Plateau Indian Treaties

in the foregoing treaty, to the provisions of this treaty, this day in convention, accede to all the terms therein expressed. 1856.

In witness whereof, we do severally hereto set our names and seals, the day and date written in the foregoing treaty.

Louis la Pe Cinque, his x mark, Peter, his x mark, Tom, his x mark, Billy, his x mark, Nessick, his x mark, George, his x mark, Bogus, his x mark, Cars, his x mark

Done in the presence of the undersigned witnesses
C. M. Walker, T. R. Magruder, John Flett, interpreter.

TREATY WITH THE STOCKBRIDGE AND MUNSEE {1856, Feb. 5} Ratified Apr. 18, 1856. Proclaimed Sept. 8, 1856.

Whereas by Senate amendment to the treaty with the Menomonees of February (twenty) eighth, one thousand eight hundred and thirty-one, two townships of land on the east side of Winnebago Lake, Territory of Wisconsin, were set aside for the use of the Stockbridge and Munsee tribes of Indians, all formerly of the State of New York, but a part of whom had already removed to Wisconsin; and

Whereas said Indians took possession of said lands, but dissensions existing among them led to the treaty of September third, one thousand eight hundred and thirty-nine, by which the east half of said two townships was retroceded to the United States, and in conformity to which a part of said Stockbridges and Munsees emigrated west of the Mississippi; and

Whereas to relieve them from dissensions still existing by "An act for the relief of the Stockbridge tribe of Indians in the Territory of Wisconsin," approved March third, one thousand eight hundred and forty-three, it was provided, that the remaining townships of land should be divided into lots and allotted between the individual members of said tribe; and

Whereas a part of said tribe refused to be governed by the provisions of said act, and a subsequent act was passed on the sixth day of August, one thousand eight hundred and forty-six, repealing the aforementioned act, but without making provision for bona fide purchasers of lots in the townships subdivided in conformity to the said first-named act; and

Whereas it was found impracticable to carry into effect the provisions of the last-mentioned act, and to remedy all difficulties, a treaty was entered into on the twenty-fourth of November, one thousand eight hundred and forty-eight,

Plains, West and Northwest Plateau Indian Treaties

wherein among other provisions, the tribe obligated itself to remove to the country west of the Mississippi set apart for them by the amendment to said treaty; and

Whereas dissensions have yet been constantly existing amongst them, and many of the tribe refused to remove, when they were offered a location in Minnesota, and applied for a retrocession to them of the township of Stockbridge, which has been refused by the United States; and

Whereas a majority of the said tribe of Stockbridges and the Munsees are averse to removing to Minnesota and prefer a new location in Wisconsin, and are desirous soon to remove and to resume agricultural pursuits, and gradually to prepare for citizenship, and a number of other members of the said tribe desire at the present time to sever their tribal relations and to receive patents for the lots of land at Stockbridge now occupied by them; and

Whereas the United States are willing to exercise the same liberal policy as heretofore, and for the purpose of relieving these Indians from the complicated difficulties, by which they are surrounded, and to establish comfortably together all such Stockbridges and Munseeswherever they may be now located, in Wisconsin, in the State of New York, or west of the Mississippias were included in the treaty of September third, one thousand eight hundred and thirty-nine, and desire to remain for the present under the paternal care of the United States Government; and for the purpose of enabling such individuals of said tribes as are now qualified and desirous to manage their own affairs, to exercise the rights and to perform the duties of the citizen, these articles of agreement have been entered into:

Articles of agreement and convention made and concluded at Stockbridge in the State of Wisconsin, on the fifth day of February, in the year of our Lord one thousand eight hundred and fifty-six, between Francis Huebschmann, commissioner on the part of the United States, and the Stockbridge and Munsee tribes of Indians assembled in general council, and such of the Munsees who were included in the treaty of September third, one thousand eight hundred and thirty-nine, but are yet residing in the State of New York, by their duly authorized delegates, William Mohawk and Joshua Willson.

ARTICLE 1. The Stockbridge and Munsee tribes, who were included in the treaty of September third, one thousand eight hundred and thirty-nine, and all the individual members of said tribes, hereby jointly and severally cede and relinquish to the United States all their remaining right and title in the lands at the town of Stockbridge, State of Wisconsin, the seventy-two sections of land in Minnesota set aside for them by the amendment to the treaty of November twenty-fourth, one thousand eight hundred and forty-eight, the twenty thousand dollars stipulated to be paid to them by the said amendment, the sixteen thou-

Plains, West and Northwest Plateau Indian Treaties

sand five hundred dollars invested by the United States in stocks for the benefit of the Stockbridge tribe in conformity to Article 9 of the said treaty, and all claims set up by and for the Stockbridge and Munsee tribes, or by and for the Munsees separately, or by and for any individuals of the Stockbridge tribe who claim to have been deprived of annuities since the year one thousand eight hundred and forty-three, and all such and other claims set up by or for them or any of them are hereby abrogated, and the United States released and discharged therefrom.

ARTICLE 2. In consideration of such cession and relinquishment by said Stockbridges and Munsees, the United States agree to select as soon as practicable and to give them a tract of land in the State of Wisconsin, near the southern boundary of the Menomonee reservation, of sufficient extent to provide for each head of a family and others lots of land of eighty and forty acres, as hereinafter provided: every such lot to contain at least one-half of arable land, and to pay to be expended for improvements for the said Stockbridges and Munsees as provided in article 4, the sum of forty-one thousand one hundred dollars, and a further sum of twenty thousand five hundred and fifty dollars to enable them to remove, and the further sum of eighteen thousand dollars, (twelve thousand for the Stockbridges and six thousand for the Munsees) to be expended, at such time, and in such manner, as may be prescribed by the Secretary of the Interior, in the purchase of stock and necessaries, the discharge of national or tribal debts, and to enable them to settle their affairs.

ARTICLE 3. As soon as practicable after the selection of the lands set aside for these Indians by the preceding article, the United States shall cause the same to be surveyed into sections, half and quarter sections, to correspond with the public surveys, and the council of the Stockbridges and Munsees shall under the direction of the superintendent of Indian affairs for the northern superintendency, make a fair and just allotment among the individuals and families of their tribes. Each head of a family shall be entitled to eighty acres of land, and in case his or her family consists of more than four members, if thought expedient by the said council, eighty acres more may be allotted to him or her; each single male person above eighteen years of age shall be entitled to eighty acres; and each female person above eighteen years of age, not belonging to any family, and each orphan child, to forty acres; and sufficient land shall be reserved for the rising generation.

After the said allotment is made, the persons entitled to land may take immediate possession thereof, and the United States will thenceforth and until the issuing of the patents, as hereinafter provided, hold the same in trust for such persons, and certificates shall be issued, in a suitable form, guaranteeing and securing to the holders their possession and an ultimate title to the land; but such certificates shall not be assignable, and shall contain a clause expressly prohibiting the sale or transfer by the holder of the land described therein. After

379

Plains, West and Northwest Plateau Indian Treaties

the expiration of ten years upon the application of the holder of such certificate, made with the consent of the said Stockbridge and Munsee council, and-when it shall appear prudent and for his or her welfare, the President of the United States may direct, that such restriction on the power of sale shall be withdrawn and a patent issued in the usual form.

Should any of the heads of families die before the issuing of the certificates or patents herein provided for, the same shall issue to their heirs; and if the holder of any such certificate shall die without heirs, his or her land shall not revert to the United States, unless on petition of the Stockbridge and Munsee council for the issuing of a new certificate for the land of such deceased person, to the holder of any other certificate for land, and on the surrendering to the United States of such other certificate, by the holder thereof, the President shall direct the issuing of a new certificate for such land; and in like manner new certificates, may be given for lots of land, the prior certificates for which have been surrendered by the holders thereof.

ARTICLE 4. Of the monies set aside for improvements by the second of these articles, not exceeding one-fourth shall be applied to the building of roads leading to, and through said lands: to the erection of a school-house, and such other improvements of a public character, as will be deemed necessary by the said Stockbridge and Munsee council, and approved by the superintendent of the northern superintendency. The residue of the said fund shall be expended for improvements to be made by and for the different members and families composing the said tribes, according to a system to be adopted by the said council, under the direction of the superintendent aforesaid, and to be first approved by the Commissioner of Indian Affairs.

ARTICLE 5. The persons to be included in the apportionment of the land and money to be divided and expended under the provisions of this agreement, shall be such only, as are actual members of the said Stockbridge and Munsee tribes, (a roll or census of whom shall be taken and appended to this agreement) their heirs, and legal representatives; and hereafter, the adoption of any individual amongst them shall be null and void, except it be first approved by the Commissioner of Indian Affairs.

ARTICLE 6. In case the United States desire to locate on the tract of land to be selected as herein provided, the Stockbridges and Munsees emigrated to the west of the Mississippi in conformity to the treaty of September third, one thousand eight hundred and thirty-nine, the Stockbridges and Munsees, parties to this treaty, agree to receive them as brethren: Provided, That none of the said Stockbridges and Munsees, whether now residing at Stockbridge, in the State of Wisconsin, in the State of New York, or west of the Mississippi, shall be entitled to any of these lands or the money stipulated to be expended by these

Plains, West and Northwest Plateau Indian Treaties

articles, unless they remove to the new location within two years from the ratification hereof.

ARTICLE 7. The said Stockbridges and Munsees hereby set aside, for educational purposes exclusively, their portion of the annuities under the treaties of November the eleventh, one thousand seven hundred and ninety-four; August eleventh, one thousand eight hundred and twenty-seven; and September third, one thousand eight hundred and thirty-nine.

ARTICLE 8. One hundred and fifty dollars valuation of the schoolhouse at Stockbridge made in conformity to article 6 of the treaty of November twenty-fourth, one thousand eight hundred and forty-eight, and remaining unpaid, shall be expended in the erection of a schoolhouse, with the other funds set aside for the same purpose by article 4 of this agreement.

ARTICLE 9. About seven and two-fifths acres bounded as follows: Beginning at the northeast corner of lot eighty-nine, in the centre of the military road; thence west, along the north line of said lot, fifty-four and a quarter rods; thence south, thirty-eight and a quarter rods; thence east twenty-eight and a quarter rods; thence north thirty four and a quarter rods; thence east twenty-six rods; thence north, four rods, to the place of beginning, comprising the ground heretofore used by the Stock bridges to bury their dead, shall be patented to the supervisors of the town of Stockbridge, to be held by them and their successors in trust for the inhabitants of said town, to be used by them as a cemetery, and the proceeds from cemetery lots and burial-places to be applied in fencing, clearing, and embellishing the grounds.

ARTICLE 10. It is agreed that all roads and highways laid out by authority of law shall have right of way through the lands set aside for said Indians, on the same terms as are provided by law for their location through lands of citizens of the United States.

ARTICLE 11. The object of this instrument being to advance the welfare and improvement of said Indians, it is agreed, if it prove insufficient from causes which cannot now be foreseen, to effect these ends, that the President of the United States may, by and with the advice and consent of the Senate, adopt such policy in the management of their affairs, as in his judgment may be most beneficial to them; or Congress may, hereafter, make such provision by law, as experience shall prove to be necessary.

ARTICLE 12. The said Stockbridges and Munsees agree to suppress the use of ardent spirits among their people and to resist by all prudent means, its introduction in their settlements.

Plains, West and Northwest Plateau Indian Treaties

ARTICLE 13. The Secretary of the Interior, if deemed by him expedient and proper, may examine into the sales made by the Stockbridge Indians, to whom lots of land were allotted in conformity to the acts of Congress, entitled "An act for the relief of the Stockbridge tribe of Indians in the Territory of Wisconsin." approved March third, one thousand eight hundred and forty-three; and if it shall be found that any of the said sales have been improperly made, or that a proper consideration has not been paid, the same may be disapproved or set aside. By the direction of the said Secretary, patents to such lots of land shall be issued to such persons as shall be found to be entitled to the same.

ARTICLE 14. The lots of land the equitable title to which shall be found not to have passed by valid sales from the Stockbridge Indians to purchasers, and such lots as have, by the treaty of November twenty-fourth, one thousand eight hundred and forty-eight, been receded to the United States, shall be sold at the minimum price of ten dollars per acre for lots fronting on Lake Winnebago, on both sides of the military road, and all the lands in the three tiers of lots next to Lake Winnebago, and at five dollars per acre for the residue of the lands in said township of Stockbridge.

Purchasers of lots, on which improvements were made by. Stockbridge Indians shall pay, in addition to the said minimum price, the appraised value of such improvements. To actual settlers on any of said lots possessing the qualifications requisite to acquire pre-emption rights, or being civilized persons of Indian descent, not members of any tribe, who shall prove, to the satisfaction of the register of the land district to which the township of Stockbridge shall be attached, that he or she has made improvements to the value of not less than fifty dollars on such lot, and that he or she is actually residing on it; the time of paying the purchase-price may be extended for a term not exceeding three years from the ratification hereof, as shall be deemed advisable by the President of the United States, provided, that no such actual settler shall be permitted to pre-empt, in the manner aforesaid, more than one lot, or two contiguous lots, on which he has proved to have made improvements exceeding the value of one hundred dollars.

The residue of said lots shall be brought into market as other Government lands are offered for sale, and shall not be sold at a less price than the said minimum, price; and all said sales shall be made, and the patents provided for in these articles shall be issued in accordance with the survey made in conformity to said act of March third, one thousand eight hundred and forty-three, unless, in the opinion of the Secretary of the Interior, a new survey shall be deemed necessary and proper.

ARTICLE 15. The United States agree to pay, within one year after the ratification of this agreement, the appraised value of the improvements upon the lands herein ceded and relinquished to the United States, to the individuals

382

Plains, West and Northwest Plateau Indian Treaties

claiming the same, the valuation of such improvements, to be made by a person to be selected by the superintendent of Indian affairs for the northern superintendency, and not to exceed, in the aggregate, the sum of five thousand dollars.

ARTICLE 16. The hereinafter named Stockbridge Indians, having become sufficiently advanced in civilization, and being desirous of separating from the Stockbridge tribe, and of enjoying the privileges granted to persons of Indian descent by the State of Wisconsin, and in consideration of ceding and relinquishing to the United States all their rights in the lands and annuities of the Stockbridge tribe of Indians, and in the annuities, money, or land, to which said Indians now are or may hereafter be entitled, the United States agree to issue patents in fee-simple to the said Stockbridge Indians to the lots of land, at the town of Stockbridge, described and set opposite their names.

Names of persons Lots to be patented to them Lots, the privilege of entering which on the same terms of pay-merit as prescribed for actual settlers in article 14 is granted.

Names of persons	Lots to be patented to them	Lots, the privilege of entering
John Moore	9, 38, and 105	226 and 187
Job Moore	69, 176 and 191	280
Sopha Moore	177	
Caleb Moore	223	
Elizabeth Moore	234	
Henry Moore	264	233
Daniel Davids' heirs		47, N. half 48, 60
John Littleman's heirs		113
Jane Dean's heirs	30	
A. Miller's heirs	14	
Mary McAllister	N. half 280	S. half 280
Hope Welch	284	
Catharine Mills	S. half 194	N. half 194
Nancy Hom	N. half 270	S. half 270
Margaret Beaulieu	N. half 238	S. half 238
Sally Shenandoah	76	
Jacob Moore	233	190
Martha Moore, wife of Jacob Moore		253
Betsey Manague	N. half 349	S. half 349
Levy Konkapot	61, 152	
Mary Hendrick	78	
John W. Abrams	59	

The said Mary Hendrick, and Levy Konkapot, John W. Abrams to have the privilege of joining again the said Stockbridges and Munsees in their new location.

383

Plains, West and Northwest Plateau Indian Treaties

ARTICLE 17. So much of the treaties of September third, one thousand eight hundred and thirty-nine, and of November twenty-fourth, one thousand eight hundred and forty-eight, as is in contravention or in conflict with the stipulations of this agreement, is hereby abrogated and annulled.

ARTICLE 18. This instrument shall be binding upon the contracting parties whenever the same shall be ratified by the President and the Senate of the United States.

In testimony whereof, the said Francis Huebschmann, commissioner as aforesaid, and the chiefs, headmen, and members of the said Stockbridge and Munsee tribes, and the said delegates of the Munsees of New York, have hereunto set their hands and seals at the place and on the day and year hereinbefore written.

Francis Huebschmann, Commissioner on the part of the United States.

Ziba T. Peters, sachem, John N. Chicks.
Jeremiah Slingerland, John W. Abrams, Levi Konkapot, Counsellors
Joshua Willson, his x mark, Delegate of Munsees of New York.
Thomas S. Branch, Jacob Davids, his x mark, John W. Quinney, jr. his x mark, Timothy Jourden, his x mark, John Yoeeom, his x mark, William Mohawk, his x mark, Delegate of Munsees of New York.
Benjamin Pye, 3d, his x mark, Abram Pye, sr., his x mark, Abram Pye, jr., his x mark,

Mary Jane Dean, Daniel P. Dean, John W. Dean, heirs of Jane Dean.
Cornelius Yoccom, his x mark, Harriet Jourden, her x mark, Peter D. Littleman, his x mark, Lovina Pye, her x mark, Charlotte Palmer, her x mark, Ramona Miller, her x mark, Hannah Turkey, her x mark, Didema Miller, Dr. Big Deer, his x mark, Elizabeth Wilber, her x mark, Darius Davids, his x mark, Harvy Johnston, his x mark,

Signed and sealed in presence of
Theodore Koven, Secretary to Commissioner.
Saml. W. Beall, Adam Scherff, James Christie, Lemuel Goodell, Enos McKenzie, Elam C. Pease.

Roll and census made in conformity to Article 5 of the foregoing treaty.
Census of the Munsees of New York, included in the treaty of September 3, 1839:

Names	Men	Women	Children	Total
Isaac Durkee	1	1	2	4
William Mohawk	1	1	2	4

Plains, West and Northwest Plateau Indian Treaties

Titus Mohawk	---	---	1	1	
Thomas Snake's widow	---	1	1		2
Austin Half White	---	---	1	1	
Clarissa Spragg	---	1	7	9	
George Moses	---	1	2	4	
Jonathan Waterman	1	1	5	7	
Jonathan Titus	1	---	---	1	
Levy Halftown	1	1	7	9	
Jefferson Halftown	1	1	---	2	
Eunice Red Eye	1	1	5	6	
John Wilson	1	1	3	5	
Joshua Wilson	1	1	2	4	

Census of Stockbridges and Munsees at Stockbridge, Wisconsin:

Names	Men	Women	Children	Total	
John N. Chicks	1	---	3	4	
Jeremiah Slingerland		1	1	3	5
John W. Abrams	1	1	4	6	
Ziba T. Peters	1	1	2	4	
Levy Konkapot	1	---	---	1	
Thomas S. Branch	1	1	2	4	
Jacob Davids	1	1	4	6	
John W. Quinney, jr	1	1	1	2	4
Timothy Jourdan	1	1	3	5	
John Yoccum	1	1	4	6	
George T. Bennet	1	1	3	5	
Jacob Konkapot	1	1	3	5	
,Jesse Jourdan	1	1	2	4	
Jeremiah Bennet	1	1	2	---	
Isaac Jacobs	1	1	1	3	
James Joshua	1	---	---	1	
Benjamin Pye, 2d	1	2	4	7	
John P. Hendricks	1	1	2	4	
Eli Williams	1	1	3	5	
Cornelius Anthony	1	1	2	4	
Lewis Hendrick	1	---	---	---	
Adam Davids	1	1	2	---	
Elias Konkapot	1	---	---	1	
Jedediah Wilber	1	---	---	1	
William Gardner	1	1	3	5	
Stephen Gardner	1	1	1	3	
Simeon Gardner	1	1	1	3	
Polly Bennett	---	1	2	3	
Eleanor Charles	---	1	---	1	

Plains, West and Northwest Plateau Indian Treaties

Mary Henririck	---	1	---	1
Susannab Hendrick	---	1	---	1
Joseph Doxtater	1	1	---	2
Joseph L. Chicks	1	3	4	---
James Chicks	---	1	1	---
Solomon Davids	1	1	1	3
Elizabeth Bowman	---	1	3	4
Humble Jourdan	1	1	---	2
Phebe Pye	---	1	---	1
Jacob Jacobs	1	---	---	1
Aaron Konkapot	1	---	---	1
Jeremiah Gardiner	1	---	---	1
Andrew Wilber	1	---	---	1
Prudence Quinney	---	1	---	1
Bethseba Wright	---	1	---	1
Alonzo Quinney	1	---	---	1
Rebecca Thompson	---	1	---	1
Peter Bennett, sen	1	1	4	6
Peter Bennett, jr	1	1	---	2
Daniel Gardner	1	---	---	---
Bathseba Brown	---	1	---	1
Dennis T. Turkey	1	1	---	2
Benjamin Pye, 3d	1	1	4	6
Abram Pye, sen	1	---	2	3
Abram Pye, jr	1	---	---	1
David Pye	1	---	---	1
Elizabeth Doxtater	---	1	4	5
Margaret Davids	---	1	1	2
Cornelius Aaron	1	1	1	3
Anna Turkey	---	1	---	1
Phebe Skicket	---	1	---	1
Louisa Konkapot	---	1	---	1
Elizabeth Aaron	---	1	---	1
Rebecca Aaron	---	1	---	1
Benjamin Pye, 4th	1	1	3	5
Paul Pye	1	---	---	1
Jackson Chicks and one other orphan, heirs of Josiah Chicks				---
	---	2	2	
Electa W. Candy	1	1	4	6
Cornelius Yoccum	1	1	3	5
Harriet Jourdan	---	1	---	1
Levina Pye	---	1	---	1
Charlotte Palmer	---	1	3	4
Remona Miller	---	1	2	3
Hannah Turkey	---	1	3	4

Bigdeer	1	---	---	1	
Elizabeth Wilber	---	1	2	3	
Harvey Johnson	1	1	7	9	
Mary Eliza Butler	---	1	3	4	
Thomas Tousey	1	1	6	8	
Chester Tousey	1	1	5	7	
Daniel Tousey	1	---	---	1	
Sarah Tousey	---	1	---	1	
Philena Pye, 1st	---	1	---	1	
Lucinda Quinney	---	1	2	3	
Eliza Franks	---	1	1	2	
Lucinda Gardner	---	1	1	2	
Mary Jane Bowman		---	1	---	1
Debby Baldwin	---	1	2	3	
Edward Bowman	1	1	1	3	
Moses Smith	1	1	2	4	
Dolly Doxtater	---	1	1	2	
Polly Smith	---	1	---	1	
Aaron Smith, (Hannah Smith)		1	1	2	4
Polly Konkapot	---	1	---	1	
John Lewis	1	---	---	1	
Peter D. Littleman	1	1	4	6	
Clarissa Miller	1	---	---	1	
John P. Quinney, (absent)	1	1	---		2
Paul Quinney, (absent)	1	1	1		3
Charles Stevens	1	---	---	1	
Samuel Stevens	1	1	---	2	
Samuel Miller	---	1	4	5	
John Metoxen, sen	1	1	---	2	
Simeon S. Metoxen	1	1	4	6	
Nicholas Palmer	1	1	2	4	
Daniel Metoxen	1	---	---	1	
Moses Doxtator	1	1	2	4	
Darius Charles	1	---	2	3	
Catharine Butterfield		---	1	1	2
Washington Quinney	1	1	3		5
Ezekiel Robinson	1	---	---	1	
Sally Pye ---	1	2	3		
James Palmer	1	---	2	3	
Jonas Thompson	1	1	3	5	
William Thompson	1	---	---	1	
Austin E. Quinney	1	1	3	5	
John Beaman	1	---	---	1	
Simeon Quinney	1	1	1	3	
Elizabeth Palmer	---	1		1	

Plains, West and Northwest Plateau Indian Treaties

Margaret Miller	---	1	2	3	
William Miller	1	---	---	1	
Zachariah Miller	1	1	---	2	
Solomon Duchamp	1	---	---	1	
John Metoxen, jr	1	---	---	1	
Joseph M. Quinney	1	1	1	3	
Mary Quinney	---	1	---	1	
Frelinghuysen Quinney	1	---	---		1
Bartholomew Bowman	1	---	---		1
Lewis Bowman	1	---	---	1	

Francis Huebschmann, Commissioner on the part of the United States.
Ziba T. Peters, Sachem.

Roll and census of Stockbridges and Munsees who prefer to remain at Stockbridge according to article 16.

Name	Men	Women	Children	Total	
John Moore	1	---	---	1	
Job Moore	1	1	6	8	
Sophia Moore	---	1	---	1	
Caleb Moore	---	---	---	---	
Elizabeth Moore	---	---	---	---	
Henry Moore	1	---	1	2	
Diana Davids	1	---	1		
Mary Ann Littleman		---	1	1	2
Mary Jane Dean,Daniel P. Dean,John W. Dean,(Children of Jane Dean)					
Dideema Miller	---	1	---	1	
Darius Davids	1	---	---	1	
Mary McAllister	---	1	1	---	
Hope Welch	---	1	---	1	
Catharine Mills	---	1	---	1	
Nancy Hom	---	1	---	1	
Margaret Beaulieu	---	1	5	6	
Sally Schenandoah	---	1	2	3	
Betsey Manague	---	1	5	6	
Jacob Moore	1	1	2	4	

Francis Huebschmann, Commissioner on the part of the United States.
Ziba T. Peters, Sachem.

Plains, West and Northwest Plateau Indian Treaties

TREATY WITH THE MENOMINEE {1856, Feb. 11}
Ratified Apr. 18, 1856.
Proclaimed Apr. 24, 1856.

Whereas a treaty was entered into at Stockbridge, in the State of Wisconsin, on the fifth of the present month, between the United States of America on the one part, and the Stockbridge and Munsee tribes of Indians on the other, stipulating that a new home shall be furnished to the said Stockbridge and Munsee Indians, near the south line of the Menomonee reservation; and

Whereas the United States desire to locate said Stockbridges and Munsees near the said line in the western part of the said reservation, on lands on which no permanent settlements have been made by the Menomonees; and

Whereas there is no objection on the part of the Menomonees to the location of the Stockbridges and Munsees in their neighborhood, therefore this agreement and convention has been entered into.

Articles of agreement made and concluded at Keshena, State of Wisconsin, on the eleventh day of February, in the year of our Lord eighteen hundred and fifty-six, between Francis Huebschmann, commissioner on the part of the United States, and the Menomonee tribe of Indians, assembled in general council.

ARTICLE 1. The Menomonee tribe of Indians cede to the United States a tract of land, not to exceed two townships in extent, to be selected in the western part of their present reservation on its south line, and not containing any permanent settlements made by any of their number, for the purpose of locating thereon the Stockbridge and Munsee Indians, and such others of the New York Indians as the United States may desire to remove to the said location within two years from the ratification hereof.

ARTICLE 2. The United States agree to pay for the said cession, in case the said New York Indians will be located on the said lands, at the rate of sixty cents per acre; and it is hereby stipulated, that the monies so to be paid shall be expended in a like manner, to promote the improvement of the Menomonees, as is stipulated by the third article of the treaty of May twelfth, eighteen hundred and fifty-four, for the expenditure of the forty thousand dollars which had been set aside for their removal and subsistence, west of the Mississippi, by the treaty of October eighteenth, eighteen hundred and forty-eight.

ARTICLE 3. To promote the welfare and the improvement of the said Menomonees, and friendly relations between them and the citizens of the United States, it is further stipulated.
First. That in case this agreement and the treaties made previously with the Menomonees should prove insufficient, from causes which cannot now been

389

Plains, West and Northwest Plateau Indian Treaties

(be) foreseen, to effect the said objects, the President of the United States may, by and with the advice and consent of the Senate, adopt such policy in the management of the affairs of the Menomonees as in his judgment may be most beneficial to them; or Congress may, hereafter, make such provision by law as experience shall prove to be necessary.

Second. That the Menomonees will suppress the use of ardent spirits among their people, and resist, by all prudent means, its introduction in their settlements.

Third. That the President of the United States, if deemed by him conducive to the welfare of the Menomonees, may cause their annuity monies to be paid to them in semi-annual or quarterly instalments.
Fourth. That all roads and highways, laid out by authority of law, shall have right of way through the lands of the said Indians on the same terms as are provided by law for their location through lands of citizens of the United States.

ARTICLE 4. This instrument shall be binding upon the contracting parties whenever the same shall be ratified by the President and Senate of the United States.

In testimony whereof, the said Francis Huebschmann, commissioner as aforesaid, and the chiefs and headmen of the said Menomonee tribe, in presence and with the consent of the warriors and young men of the said tribe, assembled in general council, have hereunto set their hands and seals at the place and on the day and year hereinbefore written.

Francis Huebschmann, Commissioner on the part of the United States.

Osh-kosh, his x mark, Sho-ne-niew, his x mark, Ke-she-na, his x mark, La-motte, his x mark, Pe-quah-kaw-nah, his x mark, Car-ron, his x mark, Wau-ke-chon, his x mark, Ah-kamote, his x mark, A h-yah-metah, his x mark, Osh-ke-he-na-niew, his x mark, Kotch-kaw-no-naew, his x mark, Sho-ne-on, his x mark, Wa-pa-massaew, his x mark, Naw-no-ha-toke, his x mark, Match-a-kin-naew, his x mark, Mah-mah-ke-wet, his x mark, Ko-man-e-kim, his x mark, Shaw-puy-tuck, his x mark,

Signed and sealed in presence of
Benja Hunkins, Indian agent, Talbot Pricket, United States interpreter, Benjamin Rice, John Werdchaff, Stephen Canfield, Thomas Heaton.

Plains, West and Northwest Plateau Indian Treaties

TREATY WITH THE PAWNEE {1857, Sept. 24}
Ratified, Mar. 31, 1858
Proclaimed May 26, 1858.

Articles of agreement and convention made this twenty-fourth day of September A D 1857 at Table Creek, Nebraska Territory, between James W. Denver, commissioner on behalf of the United States, and the chiefs and head-men of the four confederate bands of Pawnee Indians, viz: Grand Pawnees, Pawnee Loups, Pawnee Republicans, and Pawnee Tappahs, and generally known as the Pawnee tribe.

ARTICLE 1. The confederate bands of the Pawnees aforesaid, hereby cede and relinquish to the United States all their right, title, and interest in and to all the lands now owned or claimed by them, except as hereinafter reserved, and which are bounded as follows, viz: On the east by the lands lately purchased by the United States from the Omahas; on the south by the lands heretofore ceded by the Pawnees to the United States; on the west by a line running due north from the junction of the North with the South Fork of the Platte River, to the Keha-Paha River; and on the north by the Keha-Paha River to its junction with the Niobrara, L'eauqi Court, or Running-Water River, and thence, by that river, to the western boundary of the late Omaha cession.

Out of this cession the Pawnees reserve a tract of country, thirty miles long from east to west, by fifteen miles wide from north to south, including both banks of the Loup Fork of the Platte River; the east line of which shall be at a point not further east than the mouth of Beaver Creek. If, however, the Pawnees, in conjunction with the United States agent, shall be able to find a more suitable locality for their future homes, within said cession, then, they are to have the privilege of selecting an equal quantity of land there, in lieu of the reservation herein designated, all of which shall be done as soon as practicable; and the Pawnees agree to remove to their new homes, thus reserved for them, without cost to the United States, within one year from the date of the ratification of this treaty by the Senate of the United States, and, until that time, they shall be permitted to remain where they are now residing, without molestation.

ARTICLE 2. In consideration of the foregoing cession, the United States agree to pay to the Pawnees the sum of forty thousand dollars per annum, for five years, commencing on the first day of January, A. D. eighteen hundred and fifty-eight; and, after the end of five years, thirty thousand dollars per annum, as a perpetual annuity, at least one-half of which annual payments shall be made in goods, and such articles as may be deemed necessary for them.

And it is further agreed that the President may, at any time, in his discretion, discontinue said perpetuity, by causing the value of a fair commutation thereof

Plains, West and Northwest Plateau Indian Treaties

to be paid to, or expended for the benefit of, said Indians, in such manner as to him shall seem proper.

ARTICLE 3. In order to improve the condition of the Pawnees, and teach them the arts of civilized life, the United States agree to establish among them, and for their use and benefit, two manual-labor schools, to be governed by such rules and regulations as may be prescribed by the President of the United States, who shall also appoint the teachers, and, if he deems it necessary, may increase the number of schools to four. In these schools, there shall be taught the various branches of a common-school education, and, in addition, the arts of agriculture, the most useful mechanical arts, and whatever else the President may direct. The Pawnees, on their part, agree that each and every one of their children, between the ages of seven and eighteen years, shall be kept constantly at these schools for, at least, nine months in each year; and if any parent or guardian shall fail, neglect, or refuse to so keep the child or children under his or her control at such school, then, and in that case, there shall be deducted from the annuities to which such parent or guardian would be entitled, either individually or as parent or guardian, an amount equal to the value, in time, of the tuition thus lost; but the President may at any time change or modify this clause as he may think proper.

The chiefs shall be held responsible for the attendance of orphans who have no other guardians; and the United States agree to furnish suitable houses and farms for said schools, and whatever else may be necessary to put them in successful operation; and a sum not less than five thousand dollars per annum shall be applied to the support of each school, so long as the Pawnees shall, in good faith, comply with the provisions of this article; but if, at any time, the President is satisfied they are not doing so, he may, at his discretion, discontinue the schools in whole or in part.

ARTICLE 4. The United States agree to protect the Pawnees in the possession of their new homes. The United States also agree to furnish the Pawnees:
First, with two complete sets of blacksmith, gunsmith, and tinsmith tools, not to exceed in cost seven hundred and fifty dollars; and erect shops at a cost not to exceed five hundred dollars; also five hundred dollars annually, during the pleasure of the President, for the purchase of iron, steel, and other necessaries for the same. The United States are also to furnish two blacksmiths, one of whom shall be a gunsmith and tinsmith; but the Pawnees agree to furnish one or two young men of their tribe to work constantly in each shop as strikers or apprentices, who shall be paid a fair compensation for their labor.

Second. The United States agree to furnish farming utensils and stock, worth twelve hundred dollars per annum, for ten years, or during the pleasure of the President, and for the first year's purchase of stock, and for erecting shelters for

Plains, West and Northwest Plateau Indian Treaties

the same, an amount not exceeding three thousand dollars, and also to employ a farmer to teach the Indians the arts of agriculture.

Third. The United States agree to have erected on said reservation a steam-mill, suitable to grind grain and saw lumber, which shall not exceed in cost six thousand dollars, and to keep the same in repair for ten years; also, to employ a miller and engineer for the same length of time, or longer, at the discretion of the President; the Pawnees agreeing to furnish apprentices, to assist in working the mill, who shall be paid a fair compensation for their services.

Fourth. The United States agree to erect dwelling-houses for the interpreter, blacksmiths, farmer, miller and engineer, which shall not exceed in cost five hundred dollars each; and the Pawnees agree to prevent the members of their tribe from injuring or destroying the houses, shops, machinery, stock farming utensils, and all other things furnished by the Government, and if any such shall be carried away, injured, or destroyed, by any of the members of their tribe, the value of the same shall be deducted from the tribal annuities. Whenever the President shall become satisfied that the Pawnees have sufficiently advanced in the acquirement of a practical knowledge of the arts and pursuits to which this article relates, then, and in that case, he may turn over the property to the tribe, and dispense with the services of any or all of the employees herein named.

ARTICLE 5. The Pawnees acknowledge their dependence on the Government of the United States, and promise to be friendly with all the citizens thereof, and pledge themselves to commit no depredations on the property of such citizens, nor on that of any other person belonging to any tribe or nation at peace with the United States. And should any one or more of them violate this pledge, and the fact be satisfactorily proven before the agent, the property taken shall be returned, or in default thereof, or if injured or destroyed, compensation may be made by the Government out of their annuities. Nor will they make war on any other tribe, except in self-defence, but will submit all matters of difference between them and other Indians to the Government of the United States, or its agent, for decision, and abide thereby.

ARTICLE 6. The United States agent may reside on or near the Pawnee reservation; and the Pawnees agree to permit the United States to build forts and occupy military posts on their lands, and to allow the whites the right to open roads through their territories; but no white person shall be allowed to reside on any part of said reservation unless he or she be in the employ of the United States, or be licensed to trade with said tribe, or be a member of the family of such employe or licensed trader; nor shall the said tribe, or any of them, alienate any part of said reservation, except to the United States; but, if they think proper to do so, they may divide said lands among themselves, giving to each person, or each head of a family, a farm, subject to their tribal regulations, but

Plains, West and Northwest Plateau Indian Treaties

in no instance to be sold or disposed of to persons outside, or not themselves of the Pawnee tribe.

ARTICLE 7. The United States agree to furnish, in addition to the persons heretofore mentioned, six laborers for three years, but it is expressly understood that while these laborers are to be under the control, and subject to the orders, of the United States agent, they are employed more to teach the Pawnees how to manage stock and use the implements furnished, than as merely laboring for their benefit; and for every laborer thus furnished by the United States, the Pawnees engage to furnish at least three of their tribe to work with them, who shall also be subject to the orders of the agent, and for whom the chiefs shall be responsible.

ARTICLE 8. The Pawnees agree to deliver up to the officers of the United States all offenders against the treaties, laws, or regulations of the United States, whenever they may be found within the limits of their reservation; and they further agree to assist such officers in discovering, pursuing, and capturing any such offender or offenders, anywhere, whenever called on so to do; and they agree, also, that, if they violate any of the stipulations contained in this treaty, the President may, at his discretion, withhold a part, or the whole, of the annuities herein provided for.

ARTICLE 9. The Pawnees desire to have some provision made for the half-breeds of their tribe. Those of them who have preferred to reside, and are now residing, in the nation, are to be entitled to equal rights and privileges with other members of the tribes, but those who have chosen to follow the pursuits of civilized life, and to reside among the whites, viz: Baptiste Bayhylle, William Bayhylle, Julia Bayhylle, Frank Tatahyee, William Nealis, Julia Nealis, Catharine Papan, Politte Papan, Rousseau Papan, Charles Papan, Peter Papan, Emily Papan, Henry Geta, Stephen Geta, James Cleghorn, Eliza Deroine, are to be entitled to scrip for one hundred and sixty acres, or one quarter section, of land for each, provided application shall be made for the same within five years from this time, which scrip shall be receivable at the United States land-offices, the same as military bounty-land warrants, and be subject to the same rules and regulations.

ARTICLE 10. Samuel Allis has long been the firm friend of the Pawnees, and in years gone by has administered to their wants and necessities. When in distress, and in a state of starvation, they took his property and used it for themselves, and when the small-pox was destroying them, he vaccinated more than two thousand of them; for all these things, the Pawnees desire that he shall be paid, but they think that the Government should pay a part. It is, therefore, agreed that the Pawnees will pay to said Allis one thousand dollars, and the United States agree to pay him a similar sum of one thousand dollars as a full remuneration for his services and losses.

Plains, West and Northwest Plateau Indian Treaties

ARTICLE 11. Ta-ra-da-ka-wa, head-chief of the Tappahs band, and four other Pawnees, having been out as guides for the United States troops, in their late expedition against the Cheyennes, and having to return by themselves, were overtaken and plundered of everything given them by the officers of the expedition, as well as their own property, barely escaping with their lives; and the value of their services being fully acknowledged, the United States agree to pay to each of them one hundred dollars, or, in lieu thereof, to give to each a horse worth one hundred dollars in value.

ARTICLE 12. To enable the Pawnees to settle any just claims at present existing against them, there is hereby set apart, by the United States, ten thousand dollars, out of which the same may be paid, when presented, and proven to the satisfaction of the proper department; and the Pawnees hereby relinquish all claims they may have against the United States under former treaty stipulations. In testimony whereof, the said James W. Denver, Commissioner, as aforesaid, and the undersigned, chiefs and head-men of the four confederate bands of Pawnee Indians, have hereunto set their hands and seals, at the place and on the day and year hereinbefore written.

James W. Denver, U. S. Commissioner.

Grand Pawnees:
Pe-ta-na-sharo, or the Man and the Chief, his x mark, Sa-ra-cherish, the Cross Chief, his x mark, Te-ra-ta-puts, he who Steals Horses, his x mark, Le-ra-kuts-a-nasharo, the Grey Eagle Chief, his x mark,
Pawnee Loups:
La-le-ta-ra-nasharo, the Comanche Chief, his x mark, Te-ste-de-da-we-tel, the Man who Distributes the Goods, his x mark, Le-ta-kuts-nasharo, the Grey Eagle Chief, his x mark, A-sa-na-sharo, the Horse Chief, his x mark,
Pawnee Republicans:
Na-sharo-se-de-ta-ra-ko, the one the Great Spirit smiles on, his x mark, Na-sharo-eha-hicko, a Man, but a Chief, his x mark, Da-lo-le-kit-ta-to-kah, the Man the Enemy steals from, his x mark, Da-lo-de-na-sharo, the Chief like an Eagle, his x mark,
Pawnee Tappahs:
Ke-we-ko-na-sharo, theBuffalo Bull Chief, his x mark, Na-sharo-la-da-hoo, the Big Chief, his x mark, Na-sharo, the Chief, his x mark, Da-ka-to-wa-kuts-o-ra-na-sharo, the Hawk Chief, his x mark,

Signed and sealed in presence of
Wm. W. Dennison, United States Indian Agent.
A. S. H. White, secretary to commissioner.

Plains, West and Northwest Plateau Indian Treaties

TREATY WITH THE PONCA {1858, Mar. 12}
Ratified Mar. 8, 1859.
Proclaimed Apr. 11, 1859.

Articles of agreement and convention made and concluded at the city of Washington, on the twelfth day of March, one thousand eight hundred and fifty-eight, by Charles E. Mix, commissioner on the part of the United States, and Wa-gah-sah-pi, or Whip; Gish-tah-wah-gu, or Strong Walker; Mitchell P. Cera, or Wash-kom-moni; A-shno-ni-kah-gah-hi, or Lone Chief; Shu-kah-bi, or Heavy Clouds; Tah-tungah-nushi, or Standing Buffalo, on the part of the Ponca tribe of Indians; they being thereto duly authorized and empowered by said tribe.

ARTICLE 1. The Ponca tribe of Indians hereby cede and relinquish to the United States all the lands now owned or claimed by them wherever situate, except the tract bounded as follows, viz: Beginning at a point on the Neobrara River and running due north, so as to intersect the Ponca River twenty-five miles from its mouth; thence from said point of intersection, up and along the Ponca River, twenty miles; thence due south to the Neobrara River; and thence down and along said river to the place of beginning; which tract is hereby reserved for the future homes of said Indians; and to which they agree and bind themselves to remove within one year from the date of the ratification of this agreement by the Senate and President of the United States.

ARTICLE 2. In consideration of the foregoing cession and relinquish-meet, the United States agree and stipulate as follows, viz:

First. To protect the Poncas in the possession of the tract of land reserved for their future homes, and their persons and property thereon, during good behavior on their part.

Second. To pay to them, or expend for their benefit, the sum of twelve thousand dollars ($12,000) per annum for five years; commencing with the year in which they shall remove to and settle upon the tract reserved for their future homes; ten thousand dollars ($10,000) per annum for ten years, from and after the expiration of the said five years; and thereafter eight thousand dollars ($8,000) per annum, for fifteen years; of which sums the President of the United States shall, from time to time, determine what proportion shall be paid to the Poncas in cash, and what proportion shall be expended for their benefit; and also in what manner or for what objects such expenditure shall be made. He shall likewise exercise the power to make such provision out of the same, as he may deem to be necessary and proper for the support and comfort of the aged and infirm members of the tribe.

Plains, West and Northwest Plateau Indian Treaties

In case of any material decrease of the Poncas in number, the said amounts shall be reduced and diminished in proportion thereto, or they may, at the discretion of the President, be discontinued altogether should said Indians fail to make satisfactory efforts to advance and improve their condition; in which case such other provision shall be made for them as the President and Congress may judge to be suitable and proper.

Third. To expend the sum of twenty thousand dollars ($20,000) in maintaining and subsisting the Poncas during the first year after their removal to their new homes, purchasing stock and agricultural implements, breaking up and fencing land, building houses, and in making such other improvements as may be necessary for their comfort and welfare.

Fourth. To establish, and to maintain for ten years, at an annual expense not to exceed five thousand dollars, ($5,000) one or more manual-labor schools for the education and training of the Ponca youth in letters, agriculture, the mechanic arts, and housewifery; which school or schools shall be managed and conducted in such manner as the President of the United States shall direct; the Poncas hereby stipulating to constantly keep thereat, during at least nine months in every year, all their children between the ages of seven and eighteen years; and that, if this be not done, there shall be deducted from the shares of the annuities due to the parents, guardians, or other persons having control of the children, such amounts as may be proportioned to the deficiency in their time of attendance, compared with the said nine months, and the cost of maintaining and educating the children during that period. It is further agreed that such other measures may be adopted, to compel the attendance of the children at the school or schools as the President may think proper and direct; and whenever he shall be satisfied of a failure to fulfil the aforesaid stipulation on the part of the Poncas, he may, at his discretion, diminish or wholly discontinue the allowance and expenditure of the sum herein set apart for the support and maintenance of said school or schools.

Fifth. To provide the Poncas with a mill suitable for grinding grain and sawing timber, one or more mechanic shops, with the necessary tools for the same, and dwelling-houses for an interpreter, miller, engineer for the mill, if one be necessary, farmer, and the mechanics that may be employed for their benefit, the whole not to exceed in cost the sum of ten thousand five hundred dollars, ($10,500;) and also to expend annually, for ten years, or during the pleasure of the President, an amount not exceeding seven thousand five hundred dollars, ($7,500.) for the purpose of furnishing said Indians with such aid and assistance in agricultural and mechanical pursuits, including the working of said mill, as the Secretary of the Interior may consider advantageous and necessary for them; the Poncas hereby stipulating to furnish from their tribe the number of young men that may be required as apprentices and assistants in the mill and mechanic shops, and at least three persons to work constantly with each laborer

Plains, West and Northwest Plateau Indian Treaties

employed for them in agricultural pursuits, it being understood that such laborers are to be employed more for the instruction of the Indians than merely to work for their benefit. The persons so to be furnished by the tribe shall be allowed a fair and just compensation for their services, to be fixed by the Secretary of the Interior.

The Poncas further stipulate and bind themselves to prevent any of the members of their tribe from destroying or injuring the said houses, shops, mill, machinery, stock, farming utensils, or any other thing furnished them by the Government; and in case of any such destruction or injury, or of any of the things so furnished being carried off by any member or members of their tribe, the value of the same shall be deducted from the tribal annuities. And whenever the President shall be satisfied that the Poncas have become sufficiently confirmed in habits of industry, and advanced in acquiring a practical knowledge of agriculture and the mechanic arts, he may, at his discretion, cause to be turned over to the tribe all of the said houses and other property furnished them by the United States, and dispense with the services of any or all of the persons hereinbefore stipulated to be employed for their benefit and assistance.

Sixth. To provide and set apart the sum of twenty thousand dollars ($20,000) to enable the Poncas to adjust, and settle their existing obligations and engagements, including depredations committed by them on property of citizens of the United States prior to the date of the ratification of this agreement, so far as the same may be found and decided by their agent to be valid and just, subject to the approval of the Secretary of the Interior; and in consideration of the long continued friendship and kindness of Joseph Hollman and William G. Crawford toward the Poncas, of their furnishing them, when in distress, with large quantities of goods and provisions, and of their good counsel and advice, in consequence of which peace has often been preserved between the Poncas and other Indians and the whites, it is agreed that out of the above-mentioned amount they shall be paid the sum of three thousand five hundred dollars, ($3,500) and the sum of one thousand dollars ($1,000) shall in like manner be paid to Jesse Williams of Iowa, in full for his claim, as such has been admitted by the Poncas for depredations committed by them on his property.

ARTICLE 3. The Poncas being desirous of making provision for their half-breed relatives, it is agreed that those who prefer and elect to reside among them shall be permitted to do so, and be entitled to and enjoy all the rights and privileges of members of the tribe; but to those who have chosen and left the tribe to reside among the whites and follow the pursuits of civilized life, viz: Charles Leclaire, Fort Piere, N. T.; Cillaste Leclaire, Pottowattomie, K. T.; Ciprian Leclaire. St. Louis, Missouri; Julia Harvey, Omaha, N. T.; Jenny Ruleau, Sioux City, Iowa; David Leclaire, Amelia Deloge, and Laura Deloge, at the Omaha mission, there shall be issued scrip for one hundred and sixty acres of land each, which shall be receivable at the United States land-offices in the

Plains, West and Northwest Plateau Indian Treaties

same manner, and be subject to the same rules and regulations as military bounty and warrants. And in consideration of the faithful services rendered to the Poncas by Francis Roy, their interpreter, it is agreed that scrip shall, in the like manner and amount, be issued to his wife and to each of his six children now living, without their being required to leave the nation. Provided, That application for the said scrip shall be made to the Commissioner of Indian Affairs within five years from and after the date of the ratification of this agreement.

ARTICLE 4. The United States shall have the right to establish and maintain such military posts, roads, and Indian agencies as may be deemed necessary within the tract of country hereby reserved for the Poncas, but no greater quantity of land or timber shall be used for said purposes than shall be actually requisite; and if, in the establishment or maintenance of such posts, roads, and agencies, the-property of any Ponca shall be taken, injured, or destroyed, just and adequate compensation shall be made therefor by the United States. And all roads or highways authorized by competent authority, other than the United States, the lines of which shall lie through said tract, shall have the right of way through the same; the fair and just value of such right being paid to the Poncas therefor by the party or parties authorizing the same or interested therein; to be assessed and determined in such manner as the President of the United States shall direct.

ARTICLE 5. No white person, unless in the employment of the United States, or duly licensed to trade with the Poncas, or members of the family of such persons, shall be permitted to reside, or to make any settlement, upon any part of the tract herein reserved for said Indians, nor shall the latter alienate, sell, or in manner dispose of any portion thereof, except to the United States; but, whenever they may think proper, they may divide said tract among themselves, giving to each head of a family or single person a farm, with such rights of possession, transfer to any other member of the tribe, or of descent to their heirs and representatives, as may be in accordance with the laws, customs, and regulations of the tribe.

ARTICLE 6. Such persons as are now lawfully residing on the lands herein ceded by the Poncas shall each have the privilege of entering one hundred and sixty acres thereof, to include any improvements they may have, at one dollar and twenty-five cents per acre.

ARTICLE 7. The Poncas acknowledge their dependence upon the Government of the United States, and do hereby pledge and bind themselves to preserve friendly relations with the citizens thereof, and to commit no injuries or depredations on their persons or property, nor on those of members of any other tribe; but, in case of any such injury or depredation, full compensation shall, as far as practicable, be made therefor out of their tribal annuities; the amount in all cases to be determined by the Secretary of the Interior. They further pledge

Plains, West and Northwest Plateau Indian Treaties

themselves not to engage in hostilities with any other tribe, unless in self-defence, but to submit, through their agent, all matters of dispute and difficulty between themselves and other Indians for the decision of the President of the United States, and to acquiesce in and abide thereby. They also agree, whenever called upon by the proper officer, to deliver up all offenders against the treaties, laws, or regulations of the United States, who may be within the limits of their reservation, and to assist in discovering, pursuing, and capturing all such offenders, whenever required to do so by such officer.

ARTICLE 8. To aid in preventing the evils of intemperance, it is hereby stipulated that if any of the Poncas shall drink, or procure for others, intoxicating liquor, their proportion of the tribal annuities shall be withheld from them for at least one year; and for a violation of any of the stipulations of this agreement on the part of the Poncas, they shall be liable to have their annuities withheld, in whole or in part, and for such length of time as the President of the United States shall direct.

ARTICLE 9. No part of the annuities of the Poncas shall be taken to pay any claims or demands against them, except such as may arise under this agreement, or under the trade and intercourse laws of the United States; and the said Indians do hereby fully relinquish and release the United States from all demands against them on the part of the tribe or any individuals thereof, except such as are herein stipulated and provided for.

ARTICLE 10. The expenses connected with the negotiation of this agreement shall be paid by the United States.

In testimony whereof, the said Charles E. Mix, commissioner, as aforesaid, and the undersigned delegates and representatives of the Ponca tribes of Indians, have hereunto set their names and seals, at the place and on the day hereinbefore written.

Charles E. Mix, Commissioner.

Wah-gah-sah-pi, or Whip, his x mark, Gish-tah-wah-gn, or Strong Walker, his x mark, Mitchell P. Cera, or Wash-kom-mo-ni, his x mark, A-shno-ni-kah-gah-hi, or Lone Chief, his x mark, Shu-kah-bi, or Heavy Clouds, his x mark, Tah-tungah-nushi, or Standing Buffalo, his x mark,

Executed in the presence of
Edward Hanrick, E. B. Grayson, James R. Roche, Moses Kelly, Joseph Hollman, Jno. Wm. Wells, J. B. Robertson, United States Indian agent, Henry Fontenelle, United States interpreter, Francis Roy, his x ,

Plains, West and Northwest Plateau Indian Treaties

TREATY WITH THE YANKTON SIOUX {1858, Apr. 19}
Ratified Feb.16, 1859.
Proclaimed Feb. 26, 1859.

Articles of agreement and convention made and concluded at the city of Washington, this nineteenth day of April, A. D. one thousand eight hundred and fifty-eight, by Charles E. Mix, commissioner on the part of the United States, and the following-named chiefs and delegates of the Yancton tribe of Sioux or Dacotah Indians, viz: Pa-la-ne-a-pa-pe, the man that was struck by the Ree. Ma-to-sa-be-che-a, the smutty bear. Charles F. Picotte, Eta-ke-cha. Ta-ton-ka-wete-co, the crazy bull. Pse-cha-wa-kea, the jumping thunder. Ma-ra-ha-ton, the iron horn. Mombe-kah-pah, one that knocks down, two. Ta-ton-ka-e-yah-ka, the fast bull. A-ha-ka-ma-ne, the walking elk. A-ha-ka-ka-zhe, the standing elk. A-ha-ka-ho-che-cha, the elk with a bad voice. Cha-ton-wo-ka-pa, the grabbing hawk. E-ha-we-cha-sha, the owl man. Pla-son-wa-kan-na-ge, the white medicine cow that stands. Ma-ga-scha-che-ka, the little white swan. Oke-che-la-wash-ta, the pretty boy. (The three last names signed by their duly-authorized agent and representative, Charlee F. Picotte) they being thereto duly authorized empowered by said tribe of Indians.

ARTICLE 1. The said chiefs and delegates of said tribe of Indians do hereby Cede and relinquish to the United States all the lands now owned, possessed, or claimed by them, wherever situated, except four hundred thousand acres thereof, situated and described as follows, to witBeginning at the mouth of the Naw-izi-wa-koo-pah or Chouteau River and extending up the Missouri River thirty miles; thence due north to a point; thence easterly to a point on the said Chouteau River; thence down said river to the place of beginning, so as to include the said quantity of four hundred thousand acres. They, also, hereby relinquish and abandon all claims and complaints about or growing out of any and all treaties heretofore made by them or other Indians, except their annuity rights under the treaty of Laramie, of September 17, A. D. 1851.

ARTICLE 2. The land so ceded and relinquished by the said chiefs and delegates of the said tribe of Yanctons is and shall be known and described as follows, to wit-
"Beginning at the mouth of the Tchan-kas-an-data or Calumet or Big Sioux River; thence up the Missouri River to the mouth of the Pa-hah-wa-kan or East Medicine Knoll River; thence up said river to its head; thence in a direction to the head of the main fork of the Wan-dush-kah-for or Snake River; thence down said river to its junction with the Tchan-san-san or Jaques or James River; thence in a direct line to the northern point of Lake Kampeska; thence along the northern shore of said lake and its outlet to the junction of said outlet with the said Big Sioux River; thence down the Big Sioux River to its junction with the Missouri River."

Plains, West and Northwest Plateau Indian Treaties

And they also cede and relinquish to the United States all their right and title to and in all the islands of the Missouri River, from the mouth of the Big Sioux to the mouth of the Medicine Knoll River.

And the said chiefs and delegates hereby stipulate and agree that all the lands embraced in said limits are their own, and that they have full and exclusive right to cede and relinquish the same to the United States.

ARTICLE 3. The said chiefs and delegates hereby further stipulate and agree that the United States may construct and use such roads as may be hereafter necessary across their said reservation by the consent and permission of the Secretary of the Interior, and by first paying the said Indians all damages and the fair value of the land so used for said road or roads, which said damages and value shall be determined in such manner as the Secretary of the Interior may direct. And the said Yanctons hereby agree to remove and settle and reside on said reservation within one year from this date, and, until they do so remove, (if within said year) the United States guarantee them in the quiet and undisturbed possession of their present settlements.

ARTICLE 4. In consideration of the foregoing cession, relinquishment, and agreements, the United States do hereby agree and stipulate as follows, to wit:

First. To protect the said Yanctons in the quiet and peaceable possession of the said tract of four hundred thousand acres of land so reserved for their future home, and also their persons and property thereon during good behavior on their part.

Second. To pay to them, or expend for their benefit, the sum of sixty-five thousand dollars per annum, for ten years, commencing with the year in which they shall remove to, and settle and reside upon, their said reservation   forty thousand dollars per annum for and during ten years thereafter twenty-five thousand dollars per annum for and during ten years thereafter and fifteen thousand dollars per annum for and during twenty years thereafter; making one million and six hundred thousand dollars in annuities in the period of fifty years, of which sums the President of the United States shall, from time to time, determine what proportion shall be paid to said Indians, in cash, and what proportion shall be expended for their benefit, and, also, in what manner and for what objects such expenditure shall be made, due regard being had in making such determination to the best interests of said Indians.

He shall likewise exercise the power to make such provision out of said sums as he may deem to be necessary and proper for the support and comfort of the aged or infirm, and helpless orphans of the said Indians. In case of any material decrease of said Indians, in number, the said amounts may, in the discretion of the President of the United States, be diminished and reduced in proportion thereto or they may, at the discretion of the President of the United States, be

Plains, West and Northwest Plateau Indian Treaties

discontinued entirely, should said Indians fail to make reasonable and satisfactory efforts to advance and improve their condition, in which case, such other provisions shall be made for them as the President and Congress may judge to be suitable and proper.

Third. In addition to the foregoing sum of one million and six hundred thousand dollars as annuities, to be paid to or expended for the benefit of said Indians, during the period of fifty years, as before stated, the United States hereby stipulate and agree to expend for their benefit the sum of fifty thousand dollars more, as follows, to wit: Twenty-five thousand dollars in maintaining and subsisting the said Indians during the first year after their removal to and permanent settlement upon their said reservation; in the purchase of stock, agricultural implements, or other articles of a beneficial character, and in breaking up and fencing land; in the erection of houses, store-houses, or other needful buildings, or in making such other improvements as may be necessary for their comfort and welfare.

Fourth. To expend ten thousand dollars to build a school-house or school-houses, and to establish and maintain one or more normal-labor schools (so far as said sum will go) for the education and training of the children of said Indians in letters, agriculture, the mechanic arts, and housewifery, which school or schools shall be managed and conducted in such manner as the Secretary of the Interior shall direct.

The said Indians hereby stipulating to keep constantly thereat, during at least nine months in the year, all their children between the ages of seven and eighteen years; and if any of the parents, or others having the care of children, shall refuse or neglect to send them to school, such parts of their annuities as the Secretary of the Interior may direct, shall be withheld from them and applied as he may deem just and proper; and such further sum, in addition to the said ten thousand dollars, as shall be deemed necessary and proper by the President of the United States, shall he reserved and taken from their said annuities, and applied annually, during the pleasure of the President to the support of said schools, and to furnish said Indians with assistance and aid and instruction in agricultural and mechanical pursuits, including the working of the mills, hereafter mentioned, as the Secretary of the Interior may consider necessary and advantageous for said Indians; and all instruction in reading shall be in the English language.

And the said Indians hereby stipulate to furnish, from amongst themselves, the number of young men that may be required as apprentices and assistants in the mills and mechanic shops, and at least three persons to work constantly with each white laborer employed for them in agriculture and mechanical pursuits, it being understood that such white laborers and assistants as may be so employed are thus employed more for the instruction of the said Indians than merely to

403

Plains, West and Northwest Plateau Indian Treaties

work for their benefit; and that the laborers so to be furnished by the Indians may be allowed a fair and just compensation for their services, to be fixed by the Secretary of the Interior, and to be paid out of the shares of annuity of such Indians as are able to work, but refuse or neglect to do so. And whenever the President of the United States shall become satisfied of a failure, on the part of said Indians, to fulfil the aforesaid stipulations, he may, at his discretion, discontinue the allowance and expenditure of the sums so provided and set apart for said school or schools, and assistance and instruction.

Fifth. To provide the said Indians with a mill suitable for grinding grain and sawing timber; one or more mechanic shops, with the necessary tools for the same; and dwelling-houses for an interpreter, miller, engineer for the mill, (if one be necessary) a farmer, and the mechanics that may be employed for their benefit, and to expend therefor a sum not exceeding fifteen thousand dollars.

ARTICLE 5. Said Indians further stipulate and bind themselves to prevent any of the members of their tribe from destroying or injuring the said houses, shops, mills, machinery, stock, farming-utensils, or any other thing furnished them by the Government, and in case of any such destruction or injury of any of the things so furnished, or their being carried off by any member or members of their tribe, the value of the same shall be deducted from their general annuity; and whenever the Secretary of the Interior shall be satisfied that said Indians have become sufficiently confirmed in habits of industry and advanced in the acquisition of a practical knowledge of agriculture and the mechanic arts to provide for themselves, he may, at his discretion, cause to be turned over to them all of the said houses and other property furnished them by the United States, and dispense with the services of any or all persons hereinbefore stipulated to be employed for their benefit, assistance, and instruction.

ARTICLE 6. It is hereby agreed and understood that the chiefs and head-men of said tribe may, at their discretion, in open council, authorize to be paid out of their said annuities such a sum or sums as may be found to be necessary and proper, not exceeding in the aggregate one hundred and fifty thousand dollars, to satisfy their just debts and obligations, and to provide for such of their half-breed relations as do not live with them, or draw any part of the said annuities of said Indians: Provided, however, That their said determinations shall be approved by their agent for the time being, and the said payments authorized by the Secretary of the Interior: Provided, also, That there shall not be so paid out of their said annuities in any one year, a sum exceeding fifteen thousand dollars.

ARTICLE 7. On account of their valuable services and liberality to the Yanctons, there shall be granted in fee to Charles F. Picotte and Zephyr Rencontre, each, one section of six hundred and forty acres of land, and to Paul Dorian one-half a section; and to the half-breed Yancton, wife of Charles Reulo, and

Plains, West and Northwest Plateau Indian Treaties

her two sisters, the wives of Eli Bedaud and Augustus Traverse, and to Louis Le Count, each, one-half a section. The said grants shall be selected in said ceded territory, and shall not be within said reservation, nor shall they interfere in any way with the improvements of such persons as are on the lands ceded above by authority of law; and all other persons (other than Indians, or mixed-bloods) who are now residing within said ceded country, by authority of law, shall have the privilege of entering one hundred and sixty acres thereof, to include each of their residences or improvements, at the rate of one dollar and twenty-five cents per acre.

ARTICLE 8. The said Yancton Indians shall be secured in the free and unrestricted use of the red pipe-stone quarry, or so much thereof as they have been accustomed to frequent and use for the purpose of procuring stone for pipes; and the United States hereby stipulate and agree to cause to be surveyed and marked so much thereof as shall be necessary and proper for that purpose, and retain the same and keep it open and free to the Indians to visit and procure stone for pipes so long as they shall desire.

ARTICLE 9. The United States shall have the right to establish and maintain such military posts, roads, and Indian agencies as may be deemed necessary within the tract of country herein reserved for the use of the Yanctons; but no greater quantity of land or timber shall be used for said purposes than shall be actually requisite; and if, in the establishment or maintenance of such posts, roads, and agencies, the property of any Yancton shall be taken, injured, or destroyed, just and adequate compensation shall be made therefor by the United States.

ARTICLE 10. No white person, unless in the employment of the United States, or duly licensed to trade with the Yanctons, or members of the families of such persons, shall be permitted to reside or make any settlement upon any part of the tract herein reserved for said Indians, nor shall said Indians alienate, sell, or in any manner dispose of any portion thereof, except to the United States. Whenever the Secretary of the Interior shall direct, said tract shall be surveyed and divided as he shall think proper among said Indians, so as to give to each head of a family or single person a separate farm, with such rights of possession or transfer to any other member of the tribe or of descent to their heirs and representatives as he may deem just.

ARTICLE 11. The Yanctons acknowledge their dependence upon the Government of the United States, and do hereby pledge and bind themselves to preserve friendly relations with the citizens thereof, and to commit no injuries or depredations on their persons or property, nor on those of members of any other tribe or nation of Indians; and in case of any such injuries or depredations by said Yanctons, full compensation shall, as far as possible, be made therefor out of their tribal annuities, the amount in all cases to be determined by the Secre-

Plains, West and Northwest Plateau Indian Treaties

tary of the Interior. They further pledge themselves not to engage m hostilities with any other tribe or nation, unless in self-defence, but to submit, through their agent, all matters of dispute and difficulty between themselves and other Indians for the decision of the President of the United States, and to acquiesce in and abide thereby. They also agree to deliver, to the proper officer of the United States all offenders against the treaties, laws, or regulations of the United States, and to assist in discovering, pursuing, and capturing all such offenders, who may be within the limits of their reservation, whenever required to do so by such officer.

ARTICLE 12. To aid in preventing the evils of intemperance, it is hereby stipulated that if any of the Yanctons shall drink, or procure for others, intoxicating liquor, their proportion of the tribal annuities shall be withheld from them for at least one year; and for a violation of any of the stipulations of this agreement on the part of the Yanctons they shall be liable to have their annuities withheld, in whole or in part, and for such length of time as the President of the United States shall direct.

ARTICLE 13. No part of the annuities of the Yanctons shall be taken to pay any debts, claims, or demands against them, except such existing claims and demands as have been herein provided for, and except such as may arise under this agreement, or under the trade and intercourse laws of the United States.

ARTICLE 14. The said Yanctons do hereby fully acquit and release the United States from all demands against them on the part of said tribe, or any individual thereof, except the beforementioned right of the Yanctons to receive an annuity under said treaty of Laramie, and except, also, such as are herein stipulated and provided for.

ARTICLE 15. For the special benefit of the Yanctons, parties to this agreement, the United States agree to appoint an agent for them, who shall reside on their said reservation, and shall have set apart for his sole use and occupation, at such a point as the Secretary of the Interior may direct, one hundred and sixty acres of land.

ARTICLE 16. All the expenses of the making of this agreement, and of surveying the said Yancton reservation, and of surveying and marking said pipestone quarry, shall be paid by the United States.

ARTICLE 17. This instrument shall take effect and be obligatory upon the contracting parties whenever ratified by the Senate and the President of the United States.

In testimony whereof, the said Charles E. Mix, commissioner, as aforesaid, and the undersigned chiefs, delegates, and representatives of the said tribe of

Plains, West and Northwest Plateau Indian Treaties

Yancton Indians, have hereunto set their hands and seals at the place and on the day first above written.

Charles E. Mix, Commissioner.

Pa-la-ne-apa-pe, or the Man that was struck by the Tree, his x mark, Ma-to-sa-be-ehe-a, or the Smutty Bear, his x mark, Charles F. Piecite, or Eta-ke-cha, Ta-ton-ka-wete-eo, or the Crazy Bull, his x mark, Pse-cha-wa-kea, or the Jumping Thunder, his x mark, Ma-ra-ha-ton, or the Iron Horn, his x mark, Nombe-kah-pah, or One that knocks down two, his x mark, Ta-ton-ka-e-yah-ka,or the Fast Bull, his x mark, A-ha-ka Ma-ne, orthe Walking Elk, his x mark, O-ke-cheda-wash-ta, or the Pretty Boy, by his duly authorized delegate and representative, Chas. F. Picotte.

Executed in the presence of-
A. H. Redfield, agent, J. B. S. Todd, Theophile Bruguier.

TREATY WITH THE SIOUX {1858, June 19}
Ratified Mar, 9, 1859.
Proclaimed Mar. 31, 1859.

Articles of agreement and convention made and concluded at the city of Washington, on the nineteenth day of June, one thousand eight hundred and fifty-eight, by Charles E. Mix, commissioner on the part of the United States, and the following named chiefs and headmen of the Mendawakanton and Wahpahoota bands of the Dakota or Sioux tribe of Indians, viz, Wabashaw, Chhetanakooamonee, Washuhiyahi-dan, Shakopee, Wamindeetonkee, Muzza-janjan, and Makawto, chiefs, and Hinhanduta, Ha-raka-Muzza, Wakanojanjan, Tachunr-pee-muz-za, Wakinyantowa, Chunrpiyuha, Onkeeterhidan, and Wa-mouisa, braves, on the part of the Mendawantons, and Hushaw-shaw, chief, and Pa-Pa and Tataebomdu, braves, on the part of the Wahpakootas, they being duly authorized and empowered to act for said bands.

ARTICLE 1. It is hereby agreed and stipulated that, as soon as practicable after the ratification of this agreement, so much of that part of the reservation or tract of land now held and possessed by the Mendawakanton and Wahpakoota bands of the Dakota or Sioux Indians, and which is described in the third article of the treaty made with them on the fifth day of August, one thousand eight hundred and fifty-one, which lies south or southwestwardly of the Minnesota River, shall constitute a reservation for said bands, and shall be surveyed and eighty acres thereof, as near as may be in conformity with the public surveys, be allotted in severalty to each head of a family, or single person over the age of twenty-one years, in said band of Indians, said allotments to be so made as to

Plains, West and Northwest Plateau Indian Treaties

include a proper proportion of timbered land, if the same be practicable, in each of said allotments.

The residue of said part of said reservation not so allotted, shall be held by said bands in common, and as other Indian lands are held: Provided, however, That eighty acres, as near as may be, shall, in like manner as above provided for, be allotted to each of the minors of said bands on his or her attaining their majority, or on becoming heads of families by contracting marriage, if neither of the parties shall have previously received land.

All the necessary expenses of the surveys, and allotments thus provided, for shall be defrayed out of the funds of said bands of Indians in the hands of the Government of the United States.

As the members of said bands become capable of managing their business and affairs, the President of the United States may, at his discretion, cause patents to be issued to them, for the tracts of land allotted to them, respectively, in conformity with this article; said tracts to be exempt from levy, taxation, sale or forfeiture, until otherwise provided for by the legislature of the State in which they are situated with the assent of Congress; nor shall they be sold or alienated in fee, or be in any other manner disposed of except to the United States or to members of said bands.

ARTICLE 2. Whereas by the treaty with the Mendawakanton and Wahpakoota bands of Sioux Indians, concluded at Mendota on the fifth day of August, one thousand eight hundred and fifty-one, said bands retained for their "future occupancy and home," "to be held by them as Indian lands are held, a tract of country of the average width of ten miles on either side of the Minnesota River," extending from Little Rock River to the Tchatamba and Yellow Medicine Rivers, which land was to "be held by said bands in common."

And whereas the Senate of the United States so amended said treaty as to strike therefrom the provision setting apart said land as a home for said bands, and made provision for the payment to said bands "at the rate of ten cents per acre for the lands included in the" said tract so reserved and set apart for the "occupancy and home" of said bands, and also provided in addition thereto, that there should be "set apart, by appropriate landmarks and boundaries, such tracts of country without the limits of the cession made by the first article of the" said treaty as should "be satisfactory for their future occupancy and home," said Senate amendment providing also "that the President may, with the consent of these Indians, vary the conditions aforesaid, if deemed expedient;" all of which provisions in said amendment were assented to by said Indians.

And whereas the President so far varied the conditions of said Senate amendment, as to permit said bands to locate for the time being, upon the tract originally reserved by said bands for a home, and no "tracts of country without the

Plains, West and Northwest Plateau Indian Treaties

limits of the cession" made in the said treaty has (have) ever been provided for, or offered to, said bands:

And whereas by the "act making appropriations for the current and contingent expenses of the Indian Department and for fulfilling treaty stipulations with various Indian tribes," approved July 31, 1854, the President was authorized to confirm to the Sioux of Minnesota forever, the reserve on the Minnesota River now occupied by them, upon such conditions as he may deem just:

And whereas, although the President has not directly confirmed said reserve to said Indians, they claim that as they were entitled to receive "such tracts of country" as should "be satisfactory for their future occupancy and home," and as no such country has been provided for, or offered to, said bands, it is agreed and stipulated that the question shall be submitted to the Senate for decision whether they have such title: and if they have, what compensation shall be made to them for that part of said reservation or tract of land lying on the north side of the Minnesota Riverwhether they shall be allowed a specific sum of money therefor, and if so, how much; or whether the same shall be sold for their benefit, they to receive the proceeds of such sale, deducting the necessary expenses incident thereto. Such sale, if decided in favor of by the Senate, shall be made under and according to regulations to be prescribed by the Secretary of the Interior, and in such manner as will secure to them the largest sum it may be practicable to obtain for said land.

ARTICLE 3. It is also agreed that if the Senate shall authorize the land designated in article two of this agreement to be sold for the benefit of the said Mendawakanton and Wahpakoota bands, or shall prescribe an amount to be paid said bands for their interest in said tract, provision shall be made by which the chiefs and head-men of said bands may, in their discretion, in open council, authorize to be paid out of the proceeds of said tract, such sum or sums as may be found necessary and proper, not exceeding seventy thousand dollars, to satisfy their just debts and obligations, and to provide goods to be taken by said chiefs and head-men to the said bands upon their return: Provided, however, That their said determinations shall be approved by the superintendent of Indian affairs for the northern superintendency for the time being, and the said payments be authorized by the Secretary of the Interior.

ARTICLE 4. The lands retained and to be held by the members of the Mendawakanton and Wahpakoota bands of the Dakota or Sioux Indians, under and by virtue of the first article of this agreement, shall, to all intents and purposes whatever, be deemed and held to be an Indian reservation; and the laws which have been, or may hereafter be enacted by Congress, to regulate trade and intercourse with the Indian tribes, shall have full force and effect over and within the limits of the same; and no person other than the members of the said bands, to be ascertained and defined under such regulations as the Secretary of the In-

409

Plains, West and Northwest Plateau Indian Treaties

terior shall prescribe, unless such as may be duly licensed to trade with said bands, or employed for their benefit, or members of the family of such persons, shall be permitted to reside or make any settlement upon any part of said reservation; and the timbered land allotted to individuals, and also that reserved for subsequent distribution as provided in the first article of this agreement, shall be free from all trespass, use, or occupation, except as hereinafter provided.

ARTICLE 5. The United States shall have the right to establish and maintain upon said reservation such military posts, agencies, schools, mills, shops, roads, and agricultural or mechanical improvements, as may be deemed necessary, but no greater quantity of land or timber shall be taken and used for said purposes than shall be actually requisite therefor. And if in the establishment or maintenance of such posts, agencies, roads or other improvements, the timber or other property of any individual Indian shall be taken, injured, or destroyed, just and adequate compensation shall be made therefor by the United States. Roads or highways authorized by competent authority other than the United States, the lines of which shall lie through said reservation, shall have the right of way through the same, upon the fair and just value of such right being paid to the said Mendawakanton and Wapakoota bands by the party or parties authorizing or interested in the same, to be assessed and determined in such manner as the Secretary of the Interior shall direct.

ARTICLE 6. The Mendawakanton and Wahpakoota bands of Dakota or Sioux Indians acknowledge their dependence on the Government of the United States, and do hereby pledge and bind themselves to preserve friendly relations with the citizens thereof, and to commit no injuries or depredations on their persons or property, nor on those of the members of any other tribe; but in case of any such injury or depredation, full compensation shall, as far as practicable be made therefor out of their moneys in the hands of the United States; the amount in all cases to be determined by the Secretary of the Interior. They further pledge themselves not to engage in hostilities with the Indians of any other tribe unless in self-defence, but to submit, through their agent, all matters of dispute and difficulty between themselves and other Indians, for the decision of the President of the United States, and to acquiesce in and abide thereby. They also agree to deliver to the proper officers all persons belonging to their said bands who may become offenders against the treaties, laws, or regulations of the United States, or the laws of the State of Minnesota, and to assist in discovering, pursuing, and capturing all such offenders whenever required so to do by such officers, through the agent or other proper officer of the Indian Department.

ARTICLE 7. To aid in preventing the evils of intemperance, it is hereby stipulated that if any of the members of the said Mendawakanton and Wahpakoota bands of Sioux Indians shall drink, or procure for others, intoxicating liquors, their proportion of the annuities of said bands shall, at the discretion of

Plains, West and Northwest Plateau Indian Treaties

the Secretary of the Interior, be withheld from them for the period of at least one year; and for a violation of any of the stipulations of this agreement on the part of any members of said bands, the persons so offending shall be liable to have their annuities withheld and to be subject to such other punishment as the Secretary of the Interior may prescribe.

ARTICLE 8. Such of the stipulations of former treaties as provided for the payment of particular sums of money to the said Mendawakanton and Wahpakoota bands, or for the application or expenditure of specific amounts for particular objects or purposes, shall be, and hereby are, so amended and changed as to invest the Secretary of the Interior with discretionary power in regard to the manner and objects of the annual expenditure of all such sums or amounts which have accrued and are now due to said bands, together with the amount the said bands shall become annually entitled to under and by virtue of the provisions of this agreement: Provided, The said sums or amounts shall be expended for the benefit of said bands at such time or times and in such manner as the said Secretary shall deem best calculated to promote their interests, welfare, and advance in civilization. And it is further agreed, that such change may be made in the stipulations of former treaties which provide for the payment of particular sums for specified purposes, as to permit the chiefs and braves of said bands or any of the subdivisions of said bands, with the sanction of the Secretary of the Interior, to authorize such payment or expenditures of their annuities, or any portion thereof, which are to become due hereafter, as may be deemed best for the general interests and welfare of the said bands or subdivisions thereof.

ARTICLE 9. As the Senate struck front the treaty with the Mendawakanton band of Sioux on the twenty-ninth day of September, one thousand eight hundred and thirty-seven, the ninth clause of the second article and the whole of the third article of said treaty, which provided for the payment of four hundred and fifty (450) dollars annually, for twenty years, to Scott Campbell, and confirmed to the said Scott Campbell a title to five hundred (500) acres of land which he then occupied, said payment and land, being deemed by said Indians to form a part of the consideration for which they ceded to the United States a certain tract of land in said treaty specified, which reduction, in the consideration for said land, has never been sanctioned by said Indians, the said Mendawakantons and Wahpakoota bands now request that provision be made for the payment of the sum of ten thousand (10,000) dollars to A. J. Campbell, the son of said Scott Campbell, now deceased, in full consideration of the money stipulated to be paid and land confirmed to said Scott Campbell in the original draft of said treaty aforesaid; which subject is hereby submitted to the Senate for its favorable consideration.

ARTICLE 10. The expenses attending the negotiation of this agreement shall be defrayed by the United States.

Plains, West and Northwest Plateau Indian Treaties

In testimony whereof, the said Charles E. Mix, Commissioner, as aforesaid, and the undersigned chiefs and headmen of the said Mendawakanton and Wahpakoota bands, have hereunto set their hands and seals at the place and on the day first above written.

Charles E. Mix, Commissioner,
Wa-bash-aw, his x mark, Che-tan-a-koo-a-mo-nee, (Little Crow) his x mark, Wa-su-hi-ya-hi-dan, his x mark, Sha-ko-pee, (Six) his x mark, Wa-min-dee-ton-kee, (Large War Eagle) his x mark, Muz-za-o-jan-jan, (Iron Light)his x mark, Ma-kaw-to, (Blue Earth) his x mark, Hu-shaw-shaw, (Red Legs) his x mark, Hin-han-du-ta, (Scarlet Owl) his x mark, Ha-raka-muz-za, (Iron Elk) his x mark, Wu-ka-no-jan-jan,(Medicine Light) his x mark,

Signed, sealed and delivered in presence of
Joseph R. Brown, Sioux agent, James R. Roche, A. J. Campbell, interpreter.

(Note. By the first section of the act of February 16, 1863, 12th Statutes at Large, page 652, it is provided as follows: That all treaties heretofore made and entered into by the Sisseton, Wahpaton, Medawakanton, and Wahpakoota bands of Sioux or Dakota Indians, or any of them, with the United States, are hereby declared to be abrogated and annulled, so far as said treaties or any of them purport to impose any future obligation on the United States, and all lands and rights of occupancy within the State of Minnesota, and all annuities and claims heretofore accorded to said Indians, or any of them, to be forfeited to the United States.)

TREATY WITH THE SIOUX {1858, June 19}
Ratified Mar. 9, 1859.
Proclaimed Mar. 31. 1859.

Articles of agreement and convention made and concluded at the city of Washington on the nineteenth day of June, one thousand eight hundred and fifty-eight, by Charles E. Mix, commissioner on the part of the United States, and the following-named chiefs and head-men of the Sisseeton and Wahpaton bands of the Dakota or Sioux tribe of Indians, viz: Maz-zah-shaw, Wamdupi-dutah, Ojupi, and Hahutanai, on the part of the Sisseetons, and Maz-zomanee, Muz-zakoote-manee, Upiyahideyaw, Umpedutokechaw, and Tachandupaho-tanka, on the part of the Wahpatons, they being duly authorized and empowered to act for said bands.

ARTICLE 1. It is hereby agreed and stipulated that as soon as practicable after the ratification of this agreement, so much of that part of the reservation or tract of land now held and possessed by the Sisseeton and Wahpaton bands of the

412

Plains, West and Northwest Plateau Indian Treaties

Dakota or Sioux Indians, and which is described in the third article of the treaty made with them on the twenty-third day of July, one thousand eight hundred and fifty-one, which lies south or south westwardly of the Minnesota River, shall constitute a reservation for said bands, and shall be surveyed, and eighty acres thereof, as near as may be in conformity with the public surveys, be allotted in severalty to each head of a family or single person over the age of twenty-one years, in said bands of Indians; said allotments to be so made as to include a proper proportion of timbered land, if the same be practicable, in each of said allotments.

The residue of said part of said reservation not so allotted shall be held by said bands in common, and as other Indian lands are held: Provided, however, That eighty acres thereof, as near as may be, shall in like manner, as above provided for, be allotted to each of the minors of said bands on his or her attaining their majority, or on becoming heads of families, by contracting marriage, if neither of the parties shall have previously received land. All the necessary expenses of the surveys and allotments thus provided for shall be defrayed out of the funds of said bands of Indians in the hands of the Government of the United States.

As the members of said bands become capable of managing their business and affairs, the President of the United States may at his discretion, cause patents to be issued to them for the tracts of lands allotted to them respectively, in conformity with this article; said tracts to be exempt from levy, taxation, sale, or forfeiture, until otherwise provided for by the legislature of the State in which they are situated, with the assent of Congress; nor shall they be sold or alienated in fee, or be in any other manner disposed of, except to the United States or to members of said bands.

ARTICLE 2. Whereas, by the treaty with the Sisseeton and Wahpaton bands of Sioux Indians, concluded at Traverse des Sioux on the twenty-third day of July, one thousand eight hundred and fifty-one, said bands retained for their "future occupancy and home," "to be held by them as Indian lands are held, all that tract of country on the Minnesota River, from the western boundary" of the cession therein made "east to the Tcha-tam-ba river on the north, and to the Yellow Medicine River on the south side, to extend on each side a distance of not less than ten miles from the general course of said Minnesota River,"

And whereas the Senate of the United States so amended said treaty as to strike therefrom the provision setting apart the said land as a home for said bands, and made provision for the payment to said bands, "at the rate of ten cents per acre for the land included in the said tract so retained and set apart for the occupancy and home" of said bands, and also provided, in addition thereto, that there should be "set apart by appropriate landmarks and boundaries such tracts of country without the limits of the cession made by the first article of the said treaty as shall be satisfactory for their future occupancy and home;" said Senate

413

Plains, West and Northwest Plateau Indian Treaties

amendment providing also "that the President may, with the consent of these Indians, vary the conditions aforesaid, if deemed expedient;" all of which provisions in said amendment were assented to by said Indians;

And whereas the President so far varied the conditions of said Senate amendment as to permit said bands to locate for the time being upon the tract originally reserved by said bands for a home, and 'no tract of country, without the limits of the cession" made in the said treaty, has ever been provided for or offered to said bands;

And whereas, by the act making appropriations for the current and contingent expenses of the Indian Department, and for fulfilling treaty stipulations with various Indian tribes, approved July 31., 1854, the President was authorized "to confirm to the Sioux of Minnesota, forever, the reserve on the Minnesota River now occupied by them, upon such conditions as he may deem just;"

And whereas, although the President has not directly confirmed said reserve to said Indians, they claim that, as they were entitled to receive "such tracts of country" as should "be satisfactory for their future occupancy and home," and as no other country than this reservation was ever provided for or offered to them, and as valuable improvements have been made on said reservation with the moneys belonging to said bands, it is agreed and stipulated that the question shall be submitted to the Senate for decision whether they have such title, and if they have, what compensation shall be made to them for that part of said reservation or tract of land lying on the north side of the Minnesota River; whether they shall be allowed a specific sum of money therefor, and if so, how much; or whether the same shall be sold for their benefit, they to receive the proceeds of such sale, deducting the necessary expenses incident thereto. Such sale, if decided in favor of by the Senate, shall be made under and according to regulations to be prescribed by the Secretary of the Interior, and in such manner as will secure to them the largest sum it may be practicable to obtain for said land.

ARTICLE 3. It is also agreed that if the Senate shall authorize the land designated in article two of this agreement to be sold for the benefit of the said Sisseeton and Wahpaton bands, or shall prescribe an amount to be paid to said bands for their interest in said tract, provision shall be made by which the chiefs and head-men of said bands may, in their discretion, in open council, authorize to be paid out of the proceeds of said tract such sum or sums as may be found necessary and proper, not exceeding seventy thousand dollars, to satisfy their just debts and obligations, and to provide goods to be taken by said chiefs and headmen to the said bands on their return: Provided, however, That their said determinations shall be approved by the superintendent of Indian affairs for the northern superintendency for the time being, and the said payments be authorized by the Secretary of the Interior.

414

Plains, West and Northwest Plateau Indian Treaties

ARTICLE 4. The lands retained and to be held by the members of the Sisseeton and Wahpaton bands of Dakota or Sioux Indians, under and by virtue of the first article of this agreement, shall, to all intents and purposes whatever be deemed and held to be an Indian reservation, and the laws which have been or may hereafter be enacted by Congress to regulate trade and intercourse with the Indian tribes, shall have full force and effect over and within the limits of the same; and no person other than the members of said bands, to be ascertained and defined under such regulations as the Secretary of the Interior shall prescribeunless such as may be duly licensed to trade with said bands, or employed for their benefit, or members of the family of such personsshall be permitted to reside or make any settlement upon any part of said reservation; and the timbered land allotted to individuals, and also that reserved for subsequent distribution, as provided in the first article of this agreement, shall be free from all trespass, use or occupation, except as hereinafter provided.

ARTICLE 5. The United States shall have the right to establish and maintain upon said reservation such military posts, agencies, schools, mills, shops, roads, and agricultural or mechanical improvements as may be deemed necessary; but no greater quantity of land or timber shall be taken and used for said purposes than shall be actually requisite therefor. And if in the establishment or maintenance of such posts, agencies, roads, or other improvements, the timber or other property of any individual Indian shall be taken, injured, or destroyed, just and adequate compensation shall be made therefor by the United States. Roads or highways authorized by competent authority other than the United States, the lines of which shall lie through said reservation, shall have the right of way through the same upon the fair and just value of such right being paid to the said Sisseeton and Wahpeton bands by the party or parties authorizing or interested in the same, to be assessed and determined in such manner as the Secretary of the Interior shall direct.

ARTICLE 6. The Sisseeton and Wahpeton bands of Dakota or Sioux Indians acknowledge their dependence on the Government of the United States, and do hereby pledge and bind themselves to preserve friendly relations with the citizens thereof, and to commit no injuries or depredations on their persons or property, nor on those of the members of any other tribe; but in case of any such injury or depredation, full compensation shall, as far as practicable, be made therefor out of their moneys in the hands of the United States, the amount in all cases to be determined by the Secretary of the Interior.

They further pledge themselves not to engage in hostilities with the Indians of any other tribe, unless in self-defence, but to submit, through their agent, all matters of dispute and difficulty between themselves and other Indians for the decision of the President of the United States, and to acquiesce in and abide thereby. They also agree to deliver to the proper officers all persons belonging to their said bands who may become offenders against the treaties, laws, or

Plains, West and Northwest Plateau Indian Treaties

regulations of the United States, or the laws of the State of Minnesota, and to assist in discovering, pursuing, and capturing all such offenders whenever required so to do by such officers, through the agent or other proper officer of the Indian Department.

ARTICLE 7. To aid in preventing the evils of intemperance, it is hereby stipulated that if any of the members of the said Sisseeton and Wahpaton bands of Sioux Indians shall drink or procure for others intoxicating liquors, their proportion of the annuities of said bands shall, at the discretion of the Secretary of the Interior, be withheld from them for the period of at least one year; and for a violation of any of the stipulations of this agreement on the part of any member of said bands, the persons so offending shall be liable to have their annuities withheld, and to be subject to such other punishment as the Secretary of the Interior may prescribe.

ARTICLE 8. Any members of said Sisseeton and Wahpaton bands who may be desirous of dissolving their tribal connection and obligations, and of locating beyond the limits of the reservation provided for said bands, shall have the privilege of so doing, by notifying the United States agent of such intention, and making an actual settlement beyond the limits of said reservation; shall be vested with all the rights, privileges, and immunities, and be subject to all the laws, obligations, and duties, of citizens of the United States; but such procedure shall work no forfeiture on their part of the right to share in the annuities of said bands.

ARTICLE 9. Such Of the stipulations of the former treaties as provide for the payment of particular sums of money to the said Sisseeton and Wahpaton bands, or for the application or expenditure of specific amounts for particular objects or purposes, shall be, and hereby are, so amended and changed as to invest the Secretary of the interior with discretionary power in regard to the manner and objects of the annual expenditure of all such sums or amounts which have accrued and are now due to said bands, together with the amount the said bands shall become annually entitled to under and by virtue of the provisions of this agreement: Provided, The said sums or amounts shall be expended for the benefit of said bands at such time or times and in such manner as the said Secretary shall deem best calculated to promote their interests, welfare, and advance in civilization

And if is further agreed that such change may be made in the stipulations of former treaties, which provide for the payment of particular sums for specified purposes, as to permit the chiefs and braves of said bands, or any of the subdivisions of said bands, with the sanction of the Secretary of the Interior, to authorize such payment or expenditure of their annuities, or any portion thereof, which are to become due hereafter, as may be deemed best for the general interests and welfare of the said bands or subdivisions thereof.

Plains, West and Northwest Plateau Indian Treaties

ARTICLE 10. The expenses attending the negotiation of this agreement shall be defrayed by the United States.

In testimony whereof, the said Charles E. Mix, Commissioner, as aforesaid, and the undersigned chiefs and headmen of the said Sisseeton and Wahpaton bands, have hereunto set their hands and seals at the place and on the day first above written.

Charles E. Mix, Commissioner.

Muz-zah-shaw, (Red Iron) his x mark, Wam-du-pi-du-tah, (War Eagle's Scarlet Tail) his x mark, Ojupi, (The Planter) his x mark, Ha-hu-ta-nai, (The Stumpy Horn) his x mark, Maz-zo-ma-nee, (Walking Iron) his x mark, Maz-za-koote-manee, (Shoots Iron as he Walks) his x mark, Upi-ya-hi-de-yaw, (Chief of Lac qui Parle) his x mark, Umpe-du-to-ke-chaw, (Other Day) his x mark, Ta-chan-du-pa-ho-tan-ka, (His Pipe with Strong Voice) his x mark.

Signed, sealed and delivered in presence of
Joseph R. Brown, Sioux agent, A. J. Campbell, interpreter, A. Robertson.

RESOLUTION OF THE SENATE OF THE UNITED STATES.
June 27, 1860.
12 Stat., 1042.

Right and title of certain bands of Sioux Indians, to the lands embraced in reservation on the Minnesota River.

IN THE SENATE OF THE UNITED STATES, June 27th, 1860. Whereas by the second articles of the treaties of June 19, 1858, with the Med-a-wa-kanton and Wah-pa-koo-ta, and the Sisseeton and Wah-pa-ton bands of the Dacotah or Sioux Indians, it is submitted to the Senate to decide as to the right or title of said bands of Indians to the lands embraced in the reservation occupied-by them on the Minnesota River, in the State of Minnesota, and what compensation shall be made to them for those portions of said reservation lying on the north side of that river, which they agreed by said treaties to surrender and relinquish to the United States; "whether they shall be allowed a specified sum in money therefor, and if so, how much, or whether the same shall be sold for their benefit, they to receive the proceeds of such sale, deducting the necessary expenses incident thereto;" and whereas said Indians were permitted to retain and occupy said reservations in lieu of other lands which they were entitled to under the amendments of the Senate to the treaties made with them in the year 1851, and large amounts of the money of said Indians have been expended by the government in improvements and otherwise upon the lands contained in

417

Plains, West and Northwest Plateau Indian Treaties

said reservations; and whereas by act of Congress of July 31, 1854, said reservations were authorized to be confirmed to those Indians:

Resolved, That said Indians possessed a just and valid right and title to said reservations, and that they be allowed the sum of thirty cents per acre for the lands contained in that portion thereof lying on the north side of the Minnesota River, exclusive of the cost of survey and sale, or any contingent expense that may accrue whatever, which by the treaties of June, 1858, they have relinquished and given up to the United States, Resolved, further, That all persons who have in good faith settled and made improvements upon any of the lands contained in said reservations, believing the same to be government lands, shall have the right of preemption to one hundred and sixty acres thereof, to include their improvements, on paying the sum of one dollar and twenty-five cents per acre therefor: Provided, That when such settlements have been made on the lands of the Indians on the south side of the Minnesota River, the assent of the Indians shall first be obtained, in such a manner as the Secretary of the Interior shall prescribe, and that the amount which shall be so paid for their lands, shall be paid into the treasury of the United States.

TREATY WITH THE WINNEBAGO {1859, Apr. 15}
Ratified Mar. 16, 1861.
Proclaimed Mar. 23, 1861.

Articles of agreement and convention made and concluded at Washington City on the fifteenth day of April, eighteen hundred and fifty-nine, by and between Charles E. Mix, commissioner on the part of the United States, and the following-named chiefs and delegates, representing the Winnebago tribes of Indians, viz: Baptiste Lassalleur, Little Hill, Little De-Corie, Prophet, Wakon, Cono-hutta-kau, Big Bear, Rogue, Young Frenchman, One Horn, Yellow Banks, and O-o-kau, they being thereto duly authorized by said tribe.

ARTICLE 1. The Winnebago Indians having now more lands than are necessary for their occupancy and use, and being desirous of promoting settled habits of industry and enterprise amongst, themselves by abolishing the tenure in common by which they now hold their lands, and by assigning limited quantities thereof, in severalty, to the members of the tribe, including their half or mixed blood relatives now residing with them, to be cultivated and improved for their own individual use and benefit, it is hereby agreed and stipulated that the eastern portion of their present reservation, embracing townships one hundred and six, (106) and one hundred and seven, (107) range twenty-four (24) and one hundred and six (106) and one hundred and seven, (107) range twenty-five (25)and the two strips of land immediately adjoining them on the east and north, shall be set apart and retained by them for said purposes; and that out of the same there shall be assigned to each head of a family not exceeding eighty

418

Plains, West and Northwest Plateau Indian Treaties

acres, and to each male person eighteen years of age and upwards, without family, not exceeding forty acres of land, to include, in every case, as far as practicable, a reasonable proportion of timber; one hundred and sixty acres of said retained lands in a suitable locality shall also be set apart and appropriated to the occupancy and use of the agency for said Indians.

The lands to be so assigned, including those for the use of the agency, shall be in as regular and compact a body as possible, and so as to admit of a distinct and well-defined exterior boundary, embracing the whole of them and any intermediate portions or parcels of land or water not included in or made part of the tracts assigned in severalty. Any such intermediate parcels of land and water shall be owned by the Winnebagoes in common; but in case of increase in the tribe, or other cause, rendering it necessary or expedient, the said intermediate parcels of land shall be subject to distribution and assignment, in severalty, in such manner as the Secretary of the Interior shall prescribe and direct.

The whole of the lands assigned or unassigned in severalty, embraced within the said exterior boundary, shall constitute and be known as the Winnebago reservation, within and over which all laws passed or which may be passed by Congress regulating trade and intercourse with the Indian tribes shall have full force and effect. And no white person, except such as shall be in the employment of the United States, shall be allowed to reside or go upon any portion of said reservation, without the written permission of the superintendent of Indian affairs, or of the agent for the tribe. Said division and assignment of lands to the Winnebagoes in severalty shall be made under the direction of the Secretary of the Interior, and when approved by him shall be final and conclusive. Certificates shall be issued by the Commissioner of Indian Affairs for the tracts so assigned, specifying the names of the individuals to whom they have been assigned, respectively, and that they are for the exclusive use and benefit of themselves, their heirs, and descendants.

And said tracts shall not be alienated in fee, leased, or otherwise disposed of, except to the United States, or to other members of the tribe, under such rules and regulations as may be prescribed by the Secretary of the Interior; and they shall be exempt from taxation, levy, sale, or forfeiture until otherwise provided for by Congress Prior to the issue of said certificates, the Secretary of the Interior shall make such rules and regulations as he may deem necessary and expedient respecting the disposition of any of said tracts, in case of the death of the person, or persons to whom they may be assigned, so that the same shall be secured to the families of such deceased persons; and should any of the Indians to whom tracts shall be assigned abandon them, the said Secretary may take such action in relation to the proper disposition thereof as in his judgment may be necessary and proper.

Plains, West and Northwest Plateau Indian Treaties

ARTICLE 2. For the purpose of procuring the means of comfortably establishing the Winnebagoes upon the lands to be assigned to then, in severalty, by building them houses, and by furnishing them with agricultural implements, stock-animals, and other necessary aid and facilities for commencing agricultural pursuits under favorable circumstances, the lands embraced in that portion of their reservation not stipulated to be retained and divided, as aforesaid, shall be sold, under the direction of the Secretary of the Interior, in parcels not exceeding one hundred and sixty acres each, to the highest bidder, for cash; the sales to be made upon sealed proposals to be duly invited by public advertisement.

And should any of the tracts so to be sold have upon them improvements of any kind which were made by or for the Indians, or for Government purposes, the proposals therefor must state the price for both the land and improvements. And if, after assigning to all the members of the tribe entitled thereto their proportions of land in severalty, there shall remain a surplus of that portion of the reservation retained for that purpose, outside of the exterior boundary-line of the lands assigned in severalty, the Secretary of the Interior shall be authorized and empowered, whenever he shall think proper, to cause such surplus to be sold in the same manner as the other lands to be so disposed of, and the proceeds thereof to be paid over to the Winnebagoes, or used and applied for their benefit in such manner as he shall deem to be best for them.

ARTICLE 3. The Winnebagoes being anxious to relieve themselves from the burden of their present liabilities, and it being essential to their welfare and best interests that they shall be enabled to commence their new mode of life and pursuits free from the annoyance and embarrassment thereof, or which may be occasioned thereby, it is agreed that the same shall be liquidated and paid out of the fund arising from the sale of their surplus lands, so far as found valid and just on an examination thereof, to be made by their agent and the superintendent of Indian affairs for the northern superintendency, subject to revision and confirmation by the Secretary of the Interior.

ARTICLE 4. Should the proceeds of the surplus lands of the Winnebagoes not prove to be sufficient to carry out the purposes and stipulations of this agreement, and some further aid be, from time to time, requisite, to enable said Indians to sustain themselves successfully in agricultural and other industrial pursuits, such additional means as may be necessary therefor shall be taken from the moneys due and belonging to them under the provisions of former treaties; and so much thereof as may be required to furnish them further aid, as aforesaid, shall be applied in such manner, under the direction of the Secretary of the Interior, as he shall consider best calculated to promote and advance their improvement and welfare; and, in order to render unnecessary any further treaty engagements or arrangements hereafter with the United States, it is hereby agreed and stipulated that the President, with the assent of Congress, shall have

Plains, West and Northwest Plateau Indian Treaties

full power to modify or change any of the provisions of former treaties with the Winnebagoes in such manner and to whatever extent he may judge to be necessary and expedient for their welfare and best interest.

ARTICLE 5. The Winnebagoes, parties to this agreement, are anxious that all the members of their tribe shall participate in the advantages herein provided for respecting their permanent settlement and their improvement and civilization, and to that end, to induce all that are now separated from, to rejoin and unite with them. It is therefore agreed that, as soon as practicable, the Commissioner of Indian Affairs shall cause the necessary proceeding to be adopted to have them notified of this agreement and its advantages, and to induce them to come in and unite with their brethren; and, to enable them to do so and to sustain themselves for a reasonable time thereafter, such assistance shall be provided for them, at the expense of the tribe, as may be actually necessary for those purposes: Provided, however, That those who do not rejoin and permanently re-unite themselves with the tribe within one year from the date of the ratification of this agreement shall not be entitled to the benefit of any of its stipulations.

ARTICLE 6. All the expenses connected with, and incident to, the making of this agreement, and the carrying out of its provisions, shall be defrayed out of the funds of the Winnebagoes.

In testimony whereof, the said Charles E. Mix, commissioner as aforesaid, and the said chiefs and delegates of the Winnebago tribe of Indians, have hereunto set their hands and seals at the place and on the day and year hereinbefore written.

Charles E. Mix, Commissioner, Baptiste Lassalleur, his x mark,
Little Hill, his x mark, Little De-Corrie, his x mark, Prophet, (being sick, by his representative, Big Bear) his x mark, Wakon, his x mark. Cono-hutta-kau, his x mark, Big Bear, his x mark, Rogue, his x mark, Young Frenchman, his x mark, One Horn, his x mark, Yellow Banks, his x mark, O-o-kau, his x mark,

In presence of
W. J. Cullen, superintendent Indian affairs, Charles H. Mix, United States Indian agent for the, Winnebagoes, Peter Manaize, United States interpreter, John Dowling.

Plains, West and Northwest Plateau Indian Treaties

TREATY WITH THE SAUK AND FOXES {1859, Oct. 1}
Ratified, June 27, 1860.
Proclaimed, July 9, 1860.

Articles of agreement and convention made and concluded at the Sac and Fox agency, in the Territory of Kansas, on the first day of October, in the year of our Lord one thousand eight hundred and fifty-nine, by and between Alfred B. Greenwood, commissioner the part of the United States, and the following-named chiefs and delegates, representing the confederated tribes of Sacs and Foxes of the Mississippi, viz: Ke-o-kuk, Mack-a-sah-pee, Sha-bah-caw-kah, Mat-tah-tah, My-ah-pit, Kaw-ah-kee Kah-sha-moh-mee, Maw-mee-won-e-kah, and Che-ko-skuk, they being thereto duly authorized by said confederated tribe.

ARTICLE 1. The Sacs and Foxes of the Mississippi having now more lands than are necessary for their occupancy and use, and being desirous of promoting settled habits of industry and enterprise amongst themselves by abolishing the tenure in common by which they now hold their lands, and by assigning limited quantities thereof, in severalty, to the individual members of the tribe, to be cultivated and improved for their individual use and benefit, it is hereby agreed and stipulated that the portion of their present reservation contained within the following boundaries, that is to say: beginning at a point on the northern boundary-line of their reservation, six miles west of the northeastern corner of the same; running thence due south, to the southern boundary of the same, twenty miles; thence west, and along said southern boundary, twelve miles; thence due north, to the northern boundary of said reservation, twenty miles; and thence east, along said boundary-line, twelve miles, to the place of beginningestimated to contain about one hundred and fifty-three thousand and six hundred acres shall be set apart and retained by them for the purposes aforesaid.

ARTICLE 2. Out of the lands so set apart and retained there shall be assigned to each member of said confederated tribe, without distinction of age or sex, a tract of eighty acres, to include, in every case, as far as practicable, a reasonable portion of timber. One hundred and sixty acres of said retained lands shall also be set apart and appropriated to the use and occupancy of the agent for the time being of said confederated tribe; and one hundred and sixty acres shall also be reserved for the establishment and support of a school for the education of the youth of the tribe. The location of the tracts, the assign-meet of which is provided for in this article, shall be made in as regular and compact a manner as possible, and so as to admit of a distinct and well-defined exterior boundary, embracing the whole of them and any intermediate portions or parcels of land or water not included in or made part of the tracts assigned in severalty.

All such intermediate parcels of land and water shall be owned by the Sacs and Foxes of the Mississippi in common; but, in case of increase in the tribe, or

Plains, West and Northwest Plateau Indian Treaties

other cause, rendering it necessary or expedient, the said intermediate parcels of land shall be subject to distribution and assignment in such manner as the Secretary of the Interior may prescribe and direct. The whole of the lands, assigned or unassigned, embraced within said exterior boundary, shall constitute and be known as the reservation of the Sacs and Foxes of the Mississippi; and all laws which have been, or may be, passed by the Congress of the United States regulating trade and intercourse with Indian tribes shall have full force and effect over the same, and no white person, except such as shall be in the employment of the United States, shall be allowed to reside or go upon any portion of said reservation, without the written permission of the superintendent of the central superintendency, or of the agent of the tribe.

ARTICLE 3. The division and assignment in severalty among the Sacs and Foxes of the Mississippi of the land hereinbefore reserved for that purpose shall be made under the direction of the Secretary of the Interior, and his decision of all questions arising thereupon shall be final and conclusive. Certificates shall be issued by the Commissioner of Indian Affairs for the tracts assigned in severalty, specifying the names of the individuals to whom they have been assigned, respectively, and that the said tracts are set apart for the exclusive use and benefit of the assignees and their heirs.

And said tracts shall not be alienated in fee, leased, or otherwise disposed of, except to the United States, or to members of the Sac and Fox tribe, and under such rules and regulations as may be prescribed by the Secretary of the Interior. And said tracts shall be exempt from taxation, levy, sale, or forfeiture, until otherwise provided by Congress. Prior to the issue of the certificates aforesaid, the Secretary of the interior shall make such rules and regulations as he may deem necessary or expedient respecting the disposition of any of said tracts, in case of the death of the person or persons to whom they may be assigned, so that the same shall be secured to the families of such deceased persons; and should any of the Indians to whom tracts shall be assigned abandon them, the said Secretary may take such action in relation to the proper disposition thereof as, in his judgment, may be necessary and proper.

ARTICLE 4. For the purpose of establishing the Sacs and Foxes of the Mississippi comfortably upon the lands to be assigned to them in severalty, by building them houses, and by furnishing them with agricultural implements, stock-animals, and other necessary aid and facilities for commencing agricultural pursuits under favorable circumstances, the lands embraced in that portion of their present reservation, not stipulated to be retained and divided as aforesaid, shall be sold, under the direction of the Secretary of the Interior, in parcels not exceeding one hundred and sixty acres each, to the highest bidder, for cash; the sale to be made upon sealed proposals, to be duly invited by public advertisement, and the proceeds thereof to be expended, for the purposes hereinbefore recited, in such manner as the Secretary of the Interior may think proper. And

423

Plains, West and Northwest Plateau Indian Treaties

should any of the tracts so to be sold have upon them improvements of any kind which were made by or for the Indians, or for Government purposes, the proposals therefor must state the price for both the land and the improvements.

And if, after assigning to all the members of the tribe entitled thereto their proportion of land in severalty, there shall remain a surplus of that portion of the reservation retained for that purpose, outside of the exterior boundaries of the lands assigned in severalty, the Secretary of the Interior shall be authorized and empowered, whenever he shall think proper, to cause such surplus to be sold in the same manner as the other lands to be so disposed of, and to apply the proceeds of such sale to the purposes and in the mode hereinbefore provided with respect to that portion of their present reservation not retained for distribution.

ARTICLE 5. The Sacs and Foxes of the Mississippi being anxious to relieve themselves from the burden of their present liabilities, and it being essential to their best interests that they should be allowed to commence their new mode of life, free from the embarrassments of debt, it is stipulated and agreed that debts which may be due and owing at the date of the signing and execution hereof, either by the said confederated tribes of Sacs and Foxes, or by individual members thereof, shall be liquidated, and paid out of the fund arising from the sale of their surplus lands, so far as the same shall be found to be just and valid on an examination thereof, to be made by their agent and the superintendent of Indian affairs for the central superintendency, subject to revision and correction by the Secretary of the Interior.

ARTICLE 6. Should the proceeds of the surplus lands aforesaid prove insufficient to carry out, the purposes and stipulations of this agreement, and further aid be, from time to time, requisite to enable the Sacs and Foxes of the Mississippi to sustain themselves successfully in agricultural or other industrial pursuits, such additional means as may be necessary therefor shall be taken from the ,honeys due and belonging to them under the provisions of former treaties; and so much of said moneys as may be required to furnish them further aid as aforesaid shall be applied in such manner, under the direction of the Secretary of the Interior, as he shall consider best calculated to improve and promote their welfare. And, in order to render unnecessary any further treaty engagements or arrangements hereafter with the United States, it is hereby agreed and stipulated that the President, with the assent of Congress, shall have full power to modify or change any of the provisions of former treaties with the Sacs and Foxes of the Mississippi in such manner and to whatever extent he may judge to be necessary and expedient for limit welfare and best interests.

ARTICLE 7. The Sacs and Foxes of the Mississippi, parties to this agreement, are anxious that all the members of their tribe shall participate in the advantages herein provided for respecting their improvement and civilization, and to that end to induce all that are now separated to rejoin and reunite with them. It

Plains, West and Northwest Plateau Indian Treaties

is therefore agreed that, as soon as practicable, the Commissioner of Indian Affairs shall cause the necessary proceedings to be adopted to have them notified of this agreement audits advantages, and to induce them to come in and unite with their brethren; and to enable them to do so, and to sustain themselves for a reasonable time thereafter, such assistance shall be provided for them at the expense of the tribe as may be actually necessary for that purpose: Provided, however, That those who do not rejoin and permanently re-unite themselves with the tribe within one year from the date of the ratification of this treaty shall not be entitled to the benefit of any of its stipulations.

ARTICLE 8. All the expenses connected with and incident to the making of this agreement, and the carrying out of its provisions, shall be defrayed out of the funds of the Sacs and Foxes of the Mississippi.

ARTICLE 9. It is agreed that all roads and highways laid out by authority of law shall have right of way through the lands within the reservation hereinbefore specified, on the same terms as are provided by law when roads and highways are made through lands of citizens of the United States; and railroad companies, when the lines pass through the lands of said Indians, shall have right of way on the payment of a just compensation therefor in money.

ARTICLE 10. The Sacs and Foxes of the Mississippi being anxious to make some suitable provision for their mixed and half bloods, and such of their women (whole-bloods)who have intermarried with white men, it is agreed that there shall be assigned to the mixed and half bloods of their tribe, and to such whole-blood females as have intermarried with white men, at the date of this agreement, three hundred and twenty acres each; the location and allotments of said lands to be made out of that portion relinquished by this treaty to the United States in trust, provided the mixed or half bloods, and such females of their tribes as have intermarried with white men, desire to do so.

The allotments to such of the mixed or half bloods as may be minors to be made by the agent of the tribe, subject to the confirmation and approval of the Secretary of the Interior; and in allotting lands to those provided for in this article, said allotments shall be made so as to include their improvements, (if any) provided it can be done, and at the same time make said allotments conform to the public surveys. And it is further agreed between the parties to this agreement, that Thomas Connelly, a half-breed, and a member of the tribe who has been uniformly kind to his people, shall be permitted to so locate his three hundred and twenty acres as to include Randal's dwelling and trading-house, if it can be done so as to harmonize with the public surveys; and provided the said Connelly shall pay to the owner of said improvements a fair valuation therefor. The lands granted by this article shall remain inalienable except to the United States or members of the tribe, nor shall the mixed or half bloods, or such fe-

Plains, West and Northwest Plateau Indian Treaties

males as have intermarried with white men, participate in the proceeds of the lands herein ceded.

ARTICLE 11. The United States also agree to cause to be paid to the tribe any funds that may have heretofore been withheld under the provisions of the fifth article of the treaty of one thousand eight hundred and forty-two, the same to be expended for their benefit, or paid in money, as the Secretary may direct.

ARTICLE 12. This instrument shall be obligatory on the contracting parties whenever the same shall be ratified by the President and the Senate of the United States.

In testimony whereof, the said Alfred B. Greenwood, commissioner as aforesaid, and the said chiefs and delegates of the Sacs and Foxes of the Mississippi, have hereunto set their hands and seals at the place and on the day and year hereinbefore written.

Alfred B. Greenwood.

Sacs:
Ke-o-kuk, his x mark, Mack-ah-sah-pee, his x mark, Shaw-pah-caw, his x mark, Mat-tab-tah, his x mark, My-ah-pit, his x mark, Kaw-ah-kee, his x mark, Foxes:
Ka-sha-mah-me, his x mark, Maw-me-wone-cah, his x mark, Che-co-skuk, his x mark,

In presence of
Perrey Fuller, United States agent, Thos. J. Connolly, United States interpreter, G. Bailey, secretary to commissioner.

TREATY WITH THE KANSA TRIBE {1859, Oct. 5}
Ratified June 27, 1860.
Proclaimed Nov. 17, 1860.

Articles of agreement and convention made and concluded at the Kansas agency, in the Territory of Kansas, on the fifth day of October, eighteen hundred and fifty-nine, by and between Alfred B. Greenwood, commissioner, on the part of the United States, and the following-named chiefs and headmen representing the Kansas tribe of Indians, to wit: Ke-hi-ga-wah Chuffe, Ish-tal-a-sa, Ne-hoo-ja-in-gah, Ki-hi-ga-wat-te-in-gah, Ki-he-gah-cha, Al-li-ca-wah-ho, Pah-hous-ga-tun-gah Ke-hah-lah-la-hu, Ki-ha-gah-chu, Ee-le-sun-gah, Wah-pah-jah, Ko-sah-mun-gee, Oo-ga-shama, Wah-Shumga, Wah-ti-inga,-Wah-e-la-ga, Pa-ha-ne-ga-la, Pa-ta-go, Cahulle, Ma-she-tum, Wa-no-ba-ga-ha, She-ga-wa-sa, Ma-his-pa-wa-cha, Ma-shon-o-pusha, Ja-ha-sha-watanga, Ki-he-ga-

426

Plains, West and Northwest Plateau Indian Treaties

tussa, and Ka-la-sha-wat-lumga, they being thereto duly authorized by said tribe.

ARTICLE 1. The Kansas Indians having now more lands than are necessary for their occupation and use, and being desirous of promoting settled habits of industry amongst themselves by abolishing the tenure in common by which they now hold their lands, and by assigning limited quantities thereof in severalty to the members of their tribe, owning an interest in their present reservation to be cultivated and improved for their individual use and benefit, it is agreed and stipulated that that portion of their reservation commencing at the southwest corner of said reservation, thence north with the west boundary nine miles, thence east fourteen miles, thence south nine miles, thence west with the south boundary fourteen miles to the place of beginning, shall be set apart and retained by them for said purposes; and that out of the same there shall be assigned to each head of a family not exceeding forty acres, and to each member thereof not exceeding forty acres, and to each single male person of the age of twenty-one years and upwards not exceeding forty acres of land, to include in every case, as far as practicable, a reasonable proportion of timber.

One hundred and sixty acres of said retained lands, in a suitable locality, shall also be set apart and appropriated to the occupancy and use of the agency of said Indians, and one hundred and sixty acres of said lands shall also be reserved for the establishment of a school for the education of the youth of the tribe.

ARTICLE 2. The lands to be so assigned, including those for the use of the agency, and those reserved for school purposes, shall be in as regular and compact a body as possible, and so as to admit of a distinct and well-defined exterior boundary, embracing the whole of them, and any intermediate portions or parcels of land or water not included in or made part of the tracts assigned in severalty. Any such intermediate parcels of land and water shall be owned by the Kansas tribe of Indians in common; but in case of increase in the tribe, or other cause rendering it necessary or expedient, the said intermediate parcels of land shall be subject to distribution and assignment in such manner as the Secretary of the Interior shall prescribe and direct.

The whole of the lands assigned or unassigned in severalty, embraced within the said exterior boundary, shall constitute and be known as the Kansas reservation, within and over which all laws passed, or which may be passed by Congress, regulating trade and intercourse with the Indian tribes, shall have full force and effect. And no white person, except such as shall be in the employment of the United States, shall be allowed to reside or go upon any portion of said reservation without the written permission of the superintendent of Indian affairs, or of the agent for the tribe.

Plains, West and Northwest Plateau Indian Treaties

ARTICLE 3. Said division and assignment of lands to the Kansas tribe of Indians in severalty shall be made under the direction of the Secretary of the Interior, and when approved by him shall be final and conclusive. Certificates shall be issued by the Commissioner of Indian Affairs for the tracts so assigned, specifying the names of the individuals to whom they have been assigned respectively and that they are for the exclusive use and benefit of themselves, their heirs and descendants, and said tracts shall not be alienated in fee, leased or otherwise disposed of, except to the United States or to other members of the tribe, under such rules and regulations as may be prescribed by the Secretary of the Interior; and they shall be exempt from taxation, levy, sale, or forfeiture, until otherwise provided by Congress. Prior to the issue of said certificates, the Secretary of the Interior shall make such rules and regulations, as he may deem necessary and expedient respecting the disposition of any of said tracts, in case of the death of the person or persons to whom they may be assigned, so that the same shall be secured to the families of such deceased persons; and should any of the Indians to whom tracts shall be assigned abandon them, the said Secretary may take such action in relation to the proper disposition thereof as in his judgment may be necessary and proper.

ARTICLE 4. For the purpose of procuring the means of comfortably establishing the Kansas tribe of Indians upon the lands to be assigned to them in severalty, by building them houses, and by furnishing them with agricultural implements, stock animals, and other necessary aid and facilities for commencing agricultural pursuits under favorable circumstances, the lands embraced in that portion not stipulated to be retained and divided as aforesaid shall be sold, under the direction of the Secretary of the Interior, in parcels not exceeding one hundred and sixty acres each, to the highest bidder for cash, the sale to be made upon sealed proposals to be duly invited by public advertisement, and should any of the tracts so to be so sold have upon them improvements of any kind, which were made by or for the Indians, or for Government purposes, the proposals therefor must state the price for both the land and improvements.

If, after assigning to all the members of the tribe entitled thereto, their proportions in severalty, there shall remain a surplus of that portion of the reservation retained for that purpose, outside of the exterior boundary-line of the lands assigned in severalty, the Secretary of the Interior shall be authorized and empowered, whenever he shall think proper, to cause such surplus to be sold in the same manner as the other lands to be so disposed of, and the proceeds thereof to be expended for their benefit in such manner as the Secretary of the Interior may deem proper: Provided, That all those who had in good faith settled and made improvements upon said reservation prior to the second day of December, eighteen hundred and fifty-six, (that being the day when the survey was certified by the agent of the tribe), and who would have been entitled to enter their improvements under any general or special pre-emption law, (had their

Plains, West and Northwest Plateau Indian Treaties

improvements not fallen within the reservation) such settlers shall be permitted to enter their improvements at the sum of one dollar and seventy-five cents per acre, m cash; said entries to be made in legal subdivisions and in such quantities as the pre-emption laws under which they may claim entitle them to locate: payments to be made On or before a day to be named by the Secretary of the Interior.

And provided, further, That all those who had in good faith settled upon that portion of the reservation retained by this treaty for the future homes of the Kansas tribe of Indians, and had made bona fide improvements thereon prior to the second day of December, eighteen hundred and fifty-six, aforesaid, and who would have been entitled to enter their lands, under the general pre-emption law, at one dollar and twenty-five cents per acre, had their improvements not fallen upon the reservation, such settlers shall be entitled to receive a fair compensation for their improvements, to be ascertained by the Commissioner of Indian Affairs, under the direction of the Secretary of the Interior; such compensation to be paid out of the proceeds of the lands sold in trust for said tribe of Indians.

All questions growing out of amendment, and rights claimed in consequence thereof, shall be determined by the Commissioner of Indian Affairs, to be approved by the Secretary of the Interior. And in all cases where licensed traders, or others lawfully there, may have made improvements upon said reservation, the Secretary of the Interior shall have power to adjust the claims of each upon fair and equitable terms, they paying a fair value for the lands awarded to such persons, and shall cause patents to issue in pursuance of such award.

ARTICLE 5. The Kansas tribe of Indians being anxious to relieve themselves from the burden of their present liabilities, and it being very essential to their welfare that they shall be enabled to commence their new mode of life and pursuits free from the annoyance and embarrassment thereof, or which may be occasioned thereby, it is agreed that the same shall be liquidated and paid out of the fund arising from the sale of their surplus lands so far as found valid and just, (if they have the means)on an examination thereof, to be made by their agent and the superintendent of Indian affairs for the central superintendency, subject to revision and confirmation by the Secretary of the Interior.

ARTICLE 6. Should the proceeds of the surplus lands of the Kansas tribe of Indians not prove to be sufficient to carry out the purposes and stipulations of this agreement, and some further aid be necessary, from time to time, to enable said Indians to sustain themselves successfully in agricultural and other industrial pursuits, such additional means may be taken, so far as may be necessary, from the moneys due and belonging to them under the provisions of former treaties, and so much thereof as may be required to furnish further aid as aforesaid shall be applied in such manner, under the direction of the Secretary of the

Plains, West and Northwest Plateau Indian Treaties

Interior, as he shall consider best calculated to promote and advance their improvement and welfare.

ARTICLE 7. In order to render unnecessary any further treaty engagements or arrangements hereafter with the United States, it is hereby agreed and stipulated that the President, with the assent of Congress, shall have full power to modify or change any of the provisions of former treaties with the Kansas tribes of Indians in such manner and to whatever extent he may judge to be necessary and expedient for their welfare and best interest.

ARTICLE 8. All the expenses connected with and incident to the making of this agreement, and the carrying out its provisions, shall be defrayed out of the funds of the Kansas tribe of Indians.

ARTICLE 9. The Kansas tribe of Indians being desirous of manifesting their good-will towards the children of their half-breed relatives now residing upon the half-breed tract on the north side of the Kansas River, agree that out of the tract retained by this agreement there shall also be assigned, in severalty, to the eight children of Julia Pap-pan forty acres each, to the three children of Adel Bellmard, to the four children of Jasette Gouville, to the child of Lewis Pappan, to the four children of Pelagia Obrey, to the child of Acaw Pappan, to the two children of Victoria Pappan, to the two children of Elizabeth Carboneau, to the child of Victoria Williams, to the child of Joseph Butler, to the child of Joseph James, to the two children of Pelagia Pushal, Frank James, and Batest Gouville, forty acres each, but the land so to be assigned under this article shall not be alienated in fee, leased, or otherwise disposed of, except to the United States, or to other members of the tribe, tinder such regulations as may be prescribed by the Secretary of (the) Interior.

ARTICLE 10. It is agreed that all roads and highways laid out by authority of law shall have right of way through the lands within the reservation hereinbefore specified, on the same terms as are provided by law when roads and highways are made through lands of citizens of the United States; and railroad companies, when the lines pass through the lands of said Indians, shall have right of way on the payment of a just compensation therefor in money.

ARTICLE 11. This instrument shall be obligatory on the contracting parties whenever the same shall be ratified by the President and Senate of the United States.

In testimony whereof the said Alfred B. Greenwood, commissioner as aforesaid, and the said chiefs and headmen of the Kansas tribe of Indians, have hereunto set their hands and seals, at the place and on the day and year hereinbefore written.

Plains, West and Northwest Plateau Indian Treaties

In presence of (the words "upon the lands" and the word "pursuits," upon fifth page, interlined before signing)

Milton C. Dickhey, United States Indian agent, Joseph James, United States interpreter, John Goodell, Frank Lecompte, Alfred B. Greenwood.

Ki-he-ga-wah-chuffee, his x mark, Ish-tal-a-sa, his x mark, Nee-hoo-ja-in-ga, his x mark, Ki-hi-ga-wat-te-in-ga, his x mark, Ki-he-gah-cha, his x mark, Al-li-cah-wah-ho, his x mark, Pah-hous-ga-tun-gah, his x mark, Ke-hah-lah-la-hu, his x mark, Ee-he-sun-gah, his x mark, Ko-sah-mungee, his x mark, Wah-pa-jah, his x mark, Oo-gah-sha-ma, his x mark, Wah-shun-ga, his x mark,

TREATY WITH THE ARAPAHO AND CHEYENNE {1861, Feb. 18}
Ratified. Aug. 6. 1861.
Proclaimed Dec. 1861.

Articles of agreement and convention made and concluded at Fort Wise, in the Territory of Kansas, on the eighteenth day of February, in the year of our Lord one thousand eight hundred and sixty-one, by and between Albert G. Boone and F. B. Culver, commissioners on the part of the United States, and the following named chiefs and delegates, representing the confederated tribes of Arapahoe and Cheyenne Indians of the Upper Arkansas River, viz: Little Raven, Storm, Shave-Head, and Big-Mouth, (on the part of the Arapahoes), and Black Kettle, White Antelope, Lean Bear, Little Wolf, and Left Hand, or Namos (on, the part of the Cheyennes), they being thereto duly authorized by said confederated tribes of Indians.

ARTICLE 1. The said chiefs and delegates of said Arapahoe and Cheyenne tribes of Indians do hereby cede and relinquish to the United States all lands now owned, possessed, or claimed by them, wherever situated, except a tract to be reserved for the use of said tribes located within the following described boundaries, to wit: Beginning at the mouth of the Sandy Fork of the Arkansas River and extending westwardly along the said river to the mouth of Purgatory River; thence along up the west bank of the Purgatory River to the northern boundary of the Territory of New Mexico; thence west along said boundary to a point where a line drawn due south from a point on the Arkansas River, five miles east of the mouth of the Huerfano River, would intersect said northern boundary of New Mexico; thence due north from that point on said boundary of the Sandy Fork to the place of the beginning.

The Arapahoe and Cheyennes, being desirous of promoting settled habits of industry and enterprise among themselves, by abolishing the tenure in common by which they now hold their lands, and by assigning limited quantities thereof in severalty to the individual members of the respective tribes, to be cultivated

Plains, West and Northwest Plateau Indian Treaties

and improved for their individual use and benefit, it is hereby agreed and stipulated that the tract of country contained within the boundary above described shall be set apart and retained by them for the purposes aforesaid.

According to the understanding among themselves, it is hereby agreed between the United States and the said tribes that the said reservation shall be surveyed and divided by a line to be run due north from a point on the northern boundary of New Mexico fifteen miles west of Purgatory River, and extending to the Sandy Fork of the Arkansas River, which said line shall establish the eastern boundary of that portion of the reservation, to be hereafter occupied by the Cheyennes, and the western boundary of portion of said reservation to be hereafter occupied by the Arapahoes.

ARTICLE 2. Out of the lands so set apart and retained there shall be assigned to each member of said tribes, without distinction of age or sex, a tract of forty acres, to include in every case, as far as practicable, a reasonable portion of timber and water; one hundred and sixty acres of said retained lands shall also be set apart and appropriated to the use and occupancy of the agent, for the time being, of said tribes: and one hundred and sixty acres shall also be reserved out of each division of the retained tract for the establishment and support of schools for the education of the youth of the tribe. The location of the tracts, the assignment of which is provided for in this article, shall be made in as regular and compact a manner as possible, and so as to admit of a distinct and well-defined exterior boundary, embracing the whole of them, and any intermediate portions or parcels of land or water not included in or made part of the tracts assigned in severalty.

All such intermediate parcels of land and water shall be owned in common by the tribe occupying that portion of the reservation within the limits of which said parcels of land and water may be included; but in case of increase in the tribe, or other causes rendering it necessary or expedient, the said intermediate parcels of land shall be subject to distribution and assignment in such manner as the Secretary of the Interior may prescribe and direct.

The whole of the lands, assigned and unassigned, embraced within the exterior boundary herein designated, shall constitute and be known as the Reservation of the Arapahoes and Cheyennes of the Upper Arkansas; and all laws which have been or may be passed by the Congress of the United States regulating trade and intercourse with Indian tribes, shall have full force and effect over the same, and no white person, except as shall be in the employment of the United States, shall be allowed to reside or go upon any portion of said reservation without the written permission of the superintendent of the central superintendency, or of the agent of the tribes.

Plains, West and Northwest Plateau Indian Treaties

ARTICLE 3. The division and assignment in severalty among the Arapahoes and Cheyennes of the land hereinbefore reserved for that purpose, shall be made under the direction of the Secretary of the Interior, and his decision of all questions arising thereupon shall be final and conclusive. Certificates shall be issued by the Commissioner of Indian Affairs for the tracts assigned in severalty, specifying the names of the individuals to whom they have been assigned respectively-, and that the said tracts are set apart for the exclusive use and benefit of the assignees and their heirs. And said tracts shall not be alienated in fee, leased, or otherwise disposed of, except to the United States, or to members of the respective bands of Arapahoes and Cheyennes, and under such rules and regulations as may be prescribed by the Secretary of the Interior.

And said tracts shall be exempt from taxation, levy, sale, or forfeiture, until otherwise provided by Congress. Prior to the issue of the certificates aforesaid, the Secretary of the Interior shall make such rules and regulations as he may deem necessary or expedient respecting the disposition of any of said tracts, in the case of the death of the person or persons to whom they may be assigned, so that the same shall be secured to the families of such deceased persons; and should any of the Indians to whom tracts shall be assigned, abandon them, the said Secretary may take such action in relation to the proper disposition thereof as, in his judgment, may be necessary and proper.

ARTICLE 4. In consideration of the foregoing cession, relinquishment, and agreements, and for the purpose of establishing the Arapahoes and Cheyennes comfortably upon the lands to be assigned to them in severalty, by building them houses, and by furnishing them with agricultural implements, stock animals, and other necessary aid and facilities for commencing agricultural pursuits under favorable circumstances, the United States do hereby agree and stipulate as follows, to wit: 1st.

To protect the said Arapahoes and Cheyennes in the quiet and peaceful possession of the said tract of land so reserved for their future home, and also their persons and property thereon, during good behavior on their part. 2d. To pay to them, or expend for their benefit the sun, of thirty thousand dollars per annum for fifteen years; that is to say, fifteen thousand dollars per annum for each tribe for that number of years, commencing with the year in which they shall remove to and settle and reside upon their said reservation; making four hundred and fifty thousand dollars in annuities in the period of fifteen years, of which sum the Secretary of the Interior shall, from time to time, determine what proportion shall be expended for their benefit, and for what object such expenditure shall be made, due regard being had, in making such determination, to the best interests of said Indians.

He shall likewise exercise the power to make such provision out of said sums as he may deem to be necessary and proper for the support and comfort of the

Plains, West and Northwest Plateau Indian Treaties

aged or infirm and helpless orphans of the said Indians. Their annuities may, at the discretion of the President of the United States, be discontinued entirely, should said Indians fail to make reasonable and satisfactory efforts to advance and improve their condition; in which case such other provision shall be made for them as the President and Congress may judge to be suitable and proper.

3d. It is hereby agreed that the expenses to be incurred in the purchase of agricultural implements, stock animals, etc., referred to in this article, as also the cost and expenses of breaking up and fencing land, building houses, storehouses, and other needful buildings, or in making such other improvements as may be necessary for their comfort and welfare, shall be defrayed out of the aforesaid sum of four hundred and fifty thousand dollars, to be paid to or expended for the benefit of the Arapahoes and Cheyennes as annuities.

ARTICLE 5. To provide the said Indians with a mill suitable for sawing timber and grinding grain, one or more mechanic shops, with necessary tools for the same, and dwelling-houses for an interpreter, miller, engineer for the mill, (if one be necessary) farmers, and the mechanics that may be employed for their benefit, the United States agree to expend therefor a sum not exceeding five thousand dollars per annum for five years; and it is agreed that all articles of goods and provisions, stock, implements, lumber, machinery, &c., referred to in this treaty, shall be transported to the respective tribes of Arapahoes and Cheyennes, at the cost and expense of the United States.

ARTICLE 6. The Arapahoes and Cheyennes of the Upper Arkansas, parties to this Agreement, are anxious that all the members of their tribe shall participate in the advantages herein provided for respecting their improvements and civilization, and, to that end, to induce all that are now separated to rejoin and reunite with them. It is therefore agreed that, as soon as practicable, the Commissioner of Indian affairs shall cause the necessary proceedings to be adopted to have them notified of this agreement and its advantages; and to induce them to come in and unite with their brethren; and to enable them to do so, and to sustain themselves for a reasonable time thereafter, such assistance shall be provided for them, at the expense of the tribe as may be actually necessary for that purpose: Provided, however, That those who did not rejoin and permanently reunite themselves with the tribe within one year from the date of the ratification of this treaty, shall not be entitled to the benefit of any of its stipulations.

ARTICLE 7. Should any further aid from time to time be necessary to enable the Arapahoes and Cheyennes of the Upper Arkansas to sustain themselves successfully in agricultural or other industrial pursuits, such additional means as may be required therefor shall be taken from the moneys due and belonging to them under the provisions of former treaties or articles of agreement and convention, and so much of said moneys as may be required to furnish them further aid as aforesaid shall be applied in such manner, under the direction of

Plains, West and Northwest Plateau Indian Treaties

the Secretary of the Interior, as he shall consider best calculated to improve and promote their welfare.

And, in order to render unnecessary any further treaty engagements or arrangements hereafter with the United States, it is hereby agreed and stipulated that the President, with the assent of Congress, shall have full power to modify or change any of the provisions of former treaties with the Arapahoes and Cheyennes of the Upper Arkansas, in such manner and to whatever extent he may judge to be necessary and expedient for their best interests.

ARTICLE 8. All the expenses connected with and incident to the making of this agreement and carrying out its provisions shall be defrayed by the United States, except as otherwise herein provided.

ARTICLE 9. It is agreed that all roads and highways, laid out by authority of law, shall have right of way through the lands within the reservation hereinbefore specified, on the same terms as are provided by law when roads and highways are made through lands of citizens of the United States.

ARTICLE 10. It is also agreed by the United States that the annuities now paid to the Arapahoes and Cheyennes, under existing treaties or articles of agreement and convention, shall be continued to them until the stipulations of said treaties or articles of agreement and convention relating to such annuities shall be fulfilled.

ARTICLE 11. (Stricken out.)

ARTICLE 12. This instrument shall be obligatory on the contracting parties whenever the same shall be ratified by the President and the Senate of the United States.

In testimony whereof, the said Commissioner(s) as aforesaid, and the said Chiefs and Delegates of the Arapahoes and Cheyennes of the Upper Arkansas, have hereunto set their hands and seals, at the place and on the day and year hereinbefore written.

A. G. Boone, United States Indian Agent and Commissioner.
F. B. Culver, Conmfissioner and Special Agent.

On the part of the Arapahoes:
Ito-ha-ca-che, his x mark, or Little Raven, Ac-ker-ba-the, his x mark, or Storm.

On the part of the Cheyennes:
Mo-ta-va-to, his x mark, Black Kettle, Vo-ki-vokamast, his x mark, White Antelope, Avo-na-co, his x mark, Lean Bear.

Plains, West and Northwest Plateau Indian Treaties

Witnesses to the signatures:
John Sedgwick, major of Cavalry, R. Ransom, jr., lieutenant of Cavalry.

P. S. And it is further understood, before signing the above treaty, that it was the particular request and wish of the Chiefs and Councillors in general convention, in consideration of Robert Bent being one of their half-breed tribe, that he should have, as a gift from the nation, six hundred and forty acres of land, covering the valley and what is called the Sulphur Spring, lying on the north side of the Arkansas River and about five miles below the Pawnee Hills, and they wish the general government to recognize and confirm the same; and that Jack Smith, son of John S. Smith, who is also a half-breed of said nation, shall have six hundred and forty acres of land, lying seven miles above Bent's Old Fort, on the north side of the Arkansas River, including the valley and point of rock, and respectfully recommend the general government to confirm and recognize the same.

TREATY WITH THE SAUK AND FOXES, ETC. {1861, Mar. 6}
Ratified Feb. 6, 1863.
Proclaimed Mar. 26, 1863.

Articles of agreement and convention made and concluded at the of the Great Nemaha agency, Nebraska Territory, on the sixth of March, A. D. one thousand eight hundred and sixty-one, by and between Daniel Vanderslice, U.S. Indian agent, on the part of United States, and the following-named delegates of the Sacs and Foxes of Missouri, viz: Pe-ta-ok-a-ma, Ne-sour-quoit, Mo-less, and Se-se-ah-kee; and the following-named delegates of the Iowa tribe, viz: No-heart, Nag-ga-rash, Mah-hee, To-bee, Tah-ra-kee, Thur-o-mony, and White Horse; they being duly authorized thereto by their respective tribes.

ARTICLE 1. The Sacs and Foxes of Missouri hereby cede, relinquish, and convey to the United States all their right, title, and interest in and to lands within their present reservation, described as follows, viz: beginning at the mouth of the south fork of the Great Nemaha River, and thence up the southwest bank of the Great Nemaha, with its meanders, to the mouth of the west fork; thence up the west fork, with its meanders, to the line of the 40° of parallel on the west bank of creek or fork where is established the southwest corner of the Sac and Fox reserve, by erecting a stone monument, from which the following references bear, viz: A large cottonwood tree, three feet in diameter, bears S. 44° 00' E. 1.05 chains; a rock bears N. 30° 00' W. 50 links; another rock bearss. 50° 00' west 50 links; and another rock bears due north one chain; thence east along the line of the 40° of parallel to the west bank of the south fork of the Great Nemaha River, distance fourteen miles twenty-seven chains and sixty links, where is established the southeast corner of the Sac and Fox

436

Plains, West and Northwest Plateau Indian Treaties

reserve, by erecting a stone pile with a black walnut post in the center of it, from which a white elm, two feet in diameter, bears S. 33° 00' E. 22 links, and marked with the letters S. E. Cot. for the southeast corner, and another elm, 18 inch(e)s in diameter, bears S. 39° 00' E. 1.05 chains, and marked SE C B SE., for the southeast corner, bearing, and distance; and another black walnut, 9 inch(e)s in diameter, bears S. 15° 00' E. 85 links, and thence down the south fork, with its meanders, to the point of beginning, estimated to contain 32,098 acres, 3 roods and 35 perches.

ARTICLE 2. The aforesaid lands shall be surveyed in conformity with the system governing the survey of the public lands; and the same shall be sold, under the direction of the Secretary of the Interior, in parcels not exceeding one hundred and sixty acres each, to the highest bidder for cash; the sale to be made upon sealed proposals, to be duly invited by public advertisement, provided, no bid shall be favorably considered which may be less than one dollar and twenty-five cents per acre. And should any of the tracts so to be sold have upon them improvements of any kind which were made by or for the Indians, or for Government purposes, the proposals therefor must state the price for both the land and improvements.

The proceeds of the sales thereof, after deducting therefrom the expenses of surveying the lands and all other expenses incident to the negotiation of these articles of convention and the proper execution thereof, the balance shall be applied as follows, viz: One half shall be held in trust by the United States for the benefit of the Sacs and Foxes of Missouri, and interest thereon, at the rate of five per centum per annum, shall be paid annually, with the other funds to be paid said tribe, in the same manner as stipulated in the treaty of May 18th, 1854; and the other half of said balance shall be applied as hereinafter specified.

ARTICLE 3. The Iowa tribe of Indians, parties to this agreement, hereby cede, relinquish, and convey to the United States, for the use and benefit of the Sacs and Foxes of Missouri, for their permanent home, all that part of their present reservation lying and being west of Nohearts Creek, and bounded as follows, viz: Beginning at a point where the southern line of the present Iowa reserve crosses Nohearts Creek; thence with said line to the south fork of the Nemaha, (commonly known as Walnut Creek;) thence down the middle of said south fork, with the meanders thereof, to its mouth, and to a point in the middle of the Great Nemaha River; thence down the middle of said river to a point opposite the mouth of Nohearts Creek; and thence, in a southerly direction with the middle of said Nohearts Creek, to the place of beginning. And it is hereby understood and agreed that, in full consideration for said cession, the United States shall hold in trust, for the use and benefit of the Iowas, the one-half of the net proceeds of the sales of the lands described in the second article of this agreement, and interest thereon, at the rate of five per centum per annum shall be

Plains, West and Northwest Plateau Indian Treaties

paid to the Iowa tribe in the same manner as their annuities are paid under the treaty of May 17, 1854.

The reservation herein described shall be surveyed and set apart for the exclusive use and benefit of the Sacs and Foxes of Missouri, and the remainder of the Iowa lands shall be the tribal reserve of said Iowa Indians for their exclusive use and benefit.

ARTICLE 4. The Sacs and Foxes of Missouri being anxious to make full satisfaction for a just claim which Joseph Tesson holds against said tribe, it is hereby agreed by the parties to this convention that said claimant shall select a quarter section or one hundred and sixty acres of land, to include his present residence and improvements, to be located in one body, in conformity with the legal subdivisions of the public surveys, which tract of land shall be received by him in full payment of said claim, estimated at about eight hundred dollars, and all other claims or rights of every character whatsoever against said tribe; and when a relinquishment shall have been executed by said claimant in favor of said tribe for all claims that he may have against them, a patent shall be issued to him for said tract of land in fee-simple.

The following chiefs shall be entitled to select each a quarter section or one hundred and sixty acres of land in one body, In conformity with the public surveys, to include their present residences and improvements, viz: Pe-te-ok-a-ma, Ne-sour-quoit, and Mo-less: and George Gomess, a member of the Sac and Fox tribe, shall select in like manner one-eighth of a section or eighty acres of land in one body, to include his improvements, and patents shall be issued therefor in favor of said persons in fee-simple.

ARTICLE 5. In order to encourage education among the aforesaid tribes of Indians, it is hereby agreed that the United States shall expend the sum of one thousand dollars for the erection of a suitable school-house, and dwelling-house for the school teacher, for the benefit of the Sacs and Foxes, and also the additional sum of two hundred dollars per annum for school purposes, so long as the President of the United States may deem advisable. And for the benefit of the Iowa tribe of Indians there shall be expended, in like manner, at the discretion of the President, the sum of three hundred dollars per annum, for school purposes, which two last-mentioned sums shall be paid out of the funds to be appropriated for the civilization of Indians.

ARTICLE 6. There shall be set apart in one body, under the direction of the Commissioner of Indian Affairs, one section, or six hundred and forty acres of land, in harmony with the public survey, so as to include the agency-dwelling, agency-office, council-house, schoolhouse, teachers' dwelling, blacksmith's dwelling and shops, and such farming land as may be necessary for the use of the school, agency, and employees thereat.

Plains, West and Northwest Plateau Indian Treaties

ARTICLE 7. No person not a member of either of the tribes, parties to this convention, shall go upon the reservations or sojourn among the Indians without a license or written permit from the agent or superintendent of Indian affairs, except Government employees or persons connected with the public service. And no mixed-blood Indians, except those employed at some mission, or such as may be sent there to be educated, or other members of the aforesaid tribes, shall participate in the beneficial provisions of this agreement or former treaties, unless they return to and unite permanently with said tribes, and reside upon the respective reservations within six months from the date of this convention.

ARTICLE 8. It is hereby understood and agreed by the contracting parties hereto that the stipulations of the treaty with the Sacs and Foxes of Missouri of May 18th, 1854, and the treaty with the Iowa Indians of the 17th of May, 1854, which may not be inconsistent with these articles of convention, shall have full force and effect upon the contracting parties hereto.

ARTICLE 9. This instrument shall be obligatory upon the respective parties hereto, whenever the same shall be ratified by the President and the Senate of the United States.

ARTICLE 10. The Secretary of the Interior may expend a sum not exceeding three thousand five hundred dollars, ($3,500) out of the proceeds of the sales of said lands, at any time he may deem it advisable, for the purpose of erecting a toll-bridge across the Great Nemaha River, at or near Roy's Ferry, for the use of the Iowa Indians; and a like sum of three thousand five hundred dollars, ($3,500) out of the proceeds of the sales of said lands, for the purpose of erecting a toll-bridge across the Great Nemaha River, at or near Wolf Village, for the use of the Sacs and Foxes of Missouri.

Toll shall be charged and collected for the use of said bridges at such rates and under such rules and regulations as may be established by the Commissioner of Indian Affairs, with the approval of the Secretary of the Interior, the proceeds of such tolls to be expended as follows: 1st, in making necessary repairs on said bridges; 2d, for the use of said tribes, respectively.

ARTICLE 11. It is further stipulated that, whenever Congress shall by law so provide, all annuities due and to become due and payable to the said tribes of Indians under this treaty, and under all other previous treaties, may be paid in specific articles, clothing, agricultural implements, and such other articles as Congress shall direct.

Plains, West and Northwest Plateau Indian Treaties

In testimony whereof, the said commissioner as aforesaid, and the said chiefs and delegates of the Sacs and Foxes of Missouri, and of the Iowa tribe of Indians, have hereunto set their hands and seals at the place and on the day and year hereinbefore written.

D. Vanderslice, United States Indian agent.

Sac(s) and Foxes of Mo.:
Pe-te-ok-a-ma, his x mark, Ne-sour-quoit, his x mark, Modess, his x mark, Se-se-ah-kee. his x mark

Iowa Indians:
No-heart, his x mark, Nag-ga-rash, his x mark, Mah-hee, his x mark, To-bee, his x mark, Tah-ra-kee, his x mark, Thur-o-mony, his x mark, White-horse, his x mark,

Signed in the presence
George Gomess, his x mark, United States interpreter for Sac(s) and Foxes of Me.

TREATY WITH THE POTAWATOMI {1861, Nov. 15}
Ratified Apr. 15, 1862.
Proclaimed Apt. 19, 1862.

Articles of a treaty made and concluded at the agency on the Kansas River, on the fifteenth day of November, in the year of our Lord one thousand eight hundred and sixty-one, by and between Wm. W. Ross, commissioner on the part of the United States, and the undersigned chiefs, braves, and head-men of the Pottawatomie Nation, on behalf of said nation.

ARTICLE 1. The Pottawatomie tribe of Indians believing that it will contribute to the civilization of their people to dispose of a portion of their present reservation in Kansas, consisting of five hundred and seventy-six thousand acres, which was acquired by them for the sum of $87,000, by the fourth article of the treaty between the United States and the said Pottawatomies, proclaimed by the President of the United States on the 23d day of July, 1846, and to allot lands ill severalty to those of said tribe who have adopted the customs of the whites and desire to have separate tracts assigned to them, and to assign a portion of said reserve to those of the tribe who prefer to hold their lands in common.

It is therefore agreed by the parties hereto that the Commissioner of Indian Affairs shall cause the whole of said reservation to be surveyed in the same manner as the public lands are surveyed, the expense whereof shall be paid out of the sales of lands hereinafter provided for, and the quantity of land hereinafter

Plains, West and Northwest Plateau Indian Treaties

provided to be set apart to those of the tribe who desire to take their lands in severalty, and the quantity hereinafter provided to De set apart for the rest of the tribe in common; and the remainder of the land, after the special reservations hereinafter provided for shall have been made, to be sold for the benefit of said tribe.

ARTICLE 2. It shall be the duty of the agent of the United States for said tribe to take an accurate census of all the members of the tribe, and to classify them in separate lists, showing the names, ages, and numbers of those desiring lands in severalty, and of those desiring lands in common, designating chiefs and head-men, respectively; each adult choosing for himself or herself, and each head of a family for the minor children of such family, and the agent for orphans and persons of an unsound mind.

And thereupon there shall be assigned, under the direction of the Commissioner of Indian Affairs, to each chief at the signing of the treaty, one section; to each head-man, one half section; to each other head of a family, one quarter section; and to each other person eighty acres of land, to include, in every case, as far as practicable, to each family, their improvements and a reasonable portion of timber, to be selected according to the legal subdivision of survey.

When such assignments shall have been completed, certificates shall be issued by the Commissioner of Indian Affairs for the tracts assigned in severalty, specifying the names of the individuals to whom they have been assigned, respectively, and that said tracts are set apart for the perpetual and exclusive use and benefit of such assignees and their heirs. Until otherwise provided by law, such tracts shall be exempt from levy, taxation, or sale, and shall be alienable in fee or leased otherwise disposed of only to the United States, or to persons then being members of the Pottawatomie tribe and of Indian blood, with the permission of the President, and under such regulations as the Secretary of the Interior shall provide, except as may be hereinafter provided. And on receipt of such certificates, the person to whom they are issued shall be deemed to have relinquished all right to any portion of the lands assigned to others in severalty, or to a portion of the tribe in common, and to the proceeds of sale of the same whensoever made.

ARTICLE 3. At any time hereafter when the President of the United States shall have become satisfied that any adults, being males and heads of families, who may be allottees under the provisions of the foregoing article, are sufficiently intelligent and prudent to control their affairs and interests, he may, at the request of such persons, cause the lands severally held by them to be conveyed to them by patent in fee-simple, with power of alienation; and may, at the same time, cause to be paid to them, in cash or in the bonds of the United States, their proportion of the cash value of the credits of the tribe, principal and interest, then held in trust by the United States, and also, as the same may

441

Plains, West and Northwest Plateau Indian Treaties

be received, their proportion of the proceeds of the sale of lands under the provisions of this treaty.

And on such patents being issued and such payments ordered to be made by the President, such competent persons shall cease to be members of said tribe, and shall become citizens of the United States; and thereafter the lands so patented to them shall be subject to levy, taxation, and sale, in like manner with the property of other citizens: Provided, That, before making any such application to the President, they shall appear in open court in the district court of the United States for the district of Kansas, and make the same proof and take the same oath of allegiance as is provided by law for the naturalization of aliens, and shall also make proof to the satisfaction of said court that they are sufficiently intelligent and prudent to control their affairs and interests, that they have adopted the habits of civilized life, and have been able to support, for at least five years, themselves and families.

ARTICLE 4. To those members of said tribe who desire to hold their lands in common there shall be set apart an undivided quantity sufficient to allow one section to each chief, one half section to each headman, and one hundred and sixty acres to each other head of a family, and eighty acres of land to each other person, and said land shall be held by that portion of the tribe for whom it is set apart by the same tenure as the whole reserve has been held by all of said tribe under the treaty of one thousand eight hundred and forty-six. And upon such land being assigned in common, the persons to whom it is assigned shall be held to have relinquished all title to the lands assigned in severalty and in the proceeds of sales thereof whenever made.

ARTICLE 5. The Pottawatomies believing that the construction of the Leavenworth, Pawnee, and Western Railroad from Leavenworth City to the western boundary of the former reserve of the Delawares, is now rendered reasonably certain, and being desirous to have said railroad extended through their reserve in the direction of Fort Riley, so that the value of the lands retained by them may be enhanced, and the means afforded them of getting the surplus product of their farms to market, it is provided that the Leavenworth, Pawnee, and Western Railroad Company shall have the privilege of buying the remainder of their lands within six months after the tracts herein otherwise disposed of shall have been selected and set apart, provided they purchase the whole of said surplus lands at the rate of one dollar and twenty-five cents per acre.

And if said company make such purchase it shall be subject to the considerations following, to wit: They shall construct and fully equip a good and efficient railroad from Leavenworth City to a point half way between the western boundary of the said former Delaware reserve and the western boundary of the said Pottawatomie reserve, (being the first section of said road;) within six years from the date of such purchase, and shall construct and fully equip such

Plains, West and Northwest Plateau Indian Treaties

road from said last-named point to the western boundary of said Pottawatomie reserve, (being the second section of said road) within three years from the date fixed for the completion of said first section.

And no patent or patents shall issue to said company or its assigns for any of said lands purchased until the first section of said railroad shall have been completed and equipped, and then for not more than half of said lands, and no patent or patents shall issue to said company or its assigns for any of the remaining portion of said lands until said second section of said railroad shall have been completed and equipped as aforesaid; and before any patents shall issue for any part of said lands payment shall be made for the lands to be patented at the rate of one dollar and twenty-five cents per acre; and said company shall pay the whole amount of the purchase-money for said lands in gold or silver coin, to the Secretary of the Interior of the United States, in trust for said Pottawatomie Indians, within nine years from the date of such purchase, and shall also in like manner pay to the Secretary of the Interior of the United States, in trust as aforesaid, each and every year, until the whole purchase-money shall have been paid, interest from date of purchase, at six per cent. per annum, on all the purchase-money remaining unpaid.

And if said company shall fail to complete either section of such railroad in a good and efficient manner, or shall fail to pay the whole of the purchase-money for said land within the times above prescribed, or shall fail to pay all or any part of the interest upon said purchase-money each year as aforesaid within thirty days from the date when such payment of interest shall fall due, then the contract or purchase shall be deemed and held absolutely null and void, and shall cease to be binding on either of the parties thereto, and said company and its assigns shall forfeit all payments of principal and interest made on such purchase, and all right and title, legal and equitable, of any kind whatsoever, in and to all and every part of said lands which shall not have been before the date of such forfeiture earned and patented pursuant to the provisions of this treaty.

And whenever any patent shall issue to said railroad company for any part of said lands, it shall contain the condition that the said company shall sell the land described in such patent, except so much as shall be necessary for the working of the road, within five years from the issuing of such patent.

And said company shall have the perpetual right of way over the lands of the Pottawatomies not sold to it for the construction and operation of said railroad, not exceeding one hundred feet in width, and the right to enter on said lands and take and use such gravel stone, earth, water, and other material, except timber, as may be necessary for the construction and operation of said road, making compensation for any damage to improvements done in obtaining such material, and for any damages arising from the location or running of said road to improvements made before the road is located. Such damages and compen-

443

Plains, West and Northwest Plateau Indian Treaties

sation, in cases where said company and the persons whose improvements are injured or property taken cannot agree, to be ascertained and adjusted under the direction of the Commissioner of Indian Affairs

And in case said company shall not promptly pay the amount of such damages and compensation, the Secretary of the Interior may withhold patents for any part of the lands purchased by them until payment be made of the amount of such damages, with six per cent. interest thereon from the date when the same shall have been ascertained and demanded.

And in case said company shall not purchase said surplus lands, or, having purchased, shall forfeit the whole or any part thereof, the Secretary of the Interior shall thereupon cause the same to be appraised at not less than one dollar and twenty-five cents per acre, and shall sell the same, in quantities not exceeding one hundred and sixty acres, at auction to the highest bidder for cash, at not less than such appraised value.

ARTICLE 6. There shall be selected by the Commissioner of Indian Affairs three hundred and twenty acres of land, including the church, school-houses, and fields of the St. Mary's Catholic Mission, but not including the buildings and enclosures occupied and used by persons other than those connected with the mission, without the consent of such persons, which shall be conveyed by the Secretary of the Interior to John F. Diel, John Summaker, and M. Gerillain, as trustees for the use of the society under whose patronage and control the church and school have been conducted within the last fourteen years; on condition, however, that, so long as the Pottawatomie Nation shall continue to occupy its present reservation, or any portion thereof, the said land shall be used and its products devoted exclusively to the maintenance of a school and church for their benefit.

And there shall be reserved and conveyed in like manner, and upon like conditions, three hundred and twenty acres of land, including the Baptist Mission buildings and enclosures, such conveyances to be made to such persons as may be designated by the Baptist Board of Missions.

ARTICLE 7. By article eight of the treaty of June 5th, 1846, between the United States and the Pottawatomie Indians, it is stipulated "that the annual interest of their improvement fund shall be paid out promptly and fully for their benefit at their new homes. If, however, at any time thereafter, the President of the United States shall be of opinion that it would be advantageous to the Pottawatomie Nation, and they should request the same to be done, to pay them the interest of said money in lieu of the employment of persons, or the purchase of implements or machines, he is hereby authorized to pay the same, or any part thereof, in money, as their annuities are paid, at the time of the general payment of annuities."

Plains, West and Northwest Plateau Indian Treaties

It is hereby agreed that the interest arising from said improvement-fund shall, in all cases hereafter, be paid in such machines and implements as will be useful to the people in their agricultural pursuits, as long as the nation shall desire it to be done, except that the shops and mechanics and physicians, now sustained by the funds of the nation, shall continue to be maintained, as at this time, for one year after this treaty shall have been ratified.

ARTICLE 8. If at any time hereafter any band or bands of the Pottawatomie Nation shall desire to remove from the homes provided for them in this treaty, it shall be the duty of the Secretary of the Interior to have their proportionate part of the lands which may be assigned to the tribe appraised and sold, and invest such portion of the proceeds thereof as may be necessary in the purchase of a new home for such band or bands, leaving the remainder, should any remain after paying the expense of their removal, to be invested in six per cent bonds of the United States, for the benefit of such band or bands. Such band or bands so removed shall continue to receive their proportion of the annuities of the tribe.

ARTICLE 9. No provision of this treaty shall be so construed as to invalidate any claim heretofore preferred by the Pottawatomies against the United States arising out of previous treaties.

ARTICLE 10. It is hereby agreed that the Commissioner of Indian Affairs shall set apart, for the benefit of said allottees, their equal pro rata share of the improvement-fund of the tribe, which sum so set apart may be expended, in whole or in part, by the said Commissioner, and under his direction, for agricultural purposes, as he shall from time to time deem expedient and for the welfare of the said Indians.

ARTICLE 11. Should the Senate reject or amend any of the above articles, such rejection or amendment shall not affect the other provisions of this treaty, but the same shall go into effect when ratified by the Senate and approved by the President.

Wm. W. Ross, Commissioner on behalf of United States.

Peter Moose, his x mark, Jas. Levia, his x mark, Tquah-ket, his x mark, Wahs-meg-guea, his x mark, Pame-bo-go, his x mark, A-yea-nah-be, his x mark, Nah-duea, his x mark, Nau-wah-ga, his x mark, Pahs-kah-we, his x mark, Wahb-na-mid, bis x mark, Moz-wa-nwah, his x mark, Thos. L. McKenney.
Za-gah-knuk, his x mark, Che-gueah-mkuh-go, (brave) his x mark, Ain-waish-ke, his x mark, Msquah-mke, his x mark, Mko-nuih, his x mark, Oketch-gum-me, his x mark, We-zos, his x mark, A-sah-sahng-gah, his x mark, Buck, his x mark, M. B. Beaubien.

Plains, West and Northwest Plateau Indian Treaties

Signed in presence of
L. R. Palmer, S. M. Ferguson, C. N. Gray, John D. Lusby.

TREATY WITH THE KANSA INDIANS {1862, Mar. 13}
Ratified Feb. 6,1863.
Proclaimed Mar. 16, 1863.

Whereas a treaty was made and concluded at the Kansas agency, in the then Territory, but now State, of Kansas, on the fifth day of October, A. D. 1859, by and between Alfred B. Greenwood, commissioner on the part of the United States, and the chiefs and head-men representing the Kansas tribe of Indians, and authorized by said tribe for that purpose; which treaty, after having been submitted to the Senate of the United States for its constitutional action thereon, was duly accepted, ratified, and confirmed by the President of the United States, on the seventeenth day of November, A. D. 1860, with an amendment to the fourth article thereof, which amendment, first proposed and made by the Senate on the twenty-seventh day of June, A. D. 1860, was afterwards agreed to and ratified by the aforesaid chiefs and head-men of the Kansas tribe of Indians on the fourth day of October of the same year:

Now, therefore, it is further agreed and concluded on this thirteenth day of March, A. D. 1862, by and between H. W. Farnsworth, a commissioner on the part of the United States, and the said Kansas tribe of Indians, by their authorized representatives, the chiefs and headmen thereof, to wit:

ARTICLE 1. That the said treaty and the amendment thereof be further amended so as to provide that a fair and reasonable value of the improvements made by persons who settled on the diminished reserve of said Kansas Indians between the second day of December, A. D. 1859, and the fifth day of October, A. D. 1859, shall be ascertained by the Secretary of the Interior, and certificates of indebtedness by said tribe shall be issued by him to each of such persons for an amount equal to the appraisement of his or her improvements, as aforesaid, not exceeding in the aggregate the sum of fifteen thousand dollars.

And that like certificates shall be issued to the class of persons who settled on said diminished reservation prior to the second day of December, A. D. 1856, for the amounts of the respective claims as provided for and ascertained under the provisions of the amendment of said treaty, not exceeding in the aggregate the sum of fourteen thousand four hundred and twenty-one dollars; and that like certificates be issued to the owners of the same for the amounts of claims which have been examined and approved by the agent and superintendent, and revised and confirmed by the Secretary of the Interior, under the provisions of the 5th article of said treaty, not exceeding in the aggregate the sum of thirty-six thou-

446

Plains, West and Northwest Plateau Indian Treaties

sand three hundred and ninety-four dollars and forty-seven cents, and that all such certificates shall be receivable as cash, to the amount for which they may be issued, in payment for lands purchased or entered on that part of the first assigned reservation outside of said diminished reservation.

ARTICLE 2. The Kansas tribe of Indians, being desirous of making a suitable expression of the obligations the said tribe are under to Thomas S. Huffaker, for the many services rendered by said Huffaker as missionary, teacher, and friendly counsellor of said tribe of Indians, hereby authorize and request the Secretary of the Interior to convey to the said Thomas S. Huffaker the half-section of land on which he has resided and improved and cultivated since the year A. D. 1851, it being the south half of section eleven, (11)in township numbered sixteen (16) south, range numbered eight (8) east, of the sixth principal meridian, Kansas, on the payment by said Huffaker of the appraised value of said lands, at a rate not less than one dollar and seventy-five cents per acre.

In testimony whereof, the said H. W. Farnsworth, commissioner, as aforesaid, and the said chiefs and headmen of the Kansas tribe of Indians, have hereunto set their hands and seals, at the Kansas agency, in the State of Kansas, on the said thirteenth day of March, in the year of our Lord one thousand eight hundred and sixty-two.

In presence of
T. S. Huffaker, A. G. Barnett, Edward Wolcott.

Whereas, the amendments of the Senate having been fully interpreted and explained to us, the undersigned, chiefs and headmen of the Kansas tribe of Indians, we do hereby agree to and ratify the same.
Done at Kansas agency, this twenty-sixth day of February. A. D. eighteen hundred and sixty-three.

Signed in the presence of
H. W. Farnsworth, United States Indian agent, Joseph James, United States interpreter, his x mark, Joseph Dunlap, witness to signature of interpreter, Christopher Mooney. Thomas C. Hill.

Uts-ah-gah-ba, his x mark, Sah-ya, his x mark, Ge-no-in-ga, his x mark, Me-ho-je, his x mark, Mah-ku-sa-ba, his x mark, Me-o-tum-wa, his x mark, Tah-se-hah, his x mark,

Plains, West and Northwest Plateau Indian Treaties

TREATY WITH THE NEZ PERCES {1863, June 9}
Ratified Apr. 17,1867.
Proclaimed Apr. 20, 1867.

Articles of agreement made and concluded at the council-ground, in the valley of the Lapwai, W. T. on the ninth day of June, one thousand eight hundred and sixty-three; between the United States of America, by C. H. Hale, superintendent of Indian affairs, and Charles Hutchins and S. D. Howe, U. S. Indian agents for the Territory of Washington, acting on the part and in behalf of the United States, and the Nez Perce Indians, by the chiefs, head-men, and delegates of said tribe, such articles being supplementary and amendatory to the treaty made between the United States and said tribe on the 11th day of June, 1855.

ARTICLE 1. The said Nez Perce tribe agree to relinquish, and do hereby relinquish, to the United States the lands heretofore reserved for the use and occupation of the said tribe, saving and excepting so much thereof as is described in Article 2 for a new reservation.

ARTICLE 2. The United States agree to reserve for a home, and for the sole use and occupation of said tribe, the tract of land included within the following boundaries, to wit: Commencing at the northeast corner of Lake Wa-ha, and running thence, northerly, to a point on the north bank of the Clearwater River, three miles below the mouth of the Lapwai, thence down the north bank of the Clearwater to the mouth of the Hatwai Creek; thence, due north, to a point seven miles distant; thence, eastwardly, to a point on the north fork of the Clearwater, seven miles distant from its mouth; thence to a point on Oro Fino Creek, five miles above its mouth; thence to a point on the north fork of the south fork of the Clearwater, five miles above its mouth; thence to a point on the south fork of the Clearwater, one mile above the bridge, on the road leading to Elk City, (so as to include all the Indian farms now within the forks;) thence in a straight line, westwardly, to the place of beginning.

All of which tract shall be set apart, and the above-described boundaries shall be surveyed and marked out for the exclusive use and benefit of said tribe as an Indian reservation, nor shall any white man, excepting those in the employment of the Indian Department, be permitted to reside upon the said reservation without permission of the tribe and the superintendent and agent; and the said tribe agrees that so soon after the United States shall make the necessary provision for fulfilling the stipulations of this instrument as they can conveniently arrange their affairs, and not to exceed one year from its ratification, they will vacate the country hereby relinquished, and remove to and settle upon the lands herein reserved for them, (except as may be hereinafter provided.)

Plains, West and Northwest Plateau Indian Treaties

In the meantime it shall be lawful for them to reside upon any ground now occupied or under cultivation by said Indians at this time, and not included in the reservation above named. And it is provided, that any substantial improvement heretofore made by any Indian, such as fields inclosed and cultivated, or houses erected upon the lands hereby relinquished, and which he may be compelled to abandon in consequence of this treaty, shall be valued under the direction of the President of the United States, and payment therefor shall be made in stock or in improvements of an equal value for said Indian upon the lot which may be assigned to him within the bounds of the reservation, as he may choose, and no Indian will be required to abandon the improvements aforesaid, now occupied by him, until said payment or improvement shall have been made.

And it is further provided, that if any Indian living on any of the land hereby relinquished should prefer to sell his improvements to any white man, being a loyal citizen of the United States, prior to the same being valued as aforesaid, he shall be allowed so to do, but the sale or transfer of said improvements shall be made in the presence of, and with the consent and approval of, the agent or superintendent, by whom a certificate of sale shall be issued to the party purchasing, which shall set forth the amount of the consideration in kind.

Before the issue of said certificate, the agent or superintendent shall be satisfied that a valuable consideration is paid, and that the party purchasing is of undoubted loyalty to the United States Government. No settlement or claim made upon the improved lands by any Indian will be permitted, except as herein provided, prior to the time specified for their removal. Any sale or transfer thus made shall be in the stead of payment for improvements from the United States.

ARTICLE 3. The President shall, immediately after the ratification of this treaty, cause the boundary-lines to be surveyed, and properly marked and established; after which, so much of the lands hereby reserved as may be suitable for cultivation shall be surveyed into lots of twenty acres each, and every male person of the tribe who shall have attained the age of twenty-one years, or is the head of a family, shall have the privilege of locating upon one lot as a permanent home for such person, and the lands so surveyed, shall be allotted under such rules and regulations as the President shall prescribe, having such reference to their settlement as may secure adjoining each other the location of the different families pertaining to each band, so far as the same may be practicable. Such rules and regulations shall be prescribed by the President, or under his direction, as will insure to the family, in case of the death of the head thereof, the possession and enjoyment of such permanent home, and the improvements thereon.

When the assignments as above shall have been completed, certificates shall be issued by the Commissioner of Indian Affairs, or under his direction, for the tracts assigned in severalty, specifying the names of the individuals to whom

Plains, West and Northwest Plateau Indian Treaties

they have been assigned respectively, and that said tracts are set apart for the perpetual and exclusive use and benefit of such assignees and their heirs.

Until otherwise provided by law, such tracts shall be exempt from levy, taxation, or sale, and shall be alienable in fee, or leased, or otherwise disposed of, only to the United States, or to persons then being members of the Nez Perce tribe, and of Indian blood, with the permission of the President, and under such regulations as the Secretary of the Interior or the Commissioner of Indian Affairs shall prescribe; and if any such person or family shall at any time neglect or refuse to occupy and till a portion of the land so assigned, and on which they have located, or shall rove from place to place, the President may cancel the assignment, and may also withhold from such person or family their proportion of the annuities or other payments due them until they shall have returned to such permanent home, and resumed the pursuits of industry; and in default of their return, the tract may be declared abandoned, and thereafter assigned to some other person or family of such tribe.

The residue of the land hereby reserved shall be held in common for pasturage for the sole use and benefit of the Indians: Provided, however, That from time to time, as members of the tribe may come upon the reservation, or may become of proper age, after the expiration of the time of one year after the ratification of this treaty, as aforesaid, and claim the privileges granted under this article, lots may be assigned from the lands thus held in common, wherever the same may be suit able for cultivation. No State or territorial legislature shall remove the restriction herein provided for, without the consent of Congress, and no State or territorial law to that end shall be deemed valid until the same has been specially submitted to Congress for its approval.

ARTICLE 4. In consideration of the relinquishment herein made the United States agree to pay to the said tribe, in addition to the annuities provided by the treaty of June 11, 1855, and the goods and provisions distributed to them at the time of signing this treaty, the sum of two hundred and sixty-two thousand and five hundred dollars, in manner following, to wit:

First. One hundred and fifty thousand dollars, to enable the Indians to remove and locate upon the reservation, to be expended in the ploughing of land, and the fencing of the several lots, which may be assigned to those individual members of the tribe who will accept the same in accordance with the provisions of the preceding article, which said sum shall be divided into four annual instalments, as follows: For the first year after the ratification of this treaty, seventy thousand dollars; for the second year, forty thousand dollars; for the third year, twenty-five thousand dollars; for the fourth year, fifteen thousand dollars.

Plains, West and Northwest Plateau Indian Treaties

Second. Fifty thousand dollars to be paid the first year after the ratification of this treaty in agricultural implements, to include wagons or carts, harness, and cattle, sheep, or other stock, as may be deemed most beneficial by the superintendent of Indian affairs, or agent, after ascertaining the wishes of the Indians in relation thereto.

Third. Ten thousand dollars for the erection of a saw and flouring mill, to be located at Kamia, the same to be erected within one year after the ratification hereof.

Fourth. Fifty thousand dollars for the boarding and clothing of the children who shall attend the schools, in accordance with such rules or regulations as the Commissioner of Indian Affairs may prescribe, providing the schools and boarding-houses with necessary furniture, the purchase of necessary wagons, teams, agricultural implements, tools, &c., for their use, and for the fencing of such lands as may be needed for gardening and farming purposes, for the use and benefit of the schools, to be expended as follows: The first year after the ratification of this treaty, six thousand dollars; for the next fourteen years, three thousand dollars each year; and for the succeeding year, being the sixteenth and last instalment, two thousand dollars.

Fifth. A further sum of two thousand five hundred dollars shall be paid within one year after the ratification hereof, to enable the Indians to build two churches, one of which is to be located at some suitable point on the Kamia, and the other on the Lapwai.

ARTICLE 5. The United States further agree, that in addition to a head chief the tribe shall elect two subordinate chiefs, who shall assist him in the performance of his public services, and each subordinate chief shall have the same amount of land ploughed and fenced, with comfortable house and necessary furniture, and to whom the same salary shall be paid as is already provided for the head chief in article 5 of the treaty of ,June 11, 1855, the salary to be paid and the houses and land to be occupied during the same period and under like restrictions as therein mentioned.

And for the purpose of enabling the agent to erect said buildings, and to plough and fence the land, as well as to procure the necessary furniture, and to complete and furnish the house, &e., of the head chief, as heretofore provided, there shall be appropriated, to be expended within the first year after the ratification hereof, the sum of two thousand five hundred dollars.

And inasmuch as several of the provisions of said art. 5th of the treaty of June 11, 1855, pertaining to the erection of school-houses, hospital, shops, necessary buildings for employe(e)s and for the agency, as well as providing the same with necessary furniture, tools, &c., have not yet been complied with, it is

451

Plains, West and Northwest Plateau Indian Treaties

hereby stipulated that there shall be appropriated, to be expended for the purposes herein specified during the first year after the ratification hereof, the following sums, to wit:

First. Ten thousand dollars for the erection of the two schools, including boarding-houses and the necessary out-buildings; said schools to be conducted on the manual-labor system as far as practicable.

Second. Twelve hundred dollars for the erection of the hospital, and providing the necessary furniture for the same.

Third. Two thousand dollars for the erection of a blacksmith's shop, to be located at Kamia, to aid in the completion of the smith's shop at the agency, and to purchase the necessary tools, iron, steel, &c.; and to keep the same in repair and properly stocked with necessary tools and materials, there shall be appropriated thereafter, for the fifteen years next succeeding, the sum of five hundred dollars each year.

Fourth. Three thousand dollars for erection of houses for employe(e)s, repairs of mills, shops, &c., and providing necessary furniture, tools, and materials. For the same purpose, and to procure from year to year the necessary articlesthat is to say, saw-logs, nails, glass, hardware, &c.-there shall be appropriated thereafter, for the twelve years next succeeding, the sum of two thousand dollars each year; and for the next three years, one thousand dollars each year.

And it is further agreed that the United States shall employ, in addition to those already mentioned in art. 5th of the treaty of June 11, 1855, two matrons to take charge of the boarding-schools, two assistant teachers, one farmer, one carpenter, and two millers.
All the expenditures and expenses contemplated in this treaty, and not otherwise provided for, shall be defrayed by the United States.

ARTICLE 6. In consideration of the past services and faithfulness of the Indian chief, Timothy, it is agreed that the United States shall appropriate the sum of six hundred dollars, to aid him in the erection of a house upon the lot of land which may be assigned to him, in accordance with the provisions of the third article of this treaty.

ARTICLE 7. The United States further agree that the claims of certain members of the Nez Perce tribe against the Government for services rendered and for horses furnished by them to the Oregon mounted volunteers, as appears by certificate issued by W. H. Fauntleroy, A. R. Qr. M. and Com. Oregon volunteers, on the 6th of March, 1856, at Camp Cornelius, and amounting to the sum of four thousand six hundred and sixty-five dollars, shall be paid to them in full, in gold coin.

Plains, West and Northwest Plateau Indian Treaties

ARTICLE 8. It is also understood that the aforesaid tribe do hereby renew their acknowledgments of dependence upon the Government of the United States, their promises of friendship, and other pledges, as set forth in the eighth article of the treaty of June 11, 1855; and further, that all the provisions of said treaty which are not abrogated or specifically changed by any article herein contained, shall remain the same to all intents and purposes as formerly, the same obligations resting upon the United States, the same privileges continued to the Indians outside of the reservation, and the same rights secured to citizens of the U. S. as to right of way upon the streams and over the roads which may run through said reservation, as are therein set forth

But it is further provided, that the United States is the only competent authority to declare and establish such necessary roads and highways, and that no other right is intended to be hereby granted to citizens of the United States than the right of way upon or over such roads as may thus be legally established: Provided, however, That the roads now usually travelled shall, in the mean time, be taken and deemed as within the meaning of this article, until otherwise enacted by act of Congress or by the authority of the Indian Department.

And the said tribe hereby consent, that upon the public roads which may run across the reservation there may be established, at such points as shall be necessary for public convenience, hotels, or stage-stands, of the number and necessity of which the agent or superintendent shall be the sole judge, who shall be competent to license the same, with the privilege of using such amount of land for pasturage and other purposes connected with such establishment as the agent or superintendent shall deem necessary, it being understood that such lands for pasturage are to be enclosed, and the boundaries thereof described in the license.

And it is further understood and agreed that all ferries and bridges within the reservation shall be held and managed for the benefit of said tribe.

Such rules and regulations shall be made by the Commissioner of Indian Affairs, with the approval of the Secretary of the interior, as shall regulate the travel on the highways, the management of the ferries and bridges, the licensing of public houses, and the leasing of lands, as herein provided, so that the rents, profits, and issues thereof shall inure to the benefit of said tribe, and so that the persons thus licensed, or necessarily employed in any of the above relations, shall be subject to the control of the Indian Department, and to the provisions of the act of Congress "to regulate trade and intercourse with the Indian tribes, and to preserve peace on the frontiers."

All timber within the bounds of the reservation is exclusively the property of the tribe, excepting that the U. S. Government shall be permitted to use thereof

Plains, West and Northwest Plateau Indian Treaties

for any purpose connected with its affairs, either in carrying out any of the provisions of this treaty, or in the maintaining of its necessary forts or garrisons.
The United States also agree to reserve all springs or fountains not adjacent to, or directly connected with, the streams or rivers within the lands hereby relinquished, and to keep back from settlement or entry so much of the surrounding land as may be necessary to prevent the said springs or fountains being enclosed; and, further, to preserve a perpetual right of way to and from the same, as watering places, for the use in common of both whites and Indians.

ARTICLE 9. Inasmuch as the Indians in council have expressed their desire that Robert Newell should have confirmed to him a piece of land lying between Snake and Clearwater Rivers, the same having been given to him on the 9th day of June, 1861, and described in an instrument of writing bearing that date, and signed by several chiefs of the tribe, it is hereby agreed that the said Robert Newell shall receive from the United States a patent for the said tract of land.

ARTICLE 10. This treaty shall be obligatory upon the contracting parties as soon as the same shall be ratified by the President and Senate of the United States.

In testimony whereof the said C. H. Hale, superintendent of Indian affairs, and Charles Hutchins and S. D. Howe, United States Indian agents in the Territory of Washington, and the chiefs, headmen, and delegates of the aforesaid Nez Perce tribe of Indians, have hereunto set their hands and seals at the place and on the day and year hereinbefore written.

Calvin H. Hale, Superintendent Indian Affairs, Wash.
T. Chas. Hutchins, United States Indian agent, Wash. T.
S. D. Howe, United States Indian agent, Head Chief Nez Perces Nation, Utesin-male-e-cum, x, Ha-harch-tuesta, x, Tip-ulania-timecca, x, Kup-kup-pellia x, Wap-tas-ta-mana, x

Signed and sealed in presence of-
George F. Whitworth, Secretary.
Justus Steinberger, Colonel U. S. Volunteers.
R. F. Malloy, Colonel Cavalry, O.V.

TREATY WITH THE EASTERN SHOSHONI {1863, July 2}
Ratified Mar. 7, 1864.
Proclaimed June 7, 1869.

Articles of Agreement made at Fort Bridget, in Utah Territory, this second day of July, A. D. one thousand eight hundred and sixty-three, by and between the United States of America, represented by its Commissioners, and the Shoshone

Plains, West and Northwest Plateau Indian Treaties

nation of Indians, represented by its Chiefs and Principal Men And Warriors of the Eastern Bands, as follows:

ARTICLE 1. Friendly and amically relations are hereby re-established between the bands of the Shoshonee nation, parties hereto, and the United States; and it is declared that a firm and perpetual peace shall be henceforth maintained between the Shoshonee nation and the United States.

ARTICLE 2. The several routes of travel through the Shoshonee country, now or hereafter used by white men, shall be and remain forever free and safe for the use of the government of the United States, and of all emigrants and travellers under its authority and Protection, without molestation or injury from any of the people of the said nation. And if depredations should at any time be committed by bad men of their nation, the offenders shall be immediately seized and delivered up to the proper officers of the United States, to be punished as their offences shah deserve; and the safety of all travellers passing peaceably over said routes is hereby guaranteed by said nation.

Military agricultural settlements and military posts may be established by the President of the United States along said routes; ferries may be maintained over the rivers wherever they may be required; and houses erected and settlements formed at such points as may be necessary for the comfort and convenience of travellers.

ARTICLE 3. The telegraph and overland stage lines having been established and operated through a part of the Shoshonee country, it is expressly agreed that the same may be continued without hindrance, molestation, or injury from the people of said nation; and that their property, and the lives of passengers in the stages, and of the employes of the respective companies, shall be protected by them.
And further, it being understood that provision has been made by the Government of the United States for the construction of a railway from the plains west to the Pacific ocean, it is stipulated by said nation that said railway, or its branches, may be located, constructed, and operated, without molestation from them, through any portion of the country claimed by them.

ARTICLE 4. It is understood the boundaries of the Shoshonee country, as defined and described by said nation, is as follows: On the north, by the mountains on the north side of the valley of Shoshonee or Snake River; on the east, by the Wind River mountains, Peenahpah river, the north fork of Platte or Koochin-agah, and the north Park or Buffalo House; and on the south, by Yampah river and the Uintah mountains. The western boundary is left undefined, there being no Shoshonees from that district of country present; but the bands now present claim that their own country is bounded on the west by Salt Lake.

455

Plains, West and Northwest Plateau Indian Treaties

ARTICLE 5. The United States being aware of the inconvenience resulting to the Indians in consequence of the driving away and destruction of game along the routes travelled by whites, and by the formation of agricultural and mining settlements, are willing to fairly compensate them for the same; therefore, and in consideration of the preceding stipulations, the United States promise and agree to pay to the bands of the Shoshonee nation, parties hereto, annually for the term of twenty years, the sum of ten thousand dollars, in such articles as the President of the United States may deem suitable to their wants and condition, either as hunters or herdsmen. And the said bands of the Shoshonee nation hereby acknowledge the reception of the said stipulated annuities, as a full compensation and equivalent for the loss of game, and the rights and privileges hereby conceded.

ARTICLE 6. The said bands hereby acknowledge that they have received from said Commissioners provisions and clothing amounting to six thousand dollars, as presents, at the conclusion of this treaty.

ARTICLE 7. Nothing herein contained shall be construed or taken to admit any other or greater title or interest in the lands embraced within the territories described in said Treaty with said tribes or bands of Indians than existed in them upon the acquisition of said territories from Mexico by the laws thereof.

James Duane Doty, Luther Mann, jr., Commissioners.

Washakee, his x mark, Wanapitz, his x mark, Toopsapowet, his x mark, Panto-shiga, his x mark, Ninabitzee, his x mark, Narkawk, his x mark, Taboonshea, his x mark, Weerango, his x mark, Tootsahp, his x mark, Weeahyukee, his x mark, Bazile, his x mark,

In the presence of
Jack Robertson, interpreter. Samuel Dean.

TREATY WITH THE SHOSHONI NORTHWESTERN BANDS
{1863, July 30}
Ratified Mar. 7. 1864.
Proclaimed Jan. 17, 1865.

Articles of agreement made at Box Elder, in Utah Territory, this thirtieth day of July, A. D. one thousand eight hundred and sixty-three, by and between the United States of America, represented by Brigadier-General P. Edward Connor, commanding the military district of Utah, and James Duane Dory, commissioner, and the northwestern bands of the Shoshonee Indians, represented by their chiefs and warriors.

Plains, West and Northwest Plateau Indian Treaties

ARTICLE 1. It is agreed that friendly and amicable relations shall be reestablished between the bands of the Shoshonee Nation, parties hereto, and the United States, and it is declared that a firm and perpetual peace shall be henceforth maintained between the said bands and the United States.

ARTICLE 2. The treaty concluded at Fort Bridger on the 2nd day of July, 1863, between the United States and the Shoshonee Nation, being read and fully interpreted and explained to the said chiefs and warriors, they do hereby give their full and free assent to all of the provisions of said treaty, and the same are hereby adopted as a part of this agreement, and the same shall be binding upon the parties hereto.

ARTICLE 3. In consideration of the stipulations in the preceding articles, the United States agree to increase the annuity to the Shoshonee Nation five thousand dollars, to be paid in the manner provided in said treaty. And the said northwestern bands hereby acknowledge to have received of the United States, at the signing of these articles, provisions and goods to the amount of two thousand dollars, to relieve their immediate necessities, the said bands having been reduced by the war to a state of utter destitution.

ARTICLE 4. The country claimed by Pokatello, for himself and his people, is bounded on the west by Raft River and on the east by the Porteneuf Mountains.

ARTICLE 5. Nothing herein contained shall be construed or taken to admit any other or greater title or interest in the lands embraced within the territories described in said treaty in said tribes or bands of Indians than existed in them upon the acquisition of said territories from Mexico by the laws thereof.

Done at Box Elder, this thirtieth day of July, A. D. 1863.

James Duane Dory, Governor and acting superintendent of Indian affairs in Utah Territory.
P. Edw. Connor, Brigadier-General U. S. Volunteers, commanding District of Utah.

Pokatello, his x mark, chief, Toomontso, his x mark, chief, Sanpitz, his x mark, chief, Tosowitz, his x mark, chief.

Witnesses:
Robt. Pollock, colonel Third Infantry, C. V. M. G. Lewis, captain Third Infantry, C. V.
S. E. Jocelyn, first lieutenant Third Infantry, C. V. Jos. A. Gebone, Indian interpreter.

Plains, West and Northwest Plateau Indian Treaties

TREATY WITH THE WESTERN SHOSHONI {1863, Oct. 1}
Ratified June 26, 1866.
Proclaimed Oct. 21, 1869.

Treaty of Peace and Friendship made at Ruby Valley, in rite of Territory of Nevada, this first day of October, A. D. one thousand eight hundred and sixty-three, between the United States of America, represented by the undersigned commissioners, and the Western Bands of the Shoshonee Nation of Indians, represented by their Chiefs and Principal Men and Warriors, as follows:

ARTICLE 1. Peace and friendship shall be hereafter-established and maintained between the Western Bands of the Shoshonee nation and the people and Government of the United States; and the said bands stipulate and agree that hostilities and all depredations upon the emigrant trains, the mail and telegraph lines, and upon the citizens of the United States within their country, shall cease.

ARTICLE 2. The several routes of travel through the Shoshonee country, now or hereafter used by white men, shall be forever free, and unobstructed by the said bands, for the use of the government of the United States, and of all emigrants and travellers under its authority and protection, without molestation or injury from them. And if depredations are at any time committed by bad men of their nation, the offenders shall be immediately taken and delivered up to the proper officers of the United States, to be punished as their offences shall deserve; and the safety of all travellers passing peaceably over either of said routes is hereby guarantied by said bands.

Military posts may be established by the President of the United States along said routes or elsewhere in their country; and station houses may be erected and occupied at such points as may be necessary for the comfort and convenience of travellers or for mail or telegraph companies.

ARTICLE 3. The telegraph and overland stage lines having been established and operated by companies under the authority of the United States through a part of the Shoshonee country, it is expressly agreed that the same may be continued without hindrance, molestation, or injury from the people of said bands, and that their property and the lives and property of passengers in the stages and of the employes of the respective companies, shall be protected by them. And further, it being understood that provision has been made by the government of the United States for the construction of a railway from the plains west to the Pacific ocean, it is stipulated by the said bands that the said railway or its branches may be located, constructed, and operated, and without molestation from them, through any portion of country claimed or occupied by them.

Plains, West and Northwest Plateau Indian Treaties

ARTICLE 4. it is further agreed by the parties hereto, that the Shoshonee country may be explored and prospected for gold and silver, or other minerals; and when mines are discovered, they may be worked, and mining and agricultural settlements formed, and ranches established whenever they may be required. Mills may be erected and timber taken for their use, as also for building and other purposes in any part of the country claimed by said bands.

ARTICLE 5. It is understood that the boundaries of the country claimed and occupied by said bands are defined and described by them as follows:

On the north by Wong-goga-da Mountains and Shoshonee River Valley; on the west by Su-non-to-yah Mountains or Smith Creek Mountains; on the south by Wi-co-bah and the Colorado Desert; on the east by Po-ho-no-be Valley or Steptoe Valley and Great Salt Lake Valley.

ARTICLE 6. The said bands agree that whenever the President of the United States shall deem it expedient for them to abandon the roaming life, which, they now lead, and become herdsmen or agriculturalists, he is hereby authorized to make such reservations for their use as he may deem necessary within the country above described; and they do also hereby agree to remove their camps to such reservations as he may indicate, and to reside and remain therein.

ARTICLE 7. The United States, being aware of the inconvenience resulting to the Indians in consequence of the driving away and destruction of game along the routes travelled by white men, and by the formation of agricultural and mining settlements, are willing to fairly compensate them for the same; therefore, and in consideration of the preceding stipulations, and of their faithful observance by the said bands, the United States promise and agree to pay to the said bands of the Shoshonee nation parties hereto, annually for the term of twenty years, the sum of five thousand dollars in such articles, including cattle for herding or other purposes, as the, President of the United States shall deem suitable for their wants and condition, either as hunters or herdsmen. And the said bands hereby acknowledge the reception of the said stipulated annuities as a full compensation and equivalent for the loss of game and the rights and privileges hereby conceded.

ARTICLE 8. The said bands hereby acknowledge that they have received from said commissioners provisions and clothing amounting to five thousand dollars as presents at the conclusion of this treaty.

Done at Ruby Valley the day and year above written.

Plains, West and Northwest Plateau Indian Treaties

James W. Nye, James Duane Doty, Te-moak, his x mark, Mo-ho-a, Kirk-weedgwa, his x mark, To-nag, his x mark, To-so-wee-so-op, his x mark, Sow-er-e-gah, his x mark,

Witnesses:
Po-on-go-sah, his x mark, Par-a-woat-ze, his x mark, Ga-ha-dier, his x mark, Ko-ro-kout-ze, his x mark, Pon-ge-mah, his x mark, Buck, his x mark, J. B. Moore, lieutenant-colonel Third Infantry California Volunteers, Jacob T. Lockhart, Indian agent Nevada Territory, Henry Butterfield, interpreter.

TREATY WITH THE UTAH TABEGUACHE BAND {1863, Oct. 7}
Ratified Mar. 25, 1864.
Proclaimed Dec. 14, 1864.

Whereas the Tabeguache band of Utah Indians claim as against all other Indian tribes an exclusive right to the following-described country as their lands and hunting grounds within the territory of the United States of America, being bounded and described as follows, to wit:

"Beginning on the 37th degree of north latitude, at the eastern base of the Sierra Madre Mountain; running thence northerly with the base of the Rocky Mountains to the forty-first parallel of north latitude: thence west with the line of said forty-first parallel of north latitude to its intersection with the summit of the Snowy range northwest of the North Park; thence with the summit of the Snowy range southerly to the Rabbit-Ear Mountains; thence southerly with the summit of said Rabbit-Ear range of Mountains, west of the Middle Park, to the Grand River.

Thence with the said Grand River to its confluence with the Gunnison River; thence with the said Gunnison River to the mouth of the Uncompahgre River; thence with the said Uncompahgre River to its source in the summit of the Snowy range, opposite the source of the Rio Grande del Norte; thence in a right line south to the summit of the Sierra La Plata range of mountains, dividing the waters of the San Juan River from those of the Rio Grande del Norte; thence with the summit of said range southeasterly to the thirty-seventh parallel of north latitude; thence with the line of said parallel of latitude to the place of beginning:"

The President of the United States of America, by John Evans, governor of Colorado Territory, and ex-officio superintendent of Indian affairs for the same; Michael Steck, superintendent of Indian affairs for the Territory of New Mexico; Simeon Whiteley and Lafayette Head, Indian agents, duly authorized and appointed as commissioners for the purpose, of the one part, and the undersigned chiefs and war-riots of the Tabeguache band of Utah Indians, of the

Plains, West and Northwest Plateau Indian Treaties

other part, have made and entered into the following treaty, which, when ratified by the President of the United States, by and with the advice and consent of the Senate, shall be binding on both parties, to wit:

ARTICLE 1. It is admitted by the Tabeguache band of Utah Indians that they reside within the territorial limits of the United States, acknowledging their supremacy, and claim their protection. The said band also admits the right of the United States to regulate all trade and intercourse with them.

ARTICLE 2. Said Tabeguache band of Utah Indians hereby cede, convey, and relinquish all of their claims, right, title, and interest in and to any and all lands within the territory of the United States wherever situated, excepting that which is included within the following boundaries, which are hereby reserved as their hunting-grounds, viz:

Beginning at the mouth of the Uncompahgre River; thence down Gunnison River to its confluence with Bunkara River; thence up the Bunkara River to the Roaring Fork of the same; thence up the Roaring Fork to its source; thence along the summit of the range dividing the waters of the Arkansas from those of the Gunnison River to its intersection with the range dividing the waters of the San Luis Valley from those of the Gunnison's Fork of the Great Colorado River; thence along the summit of said range to the source of the Uncompahgre River; thence from said source and down the main channel of said Uncompahgre River to its mouth, the place of beginning. Nothing contained in this treaty shall be construed or taken to admit on the part of the United States any other or greater title or interest in the lands above excepted and reserved in said tribe or band of Indians than existed in them upon the acquisition of said Territory from Mexico by the laws thereof.

ARTICLE 3. And it is further agreed that the United States shall have the right to establish one or more military posts, with their needful reservations, upon the lands and hunting-grounds not ceded by the Tabeguache band in this treaty; also the right to locate, construct, and maintain railroads and other roads and highways through the same, and along routes of United States mail-lines, at suitable points, to establish and maintain stations.

Any citizen of the United States may mine, without interference or molestation, in any part of the country hereby reserved to said Indians where gold or other metals or minerals may be found.

ARTICLE 4. And the said Tabeguache band hereby gives its consent that the Mohuache band of Utah Indians may also be settled with them upon the lands and hunting-grounds reserved in this treaty.

Plains, West and Northwest Plateau Indian Treaties

ARTICLE 5. And-the said Tabeguache band further agrees to give safe-conduct to all persons who may be legally authorized by the United States to pass through their reservation, and to protect in their persons and property all agents or other persons sent by the United States to reside temporarily among them.

ARTICLE 6. That the friendship which is now established between the United States and the Tabeguache band of Utah Indians should not be interrupted by the misconduct of individuals, it is hereby agreed that for injuries done no private revenge or retaliation shall take place, but, instead thereof, complaint shall be made by the party injured to the superintendent or agent of Indian affairs, or other person appointed by the President. And it shall be the duty of the chiefs of said Tabeguache band, upon complaint being made as aforesaid, to deliver up the person or persons against whom the complaint is made, to the end that he or they may be punished agreeably to the laws of the United States. And in like manner, if any robbery, violence, or murder shall be committed on any Indian or Indians belonging to said band, the person or persons so offending shall be tried, and if found guilty, shall be punished in like manner as if the injury had been done to a white man.

And it is agreed that the chiefs of said Tabeguache band shall, to the utmost of their power, exert themselves to recover horses or other property which may be stolen or taken from any citizen or citizens or white residents of the United States by any individual or individuals of said band; and the property so recovered shall be forthwith delivered to the agents or other persons authorized to receive it, that it may be restored to the proper owner. And for such property as any Indian or Indians belonging to said band may have taken from citizens or white residents of the United States which cannot be restored, payment shall be reserved from the annuities which the said band is to receive, upon sufficient proof of the fact. And the United States hereby guarantee to any Indian or Indians of said band a full indemnification for any horses or other property which may be stolen from them by any of their citizens or white residents: Provided, That the property so stolen cannot be recovered, and that sufficient proof is produced that it was actually stolen by a citizen or white resident of the United States. And the said Tabeguache band engages, on the requisition or demand of the President of the United States, or of the agents, to deliver up any white man resident among them.

ARTICLE 7. And the chiefs and warriors as aforesaid promise and engage their band will never, by sale, exchange, or as presents, supply any nation or tribe of Indians, not in amity with the United States, with guns, ammunition, or other implements of war.

Plains, West and Northwest Plateau Indian Treaties

ARTICLE 8. For the period of ten years the said band shall receive, annually, by such distribution as the Secretary of the interior may direct, ten thousand dollars' worth of goods, and also ten thousand dollars' worth of provisions.

ARTICLE 9. For the purpose of improving their breed of horses, the band shall receive five American stallions the first year after the ratification of this treaty.

ARTICLE 10. That in case the chiefs of said band shall announce to the agent a willingness and determination on their part, and on the part of their people, to begin and follow agricultural or pastoral pursuits by farming or raising stock, and growing wool upon such lands to be selected and set apart within said reservation, and according to such regulations as the Secretary of the Interior may prescribe, they shall receive the following donations of stock to aid them in their endeavor to gain a livelihood by such new pursuits, viz:

Of cattle, not exceeding one hundred and fifty head annually during five years, beginning with the ratification of this treaty. Of sheep, not exceeding one thousand head annually during the first two years after the ratification of this treaty, and five hundred head annually during the three years thereafter.
The Secretary of the Interior may also direct that their share of annuity goods and provisions shall be of a character suited to such change of life: Provided, however, That such stock shall only be donated as long as such chiefs shall in good faith keep and use the same for the purpose indicated in this article, and provided that the amount expended under this article shall not exceed ten thousand dollars annually.

All the Indians of said band who may adopt and conform to the provisions of this article shall be protected in the quiet and peaceable possession of their said lands and property.

The Government also agrees to establish and maintain a blacksmith-shop, and employ a competent blacksmith, for the purpose of repairing the guns and agricultural implements which may be used by said band of Indians.

In testimony whereof, the said commissioners, as aforesaid, and the said chiefs and warriors of the Tabeguache band of Utah Indians, have hereunto set their hands and seals, at the Tabeguache agency, at Conejos, Colorado Territory, on this the seventh day of October, in the year of our Lord one thousand eight hundred and sixty-three.

Jno. Evans, Governor C. T., Superintendent Indian Affairs, and Commissioner.
M. Steck, Superintendent Indian Affairs New Mexico and Commissioner.
Simeon Whiteley, U. S. Agent to the Grand River and Uintah, Bands of Utah Indians and Commissioner, Lafayette Head, U. S. Indian Agent and Commissioner.

Plains, West and Northwest Plateau Indian Treaties

Un-cow-ra-gut, or Red Color, his x mark, Sha-wa-she-yet, or Blue Flower, his x mark, Colorado, his x mark, U-ray, or Arrow, his x mark, No-va-ve-tu quar-et, or One that Slides under the Snow, his x mark, Sa-wa-wat-se-wich, or Blue. River, his x mark, A-ca-mu-che-ne, or Red Wind, his x mark, Mu-chu-chop, or Lock of Hair, his x mark, Sa-patch, or White Warm, his x mark, Cinche, or Left. Hand.

Witnesses to the treaty:
J no. G. Nicolay, Secretary to the Commission, Chas. E. Phillips, Assistant Sec-retary to Commission, J. W. Chroughton, Colonel First Cavalry of Colorado, Commanding District, Samuel F. Tappan, Lieutenant-Colonel First Cavalry of Colorado, Charles Kerber, Captain, First Cavalry of Colorado, J. P. Benesteel, Captain, First Cavalry of Colorado.

Interpreters:
Juan V. Valdes, Bernardo Sanchcz, his x mark, Areadot Sanchez, his x mark,

TREATY WITH THE SHOSHONI-GOSHIP {1863, Oct. 12}
Ratified Mar. 7, 1864
Proclaimed Jan. 17, 1865.

Treaty of peace and friendship made at Tuilla Valley, in the Territory of Utah, this twelfth day of October, A. D. one thousand eight hundred and sixty-three, between the United States of America, represented by the undersigned commis-sioners, and the Shoshonee-Goship bands of Indians, represented by their chiefs, principal men, and warriors, as follows:

ARTICLE 1. Peace and friendship is hereby established and shall be hereafter maintained between the Shoshonee-Goship bands of Indians and the citizens and Government of the United States; and the said bands stipulate and agree that hostilities and all depredations upon the emigrant trains, the mail and tele-graph lines, and upon the citizens of the United States, within their country, shall cease.

ARTICLE 2. It is further stipulated by said bands that the several routes of travel through their country now or hereafter used by white men shall be for-ever free and unobstructed by them, for the use of the Government of the United States, and of all emigrants and travellers within it under its authority and protection, without molestation or injury from them.

And if depredations are at any time committed by bad men of their own or other tribes within their country, the offenders shall be immediately taken and delivered up to the proper officers of the United States, to be punished as their

Plains, West and Northwest Plateau Indian Treaties

offences may deserve; and the safety of all travellers passing peaceably over either of said routes is hereby guaranteed by said bands.

Military posts may be established by the President of the United States along said routes, or elsewhere in their country; and station-houses may be erected and occupied at such points as may be necessary for the comfort and convenience of travellers or for the use of the mail or telegraph companies.

ARTICLE 3. The telegraph and overland stage lines having been established and operated by companies under the authority of the United States through the country occupied by said bands, it is expressly agreed that the same may be continued without hindrance, molestation, or injury from the people of said bands, and that their property, and the lives and property of passengers in the stages, and of the employees of the respective companies, shall be protected by them.

And further, it being understood that provision has been made by the Government of the United States for the construction of a railway from the plains west to the Pacific Ocean, it is stipulated by said bands that the said railway or its branches may be located, constructed, and operated, and without molestation from them, through any portion of the country claimed or occupied by them.

ARTICLE 4. It is further agreed by the parties hereto that the country of the Goship tribe may be explored and prospected for gold and silver, or other minerals and metals; and when mines are discovered they may be worked, and mining and agricultural settlements formed and ranchos established wherever they may be required. Mills may be erected and timber taken for their use, as also for building and other purposes, in any part of said country.

ARTICLE 5. It is understood that the boundaries of the country claimed and occupied by the Goship tribe, as defined and described by said bands, are as follows: On the north by the middle of the Great Desert; on the west by Steptoe Valley; on the south by Tooedoe or Green Mountains; and on the east by Great Salt Lake, Tuilla, and Rush Valleys.

ARTICLE 6. The said bands agree that whenever the President of United States shall deem it expedient for them to abandon the roaming life which they now lead, and become settled as herdsmen or agriculturists, he is hereby authorized to make such reservations for their use as he may deem necessary; and they do also agree to remove their camps to such reservations as he may indicate, and to reside and remain thereon.

ARTICLE 7. The United States being aware of the inconvenience resulting to the Indians, in consequence of the driving away and destruction of game along the routes travelled by white men, and by the formation of agricultural and

Plains, West and Northwest Plateau Indian Treaties

mining settlements, are willing to fairly compensate them for the same. Therefore, and in consideration of the preceding stipulations, and of their faithful observance by said bands, the United States promise and agree to pay to the said Goship tribe, or to the said bands, parties hereto, at the option of the President of the United States, annually, for the term of twenty years, the sum of one thousand dollars, in such articles, including cattle for herding or other purposes, as the President shall deem suitable for their wants and condition either as hunters or herdsmen.

And the said bands, for themselves and for their tribe, hereby acknowledge the reception of the said stipulated annuities as a full compensation and equivalent for the loss of game and the rights and privileges hereby conceded; and also one thousand dollars in provisions and goods at and before the signing of this treaty.

ARTICLE 8. Nothing herein contained shall be construed or taken to admit any other or greater title or interest in the lands embraced within the territories described in said treaty in said tribes or bands of Indians than existed in them upon the acquisition of said territories from Mexico by the laws thereof.

James Duane Dory, commissioner, Brigadier-General U. S. Volunteers, Commanding District of Utah.

P. Edw. Connor, Tabby, his x mark, Adaseim, his x mark, Tintsa-pa-gin, his x mark, Harray-nup, his x mark,

Witnesses
Amos Reed, Chas. H. Hempstead, captain and chief commissary district of Utah, William Lee, interpreter,

TREATY WITH THE KLAMATH, ETC. {1864, Oct. 14}
Ratified, July 2, 1866.
Proclaimed Feb. 17, 1870.

Articles of agreement and convention made and concluded at Klamath Lake, Oregon, on the fourteenth day of October, A. D. one thousand eight hundred and sixty-four, by J. W. Petit Huntington, superintendent of Indian affairs in Oregon, and William Logan, United States Indian agent for Oregon, on the part of the United States, and the chiefs and head-men of the Klamath and Moadoc tribes, and Yahooskin band of Snake Indians, hereinafter named, to wit, La-Lake, Chil-o-que-nas, Kellogue, Mo-ghen-kas-kit, Blow, Le-lu, Palmer, Jack, Que-as, Poo-sak-sult, Che-mult, No-ak-sum, Mooch-kat-allick, Toon-tuck-tee, Boos-ki-you, Ski-a-tic, Shol-las-loos, Ta-tet-pas,-Muk-has, Herman-koos-mam, chiefs and head-men of the Klamaths; Schon-chin, Stat-it-ut, Keint-poos,

466

Plains, West and Northwest Plateau Indian Treaties

Chuck-e-i-ox, chiefs and head-men of the Moadocs, and Kile-to-ak and Sky-te-ock-et, chlefs of the Yahooskin band of Snakes.

ARTICLE 1. The tribes of Indians aforesaid cede to the United States all their right, title, and claim to all the country claimed by them, the same being determined by the following boundaries, to wit: Beginning at the point where the forty fourth parallel of north latitude crosses the summit of the Cascade Mountains; thence following the main dividing-ridge of said mountains in a southerly direction to the ridge which separates the waters of Pitt and McCloud Rivers from the waters on the north; thence along said dividing-ridge in an easterly direction to the southern end of Goose Lake; thence northeasterly to the northern end of Harney Lake; thence due north to the forty-fourth parallel of north latitude; thence west to the place of beginning: Provided, That the following-described tract, within the country ceded by this treaty, shall, until otherwise directed by the President of the United States, be set apart as a residence for said Indians, (and) held and regarded as an Indian reservation, to wit:

Beginning upon the eastern shore of the middle Klamath Lake, at the Point of Rocks, about twelve miles below the mouth of Williamson's River; thence following up said eastern shore to the mouth of Wood River; thence up Wood River to a point one mile north of the bridge at Fort Klamath; thence due east to the summit of the ridge which divides the upper and middle Klamath Lakes; thence along said ridge to a point due east of the north end of the upper lake; thence due east, passing the said north end of the upper lake, to the summit of the mountains on the east side of the lake; thence along said mountain to the point where Sprague's River is intersected by the Ish-tish-ea-wax Creek; thence in a southerly direction to the summit of the mountain, the extremity of which forms the Point of Rocks; thence along said mountain to the place of beginning. And the tribes aforesaid agree and bind themselves that, immediately after the ratification of this treaty, they will remove to said reservation and remain thereon, unless temporary leave of absence be granted to them by the superintendent or agent having charge of the tribes.

it is further stipulated and agreed that no white person shall be permitted to locate or remain upon the reservation, except the Indian superintendent and agent, employes of the Indian department, and officers of the Army of the United States, and that m case persons other than those specified are found upon the reservation, they shall be immediately expelled therefrom; and the exclusive right of taking fish in the streams and lakes, included in said reservation, and of gathering edible roots, seeds, and berries within its limits, is hereby secured to the Indians aforesaid: Provided, also, That the right of way for public roads and railroads across said reservation is reserved to citizens of the United States.

Plains, West and Northwest Plateau Indian Treaties

ARTICLE 2. In consideration of, and in payment for the country ceded by this treaty, the United States agree to pay to the tribes conveying the same the several sums of money hereinafter enumerated, to wit: Eight thousand dollars per annum for a period of five years, commencing on the first day of October, eighteen hundred and sixty-five, or as soon thereafter as this treaty may be ratified; five thousand dollars per annum for the term of five years next succeeding the first period of five years; and three thousand dollars per annum for the term of five years next succeeding the second period; all of which several sums shall be applied to the use and benefit of said Indians by the superintendent or agent having charge of the tribes, under the direction of the President of the United States, who shall, from time to time, in his discretion, determine for what objects the same shall be expended, so as to carry out the design of the expenditure, (it) being to promote the well-being of the Indians, advance them in civilization, and especially agriculture, and to secure their moral improvement and education.

ARTICLE 3. The United States agree to pay said Indians the additional sum of thirty-five thousand dollars, a portion whereof shall be used to pay for such articles as may be advanced to them at the time of signing this treaty, and the remainder shall be applied to subsisting the Indians during the first year after their removal to the reservation, the purchase of teams, farming implements, tools, seeds, clothing, and provisions, and for the payment of the necessary employes.

ARTICLE 4. The United States further agree that there shall be erected at suitable points on the reservation, as soon as practicable after the ratification of this treaty, one saw-mill, one flouring-mill, suitable buildings for the use of the blacksmith, carpenter, and wagon and plough maker, the necessary buildings for one manual-labor school, and such hospital buildings as may be necessary, which buildings shall be kept in repair at the expense of the United States for the term of twenty years; and it is further stipulated that the necessary tools and material for the saw-mill, flour-mill, carpenter, blacksmith, and wagon and plough maker's shops, and books and stationery for the manual-labor school, shall be furnished by the United States for the period of twenty years.

ARTICLE 5. The United States further engage to furnish and pay for the services and subsistence, for the term of fifteen years, of one superintendent of farming operations, one farmer, one blacksmith, one sawyer, one carpenter, and one wagon and plough maker, and for the term of twenty years of one physician, one miller, and two schoolteachers.

ARTICLE 6. The United States may, in their discretion, cause a part or the whole of the reservation provided for in Article 1 to be surveyed into tracts and assigned to members of the tribes of Indians, parties to this treaty, or such of them as may appear likely to be benefited by the same, under the following re-

Plains, West and Northwest Plateau Indian Treaties

strictions and limitations, to wit: To each head of a family shall be assigned and granted a tract of not less than forty nor more than one hundred and twenty acres, according to the number of persons in such family; and to each single man above the age of twenty-one years a tract not exceeding forty acres. The Indians to whom these tracts are granted are guaranteed the perpetual possession and use of the tracts thus granted and of the improvements which may be placed thereon; but no Indian shall have the right to alienate or convey any such tract to any person whatsoever, and the same shall be forever exempt from levy, sale, or forfeiture: Provided, That the Congress of the United States may hereafter abolish these restrictions and permit the sale of the lands so assigned, if the prosperity of the Indians will be advanced thereby: And Provided further, If any Indian, to whom an assignment of land has been made, shall refuse to reside upon the tract so assigned for a period of two years, his right to the same shall be deemed forfeited.

ARTICLE 7. The President of the United States is empowered to declare such rules and regulations as will secure to the family, in case of the death of the head thereof, the use and possession of the tract assigned to him, with the improvements thereon.

ARTICLE 8. The antiquities of the tribes mentioned in this treaty shall not be held liable or taken to pay the debts of individuals.

ARTICLE 9. The several tribes of Indians, parties to this treaty, acknowledge their dependence upon the Government of the United States, and agree to be friendly with all citizens thereof, and to commit no depredations upon the person or property of said citizens, and to refrain from carrying on any war upon other Indian tribes; and they further agree that they will not communicate with or assist any persons or nation hostile to the United States, and, further, that they will submit to and obey all laws and regulations which the United States may prescribe for their government and conduct.

ARTICLE 10. It is hereby provided that if any member of these tribes shall drink any spirituous liquor, or bring any such liquor upon the reservation, his or her proportion of the benefits of this treaty may be withheld for such time as the President of the United States may direct.

ARTICLE 11. It is agreed between the contracting parties that if the United States, at any future time, may desire to locate other tribes upon the reservation provided for in this treaty, no objection shall be made thereto; but the tribes, parties to this treaty, shall not, by such location of other tribes, forfeit any of their rights or privileges guaranteed to them by this treaty.

ARTICLE 12. This treaty shall bind the contracting parties whenever the same is ratified by the Senate and President of the United States.

Plains, West and Northwest Plateau Indian Treaties

In witness of which, the several parties named in the foregoing treaty have hereunto set their hands and seals at the place and date above written.

J. W. Perit Huntington, Superintendent Indian Affairs.
William Logan, United States Indian Agent.

La-lake, his x mark, Chil-o-que-nas, his x mark, Kellogue, his x mark, Moghen-kas-kit, his x mark, Blow, his x mark, Le-lu, his x mark, Palmer, his x mark, Jack, his x mark, Que-ass, his x mark, Poo-sak-sult, his x mark, Chemult, his x mark, No-ak-sum, his x mark, Mooch-kat-allick, his x mark, Toontuc-tee, his x mark, Boss-ki-you, his x mark,

Signed in the presence of
R. P. Earhart, secretary, Wm. Kelly, captain First Cavalry, Oregon Volunteers.

TREATY WITH THE OMAHA {1865, Mar. 6}
Ratified, Feb. 13, 1866.
Proclaimed Feb. 15, 1866.

Articles of treaty made and concluded at Washington, D.C., on the sixth day of March, A.D. 1865, between the United of America, by their commissioners, Clark W. Thompson, Robert W. Furnas, and the Omaha tribe of Indians by their chiefs, E-sta-mah-za, or Joseph La Flesche, Gra-ta-mah-zhe, or Standing Hawk; Ga-he-ga-zhinga, or Little Chief; Tah-wah-gah-ha, or Village Maker; Wah-no-ke-ga, or Noise; Sha-da-na-ge, or Yellow Smoke; Wastch-com-ma-nu, or Hard Walker; Pad-a-ga-he, or Fire Chief; Ta-su, or White Crow; Ma-ha-nin-ga, or No Knife.

ARTICLE 1. The Omaha tribe of Indians do hereby cede, sell, and convey to the United States a tract of land from the north side of their present reservation, defined and bounded as follows, viz: commencing at a point on the Missouri River four miles due south from the north boundary line of said reservation, thence west ten miles, thence south four miles, thence west to the western boundary line of the reservation, thence north to the northern boundary line, thence east to the Missouri River, and thence south along the river to the place of beginning: and that the said Omaha tribe of Indians will vacate and give possession of the lands ceded by this treaty immediately after its ratification: Provided, That nothing herein contained shall be construed to include any of the lands upon which the said Omaha tribe of Indians have now improvements, or any land or improvements belonging to, connected with, or used for the benefit of the Missouri school now in existence upon the Omaha reservation.

Plains, West and Northwest Plateau Indian Treaties

ARTICLE 2. In consideration of the foregoing cession, the United States agree to pay to the said Omaha tribe of Indians the sum of fifty thousand dollars, to be paid upon the ratification of this treaty, and to be expended by their agent, under the direction of the Commissioner of Indian Affairs, for goods, provisions, cattle, horses, construction of buildings, farming implements, breaking up lands, and other improvements on their reservation.

ARTICLE 3. In further consideration of the foregoing cession, the United States agree to extend the provisions of article 8 of the treaty between the Omaha tribe of Indians and the United States, made the 16th day of March, A. D. 1854, for a term of ten years from after the ratification of this treaty; and the United States further agree to pay to the said Omaha tribe of Indians, upon the ratification of this treaty, the sum of seven thousand dollars as damages in consequence of the occupancy of a portion of the Omaha reservation not hereby ceded, and use and destruction of timber by the Winnebago tribe of Indians while temporarily residing thereon.

ARTICLE 4. The Omaha Indians being desirous of promoting settled habits of industry and enterprise amongst themselves by abolishing the tenure in common by which they now hold their lands, and assigning limited quantities thereof in severalty to the members of the tribe, including their half or mixed blood relatives now residing with them, to be cultivated and improved for their own individual use and benefit, it is hereby agreed and stipulated that the remaining portion of their present reservation shall be set apart for said purposes; and that out of the same there shall be assigned to each head of a family not exceeding one hundred and sixty acres, and to each male person, eighteen years of age and upwards, without family, not exceeding forty acres of land to include in every case, as far as practicable, a reasonable proportion of timber; six hundred and forty acres of said lands, embracing and surrounding the present agency improvements, shall also be set apart and appropriated to the occupancy and use of the agency for said Indians.

The lands to be so assigned, including those for the use of the agency, shall be in as regular and compact a body as possible, and so as to admit of a distinct and well-defined exterior boundary. The whole of the lands, assigned or unassigned, in severalty, shall constitute and be known as the Omaha reservation, within and over which all laws passed or which may be passed by Congress regulating trade and intercourse with the Indian tribes shall have full force and effect, and no white person, except such as shall be in the employ of the United States, shall be allowed to reside or go upon any portion of said reservation without the written permission of the superintendent of Indian affairs or the agent for the tribe. Said division and assignment of lands to the Omahas in severalty shall be made under the direction of the Secretary of the Interior, and when approved by him, shall be final and conclusive.

Plains, West and Northwest Plateau Indian Treaties

Certificates shall be issued by the Commissioner of Indian Affairs for the tracts so assigned, specifying the names of individuals to whom they have been assigned respectively, and that they are for the exclusive use and benefit of themselves, their heirs, and descendants; and said tracts shall not be alienated in fee, leased, or otherwise disposed of except to the United States or to other members of the tribe, under such rules and regulations as may be prescribed by the Secretary of the Interior, and they shall be exempt from taxation, levy, sale, or forfeiture, until otherwise provided for by Congress.

ARTICLE 5. It being understood that the object of the Government in purchasing the land herein described is for the purpose of locating the Winnebago tribe thereon, now, therefore, should their location there prove detrimental to the peace, quiet, and harmony of the whites as well as of the two tribes of Indians, then the Omahas shall have the privilege of repurchasing the land herein ceded upon the same terms they now sell.

In testimony whereof, the said Clark W. Thompson and Robert W. Furnas, Commissioners as aforesaid, and the said chiefs and delegates of the Omaha tribe of Indians, have hereunto set their hands and seals at the place and on the day and year hereinbefore written.

Clark W. Thompson, R. W. Furnas, Commissioners.

E-sta-mah-zha, or Joseph La Flesche, his x mark, Gra-ta-rnah-zhe, or Standing Hawk, his x mark, Ga-he-ga-zhin-ga, or Little Chief, his x mark, Tah-wah-ga-ha, or Village Maker, his x mark, Wah-no-ke-ga, or Noise, his x mark, Sha-da-na-ge, or Yellow Smoke, his x mark, Wastch-com-ma-nu, or Hard Walker, his x mark, Pad-a-ga-he, or Fire Chief, his x mark, Ta-su, or White Cow, his x mark, Ma-ha-nin-ga, or No Knife, his x mark,

In presence of
H. Chase, United States interpreter.
Lewis Saunsoci, interpreter.

TREATY WITH THE WINNEBAGO {1865, Mar. 8}
Ratified Feb. 13, 1866.
Proclaimed Mar. 28, 1866.

Articles of treaty made and concluded at Washington, D.C., between the United States of America, by their commissioners, Wm. P. Dole, C W. Thompson, and St. A. D. Balcombe, and the Winnebago tribe of Indians, by their chiefs, Little Hill, Little Decoria, Whirling Thunder, Young Prophet, Good Thunder, and White Breast, on the 8th day of March, 1865.

Plains, West and Northwest Plateau Indian Treaties

ARTICLE 1. The Winnebago tribe of Indians hereby cede, sell, and convey to the United States all their right, title, and interest in and to their present reservation in the Territory of Dakota, at Usher's Landing, on the Missouri River, the metes and bounds whereof being on file in the Indian Department.

ARTICLE 2. In consideration of the foregoing cession, and the valuable improvements thereon, the United States agree to set apart for the occupation and future home of the Winnebago Indians, forever, all that certain tract or parcel of land ceded to the United States by the Omaha tribe of Indians on the sixth day of March, A. D. 1865, situated in the Territory of Nebraska, and described as follows, viz: Commencing at a point on the Missouri River four miles due south from the north boundary-line of said reservation; thence west ten miles; thence south four miles; thence west to the western boundary-line of the reservation; thence north to the northern boundary-line; thence east to the Missouri River, and thence south along the river to the place of beginning.

ARTICLE 3. In further consideration of the foregoing cession, and in order that the Winnebagos may be as well situated as they were when they were moved from Minnesota, the United States agree to erect on their reservation, hereby set apart, a good steam saw-mill with a grist-mill attached, and to break and fence one hundred acres of land for each band, and supply them with seed, to sow and plant the same, and shall furnish them with two thousand dollars' worth of guns, four hundred horses, one hundred cows, twenty yoke of oxen and wagons, two chains each, and five hundred dollars' worth of agricultural implements, in addition to those on the reserve hereby ceded.

ARTICLE 4. The United States further agree to erect on said reservation an agency building, school-house, warehouse, and suitable buildings for the physician, interpreter, miller, engineer, carpenter, and blacksmith, and a house 18 by 24 feet, one and a half story high, well shingled and substantially finished, for each chief.

ARTICLE 5. The United States also stipulate and agree to remove the Winnebago tribe of Indians and their property to their new home, and to subsist the tribe one year after their arrival there.

In testimony whereof, the said Wm. P. Dole, Clark W. Thompson, and St. A. D. Balcombe, Commissioners as aforesaid, and the undersigned chiefs and delegates of the Winnebago Tribe of Indians, have hereunto set their hands and seals at the place and on the day hereinbefore written.

W. P. Dole, Clark W. Thompson, St. A. D. Balcombe, Commissioners.

Plains, West and Northwest Plateau Indian Treaties

Little Hill, his x mark, Little Dacoria, his x mark, Whirling Thunder, his x mark, Young Prophet, his x mark, Good Thunder, his x mark, Young Crane, his x mark, White Breast, his x mark,

In the presence of
Mitchell St. Cyr, United State(s) interpreter, Alexander Payn, United State(s) interpreter, R. W. Furnas, United States agent for Omahas.

TREATY WITH THE PONCA {1865, Mar. 10}
Ratified Mar. 2. 1867.
Proclaimed Mar. 1867.

Supplementary treaty between the United States of America and the Ponca tribe of Indians, made at the city of Washington on the tenth day of March, A.D. 1865, between William P. Dole, commissioner on the part of the United States, and Wah-gah-sap-pi, or Iron Whip; Gist-tah-wah-gu, or Strong Walker; Wash-com-mo-ni, or Mitcell P. Cerre; Ash-nan-e-kah-gah-ge, or Lone Chief; Tah-ton-ga-nuz-zhe, or Standing Buffalo; on the part of the Ponca tribe of Indians, they being duly authorized and empowered by the said tribe, as follows, viz:

ARTICLE 1. The Ponca tribe of Indians hereby cede and relinquish to the United States all that portion of their present reservation as described in the first article of the treaty of March 12th, 1858, lying west of the range line between townships numbers (32) thirty-two and (33) thirty-three north, ranges (10) ten and (11) eleven west of the (6) sixth principal meridian, according to the Kansas and Nebraska survey; estimated to contain thirty thousand acres, be the same more or less.

ARTICLE 2. In consideration of the cession or release of that portion of the reservation above described by the Ponca tribe of Indians to the Government of the United States, the Government of the United States, by way of rewarding them for their constant fidelity to the Government and citizens thereof, and with a view of returning to the said tribe of Ponca Indians their old burying-grounds and corn-fields, hereby cede and relinquish to the tribe of Ponca Indians the following-described fractional townships, to wit: township (31) thirty-one north, range (7) seven west; also, fractional township (32)thirty-two north, ranges (6) six, (7) seven, (8) eight, (9) nine, and (10) ten west; also, fractional township (33) thirty-three north, ranges (7) seven and (8) eight west; and also all that portion of township (33) thirty-three north, ranges (9) nine and (10) ten west, lying south of Ponca Creek; and also all the islands in the Niobrara or Running Water River, lying in front of lands or townships above ceded by the United States to the Ponca tribe of Indians.

Plains, West and Northwest Plateau Indian Treaties

But it is expressly understood and agreed that the United States shall not be called upon to satisfy or pay the claims of any settlers for improvements upon the lands above ceded by the United States to the Poncas, but that the Ponca tribe of Indians shall, out of their own funds, and at their own expense, satisfy said claimants, should any be found upon said lands above ceded by the United States to the Ponca tribe of Indians.

ARTICLE 3. The Government of the United States, in compliance with the first paragraph of the second article of the treaty of March 12th, 1858, hereby stipulate and agree to pay to the Ponca tribe of Indians for indemnity for spoliation committed upon them, satisfactory evidence of which has been lodged in the office of the Commissioner of Indian Affairs, and payment recommended by that officer, and also by the Secretary of the Interior, the sum of fifteen thousand and eighty dollars.

ARTICLE 4. The expenses attending the negotiation of this treaty or agreement shall be paid by the United States.

In testimony whereof, the said Wm. P. Dole, Commissioner as aforesaid, and the undersigned, chiefs of the Ponca tribe of Indians, have hereunto set their hands and seals at the place and on the day hereinbefore written.

Wm. P. Dole.

Wah-gah-sap-pi, or Iron Whip, his x mark, Gist-tah-wah-gu, or Strong Walker, his x mark, Wash-corn-too-hi, or Mitchell P. Cerre, his x mark, Ash-nan-e-kah-gah-he, or Lone Chief, his x mark, Tah-ton-ga-nuz-zhe, or Standing Buffalo, his x mark,

Executed in the presence of
Chas. Sims.
Stephen A. Dole.

TREATY WITH THE SNAKE {1865, Aug. 12}
Ratified July 5, 1866.
Proclaimed July 10, 1866.

Articles of agreement and convention made and concluded at Sprague River Valley, on this twelfth day of August, in the year one thousand eight hundred and sixty-five, by J. W. Perit Huntington, superintendent of Indian affairs in Oregon, on the part of the United States, and the undersigned chiefs and headmen of the Woll-pah-pe tribe of Snake Indians, acting in behalf of said tribe, being duly authorized so to do.

Plains, West and Northwest Plateau Indian Treaties

ARTICLE 1. Peace is declared henceforth between the United States and the Woll-pah-pe tribe of Snake Indians, and also between said tribe and all other tribes in amity with the United States. All prisoners and slaves held by the Woll-pah-pe tribe, whether the same are white persons or members of Indian tribes in amity with the United States, shall be released; and all persons belonging to the said Woll-pah-pe tribe now held as prisoners by whites, or as slaves by other Indian tribes, shall be given

ARTICLE 2. The said tribe hereby cedes and relinquishes to the United States all their right, title, and interest to the country occupied by them, described as follows, to wit: Beginning at the Snow Peak in the summit of the Blue Mountain range, near the heads of the Grande Ronde River and the north fork of John Day's River; thence down said north fork of John Day's River to its junction with the south fork; thence due south to Crooked River; thence up Crooked River and the south fork thereof to its source; thence southeasterly to Harney Lake; thence northerly to the heads of Malheur and Burnt Rivers; thence continuing northerly to the place of beginning.

ARTICLE 3. The said tribe agree to remove forthwith to the reservation designated by the treaty concluded on the 14th (15th) of October, 1864, with the Klamath, Moadoc, and Yahooskiu Snake Indians, there to remain under the authority and protection of such Indian agent, or other officer, as the Government of the United States may assign to such duty, and no member of said tribe shall leave said reservation for any purpose without the written consent of the agent or superintendent having jurisdiction over said tribe.

ARTICLE 4. The said Woll-pah-pe tribe promise to be friendly with the people of the United States, to submit to the authority thereof, and to commit no depredations upon the persons or property of citizens thereof, or of other Indian tribes; and should any member of said tribe commit any such depredations, he shall be delivered up to the agent for punishment, and the property restored. If after due notice the tribe neglect or refuse to make restitution, or the property is injured or destroyed, compensation may be made by the Government out of the annuities hereinafter provided. In case of any depredation being committed upon the person or property of any member of the aforesaid Woll-pah-pe tribe, it is stipulated that no attempt at revenge, retaliation, or reclamation shall be made by said tribe; but the case shall be reported to the agent or superintendent in charge, and the United States guarantee that such depredation shall be punished in the same manner as if committed against white persons, and that the property shall be restored to the owner.

ARTICLE 5. The said tribe promise to endeavor to induce the Hoo-ne-boo-ey and Wa-tat-kah tribes of Snake Indians to cease hostilities against the whites; and they also agree that they will, in no case, sell any arms or ammunition to them nor to any other tribe hostile to the United States.

476

Plains, West and Northwest Plateau Indian Treaties

ARTICLE 6. The United States agree to expend, for the use and benefit of said tribe, the sum of five thousand dollars to enable the Indians to fence, break up, and cultivate a sufficient quantity of land for their use, to supply them with seeds, farming-implements, domestic animals, and such subsistence as may be necessary during the first year of their residence upon the reservation.

ARTICLE 7. The United States also agree to expend, for the use and benefit of said tribe, the sum of two thousand dollars per annum for five years next succeeding the ratification of this treaty, and twelve hundred dollars per annum for the next ten years following, the same to be expended under the direction of the President of the United States for such objects as, in his judgment, will be beneficial to the Indians, and advance them in morals and knowledge of civilization.

ARTICLE 8. The said tribe, after their removal to the reservation, are to have the benefit of the services of the physician, mechanics, farmers, teachers, and other employes provided for in the treaty of the 15th October, 1864, in common with the Klamaths, Moadocs, and Yahooskiu Snakes, and are also to have the use of the mills and schoolhouses provided for in said treaty, so far as may be necessary to them, and not to the disadvantage of the other tribes; and, in addition, an interpreter who understands the Snake language shall be provided by the Government. Whenever, in the judgment of the President, the proper time shall have arrived for an allotment of land in severalty to the Indians upon the said reservation, a suitable tract shall be set apart for each family of the said Woll-pah-pe tribe, and peaceable possession of the same is guaranteed to them.

ARTICLE 9. The tribe are desirous of preventing the use of ardent spirits among themselves, and it is therefore provided that any Indian who brings liquor on to the reservation, or who has it in his possession, may in addition to the penalties affixed by law, have his or her proportion of the annuities withheld for such time as the President may determine.

ARTICLE 10. This treaty shall be obligatory upon the contracting parties as soon as the same shall be ratified by the Senate of the United States.

In testimony whereof, the said J. W. Perit Huntington, superintendent of Indian affairs, and the undersigned chiefs and headmen of the tribe aforesaid, have hereunto set their signatures and seals, at the place and on the day and year above written.

J. W. Perit Huntington, Superintendent Indian Affairs in Oregon.

Pah-ni-ne, his x mark, Hau-ni-noo-ey, his x mark, Ki-nau-ney, his x mark, Wa-ak-chau, his x mark., Chok-ko-si, his x mark, She-zhe, his x mark, Che-em-ma,

Plains, West and Northwest Plateau Indian Treaties

his x mark, Now-hoop-a-cow-e. his x mark, Ki-po-weet-ka, his x mark, Hau-ne, or Shas-took, his x mark, Sah-too-too-we, his x mark,

Executed in our presence
W. V. Rinehart, major First Oregon Infantry, Wm. Kelly, captain First Cavalry, Oregon Volunteers.

TREATY WITH THE OSAGE {1865, Sept. 29}
Ratified June 26, 1866.
Proclaimed, Jan. 21, 1867.

Articles of treaty and convention, made and concluded at Canville Trading Post, Osage Nation, within the boundary of the State of Kansas, on the twenty-ninth day of September, hundred and sixty-five, by and between D.C. Cooley, Commissioner of Indian Affairs, and Elijah Sells, superintendent of Indian Affairs for the southern superintendency, commissioners on the part of the United States, and the chiefs of the tribe of Great and Little Osage Indians, the said chiefs being duly authorized to negotiate and treat by said tribes.

ARTICLE 1. The tribe of the Great and Little Osage Indians, having now more lands than are necessary for their occupation, and all payments from the Government to them under former treaties having ceased, leaving them greatly impoverished, and being desirous of improving their condition by disposing of their surplus lands, do hereby grant and sell to the United States the hinds contained within the following boundaries, that is to say: Beginning at the southeast corner of their present reservation, and running thence north with the eastern boundary thereof fifty miles to the northeast cornet'; thence west with the northern line thirty miles; thence south fifty miles, to the southern boundary of said reservation; and thence east with said southern boundary to the place of beginning: Provided, That the western boundary of said land herein ceded shall not extend further westward than upon a line commencing at a point on the southern boundary of said Osage country one mile east of the place where the Verdigris River crosses the southern boundary of the State of Kansas.

And, in consideration of the grant and sale to them of the above-described lands, the United States agree to pay the sum of three hundred thousand dollars, which sum shall be placed to the credit of said tribe of Indians in the Treasury of the United States, and interest thereon at the rate of five per centum per annum shall be paid to said tribes semi-annually, in money, clothing, provisions, or such articles of utility as the Secretary of the Interior may, from time to time, direct. Said lands shall be surveyed and sold, under the direction of the Secretary of the Interior, on the most advantageous terms, for cash, as public lands are surveyed and sold under existing laws, including any act granting lands to the State of Kansas in aid of the construction of a railroad through said lands;

Plains, West and Northwest Plateau Indian Treaties

but no preemption claim or homestead settlement shall be recognized: and after re-imbursing the United States the cost of said survey and sale, and the said sum of three hundred thousand dollars placed to the credit of said Indians, the remaining proceeds of sales shall be placed in the Treasury of the United States to the credit Of the "civilization fund," to be used, under the direction of the Secretary of the Interior, for the education and civilization of Indian tribes residing within the limits of the United States.

ARTICLE 2. The said tribe of Indians also hereby cede to the United States a tract of land twenty miles in width from north to south, off the north side of the remainder of their present reservation, and extending its entire length from east to west; which land is to be held in trust for said Indians, and to be surveyed and sold for their benefit under the direction of the Commissioner of the General Land-Office, at a price not less than one dollar and twenty-five cents per acre, as other lands are surveyed and sold, under such rules and regulations as the Secretary of the Interior shall from time to time prescribe

The proceeds of such sales, as they accrue, after deducting all expenses incident to the proper execution of the trust, shall be placed in the Treasury of the United States to the credit of said tribe of Indians; and the interest thereon, at the rate of five per centum per annum, shall be expended annually for building houses, purchasing agricultural implements and stock animals, and for the employment of a physician and mechanics, and for providing such other necessary aid as will enable said Indians to commence agricultural pursuits under favorable circumstances: Provided, That twenty-five per centum of the net proceeds arising from the sale of said trust lands, until said percentage shall amount to the sum of eighty thousand dollars, shall be placed to the credit of the school fund of said Indians; and the interest thereon, at the rate of five per centum per annum, shall be expended semi-annually for the boarding, clothing, and education of the children of said tribe.

ARTICLE 3. The Osage Indians, being sensible of the great benefits they have received from the Catholic mission, situate in that portion of their reservation herein granted and sold to the United States, do hereby stipulate that one section of said land, to be selected by the Commissioner of Indian Affairs so as to include the improvements of said mission, shall be granted in fee-simple to John Shoenmaker, in trust, for the use and benefit of the society sustaining said mission, with the privilege to said Shoenmaker, on the payment of one dollar and twenty-five cents per acre, of selecting and purchasing two sections of land adjoining the section above granted; the said selection to be held in trust for said society, and to be selected in legal subdivisions of surveys, and subject to the approval of the Secretary of the Interior.

ARTICLE 4. All loyal persons, being heads of families and citizens of the United States, or members of any tribe at peace with the United States, having

Plains, West and Northwest Plateau Indian Treaties

made settlements and improvements as provided by the pre-emption laws of the United States, and now residing on the lands provided to be sold by the United States, in trust for said tribe, as well as upon the said lands herein granted and sold to the United States, shall have the privilege, at any time within one year after the ratification of this treaty, of buying a quarter section each, at one dollar and twenty-five cents per acre; such quarter section to be selected according to the legal subdivisions of surveys, and to include, as far as practicable, the improvements of the settler.

ARTICLE 5. The Osages being desirous of paying their just debts to James N. Coffey and A. B. Canville, for advances in provisions, clothing, and other necessaries of life, hereby agree that the superintendent of Indian affairs for the southern superintendency and the agent of the tribe shall examine all claims against said tribe, and submit the same to the tribe for approval or disapproval, and report the same to the Secretary of the Interior, with the proofs in each case, for his concurrence or rejection; and the Secretary may issue to the claimants scrip for the claims thus allowed, which shall be receivable as cash in payment for any of the lands sold in trust for said tribe: Provided, The aggregate amount thus allowed by the Secretary of the Interior shall not exceed five thousand dollars.

ARTICLE 6. In consideration of the long and faithful services rendered by Charles Mograin, one of the principal chiefs of the Great Osages, to the people, and in consideration of improvements made and owned by him on the land by this treaty sold to the United States, and in lieu of the provision made in article fourteen for the half-breed Indians, the heirs of the said Charles Mograin, dec(ease)d, may select one section of land, including his improvements, from the north half of said land, subject to the approval of the Secretary of the Interior, and upon his approval of such selection it shall be patented to the heirs of the said Mograin, dec(ease)d, in fee-simple.

ARTICLE 7. It is agreed between the parties hereto that the sum of five hundred dollars shall be set apart each year from the moneys of said tribe, and paid by the agent to the chiefs.

ARTICLE 8. The Osage Indians being anxious that a school should be established in their new home, at their request it is agreed and provided that John Shoenmaker may select one section of land within their diminished reservation, and upon the approval of such selection by the Secretary of the Interior, such section of land shall be set apart to the said Shoenmaker and his successors, upon condition that the same shall be used, improved, and occupied for the support and education of the children of said Indians during the occupancy of said reservation by said tribe: Provided, That said lands shall not be patented, and upon the discontinuance of said school shall revert to said tribe and to the United States as other Indian lands.

Plains, West and Northwest Plateau Indian Treaties

ARTICLE 9. It is further agreed that, in consideration of the services of Darius Rogers to the Osage Indians, a patent shall be issued to him for one hundred and sixty acres of land, to include his mill and improvements, on paying one dollar and twenty-five cents per acre; and said Rogers shall also have the privilege of purchasing, at the rate of one dollar and twenty-five cents per acre, one quarter section of land adjoining the tract above mentioned, which shall be patented to him in like manner; said lands to be selected subject to the approval of the Secretary of the Interior.

ARTICLE 10. The Osages acknowledge their dependence on the Government of the United States, and invoke its protection and care; they desire peace, and promise to abstain from war, and commit no depredations on either citizens or Indians; and they further agree to use their best efforts to suppress the introduction and use of ardent spirits in their country.

ARTICLE 11. It is agreed that all roads and highways laid out by the State or General Government shall have right of way through the remaining lands of said Indians, on the same terms as are provided by law, when made through lands of citizens of the United States; and railroad companies, when the lines of their roads necessarily pass through the lands of said Indians, shall have right of way upon the payment of fair compensation therefor.

ARTICLE 12. Within six months after the ratification of this treaty the Osage Indians shall remove from the lands sold and ceded in trust, and settle upon their diminished reservation.

ARTICLE 13. The Osage Indians having no annuities from which it is possible for them to pay any of the expenses of carrying this treaty into effect, it is agreed that the United States shall appropriate twenty thousand dollars, or so much thereof as may be necessary, for the purpose of defraying the expense of survey and sale of the lands hereby ceded in trust, which amount so expended shall be re-imbursed to the Treasury of the United States from the proceeds of the first sales of said lands.

ARTICLE 14. The half-breeds of the Osage tribe of Indians, not to exceed twenty-five in number, who have improvements on the north half of the lands sold to the United States, shall have a patent issued to them, in fee-simple, for eighty acres each, to include, as far as practicable, their improvements, said half-breeds to be designated by the chiefs and head-men of the tribe; and the heirs of Joseph Swiss, a half-breed, and a former interpreter of said tribe, shall, in lieu of the above provision, receive a title, in fee-simple, to a half section of land, including his house and improvements, if practicable, and also to a half section of the trust lands; all of said lands to be selected by the parties, subject to the approval of the Secretary of the Interior.

Plains, West and Northwest Plateau Indian Treaties

ARTICLE 15. It is also agreed by the United States that said Osage Indians may unite with any tribe of Indians at peace with the United States, residing in said Indian Territory, and thence afterwards receive an equitable proportion, according to their numbers, of all moneys, annuities, or property payable by the United States to said Indian tribe with which the agreement may be made; and in turn granting to said Indians, in proportion to their numbers, an equitable proportion of all moneys, annuities, and property payable by the United States to said Osages.

ARTICLE 16. It is also agreed by said contracting parties, that if said Indians should agree to remove from the State of Kansas, and settle on lands to be provided for them by the United States in the Indian Territory on such terms as may be agreed on between the United States and the Indian tribes now residing in said Territory or any of them, then the diminished reservation shall be disposed of by the United States in the same manner and for the same purposes as hereinbefore provided in relation to said trust lands, except that 50 per cent. of the proceeds of the sale of said diminished reserve may be used by the United States in the purchase of lands for a suitable home for said Indians in said Indian Territory.

ARTICLE 17. Should the Senate reject or amend any of the above articles, such rejection or amendment shall not affect the other provisions of this treaty, but the same shall go into effect when ratified by the Senate and approved by the President.

D. N. Cooley, Commissioner of Indian Affairs.
Elijah Sells, Superintendent Indian Affairs Southern Superintendency, and Commissioner.

Me-tso-shin-ca, (Little Bear.) his x mark, Chief Little Osages, No-pa-wah-la, his x mark, Second Chief to, Little Bear, Pa-tha-hun-kah, his x mark, Little Chief L. B. Band, White Hair, his x mark, Principal Chief Osage Nation.

Witnesses:
Ma-sho-hun-ca, counsellor Little Bear Band, his x mark, Wa-sha-pa-wa-ta-ne-ca, his x mark, Wa-du-ha-ka, his x mark, Shin-ka-wa-ta-ne-kah, his x mark, She-wch-tch, his x mark, Gra-ma, his x mark, Hu-la-wah-sho-sha, his x mark, Na-ta-ton-ca-wa-ki, his x mark, Num-pa-wah-cu, his x mark, Ha-ska-mon-ne, his x mark,

Attest:
G. C. Snow, U. S. Neosho Indian agent.
Milton W. Reynolds, acting clerk.

Plains, West and Northwest Plateau Indian Treaties

Witnesses, Little Bear's Band:
Ka-wah-ho-tza, his x mark, O-ke-pa-hola, his x mark, Me-he-tha, his x mark,
White Hair's band of witnesses:
Shin-ka-wa-sha, councillor of White Hair's, his x mark, Wa-sha-wa, his x mark,
Ka-he-ka-stza-jeh, his x

We the undersigned, chiefs and headmen of the Clermont and Black Dog Band
of the Great Osage nation, in council at Fort Smith, Ark., have had the foregoing treaty read and explained in full by our interpreter, L. P. Chouteau, and
fully approve the provisions of said treaty made by our brothers the Osages,
and by this signing make it our act and deed.

Clermont, chief of Clermont Band, his x mark, Palley, second chief of Cler-
mont Band, his x mark, Hah-ti-in-gah, (Dry Feather)counsellor, his x mark,
Kah-ha-che-la-ton, brave, his x mark, Do-tah-cah-she, brave, his x mark, Black
Dog, chief Black Dog Band, his x mark, William Penn, second chief Black Dog
Band, his x mark, Broke Arm, counsellor, his x mark, Ne-kah-ke-pon-nah,
brave, his x mark, Ne-kah-gah-hee, brave, his x mark,

Witnesses:
Wah-skon-mon-ney, his x mark, Wah-kon-che-la, his x mark, Wah-sha-sha-
wah-ti-in-gah, his x mark, Pah-cha-hun-gah, his x mark, Long Bow, his x mark.

TREATY WITH THE SIOUX-MINICONJOU BAND {1865, Oct. 10}
Ratified Mar. 5, 1866.
Proclaimed Mar. 17, 1866.

Articles of a treaty made and concluded at Fort Sully, in the Territory of Dakota, by and between Newton Edmunds, governor and ex-officio superintendency of Indian affairs of Dakota Territory; Edward B. Taylor, superintendent
of Indian affairs for the Northern superintendency; Major-General S. R. Curtis,
Brigadier-General H. H. Sibley, Henry W. Reed, and Orin Guernsey, commissioners on the part of the United States, duly appointed by the President, and
the undersigned chiefs and head-men of the Minneconjou band of Dacota or
Sioux Indians.

ARTICLE 1. The Minneconjou band of Dakota or Sioux Indians, represented
in council, hereby acknowledge themselves to be subject to the exclusive jurisdiction and authority of the United States, and hereby obligate and bind themselves individually and collectively, not only to cease all hostilities against the
persons and property of its citizens, but to use their influence, and, if requisite,
physical force, to prevent other bands of the Dakota or Sioux, or other adjacent
tribes, from making hostile demonstrations against the Government or people
of the United States.

Plains, West and Northwest Plateau Indian Treaties

ARTICLE 2. Inasmuch as the Government of the United States is desirous to arrest the effusion of blood between the Indian tribes within its jurisdiction hitherto at war with each other, the Minneconjou band of Dakotas or Sioux, represented in council, anxious to respect the wishes of the Government, hereby agree and bind themselves to discontinue for the future all attacks upon the persons or property of other tribes, unless first assailed by them, and to use their influence to promote peace everywhere in the region occupied or frequented by them.

ARTICLE 3. All controversies or differences arising between the Minneconjou band of Dakotas or Sioux, represented in council, and other tribes of Indians, involving the question of peace or war, shall be submitted to the arbitrament of the President, or such person or persons as may be designated by him, and the decision or award faithfully observed by the said band represented in council.

ARTICLE 4. The said band, represented in council, shall withdraw from the routes overland already established or hereafter to be established through their country; and in consideration thereof the Government of the United States agree to pay the said band the sum of ten thousand dollars annually for twenty years, in such articles as the Secretary of the Interior may direct: Provided, That said band, so represented in council, shall faithfully conform to the requirements of this treaty.

ARTICLE 5. Should any individual or individuals or portion of the band of the Minneconjou band of Dakotas or Sioux, represented in council, desire hereafter to locate permanently upon any part of the lands claimed by the said band for the purpose (of) agricultural or other pursuits, it is hereby agreed by the parties to this treaty that such individual or individuals shall be protected in such location against any annoyance or molestation on the part of whites or Indians.

ARTICLE 6. Any amendment or modification of this treaty by the Senate of the United States shall be considered final and binding upon the said band, represented in council, as a part of this treaty, in the same manner as if it had been subsequently presented and agreed to by the chiefs and head-men of said band.
In testimony whereof, the Commissioners on the part of the United States, and the chiefs and headmen of the said Minneconjou band of Dakota or Sioux, have hereunto set their hands, this tenth day of October, one thousand eight hundred and sixty-five, after the contents had previously been read, interpreted, and explained to the said chiefs and headmen.

Newton Edmunds, Edward B. Taylor, S. R. Curtis, Major-General, H. H. Sibley, Brigadier-General, Henry W. Reed, Orrin Guernsey, Commissioners on the part of the United States.

Plains, West and Northwest Plateau Indian Treaties

Ha-wah-zee-dan, The Lone Horn, his x mark, 1st chief, Tah-ke-chah-hoosh-tay, The Lame Deer, his x, mark, 1st chief, Kee-yam-e-i-a, One that flies when going, his x mark, chief, Ha-ilro-kah-chah-skah, White Young Bull, his x mark, chief.

Signed by the Commissioners on the part of the United States, and by the chiefs and headmen, after the treaty had been fully read, interpreted, and explained in our presence:

A. W. Hubbard, M. C. Sixth district Iowa, S. S. Curtis, Major Second Colorado Cavalry, Brevet, Lieutenant-Colonel U. S. Volunteers, Chas. C. G. Thornton, Lieutenant-Colonel Fourth U. S. Volunteers.
E. F. Ruth, Secretary of Commission.

The following chiefs came into council on the 20th Oct. and desired to sign the treaty. They are represented as always friendly to the whites, and have, therefore, been away from most of the tribe.

Hah-sah-ne-na-maza, One Iron Horse, his x mark, To-kio-wi-chack-a-ta, The One that Kills the First on Hand, his x mark,

Attest:
S. S. Curtis, Brevet Lieutenant-Colonel U. S. Volunteers.
Hez. L. Hosmer, Chief Justice of Montana Territory.

TREATY WITH THE SIOUX LOWER BRULE BAND {1865, Oct. 14}
Ratified Mar. 5, 1866.
Proclaimed Mar. 17, 1866.

Articles of a treaty made and concluded at Fort Sully, in the Territory of Dakota, by and between Newton Edmunds, governor and ex-officio superintendent of Indian affairs of Dakota Territory; Edward B. Taylor, superintendent of Indian affairs for the northern superintendency; Major-General S. R. Curtis, Brigadier-General H. H. Sibley, Henry W. Reed, and Orrin Guernsey, commissioners on the Avert of the United States, duly appointed by the President, and the undersigned chiefs and head-men of the Lower Brule' band of Dakota or Sioux Indians.

ARTICLE 1. The Lower Brule' band of Dakota or Sioux Indians, represented in council, hereby acknowledge themselves to be subject to the exclusive jurisdiction and authority of the United States, and hereby obligate and bind themselves individually and collectively, not only to cease all hostilities against the persons and property of its citizens, but to use their influence, and, if necessary, physical force, to prevent other bands of the Dakota or Sioux, or other adjacent

Plains, West and Northwest Plateau Indian Treaties

tribes, from making hostile demonstrations against the Government of the United States or its people.

ARTICLE 2. Inasmuch as the Government of the United States is desirous to arrest the effusion of blood between the Indian tribes within its jurisdiction hitherto at war with each other, the Lower Brule' band of Dakotas or Sioux, represented in council, anxious to respect the wishes of the Government, hereby agree and bind themselves to discontinue for the future all attacks upon the persons or property of other tribes, unless first assailed by them, and to use their influence to promote peace everywhere in the region occupied or frequented by them.

ARTICLE 3. All controversies or differences arising between the Lower Brule' band of Dakotas or Sioux, represented in council, and other tribes of Indians, involving the question of peace or war, shall be submitted for the arbitrament of the President, or such person or persons as may be designated by him, and the decision or award faithfully observed by the said band represented in council.

ARTICLE 4. The said band represented in council shall withdraw from the routes overland already established, or hereafter to be established through their country; and in consideration thereof the Government of the United States agree to pay to the said band the sum of six thousand dollars annually, for twenty years, in such articles as the Secretary of the Interior may direct: Provided, That said band so represented in council shall faithfully conform to the requirements of this treaty.

ARTICLE 5. Should any individual, or individuals, or portion of the Lower Brule' band of Dakotas, or Sioux, represented in council, desire hereafter to locate permanently upon any part of the lands claimed by the said band, for the purpose of agricultural or other pursuits, it is hereby agreed by the parties to this treaty that such individual or individuals shall be protected in such location against any annoyance or molestation on the part of whites or Indians.

ARTICLE 6. It is hereby agreed upon the part of the Government of the United States that the said band of Lower Brule's shall locate on a permanent reservation at or near the mouth of the White River, to include Fort Lookout, twenty miles in a straight line along the Missouri River, and ten miles in depth; and that upon the actual occupation of not less than fifty lodges or families of said reservation, and their engaging permanently in agricultural and other kindred pursuits, the Government of the United States agree to furnish at its own cost the sum of twenty-five dollars for each and every lodge or family so engaged, as a common fund, to be expended in stock, agricultural and other implements and general improvements as shall be directed by the Secretary of the Interior; the said sum to be furnished annually for five years.

486

Plains, West and Northwest Plateau Indian Treaties

It being understood that the said stock, agricultural and other implements shall be and remain the property of the United States, to be used and employed for the exclusive benefit of the lodges or families so located, and in no case to be sold or alienated by the said band or any member thereof; and the United States further engage to employ at its own cost a blacksmith and farmer for the benefit of the said lodges or families.

The United States reserve the right to construct a road or roads through the said reservation.

No white person, other than officers, agents or employes of the United States, shall be permitted to go on or remain on the said reservation, unless previously admitted as a member of the said band according to their usages.

Whenever the Secretary of the Interior may so direct, schools for the instruction of the said band may be opened on the said reservation.

ARTICLE 7. The undersigned chiefs of the Brules, hereby further agree that should the Two Kettles band of the Dakota or Sioux Indians be located adjoining them, they will cheerfully allow them to do so, and also agree that the employes secured to the Brules may be used also for the joint benefit of the said Two Kettles, at the discretion of the Government.

ARTICLE 8. Any amendment or modification of this treaty by the Senate of the United States shall be considered final and binding upon the said band, represented in council, as a part of this treaty, in the same manner as if it had been subsequently presented and agreed to by the chiefs and head-men of said band.
In testimony whereof, the Commissioners on the part of the United States, and the chiefs and headmen of the said Lower Brule band of Dakota or Sioux, have hereunto set their hands, this fourteenth day of October, one thousand eight hundred and sixty-five, after the contents had previously been read, interpreted, and explained to the said chiefs and headmen.

Newton Edmunds, Edward B. Taylor, S. R. Curtis, major-general, H. H. Sibley, brigadier-general, Henry W. Reed, Orrin Guernsey, Commissioners on the part of the United States.

Chiefs:
Muz-zah-wy-ah-tay, The Iron Nation, his x mark, Tah-ton-kah-wak-kon, Medicine Ball, his x mark, Pta-son-we-chak-tay, The One who Killed the White Buffalo Cow, his x mark, She-o-tche-kah, Little Pheasant, his x mark, Pta-san-man-nee, White Buffalo Cow that walks, his x mark, Chon-tay-o-kit-e-kah, The Brave Heart, his x mark, Tah-o-pee, The Wounded Man, his x mark, Wag-ah-mo-ah-win, The Gourd Ear Rings, his x mark, E-chap-sin-ta-muz-zah, The Iron

487

Plains, West and Northwest Plateau Indian Treaties

Whip, his x mark, Chief soldiers: Ze-te-kah-dan-sap-pah, The Blackbird, his x mark,

Signed by the Commissioners on the part of the United States, and by the chiefs and headmen, after the treaty had been fully read, interpreted, and explained in our presence:
A. W. Hubbard, M. C., Sixth district Iowa, S. S. Curtis, major, Second Colorado Cavalry, brevet lieutenant-colonel.

TREATY WITH THE CHEYENNE AND ARAPAHO {1865, Oct. 14}
Ratified May 22, 1866.
Proclaimed Feb. 2, 1867.

Articles of a treaty made and concluded at the camp on the Little Arkansas River, in the State of Kansas, on the Fourteenth day of October, in the year of our Lord one thousand eight hundred and sixty-five, by and between John B. Sanborn, William S. Harney, Thomas Murphy, Kit Carson, William W. Bent, Jesse H. Leavenworth, and James Steele, commissioners on the part of the United States, and the undersigned, chiefs and head-men of and representing the confederate tribes of Arrapahoe and Cheyenne Indians of the Upper Arkansas River, they being duly authorized by their respective tribes to act in the premises.

ARTICLE 1. It is agreed by the parties to this treaty that hereafter perpetual peace shall be maintained between the people and Government of the United States and the Indians parties hereto, and that the Indians parties hereto, shall forever remain at peace with each other, and with all other Indians who sustain friendly relations with the Government of the United States. For the purpose of enforcing the provisions of this article it is agreed that in case hostile acts or depredations are committed by the people of the United States, or by Indians on friendly terms with the United States, against the tribe or tribes, or the individual members of the tribe or tribes, who are parties to this treaty, such hostile acts or depredations shall not be redressed by a resort to arms, but the party or parties aggrieved shall submit their complaints through their agent to the President of the United States, and thereupon an impartial arbitration shall be had under his direction, and the award thus made shall be binding on all parties interested, and the Government of the United States will hi good faith enforce the same.

And the Indians, parties hereto, on their part, agree, in ease crimes or other violations of law shall be committed by any person or persons, members of their tribe, such person or persons shall, upon complaint being made, in writing, to their agent, superintendent of Indian affairs, or to other proper authority, by the party injured, and verified by affidavit, be delivered to the person duly

488

Plains, West and Northwest Plateau Indian Treaties

authorized to take such person or persons into custody, to the end that such person or persons may be punished according to the laws of the United States.

ARTICLE 2. The United States hereby agree that the district of country embraced within the following limits, or such portion of the same as may hereafter be designated by the President of the United States for that purpose, viz: commencing at the mouth of the Red Creek or Red Fork of the Arkansas River; thence up said creek or fork to its source; thence westwardly to a point on the Cimarone River, opposite the mouth of Buffalo Creek; thence due north to the Arkansas River; thence down the same to the beginning, shall be, and is hereby, set apart for the absolute and undisturbed use and occupation of the tribes who are parties to this treaty, and of such other friendly tribes as they may from time to time agree to admit among them.

And that no white person, except officers, agents, and employees of the Government, shall go upon or settle within the country embraced within said limits, unless formerly admitted and incorporated into some one of the tribes lawfully residing there, according to its laws and usages: Provided, however, That said Indians shall not be required to settle upon said reservation until such time as the United States shall have extinguished all claims of title thereto on the part of other Indians, so that the Indians parties hereto may live thereon at peace with all other tribes: Provided, however, That as soon as practicable, with the assent of said tribe, the President of the United States shall designate for said tribes a reservation, no part of which shall be within the State of Kansas, and cause them as soon as practicable to remove to and settle thereon, but no such reservation shall be designated upon any reserve belonging to any other Indian tribe or tribes without their consent.

The Indians parties hereto, on their part, expressly agree to remove to and accept as their permanent home the country embraced within said limits whenever directed so to do by the President of the United States, in accordance with the provisions of this treaty, and that they will not go from said country for hunting or other purposes without the consent in writing of their agent or other authorized person, such written consent in all cases specifying the purpose for which such leave is granted, and shall be borne with them upon their excursions as evidence that they are rightfully away from their reservation, and shall be respected by all officers, employees, and citizens of the United States as their sufficient safeguard and protection against injury or damage in person or property by any and all persons whomsoever.

It is further agreed by the Indians parties hereto that when absent from their reservation they will refrain from the commission of any depredations or injuries to the person or property of all persons sustaining friendly relations with the Government of the United States: that they will not, while so absent, encamp by day or night within ten miles of any of the main traveled routes or

489

Plains, West and Northwest Plateau Indian Treaties

roads through the country to which they go, or of the military posts, towns, or villages therein, without the consent of the commanders of such military posts, or of the civil authorities of such towns or villages; and that henceforth they will, and do hereby, relinquish all claims or rights in and to any portion of the United States or Territories, except such as is embraced within the limits aforesaid, and more especially their claims and rights in and to the country bounded as follows, viz: beginning at the junction of the north and south forks of the Platte River; thence up the north fork to the top of the principal range of the Rocky Mountains, or to the Red Buttes; thence southwardly along the summit of the Rocky Mountains to the headwaters of the Arkansas River; thence down the Arkansas River to the Cimarone crossing of the same; thence to the place of beginning; which country they claim to have originally owned, and never to have relinquished the title thereto.

ARTICLE 3. It is further agreed that until the Indians parties hereto have removed to the reservation provided for by the preceding article in pursuance of the stipulations thereof, said Indians shall be, and they are hereby, expressly permitted to reside upon and range at pleasure throughout the unsettled portions of that part of the country they claim as originally theirs, which lies between the Arkansas and Platte Rivers; and that they shall and will not go elsewhere, except upon the terms and conditions prescribed by the preceding article in relation to leaving the reservation thereby provided for: Provided, That the provisions of the preceding article in regard to encamping within ten miles of main travelled routes, military posts, towns, and villages shall be in full force as to occupancy of the country named and permitted by the terms of this article: Provided, further, That they, the said Indians, shall and will at all times during such occupancy, without delay, report to the commander of the nearest military post the presence in or approach to said country of any hostile bands of Indians whatsoever.

ARTICLE 4. It is further agreed by the parties hereto that the United States may lay off and build through the reservation, provided for by Article 2 of this treaty, such roads or highways as may be deemed necessary; and may also establish such military posts within the same as may be found necessary in order to preserve peace among the Indians, and in order to enforce such laws, rules, and regulations as are now, or may from time to time be, prescribed by the President and Congress of the United States for the protection of the rights of persons and property among the Indians residing upon said reservation; and further, that in time of war such other military posts as may be considered essential to the general interests of the United States may be established: Provided, however, That upon the building of such roads, or establishment of such military posts, the amount of injury sustained by reason thereof by the Indians inhabiting said reservation shall be ascertained under direction of the President of the United States, and thereupon such compensation shall be made to said

Plains, West and Northwest Plateau Indian Treaties

Indians as in the judgment of the Congress of the United States may be deemed just and proper.

ARTICLE 5. At the special request of the Cheyenne and Arrapahoe Indians, parties to this treaty, the United States agree to grant, by patent in fee-simple, to the following-named persons, all of whom are related to the Cheyennes or Arrapahoes by blood, to each an amount of land equal to one section of six hundred and forty acres, viz: To Mrs. Margaret Wilmarth and her children, Virginia Fitzpatrick, and Andrew Jackson Fitzpatrick; to Mrs. Mary Keith and her children, William Keith, Mary J. Keith, and Francis Keith; to Mrs. Matilda Pepperdin and her child, Miss Margaret Pepperdin; to Robert Poisal and John Poisal; to Edmund Guerrier, Rosa Guerrier, and Julia Guerrier; to William W. Bent's daughter, Mary Bent Moore, and her three children, Adia Moore, William Bent Moore, and George Moore; to William W. Bent's children, George Bent, Charles Bent, and Julia Bent; to A-me-the, the wife of John Prowers, and her children, Mary Prowers and Susan Prowers; to the children of Ote-se-ot-see, wife of John Y. Sickles, viz: Margaret, Minnie, and John.

To the children of John S. Smith, interpreter, William Gilpin Smith, and daughter Armarea; to Jenny Lind Crocker, daughter of Ne-sou-hoe, or Are-you-there, wife of Lieutenant Crocker; to-Winsor, daughter of Tow-e-nah, wife of A. T. Winsor, sutler, formerly at Fort Lyon. Said lands to be selected under the direction of the Secretary of the Interior, from the reservation established by the 1st article of their treaty of February 18. A. D. 1861: Provided, That said locations shall not be made upon any lands heretofore granted by the United States to any person, State, or corporation, for any purpose.

ARTICLE 6. The United States being desirous to express its condemnation of, and, as far as may be, repudiate the gross and wanton outrages perpetrated against certain bands of Cheyenne and Arrapahoe Indians, on the twenty-ninth day of November, A. D. 1864, at Sand Creek, in Colorado Territory, while the said Indians were at peace with the United States, and under its flag, whose protection they had by lawful authority been promised and induced to seek, and the Government being desirous to make some suitable reparation for the injuries then done, will grant three hundred and twenty acres of land by patent to each of the following-named chiefs of said bands, viz: Moke-ta-ye-to, or Black Kettle; Oh-tah-ha-ne-so-weel, or Seven Bulls; Alik-ke-home-ma, or Little Robe; Moke-tah-vo-ve-hoe, or Black White Man; and will in like manner grant to each other person of said bands made a widow, or who lost a parent upon that occasion, one hundred and sixty acres of land, the names of such persons to be ascertained under the direction of the Secretary of the Interior: Provided, That said grants shall be conditioned that all devises, grants, alienations, leases, and contracts relative to said lands, made or entered into during the period of fifty years from the date of such patents, shall be unlawful and void.

Plains, West and Northwest Plateau Indian Treaties

Said lands shall be selected under the direction of the Secretary of the Interior within the limits of country hereby set apart as a reservation for the Indians parties to this treaty, and shall be free from assessment and taxation so long as they remain inalienable. The United States will also pay in United States securities, animals, goods, provisions, or such other useful articles as may, in the discretion of the Secretary of the Interior, be deemed best adapted to the respective wants and conditions of the persons named in the schedule hereto annexed, they being present and members of the bands who suffered at Sand Creek, upon the occasion aforesaid, the sums set opposite their names, respectively, as a compensation for property belonging to them, and then and there destroyed or taken from them by the United States troops aforesaid.

ARTICLE 7. The United States agree that they will expend annually during the period of forty years, from and after the ratification of this treaty, for the benefit of the Indians who are parties hereto, and of such others as may unite with t, hem in pursuance of the terms hereof, in such manner and for such purposes as, in the judgment of the Secretary of the Interior, for the time being, will best subserve their wants and interests as a people, the following amounts, that is to say, until such time as said Indians shall be removed to their reservation, as provided for by Article 2 of this treaty, an amount which shall be equal to twenty dollars per capita for each person entitled to participate in the beneficial provisions of this treaty, and from and after the time when such removal shall have been accomplished, an amount which shall be equal to forty dollars per capita for each person entitled as aforesaid. Such proportion of the expenditure provided for by this article as may be considered expedient to distribute in the form of annuities shall be delivered to said Indians as follows, viz: one-third thereof during the spring, and two-thirds thereof during the autumn of each year.

For the purpose of determining from time to time the aggregate amount to be expended under the provisions of this article, it is agreed that the number entitled to its beneficial provisions the coming year is two thousand eight hundred, and that an accurate census of the Indians entitled shall be taken at the time of the annuity payment in the spring of each year by their agent or other person designated for that purpose by the Secretary of the Interior, which census shall be the basis on which the amount to be expended the next ensuing year shall be determined.

ARTICLE 8. The Indians parties to this treaty expressly covenant and agree that they will use their utmost endeavor to induce that portion of the respective tribes not now present to unite with them and acceed to the provisions of this treaty, which union and accession shall be evidenced and made binding on all parties whenever such absentees shall have participated in the beneficial provisions of this treaty.

Plains, West and Northwest Plateau Indian Treaties

ARTICLE 9. Upon the ratification of this treaty all former treaties are hereby abrogated.

In testimony whereof, the said Commissioners as aforesaid, and the undersigned chiefs and headmen of the confederated tribes of the Arrapahoes and Cheyennes of the Upper Arkansas, have hereunto set their hands and seals, at the place and on the day and year first hereinbefore written.

John B. Sanborn, Wm. S. Harney, Thos. Murphy, Kit Carson, Wm. W. Bent, J. H. Leavenworth, James Steele, Commissioners on the part of the United States.

Moke-ta-ve-to, or Black Kettle,head chief, his x mark, Oh-to-ah-ne-so-to-wheo, or SevenBulls, chief, his x mark, Hark-kah-o-me, or Little Robe,chief, his x mark, Moke-tah-vo-ve-ho, or BlackWhite Man, chief, his x mark, Mun-a-men-ek, or Eagle's Head,headman, his x mark, O-to-ah-nis-to, or Bull that Hears,headman, his x mark,

On the part of the Cheyennes.
Oh-has-tee, or Little Raven, headchief, his x mark, Oh-hah-mah-hah, or Storm, chief, his x mark, Pah-uf-pah-top, or BigMouth, chief, his x mark, Ah-cra-kah-tau-nah, orSpotted Wolf, chief, his x mark, Ah-nah-wat-tan, or Black Man, headman, his x mark, Nah-a-nah-cha, or Chief in Everything, headman, his x mark, Chi-e-nuk, or Haversack, headman, his x mark,

Signed and sealed in the presence of
John S. Smith, United States interpreter.
E.W. Wynkoop, W. R. Irwin, Bon. H. Van Havre, O. T. Atwood, secretaries.

N. B.The Apache tribe was brought into the provisions of the above treaty by the second article of the treaty with the Apaches, Cheyennes and Arrapahoes, proclaimed May 26, 1866.

TREATY WITH THE APACHE, CHEYENNE, AND ARAPAHO
{1865, Oct. 17}
Ratified May 22, 1866.
Proclaimed May 26, 1866.

Whereas a treaty was made and concluded, by and between the undersigned commissioners on the part of the United States, and the undersigned chiefs and head-men of the Cheyenne and Arrapahoe tribes of Indians, on the part of said tribes, on the fourteenth day of October, A. D. 1865, at the council-grounds on the Little Arkansas River, in the State of Kansas; and, whereas, the Apache Indians, who have been heretofore confederated with the Kiowa and Comanche tribes of Indians, are desirous of dissolving said confederation and uniting their

Plains, West and Northwest Plateau Indian Treaties

fortunes with the said Cheyennes and Arrapahoes; and whereas the said last-named tribes are willing to receive among themselves on an equal footing with the members of their own tribes, the said Apache Indians; and the United States, by their said commissioners, having given their assent thereto; it is therefore hereby agreed by and between the United States, by their said commissioners, and the said Cheyenne, Arrapahoe, and Apache Indians, by the undersigned chiefs and head-men of said tribes respectively, as follows, viz:

ARTICLE 1. The said Cheyenne, Arrapahoe, and Apache tribes, henceforth shall be and they are hereby united, and the United States will hereafter recognize said tribes as the confederated bands or tribes of Cheyenne, Arrapahoe, and Apache Indians.

ARTICLE 2. The several terms, stipulations and agreements to be done and performed on the part of the United States for and with the said Cheyenne and Arrapahoe tribes of Indians, and by the said Cheyenne and Arrapahoe tribes of Indians, for and with the United States, by the provisions of said treaty of October 14th, A. D. 1865, shall be done and performed by the United States for and on behalf of the said confederated tribes or bands of Cheyenne, Arrapahoe, and Apache Indians, and on their part shall be done, observed and performed to, with and for the United States in the same manner, to the same extent, and for like objects, to all intents and purposes, as would have been the case had said treaty been originally made and executed with the said confederated tribes of Cheyenne, Arrapahoe, and Apache Indians.

In testimony whereof, the undersigned, Commissioners on the part of the United states, and the chiefs and headmen of said tribes, have hereunto set their hands and seals at the council-ground on the Little Arkansas, in the State of Kansas, this 17th day of October, A. D. 1865.

John B. Sanborn, Wm. S. Harney, James Steele, Wm. W. Bent, Kit Carson, Thos. Murphy, J. H. Leavenworth, Commissioners on the part of the United States.

Kou-zhon-ta-co, or Poor Bear, head chief, his x mark., Ba-zhe-ech, or Iron Shirt, his x mark., Az-che-om-a-te-ne, or the Old Fool Man, chief, his x mark., Karn-tin-ta, or the Crow, chief, his x mark., Mah-vip-pah, or The Wolf Sleeve, chief, his x mark., Nahn-tan, or The Chief, his x mark.,

On the part of the Apaches.
Moke-ta-ve-to, or Black Kettle, head chief, his x mark., Oh-to-ah-ne-so-to-wheo, or Seven Bulls, chief, his x mark., Hark-kah-o-me, or Little Robe, chief, his x mark., Moke-tah-vo-ve-ho, or Black White Man, chief, his x mark. , Mun-a-men-ek, or Eagle's Head, headman, his x mark., O-to-ah-nis-to, or Bull that Hears, headman, his x mark.,

Plains, West and Northwest Plateau Indian Treaties

On the part of the Cheyennes.
Oh-has-tee, or Little Raven, head chief, his x mark., Oh-hah-mah-hah, or Storm, chief, his x mark., Pah-uf-pah-top, or Big Mouth, chief, his x mark., Ah-cra-ka-tau-nah, or Spotted Wolf, chief, his x mark., Ah-nah-wat-tan, or Black Man, headman, his x mark., Nah-a-nah-cha, Chief in Everything, headman, his x mark., Chi-e-nuk, or Haversack, headthan, his x mark.,
On the part of the Arrapahoes.

Signed and sealed in presence of
W. R. Irwin, Secretary.
D.C. McNeil.

TREATY WITH THE COMANCHE AND KIOWA {1865, Oct. 18}
Ratified May 22, 1866.
Proclaimed May 26, 1866.

Articles of a treaty made and concluded at the council-ground on the Little Arkansas River eight miles from the mouth of said river, in the State of Kansas, on the eighteenth day of October, in the year of our Lord one thousand eight hundred and sixty-five, by and between John. B. Sanborn, William S. Harney, Thomas Murphy, Kit Carson, William W. Bent, Jesse H. Leavenworth, and James Steele, Commissioners on the part of the United States, and the under-signed chiefs and head-men of the several bands of Comanche Indians speci-fied in connection with their signatures, and the chiefs and head-men of the Kiowa tribe of Indians, the said chiefs and head-men by the said bands and tribes being thereunto duly authorized.

ARTICLE 1. It is agreed by the parties to this treaty that hereafter perpetual peace shall be maintained between the people and Govern-meet of the United States and the Indians parties hereto, and that the Indians parties hereto shall forever remain at peace with each other and with all other Indians who sustain friendly relations with the Government of the United States.

For the purpose of enforcing the provisions of this article, it is agreed that in case hostile acts or depredations are committed by the people of the United States, or by the Indians on friendly terms with the United States, against the tribe or tribes or the individual members of the tribe or tribes who are parties to this treaty, such hostile acts or depredations shall not be redressed by a resort to arms, but the party or parties aggrieved shall submit their complaints, through their agent, to the President of the United States, and thereupon an impartial arbitration shall be had under his direction, and the award thus made shall be binding on all parties interested, and the Government of the United States will in good faith enforce the same.

Plains, West and Northwest Plateau Indian Treaties

And the Indians parties hereto, on their part, agree, in case crimes or other violations of law shall be committed by any person or persons members of their tribe, such person or persons shall, upon complaint being made in writing to their agent, superintendent of Indian affairs, or to other proper authority, by the party injured, and verified by affidavit, be delivered to the person duly authorized to take such person or persons into custody, to the end that such person or persons may be punished according to the laws of the United States.

ARTICLE 2. The United States hereby agree that the district of country embraced within the following limits, or such portion of the same as may hereafter from time to time be designated by the. President of the United States for that purpose, viz: commencing at the northeast corner of New Mexico, thence south to the southeast corner of the same: thence northeastwardly to a point on main Red River opposite the mouth of the North Fork of said river: thence down said river to the 98th degree of west longitude: thence due north on said meridian to the Cimarone river: thence up said river to a point where the same crosses the southern boundary of the State of Kansas: thence along said southern boundary of Kansas to the southwest corner of said State: thence west to the place of beginning, shall be and is hereby set apart for the absolute and undisturbed use and occupation of the tribes who are parties to this treaty, and of such other friendly tribes as have heretofore resided within said limits, or as they may from time to time agree to admit among them, and that no white person except officers, agents, and employes of the Government shall go upon or settle within the country embraced within said limits, unless formally admitted and incorporated into some one of the tribes lawfully residing there, according to its laws and usages.

The Indians parties hereto on their part expressly agree to remove to and accept as their permanent home the country embraced within said limits, whenever directed so to do by the President of the United States, in accordance with the provisions of this treaty, and that they will not go from said country for hunting purposes without the consent in writing of their agent or other authorized person, specifying the purpose for which such leave is granted, and such written consent in all cases shall be borne with them upon their excursions, as evidence that they are rightfully away from their reservation, and shall be respected by all officers, employes, and citizens of the United States, as their sufficient safeguard and protection against injury or damage in person or property, by any and all persons whomsoever.

It is further agreed by the Indians parties hereto, that when absent from their reservation, they will refrain from the commission of any depredations or injuries to the person or property of all persons sustaining friendly relations with the Government of the United States; that they will not while so absent encamp, by day or night, within ten miles of any of the main travelled-routes or roads through the country to which they go, or of the military posts, towns, or vil-

496

Plains, West and Northwest Plateau Indian Treaties

lages therein, without the consent of the commanders of such military posts, or of the civil authorities of such towns or villages, and that henceforth they will and do hereby, relinquish all claims or rights in and to any portion of the United States or territories, except such as is embraced within the limits aforesaid, and more especially their claims and rights in and to the country north of the Cimarone River and west of the eastern boundary of New Mexico.

ARTICLE 3. It is further agreed that until the Indians parties hereto have removed to the reservation provided for by the preceding article, in pursuance of the stipulations thereof, said Indians shah be and they are hereby, expressly permitted to reside upon and range at pleasure throughout the unsettled portions of that part of the country they claim as originally theirs, which lies south of the Arkansas River, as well as the country embraced within the limits of the reservation provided for by the preceding article, and that they shall and will not go elsewhere, except upon the terms and conditions prescribed by the preceding article in relation to leaving said reservation: Provided, That the provisions of the preceding article in regard to encamping within ten miles of main travelled routes, military posts, towns, and villages, shall be in full force as to the privileges granted by this article: And provided further, That they, the said Indians, shall and will at all times, and without delay, report to the commander of the nearest military post the presence in or approach to said country of any hostile band or bands of Indians whatever.

ARTICLE 4. It is further agreed by the parties hereto that the United States may lay off and build through the reservation, provided for by Article 2 of this treaty, roads or highways as may be deemed necessary, and may also establish such military posts within the same as may be found necessary, in order to preserve peace among the Indians, and in order to enforce such laws, rules, and regulations as are now or may from time to time be prescribed by the President and Congress of the United States for the protection of the rights of persons and property among the Indians residing upon said reservation, and further, that in time of war such other military posts as may be considered essential to the general interests of the United States may be established: Provided, however, That upon the building of such roads, or establishment of such military posts, the amount of injury sustained by reason thereof by the Indians inhabiting said reservation shall be ascertained under direction of the President of the United States, and thereupon such compensation shall be made to said Indians as, in the judgment of the Congress of the United States, may be deemed just and proper.

ARTICLE 5. The United States agree that they will expend annually, during the period of forty years, from and after the ratification of this treaty, for the benefit of the Indians who are parties hereto, and of such others as may unite with them in pursuance of the terms hereof, in such manner and for such purposes as, in the judgment of the Secretary of the Interior for the time being, will

Plains, West and Northwest Plateau Indian Treaties

best subserve their wants and interests as a people, the following amounts, that is to say, until such time as said Indians shall be removed to their reservations, as provided for by article two of this treaty, an amount which shall equal to ten dollars per capita for each person entitled to participate the beneficial provisions of this treaty; and from and after the time when such removal shall have been accomplished, an amount which shall be equal to fifteen dollars per capita for each person entitled as aforesaid. Such proportion of the expenditure provided for by this article as may be considered expedient to distribute in the form of annuities shall be delivered to said Indians as follows, viz: One-third thereof during the spring, and two-thirds thereof during the autumn of each year.

For the purpose of determining from time to time the aggregate amount to be expended under the provisions of this article, it is agreed that the number entitled to its beneficial provisions the coming year is four thousand, and that an accurate census of the Indians entitled shall be taken at the time of the annuity payment in the spring of each year by their agent or other person designated by the Secretary of the Interior, which census shall be the basis on which the amount to be expended the next ensuing year shall be determined.

ARTICLE 6. The Indians parties to this treaty expressly covenant and agree that they will use their utmost endeavors to induce that portion of the respective tribes not now present to unite with them and accede to the provisions of this treaty, which union and accession shall be evidenced and made binding on all parties whenever such absentees shall have participated in the beneficial provisions of this treaty.

In testimony whereof, the said Commissioners on the part of the United States, and the chiefs and headmen of the said bands of Camanche Indians and of the Kiowa tribe of Indians, hereinbefore referred to, and designated in connection with their signatures, have hereunto subscribed their names and affixed their seals on the day and year first above written.

John B. Sanborn, Wm. S. Harney, Kit Carson, Wm. W. Bent, James Steele, Thos. Murphy, J. H. Leavenworth, Commissioners on the part of the United States,

Signed and sealed in presence of-
W. R. Irwin, secretary.
Wm. T. Kittridge.

Tab-e-nan-i-kah, or Rising Sun, chief of Yampirica, or Root Eater band of Camanches, for Paddy-wah-say-mer and Ho-to-yo-koh-wat's bands, his x mark, Esh-e-tave-pa-rah, or Female Infant, headman of Yampirica band of Camanches, his x mark, A-sha-hab-beet, or Milky Way, chief Penne-taha, or Sugar Eater band of Camanches, and for Co-che-te-ka, or Buffalo Eater band, his x

Plains, West and Northwest Plateau Indian Treaties

mark, Queen-ah-e-vah, or Eagle Drink-lug, head chief of No-co-nee or Go-about band of Camanches, his x mark, Kaw-pe-ah, or Plumed Lance, his x mark, To-hau-son, or Little Mountain, his x mark, Sa-tank, or Sitting Bear, his x mark, Pawnee, or Poor Man, his x mark, Ta-ki-bull, or Stinking Saddle Cloth, chief of the Kiowa tribe, his x mark,

TREATY WITH THE SIOUX TWO-KETTLE BAND {1865, Oct. 19}
Ratified Mar. 5, 1866.
Proclaimed Mar. 17, 1866.

Articles of a treaty made and concluded at Fort Sully, in the Territory of Dakota, by and between Newton Edmunds, governor and ex-officio superintendent of Indian affairs of Dakota Territory, Edmund B. Taylor, superintendent of Indian affairs for the northern superintendency, Major-General S. R. Curtis, Brigadier-General H. H. Sibley Henry W. Reed, and Orrin Guernsey, commissioners on the part of the United States, duly appointed by the President and the undersigned, chiefs and head-men of the Two-Kettles band of Dakota or Sioux Indians.

ARTICLE 1. The Two-Kettles band of Dakota or Sioux Indians represented in council, hereby acknowledge themselves to be subject to the exclusive jurisdiction and authority of the United States, and hereby obligate and bind themselves individually and collectively, not only to cease all hostilities against the persons and property of its citizens, but to use their influence, and, if necessary, physical force, to prevent other bands of the Dakota or Sioux, or other adjacent tribes, from making hostile demonstrations against the Government of the United States, or its people.

ARTICLE 2. Inasmuch as the Government of the United States is desirous to arrest the effusion of blood between the Indian tribes within its jurisdiction, hitherto at war with each other, the Two-Kettles band of Dakota or Sioux, represented in council, anxious to respect the wishes of the Government, hereby agree and bind themselves to discontinue, for the future, all attacks upon the persons or property of other tribes, unless first assailed by them, and to use their influence to promote peace everywhere in the region occupied or frequented by them.

ARTICLE 3. All controversies or differences arising between the Two-Kettles band of Dakota or Sioux, represented in council, and other tribes of Indians, involving the question of peace or war, shall be submitted for the arbitrament of the President, or such person or persons as may be designated by him, and the decision or award faithfully observed by the said band, represented in council.

Plains, West and Northwest Plateau Indian Treaties

ARTICLE 4. The said band, represented in council, shall withdraw from the routes overland already established, or hereafter to be established, through their country; and, in consideration thereof, the Government of the United States agree to pay to the said band the sum of six thousand dollars annually, for twenty years, in such articles as the Secretary of the Interior may direct: Provided, That the said bands so represented in council shall faithfully conform to the requirements of this treaty.

ARTICLE 5. Should any individual or individuals, or portion of the band of the Two-Kettles band of Dakota and Sioux Indians, represented in council, desire her hereafter to locate permanently upon any part of the land claimed by the said band, for the purpose of agricultural or other pursuits, it is hereby agreed by the parties to this treaty that such individual or individuals shall be protected in such location against any annoyance or molestation on the part of whites or Indians; and where twenty lodges or families of the Two-Kettles band shall have located on lands for agricultural purposes, and signified the same to their agent or superintendent, they as well as other families so locating shall receive the sum of twenty-five dollars annually, for five years, for each family, in agricultural implements and improvements; and when one hundred lodges or families shall have so engaged in agricultural pursuits, they shall be entitled to a farmer and blacksmith, at the expense of the Government, also teachers, at the option of the Secretary of the Interior, when deemed necessary.

ARTICLE 6. Soldiers in the United States service having killed Ish-tah-chah-ne-aha, (Puffing Eyes) a friendly chief of the Two-Kettles band of Dakota or Sioux Indians, it is hereby agreed that the Government of the United States shall cause to be paid to the surviving widow of the deceased and his children, seventeen in number, the sum of five hundred dollars; and to the said tribe or band, in common, as indemnity for killing said chief, the sum of five hundred dollars, said payment to be made under the direction of the Secretary of the Interior.

ARTICLE 7. Any amendment or modification of this treaty by the Senate of the United States shall be considered final and binding upon the said band, represented in council, as a part of this treaty, in the same manner as if it had been subsequently presented and agreed to by the chiefs and head-men of said band.
In testimony whereof, the Commissioners on the part of the United States, and the chiefs and headmen of the said Two Kettles band of Dakota or Sioux, have hereunto set their hands, this nineteenth day of October, one thousand eight hundred and sixty-five, after the contents had previously been read, interpreted, and explained to the said chiefs and headmen.

Newton Edmunds, Edward B. Taylor, S. R. Curtis, major-general, H. H. Sibley, brigadier-general, Henry W. Reed, Orrin Guernsey Commissioners on the part of the United States.

Plains, West and Northwest Plateau Indian Treaties

Cha-tan-skah, The White Hawk, chief, his x , E-to-ke-ah, The Hump, chief, his x , Short-kah-wak-kon-ke-desh-kah, The Spotted Horse, chief, his x , Mah-to-ke-desh-kah, The Spotted Bear, chief, his x , Mah-to-to-pah, The Four Bears, his x , Chan-tay-o-me-ne-o-me-ne, The Whirling Heart, his x , Mah-to-a-cha-chah, The Bear that is like him, his x , Tah-hoo-ka-zah-nom-pub, The Two Lances, his x ,

Signed by the Commissioners on the part of the United States, and by the chiefs and headmen, after the treaty had been fully read, interpreted, and explained, in our presence :
A. W. Hubbard, M. C. Sixth district Iowa.
Hez. L. Hosmer, chief justice of Montana Territory.
Chas. C. G. Thornton, lieutenant-colonel Fourth U. S. Volunteers.

The foregoing signatures in this handwriting (that of Gen. Curtis) were made in presence of the undersigned.
Maj. A. P. Shreve, paymaster U. S. Army.
John Pattee, lieutenant-colonel Seventh Iowa Cavalry.

TREATY WITH THE BLACKFEET SIOUX {1865, Oct. 19}
Ratified Mar. 5, 1866.
Proclaimed Mar. 17, 1866.

Articles of a treaty made and concluded at Fort Sully, in the Territory of Dakota, by and between Newton Edmunds, governor and ex-officio superintendent of Indian affairs, of Dakota Territory, Edward B. Taylor, superintendent of Indian affairs for the northern superintendency, Major-General S. R. Curtis, Brigadier-General H. H. Sibley, Henry W. Reed, and Orrin Guernsey, commissioners on the part of the United States, duly appointed by the President, and the undersigned chiefs and headmen of the Blackfeet band of Dakota or Sioux Indians.

ARTICLE 1. The Blackfeet band of Dakota or Sioux Indians, represented in council, hereby acknowledge themselves to be subject to the exclusive jurisdiction and authority of the United States, and hereby obligate and bind themselves, individually and collectively, not only to cease all hostilities against the persons and property of its citizens, but to use their influence, and, if necessary, physical force to prevent other bands of the Dakota or Sioux, or other adjacent tribes from making hostile demonstrations against the Government of the United States, or its people.

ARTICLE 2. Inasmuch as the Government of the United States is desirous to arrest the effusion of blood between the Indian tribes within its jurisdiction

Plains, West and Northwest Plateau Indian Treaties

hitherto a(t) war with each other, the Blackfeet band of Dakota or Sioux, represented in council, anxious to respect the wishes of the Government, hereby agree and bind themselves to discontinue for the future all attacks upon the persons or property of other tribes, unless first assailed by them, and to use their influence to promote peace everywhere in the region occupied or frequented by them.

ARTICLE 3. All controversies or differences arising between the Blackfeet band of Dakota or Sioux, represented in council, and other tribes of Indians, involving the question of peace or war, shall be submitted for the arbitrament of the President, or such person or persons as may be designated by him, and the decision or award faithfully observed by the said band represented in council.

ARTICLE 4. The said band, represented in council, shall withdraw from the routes overland already established or hereafter to be established, through their country, and in consideration thereof, the Government Of the United States agree to pay to the said band the sum of seven thousand dollars annually, for twenty years, in such articles as the Secretary of the Interior may direct: Provided, That said band, so represented in council, shall faithfully conform to the requirements of this treaty.

ARTICLE 5. Any amendment or modification of this treaty by the (Senate of the United States shall be considered final and binding upon the) said band represented in council, as a part of this treaty, in the same manner as if it had been subsequently presented and agreed to by the chiefs and headmen of said nation. In testimony whereof the commissioners on the part of the United States, and the chiefs and headmen of the said Blackfeet band of the Dakota or Sioux, have hereunto set their hands, this nineteenth day of October, one thousand eight hundred and sixty-five, after the contents had previously been read, interpreted, and explained to the said chiefs and headmen.

Newton Edmunds, Edward B. Taylor, S. R. Curtis, major-general, H. H. Sibley, brigadier-general, Henry W. Reed, Orrin Guernsey.

Chiefs:
Wah-hah-chunk-i-ah-pee, The One that is used as a Shield, his x mark, Wah-mun-dee-wak-kon-o, The War Eagle in the Air, his x mark,
Principal braves or soldiers:
Mah-to-ko-ke-pah, He that Fears the Bear, his x mark, A-hack-ah-sap-pah, The Black Stag, his x mark, A-hack-ah-we-chash-tah, The Stag Man, his x mark, Mah-to-wash-tay, The Good Bear, his x mark, Tah-ton-kah-ho-wash-tay, The Buffalo with a Fine Voice, his x mark, Oya-hin-di-a-man-nee, The Track that Rings as it Walks, his x mark, Shon-kah-hon-skah, The Long Dog, his x mark, Shon-kah-wah-mun-dee, The Dog War Eagle, his x mark,

Plains, West and Northwest Plateau Indian Treaties

Signed by the Commissioners on the part of the United States, and by the chiefs and headmen after the treaty had been fully read, interpreted, and explained, in our presence:-

A. W. Hubbard, M. C. Sixth District Iowa.
E. F. Ruth, secretary to Commission.

TREATY WITH THE SIOUX SANS ARCS BAND {1865, Oct. 20}
Ratified Mar. 5, 1866.
Proclaimed Mar. 17, 1866.

Articles of a treaty made and concluded at Fort Sully, in the Territory of Dakota, by and between Newton Edmunds, governor and ex-officio superintendent Indian affairs of Dakota Territory, Edward B. Taylor, superintendent of Indian affairs for the northern superintendency, Major-General S. R. Curtis, Brigadier-General H. H. Sibley, Henry W. Reed, and Orrin Guernsey, commissioners on the part of the United States, duly appointed by the President, and the undersigned chiefs and head-men of the Sans Arcs band of Dakota or Sioux Indians.

ARTICLE 1. The Sans Arcs band of Dakota or Sioux Indians, represented in council, hereby acknowledge themselves to be subject to the exclusive jurisdiction and authority of the United States, and hereby obligate and bind themselves, individually and collectively, not only to cease all hostilities against the persons and property of its citizens, but to use their influence, and, if requisite, physical force, to prevent other bands of Dakota Indians, or other adjacent tribes, from making hostile demonstrations against the Government or people of the United States.

ARTICLE 2. Inasmuch as the Government of the United States is desirous to arrest the effusion of blood between the Indian tribes within its jurisdiction hitherto at war with each other, the Sans Arcs band of Dakota or Sioux Indians, represented in council, anxious to respect the wishes of the Government, hereby agree to discontinue for the future all attacks upon the persons or property of other tribes, unless first attacked by them, and to use their influence to promote peace everywhere in the region occupied or frequented by them.

ARTICLE 3. All controversies or differences arising between the Sans Arcs band of Dakota or Sioux Indians, involving the question of peace or war, shall be submitted for the arbitrament of the President, or such person or persons as may be designated by him, and the decision or award shall be faithfully observed by the said band represented in council.

Plains, West and Northwest Plateau Indian Treaties

ARTICLE 4. The said band represented in council shall withdraw from the route overland already established, or hereafter to be established, through their country; and in consideration thereof the Government of the United States agree to pay the said band the sum of thirty dollars for each lodge or family, annually, for twenty years, in such articles as the Secretary of the Interior may direct: Provided, That said band so represented in council shall faithfully conform to the requirements of this treaty.

ARTICLE 5. Should any individual or individuals or portion of the band of the Sans Arcs band of Dakota or Sioux Indians, represented in council, desire hereafter to locate permanently upon any land claimed by said band for the purposes of agricultural or other similar pursuits, it is hereby agreed by the parties to this treaty, that such individuals shall be protected in such location against any annoyance or molestation on the part of whites or Indians; and whenever twenty lodges or families of the Sans Arcs band shall have located on land for agricultural purposes, and signified the same to their agent or superintendent, they, as well as other families so locating, shall receive the sum of twenty-five dollars annually, for five years, for each family, in agricultural implements and improvements; and when one hundred lodges or families shall have so engaged in agricultural pursuits they shall be entitled to a farmer and blacksmith, at the expense of the Government; as also teachers, at the option of the Secretary of the Interior, whenever deemed necessary.

ARTICLE 6. Any amendment or modification of this treaty, by the Senate of the United States, shall be considered final and binding upon the said band represented in council as a part of this treaty, in the same manner as if it had been subsequently presented and agreed to by the chiefs and head-men of said band.
In testimony whereof, the Commissioners on the part of the United States, and the chiefs and headmen of the said Sans Arcs band of Dakota or Sioux Indians, have hereunto set their hands this twentieth day of October, eighteen hundred and sixty-five, after the contents had previously been read, interpreted, and explained to the chiefs and headmen.

Newton Edmunds, Edward B. Taylor, S. R. Curtis, major-general, Henry H. Sibley, brigadier-general, Henry W. Reed, Orrin Guernsey.

Chiefs:
Wah-mun-dee-o-pee-doo-tah, The War Eagle with the Red Tail, his x mark, Cha-tau-'hne, Yellow Hawk, his x mark, Shon-kah-we-to-ko, The Fool Dog, his x mark, Chief soldiers: Chan-tay-mah-to, The Bear's Heart, his x mark, Tah-ko-ko-ke-pish-nee, The Man that Fears Nothing, his x mark, Nup-che-unk, The Nine, his x mark, Mah-to-nuk-kah, The Bear's Ears, his x mark, Chan-desh-kah-sappah, The Black Hoop, his x mark, Ze-te-kah-nah-sappcc, The Bird Necklace, his x mark.

Plains, West and Northwest Plateau Indian Treaties

Signed by the Commissioners on the part of the United States, and by the chiefs and headmen after the treaty had been fully read, interpreted, and explained, in our presence:

Hez. L. Hosmer, chief justice of Montana Territory.

S. S. Curtis, brevet lieutenant-colonel, U. S. Volunteers.

E. F. Ruth, secretary of Commission.

TREATY WITH THE SIOUX HUNKPAPA BAND {1865, Oct. 20}
Ratified Mar. 5, 1866.
Proclaimed, Mar. 17, 1866.

Articles of a treaty made and concluded at Fort Sully, in the Territory of Dakota, by and between Newton Edmunds, governor and ex-officio superintendent of Indian affairs of Dakota Territory, Edward B. Taylor, superintendent of Indian Affairs for the northern superintendency, Major-General S. R. Curtis, Brigadier-General H. H. Sibley, Henry W. Reed, and Orrin Guernsey, commissioners on the part of the United States, duly appointed by the President, and the undersigned chiefs and head-men of the Onkpahpah band of Dakota or Sioux Indians.

ARTICLE 1. The Onkpahpah band of Dakota or Sioux Indians, represented in council, hereby acknowledge themselves to be subject to the exclusive jurisdiction and authority of the United States, and hereby obligate and bind themselves, individually and collectively, not only to cease all hostilities against the persons and property of its citizens, but to use their influence, and, if requisite, physical force, to prevent other bands of Dakota Indians, or other adjacent tribes, from making hostile demonstrations against the Government or people of the United States.

ARTICLE 2. Inasmuch as the Government of the United States is desirous to arrest the effusion of blood between the Indian tribes within its jurisdiction hitherto at war with each other, the Onkpahpah band of Dakota or Sioux Indians, represented in council, anxious to respect the wishes of the Government, hereby agree to discontinue for the future all attacks upon the persons or property of other tribes, unless first attacked by them, and to use their influence to promote peace everywhere in the region occupied or frequented by-them.

ARTICLE 3. All controversies or differences arising between the Onkpahpah band of Dakota or Sioux Indians involving the question of peace or war shall be submitted for the arbitrament of the President, or such person or persons as may be designated by him, and the decision or award shall be faithfully observed by the said band represented in council.

Plains, West and Northwest Plateau Indian Treaties

ARTICLE 4. The said band represented in council shall withdraw from the routes overland already established, or hereafter to be established, through their country; and in consideration thereof the Government of the United States agree to pay the said band the sum of thirty dollars for each lodge or family, annually, for twenty years, in such articles as the Secretary of the Interior may direct:

That said band so represented in council shall faithfully conform to the requirements of this treaty.

ARTICLE 5. Should any individual or individuals, or portion of band of the Onkpahpah band of Dakota or Sioux Indians, represented in council, desire hereafter to locate permanently upon any land claimed by said band for the purposes of agricultural or other similar pursuits, it is hereby agreed by the parties to this treaty that such individuals shall be protected in such location against any annoyance or molestation on the part of whites or Indians, and whenever twenty lodges or families of the Onkpahpah band shall have located on land for agricultural purposes, and signified the same to their agents or superintendent, they as well as other families so locating shall receive the sum of twenty-five dollars annually for five years, for each family, in agricultural implements and improvements; and when one hundred lodges or families shall have so engaged in agricultural pursuits, they shall be entitled to a farmer and blacksmith, at the expense of the Government, as also teachers, at the option of the Secretary of the Interior, whenever deemed necessary.

ARTICLE 6. Any amendment or modification of this treaty by the Senate of the United States shall be considered final and binding upon the said band, represented in council, as a part of this treaty, in the same manner as if it had been subsequently presented and agreed to by the chiefs and head-men of said band.

In testimony whereof, the Commissioners on the part of the United States, and the chiefs and headmen of the said Yanktonai band of Dakota or Sioux Indians, have hereunto set their hands, this twentieth day of October, eighteen hundred and sixty-five, after the contents had previously been read, interpreted, and explained to the chiefs and headmen.

Newton Edmunds, Edward B. Taylor, S. R. Curtis, major-general, H. H. Sibley, brigadier-general, Henry Reed, Orrin Guernsey.

Chiefs:
M'doka, or The Buck, his x mark, Mah-to-wak-kouah, He that Runs the Bear, his x mark, Shon-kah-we-te-ko, The Feel Dog, his x mark,

In presence of
Hez L. Hosmer, chief justice of Montana Territory.
S. S. Curtis, brevet lieutenant-colonel U. S. Volunteers.
A. W. Hubbard, M. C. Sixth District Iowa.

Plains, West and Northwest Plateau Indian Treaties

E. F. Ruth, secretary of commission.

The foregoing signatures in this handwriting (that of General Curtis) were made in presence of the undersigned on the 28th and 29th October, 1865, at Fort Sully.
Maj. A. P. Shreve, paymaster U. S. Army.
John Pattie, lieutenant-colonel Seventh Iowa Cavalry.

TREATY WITH THE SIOUX YANKTONAI BAND {1865, Oct. 20}
Ratified, Mar. 5, 1866.
Proclaimed, Mar. 17, 1866.

Articles of a treaty made and concluded at Fort Sully, in the Territory of Dakota, by and between Newton Edmunds, governor and ex-officio superintendent of Indian affairs of Dakota Territory, Edward B. Taylor, superintendent of Indian affairs for the northern superintendency, Major-General S. R. Curtis, Brigadier-General H. H. Sibley Henry W. Reed, and Orrin Guersey, commissioners on the part of the United States, duly appointed by the President, and the undersigned chiefs and head-men of the Yanktonai band of Dakota or Sioux Indians.

ARTICLE 1. The Yanktonai band of Dakota or Sioux Indians, represented in council, hereby acknowledge themselves to be subject to the exclusive jurisdiction and authority of the United States, and hereby obligate and bind themselves, individually and collectively, not only to cease all hostilities against the persons and property of its citizens, but to use their influence, and, if requisite, physical force, to prevent other bands of Dakota Indians, or other adjacent tribes, from making hostile demonstrations against the Government or people of the United States.

ARTICLE 2. Inasmuch as the Government of the United States is desirous to arrest the effusion of blood between the Indian tribes within its jurisdiction hitherto at war with each other, the Yanktonai band of Dakota or Sioux Indians represented in council, anxious to respect the wishes of the Government, hereby agree to discontinue, for the future all attacks upon the persons or property of other tribes, unless first attacked by them, and to use their influence to promote peace everywhere in the region occupied or frequented by them.

ARTICLE 3. All controversies or differences arising between the Yanktonai band of Dakota or Sioux Indians, represented in council, and other tribes of Indians, involving the question of peace or war, shall be submitted for the arbitrament of the President, or such person or persons as may be designated by him, and the decision or award shah be faithfully observed by the said band represented in council.

507

Plains, West and Northwest Plateau Indian Treaties

ARTICLE 4. The said band, represented in council shall withdraw from the routes overland already established, or hereafter to be established, through their country; and in consideration thereof, the Government of the United States agree to pay the said band the sum of thirty dollars for each lodge or family, annually, for twenty years, in such articles as the Secretary of the Interior may direct: Provided, That said band, so represented in council, shall faithfully conform to the requirements of this treaty.

ARTICLE 5. Should any individual or individuals, or portion of the band of the Yanktonai band of Dakota or Sioux Indians represented in council, desire hereafter to locate permanently upon any land claimed by said band for the purposes of agricultural or other similar pursuits, it is hereby agreed by the parties to this treaty that such individuals shall be protected in such location against any annoyance or molestation on the part of whites or Indians; and whenever twenty lodges or families of the Yanktonai band shall have located on lands for agricultural purposes, and signified the same to their agents or superintendent, they, as well as other families so locating, shall receive the sum of twenty-five dollars annually, for five years, for each family, in agricultural implements and improvements; and when one hundred lodges or families shall have so engaged in agricultural pursuits, they shall be entitled to a farmer and blacksmith, at the expense of the Government, as also teachers, at the option of the Secretary of the Interior, whenever deemed necessary.

ARTICLE 6. Any amendment or modification of this treaty by the Senate of the United States shall be considered final and binding upon the said band, represented in council, as a part of this treaty, in the same manner as if it had been subsequently presented and agreed to by the chiefs and head-men of said band.
In testimony whereof, the Commissioners on the part of the United States, and the chiefs and headmen of the said Onkpahpah band of Dakota or Sioux Indians, have hereunto set their hands this twentieth day of October, eighteen hundred and sixty-five, after the contents had previously been read, interpreted, and explained to the chiefs and headmen.

Newton Edmunds, Edward B. Taylor, S. R. Curtis, major-general, H. H. Sibley, brigadier-general, Henry W. Reed, Orrin Guernsey.

Chiefs:
Ah-ke-tche-tah-hon-skah, The Tall Soldier, his x mark, Mah-to-che-kah, The Little Bear, his x mark, Muzzah-e-nom-pah, The Iron that Comes Out, his x mark, Wak-ke-an-skah, The White Thunder, his x mark, Chief Soldiers: Mah-to-nom-pah, The Two Bears, his x mark, Cha-tan-me-ne-o-me-nec, The Whirling Heart, his x mark, Chiefs: Ma-to-chewicksa, Bear's Rib, his x mark, Running Antelope, Ta-to-kee-un, his x mark, The Man that Has a Heart for All, O-en-e-chan-ta-u-can, his x mark,

Plains, West and Northwest Plateau Indian Treaties

Signed by the Commissioners on the part of the United States, and by the chiefs and headmen, after the treaty had been fully read, interpreted, and explained in our presence:-

Hez. L. Hosmer, chief justice of Montana Territory.

S. S. Curtis, brevet lieutenant colonel U. S. Volunteers.

TREATY WITH THE SIOUX UPPER YANKTONAI BAND
{1865, Oct. 28}
Ratified Mar. 5, 1866.
Proclaimed, Mar. 17, 1866.

Articles of a treaty made and concluded at Fort Sully, in the Territory of Dakota, by and between Newton Edmunds, governor and ex-officio superintendent of Indian affairs of Dakota Territory, Edward B. Taylor, superintendent of Indian affairs for the northern superintendency, Major-General S. R. Curtis, Brigadier-General H. H. Sibley, Henry W. Reed and Orrin Guernsey, commissioners on the part of the United States, duly appointed by the President, and the undersigned chiefs and head-men of the Upper Yanktonais band of Dakota or Sioux Indians.

ARTICLE 1. The Upper Yanktonais band of Dakota or Sioux Indians, represented in council, hereby acknowledge themselves to be subject to the exclusive jurisdiction and authority of the United States, and hereby obligate and bind themselves, individually and collectively, not only to cease all hostilities against the persons and property of its citizens, but to use their influence, and, if necessary, physical force, to prevent other bands of the Dakota Indians, or other adjacent tribes, from making hostile demonstrations against the Government or people of the United States.

ARTICLE 2. Inasmuch as the Government of the United States is desirous to arrest the effusion of blood between the Indian tribes within its jurisdiction hitherto at war with each other, the Upper Yanktonais band of Dakota or Sioux Indians, represented in council, anxious to respect the wishes of the Government, hereby agree to discontinue for the future all attacks upon the persons or property of other tribes, unless first attacked by them, and to use their influence to promote peace everywhere in the region occupied or frequented by them.

ARTICLE 3. All controversies or differences arising between the Upper Yanktonais band of Dakota or Sioux Indians, represented in council, and other tribes of Indians, involving the question of peace or war, shall be submitted for the arbitrament of the President, or such person or persons as may be designated by him, and the decision or award faithfully observed by the said band represented in council.

509

Plains, West and Northwest Plateau Indian Treaties

ARTICLE 4. The said band represented in council shall withdraw from the routes overland already established, or hereafter to be established, through their country; and in consideration thereof, and of their non-interference with the persons and property of citizens of the United States travelling thereon, the Government of the United States agree to pay the said band the sum of ten thousand dollars, annually, for twenty years, in such articles as the Secretary of the Interior may direct: Provided, That said band so represented in council shall faithfully conform to the requirements of this treaty.

ARTICLE 5. Should any individual or individuals, or portion of the band of the Upper Yanktonais band of Dakota or Sioux Indians, represented in council, desire hereafter to locate permanently upon any land claimed by said band for the purposes of agricultural or other similar pursuits, it is hereby agreed by the parties to this treaty that said individuals shall be protected in such location against any annoyance or molestation on the part of whites or Indians, and whenever twenty lodges or families of the Upper Yanktonais band shall have located on land for agricultural purposes, and signified the same to their agent or superintendent, they, as well as other families so locating, shall receive the sum of twenty-five dollars annually for five years, for each family, in agricultural implements and improvements; and when one hundred lodges or families shall have so engaged in agricultural pursuits they shall be entitled to a farmer and blacksmith at the expense of the Government, as also teachers, at the option of the Secretary of the Interior, whenever deemed necessary.

ARTICLE 6. Any amendment or modification of this treaty by the Senate of the United States shall be considered final and binding upon the said band, represented in council, as a part of this treaty, in the same manner as if it had been subsequently presented and agreed to by the chiefs and head-men of said band. In testimony whereof, the Commissioners on the part of the United States, and the chiefs and headmen of the said Upper Yanktonais band of Dakota or Sioux Indians, have hereunto set their hands this twenty-eighth day of October, eighteen hundred and sixty-five, after the contents had previously been read, interpreted, and explained to the chiefs and headmen.

Newton Edmunds, Edward B. Taylor, S. R. Curtis, major-general, H. H. Sibley, brigadier-general, Henry W. Reed, Orrin Guernsey.

The above signatures were made in our presence:
Geo. D. Hill.
S. L. Spink.
A. W. Hubbard.

Plains, West and Northwest Plateau Indian Treaties

TREATY WITH THE SIOUX OGLALA BAND {1865, Oct. 28}
Ratified, Mar. 5, 1866.
Proclaimed Mar. 17, 1866.

Articles of a treaty made and concluded at Fort Sully, in the Territory of Dakota, by and between Newton Edmunds, governor and ex-officio superintendent of Indian affairs of Dakota Territory, Edward B. Taylor, superintendent of Indian affairs for the northern superintendency, Major-General S. R. Curtis, Brigadier-General, H. H. Sibley, Henry W. Reed, and Orrin Guernsey, commissioners on the part of the United States, duly appointed by the President, and the undersigned chiefs and head-men of the O'Galla band of Dacota or Sioux Indians.

ARTICLE 1. The O'Gallala band of Dakota or Sioux Indians, represented in council, hereby acknowledge themselves to be subject to the exclusive jurisdiction and authority of the United States, and hereby obligate and bind themselves, individually and collectively, not only to cease all hostilities against the persons and property of its citizens, but to use their influence, and, if necessary, physical force, to prevent other bands of the Dakota Indians, or other adjacent tribes, from making hostile demonstrations against the Government or people of the United States.

ARTICLE 2. Inasmuch as the Government of the United States is desirous to arrest the effusion of blood between the Indian tribes within its jurisdiction hitherto at war with each other, the O'Gallala band of Dakota or Sioux Indians, represented in council, anxious to respect the wishes of the Government, hereby agree to discontinue for the future all attacks upon the persons or property of other tribes, unless first attacked by them, and to use their influence to promote peace everywhere in the region occupied or frequented by them.

ARTICLE 3. All controversies or differences arising between the O'Gallala band of Dakota or Sioux Indians, represented in council, and other tribes of Indians, involving the question of peace or war, shall be submitted shall be submitted for the arbitrament of the arbitrament of the President, or such person or persons as may be designated by him, and the decision or award faithfully observed by the said band represented in council.

ARTICLE 4. The said band represented in council shall withdraw from the routes overland already established or hereafter to be established through their country: and in consideration thereof, the Government of the United States agree to pay to the said band the sum of ten thousand dollars annually for twenty years, in such articles as the Secretary of the Interior may direct: Provided, That said band, so represented in council, shall faithfully conform to the requirements of this treaty.

511

Plains, West and Northwest Plateau Indian Treaties

ARTICLE 5. Should any individual or individuals, or portion of the band of the (O'Gallala) band of Dakota or Sioux Indians, represented in council, desire hereafter to locate permanently upon any land claimed by said band for the purposes of agricultural or other similar pursuits, it is hereby agreed by the parties to this treaty, that such individuals shall be protected in such location against any annoyance or molestation on the part of whites or Indians; and whenever twenty lodges or families of the O'Gallala band shall have located on land for agricultural purposes, and signified the same to their agent or superintendent, they as well as other families so locating shall receive the sum of twenty-five dollars annually, for five years, for each family, in agricultural implements and improvements; and when one hundred lodges or families shall have so engaged in agricultural pursuits they shall be entitled to a farmer and blacksmith, at the expense of the Government, as also teachers, at the option of the Secretary of the Interior, whenever deemed necessary.

ARTICLE 6. Any amendment or modification of this treaty by the Senate of the United States shall be considered final and binding upon the said band, represented in council, as a part of this treaty, in the same manner as if it had been subsequently presented and agreed to by the chiefs and head-men of said band.
In testimony whereof, the Commissioners on the part of the United States, and the chiefs and headmen of the said O'Gallala band of Dakota or Sioux Indians, have hereunto set their hands this twenty-sixth day of October, eighteen hundred and sixty-five after the contents had previously been read, interpreted, and explained to the chiefs and headmen.

Newton Edmunds, Edward B. Taylor, S.R. Curtis, major-general, H. H. Sibley, brigadier-general, Henry W. Reed, Orrin Guernsey.

Signed on the part of the Commission, in our presence:
S. L Spink, Geo. D. Hill, A. W. Hubbard, G. C. Moody.
Chief Long Bull, Tan-tan-ka-has-ka, his x mark, The Charging Bear, Ma-lo-wa-ta-khe, his x mark, The Man that Stands on a Hill, Pa-ha-to-na-je, his x mark,

The foregoing signatures in this handwriting (that of General Curtis) were made in presence of the undersigned on the 28th and 29th Oct., 1865, at Fort Sully.
Maj. A. P. Shreve, Paymaster U. S. Army.
John Pattee, Lieutenant-Colonel Seventh Iowa Cavalry.

Plains, West and Northwest Plateau Indian Treaties

TREATY WITH THE MIDDLE OREGON TRIBES {1865, Nov. 15}
Ratified, Mar. 2, 1867.
Proclaimed Mar. 28, 1867.

Articles of agreement and convention entered into at the Warm Springs Agency, Oregon, by J. W. Perit Huntington, sup't Indian affairs for Oregon, on behalf of the United States, and the undersigned, chief and head-men of the confederated tribes and bands of Middle Oregon, the same being amendatory of and supplemental to the treaty negotiated with the aforesaid tribes on the twenty-fifth day of June, eighteen hundred and fifty-five, and ratified by the Senate of the United States on the eighteenth day of April, eighteen hundred and fifty-nine.

ARTICLE 1. It having become evident from experience that the provision of article 1 of the treaty of the twenty-fifth of June, A. D. eighteen hundred and fifty-five, which permits said confederated tribes to fish, hunt, gather berries and roots, pasture stock, and erect houses on lands outside the reservation, and which have been ceded to the United States, is often abused by the Indians to the extent of continuously residing away from the reservation, and is detrimental to the interests of both Indians and whites; therefore it is hereby stipulated and agreed that all the rights enumerated in the third proviso of the first section of the before-mentioned treaty of the twenty-fifth of June, eighteen hundred and fifty-fivethat is to say, the right to take fish, erect houses, hunt game, gather roots and berries, and pasture animals upon lands without the reservation set apart by the treaty aforesaid are hereby relinquished by the confederated Indian tribes and bands of Middle Oregon, parties to this treaty.

ARTICLE 2. The tribes aforesaid covenant and agree that they will hereafter remain upon said reservation, subject to the laws of the United States, the regulations of the Indian Department, and the control of the officers thereof; and they further stipulate that if any of the members of said tribes do leave, or attempt to leave, said reservation in violation of this treaty, they will assist in pursuing and returning them, when called upon to do so by the superintendent or agent in charge.

ARTICLE 3. In cases which may arise which make it necessary for any Indian to go without the boundaries of said reservation, the superintendent or agent in charge may, in his discretion, give to such Indian a written permit or pass, which shall always be for a short period and the expiration definitely fixed in said paper. Any Indian who, having gone out with a written pass, shall remain beyond the boundaries for a longer period than the time named in said pass, (shall) be deemed to have violated this treaty to the same extent as if he or she had gone without a pass.

Plains, West and Northwest Plateau Indian Treaties

ARTICLE 4. An infraction of this treaty shall subject the Indian guilty thereof to a deprivation of his or her share of the annuities, and to such other punishment as the President of the United States may direct.

ARTICLE 5. It is stipulated and agreed on the part of the United, States, as a consideration for the relinquishment of the rights herein enumerated, that the sum of three thousand five hundred dollars shall be expended in the purchase of teams, agricultural implements, seeds, and other articles calculated to advance said confederated tribes in agriculture and civilization.

ARTICLE 6. It is further agreed that the United States shall cause to be alloted to each head of a family in said confederated tribes and bands a tract of land sufficient for his or her use, the possession of which shall be guaranteed and secured to said family and the heirs thereof forever.

ARTICLE 7. To the end that the vice of intemperance among said tribes may be checked, it is hereby stipulated that when any members thereof shall be known to drink ardent spirits, or to have the same in possession, the facts shall be immediately reported to the agent or superintendent, with the name of the person or persons from whom the liquor was obtained; and the Indians agree to diligently use, under the direction of the superintendent or agent, all proper means to secure the identification and punishment of the persons unlawfully furnishing liquor as aforesaid.

In testimony whereof, the said J. W. Perit Huntington, superintendent of Indian affairs, on the part of the United States, and the undersigned chiefs and head confederated tribes and bands aforesaid, have hereunto, in the presence of the subscribing witnesses and of each other, affixed our signatures and seals on this fifteenth day of November, in the year one thousand eight hundred and sixty-five.

J. W. Perit Huntington, Sup't Indian Affairs in Oregon, and acting Commissioner on behalf of the United States.

Mark, head chief, his x mark. Wm. Chinook, his x mark, Kuck-up, his x mark, Ponst-am-i-ne, his x mark, Alex-zan, his x mark, Tas-simk, his x mark, John Mission, his x mark, Lock-squis-squis-sa, his x mark, Kuck-ups, his x mark.Hote, his x mark, I-palt-pel, his x mark, Sin-ne-wah, his x mark, Ump-chil-le-poo, his x mark, Shooley, his x mark, Tah-koo, his x mark, Tum-tsche-cus, his x mark, Tou-wacks, his x mark, Hul-le-quil-la, his x mark, Te-ah-ki-ak,-his x mark, Chok-te, his x mark, Kootsh-ta, his x mark,

Done in presence of
Tallax, his x mark, interpreter, Donald McKay, his x mark, interpreter.
Charles Lafollett, captain, First Oregon Infantry.

Plains, West and Northwest Plateau Indian Treaties

TREATY WITH THE POTAWATOMI {1866, Mar. 29}
Ratified Apr. 26, 1866.
Proclaimed May 5, 1866.

Whereas certain amendments are desired by the Pottawatomie Indians to their treaty concluded at the Pottawatomie agency on the fifteenth day of November, A. D. 1861, and amended by resolution of the Senate of the United States dated April the fifteenth, A. D. 1862; and whereas the United States are willing to assent to such amend-meats, it is therefore agreed by and between Dennis N. Cooley, commissioner, on the part of the United States, thereunto duly authorized, and the undersigned business committee, acting on behalf of said tribe, and being thereunto duly authorized, in manner and form following, that is to say:

ARTICLE 1. The beneficial provisions in behalf of the more prudent and intelligent members of said tribe, contained in the third article of the amended treaty above recited, shall not hereafter be confined to males and heads of families, but the same shall be and are hereby extended to all adult persons of said tribe, without distinction of sex, whether such persons are or shall be heads of families or otherwise, in the same manner, to the same extent, and upon the same terms, conditions, and stipulations as are contained in said third article of said treaty with reference to "males and heads of families."

In testimony whereof the said parties by their Commissioner and Business Committee aforesaid have hereunto set their hands and seals at Washington City, District of Columbia, this 29th day of March, in the year of our Lord one thousand eight hundred and sixty-six.

Dennis N. Cooley, Commissioner.
J. N. Bourassa, U. F. Navane, B. N. Bertrand, Business Committee.

Signed in presence of
L. R. Palmer, James Steele.

TREATY WITH THE KIOWA, COMANCHE, AND APACHE
{1867, Oct. 21}
Ratified, July 25, 1868.
Proclaimed Aug. 25 1868.

Articles of a treaty concluded at the Council Camp on Medicine Lodge Creek, seventy miles south of Fort Larned, in the State of Kansas, on the twenty-first day of October, eighteen hundred and sixty-seven, by and between the United

Plains, West and Northwest Plateau Indian Treaties

States of America, represented by its commissioners duly appointed thereto to-wit: Nathaniel G. Taylor, William S. Harney, C. C. Augur, Alfred S. (H.) Terry, John B. Sanborn, Samuel F. Tappan, and J. B. Henderson, of the one part, and the Kiowa, Comanche, and Apache Indians, represented by their chiefs and headmen duly authorized and empowered to act for the body of the people of said tribes (the names of said chiefs and headmen being hereto subscribed) of the other part, witness:

Whereas, on the twenty-first day of October, eighteen hundred and sixty-seven, a treaty of peace was made and entered into at the Council Camp, on Medicine Lodge Creek, seventy miles south of Fort Larned, in the State of Kansas, by and between the United States of America, by its commissioners Nathaniel G. Taylor, William S. Harney, C. C. Augur, Alfred H. Terry, John B. Sanborn, Samuel F. Tap-pan, and J. B. Henderson, of the one part, and the Kiowa and Comanche tribes of Indians, of the Upper Arkansas, by and through their chiefs and headmen whose names are subscribed thereto, of the other part, reference being had to said treaty; and whereas, since the making and signing of said treaty, at a council held at said camp on this day, the chiefs and headmen of the Apache nation or tribe of Indians express to the commissioners on the part of the United States, as aforesaid, a wish to be confederated with the said Kiowa and Comanche tribes, and to be placed, in every respect, upon an equal footing with said tribes; and whereas, at a council held at the same place and on the same day, with the chiefs and headmen of the said Kiowa and Comanche Tribes, they consent to the confederation of the said Apache tribe, as desired by it, upon the terms and conditions hereinafter set forth in this supplementary treaty.

Now, therefore, it is hereby stipulated and agreed by and between the aforesaid commissioners, on the part of the United States, and the chiefs and headmen of the Kiowa and Comanche tribes, and, also, the chiefs and headmen of the said Apache tribe, as follows, to wit:

ARTICLE 1. The said Apache tribe of Indians agree to confederate and become incorporated with the said Kiowa and Comanche Indians, and to accept as their permanent home the reservation described in the aforesaid treaty with said Kiowa and Comanche tribes, concluded as aforesaid at this place, and they pledge themselves to make no permanent settlement at any place, not on any lands, outside of said reservation.

ARTICLE 2. The Kiowa and Comanche tribes, on their part, agree that all the benefits and advantages arising from the employment of physicians, teachers, carpenters, millers, engineers, farmers, and blacksmiths, agreed to be furnished under the provisions of their said treaty, together with all the advantages to be derived from the construction of agency buildings, warehouses, mills, and other structures, and also from the establishment of schools upon their said reserva-

Plains, West and Northwest Plateau Indian Treaties

tion, shall be jointly and equally shared and enjoyed by the said Apache Indians, as though they had been originally a part of said tribes; and they further agree that all other benefits arising from said treaty shall be jointly and equally shared as aforesaid.

ARTICLE 3. The United States, on its part, agrees that clothing and other articles named in Article X. of said original treaty, together with all money or other annuities agreed to be furnished under any of the provisions of said treaty, to the Kiowa and Comanches, shall be shared equally by the Apaches. In all cases where specific articles of clothing are agreed to be furnished to the Kiowas and Comanches, similar articles shall be furnished to the Apaches, and a separate census of the Apaches shall be annually taken and returned by the agent, as provided for the other tribes. And the United States further agrees, in consideration of the incorporation of said Apaches, to increase the annual appropriation of money, as provided for in Article X. of said treaty, from twenty-five thousand to thirty thousand dollars; and the latter amount shall be annually appropriated-, for the period therein named, for the use and benefit of said three tribes, confederated as herein declared; and the clothing and other annuities, which may from time to time be furnished to the Apaches, shall be based upon the census of the three tribes, annually to be taken by the agent, and shall be separately marked, forwarded, and delivered to them at the agency house, to be built trader the provisions of said original treaty.

ARTICLE 4. In consideration of the advantages conferred by this supplementary treaty upon the Apache tribe of Indians, they agree to observe and faithfully comply with all the stipulations and agreements entered into by the Kiowas and Comanches in said original treaty. They agree, in the same manner, to keep the peace toward the whites and all other persons under the jurisdiction of the United States, and to do and perform all other things enjoined upon said tribes by the provisions of said treaty; and they hereby give up and forever relinquish to the United States all rights, privileges, and grants now vested in them, or intended to be transferred to them, by the treaty between the United States and the Cheyenne and Arapahoe tribes of Indians, concluded at the camp on the Little Arkansas River, in the State of Kansas, on the fourteenth day of October, one thousand eight hundred and sixty-five, and also by the supplementary treaty, concluded at the same place on the seventeenth day of the same month, between the United States, of the one part, and the Cheyenne, Arapahoe, and Apache tribes, of the other part.

In testimony of all which, the said parties have hereunto set their hands and seals at the place and on the day hereinbefore stated.

N. G. Taylor, President of Indian Commission.
Wm. S. Harney, Brevet Major-General, Commissioner, &c.
C. C. Augur, Brevet Major-General.

Plains, West and Northwest Plateau Indian Treaties

On the part of the Kiowas:
Satanka, or Sitting Bear, his x mark, Sa-tan-ta, or White Bear, his x mark, Wah-toh-konk, or Black Eagle, his x mark, Ton-a-en-ko, or Kicking Eagle, his x mark, Fish-e-more, or Stinking Saddle, his x mark, Ma-ye-tin, or Woman's Heart, his x mark, Sa-tim-gear, or Stumbling Bear, his x mark, Sa-pa-ga, or One Bear, his x mark, Cor-beau, or The Crow, his x mark, Sa-ta-more, or Bear Lying Down, his x mark,

On the part of the Comariches:
Parry-wah-say-men, or Ten Bears, his x mark, Tep-pe-navon, or Painted Lips, his x mark, To-she-wi, or Silver Brooch, his x mark, Cear-chi-neka, or Standing Feather, his x mark, Ho-we-ar, or Gap in the Woods, his x mark, Tir-ha-yah-gua-hip, or Horse's Back, his x mark, Es-a-man-a-ca, or Wolf's Name, his x mark, Ah-te-es-ta, or Little Horn, his x mark, Pooh-yah-to-yeh-be, or Iron Mountain, his x mark, Sad-dy-yo, or Dog Fat, his x mark,

On the part of the Apaches:
Mah-vip-pah, Wolfe Sleeve, his x mark, Kon-zhon-ta-co, Poor Bear, his x mark, Cho-se-ta, or Bad Back, his x mark, Nab-tan, or Brave Man, his x mark, Ba-zhe-ech, Iron Shirt, his x mark, Til-la-ka, or White Horn, his x mark,

TREATY WITH THE CHEYENNE AND ARAPAHO {1867, Oct. 28}
Ratified July 25, 186i8.
Proclaimed Aug. 19, 1868

Articles of a treaty and agreement made and entered into at the Council Camp on Medicine Lodge Creek, seventy miles south of Fort Larned, in the State of Kansas, on the twenty-eight day of October, eighteen hundred and sixty-seven, by and between the United States of America, represented by its commissioners duly appointed thereto, to wit: Nathaniel G. Taylor, William S. Harney, C. C. Augur, Alfred H. Terry, John B. Sanborn, Samuel F. Tappan and John B. Henderson, of the one part, and the Cheyenne and Arapahoe tribes of Indians, represented by their chiefs and head-men duly authorized and empowered to act for the body of the people of said tribesthe names of said chiefs and head-men being hereto subscribed of the other part, witness:

ARTICLE 1. From this day forward all war between the parties to this agreement shall forever cease. The Government of the United States desires peace, and its honor is here pledged to keep it. The Indians desire peace, and they now pledge their honor to maintain it.
If bad men among the whites, or among other people subject to the authority of the United States, shall commit any wrong upon the person or property of the Indians, the United States will, upon proof made to the agent and forwarded to

518

Plains, West and Northwest Plateau Indian Treaties

the Commissioner of Indian Affairs at Washington City, proceed at once to cause the offender to be arrested, and punished according to the laws of the United States, and also reimburse the injured person for the loss sustained.

If bad men among the Indians shall commit a wrong or depredation upon the person or property of any one, white, black, or Indian, subject to the authority of the United States and at peace therewith, the tribes herein named solemnly agree that they will, on proof made to their agent, and notice by him, deliver up the wrongdoer to the United States, to be tried and punished according to its laws; and in case they wilfully refuse so to do, the person injured shall be re-imbursed for his loss from the annuities or other moneys due or to become due to them under this or other treaties made with the United States. And the President, on advising with the Commissioner of Indian Affairs, shall prescribe such rules and regulations for ascertaining damages, under the provisions of this article, as in his judgment may be proper. But no such damages shall be adjusted and paid until thoroughly examined and passed upon by the Commissioner of Indian Affairs and the Secretary of the Interior, and no one sustaining loss, while violating, or because of his violating, the provisions of this treaty or the laws of the United States, shall be re-imbursed therefor.

ARTICLE 2. The United States agrees that the following district of country, to wit: commencing at the point where the Arkansas River crosses the 37th parallel of north latitude, thence west on said parallel the said line being the southern boundary of the State of Kansas to the Cimarone River; (sometimes called the Red Fork of the Arkansas River), thence down said Cimarone River, in the middle of the main channel thereof, to the Arkansas River; thence up the Arkansas River, in the middle of the main channel thereof, to the place of beginning, shall be and the same is hereby set apart for the absolute and undisturbed use and occupation of the Indians herein named, and for such other friendly tribes or individual Indians, as from time to time they may be willing, with the consent of the United States, to admit among them; and the United States now solemnly agrees that no persons except those herein authorized so to do, and except such officers, agents, and employes of the Government as may be authorized to enter upon Indian reservations in discharge of duties enjoined by law, shall ever be permitted to pass over, settle upon, or reside in the territory described in this article, or in such territory as may be added to this reservation for the use of said Indians.

ARTICLE 3. If it should appear from actual survey or other examination of said tract of land, that it contains less than one hundred and sixty acres of tillable land for each person who at the time may be authorized to reside on it, under the provisions of this treaty, and a very considerable number of such persons shall be disposed to commence cultivating the soil as farmers, the United States agrees to set apart for the use of said Indians as herein provided, such

519

Plains, West and Northwest Plateau Indian Treaties

additional quantity of arable land adjoining to said reservation, or as near the same as it can be obtained, as may be required to provide the necessary amount.

ARTICLE 4. The United States agrees at its own proper expense to construct at some place near the center of said reservation, where timber and water may be convenient, the following buildings, to wit: a warehouse or store-room for the use of the agent in storing goods belonging to the Indians, to cost not exceeding fifteen hundred dollars; an agency-building for the residence of the agent, to cost not exceeding three thousand dollars; a residence for the physician, to cost not more than three thousand dollars; and five other buildings, for a carpenter, farmer, blacksmith, miller, and engineer, each to cost not exceeding two thousand dollars; also a school-house or mission-building, so soon as a sufficient number of children can be induced by the agent to attend school, which shall not cost exceeding five thousand dollars. The United States agrees, further, to cause to be erected on said reservation, near the other buildings herein authorized, a good steam circular saw-mill, with a grist-mill and shingle machine attached: the same to cost not exceeding eight thousand dollars.

ARTICLE 5. The United States agrees that the agent for said Indians in the future shall make his home at the agency building; that he shall reside among them, and keep an office open at all times for the purpose of prompt and diligent inquiry into such matters of complaint by and against the Indians as may be presented for investigation, under the provisions of their treaty stipulations, as also for the faithful discharge of other duties enjoined on him by law. In all cases of depredation on person or property, he shall cause the evidence to be taken in writing and forwarded, together with his finding, to the Commissioner of Indian Affairs, whose decision, subject to the revision of the Secretary of the Interior, shall be binding on the parties to this treaty.

ARTICLE 6. If any individual, belonging to said tribes of Indians, or legally incorporated with them, being the head of a family, shall desire to commence farming, he shall have the privilege to select, in the presence and with the assistance of the agent then in charge, a tract of land within said reservation not exceeding three hundred and twenty acres in extent, which tract when so selected, certified, and recorded in the land-book as herein directed, shall cease to be held in common, but the same may be occupied and held in the exclusive possession of the person selecting it, and of his family, so long as he or they may continue to cultivate it. Any person over eighteen years of age, not being the head of a family, may in like manner select and cause to be certified to him, or her, for purposes of cultivation, a quantity of land not exceeding eighty acres in extent, and thereupon be entitled to the exclusive possession of the same as above directed.

Plains, West and Northwest Plateau Indian Treaties

For each tract of land so selected, a certificate containing a description thereof, and the name of the person selecting it, with a certificate indorsed thereon, that the same has been recorded, shall be delivered to the party entitled to it by the agent, after the same shall have been recorded by him in a book to be kept in his office, subject to inspection, which said book shall be known as the "Cheyenne and Arapahoe Land Book." The President may at any time order a survey of the reservation, and, when so surveyed, Congress shall provide for protecting the rights of settlers in their improvements, and may fix the character of the title held by each.

The United States may pass such laws on the subject of alienation and descent of property, and on all subjects connected with the government of the Indians on said reservations, and the internal police thereof as may be thought proper.

ARTICLE 7. In order to insure the civilization of the tribes entering into this treaty, the necessity of education is admitted, especially by such of them as are or may be settled on said agricultural reservation, and they therefore pledge themselves to compel their children, male and female, between the ages of six and sixteen years, to attend school; and it is hereby made the duty of the agent for said Indians to see that this stipulation is strictly complied with; and the United States agrees that for every thirty children between said ages, who can be induced or compelled to attend school, a house shall be provided, and a teacher competent to teach the elementary branches of an English education shall be furnished, who will reside among said Indians, and faithfully discharge his or her duties as a teacher. The provisions of this article to continue for not less than twenty years.

ARTICLE 8. When the head of a family or lodge shall have selected lands and received his certificate as above directed, and the agent shall be satisfied that he intends in good faith to commence cultivating the soil for a living, he shall be entitled to receive seeds and agricultural implements for the first year, not exceeding in value one hundred dollars; and for each succeeding year he shall continue to farm for a period of three years more, he shall be entitled to receive seeds and implements as aforesaid, not exceeding in value twenty-five dollars.

And it is further stipulated that such persons as commence farming shall receive instruction from the farmer herein provided for; and whenever more than one hundred persons shall enter upon the cultivation of the soil, a second blacksmith shall be provided, with such iron, steel, and other material as may be needed.

ARTICLE 9. At any time after ten years from the making of this treaty the United States shall have the privilege of withdrawing the physician, farmer, blacksmith, carpenter, engineer, and miller, herein provided for, but in case of such withdrawal, an additional sum, thereafter, of ten thousand dollars per an-

521

Plains, West and Northwest Plateau Indian Treaties

num shall be devoted to the education of said Indians, and the Commissioner of Indian Affairs shall upon careful inquiry into their condition make such rules and regulations for the expenditure of said sum as will best promote the educational and moral improvement of said tribes.

ARTICLE 10. In lieu of all sums of money or other annuities provided to be paid to the Indians herein named, under the treaty of October fourteenth, eighteen hundred and sixty-five, made at the mouth of Little Arkansas, and under all treaties made previous thereto, the United States agrees to deliver at the agency house on the reservation herein named, on the fifteenth day of October, of each year, for thirty years, the following articles, to wit:

For each male person over fourteen years of age, a suit of good, substantial woolen clothing, consisting of coat, pantaloons, flannel shirt, hat, and a pair of home-made socks.

For each female over twelve years of age, a flannel skirt, or the goods necessary to make it, a pair of woolen hose, twelve yards of calico and twelve yards of cotton domestics.

For the boys and girls under the ages named, such flannel and cotton goods as may be needed to make each a suit as aforesaid, together with a pair of woolen hose for each.

And in order that the Commissioner of Indian Affairs may be able to estimate properly for the articles herein named, it shall be the duty of the agent each year to forward to him a full and exact census of the Indians on which the estimate from year to year can be based.

And, in addition to the clothing herein named, the sum of twenty thousand dollars shall be annually appropriated for a period of thirty years, to be used by the Secretary of the Interior in the purchase of such articles as, from time to time, the condition and necessities of the Indians may indicate to be proper. And if at any time, within the thirty years, it shall appear that the amount of money needed for clothing, under this article, can be appropriated to better uses for the tribe herein named, Congress may, by law, change the appropriation to other purposes; but, in no event, shall the amount of this appropriation be withdrawn or discontinued for the period named. And the President shall, annually, detail an officer of the Army to be present, and attest the delivery of all the goods herein named to the Indians, and he shall inspect and report on the quantity and quality of the goods and the manner of their delivery.

ARTICLE 11. In consideration of the advantages and benefits conferred by this treaty, and the many pledges of friendship by the United States, the tribes who are parties to this agreement hereby stipulate that they will relinquish all

Plains, West and Northwest Plateau Indian Treaties

right to occupy permanently the territory outside of their reservation as herein defined, but they yet reserve the right to hunt on any lands south of the Arkansas so long as the buffalo may range thereon in such numbers as to justify the chase; and no white settlements shall be permitted on any part of the lands contained in the old reservation as defined by the treaty made between the United States and the Cheyenne, Arapahoe, and Apache tribes of Indians, at the mouth of the Little Arkansas, under date of October fourteenth, eighteen hundred and sixty-five, within three years from this date, and they, the said tribes, further expressly agree:

First. That they will withdraw all opposition to the construction of the railroad now being built on the Smoky Hill River, whether it be built to Colorado or New Mexico.

Second. That they will permit the peaceable construction of any railroad not passing over their reservation, as herein defined.

Third. That they will not attack any persons at home or travelling, nor molest or disturb any wagon-trains, coaches, mules, or cattle belonging to the people of the United States or to persons friendly therewith.

Fourth. They will never capture or carry off from the settlements white women or children.

Fifth. They will never kill or scalp white men, nor attempt to do them harm.

Sixth. They withdraw all pretense of opposition to the construction of the railroad now being built along the Platte River, and westward to the Pacific Ocean; and they will not in future object to the construction of railroads, wagon-roads, mail-stations, or other works of utility or necessity, which may be ordered or permitted by the laws of the United States. But should such roads or other works be constructed on the lands of their reservation, the Government will pay the tribe whatever amount of damage may be assessed by three disinterested commissioners to be appointed by the President for that purpose, one of said commissioners to be a chief or head-man of the tribe.

Seventh. They agree to withdraw all opposition to the military posts or roads now established, or that may be established, not in violation of treaties heretofore made or hereafter to be made with any of the Indian tribes.

ARTICLE 12. No treaty for the cession of any portion or part of the reservation herein described, which may be held in common, shall be of any validity or force as against the said Indians unless executed and signed by at least three-fourths of all the adult male Indians occupying or interested in the same; and no cession by the tribe shall be understood or construed in such manner as to de-

Plains, West and Northwest Plateau Indian Treaties

prive without his consent any individual member of the tribe of his rights to any tract of land selected by him as provided in Article 6 of this treaty.

ARTICLE 13. The United States hereby agree to furnish annually to the Indians the physician, teachers, carpenter, miller, engineer, farmer, and blacksmiths, as herein contemplated, and that such appropriations shall be made from time to time, on the estimates of the Secretary of the Interior, as will be sufficient to employ such persons.

ARTICLE 14. It is agreed that the sum of five hundred dollars, annually, for three years from date, shall be expended in presents to the ten persons of said tribe who, in the judgment of the agent, may grow the most valuable crops for the respective year.

ARTICLE 15. The tribes herein named agree that when the agency-house and other buildings shall be constructed on the reservation named, they will regard and make said reservation their permanent home, and they will make no permanent settlement elsewhere, but they shall have the right, subject to the conditions and modifications of this treaty, to hunt on the lands south of the Arkansas River, formerly called theirs, in the same manner as agreed on by the treaty of the "Little Arkansas," concluded the fourteenth day of October, eighteen hundred and sixty-five.

In testimony of which, we have hereunto set our hands and seals, on the day and year aforesaid.

N. G. Taylor, ,President of Indn. Commission.
Wm. S. Harney, Major-General, Brevet, &c.
C. C. Augur, Brevet Major-General.

Attest:
Ashton S. H. White, secretary.
Geo. B. Willis, phonographer.

On the part of the Cheyennes:
O-to-ah-nac-co, Bull Bear, his x mark, Moke-tav-a-to, Black Kettle, his x mark, Nac-co-hah-ket, Little Bear, his x mark, Mo-a-vo-va-ast, Spotted Elk, his x mark, Is-se-von-ne-ve, Buffalo Chief, his x mark, Vip-po-nah, Slim Face, his x mark, Wo-pah-ah, Gray Head, his x mark, O-ni-hah-ket., Little Rock, his x mark, Ma-mo-ki, or Curly Hair, his x mark, O-to-ah-has-tis, Tall Bull, his x mark,

On the part of the Arapahoes:

Plains, West and Northwest Plateau Indian Treaties

Little Raven, his x mark, Yellow Bear, his x mark, Storm, his x mark, White Rabbit, his x mark, Spotted Wolf, his x mark, Little Big Mouth, his x mark, Young Colt, his x mark, Tall Bear, his x mark,

Attest:
C. W. Whitaker, interpreter.
H. Douglas, major, Third Infantry.

TREATY WITH THE SAUK AND FOXES {1867, Feb. 18}
Ratified July 25, 1868.
Proclaimed Oct. 14, 1868.

Articles of agreement made and concluded this eighteenth day of February, one thousand eight hundred and sixty-seven, between the United States, represented by Lewis E Bogy, Commissioner of Indian Affairs; William H. Watson, special commissioner Thomas Murphy, superintendent of Indian Affairs for Kansas; and Henry W. Martin, United States Indian agent, duly authorized, and the tribes of Sacs and Foxes of the Mississippi, represented by Keokuk, Che-kus-kuk, Uc-quaw-ho-ko, Mut-tut-tah, and Man-ah-to-wah, chiefs of said tribes.

ARTICLE 1. The Sacs and Foxes of the Mississippi cede to the Government of the United States all the lands, with the improvements thereon, contained in their unsold portion of their diminished reserve defined in the first article of their treaty ratified July ninth, one thousand eight hundred and sixty, (the said tract containing about eighty-six thousand and four hundred acres, and being more particularly described by the survey and plats on file in the Department of the Interior) except as reserved in previous treaties, or in this treaty.

ARTICLE 2. The said Indians also cede to the United States a full and complete title to the land, with the improvements thereon, now remaining unsold in that portion of their old reservation provided by article four of the treaty of July ninth, one thousand eight hundred and sixty, to be sold by the Government for their benefit, the cession herein made being subject to the exceptions defined in this treaty.

ARTICLE 3. The United States agree to pay to the Sac and Fox Indians, parties to this treaty, at the rate of one dollar an acre for the whole of the land ceded in the two preceding sections, being about one hundred and fifty-seven thousand acres of land, less the amount of land set apart for individuals; and further agree to pay the outstanding indebtedness of the said tribe, now represented by scrip issued under the provisions of previous treaties, and amounting, on the first of November, eighteen hundred and sixty-five, to twenty-six thousand five hundred and seventy-four dollars, besides the interest thereon; out of the proceeds of the sale of lands ceded in this treaty, and the amount herein

525

Plains, West and Northwest Plateau Indian Treaties

provided to be paid to said Indians, after deducting such sums as, under the provisions of this treaty, are to be expended for their removal, subsistence, and establishing them in their new country, shall be added to their invested funds, and five per cent. interest paid thereon in the same manner as the interest of their present funds is now paid.

ARTICLE 4. At any time after the ratification of this treaty, the lands ceded in the first article shall be held and considered at the disposal of the United States, except that, until the time for the removal of the Indians is fixed by public notice, under the provisions of this treaty, no interference shall be made with the rights of the Indians as the occupants of the lands, but they shall remain in all respects without molestation, in the same manner as if this treaty had not been made: And provided further, That inasmuch as there are valuable improvements upon said reservation, such improvements shall be appraised under the direction of the Secretary of the Interior, and the appraised value of the same shall be paid to the United States, before title is given to any individual or corporation for the lands upon which such improvements are situated.

ARTICLE 5. The lands ceded in the second article of this treaty, being the unsold remainder of the lands provided in the fourth article of the treaty of July ninth, one thousand eight hundred and sixty, to be sold in trust for said Indians, shall, immediately upon the ratification of this treaty, become the property of the United States, and shall be open to entry and settlement, and the lands in the second article ceded, as well as those ceded in the first article, shall be subject to all the laws and regulations of the General Land-Office the same as other public lands, except as relates to the provisions in the next preceding article relating to the time when they shall be open for settlement, and the requirement of payment for the improvements; and should there be any improvements upon the land ceded in the second article, they shall be appraised, and payment shall be required therefor: Provided, That such lands shall be subject to sale, tracts of not exceeding one hundred and sixty acres to any one person, and at a price not less than one dollar and fifty cents per acre.

ARTICLE 6. The United States agree, in consideration of the improvements upon the said reservation, to give to the Sacs and Foxes for their future home a tract of land in the Indian country south of Kansas, and south of the Cherokee lands, not exceeding seven hundred and fifty square miles in extent. The selection of such new reservation shall be made under the direction of the Secretary of the Interior, and with his approval, by commissioners appointed by the said Secretary, who shall visit the Indian country, with delegations from all the tribes proposing to remove thereto, as soon as practicable after the ratification of this treaty; and said reservation shall be surveyed as to its exterior lines, at the cost of the United States, under the direction of the Commissioner of Indian Affairs, not to exceed three thousand dollars: Provided, That if it shall be found impracticable to select a suitable home for the tribe except by purchase from

526

Plains, West and Northwest Plateau Indian Treaties

the Cherokees, the United States will pay toward the said purchase the same amount that would have been payable to the Creeks if the reservation had been selected upon the former Creek lands; and in that case the balance of the money payable to the Cherokees shall be deducted from the amount due the Sacs and Foxes under this treaty.

ARTICLE 7. As soon as practicable after the selection of the new reservation herein provided for, there shall be erected thereon, at the cost of the United States, a dwelling-house for the agent of the tribe, a house and shop for a blacksmith, and dwelling-house for a physician, the aggregate cost of which shall not exceed ten thousand dollars; and also, at the expense of the tribe, five dwelling-houses for the chiefs, to cost in all not more than five thousand dollars.

As soon as practicable after such selection of a reservation as it may, in the discretion of the Secretary of the Interior, be deemed advisable for the Indians to remove thereto, regard being had to the proper season of the year for such removal, notice shall be given to their agent, directing such removal; and whenever such time shall be fixed, public notice thereof shall be given in three leading newspapers of Kansas, and thereafter the land ceded to the United States by the first article of this treaty, shall be open to entry and settlement under the provisions of the fourth article.

ARTICLE 8. No part of the invested funds of the tribe, or of any moneys which may be due to them under the provisions of previous treaties, nor of any moneys provided to be paid to them by this treaty, shall be used in payment of any claims against the tribe accruing previous to the ratification of this treaty unless herein expressly provided for.

ARTICLE 9. In order to promote the civilization of the tribe, one section of land, convenient to the residence of the agent, shall be selected by said agent, with the approval of the Commissioner of Indian Affairs, and set apart for a manual-labor school; and there shall also be set apart, from the money to be paid to the tribe under this treaty, the sum of ten thousand dollars for the erection of the necessary school-buildings and dwelling for teacher, and the annual amount of five thousand dollars shall be set apart from the income of their funds after the erection of such school-buildings, for the support of the school; and after settlement of the tribe upon their new reservation, the sum of five thousand dollars of the income of their funds may be annually used, under the direction of the chiefs, in the support of their national government, out of which last-mentioned amount the sum of five hundred dollars shall be annually paid to each of the chiefs.

ARTICLE 10. The United States agree to pay annually, for five years after the removal of the tribe, the sum of fifteen hundred dollars for the support of a physician and purchase of medicines, and also the sum of three hundred and

Plains, West and Northwest Plateau Indian Treaties

fifty dollars annually for the same time, in order that the tribe may provide itself with tobacco and salt.

ARTICLE 11. In consideration of certain improvements made by John Goodell upon the lands of the nation within their present reservation, and of his services as their interpreter, he shall be allowed to select therefrom a half section of land; and it is further provided that of said land, Sarah A. Whistler and Pash-e-ca-cah, or Amelia Mitchell, shall each be allowed to select a half section of land, the latter selection to include the house in which she lives; and Julia A. Goodell one quarter section, besides the land, not exceeding eight acres, upon which her house and improvements are situated; and Mary A. Means, one quarter section, to includ(e) the improvements occupied by her; and there shall also be allowed to Antoine Gokey and William Avery, each one hundred and sixty acres, to Leo Whistler and Gertrude Whistler, each three hundred and twenty acres, and to James Thorpe, Virginia Thorpe, and Cassandra Thorpe, Thomas J. Miles, Hattie Miles, Ema-Ke-O-Kuck, Hannie Ke-O-Kuck, Mo-Co-P-quah, each eighty acres; Man-a-tah, Pah-me-che-kaw-paw, Henry Jones, Wilson McKinney, and Carrie C. Capper, each one hundred and sixty acres, to be selected from unimproved lands.

Provided, That the parties herein named shall pay to the Secretary of the Interior, within three months after the ratification of this treaty, the sum of one dollar per acre for said lands, the avails of which shall be used for the benefit of the Sacs and Foxes in the same manner as the other funds arising from the sales of their lands: Provided also, That George Powers, the present Government interpreter, for valuable services rendered and uniform kindness toward the nation, shall have patented to him, in fee-simple, three hundred and twenty acres of land, to be located by the agent: Provided also, That they may select from land upon which improvements exist, by paying the appraised value of such improvements; but no selection shall include the agency, mission, or mill buildings; and upon the approval by the Secretary of the Interior of such selections, and on payment therefor as hereinbefore provided, patents in fee-simple shall be issued to the respective parties, their heirs or assigns.

ARTICLE 12. In consideration of the faithful services of Samuel Black in protecting their houses and timber from trespass and depredation, there shall be patented to him in fee-simple the tract of land upon which he lives, being the west half of the northwest quarter-section four, town(ship) seventeen, range sixteen.

ARTICLE 13. John K. Rankin, licensed traders, having erected valuable building at the agency, it is agreed that (he) may have a patent for the land, not exceeding eight acres, upon which such improvements are built, and not to include any other improvements, on the payment of two dollars and fifty cents per acre.

Plains, West and Northwest Plateau Indian Treaties

ARTICLE 14. The Sacs and Foxes, parties to this treaty, agree that the Sacs and Foxes of Missouri, if they shall so elect, with the approval of the Secretary of the Interior, may unite with them and become a part of their people, upon their contributing to the common fund such a portion of their funds as will place them on an equal footing in regard to annuities.

ARTICLE 15. The claims of the Sacs and Foxes against the United States for stealing of stock, which have heretofore been adjusted, amounting to sixteen thousand four hundred dollars, shall be paid by the United States, and the amount disbursed and expended for the benefit of the tribe in such objects for their improvement and comfort upon the new reservation as the chiefs, through their agent, shall desire; and whereas the Indians claim that one full payment due under previous treaty has never been made to them, it is agreed that a careful examination of the books of the Commissioner of Indian Affairs shall be made, and if any sum is found to be still due and unpaid, the same shall be paid to them per capita in the same manner as their annuities are paid.

ARTICLE 16. The United States will advance to the said tribe of Indians the sum of twenty thousand dollars, or so much thereof as may be necessary, to pay the expenses of their subsistence for the first year after their arrival at their new home in the Indian country, and to pay the necessary expenses of removal, and furnish necessary rations for the journey during such removal; said removal to be made under direction of the superintendent or agent, to be designated by the Secretary of the Interior; the moneys thus expended to be deducted from the whole amount provided to be paid for their lands herein ceded.

ARTICLE 17. It is hereby provided that the half-breeds and full-bloods of the tribe, who were entitled to selections of land under the Sac and Fox treaty, ratified July ninth, one thousand eight hundred and sixty, and which selections have been approved by the Secretary of the Interior, shall be entitled to patents in fee-simple for the lands heretofore selected, according to the schedule annexed to this treaty: Provided, That where such selections have been made and the allottees have sold their lands for a valuable consideration, not less than one dollar and twenty-five cents per acre, the Secretary of the Interior shall, upon full proof being made, cause patents to issue to the purchasers or their assigns.

ARTICLE 18. All sales hereafter made by or on behalf of persons to whom lands are assigned in this treaty shall receive the approval of the Secretary of the Interior before taking effect in conveying titles to lands so sold.

ARTICLE 19. The United States agree to pay the expenses of negotiating this treaty, not to exceed the sum of fifteen hundred dollars.

Plains, West and Northwest Plateau Indian Treaties

ARTICLE 20. The chiefs and head-men of the Sacs and Foxes having permitted their employees to cultivate farms, which, together with the farms of Ke-o-kuck and other chiefs, are embraced within an area two miles by four, and the said Sacs and Foxes believing that the lands comprising the said area having been made valuable by reason of said occupancy, and in order that they may receive a fair compensation for said area of land, bounded and described as follows, except as heretofore specially excepted, and the mill and mission building, to wit: commencing at the northwest corner of section thirty-three, township sixteen, range seventeen, thence east two and a quarter (2 1/4) miles to the reservation line; thence south along said line four miles; thence west two and a fourth (2¼)miles to the southwest corner of section sixteen, township seventeen, range seventeen; thence north along the section line to the place of beginning, are hereby withdrawn from sale, as is provided for the sale of their lands in this treaty, and the said area of land, as above described, shall be sold by the chiefs and agent for the tribe at the best price obtainable; and they are hereby empowered to make warrantee deeds for the same, subject to the approval of the Secretary of the Interior, at not less than two dollars per acre in addition to the appraised value of the improvements. The avails of said lands shall be expended by the agent, under the direction of the chiefs, for the benefit of the nation.

ARTICLE 21. The Sacs and Foxes of the Mississippi, parties to this agreement, being anxious that all the members of their tribe shall participate in the advantages to be derived from the investment of their national funds, sales of lands, and so forth, it is therefore agreed that, as soon as practicable, the Commissioner of Indian Affairs shall cause the necessary proceedings to be adopted, to have such members of the tribe as may be absent notified of this agreement and its advantages, and to induce them to come in and permanently unite with their brethren; and that no part of the funds arising from or due the nation under this or previous treaty stipulations shall be paid to any bands or parts of bands who do not permanently reside on the reservation set apart to them by the Government in the Indian Territory, as provided in this treaty, except those residing in the State of Iowa; and it is further agreed that all money accruing from this or former tribes, (treaties,) now due or to become due said nation, shall be paid them on their reservation in Kansas; and after their removal, as provided in this treaty, payments shall be made at their agency, on their lands as then located.

List of Sac and Fox lands selected for individuals referred to in Article XVII of the above treaty, selected by Perry Fuller, agent.

Names of persons	Description	Sec(tion)	Town(ship)		Range
Alvira Connolly	S. ½ NW. ¼	5	17	18	
Alvira Connolly	SW. ¼ 5	17	18		
Alvira Connolly	N. ½ NW. ¼	8	17	18	

Plains, West and Northwest Plateau Indian Treaties

Name	Description			
Alexander Connolly	E. ½	4	17	18
Cordella Connolly	E. ½ 35	16	17	
Isaac Goodell	W. ½ 3	17	18	
Kish-Kah-Iwah	S. ½ 16	17	18	
Mary I. Thorp	E. ½ 12	17	17	
Hiram P. Thorp	E. ½ 1	17	17	
Francis A. Thorp	W. ½ 6	17	18	
Amelia McPherson	W. ½, 1	17	17	
Sarah A. Whistler	SW. ¼ 34	16	18	
Sarah A. Whistler	SW. ¼ SW. ¼ 35	16	18	
Sarah A. Whistler	W. ½ NW. 1 2	17	18	
Sarah A. Whistler	NW. ¼ SW. ¼ 2	17	18	
Julia A. Goodell	N. ½ 21	17	18	
Susan J. Goodell	E. ½ 3	17	1S	
John Goodell, jr	E. ½ 17	17	18	
Jane Goodell	NE. ¼ 10	17	18	
Jane Goodell	NW. ¼ NW. ¼ 10	17	18	
Jane Goodell	E. 1/2 NW. ¼ 10	17	18	
,lane Goodell	NW. ¼ NW. ¼ 11	17	18	
Mary A. Byington	E. ½ NE. ¼ 9	17	18	
Mary A. Byington	E. ½ SE. ¼ 9	17	18	
Mary A. Byington	W. ½ SW. ¼ 10	17	18	
Mary A. Byington	SW. ¼ NW. ¼ 10	17	18	
Mary A. Byington	NE. ¼ NE. 1 16	17	1S	
Margaret Miles	W. ½ 4	17	18	
Thomas J. Connoily	SW. ¼ SE. ¼	9	17	18
Thomas ,1. Connoily	SE. ¼ NE. ¼	16	17	18
Thomas J. ConnollY	W. ½ NE. ¼	16	17	18
Thomas J. Connolly	NW. ¼ 16	17	18	
Charles T. Connolly	E. ½ NW. ¼	9	17	18
Charles T. Connolly	W. ½ NE. ¼	9	17	18
Charles T. Connoily	NW. ¼ SE. ¼	9	17	18
Charles T. Connolly	SE. ¼ SW. ¼	9	17	18
Charles T. Connolly	S. ½ SW. ¼	9	17	18
Kaw-Kol-we-nah	E. ½ 2	17	17	
George Powers	NE. ¼ 8	17	18	
George Powers	S. ½ NW. ¼ 8	17	18	
George Powers	N. ½ SW. ¼ 8	17	18	
Joseph Gokey	W. ½ SE. ¼ 21	17	18	
Joseph Gokey	N. ½ NW. ¼ 28	17	18	
Joseph Gokey	SW. ¼ NW. ¼ 28	17	18	
Joseph Gokey	NW. ¼ NE. ¼ 28	17	18	
Joseph Gokey	W. ½ SE. ¼ 29	17	18	
Met-tach-ah-pack-o-tah	E. ½ 7	17	18	
Mack-oh-tach-o-quit	W. ½ 7	17	18	

Plains, West and Northwest Plateau Indian Treaties

In testimony whereof, the parties hereinbefore named have hereunto set their hands and seals the day and year first above mentioned.
Lewis V. Bogy, Commissioner of Indian Affairs.
W. H. Watson, Special Commissioner.
Thos. Murphy, Superintendent of Indian Affairs.

In presence of
Antoine Gokey, his x mark, United States interpreter.
Charles E. Mix, Thos. E. McGraw, Wm. Whistler.

TREATY WITH THE SIOUX SISSETON AND WAHPETON BANDS
{1867, Feb. 19}
Ratified April 15, 1867.
Proclaimed May 2, 1867.

Whereas it is understood that a portion of the Sissiton and Warpeton bands of, Santee Sioux Indians, numbering from twelve hundred to fifteen hundred persons, not only preserved their obligations to the Government of the United States, during and since the outbreak of the Medewakantons and other bands of Sioux in 1862, but freely perilled their lives during that outbreak to rescue the residents on the Sioux reservation, and to obtain possession of white women and children made captives by the hostile bands; and that another portion of said Sissiton and Warpeton bands, numbering from one thousand to twelve hundred persons, who did not participate in the massacre of the whites in 1862, fearing the indiscriminate vengeance of the whites, fled to the great prairies of the Northwest, where they still remain; and

Whereas Congress, in confiscating the Sioux annuities and reservations, made no provision for the support of these, the friendly portion of the Sissiton and Warpeton bands, and it is believed (that) they have been suffered to remain homeless wanderers, frequently subject to intense sufferings from want of subsistence and clothing to protect them from the rigors of a high northern latitude, although at all times prompt in rendering service when called upon to repel hostile raids and to punish depredations committed by hostile Indians upon the persons and property of the whites; and

Whereas the several subdivisions of the friendly Sissitons and Warpeton bands ask, through their representatives, that their adherence to their former obligations of friendship to the Government and people of the United States be recognized, and that provision be made to enable them to return to an agricultural life and be relieved from a dependence upon the chase for a precarious subsistence: Therefore, A treaty has been made and entered into, at Washington City, District of Columbia, this nineteenth day of February, A. D. 1867, by and be-

Plains, West and Northwest Plateau Indian Treaties

tween Lewis V. Bogy, Commissioner of Indian Affairs, and William It. Watson, commissioners, on the part of the United States, and the undersigned chiefs and head-men of the Sissiton and Warpeton bands of Dakota or Sioux Indians, as follows, to wit:

ARTICLE 1. The Sissiton and Warpeton bands of Dakota Sioux Indians, represented in council, will continue their friendly relations with the Government and people of the United States, and bind themselves individually and collectively to use their influence to the extent of their ability to prevent other bands of Dakota or other adjacent tribes from making hostile demonstrations against the Government or people of the United States.

ARTICLE 2. The said bands hereby cede to the United States the right to construct wagon-roads, railroads, mail stations, telegraph lines, and such other public improvements as the interest of the Government may require, over and across the lands claimed by said bands, (including their reservation as hereinafter designated) over any route or routes that that may be selected by the authority of the Government, said lands so claimed being bounded on the south and east by the treaty-line of 1851, and the Red River of the North to the mouth of Goose River; on the north by the Goose River and a line running from the source thereof by the most westerly point of Devil's Lake to the Chief's Bluff at the head of James River, and on the west by the James River to the mouth of Mocasin River, and thence to Kampeska Lake.

ARTICLE 3. For and in consideration of the cession above mentioned, and in consideration of the faithful and important services said to have been rendered by the friendly bands of Sissitons and Warpetons Sioux here represented, and also in consideration of the confiscation of all their annuities, reservations, and improvements, it is agreed that there shall be set apart for the member's of said bands who have heretofore surrendered to the authorities of the Government, and were not sent to the Crow Creek reservation, and for the members of said bands who were released from prison in 1866, the following-described lands as a permanent reservation, viz:

Beginning at the head of Lake Travers(e), and thence along the treaty-line of the treaty of 1851 to Kampeska Lake; thence in a direct line to Reipan or the northeast point of the Coteau des Prairie(s), and thence passing north of Skunk Lake, on the most direct line to the foot of Lake Traverse, and thence along the treaty-line of 1851 to the place of beginning.

ARTICLE 4. It is further agreed that a reservation be set apart for all other members of said bands who were not sent to the Crow Creek reservation, and also for the Cut-Head bands of Yanktonais Sioux, a reservation bounded as follows, viz:

Plains, West and Northwest Plateau Indian Treaties

Beginning at the most easterly point of Devil's Lake; thence along the waters of said lake to the most westerly point of the same; thence on a direct line to the nearest point on the Cheyenne River; thence down said river to a point opposite the lower end of Aspen Island, and thence on a direct line to the place of beginning.

ARTICLE 5. The said reservations shall be apportioned in tracts of (160) one hundred and sixty acres to each head of a family or single person over the age of (21) twenty-one years, belonging to said bands and entitled to locate thereon, who may desire to locate permanently and cultivate the soil as a means of subsistence: each (160) one hundred and sixty acres so allotted to be made to conform to the legal subdivisions of the Government surveys when such surveys shall have been made; and every person to whom lands may be allotted under the provisions of this article, who shall occupy and cultivate a portion thereof for five consecutive years shall thereafter be entitled to receive a patent for the same so soon as he shall have fifty acres of said tract fenced, ploughed, and in crop: Provided, (That) said patent shall not authorize any transfer of said lands, or portions thereof, except to the United States, but said lands and the improvements thereon shall descend to the proper heirs of the persons obtaining a patent.

ARTICLE 6. And, further, in consideration of the destitution of said bands of Sissiton and Warpeton Sioux, parties hereto, resulting from the confiscation of their annuities and improvements, it is agreed that Congress will, in its own discretion, from time to time make such appropriations as may be deemed requisite to enable said Indians to return to an agricultural life under the system in operation on the Sioux reservation in 1862; including, if thought advisable, the establishment and support of local and manual-labor schools; the employment of agricultural, mechanical, and other teachers; the opening and improvement of individual farms; and generally such objects as Congress in its wisdom shall deem necessary to promote the agricultural improvement and civilization of said bands.

ARTICLE 7. An agent shall be appointed for said bands, who shall be located at Lake Traverse; and whenever there shall be five hundred (500) persons of said bands permanently located upon the Devil's Lake reservation there shall be an agent or other competent person appointed to superintend at that place the agricultural, educational, and mechanical interests of said bands.

ARTICLE 8. All expenditures under the provisions of this treaty shall be made for the agricultural improvement and civilization of the members of said bands authorized to locate upon the respective reservations, as hereinbefore specified, in such manner as may be directed by law; but no goods, provisions, groceries, or other articlesexcept materials for the erection of houses and articles to facilitate the operations of agricultureshall be issued to Indians or mixed-bloods

Plains, West and Northwest Plateau Indian Treaties

on either reservation unless it be in payment for labor performed or for produce delivered: Provided, That when persons located on either reservation, by reason of age, sickness, or deformity, are unable to labor, the agent may issue clothing and subsistence to such persons from such supplies as may be provided for said bands.

ARTICLE 9. The withdrawal of the Indians from all dependence upon the chase as a means of subsistence being necessary to the adoption of civilized habits among them, it is desirable that no encouragement be afforded them to continue their hunting operations as means of support, and, therefore, it is agreed that no person will be authorized to trade for furs or peltries within the limits of the land claimed by said bands, as specified in the second article of this treaty, it being contemplated that the Indians will rely solely upon agricultural arid mechanical labor for subsistence, and that the agent will supply the Indians and mixed-bloods on the respective reservations with clothing, provisions, &c., as set forth in article eight, so soon as the same shall be provided for that purpose. And it is further agreed that no person not a member of said bands, parties hereto whether white, mixed-blood, or Indian, except persons in the employ of the Government or located under its authority, shall be permitted to locate upon said lands, either for hunting, trapping, or agricultural purposes.

ARTICLE 10. The chiefs and head-men located upon either of the reservations set apart for said bands are authorized to adopt such rules, regulations, or laws for the security of life and property, the advancement of civilization, and the agricultural prosperity of the members of said bands upon the respective reservations, and shall have authority, under the direction of the agent, and without expense to the Govern-meat, to organize a force sufficient to carry out all such rules, regulations, or laws, and all rules and regulations for the government of said Indians, as may be prescribed by the Interior Department: Provided, That all rules, regulations, or laws adopted or amended by the chiefs and head-men on either reservation shall receive the sanction of the agent.

In testimony whereof, we, the commissioners representing the United States, and the delegates representing the Sissiton and Warpeton bands of Sioux Indians, have hereunto set our hands and seals, at the place and on the day and year above written.

Lewis V. Bogy, Commissioner of Indian Affairs.
W. H. Watson.

Signed in the presence of
Charles E. Mix.

Gabriel Renville, head chief Siss(i)ton and Wa(r)peton bands.
Wamdiupiduta, his x mark, head Siss(i)ton chief.

Plains, West and Northwest Plateau Indian Treaties

Tacandupahotanka, his x mark, head Wa(r) peton chief.
Oyehduze, his x mark, chief Sissiton.

Witness
Charles E. Mix, Benj'n Thompson, J. R. Brown.

TREATY WITH THE POTAWATOMI {1867, Feb. 27}
Ratified July 25, 1868.
Proclaimed, Aug. 7, 1,868.

Articles of agreement concluded at Washington, D.C., on the twenty-seventh day of February, 1867, between the United States, represented by Lewis G. Bogy, Commissioner of Indian Affairs, W.H. Watson , special commissioner, Thos. Murphy, supt. of Indian affairs for Kansas, and Luther R. Palmer, U. S. Indian agent, duly authorized, and the Pottawatomie tribe of Indians, represented by their chiefs, braves, and head-men, to wit: Mazhee, Mianco, Shawgwe, B. H. Bertrand, J. N. Bourassa, M. B. Beaubien, L. H. Ogee, and G. L. Hawgenschleimer.

Whereas the Pottawatomies believe that it is for the interest of their tribe that a home should be secured for them in the Indian country south of Kansas, while there is yet an opportunity for the selection of a suitable reservation; and whereas the tribe has the means of purchasing such reservation from funds to arise from the sale of lands under the provisions of this treaty, without interfering with the exclusive rights of those of their people who hold their lands in common to the ownership of their diminished reserve, held by them in common, or with their right to receive their just proportion of the moneys arising from the sale of unallotted lands, known as surplus lands: Now, therefore, it is agreed

ARTICLE 1. It being the intention of the Government that a commission shall visit the Indian country as soon as practicable after the ratification of the treaties contemplating the removal of certain tribes from Kansas, accompanied by delegates from the several tribes proposing to remove, it is agreed that a delegation Of the Pottawatomies may accompany said commission in order to select, if possible, a suitable location for their people without interfering with the locations made for other Indians; and if such location shall be found satisfactory to the Pottawatomies, and approved by the Secretary of the Interior, such tract of land, not exceeding thirty miles square, shall be set apart as a reservation for the exclusive use and occupancy of that tribe; and upon the survey of its lines and boundaries, and ascertaining of its area, and payment to the United States for the same, as hereinafter mentioned and set forth, the said tract shall be patented to the Pottawatomie Nation: Provided, That if the said Pottawatomies shall prefer to select a new home among the Cherokees, by agreement

Plains, West and Northwest Plateau Indian Treaties

with the said Cherokees, for a price within the means of the Pottawatomies, the Government will confirm such agreement.

ARTICLE 2. In case the new reservation shall be selected upon the lands purchased by the Government from the Creeks, Seminoles, or Choctaws, the price to be paid for said reservation shall not exceed the cost of the same to the Government of the United States; and the sum to be paid by the tribe for said reservation shall be taken from the amount which may be received for the lands which were offered for sale to the Leavenworth, Pawnee, and Western Railroad Company, under the treaty dated November fifteen, eighteen hundred and sixty-one, which amount shall be the common property of the tribe, except the Prairie band, who shall have no interest in said reservation to be purchased as aforesaid, but in lieu thereof shall receive their pro rata share of the proceeds of the sale of said land in money, as the same may be received.

Provided, That if the United States shall advance the amount necessary to purchase the said reservation, the interest due upon the deferred payments for said lands, sold as hereinafter provided, shall, when received by the United States, be retained and credited to said tribe interested in said reservation, or so much of said interest as may be due said tribe under this treaty: And provided further, That the Leavenworth, Pawnee and Western Railroad Company, their successors and assigns, having failed to purchase said lands, the Atchison, Topeka and Santa Fe Railroad Company may, within thirty days after the promulgation of this treaty, purchase of the said Pottawatomies their said unallotted lands, except as hereinafter provided, to St. Mary's Mission, at the price of one dollar per acre, lawful money of the United States, and upon filing their bond for the purchase and payment of said lands in due form, to be approved by the Secretary of the Interior within the time above named, the Secretary of the Interior shall issue to the last-named railroad company certificates of purchase, and such certificates of purchase shall be deemed and holden, in all courts, as evidence of title and possession in the said railroad company to all or any part of said lands, unless the same shall be forfeited as herein provided.

The said purchase-money shall be paid to the Secretary of the Interior in trust for said Indians within five years from the date of such purchase, with interest at the rate of six per cent. per annum on all deferred payments, until the whole purchase-money shall have been paid; and before any patents shall issue for any part of said lands, one hundred thousand dollars shall be deposited with the Secretary of the Interior, to be forfeited in case the whole of the lands are not paid for as herein provided; (said money may be applied as the payment for the last one hundred thousand acres of said land;) payments shall also be made for at least one-fourth of said unallotted lands at the rate of one dollar per acre, and when so paid the President is authorized hereby to issue patents for the land so paid for; and then for every additional part of said land upon the payment of

537

Plains, West and Northwest Plateau Indian Treaties

one dollar per acre. The interest on said purchase-money shall be paid annually to the Secretary of the Interior for the use of said Indians.

If the said company shall fail to pay the principal when the same shall become due, or to pay all or any part of the interest upon such purchase-money within thirty (30) days after the time when such payment of interest shall fall due, then this contract shall be deemed and held absolutely null and void, and cease to be binding upon either of the parties thereto, and said company and its assigns shall forfeit all payments of principal and interest made on such purchase, and all right and title, legal and equitable, of any kind whatsoever, in and to all and every part of said lands which shall not have been, before the date of such forfeiture, paid for as herein provided: Provided, however, That in case any of said lands have been conveyed to bona-fide purchasers by said Atchison, Topeka and Santa Fe Railroad Company, such purchasers shall be entitled to patents for said land so purchased by them upon the payment of one dollar and twenty-five cents per acre therefor, under such rules and regulations as may be prescribed by the Secretary of the Interior.

ARTICLE 3. After such reservation snail nave been selected and set apart for the Pottawatomies, it shall never be included within the jurisdiction of any State or Territory, unless an Indian Territory shall be organized, as provided for in certain treaties made in eighteen hundred and Sixty-six with the Choctaws and other tribes occupying "Indian country;" in which case, or in case of the organization of a legislative council or other body, for the regulation of matters affecting the relations of the tribes to each other, the Pottawatomies resident thereon shall have the right to representation, according to their numbers, on equal terms with the other tribes.

ARTICLE 4. A register shall be made, under the direction of the agent and the business committee of the tribe, within two years after the ratification of this treaty, which shall show the names of all members of the tribe who declare their desire to remove to the new reservation, and of all who desire to remain and to become citizens of the, United States; and after the filing of such register in the office of the Commissioner of Indian Affairs, all existing restrictions shall be removed from the sale and alienation of lands by adults who shall have declared their intention to remove to the new reservation.

But, provided, That no person shall be allowed to receive to his own use the avails of the sale of his land, unless he shall have received the certificate of the agent and business committee that he is fully competent to manage his own affairs; nor shall any person also be allowed to sell and receive the proceeds of the sale of the lands belonging to his family, unless the certificate of the agent and business committee shall declare him competent to take the charge of their property; but such persons may negotiate for the sales of their property and that of their families, and any contracts for sales so made, if certified by the agent

Plains, West and Northwest Plateau Indian Treaties

and business committee to be at reasonable rates, shall be confirmed by the Secretary of the Interior, and patents shall issue to the purchaser upon full payment; and all payments for such land shall be made to the agent, and the funds by him deposited on the first of each month in some Government depository to be designated by the Secretary of the Treasury, and triplicate certificates of deposit taken therefor, one to be forwarded to the Commissioner of Indian Affairs, one to be retained at the agency, and the third to be sent to the superintendent of Indian affairs for Kansas; after which deposit the United States will be responsible for said funds until drawn out for use as hereinafter provided, and the bonds of the agent shall be increased to a sufficient amount to cover his increased liabilities under this section.

ARTICLE 5. The moneys received and deposited as provided in the preceding article shall be retained until the party on whose behalf it is held shall be ready to remove to the new reservation, and shall then, or such part thereof as may from time to time be necessary, be drawn out, under the direction of the Commissioner of Indian Affairs, by the agent, and expended for the benefit of the owner in providing for his removal and that of his family to the new reservation, and in such articles and for such uses as may, with the advice of the business committee, be deemed for his best interest at his new home.

ARTICLE 6. The provisions of article third of the treaty of November fifteenth, eighteen hundred and sixty-one (April nineteenth, eighteen hundred and sixty-two), relative to Pottawatomies who desire to become citizens, shall continue in force, with the additional provisions that, before patents shall issue and full payments be made to such persons, a certificate shall be necessary from the agent and business committee that the applicant is competent to manage his own affairs; and when computation is made to ascertain the amount of the funds to the tribe to which such applicants are entitled, the amounts invested in the new reservation provided for in the treaty shall not be taken into account; and where any member of the tribe shall become a citizen under the provisions of the said treaty of eighteen hundred and sixty-two, the families of said parties shall also be considered as citizens, and the head of the family shall be entitled to patents and the proportional share of funds belonging to his family; and women who are also heads of families, and single women of adult age, may become citizens in the same manner as males.

ARTICLE 7. (Stricken out.)

ARTICLE 8. Where allottees under the treaty of eighteen hundred and sixty-one shall have died, or shall hereafter decease, such allottees shall be regarded, for the purpose of a careful and just settlement of their estates, as citizens of the United States, and of the State of Kansas, and it shall be competent for the proper courts to take charge of the settlement of their estates under all the forms and in accordance with the laws of the State, as in the case of other citizens de-

Plains, West and Northwest Plateau Indian Treaties

ceased: and in cases where there are children of allottees left orphans, guardians for such orphans may be appointed by the probate court of the county in which such orphans may reside, and such guardians shall give bonds, to be approved by the said court, for the proper care of the person and estate of such orphans, as provided by law.

ARTICLE 9. It is agreed that an examination shall be made of the books of the Indian Office in order to ascertain what amount is justly due to the Pottawatomies under the provisions of their treaties of eighteen hundred and eighteen and eighteen hundred and twenty-nine, providing for the payment of their annuities in coin, whereas they have been paid for several years in currency; and the result of such examination shall be reported to Congress, and the difference in amount due to said Indians shall be paid to them.

ARTICLE 10. It is further agreed that, upon the presentation to the Department of the Interior of the claims of said tribe for depredations committed by others upon their stock, timber, or other property, accompanied by evidence thereof, examination and report shall be made to Congress of the amount found to be equitably due, in order that such action may be taken as shall be just in the premises.

And it is further agreed that the claims of the Pottawatomies heretofore examined and reported on by the Secretary of the Interior under the act of Congress of March two, eighteen hundred and sixty-one, shall be submitted to two commissioners, to be named by the President of the United States, for examination, and said commissioners, after being sworn impartially to decide on said claims, shall make report of their judgment in the premises, together with the evidence taken, to the Secretary of the Interior, and the same shall be communicated to Congress at its next session: Provided, That no part of the money reported due by the said commissioners shall be paid until the same shall be appropriated by Congress.

ARTICLE 11. The half sections of land heretofore set apart for the mission-schools, to wit, those of the St. Mary's mission, and the American Baptist mission, shall be granted in fee-simple, the former to John F. Diels, John Schoenmaker and M. Gillaud, and the latter to such party as the American Baptist Board of Missions shall designate.

And the said John F. Deils, John Shoemaker, and M. C. Gillaud shall have the right to purchase in a compact body ten hundred and thirteen 54-100 acres of the unallotted lands at the price of one dollar per acre, to be paid to the Secretary of the Interior, for the use of said tribe, and when the consideration shall be paid as aforesaid the President shall issue patents to said purchasers therefor; and in selecting said ten hundred and thirteen 54-100 acres, said purchasers shall have the preference over all other parties.

Plains, West and Northwest Plateau Indian Treaties

ARTICLE 12. No provisions of this treaty shall be held to apply in such manner as to authorize any interference with the exclusive rights in their own lands of those members of the tribe who hold their lands in common; but such Indians shall be entitled to their share in the ownership of the new reservation; and it shall not be necessary at any future time to treat with the representatives of the whole people for a cession of the lands of those who hold in common, but special treaty arrangements may be made at any time with the class of persons last named for the sale of their lands, and the disposition to be mane of the proceeds thereof.

ARTICLE 13. All provisions of former treaties inconsistent with the provisions of this treaty shall be hereafter null and void.

ARTICLE 14. The expenses of negotiating this treaty shall be paid by the United States, not to exceed six thousand dollars.

In testimony whereof, the aforenamed commissioners on behalf of the United States, and on behalf of the Pottawatomies the aforenamed chiefs, braves, and headmen, have hereunto set their hands and seals the day and year first above mentioned.

Lewis V. Bogy, Commissioner of Indian Affairs.
W. H. Watson, Special Commissioner.
Thos. Murphy, Superintendent of Indian Affairs.
L. R. Palmer, United States Indian agent.

Mazhee, his x mark, Mianco, his x mark, Shawgwe, his x mark, B. H. Bertrand, J. N. Bourassa, M. B. Beaubien, L. H. Ogee, George L. Young.

In presence of
J. N. Bourassa, United States interpreter, Lewis S. Hayden, H. W. Farnsworth, Vital Jarrot, W. R. Irvin.

TREATY WITH THE KIOWA AND COMANCHE {1867, Oct. 21}
Ratified. July 25, 1868.
Proclaimed, Aug. 25. 1868.

(NOTE BY THE DEPARTMENT OF STATE.The words of this treaty which are put in parens with an asterisk are written in the original with black pencil, the rest of the original treaty being written with black ink.)

Articles of a treaty and agreement made and entered into at the Council Camp, on Medicine Lodge Creek, seventy miles south of Fort Larned, in the State of

Plains, West and Northwest Plateau Indian Treaties

Kansas on the twenty-first day of October, one thousand eight hundred and sixty-seven, by and between the United States of America, represented by its commissioners duly appointed thereto, to wit, Nathaniel G. Taylor, William S. Harney, C. C. Augur, Alfred S. (II) Terry, John B. Sanborn, Samuel F Tappan, and J. B. Henderson, of the one part, and the confederated tribes of Kiowa and Comanche Indians, represented by their chiefs and headmen, duly authorized and empowered to act for the body of the people of said tribes, (the names of said chiefs and head-men being hereto subscribed.) of the other part, witness:

ARTICLE 1. From this day forward all war between the parties to this agreement shall forever cease.
The Government of the United States desires peace, and its honor is here pledged to keep it. The Indians desire peace, and they now pledge their honor to maintain it. If bad men among the whites, or among other people subject to the authority of the United States, shall commit any wrong upon the person or property of the Indians, the United States will, upon proof made to the agent and forwarded to the Commissioner of Indian Affairs at Washington City, proceed at once to cause the offender to be arrested and punished according to the laws of the United States, and also re-imburse the injured person for the loss sustained.

If bad men among the Indians shall commit a wrong or depredation upon the person or property of any one, white, black, or Indians, subject to the authority of the United States and at peace therewith, the tribes herein named solemnly agree that they will, on proof made to their agent and notice by him, deliver up the wrong-doer to the United States, to be tried and punished according to its laws, and in case they wilfully refuse so to do, the person injured shall be re-imbursed for his loss from the annuities or other moneys due or to become due to them under this or other treaties made with the United States. And the President, on advising with the Commissioner of Indian Affairs shall prescribe such rules and regulations for ascertaining damages under the provisions of this article as, in his judgment, may be proper; last no such damages shall be adjusted and paid until thoroughly examined and passed upon by the Commissioner of Indian Affairs and the Secretary of the Interior; and no one sustaining loss, while violating or because of his violating, the provisions of this treaty or the laws of the United States, shall be re-imbursed therefor.

ARTICLE 2. The United States agrees that (the*) following district of country, to wit: commencing at a point where the Washita River crosses the 98th meridian, west from Greenwich; thence up the Washita River, in the middle of the main channel thereof, to a point thirty miles, by river, west of Fort Cobb, as now established; thence, due west to the north fork of Red River, provided said line strikes said river east of the one hundredth meridian of west longitude; if not, then only to said meridian-line, and thence south, on said meridian-line, to the said north fork of Red River; thence down said north fork, in the middle of

Plains, West and Northwest Plateau Indian Treaties

the main channel thereof, from the point where it may be first intersected by the lines above described, to the main Red River; thence down said river, in the middle of the main channel thereof to its intersection with the ninety-eighth meridian of longitude west from Greenwich.

Thence north, on said meridian-line, to the place of beginning, shall be and the same is hereby set apart for the absolute and undisturbed use and occupation of the tribes herein named, and for such other friendly tribes or individual Indians as, from time to time, they may be willing (with the consent of the United States*) to admit among them; and the United States now solemnly agrees that no persons except those herein authorized so to do and except such officers, agents, and employes of the Government as may be authorized to enter upon Indian reservation in discharge of duties enjoined by law, shall ever be permitted to pass over, settle upon, or reside in the territory described in this article, or in such territory as may be added to this reservation, for the use of said Indians.

ARTICLE 3. If it should appear from actual survey or other satisfactory examination of said tract of land, that it contains less than one, hundred and sixty acres of tillable land, for each person, who at the time may be authorized to reside on it under the provisions of this treaty, and a very considerable number of such persons shall be disposed to commence cultivating the soil as farmers, the United States agrees to set apart for the use of said Indians, as herein provided, such additional quantity of arable land adjoining to said reservation, or as near the same as it can be obtained, as may be required, to provide the necessary amount.

ARTICLE 4. The United States agrees at its own proper expense to construct at some place, near the centre of said reservation, where timber and water may be convenient, the following buildings, to wit: A warehouse or store-room for the use of the agent, in storing goods belonging to the Indians, to cost not exceeding fifteen hundred dollars: an agency-building for the residence of the agent, to cost not exceeding three thousand dollars; a residence for the physician, to cost not more than three thousand dollars; and five other buildings, for a carpenter, farmer, blacksmith, miller, and engineer, each to cost not exceeding two thousand dollars; also a school-house or mission-building, so soon as a sufficient number of children can be induced by the agent to attend school, which shall not cost exceeding five thousand dollars.

The United States agrees further to cause to be erected on said reservation, near the other buildings herein authorized, a good steam circular saw mill, with a grist-mill and shingle-machine attached: the same to cost not exceeding eight thousand dollars.

ARTICLE 5. The United States agrees that the agent for the said Indians in the future shall make his home at the agency-building; that he shall reside among

Plains, West and Northwest Plateau Indian Treaties

them, and keep an office open at all times, for the purpose of prompt and diligent inquiry into such matters of complaint by and against the Indians as may be presented for investigation under the provisions of their treaty stipulations, as also for the faithful discharge of other duties enjoined on him by law. In all cases of depredation on person or property, he shall cause the evidence to be taken in writing and forwarded, together with his findings to the Commissioner of Indian Affairs, whose decision, subject to the revision of the Secretary of the Interior, shall be binding on the parties to this treaty.

ARTICLE 6. If any individual belonging to said tribes of Indians, or legally incorporated with them, being the head of a family, shall desire to commence farming, he shall have the privilege to select, in the presence and with the assistance of the agent then in charge, a tract of land within said reservation, not exceeding three hundred and twenty acres in extent, which tract, when so selected, certified, and recorded in the "land book" as herein directed, shall cease to be held in common, but the same may be occupied and held in the exclusive possession of the person selecting it, and of his family so long as he or they may continue to cultivate it. Any person over eighteen years of age, not being the head of a family, may in like manner select and cause to be certified to him or her, for purposes of cultivation, a quantity of land not exceeding eighty acres in extent, and thereupon, be entitled to the exclusive possession of the same as above directed.

For each tract of land so selected, a certificate, containing a description thereof and the name of the person selecting it, with a certificate indorsed thereon that the same has been recorded, shall be delivered to the party entitled to it, by the agent, after the same shall have been recorded by him in a book to be kept in his office, subject to inspection, which said book shall be known as the "Kiowa and Comanche land book." The President may, at any time, order a survey of the reservation, and, when so surveyed, Congress shall provide for protecting the rights of settlers, in their improvements, and may fix the character of the title held by each. The United States may pass such laws, on the subject of alienation and descent of property and on all subjects connected with the government of the said Indians on said reservations, and the internal police thereof, as may be thought proper.

ARTICLE 7. In order to insure the civilization of the tribes, entering into this treaty, the necessity of education is admitted, especially by such of them as are or may be settled on said agricultural reservations; and they therefore pledge themselves to compel their children, male and female, between the ages of six and sixteen years, to attend school; and it is hereby made the duty of the agent for said Indians to see that this stipulation is strictly complied with; and the United States agrees that for every thirty children between said ages, who can be induced or compelled to attend school, a house shall be provided, and a teacher competent to teach the elementary branches of an English education,

544

Plains, West and Northwest Plateau Indian Treaties

shall be furnished, who will reside among said Indians, and faithfully discharge his or her duties as a teacher. The provisions of this article to continue for not less than twenty years.

ARTICLE 8. When the head of a family or lodge shall have selected lands and received his certificate as above directed, and the agent shall be satisfied that he intends in good faith to commence cultivating the soil for a living, he shall be entitled to receive seeds and agricultural implements for the first year not exceeding in value one hundred dollars, and for each succeeding year he shall continue to farm for a period of three years more, he shall be entitled to receive seeds and implements as aforesaid not exceeding in value twenty-five dollars. And it is further stipulated that such persons as commence farming shall receive instruction from the farmer herein provided for, and whenever more than one hundred persons shall enter upon the cultivation of the soil a second blacksmith shall be provided, together with such iron, steel, and other material as may be needed.

ARTICLE 9. At any time after ten years from the making of this treaty the United States shall have the privilege of withdrawing the physician, farmer, blacksmiths, carpenter, engineer, and miller herein provided for; but, in case of such withdrawal, an additional sum thereafter of ten thousand dollars per annum shall be devoted to the education of said Indians, and the Commissioner of Indian Affairs shall, upon careful inquiry into the condition of said Indians, make such rules and regulations for the expenditure of said sum as will best promote the educational and moral improvement of said tribes.

ARTICLE 10. In lieu of all sums of money or other annuities provided to be paid to the Indians, herein named, under the treaty of October eighteenth, one thousand eight hundred and sixty-five, made at the mouth of the "Little Arkansas," and under all treaties made previous thereto, the United States agrees to deliver at the agency-house on the reservation herein named, on the fifteenth day of October of each year, for thirty years, the following articles, to wit:

For each male person over fourteen years of age, a suit of good substantial woollen clothing, consisting of coat, pantaloons, flannel shirt, hat, and a pair of home-made socks. For each female over twelve years of age, a flannel skirt, or the goods necessary to make it, a pair of woolen hose, and twelve yards of calico, and twelve yards of "domestic."

For the boys and girls under the ages named, such flannel and cotton goods as may be needed, to make each a suit as aforesaid, together with a pair of woollen hose for each; and in order that the Commissioner of Indian Affairs may be able to estimate properly for the articles herein named, it shall be the duty of the agent, each year, to forward him a full and exact census of the Indians on which the estimates from year to year can be based; and, in addition to the

545

Plains, West and Northwest Plateau Indian Treaties

clothing herein named, the sum of twenty-five thousand dollars shall be annually appropriated for a period of thirty years, to be used by the Secretary of the Interior in the purchase of such articles, upon the recommendation of the Commissioner of Indian Affairs, as from time to time the condition and necessities of the Indians may indicate to be proper; and if at any time within the thirty years it shall appear that the amount of money needed for clothing under this article can be appropriated to better uses for the tribes herein named, Congress may by law change the appropriation to other purposes, but in no event shall the amount of this appropriation be withdrawn or discontinued for the period named; and the President shall, annually, detail an officer of the Army to be present and attest the delivery of all the goods herein named to the Indians, and he shall inspect and report on the quantity and quality of the goods and the manner of their delivery.

ARTICLE 11. In consideration of the advantages and benefits conferred by this treaty and the many pledges of friendship by the United States, the tribes who are parties to this agreement hereby stipulate that they will relinquish all right to occupy permanently the territory outside of their reservation, as herein defined, but they yet reserve the right to hunt on any lands south of the Arkansas (River*) so long as the buffalo may range thereon in such numbers as to justify the chase, (and no white settlements shall be permitted on any part of the lands contained in the old reservation as defined by the treaty made between the United States and the Cheyenne, Arapahoe, and Apache tribes of Indians at the mouth of the Little Arkansas, under date of October fourteenth, one thousand eight hundred and sixty-five, within three years from this date;*) and they, (the said tribes,*) further expressly agree-

First. That they will withdraw all opposition to the construction of the railroad now being built on the Smoky Hill River, whether it be built to Colorado or New Mexico.

Second. That they will permit the peaceable construction of any railroad not passing over their reservation as herein defined.

Third. That they will not attack any persons at home, nor travelling, nor molest or disturb any wagon-trains, coaches, mules, or cattle belonging to the people of the United States, or to persons friendly therewith.

Fourth. They will never capture or carry off from the settlements white women or children.

Fifth. They will never kill nor scalp white men nor attempt to do them harm.

Sixth. They withdraw all pretence of opposition to the construction of the railroad now being built along the Platte River and westward to the Pacific Ocean;

Plains, West and Northwest Plateau Indian Treaties

and they will not, in future, object to the construction of railroads, wagon-roads, mail-stations, or other works of utility or necessity which may be ordered or permitted by the laws of the United States. But should such roads or other works be constructed on the lands of their reservation, the Government will pay the tribes whatever amount of damage may be assessed by three disinterested commissioners, to be appointed by the President for that purpose; one of said commissioners to be a chief or head-man of the tribes.

Seventh. They agree to withdraw all opposition to the military posts now established in the western Territories.

ARTICLE 12. No treaty for the cession of any portion or part of the reservation herein described, which may be held in common, shall be of any validity or force as against the said Indians, unless executed and signed by at least three-fourths of all the adult male Indians occupying the same, and no cession by the tribe shall be understood or construed in such manner as to deprive, without his consent, any individual member of the tribe of his rights to any tract of land selected by him as provided in Article 3 (6) of this treaty.

ARTICLE 13. The Indian agent, in employing a farmer, blacksmith, miller, and other employes herein provided for, qualifications being equal, shall give the preference to Indians.

ARTICLE 14. The United States hereby agrees to furnish annually to the Indians the physician, teachers, carpenter, miller, engineer, farmer, and blacksmiths, as herein contemplated, and that such appropriations shall be made from time to time, on the estimates of the Secretary of the Interior, as will be sufficient to employ such persons.

ARTICLE 15. It is agreed that the sum of seven hundred and fifty dollars be appropriated for the purpose of building a dwelling-house on the reservation for "Tosh-e-wa," (or the Silver Brooch) the Comanche chief who has already commenced farming on the said reservation. And the sum of five hundred dollars annually, for three years from date, shall be expended in presents to the ten persons of said tribes who in the judgment of the agent may grow the most valuable crops for the period named.

ARTICLE 16. The tribes herein named agree, when the agency-house and other buildings shall be constructed on the reservation named, they will make said reservation their permanent home and they will make no permanent settlement elsewhere, but they shall have the right to hunt on the lands south of the Arkansas River, formerly called theirs, in the same manner, subject to the modifications named in this treaty, as agreed on by the treaty of the Little Arkansas, concluded the eighteenth day of October, one thousand eight hundred and sixty-five.

Plains, West and Northwest Plateau Indian Treaties

In testimony of which, we have hereunto set our hands and seals on the day and year aforesaid.

N. G. Taylor, President of Indian Commission.
Wm. S. Harney, Brevet Major-General, C. C. Augur, Brevet Major-General, Alfred H. Terry, Brigadier and Brevet Major-General.

Attest: Ashton S. H. White, secretary.

Kioways:
Satank, or Sitting Bear, his x mark, Sa-tan-ta, or White Bear, his x mark, Wa-toh-konk, or Black Eagle, his x mark, Ton-a-en-ko, or Kicking Eagle, his x mark, Fish-e-more, or Stinking Saddle, his x mark, Ma-ye-tin, or Woman's Heart, his x mark, Sa-tim-gear, or Stumbling Bear, his x mark, Sit-par-ga, or One Bear, his x mark, Corbeau, or The Crow, his x mark, Sa-ta-more, or Bear Lying Down.

Comanches:
Parry-wah-say-men, or Ten Bears, his x mark, Tep-pe-navon, or Painted Lips, his x mark, To-sa-in, or Silver Brooch, his x mark, Cear-chi-neka, or Standing Feather, his x mark, Ho-we-ar, or Gap in the Woods, his x mark, Tir-ha-yah-guahip, or Horse's Back, his x mark, Es-a-nanaca, or Wolf's Name, his x mark, Ah-te-es-ta, or Little Horn, his x mark, Pooh-yah-to-yeh-be, or Iron Mountain, his x mark, Sad-dy-yo, or Dog Fat, his x mark

TREATY WITH THE UTE {1868, Mar. 2}
Ratified, July 25, 1868.
Proclaimed, Nov. 6, 1868.

Articles of a treaty and agreement made and entered into at Washington City, D. C., on the second day of March, one thousand eight hundred and sixty-eight, by and between Nathaniel G. Taylor, Commissioner of Indian Affairs, Alexander C. Hunt, governor of Colorado Territory and ex-officio superintendent of Indian affairs, and Kit Carson, duly authorized to represent the United States, of the elite part, and the representatives of the Tabaquache, Muache, Capote, Weeminuehe, Yampa, Grand River, and Uintah bands of Ute Indians, (whose names are hereto subscribed) duly authorized and empowered to act for the body of the people of said bands, of the other part, witness:

ARTICLE 1. All of the provisions of the treaty concluded with the Tabequache band of Utah Indians October seventh, one thousand eight hundred and sixty-three, as amended by the Senate of the United States and proclaimed December fourteenth, one thousand eight hundred and sixty-four, which are not inconsis-

Plains, West and Northwest Plateau Indian Treaties

tent with the provisions of this treaty, as hereinafter provided, are hereby re-affirmed and declared to be applicable and to continue in force as well to the other bands, respectively, parties to this treaty, as to the Tabequache band of Utah Indians.

ARTICLE 2. The United States agree that the following district of country, to wit: Commencing at that point on the southern boundary-line of the Territory of Colorado where the meridian of longitude 107 degrees west from Greenwich crosses the same; running thence north with said meridian to a point fifteen miles due north of where said meridian intersects the fortieth parallel of north latitude; thence due west, to the western boundary-line of said Territory; thence south with said western boundary-line of said Territory to the southern bound-ary-line of said Territory; thence east with said southern boundary-line to the place of beginning, shall be, and the same is hereby, set apart for the absolute and undisturbed use and occupation of the Indians herein named, and for such other friendly tribes or individual Indians as from time to time they may be willing, with the consent of the United States, to admit among them; and the United States now solemnly agree that no persons, except those herein author-ized so to do, and except such officers, agents, and employees of the Govern-ment as may be authorized to enter upon Indian reservations in discharge of duties enjoined by law shall ever be permitted to pass over, settle upon, or re-side in the Territory described in this article, except as herein other-wise pro-vided.

ARTICLE 3. It is further agreed by the Indians, parties hereto, that henceforth they will and do hereby relinquish all claims and rights in and to any portion of the United States or Territories, except such as are embraced in the limits de-fined in the preceding article.

ARTICLE 4. The United States agree to establish two agencies on the reserva-tion provided for in article two, one for the Grand River, Yampa, and Uintah bands, on White River, and the other for the Tabequache, Muache, Weeminuche, and Capote bands, on the Rio de los Pinos, on the reservation, and at its own proper expense to construct at each of said agencies a ware-house, or store-room, for the use of the agent in storing goods belonging to the Indians, to cost not exceeding fifteen hundred dollars; an agency-building for the residence of the agent, to cost not exceeding three thousand dollars; and four other buildings for a carpenter, farmer, blacksmith, and miller, each to cost not exceeding two thousand dollars; also a school-house or mission-building, so soon as a sufficient number of children can be induced by the agent to attend school, which shall not cost exceeding five thousand dollars.

The United States agree, further, to cause to be erected on said reservation and near to each agency herein authorized, respectively, a good water-power saw-mill, with a grist-mill and a shingle-machine attached, the same to cost not ex-

Plains, West and Northwest Plateau Indian Treaties

ceeding eight thousand dollars each: Provided, The same shall not be erected until such time as the Secretary of the Interior may think it necessary to the wants of the Indians.

ARTICLE 5. The United States agree that the agents for said Indians, in the future, shall make their homes at the agency-buildings; that they shall reside among the Indians, and keep an office open at all times for the purpose of prompt and diligent inquiry into such matters of complaint by and against the Indians, as may be presented for investigation under the provisions of their treaty stipulations, as also for the faithful discharge of other duties enjoined on them by law. In all cases of depredation on person or property they shall cause the evidence to be taken in writing and forwarded, together with their finding, to the Commissioner of Indian Affairs, whose decision, subject to the revision of the Secretary of the Interior, shall be binding on the parties to this treaty.

ARTICLE 6. If bad men among the whites or among other people, subject to the authority of the United States, shall commit any wrong upon the person or property of the Indians, the United States will, upon proof made to the agent and forwarded to the Commissioner of Indian Affairs at Washington City, proceed at once to cause the offender to be arrested and punished according to the laws of the United States, and also re-imburse the injured person for the loss sustained.

If bad men among the Indians shall commit a wrong or depredation upon the person or property of any one, white, black, or Indian, subject to the authority of the United States and at peace therewith, the tribes herein named solemnly agree that they will, on proof made to their agent and notice to him, deliver up the wrong-doer to the United States, to be tried and punished according to its laws, and in case they wilfully refuse so to do, the person injured shall be re-imbursed for his loss from the annuities or other moneys due or to become due to them under this or other treaties made with the United States.

ARTICLE 7. If any individual belonging to said tribe of Indians or legally incorporated with them, being the head of a family, shall desire to commence farming, he shall have the privilege to select, in the presence and with the assistance of the agent then in charge, by metes and bounds, a tract of land within Said reservation not exceeding one hundred and sixty acres in extent, which tract, when so selected, certified, and recorded in the land-book, as herein directed, shall cease to be held in common, but the same may be occupied and held in exclusive possession of the person selecting it and his family so long as he or they may continue to cultivate it. Any person over eighteen years of age, not being the head of a family may, in like manner, select and cause to be certified to him or her for purposes of cultivation, a quantity of land not exceeding eighty acres in extent, and thereupon be entitled to the exclusive possession of the same as above directed.

Plains, West and Northwest Plateau Indian Treaties

For each tract of land so selected a certificate containing a description thereof, and the name of the person selecting it, with a certificate endorsed thereon that the same has been recorded, shall be delivered to the party entitled to it, by the agent, after the same shall have been recorded by him in a book to be kept in his office, subject to inspection, which said book shall be known as the "Ute Land-Book."

The President may at any time order a survey of the reservation; and when so surveyed Congress shall provide for protecting the rights of such Indian settlers in their improvements, and may fix the character of the title held by each.

The United States may pass such laws on the subject of alienation and descent of property, and on all subjects connected with the government of the Indians on said reservation and the internal police thereof as may be thought proper.

ARTICLE 8. In order to insure the civilization of the bands entering into this treaty, the necessity of education is admitted, especially by such of them as are or may be engaged in either pastoral, agricultural, or other peaceful pursuits of civilized life on said reservation, and they therefore pledge themselves to induce their children, male and female, between the age(s) of seven and eighteen years, to attend school; and it is hereby made the duty of the agent for said Indians to see that this stipulation is complied with to the greatest possible extent; and the United States agree that for every thirty children between said ages who can be induced to attend school a house shall be provided, and a teacher competent to teach the elementary branches of an English education shall be furnished, who will reside among said Indians, and faithfully discharge his or her duties as teacher, the provisions of this article to continue for not less than twenty years.

ARTICLE 9. When the head of a family or lodge shall have selected lands, and received his certificate as above described, and the agent shall be satisfied that he intends, in good faith, to commence cultivating the soil for a living, he shall be entitled to receive seeds and agricultural implements for the first year, not exceeding in value one hundred dollars, and for each succeeding year he shall continue to farm, for a period of three years more, he shall be entitled to receive seeds and implements as aforesaid, not exceeding in value fifty dollars; and it is further stipulated that such persons as commence farming shall receive instructions from the farmer herein provided for; and it is further stipulated that an additional blacksmith to the one provided for in the treaty of October seventh, one thousand eight hundred and sixty-three, referred to in article one of this treaty, shall be provided with such iron, steel, and other material as may be needed for the Uintah, Yampa, and Grand River agency.

Plains, West and Northwest Plateau Indian Treaties

ARTICLE 10. At any time after ten years from the making of this treaty, the United States shall have the privilege of withdrawing the farmers, blacksmiths, carpenters, and millers herein, and in the treaty of October seventh, one thousand eight hundred and sixty-three, referred to in article one of this treaty, provided for, but in case of such withdrawal, an additional sum thereafter of ten thousand dollars per annum shall be devoted to the education of said Indians, and the Commissioner of Indian Affairs shall, upon careful inquiry into their condition, make such rules and regulations, subject to the approval of the Secretary of the Interior, for the expenditure of said sum as will best promote the educational and moral improvement of said Indians.

ARTICLE 11. That a sum, sufficient in the discretion of Congress, for the absolute wants of said Indians, but not to exceed thirty thousand dollars per annum, for thirty years, shall be expended, under the direction of the Secretary of the Interior for clothing, blankets, and such other articles of utility as he may think proper and necessary upon full official reports of the condition and wants of said Indians.

ARTICLE 12. That an additional sum sufficient, in the discretion of Congress, (but not to exceed thirty thousand dollars per annum) to supply the wants of said Indians for food, shall be annually expended under the direction of the Secretary of the Interior, in supplying said Indians with beef, mutton, wheat, flour, beans, and potatoes, until such time as said Indians shall be found to be capable of sustaining themselves.

ARTICLE 13. That for the purpose of inducing said Indians to adopt habits of civilized life and become self-sustaining, the sum of forty-five thousand dollars, for the first year, shall be expended, under the direction of the Secretary of the Interior, in providing each lodge or head of a family in said confederated bands with one gentle American cow, as distinguished from the ordinary Mexican or Texas breed, and five head of sheep.

ARTICLE 14. The said confederated bands agree that whensoever, in the opinion of the President of the United States, the public interest may require it, that all roads, highways, and railroads, authorized by law, shall have the right of way through the reservations herein designated.

ARTICLE 15. The United States hereby agree to furnish the Indians the teachers, carpenters, millers, farmers, and blacksmiths, as herein contemplated, and that such appropriations shall be made from time to time, on the estimates of the Secretary of the Interior, as will be sufficient to employ such persons.

ARTICLE 16. No treaty for the cession of any portion or part of the reservation herein described, which may be held in common, shall be of any validity or force as against the said Indians, unless executed and signed by at least three-

Plains, West and Northwest Plateau Indian Treaties

fourths of all the adult male Indians occupying or interested in the same; and no cession by the tribe shall be understood or construed in such manner as to deprive, without his consent, any individual member of the tribe of his right to any tract of land selected by him, its provided in article seven of this treaty.

ARTICLE 17. All appropriations now made, or to be hereafter made, as well as goods and stock due these Indians under existing treaties, shall apply as if this treaty had not been made, and be divided proportionately among the seven bands named in this treaty, as also shall all annuities and allowances hereafter to be made: Provided, That if any chief of either of the confederated bands make war against the people of the United States, or in any manner violate this treaty in any essential part, said chief shall forfeit his position as chief and all rights to any of the benefits of this treaty: But provided further, Any Indian of either of these confederated bands who shall remain at peace, and abide by the terms of this treaty in all its essentials, shall be entitled to its benefits and provisions, notwithstanding his particular chief and band may have forfeited their rights thereto.

In testimony whereof, the commissioners as aforesaid on the part of the United States, and the undersigned representatives of the Tabequache, Muache, Capote, Weeminuche, Yampa, Grand River and Uintah bands of Ute Indians, duly authorized and empowered to act for the body of the people of said bands, have hereunto set their hands and seals, at the place and on the day, month and year first hereinbefore written.

N. G. Taylor, A. C. Hunt, governor, &c., Kit Carson, Commissioners on the part of the United States.

U-re, his x mark, Ka-ni-ache, his x mark, An-ka-tosh, his x mark, Jose-Maria, his x mark, Ni-ca-a-gat, or Greenleaf, his x mark, Guero, his x mark, Pa-ant, his x mark, Pi-ah, his x mark, Su-vi-ap, his x mark, Pa-bu-sat, his x mark,

Witnesses:
Daniel C. Oakes, United States Indian agent, Lafayette Head, United States Indian agent, U. M. Curtis, interpreter.

We, the chiefs and headmen of the aforesaid named bands of Ute Indians, duly authorized by our people, do hereby assent and agree to the amendment of the Senate, the same having been interpreted to us, and being fully understood by us.

Witness our hands and seals on the days and dates set opposite our names respectively.
Date of Signatures Aug. 15, 1868.

Plains, West and Northwest Plateau Indian Treaties

Grand River Ute Indians:
Sac-we-och, his x mark, White Lock of Hair, Tah-nach, his x mark, Granite Rock, Pah-ah-pitch, his x mark, Sweet Herb.

Uintah Ute Indians:
An-tro, his x mark, Rocking, Pah, his x mark, Water.

Signed in the presence of
A. Sagendorf, Uriah M. Curtis, special interpreter, E. H. Kellogg, secretary Colorado Indian superintendency.

Date of signature. Sept. 1
Yampas:
Sa-wa-wat-se-witch, his x mark, Blue River, Nick-a-a-gab, his x mark, Green Leaf.

Signed in the presence of
E. H. Kellogg, secretary Indian superintendency Colorado Territory, U. M. Curtis, special United States interpreter.

Date of signing. Sept. 14
Muaches:
Ou-ray, his x mark, Arrow, Ah-kan-ash, his x mark, Red Cloud.

Tabaguaches:
Ka-ni-ache, his x mark, Onewhowastakendown, An-ka-tosh, his x mark, Red. (Ute., Sap-po-wan-e-ri, his x mark,

Signed in the presence of
Wm. J. Godfroy , Daniel C. Oakes, United States Indian agent, Edward R. Harris, special interpreter.

To the other copy of these instruments are signed as witnesses the following names: Juan Martine Martines, (friend of Indians), Albert H. Pfeiffer, (their old agent), Manuel Lusero.

Date of signing. Sept. 24.

Ca-po-tas Utes:
So-bo-ta, his x mark, A Big Frock, I-si-dro, his x mark, Sow-wa-ch-wiche, his x mark, A Green Herb, Ba-bu-zat, his x mark, A Crystal Drop Water, Sab-ou-ichie, his x mark, Wounded in the Abdomen.

Signed in the presence of

Plains, West and Northwest Plateau Indian Treaties

Lafayette Head, Alb. H. Pfeiffer, Manuel. Lusero, E. H. Kellogg, secretary Colorado Indian superintendency.

Date of signing. Sept. 25.

We-mi-nu-ches Utes:
Pa-ja-Cho-pe, his x mark, A Claw.
Pa-no-ar, his x mark, Broad Brow.
Su-bi-to-au, his x mark, Ugly Man.

Signed in the presence of
E. H. Kellogg, secretary Colorado Indian superintendency.
Juan Martine Martines, interpreter and Indian's friend.
Daniel C. Oakes, United States Indian agent.

I hereby certify that, pursuant to the order from the Commissioner of Indian Affairs, dated August fourth, one thousand eight hundred and sixty-eight, I visited and held councils with the various bands of Ute Indians, at the times and places named in this instrument; and to all those familiar with the provisions of the treaty referred to have had the Senate amendment fully interpreted to them, and to all those not familiar with the treaty itself I have had the same fully explained and interpreted; and the forty-seven chiefs whose names are hereunto subscribed, placed their names to this instrument with the full knowledge of its contents and likewise with the provisions of the treaty itself.

Given under my hand at Denver, this fourteenth day of October, one thousand eight hundred and sixty-eight.

A. C. Hunt, Governor, Ex-officio Superintendent Indian Affairs.

TREATY WITH THE SIOUX BRULE', OGLALA, MINICONJOU, YANKTONAI, HUNKPAPA, BLACKFEET, CUTHEAD, TWO KETTLE, SANS ARCS, SANTEE AND ARAPAHO {1868, Apr. 29} Ratified, Feb. 16, 1869. Proclaimed, Feb. 24, 1869

Articles of a treaty made and concluded by and between Lieutenant-General William T. Sherman, General William S. Harney, General Alfred H. Terry, General C. C,. Augur, J. B. Henderson, Nathaniel G. Taylor, John B. Sanborn, and Samuel F. Tappan, duly appointed commissioners on the part of the United States, and the different bands of the Sioux Nation of Indians, by their chiefs and head-men, whose names are hereto subscribed, they being duly authorized to act in the premises.

Plains, West and Northwest Plateau Indian Treaties

ARTICLE 1. From this day forward all war between the parties to this agreement shall forever cease. The Government of the United States desires peace, and its honor is hereby pledged to keep it. The Indians desire peace, and they now pledge their honor to maintain it.

If bad men among the whites, or among other people subject to the authority of the United States, shall commit any wrong upon the person or property of the Indians, the United States will, upon proof made to the agent and forwarded to the Commissioner of Indian Affairs at Washington City, proceed at once to cause the offender to be arrested and punished according to the laws of the United States, and also re-imburse the injured person for the loss sustained.

If bad men among the Indians shall commit a wrong or depredation upon the person or property of any one, white, black, or Indian, subject to the authority of the United States, and at peace therewith, the Indians herein named solemnly agree that they will, upon proof made to their agent and notice by him, deliver up the wrong-doer to the United States, to be tried and punished according to its laws; and in case they wilfully refuse so to do, the person injured shall be re-imbursed for his loss from the annuities or other moneys due or to become due to them under this or other treaties made with the United States. And the President, on advising with the Commissioner of Indian Affairs, shall prescribe such rules and regulations for ascertaining damages under the provisions of this article as in his judgment may be proper. But no one sustaining loss while violating the provisions of this treaty or the laws of the United States shall be re-imbursed therefor.

ARTICLE 2. The United States agrees that the following district of country, to wit, viz: commencing on the east bank of the Missouri River where the forty-sixth parallel of north latitude crosses the same, thence along low-water mark down said east bank to a point opposite where the northern line of the State of Nebraska strikes the river, thence west across said river, and along the northern line of Nebraska to the one hundred and fourth degree of longitude west from Greenwich, thence north on said meridian to a point where the forty-sixth parallel of north latitude intercepts the same, thence due east along said parallel to the place of beginning; and in addition thereto, all existing reservations on the east bank of said river shall be, and the same is, set apart for the absolute and undisturbed use and occupation of the Indians herein named, and for such other friendly tribes or individual Indians as from time to time they may be willing, with the consent of the United States, to admit amongst them; and the United States now solemnly agrees that no persons except those herein designated and authorized so to do, and except such officers, agents, and employes of the Government as may be authorized to enter upon Indian reservations in discharge of duties enjoined by law, shall ever be permitted to pass over, settle upon, or reside in the territory described in this article, or in such territory as may be

Plains, West and Northwest Plateau Indian Treaties

added to this reservation for the use of said Indians, and henceforth they will and do hereby relinquish all claims or right in and to any portion of the United States or Territories, except such as is embraced within the limits aforesaid, and except as hereinafter provided.

ARTICLE 3. If it should appear from actual survey or other satisfactory examination of said tract of land that it contains less than one hundred and sixty acres of tillable land for each person who, at the time, may be authorized to reside on it under the provisions of this treaty, and a very considerable number of such persons shall be disposed to commence cultivating the soil as farmers, the United States agrees to set apart, for the use of said Indians, as herein provided, such additional quantity of arable land, adjoining to said reservation, or as near to the same as it can be obtained, as may be required to provide the necessary amount.

ARTICLE 4. The United States agrees, at its own proper expense, to construct at some place on the Missouri River, near the center of said reservation, where timber and water may be convenient, the following buildings, to wit: a warehouse, a store-room for the use of the agent in storing goods belonging to the Indians, to cost not less than twenty-five hundred dollars; an agency-building for the residence of the agent, to cost not exceeding three thousand dollars; a residence for the physician, to cost not more than three thousand dollars; and five other buildings, for a carpenter, farmer, blacksmith, miller, and engineer, each to cost not exceeding two thousand dollars; also a schoolhouse or mission-building, so soon as a sufficient number of children can be induced by the agent to attend school, which shall not cost exceeding five thousand dollars.

The United States agrees further to cause to be erected on said reservation, near the other buildings herein authorized, a good steam circular-saw mill, with a grist-mill and shingle-machine attached to the same, to cost not exceeding eight thousand dollars.

ARTICLE 5. The United States agrees that the agent for said Indians shall in the future make his home at the agency-building; that he shall reside among them, and keep an office open at all times for the purpose of prompt and diligent inquiry into such matters of complaint by and against the Indians as may be presented for investigation under the provisions of their treaty stipulations, as also for the faithful discharge of other duties enjoined on him by law. In all cases of depredation on person or property he shall cause the evidence to be taken in writing and forwarded, together with his findings, to the Commissioner of Indian Affairs, whose decision, subject to the revision of the Secretary of the Interior, shall be binding on the parties to this treaty.

ARTICLE 6. if any individual belonging to said tribes of Indians, or legally incorporated with them, being the head of a family, shall desire to commence

Plains, West and Northwest Plateau Indian Treaties

farming, he shall have the privilege to select, in the presence and with the as-sistance of the agent then in charge, a tract of land within said reservation, not exceeding three hundred and twenty acres in extent, which tract, when so se-lected, certified, and recorded in the "land-book," as herein directed, shall cease to be held in common, but the same may be occupied and held in the exclusive possession of the person selecting it, and of his family, so long as he or they may continue to cultivate it.

Any person over eighteen years of age, not being the head of a family, may in like manner select and cause to be certified to him or her, for purposes of culti-vation, a quantity of land not exceeding eighty acres in extent, and thereupon be entitled to the exclusive possession of the same as above directed.
For each tract of land so selected a certificate, containing a description thereof and the name of the person selecting it, with a certificate endorsed thereon that the same has been recorded, shall be delivered to the party entitled to it, by the agent, after the same shall have been recorded by him in a book to be kept in his office, subject to inspection, which said book shall be known as the "Sioux Land-Book."

The President may, at any time, order a survey of the reservation, and, when so surveyed, Congress shall provide for protecting the rights of said settlers in their improvements, and may fix the character of the title held by each. The United States may pass such laws on the subject of alienation and descent of property between the Indians and their descendants as may be thought proper. And it is further stipulated that any male Indians, over eighteen years of age, of any band or tribe that is or shall hereafter become a party to this treaty, who now is or who shall hereafter become a resident or occupant of any reservation or Territory not included in the tract of country designated and described in this treaty for the permanent home of the Indians, which is not mineral land, nor reserved by the United States for special purposes other than Indian occupation, and who shall have made improvements thereon of the value of two hundred dollars or more, and continuously occupied the same as a homestead for the term of three years, shall be entitled to receive from the United States a patent for one hundred and sixty acres of land including his said improve-meats, the same to be in the form of the legal subdivisions of the surveys of the public lands.

Upon application in writing, sustained by the proof of two disinterested wit-nesses, made to the register of the local land-office when the land sought to be entered is within a land district, and when the tract sought to be entered is not in any land district, then upon said application and proof being made to the Commissioner of the General Land-Office, and the right of such Indian or Indi-ans to enter such tract or tracts of land shall accrue and be perfect from the date of his first improvements thereon, and shall continue as long as he continues his residence and improvements, and no longer'. And any Indian or Indians re-

Plains, West and Northwest Plateau Indian Treaties

ceiving a patent for land under the foregoing provisions, shall thereby and from thenceforth become and be a citizen of the United States, and be entitled to all the privileges and immunities of such citizens, and shall, at the same time, retain all his rights to benefits accruing to Indians under this treaty.

ARTICLE 7. In order to insure the civilization of the Indians entering into this treaty, the necessity of education is admitted, especially of such of them as are or may be settled on said agricultural reservations, and they therefore pledge themselves to compel their children, male and female, between the ages of six and sixteen years, to attend school; and it is hereby made the duty of the agent for said Indians to see that this stipulation is strictly complied with; and the United States agrees that for every thirty children between said ages who can be induced or compelled to attend school, a house shall be provided and a teacher competent to teach the elementary branches of an English education shall be furnished, who will reside among said Indians, and faithfully discharge his or her duties as a teacher. The provisions of this article to continue for not less than twenty years.

ARTICLE 8. When the head of a family or lodge shall have selected lands and received his certificate as above directed, and the agent shall be satisfied that he intends in good faith to commence cultivating the soil for a living, he shall be entitled to receive seeds and agricultural implements for the first year, not exceeding in value one hundred dollars, and for each succeeding year he shall continue to farm, for a period of three years more, he shall be entitled to receive seeds and implements as aforesaid, not exceeding in value twenty-five dollars.

And it is further stipulated that such persons as commence farming shall receive instruction from the farmer herein provided for, and whenever more than one hundred persons shall enter upon the cultivation of the soil, a second blacksmith shall be provided, with such iron, steel, and other material as may be needed.

ARTICLE 9. At any time after ten years from the making of this treaty, the United States shall have the privilege of withdrawing the physician, farmer, blacksmith, carpenter, engineer, and miller herein provided for, but in case of such withdrawal, an additional sum thereafter of ten thousand dollars per annum shall be devoted to the education of said Indians, and the Commissioner of Indian Affairs shall, upon careful inquiry into their condition, make such rules and regulations for the expenditure of said sum as will best promote the educational and moral improvement of said tribes.

ARTICLE 10. In lieu of all sums of money or other annuities provided to be paid to the Indians herein named, under any treaty or treaties heretofore made, the United States agrees to deliver at the agency-house on the reservation

Plains, West and Northwest Plateau Indian Treaties

herein named, on or before the first day of August of each year, for thirty years, the following articles, to wit:

For each male person over fourteen years of age, a suit of good substantial woolen clothing, consisting of coat, pantaloons, flannel shirt, hat, and a pair of home-made socks.

For each female over twelve years of age, a flannel skirt, or the goods necessary to make it, a pair of woolen hose, twelve yards of calico, and twelve yards of cotton domestics.

For the boys and girls under the ages named, such flannel and cotton goods as may be needed to make each a suit as aforesaid, together with a pair of woolen hose for each.

And in order that the Commissioner of Indian Affairs may be able to estimate properly for the articles herein named, it shall be the duty of the agent each year to forward to him a full and exact census of the Indians, on which the estimate from year to year can be based.

And in addition to the clothing herein named, the sum of ten dollars for each person entitled to the beneficial effects of this treaty shall be annually appropriated for a period of thirty years, while such persons roam and hunt, and twenty dollars for, each person who engages in farming, to be used by the Secretary of the Interior in the purchase of such articles as from time to time the condition and necessities of the Indians may indicate to be proper. And if within the thirty years, at any time, it shall appear that the amount of money needed for clothing under this article can be appropriated to better uses for the Indians named herein, Congress may, by law, change the appropriation to other purposes; but in no event shall the amount of this appropriation be withdrawn or discontinued for the period named.

And the President shall annually detail an officer of the Army to be present and attest the delivery of all the goods herein named to the Indians, and he shall inspect and report on the quantity and quality of the goods and the manner of their delivery. And it is hereby expressly stipulated that each Indian over the age of four years, who shall have removed to and settled permanently upon said reservation and complied with the stipulations of this treaty, shall be entitled to receive from the United States, for the period of four years after he shall have settled upon said reservation, one pound of meat and one pound of flour per day, provided the Indians cannot furnish their own subsistence at an earlier date.

And it is further stipulated that the United States will furnish and deliver to each lodge of Indians or family of persons legally incorporated with them, who

Plains, West and Northwest Plateau Indian Treaties

shall remove to the reservation herein described and commence farming, one good American cow, and one good well-broken pair of American oxen within sixty days after such lodge or family shall have so settled upon said reservation.

ARTICLE 11. In consideration of the advantages and benefits conferred by this treaty, and the many pledges of friendship by the United States, the tribes who are parties to this agreement hereby stipulate that they will relinquish all right to occupy permanently the territory outside their reservation as herein defined, but yet reserve the right to hunt on any lands north of North Platte, and on the Republican Fork of the Smoky Hill River, so long as the buffalo may range thereon in such numbers as to justify the chase. And they, the said Indians, further expressly agree:

First. That they will withdraw all opposition to the construction of the railroads now being built on the plains.

Second. That they will permit the peaceful construction of any railroad not passing over their reservation as herein defined.

Third. That they will not attack any persons at home, or travelling, nor molest or disturb any wagon-trains, coaches, mules, or cattle belonging to the people of the United States, or to persons friendly therewith.

Fourth. They will never capture, or carry off from the settlements, white women or children.

Fifth. They will never kill or scalp white men, nor attempt to do them harm.

Sixth. They withdraw all pretence of opposition to the construction of the railroad now being built along the Platte River and westward to the Pacific Ocean, and they will not in future object to the construction of railroads, wagon-roads, mail-stations, or other works of utility or necessity, which may be ordered or permitted by the laws of the United States. But should such roads or other works be constructed on the lands of their reservation, the Government will pay the tribe whatever amount of damage may be assessed by three disinterested commissioners to be appointed by the President for that purpose, one of said commissioners to be a chief or head-man of the tribe.

Seventh. They agree to withdraw all opposition to the military posts or roads now established south of the North Platte River, or that may be established, not in violation of treaties heretofore made or hereafter to be made with any of the Indian tribes.

ARTICLE 12. No treaty for the cession of any portion or part of the reservation herein described which may be held in common shall be of any validity or

561

Plains, West and Northwest Plateau Indian Treaties

force as against the said Indians, unless executed and signed by at least three-fourths of all the adult male Indians, occupying or interested in the same; and no cession by the tribe shall be understood or construed in such manner as to deprive, without his consent, any individual member of the tribe of his rights to any tract of land selected by him, as provided in article 6 of this treaty.

ARTICLE 13. The United States hereby agrees to furnish annually to the Indians the physician, teachers, carpenter, miller, engineer, farmer, and blacksmiths as herein contemplated, and that such appropriations shall be made from time to time, on the estimates of the Secretary of the Interior, as will be sufficient to employ such persons.

ARTICLE 14. it is agreed that the sum of five hundred dollars annually, for three years from date, shall be expended in presents to the ten persons of said tribe who in the judgment of the agent may grow the most valuable crops for the respective year.

ARTICLE 15. The Indians herein named agree that when the agency-house or other buildings shall be constructed on the reservation named, they will regard said reservation their permanent home, and they will make no permanent settlement elsewhere; but they shall have the right, subject to the conditions and modifications of this treaty, to hunt, as stipulated in Article 11 hereof.

ARTICLE 16. The United States hereby agrees and stipulates that the country north of the North Platte River and east of the summits of the Big Horn Mountains shall be held and considered to be unceded Indian territory, and also stipulates and agrees that no white person or persons shall be permitted to settle upon or occupy any portion of the same; or without the consent of the Indians first had and obtained, to pass through the same; and it is further agreed by the United States that within ninety days after the conclusion of peace with all the bands of the Sioux Nation, the military posts now established in the territory in this article named shall be abandoned, and that the road leading to them and by them to the settlements in the Territory of Montana shall be closed.

ARTICLE 17. It is hereby expressly understood and agreed by and between the respective parties to this treaty that the execution of this treaty and its ratification by the United States Senate shall have the effect, and shall be construed as abrogating and annulling all treaties and agreements heretofore entered into between the respective parties hereto, so far as such treaties and agreements obligate the United States to furnish and provide money, clothing, or other articles of property to such Indians and bands of Indians as become parties to this treaty, but no further.

In testimony of all which, we, the said commissioners, and we, the chiefs and headmen of the Brule' band of the Sioux nation, have hereunto set our hands

562

Plains, West and Northwest Plateau Indian Treaties

and seals at Fort Laramie, Dakota Territory, this twenty-ninth day of April, in the year one thousand eight hundred and sixty-eight.

N. G. Taylor, W. T. Sherman, Lieutenant-General.

Wm. S. Harney, Brevet Major-General U. S. Army.

Executed on the part of the Brule' band of Sioux by the chiefs and headmen whose names are hereto annexed, they being thereunto duly authorized, at Fort Laramie, D. T., the twenty-ninth day of April, in the year A. D. 1868.

Ma-za-pon-kaska, his x mark, Iron Shell, Wah-pat-shah, his x mark, Red Leaf, Hah-sah-pah, his x mark, Black Horn, Zin-tah-gah-lat-skah, his x mark, Spotted Tail.

Attest:

Ashton S. H. White, secretary of commission.

George B. Withs, phonographer to commission.

Executed on the part of the Ogallalah band of Sioux by the chiefs and headmen whose names are hereto subscribed, they being thereunto duly authorized, at Fort Laramie, the twenty-fifth day of May, in the year A. D. 1868.

Tah-shun-ka-co-qui-pah, his x mark, Man-afraid-of-his-horses, Sha-ton-skah, his x mark, White Hawk, Sha-ton-sapah, his x mark, Black Hawk, E-ga-mon-ton-ka-sapah, his x mark, Black Tiger, Oh-wah-she-cha, his x mark, Bad Wound.

Attest:

S. E. Ward, Jas. C. O'Connor, J. M. Sherwood, W. C. Slicer, Lefroy Jott, interpreter.

Executed on the part of the Minneconjou band of Sioux by the chiefs and headmen whose names are hereto subscribed, they being thereunto duly authorized.

At Fort Laramie, D. T., May 26, 68, 13 names.

Heh-won-ge-chat, his x mark, One Horn.

Oh-pon-ah-tah-e-manne, his x mark, The Elk that bellows Walking.

At Fort Laramie, D. T., May 25, 68, 2 names.

Heh-ho-lah-reh-cha-skah, his x mark, Young White Bull, Wah chah chum kah coh kee-pah, his x mark, One that is afraid of Shield, He-hon-ne-shakta, his x mark, The Old Owl.

Attest:

Jas. C. O'Connor, Wm. H. Brown.

Plains, West and Northwest Plateau Indian Treaties

Executed on the part of the Yanctonais band of Sioux by the chiefs and head-men whose names are hereto subscribed, they being thereunto duly authorized. Mah-to-non-pah, his x mark, Two Bears, Ma-to-hna-skin-ya, his x mark, Mad Bear, He-o-pu-za, his x mark, Louzy, Ah-ke-che-tah-che-ca-dan, his x mark, Little Soldier, Mah-to-e-tan-chan, his x mark, Chief Bear.

Arapahoes:
Little Chief, his x mark, Tall Bear, his x mark, Top Man, his x mark, Neva, his x mark, The Wounded Bear, his x mark, Thirlwind, his x mark The Fox, his x mark, The Dog Big Mouth, his x mark, Spotted Wolf, his x mark, Sorrel Horse, his x mark, Black Coal, his x mark, Big Wolf, his x mark, Knock-knee, his x mark, Black Crow, his x mark, The Lone Old Man, his x mark, Paul, his x mark, Black Bull, his x mark, Big Track, his x mark, The Foot, his x mark,

Witnesses
Robt. P. McKibbin, captain, Fourth Infantry, brevet lieutenant-colonel, U. S. Army, commanding Fort Laramie, Wm. H. Powell, brevet major, captain, Fourth Infantry, Henry W. Patterson, captain, Fourth Infantry.

Fort Laramie, Wg. T., Nov. 6, 1868

Makh-pi-ah-lu-tah, his x mark, Red Cloud, Wa-ki-ah-we-cha-shah, his x mark, Thunder Man., Ma-zah-zah-geh, his x mark, Iron Cane.

Witnesses:
W. McE. Dye, brevet colonel, U. S. Army, commanding.
A. B. Cain, captain, Fourth Infantry, brevet major, U. S. Army.

HEADQRS., FORT LARAMIE, Novr. 6, 68.
Executed by the above on this date.
All of the Indians are Ogallalahs excepting Thunder Man and Thunder Flying Running, who are Brule's.
Wm. McE. Dye, Major Fourth Infantry, and Brevet-Colonel U. S. Army, Commanding.

Attest:
Jas. C. O'Connor.
Nicholas Janis, interpreter.

Plains, West and Northwest Plateau Indian Treaties

TREATY WITH THE CROWS {1868, May 7}
Ratified, July 25, 1868.
Proclaimed, Aug. 12, 1868.

Articles of a treaty made and concluded at Fort Laramie, Dakota Territory, on the seventh day of May, in the year of our Lord one thousand eight hundred and sixty-eight, by and between the undersigned commissioners on the part of the United States, and the undersigned chiefs and head-men of and representing the Crow Indians, they being duly authorized to act in the premises.

ARTICLE 1. From this day forward peace between the parties to this treaty shall forever continue. The Government of the United States desires peace, and its honor is hereby pledged to keep it. The Indians desire peace, and they hereby pledge their honor to maintain it. If bad men among the whites or among other people, subject to the authority of the United States, shall commit any wrong upon the person or property of the Indians, the United States will, upon proof made to the agent and forwarded to the Commissioner of Indian Affairs at Washington City, proceed at once to cause the offender to be arrested and punished according to the laws of the United States, and also reimburse the, injured person for the loss sustained.

If bad men among the Indians shall commit a wrong or depredation upon the person or property of any one, white, black, or Indian, subject to the authority of the United States and at peace therewith, the Indians herein named solemnly agree that they will, on proof made to their agent and notice by hint, deliver up the wrong-doer to the United States, to be tried and punished according to its laws; and in case they refuse willfully so to do the person injured shall be re-imbursed for his loss from the annuities or other moneys due or to become due to them under this or other treaties made with the United States. And the President, on advising with the Commissioner of Indian Affairs, shall prescribe such rules and regulations for ascertaining damages under the provisions of this article as in his judgment may be proper, But no such damages shall be adjusted and paid until thoroughly examined and passed upon by the Commissioner of Indian Affairs, and no one sustaining loss while violating, or because of his violating, the provisions of this treaty or the laws of the United States shall be re-imbursed therefor.

ARTICLE 2. The United States agrees that the following district of country, to wit: commencing where the 107th degree of longitude west of Greenwich crosses the south boundary of Montana Territory; thence north along said 107th meridian to the mid-channel of the Yellowstone River; thence up said mid-channel of the Yellowstone to the point where it crosses the said southern boundary of Montana, being the 45th degree of north latitude; and thence east along said parallel of latitude to the place of beginning, shall be, and the same is, set apart for the absolute and undisturbed use and occupation of the Indians

565

Plains, West and Northwest Plateau Indian Treaties

herein named, and for such other friendly tribes or individual Indians as from to time they may be willing, with the consent of the United States, to admit amongst them; and the United States now solemnly agrees that no persons, except those herein designated and authorized so to do, and except such officers, agents, and employees of the Government as may be authorized to enter upon Indian reservations in discharge of duties enjoined by law, shall ever be permitted to pass over, settle upon, or reside in the territory described in this article for the use of said Indians, and henceforth they will, and do hereby, relinquish all title, claims, or rights in and to any portion of the territory of the United States, except such as is embraced within the limits aforesaid.

ARTICLE 3. The United States agrees, at its own proper expense, to construct on the south side of the Yellowstone, near Otter Creek, a warehouse or store-room for the use of the agent in storing goods belonging to the Indians, to cost not exceeding twenty-five hundred dollars; an agency-building for the residence of the agent, to cost not exceeding three thousand dollars; a residence for the physician, to cost not more than three thousand dollars; and five other buildings, for a carpenter, farmer, blacksmith, miller, and engineer, each to cost not exceeding two thousand dollars; also a school-house or mission-building, so soon as a sufficient number of children can be induced by the agent to attend school, which shall not cost exceeding twenty-five hundred dollars.

The United States agrees further to cause to be erected on said reservation, near the other buildings herein authorized, a good steam circular saw-mill, with a grist-mill and shingle-machine attached, the same to cost not exceeding eight thousand dollars.

ARTICLE 4. The Indians herein named agree, when the agency-house and other buildings shall be constructed on the reservation named, they will make said reservation their permanent home, and they will make no permanent settlement elsewhere, but they shall have the right to hunt on the unoccupied lands of the United States so long as game may be found thereon, and as long as peace subsists among the whites and Indians on the borders of the hunting districts.

ARTICLE 5. The United States agrees that the agent for said Indians shall in the future make his home at the agency-building; that he shall reside among them, and keep an office open at all times for the purpose of prompt and diligent inquiry into such matters of complaint, by and against the Indians, as may be presented for investigation under the provisions of their treaty stipulations, as also for the faithful discharge of other duties enjoined on him by law. In all cases of depredation on person or property, he shall cause the evidence to be taken in writing and forwarded, together with his finding, to the Commissioner of Indian Affairs, whose decision shall be binding on the parties to this treaty.

Plains, West and Northwest Plateau Indian Treaties

ARTICLE 6. If any individual belonging to said tribes of Indians, or legally incorporated with them, being the head of a family, shall desire to commence farming, he shall have the privilege to select, in the presence and with the assistance of the agent then in charge, a tract of land within said reservation, not exceeding three hundred and twenty acres in extent, which tract, when so selected, certified, and recorded in the "land book," as herein directed, shall cease to be held in common, but the same may be occupied and held in the exclusive possession of the person selecting it, and of his family, so long as he or they may continue to cultivate it.

Any person over eighteen years of age, not being the head of a family, may in like manner select and cause to be certified to him or her, for purposes of cultivation a quantity of land not exceeding eighty acres in extent, and thereupon be entitled to the exclusive possession of the same as above directed.
For each tract of land so selected a certificate, containing a description thereof and the name of the person selecting it, with a certificate endorsed thereon that the same has been recorded, shall be delivered to the party entitled to it by the agent, after the same shall have been recorded by him in a book to be kept in his office, subject to inspection, which said book shall be known as the "Crow land book."

The President may at any time order a survey of the reservation, and, when so surveyed, Congress shall provide for protecting the rights of settlers in their improvements, and may fix the character of the title held by each. The United States may pass such laws on the subject of alienation and descent of property as between Indians, and on all subjects connected with the government of the Indians on said reservations and the internal police thereof, as may be thought proper.

ARTICLE 7. In order to insure the civilization of the tribe entering Into this treaty, the necessity of education is admitted, especially by such of them as are, or may be, settled on said agricultural reservation; and they therefore pledge themselves to compel their children, male and female, between the ages of six and sixteen years, to attend school; and it is hereby made the duty of the agent for said Indians to see that this stipulation is strictly complied with; and the United States agrees that for every thirty children, between said ages, who can be induced or compelled to attend school, a house shall be provided, and a teacher, competent to teach the elementary branches of an English education, shall be furnished, who will reside among said Indians, and faithfully discharge his or her duties as a teacher. The provisions of this article to continue for twenty years.

ARTICLE 8. When the head of a family or lodge shall have selected lands and received his certificate as above directed, and the agent shall be satisfied that he intends in good faith to commence cultivating the soil for a living, he shall be

567

Plains, West and Northwest Plateau Indian Treaties

entitled to receive seed and agricultural implements for the first year in value one hundred dollars, and for each succeeding year he shall continue to farm, for a period of three years more, he shall be entitled to receive seed and implements as aforesaid in value twenty-five dollars per annum.

And it is further stipulated that such persons as commence farming shall receive instructions from the farmer herein provided for, and whenever more than one hundred persons shall enter upon the cultivation of the soil, a second blacksmith shall be provided, with such iron, steel, and other material as may be required.

ARTICLE 9. In lieu of all sums of money or other annuities provided to be paid to the Indians herein named, under any and all treaties heretofore made with them, the United States agrees to deliver at the agency house, on the reservation herein provided for, on the first day of September of each year for thirty years, the following articles, to wit:

For each male person, over fourteen years of age, a suit of good substantial woolen clothing, consisting of coat, hat, pantaloons, flannel shirt, and a pair of woolen socks.

For each female, over twelve years of age, a flannel skirt, or the goods necessary to make it, a pair of woolen hose, twelve yards of calico, and twelve yards of cotton domestics.

For the boys and girls under the ages named, such flannel and cotton goods as may be needed to make each a suit as aforesaid, together with a pair of woollen hose for each.

And in order that the Commissioner of Indian Affairs may be able to estimate properly for the articles herein named, it shall be the duty of the agent, each year, to forward to him a full and exact census of the Indians, on which the estimate from year to year can be based.

And, in addition to the clothing herein named, the sum of ten dollars shall be annually appropriated for each Indian roaming, and twenty dollars for each Indian engaged in agriculture, for a period of ten years, to be used by the Secretary of the Interior in the purchase of such articles as, from time to time, the condition and necessities of the Indians may indicate to be proper. And if, at any time within the ten years, it shall appear that the amount of money needed for clothing, under this article, can be appropriated to better uses for the tribe herein named, Congress may, by law, change the appropriation to other purposes; but in no event shall the amount of this appropriation be withdrawn or discontinued for the period named. And the President shall annually detail an officer of the Army to be present and attest the delivery of all the goods herein

Plains, West and Northwest Plateau Indian Treaties

named to the Indians, and he shall inspect and report on the quantity and quality of the goods and the manner of their delivery; and it is expressly stipulated that each Indian over the age of four years, who shall have removed to and settled permanently upon said reservation, and complied with the stipulations of this treaty, shall be entitled to receive from the United States, for the period of four years after he shall have settled upon said reservation, one pound of meat and one pound of flour per day, provided the Indians cannot furnish their own subsistence at an earlier date. And it is further stipulated that the United States will furnish and deliver to each lodge of Indians, or family of persons legally incorporated with them, who shall remove to the reservation herein described, and commence farming, one good American cow and one good, well-broken pair of American oxen, within sixty days after such lodge or family shall have so settled upon said reservation.

ARTICLE 10. The United States hereby agrees to furnish annually to the Indians the physicians, teachers, carpenter, miller, engineer, farmer, and blacksmiths as herein contemplated, and that such appropriations shall be made from time to time on the estimates of the Secretary of the Interior, as will be sufficient to employ such persons.

ARTICLE 11. No treaty for the cession of any portion of the reservation herein described, which may be held in common, shall be of any force or validity as against the said Indians unless executed and signed by, at least, a majority of all the adult male Indians occupying or interested in the same, and no cession by the tribe shall be understood or construed in such a manner as to deprive, without his consent, any individual member of the tribe of his right to any tract of land selected by him as provided in Article 6 of this treaty.

ARTICLE 12. It is agreed that the sum of five hundred dollars annually, for three years from the date when they commence to cultivate a farm, shall be expended in presents to the ten persons of said tribe who, in the judgment of the agent, may grow the most valuable crops for the respective year.

W. T. Sherman, Lieutenant-General.
Wm. S. Harney, Brevet Major-General and Peace Commissioner.
Alfred H. Terry, Brevet Major-General.

Che-ra-pee-ish-ka-te, Pretty Bull, his x mark, Chat-sta-he, Wolf Bow, his x mark, Ah-be-che-se, Mountain Tail, his x mark, Kam-ne-but-sa, Black Foot, his x mark, De-sal-ze-cho-se, White Horse, his x mark, Chin-ka-she-arache, Poor Elk, his x mark, E-sa-woor, Shot in the Jaw, his x mark, E-sha-chose, White Forehead, his x mark, Roo-ka, Pounded Meat, his x mark, De-ka-ke-up-se, Bird in the Neck, his x mark, Me-na-che, The Swan, his x mark,

Attest: George B. Willis, phonographer, John D. Howland.

Plains, West and Northwest Plateau Indian Treaties

TREATY WITH THE NORTHERN CHEYENNE AND NORTHERN ARAPAHO {1868, May 10}
Ratified July 25, 1868.
Proclaimed Aug. 25, 1868.

Articles of a treaty made and concluded at Fort Laramie, Dakota Territory, on the tenth day of May, in the year of our Lord one thousand eight hundred and sixty-eight, by and between the undersigned commissioners on the part of the United States, and the undersigned chiefs and head-men of and representing the Northern Cheyenne and Northern Arapahoe Indians, they being duly authorized to act in the premises.

ARTICLE 1. From this clay forward peace between the parties to this treaty shall forever continue. The Government of the United States desires peace, and its honor is hereby pledged to keep it. The Indians desire peace, and they hereby pledge their honor to maintain it. If bad men among the whites, or among other people subject to the authority of the United States, shall commit any wrong upon the person or property of the Indians, the United States will, upon proof made to the agent and forwarded to the Commissioner of Indian Affairs at Washington City, proceed at once to cause the offender to be arrested and punished according to the laws of the United States, and also reimburse the injured person for the loss sustained.

If bad men among the Indians shall commit a wrong or depredation upon the person or property of any one, white, black, or Indian, subject to the authority of the United States and at peace therewith, the Indians herein named solemnly agree that they will, on proof made to their agent and notice by him, deliver up the wrong-doer to the United States, to be tried and punished according to its laws; and in case they wilfully refuse so to do, the person injured shall be reimbursed for his loss from the annuities or other moneys due or to become due to them under this or other treaties made with the United States. And the President, on advising with the Commissioner of Indian Affairs, shall prescribe such rules and regulations for ascertaining damages under the provisions of this article as in his judgment may be proper. But no such damages shall be adjusted and paid until thoroughly examined and passed upon by the Commissioner of Indian Affairs, and no one sustaining loss while violating or because of his violating the provisions of this treaty or the laws of the United States shall be reimbursed therefor.

ARTICLE 2. The Indians, parties to this treaty, hereby agree to accept for their permanent home some portion of the tract of country set apart and designated as a permanent reservation for the Southern Cheyenne and Arapahoe Indians by a treaty entered into by and between them and the United States, at Medicine

Plains, West and Northwest Plateau Indian Treaties

Lodge Creek, on the day of October, eighteen hundred and sixty-seven, or some portion of the country and reservation set apart and designated as a permanent home for the Brule' and other bands of Sioux Indians, by a treaty entered into by and between said Indians and the United States, at Fort Laramie, D. T., on the twenty-ninth day of April, eighteen hundred and sixty-eight. And the Northern Cheyenne and Arapahoe Indians do hereby relinquish, release, and surrender to the United States, all right, claim, and interest in and to all territory outside the two reservations above mentioned, except the right to roam and hunt while game shall be found in sufficient quantities to justify the chase.

And they do solemnly agree that they will not build any permanent homes outside of said reservations, and that within one year from this date they will attach themselves permanently either to the agency provided for near the mouth of Medicine Lodge Creek, or to the agency about to be established on the Missouri River, near Fort Randall, or to the Crow agency near Otter Creek, on the Yellowstone River, provided for by treaty of the seventh day of May, eighteen hundred and sixty-eight, entered into by and between the United States and said Crow Indians, at Fort Laramie, D. T.; and it is hereby expressly understood that one portion of said Indians may attach themselves to one of the aforementioned reservations, and another portion to another of said reservations, as each part or portion of said Indians may elect.

ARTICLE 3. If any individual belonging to said tribes of Indians, or legally incorporated with them, being the head of a family, shall desire to commence farming, he shall have the privilege to select, in the presence and with the assistance of the agent then in charge, a tract of land within said reservations not exceeding three hundred and twenty acres in extent, which tract, when so selected, certified, and recorded in the "Land Book" as herein directed, shall cease to be held in common, but the same may be occupied and held in the exclusive possession of the person selecting it, and of his family, so long as he or they may continue to cultivate it.

Any person over eighteen years of age, not being the head of a family, may in like manner select and cause to be certified to him or her, for purposes of cultivation, a quantity of land not exceeding eighty acres in extent, and thereupon be entitled to the exclusive possession of the same as above directed.

For each tract of land so selected a certificate containing a description thereof and the name of the person selecting it, with a certificate endorsed thereon that the same has been recorded, shall be delivered to the party entitled to it by the agent after the same shall have been recorded by him in a book to be kept in his office, subject to inspection, which said book shall be known as the "Northern Cheyenne and Arapahoe Land Book."

Plains, West and Northwest Plateau Indian Treaties

The President may, at any time, order a survey of the reservation; and when so surveyed, Congress shall provide for protecting the rights of settlers in their improvements, and may fix the character of the title held by each.

The United States may pass such laws on the subject of alienation and descent of property as between Indians and on all subjects connected with the government of the Indians on said reservations, and the internal police thereof, as may be thought proper.

ARTICLE 4. In order to insure the civilization of the tribe entering into this treaty, the necessity of education is admitted, especially by such of them as are or may be settled on said agricultural reservation, and they therefore pledge themselves to compel their children, male and female, between the ages of six and sixteen years, to attend school; and it is hereby made the duty of the agent for said Indians to see that this stipulation is strictly complied with; and the United States agrees that for every thirty children, between said ages, who can be induced or compelled to attend school, a house shall be provided, and a teacher, competent to teach the elementary branches of an English education, shall be furnished, who will reside among said Indians, and faithfully discharge his or her duties as a teacher. The provisions of this article to continue for twenty years.

ARTICLE 5. When the head of a family or lodge shall have selected lands, and received his certificate as above directed, and the agent shall be satisfied that he intends in good faith to commence cultivating the soil for a living, he shall be entitled to receive seeds and agricultural implements for the first year in value one hundred dollars, and for each succeeding year he shall continue to farm for a period of three years more he shall be entitled to receive seeds and implements as aforesaid in value twenty-five dollars per annum.

And it is further stipulated that such persons as commence farming shall receive instructions from the farmer herein provided for, and whenever more than one hundred persons shall enter upon the cultivation of the soil a second blacksmith shall be provided, with such iron, steel, and other material as may be needed.

ARTICLE 6. In lieu of all sums of money or other annuities provided to be paid to the Indians herein named, under any and all treaties heretofore made with them, the United States agrees to deliver at the agency-house, on the reservations herein provided for, on the first day of September of each year, for thirty years, the following articles, to wit:

For each male person over fourteen years of age, a suit of good substantial woolen clothing, consisting of coat, hat, pantaloons, flannel shirt, and a pair of woolen socks.

Plains, West and Northwest Plateau Indian Treaties

For each female over twelve years of age, a flannel skirt, or the goods necessary to make it, a pair of woolen hose, twelve yards of calico, and twelve yards of cotton domestics.

For the boys and girls under the ages named, such flannel and cotton goods as may be needed to make each a suit, as aforesaid, together with a pair of woolen hose for each.

And in order that the Commissioner of Indian Affairs may be able to estimate properly for the articles herein named, it shall be the duty of the agent each year to forward to him a full and exact census of the Indians, on which the estimates from year to year can be based.

And, in addition to the clothing herein named, the sum of ten dollars shall be annually appropriated for each Indian roaming, and twenty dollars for each Indian engaged in agriculture, for a period of ten years, to be used by the Secretary of the Interior in the purchase of such articles as from time to time the condition and necessities of the Indians may indicate to be proper. And if, at any time within the ten years, it shall appear that the amount of money needed for clothing under this article can be appropriated to better uses for the tribes herein named, Congress may by law change the appropriation to other purposes; but in no event shall the amount of this appropriation be withdrawn or discontinued for the period named. And the President shall annually detail an officer of the Army to be present and attest the delivery of all the goods, herein named, to the Indians, and he shall inspect and report on the quantity and quality of the goods and the manner of their delivery.

And it is expressly stipulated that each Indian over the age of four years, who shah have removed to and settled permanently upon said reservation and complied with the stipulations of this treaty, shall be entitled to receive from the United States, for the period of four years after he shall have settled upon said reservation, one pound of meat and one pound of flour per day, provided that the Indians cannot furnish their own subsistence at an earlier date; and it is further stipulated that the United States will furnish and deliver to each lodge of Indians, or family of persons legally incorporated with them, who shall remove to the reservation herein described and commence farming, one good American cow and one well-broken pair of American oxen, within sixty days after such lodge or family shall have so settled upon said reservation.

ARTICLE 7. The United States hereby agrees to furnish annually to the Indians who settle upon the reservation a physician, teachers, carpenter, miller, engineer, farmer, and blacksmiths, as herein contemplated, and that such appropriations shall be made from time to time on the estimates of the Secretary of the Interior as will be sufficient to employ such persons.

573

Plains, West and Northwest Plateau Indian Treaties

ARTICLE 8. No treaty for the cession of any portion of the reservations herein described, which may be held in common, shall be of any force or validity as against the said Indians unless executed and signed by at least a majority of all the adult male Indians, occupying or interested in the same; and no cession by the tribe shall be understood or construed in such manner as to deprive, without his consent, any individual member of the tribe of his right to any tract of land selected by him, as hereinbefore provided.

ARTICLE 9. It is agreed that the sum of five hundred dollars annually for three years, from the date when they commenced to cultivate a farm, shall be expended in presents to the ten persons of said tribe who, in the judgment of the agent, may grow the most valuable crops for the respective year.

W. T. Sherman, Lieutenant-General.
Wm. S. Harney, Brevet Major-General, U. S. Army.
Alfred H. Terry, Brevet Major-General.

Attest:
Ashton S. H. White, Secretary.

Wah-tah-nah, Black Bear, his x mark, Bah-ta-che, Medicine Man, his x mark, Oh-cum-ga-che, Little Wolf, his x mark, Iehs-tah-en, Short Hair, his x mark, Non-ne-se-be, Sorrel Horse, his x mark, Ka-te-u-nan, The Under Man, his x mark, Ah-ehe-e-wah, The Man in the Sky, his x mark, We-ah-se-vose, The Big Wolf, his x mark, Ches-ne-on-e-ah, The Beau, his x mark, Mat-ah-ne-we-tah, The Man that falls from his horse, his x mark, Oh-e-na-ku, White Crow, his x mark, A-che-kan-koo-eni, Little Shield, his x mark, Tah-meda-pash-me, or Dull Knife, his x mark,

Attest:
George B. Willis, Photographer.
John D. Howland.

TREATY WITH THE NAVAHO {1868, June 1}
Ratified July 25, 1868.
Proclaimed Aug. 12, 1868.

Articles of a treaty and agreement made and entered into at Fort Sumner, New Mexico, on the first day of June, one thousand eight hundred and sixty-eight, by and between the United States, represented by its commissioners, Lieutenant-General W. T. Sherman and Colonel Samuel F. Tappan, of the one part, and the Navajo Nation or tribe of Indians, represented by their chiefs and head-men, duly authorized and empowered to act for the whole people of said nation or

Plains, West and Northwest Plateau Indian Treaties

tribe, (the names of said chiefs and head-men being hereto subscribed) of the other part, witness:

ARTICLE 1. From this day forward all war between the parties to this agreement shall forever cease. The Government of the United States desires peace, and its honor is hereby pledged to keep it. The Indians desire peace, and they now pledge their honor to keep it.

If bad men among the whites, or among other people subject to the authority of the United States, shall commit any wrong upon the person or property of the Indians, the United States will, upon proof made to the agent and forwarded to the Commissioner of Indian Affairs at Washington City, proceed at once to cause the offender to be arrested and punished according to the laws of the United States, and also to reimburse the injured persons for the loss sustained.

If the bad men among the Indians shall commit a wrong or depredation upon the person or property of any one, white, black, or Indian, subject to the authority of the United States and at peace therewith, the Navajo tribe agree that they will, on proof made to their agent, and on notice by him, deliver up the wrongdoer to the United States, to be tried and punished according to its laws; and in case they wilfully refuse so to do, the person injured shall be reimbursed for his loss from the annuities or other moneys due or to become due to them under this treaty, or any others that may be made with the United States.

And the President may prescribe such rules and regulations for ascertaining damages under this article as in his judgment may be proper; but no such damage shall be adjusted and paid Until examined and passed upon by the Commissioner of Indian Affairs, and no one sustaining loss whilst violating, or because of his violating, the provisions of this treaty or the laws of the United States, shall be reimbursed therefor.

ARTICLE 2. The United States agrees that the following district of country, to wit: bounded on the north by the 37th degree of north latitude, south by an east and west, line passing through the site of old Fort Defiance, in Canon Bonito, east by the parallel of longitude which, if prolonged south, would pass through old Fort Lyon, or the Ojo-de-oso, Bear Spring, and west by a parallel of longitude about 109° 30' west of Greenwich, provided it embraces the outlet of the Canon-de-Chilly, which canon is to be all included in this reservation, shall be, and the same is hereby, set apart for the use and occupation of the Navajo tribe of Indians, and for such other friendly tribes or individual Indians as from time to time they may be willing, with the consent of the United States, to admit among them; and the United States agrees that no persons except those herein so authorized to do, and except such officers, soldiers, agents, and employees of the Government, or of the Indians, as may be authorized to enter upon Indian reservations in discharge of duties imposed by law, or the orders of the Presi-

Plains, West and Northwest Plateau Indian Treaties

dent, shall ever be permitted to pass over, settle upon, or reside in, the territory described in this article.

ARTICLE 3. The United States agrees to cause to be built, at some point within said reservation, where timber and water may be convenient, the following buildings: a warehouse, to cost not exceeding twenty-five hundred dollars; an agency building for the residence of the agent, not to cost exceeding three thousand dollars; a carpenter-shop and blacksmith-shop, not to cost exceeding one thousand dollars each; and a schoolhouse and chapel, so soon as a sufficient number of children can be induced to attend school, which shall not cost to exceed five thousand dollars.

ARTICLE 4. The United States agrees that the agent for the Navajos shall make his home at the agency building; that he shall reside among them, and shall keep an office open at all times for the purpose of prompt and diligent inquiry into such matters of complaint by or against the Indians as may be presented for investigation, as also for the faithful discharge of other duties enjoined by law. In all cases of depredation on person or property he shall cause the evidence to be taken in writing and forwarded, together with his finding, to the Commissioner of Indian Affairs, whose decision shall be binding on the parties to this treaty.

ARTICLE 5. If any individual belonging to said tribe, or legally incorporated with it, being the head of a family, shall desire to commence farming, he shall have the privilege to select, in the presence and with the assistance of the agent then in charge, a tract of land within said reservation, not exceeding one hundred and sixty acres in extent, which tract, when so selected, certified, and recorded in the "land-book" as herein described, shall cease to be held in common, but the same may be occupied and held in the exclusive possession of the person selecting it, and of his family, so long as he or they may continue to cultivate it.

Any person over eighteen years of age, not being the head of a family, may in like manner select, and cause to be certified to him or her for purposes of cultivation, a quantity of land, not exceeding eighty acres in extent, and thereupon be entitled to the exclusive possession of the same as above directed.
For each tract of land so selected a certificate containing a description thereof, and the name of the person selecting it, with a certificate endorsed thereon, that the same has been recorded, shall be delivered to the party entitled to it by the agent, after the same shall have been recorded by him in a book to be kept in his office, subject to inspection, which said book shall be known as the "Navajo land-book."

Plains, West and Northwest Plateau Indian Treaties

The President may at any time order a survey of the reservation, and when so surveyed, Congress shall provide for protecting the rights of said settlers in their improvements, and may fix the character of the title held by each.

The United States may pass such laws on the subject of alienation and descent of property between the Indians and their descendants as may be thought proper.

ARTICLE 6. In order to insure the civilization of the Indians entering into this treaty, the necessity of education is admitted, especially of such of them as may be settled on said agricultural parts of this reservation, and they therefore pledge themselves to compel their children, male and female, between the ages of six and sixteen years, to attend school; and it is hereby made the duty of the agent for said Indians to see that this stipulation is strictly complied with; and the United States agrees that, for every thirty children between said ages who can be induced or compelled to attend school, a house shall be provided, and a teacher competent to teach the elementary branches of an English education shall be furnished, who will reside among said Indians, and faithfully discharge his or her duties as a teacher.

The provisions of this article to continue for not less than ten years.

ARTICLE 7. When the head of a family shall have selected lands and received his certificate as above directed, and the agent shall be satisfied that he intends in good faith to commence cultivating the soil for a living, he shall be entitled to receive seeds and agricultural implements for the first year, not exceeding in value one hundred dollars, and for each succeeding year he shall continue to farm, for a period of two years, he shall be entitled to receive seeds and implements to the value of twenty-five dollars.

ARTICLE 8. In lieu of all sums of money or other annuities provided to be paid to the Indians herein named under any treaty or treaties heretofore made, the United States agrees to deliver at the agency-house on the reservation herein named, on the first day of September of each year for ten years, the following articles, to wit:

Such articles of clothing, goods, or raw materials in lieu thereof, as the agent may make his estimate for, not exceeding in value five dollars per Indianeach Indian being encouraged to manufacture their own clothing, blankets, &c.; to be furnished with no article which they can manufacture themselves. And, in order that the Commissioner of Indian Affairs may be able to estimate properly for the articles herein named, it shall be the duty of the agent each year to forward to him a full and exact census of the Indians, on which the estimate from year to year can be based.

Plains, West and Northwest Plateau Indian Treaties

And in addition to the articles herein named, the sum of ten dollars for each person entitled to the beneficial effects of this treaty shall be annually appropriated for a period of ten years, for each person who engages in farming or mechanical pursuits, to be used by the Commissioner of Indian Affairs in the purchase of such articles as from time to time the condition and necessities of the Indians may indicate to be proper; and if within the ten years at any time it shrill appear that the amount of money needed for clothing, under the article, can be appropriated to better uses for the Indians named herein, the Commissioner of Indian Affairs may change the appropriation to other purposes, but in no event shall the amount of this appropriation be withdrawn or discontinued for the period named, provided they remain at peace. And the President shall annually detail an officer of the Army to be present and attest the delivery of all the goods herein named to the Indians, and he shall inspect and report on the quantity and quality of the goods and the manner of their delivery.

ARTICLE 9. In consideration of the advantages and benefits conferred by this treaty, and the many pledges of friendship by the United States, the tribes who are parties to this agreement hereby stipulate that they will relinquish all right to occupy any territory outside their reservation, as herein defined, but retain the right to hunt on any unoccupied lands contiguous to their reservation, so long as the large game may range thereon in such numbers as to justify the chase; and they, the said Indians, further expressly agree:

First. That they will make no opposition to the construction of railroads now being built or hereafter to be built across the continent.

Second. That they will not interfere with the peaceful construction of any railroad not passing over their reservation as herein defined.

Third. That they will not attack any persons at home or travelling, nor molest or disturb any wagon-trains, coaches, mules, or cattle belonging to the people of the United States, or to persons friendly therewith.

Fourth. That they will never capture or carry off from the settlements women or children.

Fifth. They will never kill or scalp white men, nor attempt to do them harm.

Sixth. They will not in future oppose the construction of railroads, wagon-roads, mail stations, or other works of utility or necessity which may be ordered or permitted by the laws of the United States; but should such roads or other works be constructed on the lands of their reservation, the Government will pay the tribe whatever amount of damage may be assessed by three disinterested commissioners to be appointed by the President for that purpose, one of said commission-era to be a chief or head-man of the tribe.

Plains, West and Northwest Plateau Indian Treaties

Seventh. They will make no opposition to the military posts or roads now established, or that may be established, not in violation of treaties heretofore made or hereafter to be made with any of the Indian tribes.

ARTICLE 10. No future treaty for the cession of any portion or part of the reservation herein described, which may be held in common, shall be of any validity or force against said Indians unless agreed to and executed by at least three-fourths of all the adult male Indians occupying or interested in the same; and no cession by the tribe shall be understood or construed in such manner as to deprive, without his consent, any individual member of the tribe of his rights to any tract of land selected by him as provided in article 5 of this treaty.

ARTICLE 11. The Navajos also hereby agree that at any time after the signing of these presents they will proceed in such manner as may be required of them by the agent, or by the officer charged with their removal, to the reservation herein provided for, the United States paying for their subsistence en route, and providing a reasonable amount of transportation for the sick and feeble.

ARTICLE 12. It is further agreed by and between the parties to this agreement that the sum of one hundred and fifty thousand dollars appropriated or to be appropriated shall be disbursed as follows, subject to any condition provided in the law, to wit:

First. The actual cost of the removal of the tribe from the Bosque Redondo reservation to the reservation, say fifty thousand dollars.

Second. The purchase of fifteen thousand sheep and goats, at a cost not to exceed thirty thousand dollars.

Third. The purchase of five hundred beef cattle and a million pounds of corn, to be collected and held at the military post nearest the reservation, subject to the orders of the agent, for the relief of the needy during the coming winter.

Fourth. The balance, if any, of the appropriation to be invested for the maintenance of the Indians pending their removal, in such manner as the agent who is with them may determine.

Fifth. The removal of this tribe to be made under the supreme control and direction of the military commander of the Territory of New Mexico, and when completed, the management of the tribe to revert to the proper agent.

ARTICLE 13. The tribe herein named, by their representatives, parties to this treaty, agree to make the reservation herein described their permanent home, and they will not as a tribe make any permanent settlement elsewhere, reserv-

Plains, West and Northwest Plateau Indian Treaties

ing the right to hunt on the lands adjoining the said reservation formerly called theirs, subject to the modifications named in this treaty and the orders of the commander of the department in which said reservation may be for the time being; audit is further agreed and understood by the parties to this treaty, that if any Navajo Indian or Indians shall leave the reservation herein described to settle elsewhere, he or they shall forfeit all the rights, privileges, and annuities conferred by the terms of this treaty; and it is further agreed by the parties to this treaty, that they will do all they can to induce Indians now away from reservations set apart for the exclusive use and occupation of the Indians, leading a nomadic life, or engaged in war against the people of the United States, to abandon such a life and settle permanently in one of the territorial reservations set apart for the exclusive use and occupation of the Indians.

In testimony of all which the said parties have hereunto, on this the first day of June, one thousand eight hundred and sixty-eight, at Fort Sumner, in the Territory of New Mexico, set their hands and seals.

W. T. Sherman, Lieutenant-General, Indian Peace Commissioner.
S. F. Tappan, Indian Peace Commissioner.

Barboncito, chief, his x mark, Armijo, his x mark, Delgado, Manuelito, his x mark, Largo, his x mark, Herrero, his x mark, Chiqueto, his x mark, Muerto de Hombre, his x mark, Hombro, his x mark, Narbono, his x mark, Narbono Segundo, his x mark, Gañado Mucho, his x mark, Council: Riquo, his x mark, Juan Martin, his x mark, Serginto, his x mark, Grande, his x mark, Inoetenito, his x mark, Muchachos Mucho, his x mark, Chiqueto Segundo, his x mark, Cabello Amarillo, his x mark, Francisco, his x mark, Torivio, his x mark, Desdendado, his x mark, Juan, his x mark, Guero, his x mark, Gugadore, his x mark, Cabason, his x mark, Barbon Segundo, his x mark, Cabares Colorados, his x mark.

Attest:
Geo. W. G. Getty, colonel Thirty-seventh Infantry, brevet major-general U. S. Army. B. S. Roberts, brevet brigadier-general U. S. Army, lieutenant-colonel Third Cavalry.

TREATY WITH THE EASTERN BAND SHOSHONI AND BANNOCK
{1868, July 3}
Ratified Feb. 26, 1869.
Proclaimed Feb. 24, 1869.

Articles of a treaty made and concluded at Fort Bridge, Utah Territory, on the third day of July, in the year of our Lord one thousand eight hundred and sixth-eight, by and between the undersigned commissioners on the part of the United

Plains, West and Northwest Plateau Indian Treaties

States, and the undersigned chiefs and head-men of and representing the Shoshonee (eastern band) and Bannack tribes of Indians, they being duly authorized to act in the premises:

ARTICLE 1. From this day forward peace between the parties to this treaty shall forever continue. The Government of the United States desires peace, and its honor is hereby pledged to keep it. The Indians desire peace, and they hereby pledge their honor to maintain it.

If bad men among the whites, or among other people subject to the authority of the United States, shall commit any wrong upon the person or property of the Indians, the United States will, upon proof made to the agent and forwarded to the Commissioner of Indian Affairs, at Washington City, proceed at once to cause the offender to be arrested and punished according to the laws of the United States, and also re-imburse the injured person for the loss sustained.

If bad men among the Indians shall commit a wrong or depredation upon the person or property of any one, white, black, or Indian, subject to the authority of the United States, and at peace therewith, the Indians herein named solemnly agree that they will, on proof made to their agent and notice by him, deliver up the wrong-doer to the United States, to be tried and punished according to the laws; and in case they wilfully refuse so to do, the person injured shall be re-imbursed for his loss from the annuities or other moneys due or to become due to them under this or other treaties made with the United States. And the President, on advising with the Commissioner of Indian Affairs, shall prescribe such rules and regulations for ascertaining damages under the provisions of this article as in his judgment may be proper.

But no such damages shall be adjusted and paid until thoroughly examined and passed upon by the Commissioner of Indian Affairs, and no one sustaining loss while violating or because of his violating the provisions of this treaty or the laws of the United States, shall be reimbursed therefor.

ARTICLE 2. It is agreed that whenever the Bannacks desire a reservation to be set apart for their use, or whenever the President of the United States shall deem it advisable for them to be put upon a reservation, he shall cause a suitable one to be selected for them in their present country, which shall embrace reasonable portions of the "Port Neuf" and "Kansas Prairie" countries, and that, when this reservation is declared, the United States will secure to the Bannacks the same rights and privileges therein, and make the same and like expenditures therein for their benefit, except the agency-house and residence of agent, in proportion to their numbers, as herein provided for the Shoshonee reservation. The United States further agrees that the following district of country, to wit:

Plains, West and Northwest Plateau Indian Treaties

Commencing at the mouth of Owl Creek and running due south to the crest of the divide between the Sweet-water and Papo Agie Rivers; thence along the crest of said divide and the summit of Wind River Mountains to the longitude of North Fork of Wind River; thence due north to mouth of said North Fork and up its channel to a point twenty miles above its mouth; thence in a straight line to head-waters of Owl Creek and along middle of channel of Owl Creek to place of beginning, shall be and the same is set apart for the absolute and undisturbed use and occupation of the Shoshonee Indians herein named, and for such other friendly tribes or individual Indians as from time to time they may be willing, with the consent of the United States, to admit amongst them; and the United States now solemnly agrees that no persons except those herein designated and authorized so to do, and except such officers, agents, and employes of the Government as may be authorized to enter upon Indian reservations in discharge of duties enjoined by law, shall ever be permitted to pass over, settle upon, or reside in the territory described in this article for the use of said Indians, and henceforth they will and do hereby relinquish all title, claims, or rights in and to any portion of the territory of the United States, except such as is embraced within the limits aforesaid.

ARTICLE 3. The United States agrees, at its own proper expense, to construct at a suitable point of the Shoshonee reservation a warehouse or store-room for the use of the agent in storing goods belonging to the Indians, to cost not exceeding two thousand dollars; an agency building for the residence of the agent, to cost not exceeding three thousand; a residence for the physician, to cost not more than two thousand dollars; and five other buildings, for a carpenter, farmer, blacksmith, miller, and engineer, each to cost not exceeding two thousand dollars; also a school-house or mission building so soon as a sufficient number of children can be induced by the agent to attend school, which shall not cost exceeding twenty-five hundred dollars.

The United States agrees further to cause to be erected on said Shoshonee reservation, near the other buildings herein authorized, a good steam circular-saw mill, with a grist-mill and shingle-machine attached, the same to cost not more than eight thousand dollars.

ARTICLE 4. The Indians herein named agree, when the agency house and other buildings shall be constructed on their reservations named, they will make said reservations their permanent home, and they will make no permanent settlement elsewhere; but they shall have the right to hunt on the unoccupied lands of the United States so long as game may be found thereon, and so long as peace subsists among the whites and Indians on the borders of the hunting districts.

ARTICLE 5. The United States agrees that the agent for said Indians shall in the future make his home at the agency building on the Shoshonee reservation,

Plains, West and Northwest Plateau Indian Treaties

but shall direct and supervise affairs on the Ban-hack reservation; and shall keep an office open at all times for the purpose of prompt and diligent inquiry into such matters of complaint by and against the Indians as may be presented for investigation under the provisions of their treaty stipulations, as also for the faithful discharge of other duties enjoined by law. In all cases of depredation on person or property he shall cause the evidence to be taken in writing and forwarded, together with his finding, to the Commissioner of Indian Affairs, whose decision shall be binding on the parties to this treaty.

ARTICLE 6. If any individual belonging to said tribes of Indians, or legally incorported with them, being the head of a family, shall desire to commence farming, he shall have the privilege to select, in the presence and with the assistance of the agent then in charge, a tract of land within the reservation of his tribe, not exceeding three hundred and twenty acres in extent, which tract so selected, certified, and recorded in the "land-book," as herein directed, shall cease to be held in common, but the same may be occupied and held in the exclusive possession of the person selecting it, and of his family, so long as he or they may continue to cultivate it.

Any person over eighteen years of age, not being the head of a family, may in like manner select and cause to be certified to him or her, for purposes of cultivation, a quantity of land not exceeding eighty acres in extent, and thereupon be entitled to the exclusive possession of the same as above described. For each tract of land so selected a certificate, containing a description thereof, and the name of the person selecting it, with a certificate indorsed thereon that the same has been recorded, shall be delivered to the party entitled to it by the agent, after the same shall have been recorded by him in a book to be kept in his office subject to inspection, which said book shall be known as the "Shoshone (eastern band) and Bannack land-book."

The President may at any time order a survey of these reservations, and when so surveyed Congress shall provide for protecting the rights of the Indian settlers in these improvements, and may fix the character of the title held by each. The United States may pass such laws on the subject of alienation and descent of property as between Indians, and on all subjects connected with the government of the Indians on said reservations, and the internal police thereof, as may be thought proper.

ARTICLE 7. In order to insure the civilization of the tribes entering into this treaty, the necessity of education is admitted, especially of such of them as are or may be settled on said agricultural reservations, and they therefore pledge themselves to compel their children, male and female, between the ages of six and sixteen years, to attend school; and it is hereby made the duty of the agent for said Indians to see that this stipulation is strictly complied with; and the United States agrees that for every thirty children between said ages who can

Plains, West and Northwest Plateau Indian Treaties

be induced or compelled to attend school, a house shall be provided and a teacher competent to teach the elementary branches of an English education shall be furnished, who will reside among said Indians and faithfully discharge his or her duties as a teacher. The provisions of this article to continue for twenty years.

ARTICLE 8. When the head of a family or lodge shall have selected lands and received his certificate as above directed, and the agent shall be satisfied that he intends in good faith to commence cultivating the soil for a living, he shall be entitled to receive seeds and agricultural implements for the first year, in value one hundred dollars, and for each succeeding year he shall continue to farm, for a period of three years more, he shall be entitled to receive seeds and implements as aforesaid in value twenty-five dollars per annum.

And it is further stipulated that such persons as commence farming shall receive instructions from the farmers herein provided for, and whenever more than one hundred persons on either reservation shall enter upon the cultivation of the soil, a second blacksmith shall be provided, with such iron, steel, and other material as may be required.

ARTICLE 9. In lieu of all sums of money or other annuities provided to be paid to the Indians herein named, under any and all treaties heretofore made with them, the United States agrees to deliver at the agency-house on the reservation herein provided for, on the first day of September of each year, for thirty years, the following articles, to wit:

For each male person over fourteen years of age, a suit of good substantial woollen clothing, consisting of coat, hat, pantaloons, flannel shirt, and a pair of woollen socks; for each female over twelve years of age, a flannel skirt, or the goods necessary to make it, a pair of woollen hose, twelve yards of calico; and twelve yards of cotton domestics.

For the boys and girls under the ages named, such flannel and cotton goods as may be needed to make each a suit as aforesaid, together with a pair of woollen hose for each.

And in order that the Commissioner of Indian Affairs may be able to estimate properly for the articles herein named, it shall be the duty of the agent each year to forward to him a full and exact census of the Indians, on which the estimate from year to year can be based; and in addition to the clothing herein named, the sum of ten dollars shall be annually appropriated for each Indian roaming and twenty dollars for each Indian engaged in agriculture, for a period of ten years, to be used by the Secretary of the Interior in the purchase of such articles as from time to time the condition and necessities of the Indians may indicate to be proper.

584

Plains, West and Northwest Plateau Indian Treaties

And if at any time within the ten years it shah appear that the amount of money needed for clothing under this article can be appropriated to better uses for the tribes herein named, Congress may by law change the appropriation to other purposes; but in no event shall the amount of this appropriation be withdrawn or discontinued for the period named. And the President shall annually detail an officer of the Army to be present and attest the delivery of all the goods herein named to the Indians, and he shall inspect and report on the quantity and quality of the goods and the manner of their delivery.

ARTICLE 10. The United States hereby agrees to furnish annually to the Indians the physician, teachers, carpenter, miller, engineer, farmer, and blacksmith, as herein contemplated, and that such appropriations shall be made from time to time, on the estimates of the Secretary of the Interior, as will be sufficient to employ such persons.

ARTICLE 11. No treaty for the cession of any portion of the reservations herein described which may be held in common shall be of any force or validity as against the said Indians, unless executed and signed by at least a majority of all the adult male Indians occupying or interested in the same; and no cession by the tribe shall be understood or construed in such manner as to deprive without his consent, any individual member of the tribe of his right to any tract of land selected by him, as provided in Article 6 of this treaty.

ARTICLE 12. It is agreed that the sum of five hundred dollars annually, for three years from the date when they commence to cultivate a farm, shall be expended in presents to the ten persons of said tribe who, in the judgment of the agent, may grow the most valuable crops for the respective year.

ARTICLE 13. It is further agreed that until such time as the agency-buildings are established on the Shoshonee reservation, their agent shall reside at Fort Bridger, U. T., and their annuities shall be delivered to them at the same place in June of each year.

N. G. Taylor, W. T. Sherman, Lieutenant-General, Wm. S. HarLey, John B. Sanborn, S. F. Tappan, C. C. Augur, Brevet Major-General, U. S. Army, Commissioners, Alfred H. Terry, Brigadier-General and Brevet Major-General, U. S. Army.

Attest:
A. S. H. White, Secretary.

Shoshones:

Plains, West and Northwest Plateau Indian Treaties

Wash-a-kie, his x mark, Wau-ny-pitz, his x mark, Toop-se-po-wot, his x mark, Nar-kok, his x mark, Taboonshe-ya, his x mark, Bazeel, his x mark, Pan-to-she-ga, his x mark, Ninny-Bitse, his x mark,
Bannacks:
Taggee, his x mark, Tay-to-ba, his x mark, We-rat-ze-won-a-gen, his x mark, Coo-sha-gan, his x mark, Pan-sook-a-motse, his x mark, A-wite-etse, his x mark,

Witnesses:
Henry A. Morrow, Lieutenant-Colonel Thirty-sixth Infantry and Brevet Colonel U. S. Army, Commanding Fort Bridger, Luther Manpa, United States Indian agent, W. A. Carter, J. Van Allen Carter, interpreter.

TREATY WITH THE NEZ PERCÉS {1868, Aug. 13}
Ratified Feb. 16, 1869.
Proclaimed Feb. 24, 1869.

Whereas certain amendments are desired by the Nez Percé tribe of Indians to their treaty concluded at the council ground in the valley of the Lapwai, in the Territory of Washington, on the ninth day of June, in the year of our Lord one thousand eight hundred and sixty-three; and whereas the United States are willing to assent to said amendments; it is therefore agreed by and between Nathaniel G. Taylor, commissioner, on the part of the United States, thereunto duly authorized, and Lawyer, Timothy, and Jason, chiefs of said tribe, also being thereunto duly authorized, in manner and form following, that is to say:

ARTICLE 1. That all lands embraced within the limits of the tract set apart for the exclusive use and benefit of said Indians by the 2d article of said treaty of June 9th, 1863, which are susceptible of cultivation and suitable for Indian farms, which are not now occupied by the United States for military purposes, or which are not required for agency or other buildings and purposes provided for by existing treaty stipulations, shall be surveyed as provided in the 3d article of said treaty of June 9th, 1863, and as soon as the allotments shall be plowed and fenced, and as soon as schools shall be established as provided by existing treaty stipulations, such Indians now residing outside the reservation as may be decided upon by the agent of the tribe and the Indians themselves, shall be removed to and located upon allotments within the reservation: Provided, however, That in case there should not be a sufficient quantity of suitable land within the boundaries of the reservation to provide allotments for those now there and those residing outside the boundaries of the same, then those residing outside, or as many thereof as allotments cannot be provided for, may remain upon the lands now occupied and improved by them, provided, that the land so occupied does not exceed twenty acres for each and every male person who shall have attained the age of twenty-one years or is the head of a family, and

586

Plains, West and Northwest Plateau Indian Treaties

the tenure of those remaining upon lands outside the reservation shall be the same as is provided in said 3d article of said treaty of June 9th, 1863, for those receiving allotments within the reservation; and it is further agreed that those now residing outside of the boundaries of the reservation and who may continue to so reside shall be protected by the military authorities in their rights upon the allotments occupied by them, and also in the privilege of grazing their animals upon surrounding unoccupied lands.

ARTICLE 2. It is further agreed between the parties hereto that the stipulations contained in the 8th article of the treaty of June 9th, 1863, relative to timber, are hereby annulled as far as the same provides that the United States shall be permitted to use thereof in the maintaining of forts or garrisons, and that the said Indians shall have the aid of the military authorities to protect the timber upon their reservation, and that none of the same shall be cut or removed without the consent of the head-chief of the tribe, together with the consent of the agent and superintendent of Indian affairs, first being given in writing, which written consent shall state the part of the reservation upon which the timber is to be cut, and also the quantity, and the price to be paid therefor.

ARTICLE 3. It is further hereby stipulated and agreed that the amount due said tribe for school purposes and for the support of teachers that has not been expended for that purpose since the year 1864, but has been used for other purposes, shall be ascertained and the same shall be re-imbursed to said tribe by appropriation by Congress, and shall be set apart and invested in United States bonds and shall be held in trust by the United States, the interest on the same to be paid to said tribe annually for the support of teachers.

In testimony whereof the said Commissioner on the part of the United States and the said chiefs representing said Nez Percé tribe of Indians have hereunto set their hands and seals this 13th day of August, in the year of our Lord one thousand eight hundred and sixty-eight, at the city of Washington, D.C.

N. G. Taylor, Commissioner Indian Affairs.

Lawyer, Head Chief Nez Percés, Timothy, his x mark, Chief, Jason, his x mark, Chief,

In presence of:
Charles E. Mix,
Robert Newell, United States Agent.
W. R. Irwin.

Plains, West and Northwest Plateau Indian Treaties

AMENDED AGREEMENT WITH CERTAIN SIOUX INDIANS
{1873, May 2}

Ratified by acts of Feb. 14, 1873 (17 Stat., 456), and June 24, 1874 (18 Stat., 167). Indian office, Sisseton S. 128, and I. 355 (1873).

WHEREAS, the Sisseton and Wahpeton Bands of Dakota or Sioux Indians, on the 20th day of September A. D. 1872 made and entered into an agreement in writing, signed on one part by the Chiefs and headmen of said bands, with the assent and approval of the members of (said) bands, and upon the other part by Moses N. Adams, James Smith, jr., and William. H. Forbes, commissioners on the part of the United States; which said agreement is as follows, to wit:

"Whereas, the Sisseton and Wahpeton bands of Dakota or Sioux Indians made and concluded a treaty with the United States, at the city of Washington, D. C., on the 19th day of February, A. D. 1867, which was ratified, with certain amendments, by the Senate of the United States on the 15th day of April, 1867, and finally promulgated by the President of the United States on the 2d day of May, in the year aforesaid, by which the Sisseton and Wahpeton bands of Sioux Indians ceded to the United States certain privileges and rights supposed to belong to said bands in the territory described in article 2 of said treaty, and

"Whereas, it is desirable that all said territory, except the portion thereof comprised in what is termed the permanent reservations, particularly described in articles 3 and 4 of said treaty, shall be ceded absolutely to the United States, upon such consideration as in justice and equity should be paid therefor by the United States; and

"Whereas, said territory, now proposed to be ceded, is no longer available to said Indians for the purposes of the chase, and such value or consideration is essentially necessary in order to enable said bands interested therein to cultivate portions of said permanent reservations, and become wholly self-supporting by the cultivation of the soil and other pursuits of husbandry; therefore, the said bands, represented in said treaty, and parties thereto, by their chiefs and headmen, now assembled in council, do propose to M. N. Adams, William H. Forbes, and James Smith, jr., commissioners on behalf of the United States, as follows:

"First. To cede, sell, and relinquish to the United States all their right, title, and interest in and to all lands and territory, particularly described in article 2 of said treaty, as well as all lands in the Territory of Dakota to which they have title or interest, excepting the said tracts particularly described and bounded in articles 3 and 4 of said treaty, which last named tracts and territory are expressly reserved as permanent reservations for occupancy and cultivation, as contemplated by articles 8, 9, and 10 of said treaty.

Plains, West and Northwest Plateau Indian Treaties

"Second. That, in consideration of said cession and relinquishment, the United States shall advance and pay, annually, for the term of ten years from and after the acceptance by the United States of the proposition herein submitted, eighty thousand (80,000) dollars, to be expended under the direction of the President of the United States, on the plan and in accordance with the provisions of the treaty aforesaid, dated February 19, 1867, for goods and provisions, for the erection of manual-labor and public school-houses, and for the support of manual-labor and public schools, and in the erection of mills, blacksmith-shops, and other work-shops, and to aid in opening farms, breaking land, and fencing the same, and in furnishing agricultural implements, oxen, and milch-cows, and such other beneficial objects as may be deemed most conducive to the prosperity and happiness of the Sisseton and Wahpeton bands of Dakota or Sioux Indians entitled thereto according to the said treaty of February 19, 1867.

" Such annual appropriation or consideration to be apportioned to the Sisseton and Devil's Lake agencies, in proportion to the number of Indians of the said bands located upon the Lake Traverse and Devil's Lake reservations respectively. Such apportionment to be made upon the basis of the annual reports or returns of the agents in charge. Said consideration, amounting, in the aggregate, to eight hundred thousand (800,000) dollars, payable as aforesaid, without interest.

"Third. As soon as may be, the said territory embraced within said reservation described in article 4, (Devil's Lake reservation) shall be surveyed, as Government lands are surveyed, for the purpose of enabling the Indians entitled to acquire permanent rights in the soil, as contemplated by article V of said treaty.
"Fourth. We respectfully request that, in case the foregoing propositions are favorably entertained by the United States, the sale of spirituous liquors upon the territory ceded may be wholly prohibited by the United States Government.

"Fifth. The provisions of article V of the treaty of February 19, 1867, to be modified as follows: An occupancy and cultivation of five acres, upon any particular location, for a term of five consecutive years, shall entitle the party to a patent for forty acres; a like occupancy and cultivation of ten acres, to entitle the party to eighty acres; and a like occupancy and cultivation of any tract, to the extent of twenty acres, shall entitle the party so occupying and cultivating to a patent for 160 acres of land. Parties who have already selected farms and cultivated the same, may be entitled to the benefit of this modification. Patents so issued, (as hereinbefore set forth) shall authorize a transfer or alienation of such lands situate within the Sisseton agency, after the expiration of ten years from this date, and within the Devil's Lake reservation after the expiration of fifteen years, but not sooner.

"Fifth (sixth). The consideration to be paid, as hereinbefore proposed, is in addition to the provisions of Article VI of the treaty of February 19, 1867, under

Plains, West and Northwest Plateau Indian Treaties

which Congress shall appropriate from time to time, such an amount as may be required to meet the necessities of said Indians to enable them to become civilized.

"Sixth (seventh). Sections sixteen and thirty-six within the reservations shall be set apart for educational purposes, and all children of a suitable age within either reservation shall be compelled to attend school at the discretion of the agents.

"Seventh (eighth). At the expiration of ten years from this date, all members of said bands, under the age of twenty-one years shall receive forty acres of land from said permanent reservations in fee simple.

"Eighth (ninth). At the expiration of ten years, the President of the United States shall sell or dispose of all the remaining or unoccupied lands in the lake Traverse reservation, (excepting that which may hereafter be set apart for school purposes;) the proceeds of the sale of such lands to be expended for the benefit of the members of said bands located on said Lake Traverse; and, at the expiration of fifteen years, the President shall sell or dispose of all the remaining unoccupied lands (excepting that which may hereafter be set apart for school purposes) in the Devil's Lake reservation; the proceeds of the sales of such lands shall be expended for the benefit of all members of said bands who may be located on the said Devil's Lake reservation.

"Executed at Sisseton Agency, Dakota Territory, Lake Traverse reservation, this 20th day of September, A. D. 1872.

And whereas, the Congress of the United States, upon consideration of the provisions of said agreement hereinbefore recited, did, by the act making appropriations for the current and contingent expenses of the Indian department, and for fulfilling treaty stipulations with various Indian tribes, for the year ending June thirtieth, eighteen hundred and seventy-four, and for other purposes, approved February 14th, 1873, provide as follows, to wit: "For this amount, being the first of ten installments of the sum of eight hundred thousand dollars named in a certain agreement made by the commissioners appointed by the Secretary of the Interior, under the provisions of the act of June seventh, eighteen hundred and seventy-two, with the Sisseton and Wahpeton bands of Sioux Indians for the relinquishment by said Indians of their claim to, or interest in, the lands described in the second article of the treaty made with them February nineteenth, eighteen hundred and sixty-seven: the same to be expended under the direction of the President, for the benefit of said Indians, in the manner prescribed in said treaty of eighteen hundred and sixty-seven, as amended by the Senate, eighty thousand dollars.

And the said agreement is hereby confirmed, excepting so much thereof as is included in paragraphs numbered respectively, third, fourth, fifth, sixth, sev-

Plains, West and Northwest Plateau Indian Treaties

enth, eighth, and ninth: Provided, That no part of this amount shall be expended until after the ratification, by said Indians, of said agreement as hereby amended."

And whereas, the said Bands of Dakota or Sioux Indians have been duly assembled in council, and therein represented by the chiefs and head-men, and the provisions of said act of Congress, and amendments thereby made to the said above recited agreement, having been fully explained by the commissioners on the part of the United States, and the said agreement as amended having been fully interpreted, and now being understood, we the said chiefs and head-men of the said Sisseton and Wahpeton Bands, duly authorized by our people so to do, do hereby accept, assent to, confirm, ratify and agree to the said amendments, and to the said agreement as amended, and declare that the same is, and shall hereafter be binding upon us and the members of said Bands.

Witness our hands and seals at the Lac Traverse agency, Dakota Territory, this second day of May, A. D. 1873.

Gabriell Renville.

Wamdienpiduta, his x mark, Taeandupahotanka, his x mark, Wieanspinupa, Kampeska, his x mark, Simon Anawagmani, his x mark, John R. Renvill, Daniel Renville, Taokiyeota, his x mark, Mechael Paul, John Waniyarpeya, his x mark, Robert Hopkins.

We certify, on honor, that we were present and witnessed the signatures of the Indians as above.
Jno. L. Hodgman, Charles P. La Grange.

I hereby certify, on honor, that I have fully explained to the Indians in council, the above instrument, and that the Indians acknowledged the same to be well understood by them.
Thos. A Robertson, Interpreter.

Executed at Sisseton agency, Lake Traverse Reservation, D. T., this second day of May, 1873.
Mosess N. Adams, James Smith, jr. Commissioners.

Devil's Lake Reservation, Fort Totten agency, D. T., May 19, 1873.
Wah-na-ta, his x mark, Tee-oh-wash-tag, his x mark, Mah-pee-ah-keo-den, his x mark, E-ehah-na-gee-kah, his x mark, Mat-te-o-he-ehat-kah, his x mark, Ous(e)-pe-ka-ge, his x mark, Chan-te-ma-za, his x mark, Ca-do-ze, his x mark, Wa-kin-yan-ro-ta, his x mark, I-car-ta-ke, his x mark, In-im-u-sa-pa, his x mark, Mu-i-ya,to-ho-nax-te, his x mark, Ton-wau-non-pa, his x mark, Ma-ka-i-de-ya, his x mark, Xip-to, his x mark, Wa-ka-no-ki-ta, his x mark, Ta-te-o-pax-

591

Plains, West and Northwest Plateau Indian Treaties

im-a-ni, his x mark, Ru-pahn-wa-kam-a, his x mark, A-ki-ci-ta-du-ta, his x mark, Ta-wa-cin-ha, his x mark, Ru-pahu-wax-te, his x mark, Ri-o-in-yan-i-yan-ke, his x mark, Ran-in-wan-ke, his x mark, A-ki-ci-tam-a-ne, his x mark, Maza-ka-hom-ni, Wam-di-hi-ye-ya, his x mark,
Wi-cer-pi-wa-kan-na, his x mark, Wax-i-em-u-nape-wu-az-u-za, his x mark, Ha-oih-da, his x mark, Wam-di-o-ki-ga, his x.mark

Witnesses to signatures of above chiefs and soldiers, Lewis Cass Hunt, Lieut. Col. 20th Infantry.
James B. Ferguson, Act. Asst. Surgeon, U. S. A.

I hereby certify, upon honor, that I have fully explained to the Indians the above instrument and that the Indians acknowledge the same to be well understood by them.
George H. Faribault, Interpreter.

Executed at the Fort Totten agency, "Devil's Lake" reservation, this 19th day of May, 1873, in open council, by the Sisseton and Wahpeton and "Cut-Head" bands of Sioux not included in the Sisseton and Wahpeton bands of Sioux of "Lac Travers" reservation, who signed this, on the 2nd of May, 1873, as above written.
James Smith, Jr., Wm. H. Forbes, Moses N. Adams, Commissioners.

AGREEMENT WITH THE ROGUE RIVER {1853, Sept. }
Indian OfficeOregon, 1844-1858, Ore. Supt. L., 323.

Stipulations of a treaty of peace made and entered into by Joseph Lane Commanding forces of Oregon Territory, and Joe, principal Chief of the Rogue River tribe of Indians, Sam, Subordinate Chief and Jim, Subordinate Chief, on the part of the tribes under their jurisdiction.

ARTICLE 1. A treaty of peace having this day been entered into between the above named parties whereby it is agreed that all the bands of Indians living within the following boundaries to wit, commencing just below the mouth of Applegate Creek, on Rogue River, thence to the highlands which divide Applegate from Althouse creek, thence with said highlands Southeasterly to the summit of the Siskiou mountains, thence easterly along said range to the Pilot Rock, thence northeasterly following the range of mountains to Mount Pitt, thence northerly to Rogue River, thence northwesterly to the head waters of Jump-off-Joe, thence down this stream to a point due north from the mouth of Applegate Creek, thence to the mouth of Applegate Creek shall cease hostilities, and that all the property taken by them from the whites, in battle or otherwise shall be given up either to Genl. Lane or the Indian Agent

Plains, West and Northwest Plateau Indian Treaties

The Chiefs further stipulate to maintain peace and promptly deliver up to the Indian Agent for trial and punishment any one of their people who may in any way disturb the friendly relations this day entered into, by stealing property of any description or in any way interfering with the persons or property of the whites, and shall also be responsible for the amount of the property so destroyed

ARTICLE 2. It is stipulated by the Chiefs that all the different bands of Indians now residing in the Territory above described shall hereafter reside in the place to be set apart for them.

ARTICLE 3. It is further stipulated that all fire arms belonging to the Indians of the above named bands, shall be delivered to Gen. Lane, or to the Agent, for a fair consideration to be paid in blankets, clothing, &c., except Joe, principal Chief, seven guns, for hunting purposes, Sam, Subordinate Chief, five guns, Jim Subordinate Chief five guns.

ARTICLE 4. It is further stipulated, that when their right to the above described country is purchased from the Indians by the United States, a portion of the purchase money shall be reserved to pay for the property of the whites destroyed by them during the war, not exceeding fifteen thousand dollars.

ARTICLE 5. It is further stipulated that in case the above named Indians shall hereafter make war upon the whites, they shall forfeit all right to the annuities or money to be paid for the right to their lands.

ARTICLE 6. It is further stipulated, that whenever any Indians shall enter the Territory above described for the purpose of committing hostilities against the whites the chiefs above named shall immediately give information to the Agent, and shall render such other assistance as may be in their power.

ARTICLE 7. An Agent shall reside near the above named Indians to enforce the above stipulations, to whom all complaints of injuries to the Indians shall be made through their Chiefs.

Signed this 8th day of September 1853.

Joseph Lane, Joe, his x mark, Aps-er-ka-har, Principal Chief, Sam, his x mark, To-qua-he-ar Subordinate Chief, Jim, his x mark, Ana-chak-a-rah Subordinate Chief.

Witnesses:
C. B. Gray, interpreter R. B. Metcal, Y. Y. Turney, Sec.

Plains, West and Northwest Plateau Indian Treaties

AGREEMENT AT FORT BERTHOLD {1866, July 27}
Oregon Indian Office, "Treaties, box 3, 1864-1866."

Articles of agreement and convention made and concluded at Fort Berthold in the Territory of Dakota, on the twenty-seventh day of July, in the year of our Lord one thousand eight hundred and sixty-six, by and between Newton Edmunds, governor and ex-officio superintendent of Indian affairs of Dakota Territory; Major General S.R. Curtis Orrin Guernsey and Henry W. Reed, commissioners appointed on the part of the United States to make treaties with the Indians of the Upper Missouri; and the chiefs and headmen of the Arickaree tribe of Indians, Witnesseth as follows:

ARTICLE 1ST. Perpetual peace, friendship, and amity shall hereafter exist between the United States and the said Arickaree Indians.

ARTICLE 2D. The said Arickaree tribe of Indians promise and agree that they will maintain peaceful and friendly relations toward the whites; that they will in future, abstain from all hostilities against each other, and cultivate mutual good will and friendship, not only among themselves, but toward all other friendly tribes of Indians.

ARTICLE 3. The chiefs and headmen aforesaid acting as the representatives of the tribe aforesaid and being duly authorized and hereunto directed, in consideration of the payments and privileges hereinafter stated, do hereby grant and convey to the United States the right to lay out and construct roads, highways, and telegraphs through their country, and to use their efforts to prevent them from annoyance or interruption by their own or other tribes of Indians.

ARTICLE 4. No white person, unless in the employ of the United States, or duly licensed to trade with said Indians, or members of the families of such persons shall be permitted to reside or make settlement upon any part of the country belonging to said Indians, not included or described herein; nor shall said Indians sell, alienate, or in any manner dispose of any portion thereof, except to the United States.

ARTICLE 5. The said Aricara tribe of Indians hereby acknowledge their dependence on the United States and their obligation to obey the laws thereof; and they further agree and obligate themselves to submit to and obey such laws as may be made by Congress for their government and the punishment of offenders; and they agree to exert themselves to the utmost of their ability in enforcing all the laws under the superintendent of Indian affairs, or agent; and they pledge and bind themselves to preserve friendly relations with the citizens of the United States, and commit no injuries to, or depredations upon, their persons or property.

594

Plains, West and Northwest Plateau Indian Treaties

They also agree to deliver to the proper officer or officers of the United States, all offenders against the treaties, laws, or regulations of the United States, and to assist in discovering, pursuing and capturing all such offenders who may be within the limits of the country claimed by them, whenever required so to do by such officer or officers. And the said Aricara tribe of Indians further agree that they will not make war upon any other tribe or band of Indians, except in self-defence, but will submit all matters of difference between themselves and other Indians to the Government of the United States for adjustment, and will abide thereby; and if any of the Indians, party to this treaty, commit depredations upon any other Indians within the jurisdiction of the United States, the same rule shall prevail with regard to compensation and punishment as in cases of depredations against citizens of the United States.

ARTICLE 6. In consideration of the great evil of intemperance among some of the Indian tribes, and in order to prevent such consequences among ourselves, we, the said Aricara tribe of Indians agree to do all in our power to prevent the introduction or use of spirituous liquors among our people, and to this end we agree that should any of the members of our tribe encourage the use of spiritu-ous liquors, either by using it themselves, or buying and selling it, whosoever shall do so shall forfeit his claim to any annuities paid by the Government for the current year; or should they be aware of such use or sale or introduction of liquor into their country, either by whites or by persons of Indian blood and not aid by all proper means to effect its extermination and the prosecution of of-fenders, shall be liable to the forfeiture above mentioned.

ARTICLE 7. In consideration of the foregoing agreements, stipulations, ces-sions, and undertakings and of their faithful observance by the said Aricara tribe of Indians, the United States agree to expend for the said Indians, in addi-tion to the goods and provisions distributed at the time of signing this treaty, the sum of ten thousand dollars annually for twenty years, after the ratification of this treaty by the President and Senate of the United States, to be expended in such goods, provisions, and other articles as the President may in his discre-tion, from time to time determine; provided, and it is hereby agreed that the President may, at his discretion, annually expend so much of the sum of three thousand dollars as he shall deem proper, in the purchase of stock, animals, ag-ricultural implements, in establishing and instructing in agricultural and me-chanical pursuits, such of said Indians as shall be disposed thereto; and in the employment of mechanics for them, in educating their children, in providing necessary and proper medicines, medical attendance, care for and support of the aged, sick, and infirm of their number, for the helpless orphans of said Indi-ans, and in any other respect promoting their civilizations, comfort, and im-provement; provided further, that the President of the United States may, at his discretion determine in what proportion the said annuities shall be distributed among said Indians; and the United States further agree that out of the sum above stipulated to be paid to said Indians.

Plains, West and Northwest Plateau Indian Treaties

There shall be set apart and paid to the head-chief, the sum of two hundred dollars annually, and to the soldier-chiefs, fifty dollars annually in money or supplies, so long as they and their bands remain faithful to their treaty obligations; and for and in consideration of the long continued and faithful services of Pierre Garreau to the Indians of the aforesaid tribe, and his efforts for their benefit, the United States agree to give him, out of the annuities to said tribe, the sum of two hundred dollars annually, being the same amount as is paid the head chiefs as aforesaid; and also to the eight leading men presented by the said tribe as the headmen and advisers of the principal chiefs, and to their successors in orifice, the sum of fifty dollars per annum, so long as they remain faithful to their treaty obligations; and provided that the President may, at his discretion, vary the amount paid to the chiefs, if in his judgment there may be either by the fidelity or efficiency of any of said chiefs sufficient cause; yet not so as to change the aggregate amount.

ARTICLE 8. It is understood and agreed by the parties to this treaty, that if any of the bands of Indians, parties hereto, shall violate any of the agreements, stipulations, or obligations herein contained, the United States may withhold, for such length of time as the President may determine, any portion or all the annuities agreed to be paid to said Indians under the provisions of this treaty.

ARTICLE 9. The annuities of the aforesaid Indians shall not be taken to pay the debts of individuals, but satisfaction for depredations committed by them shall be made in such manner as the President may direct.

ARTICLE 10. This treaty shall be obligatory upon the aforesaid tribe of Indians from the date hereof, and upon the United States so soon as the same shall be ratified by the President and Senate.

ARTICLE 11. Any amendment or modification of this treaty by the Senate of the United States, not materially changing the nature or obligation of the same, shall be considered final and binding on said bands the same as if it had been subsequently presented and agreed to by the said chiefs and headmen, in open council.

In testimony whereof the aforesaid commissioners on the part of the United States, and the chiefs and headmen of the aforementioned tribe of Indians, have hereunto set their hands this twenty-seventh day of July, in the year of our Lord one thousand eight hundred and sixty-six, after the contents thereof had been previously read, interpreted, and explained.

Newton Edmunds, S. R. Curtis, Orrin Guernsey, Henry W. Reed.

Plains, West and Northwest Plateau Indian Treaties

White Shield, his x mark, Iron Bear, his x mark, The Son of the Star, or Rushing Bear, his x mark, The Black Trail, his x mark, The Wolf Necklace, his x mark, The one that comes out first, his x mark, The Whistling Bear, his x mark, The Yellow Knife, his x mark, The Bear of the Woods, his x mark, The Dog Chief, his x mark, Headmen: White Cow Chief, his x mark, The Walking Wolf, his x mark, The White Bear, his x mark, The Bully Head, his mark, The Young Wolf, his x mark, The Short Tail Bull, his x mark, The Lone Horse, his x mark, The War Eagle Cap, his x mark, The Sitting Night, his x mark, The Yellow Wolf, his x mark, The Old Bear, his x mark, The Brave, his x mark, The Big Head, his x mark, The Elk River, his x mark, Mahlon Wilkinson, agent, Reuben S. Pike.

U. S. Interpreters: Pierre Garreau, his x mark, Charles Papin, Charles Larpenteur.

Signed by the commissioners on the part of the United States, and by the chiefs and headmen, after the treaty had been fully read, interpreted, and explained in our presence.
Chas. A. Reed, Secy. of Commission.
M. K. Armstrong, Assist. Secty.

ADDENDA.
The chiefs and headmen of the Gros Ventres and Mandan tribes, heretofore long associated with the Arickarees named in the foregoing treaty, and anxious to continue their residence in the same community and perpetuate their friendly relations with the Arickarees and the United States, do concur in, and become parties and participants in and to all the stipulations of the foregoing treaty.

And it being made known to all the tribes thus associated that the United States may desire to connect a line of stages with the river, at the salient angle thereof about thirty miles below this point, and may desire to establish settlements and convenient supplies and mechanical structures to accommodate the growing commerce and travel, by land and river, the chiefs and headmen of the Arickarees, Gros Ventres, and Mandans, acting and uniting also with the commissioners of the United States aforesaid, do hereby convey to the United States all their right and title to the following lands, situated on the northeast side of the Missouri River, to wit: Beginning on the Missouri River at the mouth of Snake River, about thirty miles below Ft. Berthold; thence up Snake River and in a northeast direction twenty-five miles; thence southwardly parallel to the Missouri River to a point opposite and twenty-five miles east of old Ft. Clarke;

Thence west to a point on the Missouri River opposite to old Ft. Clarke; thence up the Missouri River to the place of beginning: Provided, That the premises here named shall not be a harbor for Sioux or other Indians when they are hos-

Plains, West and Northwest Plateau Indian Treaties

tile to the tribes, parties to this treaty; but it shall be the duty of the United States to protect and defend these tribes in the lawful occupation of their homes, and in the enjoyment of their civil rights, as the white people are protected in theirs.

ARTICLE 2. It is also agreed by the three tribes aforesaid, now united in this treaty as aforesaid, that in consideration of the premises named in the aforesaid treaty, and the further consideration of the cession of lands at Snake River, in addition to the payments by the United States of annuities there named to the Arickarees, there shall be paid five thousand dollars to the Gros Ventres, and five thousand dollars to the Mandans, annually, in goods, at the discretion of the President. And for the Gros Ventres and Mandan tribes twenty per cent. of their annuity may be expended for agricultural, mechanical, and other purposes as specified in the latter clause of Article Seven of the aforesaid treaty.

And also out of the aforesaid annuity to the Gros Ventres there shall be paid to the first, or principal chief, the sum of two hundred dollars each, annually, and to the six soldier chiefs the sum of fifty dollars each, annually.

There shall also be paid to the head, or principal chief, of the Mandans, out of the annuities of said tribe, the sum of two hundred dollars, annually, and to each of the nine soldier chiefs the sum of fifty dollars, annually.

In testimony whereof the aforesaid commissioners on the part of the United States, and the chiefs and headmen of the aforementioned tribes of Indians, have hereunto set their hands this twenty-seventh day of July, in the year of our Lord one thousand eight hundred and sixty-six, after the contents thereof had been previously read, interpreted, and explained to the chiefs and headmen of the aforementioned tribes.

Newton Edmunds, S. R. Curtis, Orrin Guernsey, Herny W. Reed.

Signatures of Arickarees:
White Shield, Head Chief, his x mark, Rushing Bear, Second Chief, his x mark, Wolf Necklace, Chief, his x mark, Bear of the woods, Chief, his x mark, Whistling Bear, Chief, his x mark, Iron Bear, Soldier C., his x mark, Black trail, Second Chief, his x mark, The Two Bears, Chief, his x mark, The Yellow Knife, Chief, his x mark, The Crow Chief, Chief, his x mark,

Gros Ventres Chiefs:
Crow Breast, Head Chief, his x mark, Poor Wolf, Second Chief, his x mark, Red Tail, his x mark, The War Chief, his x mark, Short Tail Bull, his x mark, One whose mouth rubbed with cherries, his x mark, The Yellow Shirt, his x mark,

598

Plains, West and Northwest Plateau Indian Treaties

Chief Soldiers:
The Flying Crow, his x mark, The Many Antelope, his x mark, One who eats no marrow, his x mark,

Mandan Chiefs:
The Red Cow, his x mark, The Running Eagle, his x mark, The Big Turtle, his x mark, The Scabby Wolf, his x mark, The Crazy Chief, his x mark, The Crow Chief, his x mark,

Chief Soldiers:
One who strikes in the back, his x mark,

Signed by the commissioners on the part of the United States, and by the chiefs and headmen after the treaty had been fully read, interpreted and explained in our presence.

Witnesses to the above signatures:
Chas. A. Reed, Secty. of Commission, Mahlon Wilkinson, Agent, M. K. Armstrong, Asst. Secy, Reuben S. Pike.

U. S. interpreters:
Charles Reader, C. F. Picotte, Charles Larpenteur, Pierre Garreau, his x mark, Charles Papin.

AGREEMENT WITH THE SISSETON AND WAHPETON BANDS OF SIOUX {1872, September 20} Unratified.

Indian Office, Sisseton, S. 247 (1872).
See 1874, c. 389, 18 Stat., 167.

Whereas, the Sisseton and Wahpeton bands of Dakota or Sioux Indians made and concluded a treaty with the United States, at the city of Washington, D.C., on the 19th day of February, A. D. 1867, which was ratified, with certain amendments, by the Senate of the United States on the 15th day of April, 1868, and finally promulgated by the President of the United States on the 2d day of May, in the year aforesaid, by which the Sisseton and Wahpeton bands of Sioux Indians ceded to the United States certain privileges and rights supposed to belong to said bands in the territory described in article two (2) of said treaty, and Whereas, it is desirable that all said territory, except the portion thereof comprised in what is termed the permanent reservations, particularly described in articles three (3) and four (4) of said treaty, shall be ceded absolutely to the United States, upon such consideration as in justice and equity should be paid therefor by the United States

599

Plains, West and Northwest Plateau Indian Treaties

And, Whereas, said territory, now proposed to be ceded, is no longer available to said Indians for the purposes of the chase, and such value or consideration is essentially necessary in order too enable said bands interested therein to cultivate portions of said permanent reservations, and become wholly self-supporting by the cultivation of the soil and other pursuits of husbandry: therefore, the said bands, represented in said treaty, and parties thereto, by their chiefs and head-men, now assembled in council, do propose to M. N. Adams, William H. Forbes, and James Smith, jr., commissioners on behalf of the United States, as follows:

First. To cede, sell, and relinquish to the United States all their right, title, and interest in and to all lands and territory, particularly described in article two (2)of said treaty, as well as all lands in the Territory of Dakota to which they have title or interest, excepting the said tracts particularly described and bounded in articles three (3) and four (4) of said treaty, which last-named tracts and territory are expressly reserved as permanent reservations for occupancy and cultivation, as contemplated by articles eight, (8) nine, (9) and ten (10) of said treaty.

Second. That, in consideration of said cession and relinquishment, the United States shall advance and pay, annually, for the term of ten (10) years from and after the acceptance by the United States of the proposition herein submitted, eighty thousand (80,000) dollars, to be expended under the direction of the President of the United States, on the plan and in accordance with the provisions of the treaty aforesaid, dated February 19, 1867, for goods and provisions, for the erection of manual-labor and public school-houses, and for the support of manual-labor and public schools, and in the erection of mills, blacksmiths-shops, and other workshops, and to aid in opening farms, breaking land, and fencing the same, and in furnishing agricultural implements, oxen, and milch-cows, and such other beneficial objects as may be deemed most conducive to the prosperity and happiness of the Sisseton and Wahpeton bands of Dakota or Sioux Indians entitled thereto according to the said treaty of February 19, 1867. Such annual appropriation or consideration to be apportioned to the Sisseton and Devil's Lake agencies, in proportion to the number of Indians of the said bands located upon the Lake Traverse and Devil's Lake reservations respectively. Such apportionment to be made upon the basis of the annual reports or returns of the agents in charge. Said consideration, amounting, in the aggregate, to eight hundred thousand (800,000) dollars, payable as aforesaid, without interest.

Third. As soon as may be, the said territory embraced within said reservation described in article four, (4) (Devil's Lake reservation) shall be surveyed, as Government lands are surveyed, for the purpose of enabling the Indians entitled

Plains, West and Northwest Plateau Indian Treaties

to acquire permanent rights in the soil, as contemplated by article five (5) of said treaty.

Fourth. We respectfully request that, in case the foregoing propositions are favorably entertained by the United States, the sale of spirituous liquors upon the territory ceded may be wholly prohibited by the United States Government.

Fifth. The provisions of article five (5) of the treaty of February 19, 1867, to be modified as follows: An occupancy and cultivation of five (5) acres, upon any particular location, for a term of (5) consecutive years shall entitle the party to a patent for forty acres; a like occupancy and cultivation of ten (10) acres, to entitle the party to a patent to eighty acres; and a like occupancy and cultivation of any tract, to the extent of twenty acres, shah entitle the party so occupying and cultivating to a patent for 160 acres of land. Parties who have already selected farms and cultivated the same may be entitled to the benefit of this modification. Patents so issued (as hereinbefore set forth) shall authorize a transfer or alienation of such lands situate within the Sisseton agency, after the expiration of ten (10) years from this date, and within the Devil's lake reservation after the expiration of fifteen (15) years, but not sooner.

Sixth. The consideration to be paid, as hereinbefore proposed, is in addition to the provision of article 6 (6) of the treaty of February 19, 1867, under which Congress shall appropriate, from time to time, such an amount as may be required to meet the necessities of said Indians, to enable them to become civilized.

Seventh. Sections sixteen (16) and thirty-six (36) within the reservations shall be set apart for educational purposes, and all children of a suitable age within either reservation shall be compelled to attend school at the discretion of the agents.

Eighth. At the expiration of ten (10) years, from this date, all members of said bands under the age of twenty-one years shall receive forty acres of land from said permanent reservations in fee simple.

Ninth. At the expiration of ten (10) years, the President of the United States shall sell or dispose of all the remaining or unoccupied lands in the lake Traverse reservation, (excepting that which may hereafter be set apart for school purposes;) the proceeds of the sale of such lands to be expended for the benefit of the members of said bands located on said lake Traverse reservation; and, at the expiration of fifteen (15) years, the President shall sell or dispose of all the remaining unoccupied lands (excepting that which may be hereafter set apart for school purposes) in the Devil's Lake reservation; the proceeds of the sale of such land shall be expended for the benefit of all members of said bands who may be located on the said Devil's Lake reservation.

Plains, West and Northwest Plateau Indian Treaties

Executed at Sisseton agency, Dakota territory, Lake Traverse reservation, this 20th day of September, A. D. 1872.
Moses N. Adams, Wm. H. Forbes, James Smith, Jr., Commissioners.

Gabriel Renville, head chief of Sissetons and Wahpetons, Wicanipinonpa, chief councilor Wahpetons and Sissetons, Wasuiciyapi, chief Sisseton band Swantain, his x mark, Hokxidanwaxte, chief councilor Sissetons, his x mark, Wasukiye, chief councilor Sissetons, his x mark, Peter Tapatatonka, hereditary chief Wahpetons. Marpiyakudan, chief Sissetons, his x mark, Matoeatka, Wahpeton soldier, his x mark, Wamdiokiya, Wahpeton soldier, his x mark, Tanwannonpa, Wahpeton soldier, his x mark, Hinhanxunna, Sisseton soldier, his x mark, Tamazakanna, Sisseton soldier, his x mark, Akacitamane, Sisseton soldier, his x mark, Wamdiupiduta, chief Sissetons, his x mark,

Witnesses to signatures of above chiefs and soldiers:
H. T. Lovett, G. H. Hawes, T. A. Robertson, G. H. Faribault, C. P. La Grange.

We hereby certify, on honor, that we have fully explained to the Indians the above instrument, and that the Indians acknowledge the same to be well understood by them.

T. A. Robertson, G. H. Faribault, Interpreters.

AGREEMENT WITH THE CROWS {1880, May 14}
Unratified.
Indian Office, Montana C. 839 (1880).

The chiefs of the Crow tribe of Indians now present in Washington hereby give their own consent and promise to use their best endeavors to procure the consent of the adult male members of said tribe to cede to the United States all that part of the present Crow reservation in the Territory of Montana described as follows, to wit:

Beginning in mid-channel of the Yellowstone River, at a point opposite the mouth of Boulder Creek; thence up the mid-channel of said river to the point where it crosses the southern boundary of Montana, being the forty-fifth degree of north latitude; thence east along said parallel of latitude to the one hundred and ninth meridian of longitude; thence north on said meridian, to a point six miles south of the first standard parallel south, being on the township-line between townships six and seven south; thence west on said township-line to the one hundred and tenth meridian of longitude; thence north along said meridian to a point either west or east of the source of the Eastern Branch of Boulder Creek; thence in a straight line to the source of the Eastern Branch of Boulder

602

Plains, West and Northwest Plateau Indian Treaties

Creek; thence down said Eastern Branch to Boulder Creek; thence down Boulder Creek, and to the place of beginning.

The said chiefs of the Crow tribe of Indians promise to obtain the consent of their people as aforesaid to the cession of the territory of their reserve as above, on the following express conditions:

First. That the Government of the United States cause the agricultural lands remaining in their reservation to be properly surveyed and divided among the said Indians in severalty in the proportions hereinafter mentioned, and to issue patents to them respectively therefor, so soon as the necessary laws are passed by Congress. Allotments in severalty of said surveyed lands shall be made as follows: To each head of a family not more than one-quarter of a section, with an additional quantity of grazing-land, not exceeding one-quarter of a section.

To each single person over eighteen years of age not more than one-eighth of a section, with an additional quantity of grazing-land not exceeding one-eighth of a section. To each orphan child under eighteen years of age not more than one-eighth of a section, with an additional quantity of grazing land not exceeding one-eighth of a section, and to each other person, under eighteen years, or who may be born prior to said allotments, one-eighth of a section, with a like quantity of grazing land. All allotments to be made with the advice of the Agent for said Indians, or such other person as the Secretary of the Interior may designate for that purpose, upon the selection of the Indians, heads of families selecting for their minor children, and the agent making the allotment for each orphan child.

The title to be acquired by the Indians shall not be subject to alienation, lease, or incumbrance, either by voluntary conveyance of the grantee or his heirs, or by the judgment, order, or decree of any court, or subject to taxation of any character, but shall be and remain inalienable, and not subject to taxation for the period of twenty-five years, and until such time thereafter as the President may see fit to remove the restriction, which shall be incorporated in the patents.

Second. That in consideration of the cession of territory to be made by the said Crow tribe, the United States, in addition to the annuities and sums for provisions and clothing stipulated and provided for in existing treaties and laws, agrees to appropriate annually for twenty-five years, the sum of thirty thousand dollars, to be expended under the direction of the President for the benefit of the said Indians, in assisting them to erect houses, to procure seeds, farming implements, stock, or in cash, as the President may direct.

Third. That if at any time hereafter the Crow Indians shall consent to permit cattle to be driven across their reservation or grazed on the same, the Secretary of the Interior shall fix the amount to be paid by parties desiring to so drive or

603

Plains, West and Northwest Plateau Indian Treaties

graze cattle; all moneys arising from this source to be paid to the Indians under such rules and regulations as the Secretary of the Interior may prescribe.
Fourth. All the existing provisions of the treaty of May seventh, 1868, shall continue in force.

Done at Washington, this fourteenth day of May, anno Domini, eighteen hundred and eighty.

Plenty Coos. his x mark, Old Crow, his x mark, Two Belly, his x mark, Long Elk, his x mark, Pretty Eagle, his x mark, Medicine Crow, his x mark,

Witnesses:
A. M. Quivly, Interpreter.
E. J. Brooks.

NOTE. This agreement was not ratified, but substituted by that of June 12, 1880, which was ratified April 11, 1882

AGREEMENT WITH THE SIOUX OF VARIOUS TRIBES {1882, Oct. 17, to 1883, Jan. 3}
See H. R. Ex. Doc. 68, 47th Congress, 2d session.

This agreement made pursuant to an item in the sundry civil act of Congress, approved August 7, 1882, by Newton Edmunds, Peter C. Shannon, and James H. Teller, duly appointed commissioners on the part of the United States, and the different bands of the Sioux Indians by their chiefs and headmen whose names are hereto subscribed, they being duly authorized to act in the premises, witnesseth that

ARTICLE 1. Whereas it is the policy of the Government of the United States to provide for said Indians a permanent home where they may live after the manner of white men, and be protected in their rights of property, person and life, therefore to carry out such policy it is agreed that hereafter the permanent of the various bands of said Indians shall be upon the separate reservations hereinafter described and set apart. Said Indians, acknowledging the right of the chiefs and headmen of the various bands at each agency to determine for themselves and for their several bands, with the Government of the United States, the boundaries of their separate reservations, hereby agree to accept and abide by such agreements and conditions as to the location and boundaries of such reservations as may be made and agreed upon by the United States and the band or bands for which such separate reservation may be made, and as the said separate boundaries may be herein set forth.

Plains, West and Northwest Plateau Indian Treaties

ARTICLE 2. The said Indians do hereby relinquish and cede to the United States all of the Great Sioux Reservationas reserved to them by the treaty of 1868, and modified by the agreement of 1876 not herein specifically reserved and set apart as separate reservations for them. The said bands do severally agree to accept and occupy the separate reservations to which they are herein assigned as their permanent homes, and they do hereby severally relinquish to the other bands respectively occupying the other separate reservations, all right, title, and interest in and to the same reserving to themselves only the reservation herein set apart for their separate use and occupation.

ARTICLE 3. In consideration of the cession of territory and rights, as herein made, and upon compliance with each and every obligation assumed by the said Indians, the United States hereby agrees that each head of a family entitled to select three hundred and twenty acres of land, under Article 6, of the treaty of 1868, may, in the manner and form therein prescribed, select and secure for purposes of cultivation, in addition to said three hundred and twenty acres, a tract of land not exceeding eighty (80) acres within his reservation, for each of his children, living at the ratification of this agreement, under the age of eighteen (18) years; and such child, upon arriving at the age of eighteen years shall have such selection certified to him or her in lieu of the selection granted in the second clause of said Article 6; but no right of alienation or encumbrance is acquired by such selection and occupation: unless hereafter authorized by act of Congress.

ARTICLE 4. The United States further agrees to furnish and deliver to the said Indians twenty-five thousand cows, and one thousand bulls, of which the occupants of each of said separate reservations shall receive such proportion as the number of Indians thereon bears to the whole number of Indian parties to this agreement. All of the said cattle and their progeny shall bear the brand of the Indian department, and shall be held subject to the disposal of said department, and shall not be sold, exchanged or slaughtered, except by consent or order of the agent in charge, until such time as this restriction shall be removed by the Commissioner of Indian Affairs.

ARTICLE 5. It is also agreed that the United States will furnish and deliver to each lodge of said Indians or family of persons legally incorporated with them, who shall, in good faith, select land within the reservation to which such lodge or family belongs, and begin the cultivation thereof, one good cow, and one well broken pair of oxen, with yoke and chain, within reasonable time after making such selection and settlement.

ARTICLE 6. The United States will also furnish to each reservation herein made and described, a physician, carpenter, miller, engineer, farmer, and blacksmith, for a period of ten years from the date of this agreement.

605

Plains, West and Northwest Plateau Indian Treaties

ARTICLE 7. It is hereby agreed that the sixteenth and thirty-sixth sections of each township in said separate reservations shall be reserved for school purposes, for the use of the inhabitants of said reservations, as provided in sections 1946 and 1947 of the revised statutes of the United States.

It is also agreed that the provisions of Article 7 of the treaty of 1868, securing to said Indians the benefits of education, shall be con-tinned in force for not less than twenty (20) years, from and after the ratification of this agreement.

ARTICLE 8. The provisions of the treaty of 1868, and the agreement of 1876, except as herein modified, shall continue in full force.
This agreement shall not be binding upon either party until it shall have received the approval of the President and Congress of the United States.
Dated and signed at Santee Agency, Nebraska, October 17th, 1882.

Newton Edmunds.
Peter C. Shannon.
James H. Teller.

The foregoing articles of agreement, having been fully explained to us in open council, we the undersigned chiefs and head-men of the Sioux Indians receiving rations and annuities at the Santee Agency, in Knox County, in the State of Nebraska, do hereby consent and agree to all the stipulations therein contained, saving and reserving all our rights, both collective and individual, in and to the Santee Reservation, in said Knox County and State of Nebraska, upon which we and our people are residing.

Witness our hands and seals at Santee Agency this 17th day of October, 1882.
Robert Hakewaste, his x mark, John Buoy.
Joseph Rouillard.
Solomon Jones.
William Dick, his x mark, Samuel Hawley.
Eli Abraham.

Attest:
Alfred L. Riggs, Missionary to the Dakotas.
W. W. Fowler, Missionary to Santee Sioux.
Isaiah Lightner, U. S. Indian Agent.

I certify that the foregoing agreement was read and explained by me, and was fully understood by the above-named Sioux Indians, before signing, and that the same was executed by said Sioux Indians, at Santee Agency, county of Knox, and State of Nebraska, on the 17th day of October, 1882.

Plains, West and Northwest Plateau Indian Treaties

Sam'l D. Hinman, Official Interpreter.

It is hereby agreed that the separate reservation for the Indians receiving rations and annuities at Pine Ridge Agency, Dakota, shall be bounded and described as follows, to wit:

Beginning at the intersection of the one hundred and third meridian of longitude with the northern boundary of the state of Nebraska, thence north along said meridian to the south fork of Cheyenne river, and down said stream to a point due west from the intersection of White River with the one hundred and second meridian; thence due east to said point of intersection and down said White River to a point in longitude one hundred and one degrees and twenty minutes west, thence due south to said north line of the State of Nebraska, thence west on said north line to the place of beginning.

Dated and signed at Pine Ridge Agency, Dakota, October 28th, 1882.

Newton Edmunds.
Peter C. Shannon.
James H. Teller.

The foregoing articles of agreement having been fully explained to us in open council, we, the undersigned chiefs and headmen of the Sioux Indians receiving rations and annuities at Pine Ridge Agency in the Territory of Dakota, do hereby consent and agree to all the stipulations therein contained.
Witness our hands and seals at Pine Ridge Agency, Dakota, this 28th day of October, 1882.

Mahpiya-luta, his x mark, Taopicikala, his x mark, Simka-luta, his x mark, Simka-wakan-hin-to, his x mark, Tatanka-hunka-sni, his x mark, Mato-sapa, his x mark, Sunanito-wankantuya, his x mark, Pehinzizi, his x mark, Canker-tanka, his x mark, Sunka-bloka, his x mark, Wapaha-sapa, his x mark, Mimwanica, his x mark, Owa-sica-hoksila, his x mark, Toicuwa, his x mark,

Sumnanito-isnala, his x mark, Kisun-sni,-his x mark, Hehaka-sapa, his x mark, Zitkala-ska, his x mark, Ogle-sa, his x mark, Sunmanito-wakpa, his x mark, Wasicum-tasunke, his x mark, Egeonge-word, Captain Polo, Akicita-injin, his x mark, Tasunko-inyauko, his x mark., Wagmu-su, his x mark, Wamli-heton, his x mark, Kangi-maza, his x mark, Sunmanito-ska, his x mark, Sunka-unzica, his x mark, Mato-sapa, his x mark, Hinho-kinyau, his x mark, Tasunka-kokipapi, sr., his x mark, Hazska-mlaska, his x mark, Tasunke-maza, his x mark, Okiksahe, his x mark, Mato-nasula, his x mark, Kangi-cikala, his x mark, Wicahhpi-yamin, his x mark, Wasicun-waukautuya, his x mark, Antoine Leiddeau, his x mark, Beaver Morto, his x mark, Sam Daon.

Plains, West and Northwest Plateau Indian Treaties

Attest:
S. S. Benedict, U. S. Indian Interpreter.
V. T. McGellycuddy, U. S. End. Ag't.

I hereby certify that the foregoing agreement was read and explained by me and was fully understood by the above named Sioux Indians, before signing, and that the same was executed by said Indians at Pine Ridge Agency, Dakota, on the 29th day of October, 1883.

Sam'l D. Hinman,Official Interpreter.

It is hereby agreed that the separate reservation for the Indians receiving rations and annuities at Rosebud Agency, Dakota, shall be bounded and described as follows, to wit:-

Beginning on the north boundary of the State of Nebraska, at a point in longitude one hundred and one degrees and twenty minutes west, and running thence due north to White River, thence down said White River to a point in longitude ninety-nine degrees and thirty minutes west, thence due south to said north boundary of the state of Nebraska, and thence west on said north boundary to the place of beginning. If any of said Indians belonging to the Rosebud agency have permanently located east of longitude ninety-nine degrees and thirty minutes, they may hold the lands so located, and have the same certified to them in accordance with the provisions of Article 6, of the treaty of 1868 and Article 3 of this agreement, or they may return to the separate reservation above described, in which case they shall be entitled to receive from the government the actual value of all improvements made on such locations.

Dated and signed at Rosebud Agency, Dakota, this 6th day of November, 1882.

Newton Edmunds.
James H. Teller.

The foregoing articles of agreement having been fully explained to us in open council, we, the undersigned chiefs and headmen of the Sioux Indians receiving rations and annuities at Rosebud Agency in, the Territory of Dakota, do hereby consent and agree to all the stipulations therein contained.
Witness our hands and seals at Rosebud Agency, Dakota, this 6th day of November, 1882.

Sinto-gleska, his x mark, Mato-luzaham, his x mark, Wakinyau-ska, his x mark, Kangi-sapa, his x mark, Mato-ohanka, his x mark, Wakinyau-ska, 2nd, his x mark, Tasunke-tokeca, his x mark, Asampi, his x mark, Mahpiya-inazin, his x mark, He-to-pa, his x mark, Tasimke-wakita, his x mark, Sunka-bloka, his x mark, Caugleska-wakinyin, his x mark, Wamniomni-akicita, his x mark,

Plains, West and Northwest Plateau Indian Treaties

Wanmli-cikala, his x mark, Wamli-waste, his x mark, Mahpiya-tatanka, his x mark, Wapashupi, his x mark, Mato-wankantuya, his x mark, Igmu-wakute, his x mark, Hohaka-gloska, his x mark, Mato-ska, his x mark, Capt. Police.
Pehan-san-mani, his x mark, Okise-wakan, his x mark, Getau-wakimyau, his x mark, Wakinyau-tomaheca, his x mark, Mloka-cikala, his x mark, Toka-kte, his x mark,

Attest:
Jas. G. Wright, U. S. Ind. Ag't.
Chas. P. Jordan, Clerk.

I hereby certify that the foregoing agreement was read and explained by me and was fully understood by the above-named Sioux Indians before signing, and that the same was executed by said Indians at Rosebud Agency, Dakota, on the 6th day of November, 1882.

Sam'l D. Hinman, Official Interpreter.

It is hereby agreed that the separate reservations for the Indians receiving rations and annuities at Standing Rock Agency, Dakota, shall be bounded and described as follows, to wit:-

Beginning at a point at low-water mark, on the east bank of the Missouri River, opposite the mouth of cannon ball river; thence down said east bank along said low-water mark to a point opposite the mouth of Grand River, thence westerly to said Grand River, and up and along the middle channel of the same to its intersection with the one hundred and second meridian of longitude; thence north along said meridian to its intersection with the south branch of Cannon Ball Riveralso known as Cedar Creek; thence down said south branch of Cannon Ball River to its intersection with the main Cannon Ball River, and down said main Cannon Ball River to the Missouri River at the place of beginning.

Dated and signed at Standing Rock Agency, Dakota, this 30th day of November, 1882.
Newton Edmunds.
James H. Teller.
Peter C. Shannon.

The foregoing articles of agreement having been fully explained to us in open council, we, the undersigned chiefs and head-men of the Sioux Indians, receiving rations and annuities at Standing Rock Agency, in the Territory of Dakota, do hereby consent and agree to all the stipulations therein contained. We also agree that the Lower Yanktonais Indians at Crow Creek, and the Indians now with Sitting Bull, may share with us the above-described separate reservation, if assigned thereto by the United States, with consent of said Indians.

Plains, West and Northwest Plateau Indian Treaties

Witness our hands and seals at Standing Rock Agency, Dakota, this 30th day of November, 1882.

Akicita-hauska, his x mark, Mato-gnaskinyan, his x mark, Mato-nonpa, his x mark, Ista-sapa, his x mark, Wanmli-waukautuya, his x mark, Wakute-mani, his x mark, Wiyaka-hanska, his x mark, Cante-peta, his x mark, John Grass, his x mark, Sasunke-luta, his x mark, Owape, his x mark, Cante-peta, sr., his x mark, Mato-wayuhi, his x mark, Pahin-ska, his x mark, Kangi-atoyapi, his x mark, Mato-kawinge, his x mark, Wakinyan-watakope, his x mark, Tasina-luta, his x mark, Tasunke-hin-zi, his x mark, Hehaka-okannazin, his x mark, Maga, his x mark, Taloka-inyauke, his x mark, Mato-wapostan, his x mark, Heton-yuha, his x mark, Sungila-luta, his x mark, Mastinca, his x mark, Sunka-maza, his x mark, Wanmli-cikala, his x mark,

Attest:
James McLaughlin, U. S. Indian Agent.
James H. Stewart, Agency Clerk.
Thomas H. Miller, Issue Clerk.

I hereby certify that the foregoing agreement was read and explained by me and was fully understood by the above-named Sioux Indians before signing, and that the same was executed by said Indians at Standing Rock Agency, Dakota, on the 30th day of November, 1882.
Sam'l D. Hinman, Official Interpreter.

It is hereby agreed that the separate reservation for the Indians receiving rations and annuities at Cheyenne River Agency, Dakota, and for such other Indians as may hereafter be assigned thereto, shall be bounded and described as follows, to wit:-

Beginning at a point at low-water mark on the east bank of the Missouri River opposite the mouth of Grand River said point being the south-easterly corner of the Standing-Rock Reservation; thence down said east bank of the Missouri River along said low-water mark to a point opposite the mouth of the Cheyenne river; thence west to said Cheyenne River and up the same to its intersection with the one hundred and second meridian of longitude; thence north along said meridian to its intersection with the Grand River; thence down said Grand River, along the middle channel thereof, to the Missouri River, at the place of beginning.

It is also agreed that said Indians shall receive all necessary aid from the government in their removal to said reservation, and when so removed, each of said Indians shall be entitled to receive from the government the full value of all improvements in buildings or on lands owned by him at the time of such

610

Plains, West and Northwest Plateau Indian Treaties

removal and lost to him thereby. Said compensation shall be given in such manner and on such appraisements as shall be ordered by the Secretary of the Interior.

Dated and signed at Cheyenne River Agency, Dakota, this 21st day of December.

Newton Edmunds.
James H. Teller.
Peter C. Shannon.

The foregoing articles of agreement having been fully explained to us in open council, we, the undersigned chiefs and headmen of the Sioux Indians receiving rations and annuities at the Cheyenne River Agency, in the Territory of Dakota, do hereby consent and agree to all the stipulations therein contained.
Witness our hands and seals at Cheyenne River Agency, Dakota, this 21st day of December, 1882.

Zitkala-kinyan, his x mark, Cetan-tokapa, his x mark, Cuwi-hda-mani, his x mark, Waumli-ohitika, his x mark, Mato-wanmli, his x mark, Wagmasa, his x mark, Toicuwa, his x mark, Cuwila, his x mark, Waumli-gleska, his x mark, Mato-nakpa, his x mark, Mato-luta, his x mark, Maste-au, his x mark, Waunatan, his x mark, Nape-wanmiomin, his x mark, Cante-wanica, his x mark,

Attest:
Wm. A. Swan, United States Indian Agent.
Rob't V. Levers, Agency Clerk.
N. G. Landmepe, Issue Clerk.

It having been understood and agreed by the undersigned commissioners and the Brule Indians at Rosebud Agency, parties to this agreement, that the reservation for the Lower Brule Indians shall be located between the Rosebud Reservation and the Missouri River, it is hereby agreed that the reservation for the said Brule Indians, now at Lower Brule Agency, Dakota, and for such other Indians as may be assigned thereto, shall consist of all that part of township No. 103, range 72, west of the 5th principal meridian, in the Territory of Dakota, lying on the north bank of the White River, together with the tract of land bounded and described as follows, to wit:

Beginning at a point at low-water mark on the east bank of the Missouri River opposite the mouth of the said White River; thence down said east bank of the Missouri River along said low-water mark to a point opposite the mouth of Pratt Creek; thence due south to the forty-third parallel of latitude; thence west along said parallel to a point in longitude ninety-nine degrees and thirty minutes west; thence due north along the eastern boundary of Rosebud Reservation

Plains, West and Northwest Plateau Indian Treaties

to the White River, and thence down said White River to the Missouri River, at the place of beginning. It is also agreed that said Indians shall receive all necessary aid from the government in their removal to said reservation, and when so removed each of said Indians shall be entitled to receive from the government the full value of all improvements, in buildings or on lands, owned by him at the time of such removal and lost to him thereby. Said compensation shall be made in such manner and on such appraisement as shall be ordered by the Secretary of the Interior.

Witness our hands and seals this 23rd day of January, 1883.
Newton Edmunds.
James H. Teller.
Peter C. Shannon.

AGREEMENT WITH THE COLUMBIA AND COLVILLE {1883, July 7} Ratified July 4, 1884,

In the conference with chief Moses and Sar-sarp-kin, of the Columbia reservation, and Tonaskat and Lot, of the Colville reservation, had this day, the following was substantially what was asked for by the Indians:
Tonasket asked for a saw and grist mill, a boarding school to be established at Bonaparte Creek to accommodate one hundred pupils (100), and a physician to reside with them, and $100. (one hundred) to himself each year.

Sar-sarp-kin asked to be allowed to remain on the Columbia reservation with his people, where they now live, and to be protected in their rights as settlers, and in addition to the ground they now have under cultivation within the limit of the fifteen mile strip cut off from the northern portion of the Columbia Reservation, to be allowed to select enough more unoccupied land in Severalty to make a total to Sar-sarp-kin of four square miles, being 2,560 acres of land, and each head of a family or male adult one square mile; or to move on to the Colville Reservation, if they so desire, and in case they so remove, and relinquish all their claims to the Columbia Reservation, he is to receive one hundred (100) head of cows for himself and people, and such farming implements as may be necessary.

All of which the Secretary agrees they should have, and that he will ask Congress to make an appropriation to enable him to perform.

The Secretary also agrees to ask Congress to make an appropriation to enable him to purchase for Chief Moses a sufficient number of cows to furnish each one of his band with two cows; also to give Moses one thousand dollars ($1,000) for the purpose of erecting a dwelling-house for himself; also to construct a saw mill and grist-mill as soon as the same shall be required for use;

Plains, West and Northwest Plateau Indian Treaties

also that each head of a family or each male adult person shall be furnished with one wagon, one double set of harness, one grain cradle, one plow, one harrow, one scythe, one hoe, and such other agricultural implements as may be necessary.

And on condition that Chief Moses and his people keep this agreement faithfully, he is to be paid in cash, in addition to all of the above, one thousand dollars ($1,000) per annum during his life.

All this on condition that Chief Moses shall remove to the Colville Reservation and relinquish all claim upon the Government for any land situated elsewhere.

Further, that the Government will secure to Chief Moses and his people, as well as to all other Indians who may go on to the Colville reservation, and engage in farming, equal rights and protection alike with all other Indians now on the Colville Reservation, and will afford him any assistance necessary to enable him to carry out the terms of this agreement on the part of himself and his people. That until he and his people are located permanently on the Colville Reservation, his status shall remain as now, and the police over his people shall be vested in the military, and all money or articles to be furnished him and his people shall be sent to some point in the locality of his people, there to be distributed as provided. All other Indians now living on the Columbia Reservation shall be entitled to 640 acres, or one square mile of land, to each head of family or male adult, in the possession and ownership of which they shall be guaranteed and protected. Or should they move on to the Colville Reservation within two years, they will be provided with such farming implements as may be required, provided they surrender all rights to the Columbia Reservation.

All of the foregoing is upon the condition that Congress will make an appropriation of funds necessary to accomplish the foregoing, and confirm this agreement; and also, with the understanding that Chief Moses or any of the Indians heretofore mentioned shall not be required to remove to the Colville Reservation until Congress does make such appropriation, etc.

Ta-Tun-Wanka, Squashed Lizard, Wa-Sa-Be, Hot Radish, No-Noo-Ki, Small-Horn

Lionel T. Fogg, Comm., Ellwood P. Suggins, Lt. U.S. Infantry, Lamar G. Gunbody, Trader, Eugene Frickert, Bureau of Indian Affairs

PLAINS

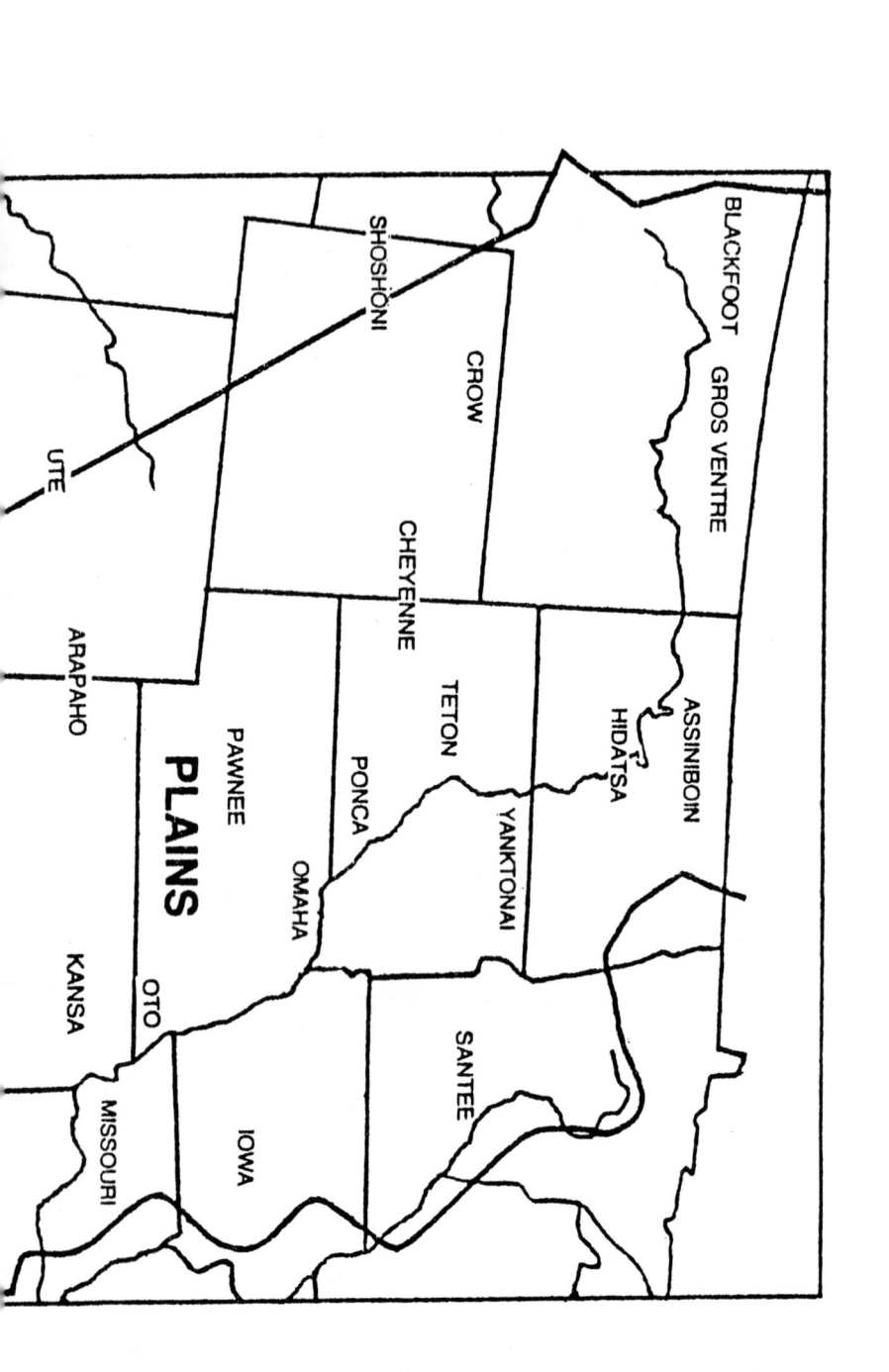

- BLACKFOOT
- GROS VENTRE
- SHOSHONI
- CROW
- UTE
- ASSINIBOIN
- CHEYENNE
- HIDATSA
- ARAPAHO
- TETON
- YANKTONAI
- PAWNEE
- PONCA
- OMAHA
- KANSA
- OTO
- SANTEE
- MISSOURI
- IOWA

Location in the 1500s

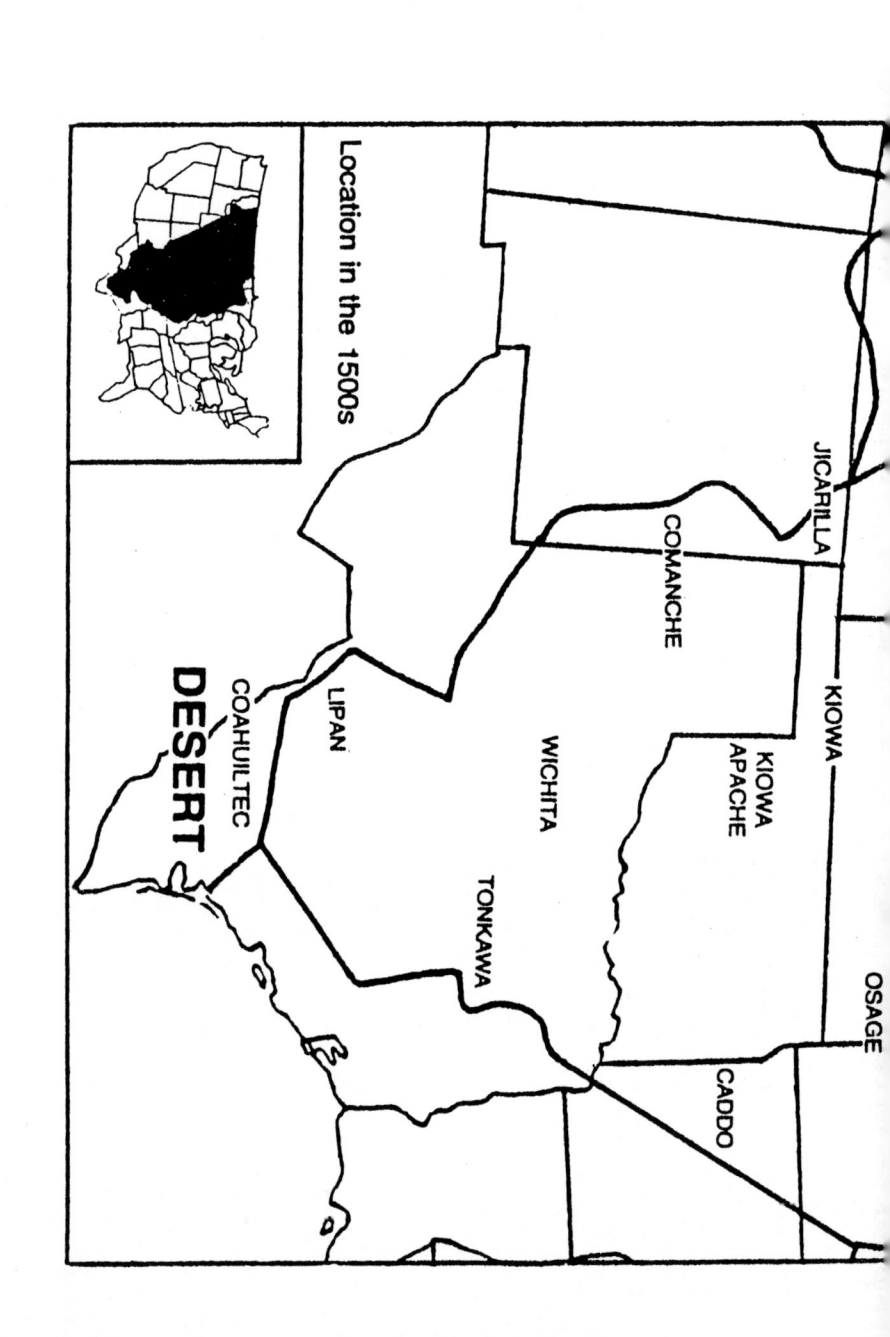

- JICARILLA
- COMANCHE
- KIOWA
- COAHUILTEC
- LIPAN
- DESERT
- WICHITA
- KIOWA APACHE
- TONKAWA
- OSAGE
- CADDO

Stafford Library WITHDRAWN
Columbia College
1001 Rogers Street
Columbia, Missouri 65216